W9-ASD-587

ART AND LIFE IN AMERICA

Oliver W. Larkin

ART AND LIFE IN AMERICA

Revised and Enlarged Edition

HOLT, RINEHART AND WINSTON, NEW YORK

TO AMERICANS OF THREE GENERATIONS:

My father, who taught me to love the things Americans have made,

My wife, whose confidence and fortitude were indispensable to this undertaking,

My son, a young American artist.

Designed by Stefan Salter

Published simultaneously in Canada by Holt, Rinehart and Winston of Canada, Limited

Revised Edition

Library of Congress Catalog Card Number: 60–6491

25148–0210

Printed in the United States of America

AUTHOR'S FOREWORD

TO THE REVISED EDITION

I introduced the first edition of this book in 1949 with a statement of its purpose, explaining that it would be

> . . . an introductory survey of the history of architecture, sculpture, painting, and to some degree of the so-called "minor arts" in the United States. It would show how these arts have expressed American ways of living and how they have been related to the development of American ideas, particularly the idea of democracy. . . . In such a book, the terms "inclusive" and "objective" could have only a relative meaning. As for the former, no survey could discuss more than a few of the thousands of creative men and women who have worked here, nor comment upon more than a fraction of the works of art they have produced. As for the latter, the fair-minded historian will direct his readers to histories and interpretations which contrast with his own; but he will write as a man with his own philosophy of art, nor will he conceal his enthusiasm for those artists who, in his opinion, have most richly contributed to the American experience.

Relying largely on the discoveries of others, with its emphasis upon interpretation and synthesis rather than upon a considerable extension of known facts, the work was written primarily, I explained, for students of American civilization who wish to know what part the visual-plastic arts have played in our society; for students of American art who may find some profit in seeing the subject as a developing whole, and some of whom may be stimulated to make contributions of their own to a rich, exciting, and inexhaustible field of knowledge; for the general reader who, knowing something of this subject, would like to know more.

Ten years later, the response of these readers has encouraged me to prepare a new edition in which previous errors have been corrected, the narrative brought up to date by new chapters, the bibliography expanded to include recent publications, and a section of color plates added with the purpose of bringing paintings more vividly before the reader with appropriate comments on their composition, color, and technical handling.

A word of explanation concerning the structure of this survey may be useful. Each Book comprises a period of art and life in America with a movement and character of its own. Each Part deals with a phase of that period, and is preceded by an Introduction. Each Introduction summarizes important cultural developments; quotes typical Americans to show what they thought they were doing and why; draws analogies between art and literature; discusses critics and art historians, the conflicts among artistic theories and practices, and the status of art patronage; and explains the constant interplay between art of the New World and the Old. In the chapters which follow these Introductions, my emphasis shifts to the lives and work of the artists themselves, many of whom make only too brief an appearance, and some of whom are rather fully delineated.

If artists have been influenced by several successive phases of life in America and Europe, I have discussed their careers in more than one chapter of this book, a procedure which has its disadvantages but also its compensations.

The illustrations in black and white are as intimately related to the text as the mechanics of book making permit, in the effort to place a picture on the page where it is discussed or on a facing page. With few exceptions, the first line of my captions identifies the work of art itself; the second line names the person or institution through whose courtesy a photograph was obtained, and also indicates the present location of the work unless that location has been specified in the first line.

The location of certain works mentioned but not illustrated has been given in abbreviated form; some of these abbreviations are explained in a table on page 490.

The bibliographical notes include references to books and articles on which I have relied and which treat in greater detail the various aspects of art discussed in these pages. Here also I have recorded the source of significant quotations, and the birth and death dates of artists.

A full acknowledgment of my indebtedness to those who helped in the preparation of the original edition or of the present revision would add another chapter to this book. A group of experts is to be thanked for reading and making helpful comments on those portions of the manuscript of the first edition which fell within their special fields of interest: John I. H. Baur and Lloyd Goodrich of the Whitney Museum of American Art; Dorothy C. Miller of the Museum of Modern Art; Prof. Hugh Morrison of Dartmouth College; Mrs. Barbara N. Parker of the Boston Museum of Fine Arts;

Prof. Chandler R. Post of Harvard University. Beaumont Newhall, an authority on American photography, scrutinized my passages on that subject; and Prof. Newton Arvin of Smith College, my comments on literary America. Other colleagues at Smith, among them Edgar Wind, Daniel Aaron, and Karl Putnam, gave indispensable criticisms. My book in its original form owed much to the moral support and material assistance of Miss Bartlett Cowdrey, an expert in more than one aspect of the subject.

For prompt and generous help I am also grateful to the museums and collectors whose names appear in the captions of my illustrations. Special thanks are due the following: Charles E. Baker, New York Historical Society; Walter R. Brown, Hampton Institute; Katherine Coffey, Newark Museum; Virginia Daiker, Hirst Milhollen, and Milton Kaplan, Library of Congress; Evelyn Grier and Janet Byrnes, Metropolitan Museum of Art; Mrs. Henry Howell, Jr., Frick Art Reference Library; Macgill James, National Gallery of Art; Jean Lipman, *Art in America;* Margaret McKellar and Rosalind Irvine, Whitney Museum of American Art; Richard McLanathan, Proctor Institute; Mrs. E. A. MacSwiggan and Miss Bessom Harris, Essex Institute of Salem; Pearl Moeller, Museum of Modern Art; Charles F. Montgomery, Winterthur Museum; Constance Moore, Wilmington Society of the Fine Arts; Paul Moore, Jr.; Dale O'Brien and Glenn Price, *Encyclopaedia Britannica;* Duncan Phillips of Washington, D.C.; Edgar P. Richardson, Detroit Institute of Arts; Josephine Setze, Yale University Art Gallery; Clifford R. Shipton, American Antiquarian Society; Frederick A. Sweet, Art Institute of Chicago; Mary B. Terwilliger, Senate House Museum, Kingston, New York; Clayton Torrence, Virginia Historical Society; Emily H. Tremaine, the Miller Co.; Walter M. Whitehill, Boston Athenaeum; Hermann W. Williams, Mrs. Russell Quandt, and Alice Phillips, Corcoran Gallery of Art; Alice Winchester, *Antiques* magazine; Carl Zigrosser, Philadelphia Museum of Art.

Of the works owned by the Museum of Modern Art and here reproduced, the following were acquired through special funds: Lehmbruck's *Kneeling Woman,* Robus' *Girl Washing Her Hair,* and Dérain's *The Window on the Park* (purchased in memory of Mrs. Cornelius J. Sullivan)—Mrs. John D. Rockefeller, Jr., Purchase Fund; Quirt's *Tranquility of Previous Existence* and Blume's *The Eternal City*—Mrs. Simon Guggenheim Fund. Gifts to the Museum: Noguchi's *Capital* from Miss Jeanne Reynal, Calder's *Lobster Trap and Fish Tail* from the Advisory Committee, and Burchfield's *The First Hepaticas* from Mrs. John D. Rockefeller, Jr.

Some of my illustrations were acquired with the help of men and women who present the work of American artists in their galleries: Herman Baron, Charles D. Childs, Edith Halpert, Samuel M. Kootz, Antoinette Kraushaar, and Bertha Schaefer. I am especially indebted in this respect to Harry Shaw Newman and Victor D. Spark.

The color plates are from photographs made by the recent Carnegie Study of the Arts of the United States. For their use I thank Florence Anderson of the Carnegie Corporation of New York; Professor Lamar Dodd, Director of the Study; Professor William Pierson and Charles B. Phelps; Sandak, Inc.; and the University of Georgia, custodian of the negatives.

On those occasions when I appealed to artists themselves, I received the help of Berenice Abbott, Leonard Baskin, George Biddle, Ernest Fiene, Robert Gwathmey, Minna Harkavy, the late Walt Kuhn, Theodore Roszak, Eero Saarinen, Charles Sheeler, Paul Strand, Abraham Walkowitz, William Zorach, and several others.

In conversations and letters, I have drawn upon the knowledge of many Americans, receiving information which in several instances had not yet appeared in print; among them Prof. Mary Ellen Chase, the late Henry W. L. Dana, Howard N. Doughty, Louisa Dresser, Prof. Samuel Green, Prof. Henry-Russell Hitchcock, Harnett T. Kane, Lincoln Kirstein, Mrs. Nina F. Little, Elizabeth McCausland, Marie de Mare, the late John Hill Morgan, the late Walter Pach, William Pierson, Dr. J. Hall Pleasants, Anna W. Rutledge, Charles C. Sellers, D. B. Steinman, and John J. Vrooman.

Mrs. Erna Huber typed these chapters not once but many times, and Stefan Salter designed this volume with a fine sense of the relation between form and content.

Oliver W. Larkin

Northampton, Mass.
June, 1960.

ACKNOWLEDGMENTS

The author is indebted to the following for permission to quote from copyrighted works:

Brandt & Brandt: The quotation from *Western Star,* published by Rinehart & Company, Inc. Copyright, 1943, by Rosemary Carr Benét.

Chatto & Windus: The quotations from Clive Bell, *Art* are reprinted by permission of the publisher, Chatto & Windus.

Doubleday & Company, Inc.: The quotation from "When 'Omer Smote 'Is Bloomin' Lyre" is from *The Seven Seas* by Rudyard Kipling. Copyright 1893, 1894, 1896, 1905, 1933 by Rudyard Kipling. Reprinted by permission of Mrs. George Bambridge, Methuen & Co., Ltd., Doubleday & Company, Inc., The Macmillan Co. of Canada, Ltd.

Duell, Sloan & Pearce, Inc.: The quotations from *Frank Lloyd Wright on Architecture* are reprinted by permission of the Publishers, Duell, Sloan & Pearce, Inc. Copyright 1941 by Duell, Sloan & Pearce, Inc.

Hamlin Garland estate: The quotation from Hamlin Garland, *Crumbling Idols* is reprinted by permission of Isabel Garland Lord and Constance Garland Doyle.

Henry George estate: The quotation from Henry George, *Progress and Poverty* is reprinted by permission of Agnes George de Mille Prude.

Harcourt, Brace and Company, Inc.: The quotations from D. B. Steinman, *Building of the Bridge;* from T. S. Eliot, *Collected Poems;* from Archibald MacLeish, *Land of the Free;* and from Carl Sandburg, *The People, Yes* are reprinted by permission of the publisher, Harcourt, Brace and Company, Inc.

Harper & Brothers: The quotations from Henry James, *The American Scene* are reprinted by permission of the publisher, Harper & Brothers.

Harvard University Press: The quotation from Georges Lemaître, *From Cubism to Surrealism in French Literature* is reprinted by permission of the publishers. Cambridge, Mass.: Harvard University Press, 1941.

Houghton Mifflin Company: The quotations from the *Letters and Journals of Samuel F. B. Morse* and from *The Education of Henry Adams* are reprinted by permission of the publishers, Houghton Mifflin Company.

Longmans, Green & Co., Inc.: The quotations from Frank Lloyd Wright's *Autobiography,* copyright 1932, are reprinted by permission of the publisher, Longmans, Green & Co., Inc.

Lund Humphries & Co., Ltd.: The quotations from Frank Lloyd Wright, *An Organic Architecture* are reprinted by permission of the publisher, Lund Humphries & Co., Ltd.

The Macmillan Company: The quotations from Lloyd Goodrich, *Winslow Homer,* copyright 1944, and his *Thomas Eakins,* copyright 1933, are reprinted by permission of the author and the publisher, The Macmillan Company.

The Museum of Modern Art: The quotations from Joseph Hirsch in *Americans, 1942* and from Lincoln Kirstein's introduction to *Gaston Lachaise* are reprinted by permission of the Museum of Modern Art.

Frederic Newlin Price: The quotations from *Edward Hicks* are reprinted by permission of the author, Frederic Newlin Price, and the publisher, the Benjamin West Society.

Random House, Inc.: The quotation from Milton Mezzrow and Bernard Wolfe, *Really the Blues,* copyright 1946, is reprinted by permission of the publisher, Random House, Inc.

Charles Scribner's Sons: The quotations from Henry James, *William Wetmore Story and His Friends* and *The American* are reprinted by permission of the publisher, Charles Scribner's Sons.

Stackpole Sons, Publishers: The quotation from Pare Lorenz, *The River* is reprinted by permission of Stackpole Sons, Publishers.

Certain material in this book was first presented in four lectures in the summer of 1948 at Northwestern University under the auspices of the Norman Wait Harris Foundation, to whom the author wishes to express his gratitude.

The Viking Press, Inc.: The quotations from Thorstein Veblen, *The Higher Learning in America* and from Marsden Hartley, *Selected Poems* are reprinted by permission of the publishers, The Viking Press, Inc.

Doorway by Samuel McIntire ▶

Museum of Fine Arts, Boston

CONTENTS

PART III / THE REVOLUTIONARY GENERATION

BOOK TWO / SELF-CONSCIOUS REPUBLIC

c. 1790-c. 1830

PART I / THE JEFFERSONIAN PROMISE

PART II / REPUBLICAN PAINTING

BOOK THREE / DEMOCRATIC VISTAS

c. 1830-c. 1870

PART I / JACKSONIAN FERMENT

PART II / AT THE FEET OF THE FAMILIAR

BOOK FOUR / BETWEEN TWO PANICS c. 1870-c. 1900

PART I / A CHROMO CIVILIZATION

PART II / CRITICS, REBELS, AND PROPHETS

PART III / COSMOPOLITANS

BOOK FIVE / PROGRESSIVISM, CULTURE, AND WAR c. 1900-c. 1930

PART I / THE VOICE OF THE CITY

PART II / ART'S COMING OF AGE

PART III / DECADE OF DISILLUSION

BOOK SIX / NEW HORIZONS

c. 1930-1960

PART I / THE AGE OF ROOSEVELT

PART II / POINT OF PROMISE AND OF DANGER

LIST OF ILLUSTRATIONS

(More complete information as to authorship, location and source of photograph will be found in the captions under these illustrations.)

LIST OF COLOR PLATES

(*Following page One Hundred Forty-three*)

BOOK ONE

THE COLONIAL ARTS

c. 1600 — c. 1790

Seventeenth century gravestone ▶

Photo Essex Institute, Salem, Mass.

PART ONE

SAINTS AND TRADERS

INTRODUCTION / A SENSIBLE PEOPLE

America was an experiment. When it began, five nations of Europe were passing none too smoothly from the stabilities of feudalism to the new beliefs, discoveries, and motivations of the modern age. In France, Spain, Portugal, Holland, and England, the power of the church-state, and with it the power of wealth, title, and property over the lives of men, was being challenged. The man of middle station was to be the prime mover in the new age; his jostling for elbow room in society was to be called Individualism. His curiosity urged him to seek provable truth, not to accept truth handed down; and his struggle to earn, to build, and to profit was the beginning of capitalism.

The new European was no simple creature, but carried inside him the conflicts and the contradictions of a society which was neither free of its past nor wholly committed to its future, as the rival imperialisms of the Old World clashed — rival economies, rival church systems, and rival courts. Sooner or later the clash was bound to be transferred to the mysterious continent waiting on this side of the Atlantic. It was only a question of time before the probing and tapping would begin, as the nations looked for new wealth in North America to carry forward their battles with one another.

The adventurers came first, and the sixteenth century saw their effort to bridge an ocean, grasp an island or a harbor, and hold it in the teeth of nature and the natives. This was a task for men whose courage was reckless and whose cupidity was unlimited; they were the hard grasping fingers of a hand whose long arm controlled them, agents of a king or a small commercial monopoly back home whose names were given to the first western forts and rivers.

Giovanni da Verrazano was a mariner and a scholar, Jacques Cartier was a skilled Breton pilot; the former

John White, *Ralph Lane's Fort,* 1585

Library of Congress photo

explored the Atlantic coast and the latter the St. Lawrence before the century was half done. Hernando de Soto, the plunderer of the Incas, came to the Indians bringing iron collars, and hacked his way from Tampa Bay to the Mississippi. Francisco de Coronado at the same moment pushed northward from Mexico to find the seven fabled cities of gold, and found only terraced pueblo villages in what is now Arizona. In the name of Castile, Pedro Menéndez de Avilés sailed from Cadiz with a sword in one hand and a cross in the other to destroy the French settlements in Florida, building the fortress at St. Augustine while his Franciscans raised a crude church and a monastery where the Matanzas flowed into the Atlantic. That politician and court favorite, Sir Walter Raleigh, dreamed of a second England in the west, a dream induced by Hakluyt's rhapsody of great undiscovered resources and of the wealth and reputation their discovery would bring. It was Raleigh who sponsored the expeditions to Roanoke Island in Albemarle Sound, where the first child of English parents was born in the New World; and it was John White, Governor of Roanoke, in whose absence the small colony disappeared forever.

When Thomas Harriot, who had seen the Roanoke venture with his own eyes in 1585, republished his *True Report* five years later, it contained the first pictures a white man had made in America. John White was not only a brilliant mathematician and competent writer, but a water colorist who accurately drew the palisaded Indian villages, the odd burial houses, the dances around fires, the fish, fruit, and flowers of the Carolina coast, and stained them with delicate color. His knowledge of the figure sufficed for the chieftain and his wife squatting before their bowl of meat, and his perspective was convincing in the barrel-shaped huts of the town of Pomeiock "all compassed abowt with smale poles stuck thick together in stedd of a wall." No painted detail on a warrior's leg escaped him, and his bird's-eye view of Ralph Lane's fort on St. John's Island was done with a relish for the geometric pattern of its pointed casemates; his brush laid down the softest of tints for the "corn newly sprung" at Secoton and the blue beads of a Horowan chieftain's daughter.

White's generation saw his pictures only in the black and white of the Flemish engraver, Theodore De Bry, under whose burin the naked redmen were given a slight resemblance to classical Renaissance athletes. Twenty years before White's Roanoke sketches, a Frenchman named Jacques Le Moyne had survived Menéndez' massacres in Florida, and his forty-odd paintings were done from memory in England and likewise engraved by De Bry for publication in 1591.

Soon after Europe saw these first pictorial expressions of the American experience, the three-cornered struggle for a continent had begun in earnest. Northward from Panama spread New Spain, with settlements in what is now Texas, California, Arizona, and New Mexico; Florida was Spanish, as was a strip along the Gulf. This was the upper half of an empire, a scattering of frontier forts with plaza, church, hospital, and a few plain houses. The rule of life was to extract work and wealth through force and taxes, to admit only Catholic settlers, and to Christianize the Indians—in short, to transplant feudalism in the wilderness. St. Augustine, a citadel against Englishmen, savages, and pirates, against fire and malaria, took the shape of the typical presidio as San Marco castle went up, block upon block laid by red and black slaves under the eyes of men who knew what a feudal moat and bastion looked like, and how to shape a casemate. The Spaniards had found a soft white stone of coral and sea shell which they called *coquina,* and out of it they built the garrison, the priest's house, the governor's palace, the hospital, and the monastery around a central plaza. In the gardens of St. Augustine grew pomegranates, figs, oranges, limes, and guavas.

The Spanish vision of sudden wealth had faded when Don Juan de Oñate's ox wagons with their four hundred colonists lumbered into the New Mexico region in 1598,

San Estevan Mission, Acoma, N. Mex.

Historic American Buildings Survey, Library of Congress

and the seventeenth-century missions of the Rio Grande Valley were the result of a shrewder and more patient policy of growth. In their southern empire the Spaniards richly developed music, literature, and the arts of building, sculpture, and painting, but not in the great forests and deserts of the north. If Spain long held its grip on this region, it was through the tenacity of her provincial governors and the faith and fervor of her priests.

Among the well-remembered building styles of the homeland were the Gothic and the Moorish, the classical of the late sixteenth and early seventeenth centuries, and the florid "churrigueresque" which succeeded it. What had been Spanish of Spain, then Spanish of Mexico, fanned out into local variations in the American Southwest, modified or transformed by frontier necessity. The development of the mission was toward self-containment: its heart was the patio, and the walled-about community held the church, shops, kitchens, refectory, guardroom, hospital, dormitory, barns, and corrals. Under its reconstructions the church of San Estevan, over three hundred feet above the New Mexico plain at Acoma, is a rugged testimonial to the fusion of Spanish modes and Indian craftsmanship in the 1600's.

The French story was not dissimilar, when Samuel de Champlain built his turreted "habitation" at Quebec and the *coureurs de bois* moved among the Hurons and the Iroquois from their posts in the Mohawk Valley, the Ohio, and the upper reaches of the Mississippi. Père Marquette with Joliet and a few *voyageurs* sailed down the Wisconsin River to make converts of the Kaskaskia tribes; the Sieur de la Salle reached the mouth of the Mississippi and shortly after 1700 a chain of forts stretched from Montreal to Mobile—Cahokia, Kaskaskia, Fort de Chartres, and Biloxi on the Gulf. These were the centers of what civilized living could be managed, and the social and cultural pattern was a feudal one. The *seigneur* and the *curé* ruled their flock in stiff paternal fashion, a tight theocracy which owned the best land and whose life alone made any pretense to be a far echo of Paris—the latest in clothes, a few pieces of imported furniture, a musician to play for the dancing—while the fur traders went up and down the rivers in hollowed-out pirogues and flat-keeled bateaux.

The Dutch enterprise began with Henry Hudson in 1609 and ended fifty-five years later when New Netherlands passed to the English. The Dutch West Indies Company, having dispatched farmers as well as traders in furs and skins to their ports along the Hudson,

New Amsterdam in 1660 (model)

Museum of the City of New York

Pioneer Village, Salem, Mass. (reconstruction)

Paul J. Weber photo

developed New Amsterdam from a walled fort to a small town, and the poet Jacob Steendam called New Netherlands a land of milk and honey. In high-pooped and broad-bottomed vessels, the Hollanders sailed from Cape Cod to Delaware Bay and up the Connecticut River. Along the Hudson were small villages and the manors of the patroons, with great stone houses for the lord and smaller cottages for his tenants. When the English took over, New Amsterdam became New York, Beverwyck was called Albany, and Wiltwyck was Kingston.

Before the Stuart restoration of 1660 there were six English centers on the Atlantic coast, two in the south and four in the north; shortly after the close of the century, twelve of them were strung along the eastern tidewater. The first James had chartered the London Company and those of Plymouth and Massachusetts Bay; the results were Jamestown in 1607, Plymouth thirteen years later, and Boston in 1630 with its scattered groups along the near-by Charles and Mystic rivers. New Hampshire was the northernmost of English settlements, and out of Massachusetts by way of pioneer enterprise and religious dissension came Connecticut and Rhode Island. From the Dutch, Finnish, Swedish, and English enterprises to the south were formed New Jersey, Pennsylvania, and Delaware. The Virginia Company had made the failure of Jamestown into the success of Virginia by heeding Captain Smith's call for fewer gentlemen and more men who could use their hands; what had been a corner of Virginia was Maryland, where the Calverts tried to reproduce the manors of England. A palisaded fort at Albemarle Point became Charles Town, thanks to a distinguished group of real-estate promoters.

The hands of Englishmen molded America more skillfully and in more enduring shapes than did those of Spaniards, French, and Dutchmen. They were more accomplished in the arts of mercantilism, and after the Roanoke fiasco they knew that more was needed for colony building than the enthusiasm of a few unprotected men and women. England was ruled by the court, the Anglican church, and the mighty landed aristocracy, and out of these came the promoters of colonization and the capital to sustain it, as the "handful of praysing saints" joined forces with merchants who "had an eye at a profitable Plantation." There were both learning and courtly experience in these leaders, both the power of wealth and the drive of intellect: in the aristocratic squire John Winthrop, who knew that the chosen few were of his sort; in Cotton Mather, keeper of other men's consciences; in Sir George Calvert, the Oxford graduate who became a convert to Catholicism and held titles in both English and Irish peerages; in humble and humane Roger Williams; in well-to-do William Penn, whose father was a courtier and who, though a radical, knew that the same land he chose for his experiment in human living could be sold or rented for profit.

The leaders were men so conspicuous and so convinced of their right to direct and dominate that it has been easy to write the colonial epic in terms of these few. Yet they were a handful only. With them were the hewers, the planters, the builders, humbler people driven westward by hard necessity; landless men of the lower middle class hungry for land; farmers and artisans; small traders; resourceless people who had to come as the servants of others and here work out their servitude. Their religious dissent was a weapon against the church-state caste in Europe, just as their respect for hard work, their insistence upon honest dealing, their shrewdness, and their temperance were virtues essential to survival, to the grasping of political power and social recognition. These were the rather stiff backbone of the American experiment, and most of them were not only Protestants but Calvinists—the Huguenots of France, the Dutch Reformed churchmen, the Scotch-Irish Presbyterians, the Puritans of England. When the Lutherans came later, and the Quakers, they differed from the earlier men in no essential way in moral earnestness, in hard thrift, in private ambition and stubborn individualism. It was these craftsmen, farmers, and small-scale businessmen, together with the more desperately poor of Europe, who not only built colonial America but sifted out, among Old World values and procedures, what was relevant to the undertaking.

The pioneers soon learned what Ferner Nuhn has called "the truth of function," as the American experience pulled one way and the European heritage the other. Colonial life developed its own patterns, but did so despite the efforts of the backward-looking to repeat, not invent, to control, not release, to preserve a past and not to create a future. For such men, whether titled lords or "Worthies of Christ," there could be no questioning the rule of the chosen few, nor the class divisions which made it workable. Neither the Calverts and Berkeleys of the South nor the Mathers of New England questioned the right of the few to rule the many; but questioners there were in growing numbers, and the conflicts of Europe found themselves transferred to a new field where many things favored the questioners.

The power of small groups of merchants and divines in Europe to direct the material and mental lives of men across the width of an ocean was bound to diminish. American land was unbelievably abundant and labor crucially needed; men could grow crops of tobacco and rice, produce superb lumber and build fisheries; the thrust of personal ambition could find play. Servants discovered that they could make their way from servitude to independence, even though slaves would take their place; artisans plied their crafts more freely and with greater reward than in crowded Europe; small merchants found that they need not be small cogs in a large commercial wheel; tenant farmers claimed and received their own pastures and fields. The old neat patterns—economic, social, religious, and political—could not for long be imposed on such a country, and the strength of the seaboard colonies, where Englishmen predominated, was in their realization of that truth, while Frenchmen clung to the seigneury, Dutchmen to the patroon system, and Spaniards to the encomienda.

The life of the mind, to be sure, was theologically directed, and booksellers ordered from Europe nothing more frivolous than *Bittner on the Psalms, Flavel on the Sacrament,* the Bible, and the Catechism. But even Protestantism, itself a quarreling with state control of men's consciences and the formalism of established ritual, had its left wing. While the Puritans, those "unspotted lambs of God," struggled to reform Anglicanism from within, the dissenters of Plymouth fought the effort of the Winthrops and the Mathers to set up their miniature absolutisms here. As time went on, to Puritan orthodoxy, to the Lutherans, and to the Calvinists were added other groups of men, dispossessed and discontented, whose colonizing motives were both religious and economic, wave upon wave of them arriving to complicate the picture and, as Samuel Butler remarked of Hudibras, to

> . . . prove their Doctrine Orthodox
> By Apostolic Blows and Knocks . . .
> As if Religion were intended
> For nothing else but to be mended.

There were even a few among the religious leaders themselves who glimpsed that the Protestant revolt had democratic implications. The mind of Cotton Mather dwelt upon them now and then, as he sought to temper his own preaching and writing to the "plainness, perspicacity and gravity" of which his father had spoken as a more suitable medium of communication with the common man. And Mather had his gadfly in John Wise of Ipswich, whose father had been an indentured servant, and who wrote that power is originally in the people. The Reverend Mr. Wise dared use the word "democracy" and to say it was a form of government "which the light of nature does highly value, and often directs to as most agreeable to the just and natural prerogatives of human beings."

While Puritan bickered with radical, and the mass of colonial mankind fought the climate and the stubborn soil, it was a foregone conclusion that the arts as Europe knew them would neither richly grow in that soil nor travel westward in the ships which, year by year, increased the numbers and diversity of the American. Culture, as Europeans thought of it, was possible only when society had its margin of leisure time, its wealth for patronage, its great central cities; and one could find none of these in seventeenth-century America. During the first two years of Plymouth Plantation, when Englishmen had "no inns to entertain and refresh their weatherbeaten bodies," Inigo Jones's superb Whitehall Banqueting House was built in London. In the year of 1642, when Adam Roelantsen, schoolmaster of New Amsterdam, moved from a log-and-bark cabin to a thatched house with several rooms, Rembrandt in old Amsterdam painted *The Night Watch.*

In Massachusetts Bay and on Manhattan Island, the first task was one of shelter, of self-defense and self-sustaining, and the farmers, artisans, and small traders to whom the task fell had been given, in the societies from which they came, meager opportunities to enjoy, possess, and patronize the arts. It had been possible for the more ambitious London merchant to get his portrait painted, to buy tapestries, to have brass and silver on his richly carved cupboards, and to pick up an occasional third-rate panel or painted allegory which the Netherlands exported for sale in the picture shops at Temple Bar and Charing Cross. Even in his less prosperous fellows, there was less than the complete artistic illiteracy which has been often presupposed: there were plays to be seen, and a rich popular literature to be enjoyed. But usefulness was the chief criterion of art in the year when Jamestown was founded and when, in England, one could read a broadside in praise of the "good hows-holder" who builds on rock, not sand, and who

> With a warie head and charie hand
> Provides (in tyme) for Hunger and for Cold:
> Not daintie Fare and Furniture of Gold,
> But handsom-holsome . . .

Nearly a century after the Plymouth landing, a New Englander reminded his fellows that use was still a first principle:

> It's more noble to be employed in serving and supplying the necessities of others, than merely in pleasing the fancy of any. The Plow-Man that raiseth Grain, is more serviceable to Mankind, than the Painter who draws only to please the Eye. The Carpenter who builds a good House to defend us from Wind and Weather, is more serviceable than the curious Carver, who employs his Art to please the Fancy.

These words betray more than a hard-headed recognition that, in a cold and hostile wilderness, first things must come first; they bear overtones of a deep-rooted suspicion of the finery, the extravagance, the amusements of the European ruling caste against which the mass of the colonists, themselves of the middle and lower levels of the old society, must fight for a life and eventually for a culture of their own.

The Protestantism of the great majority of settlers reinforced the utilitarianism which the new environment demanded, the historically bred distaste for symbols of social repression, and the poverty of aesthetic experience in men without means who had lived in provincial areas of Europe. A Protestant Europe could show Rembrandt, Cranach, Bach, and Luther's friend Dürer to prove that it was not hostile to the arts. Puritanism could be an aesthetic, but it had to be first a piety; and along with theocratic dominance of the colonial mind went theocratic insistence that Matter was of more concern than Manner. If the Protestant was suspicious of the painted metaphor, it was because his mind associated visual imagery with the pomp and magnificence of the church against which he had rebelled and the sensuous shapes and colors, both Catholic and Anglican, which diverted men's minds from the discovery of substantial truth. Calvin had warned that an image could become an end in itself. The impulse to create he acknowledged to be one of God's gifts to man, and the good servant should cultivate his talent, but truthfully and soberly: "Men should not paint or carve anything but such as can be seen with the eye; so that God's majesty, which is too exalted for human sight, may not be corrupted by fantasies which have no true agreement therewith." In this mood John Hunt complained that metaphors resembled the stained glass of popish cathedrals where the painting kept out the light.

Yet the Puritan mind was by no means closed to the beauty of the world around him; it disdained no way of discovering and proving, through the will and the probing intelligence, God's perfect creation, that total harmony which he saw in nature. It valued divine revelation but also human knowledge, and on occasion pursued the latter with an almost scientific thoroughness. Puritan literature reveals many a skirmish between a man's disciplined conscience and his instinctive delight in the natural world.

Out of those skirmishes in America came the poems of Anne Bradstreet and the flashing metaphors of Edward Johnson's *Wonder-working Providence.* In Shakespeare's England the best pictures had been written and not painted. So it was in post-Elizabethan America where Thomas Morton, that gay thorn in the side of Bradford and Winthrop, described nature's masterpiece at Massachusetts Bay in what was perhaps America's first landscape, even though it was in words, not pigment:

> I did not thinke that in all the knowne world it could be paralel'd, for so many goodly groves of trees, dainty fine round rising hillucks, delicate faire large plaines, sweete crystall fountaines, and cleare running streames that twine in fine meanders through the meads, making so sweete a murmuring noise to heare as would even lull the senses with delight a sleepe, so pleasantly doe they glide upon the pebble stones, jetting most jocundly where they doe meete and hand in hand runne downe to Neptunes Court, to pay yearely tribute which they owe him as soveraigne Lord of all the springs.

The roistering Morton of Merry Mount was scarcely the typical Puritan, and more than one generation would live and die in New England before his delight in nature would find painted expression. Meanwhile the official aesthetic would prevail, and the Protestant would avoid that ornamentation of truths which, he believed, diminished their usefulness. He would love the morally good, and that which, like God's creation, had symmetry of form, and he would refuse to cultivate the two in separation from each other. He would call beautiful the thing which pleased his eye by its shape and satisfied his sense of the appropriate by the inner fitness of its parts, the obvious and useful function of its forms. When he preached or wrote, his style attempted to be correct, masculine, nervous, and striking, not a "loose Harangue and confus'd huddle of words"; let a sermon or a tract be plain, perspicacious, and grave; let polish and ornament grace the playhouse, not degrade the pulpit or the study.

The Puritan enjoyed a restrained finery in dress and furnishings, provided men of small means did not assume the garb of gentlemen; and he built, painted, and carved in the same spirit. His churches austerely performed their function as places for congregation, not fabrics to be loaded with stone saints. His architect was the "good carpenter"; his sculptor was the man who gave a slight richness to hewn beams or provided a suitable death's-head for gravestones. His painter made coats of arms, shop signs, and coffin decorations for those who could afford them, not allegories which the human eye had never seen, nor Biblical episodes which implied a knowledge of God beyond the layman's reach. His portraits limned men as they looked and moved; in the original or in the engravings made from them, they perpetuated the valiance, austerity, and social rank of their distinguished subjects.

These forms alone, during the first century of the American experiment, testified to the fact of men's innate creative powers and their impulse to put experience into form. They also proved that the Puritans, as John Adams once said, were "a sensible people." They believed in art, but believed in it with reservations.

CHAPTER 1 / THE SERVICEABLE CARPENTER

The sequence of colonial architecture was a sequence of necessity and moved from the improvised shelter of a defensive outpost to the constructed dwelling and thence to the church or house of a planned community with a perceived future. Whenever the frontier moved forward, this sequence repeated itself: years after the coastal region had comfortably and even elegantly housed itself, the pioneer forms were built by Frenchmen along the Kaskaskia and the Wabash; at the junction of the Ohio and the Muskingum in 1788, Rufus Putnam repeated the fortress enclosure of the previous century with its corner blockhouses and its stockade. To know the log houses of the Swedes and Finns on the Delaware, which have disappeared, one must study their descendants in North Carolina and on the midwestern fringe of eighteenth-century civilization.

From the first, no pre-existing form, however greatly cherished, could be imposed on a land where the sophisticated foreigner had much to learn from the experienced aborigine, a land which yielded some materials at once and others only in time, and which had a climate and a configuration of its own. Each nation behaved in its own way: the Frenchman scarcely got beyond the frontier phase of building before his venture failed; the Spaniard's presidio and mission were a magnificent fusion of what he brought with what he found; the Hollander, the Swede, and the Englishman made little use of Indian craft, but after the first months of the new life wrought in the home style to the extent of their ability.

First there were huts and hovels while men sought a toe hold in the wilderness, digging themselves into caves and pits on hillsides and river banks, or pitching tents which they covered with ship's canvas. When Charlestown in Massachusetts had become a place of streets and houses, people would recall that Captain Green and his friends of 1630 had been glad to lodge in empty casks against the weather. John White's "necessary and decent" dwellings on Roanoke Island were probably for the most part huts whose walls were stakes driven into the earth, interwoven with branches and daubed with clay. The Dutch West India Company learned from its agent how men in New Amsterdam dug pits in the earth, floored and lined them with wood, and erected roofs of spars thatched over with sods or bark. On St. George's River in what was destined to be Maryland, the settlers simply moved into shelters which the Indians had left behind them; at Jamestown a three-sided stockade and a church were built in ancient Anglo-Saxon fashion with palisades or puncheons reinforced with wattles and clay.

There was some resemblance at Jamestown between the medieval "cruck" method of bending trees into an arc and thatching the odd shape thus made, and the building habits of the Indians. In Massachusetts Bay, where Thomas Morton envied the savages their freedom from that care which torments the minds of Christians, Morton described how the red men planted a circle of poles, curved them toward one another, lashed them with walnut bark, and covered the beehive-shaped structure with mats of reeds or flags, with an opening left for smoke.

Not otherwise did John Endecott and his sixty companions build at Naumkeag before Winthrop came, except that their wigwams early acquired a door or a window and, at one end, a log-constructed chimney with a stone fireplace. Here in the first months, as Edward Johnson described them, the Salem band "made shift to rub out the Winters cold by the Fireside . . . turning down many a drop of the Bottell, and burning Tobacco with all the ease they could, discoursing betweene one while and another, of the great progresse they would make after the Summers-Sun had changed the Earths white furr'd Gowne into a greene Mantell."

With spring would come the "breaking up of bushy ground," and the "toyl of erecting houses, for themselves and cattell, in this howling desart." From Cape Ann across the bay Governor Endecott floated his "fayre house" to the Salem shore; and already Berkeley on the James had two "English houses," and Jamestown two rows of them. At Fort Amsterdam, a Dutchman wrote in 1628 that they were beginning to build houses in place of "the hovels and huts in which heretofore they huddled rather than dwelt." The Swede soon ate his Christmas porridge and drank his Jule-skoal in a snug cabin of logs.

Whether in New England or on the James River, the form of the framed dwelling did not greatly vary. Within a few years of the first rude shelters, bricks were made in the colonies; saws were available for turning logs into planks, and lime for making mortar; glass window panes replaced oiled cloth and paper. To frame the northern or the southern dwelling, logs must be hand-hewn to a square or rectangular section; wall frames were joined as units on the ground, raised to position, and fixed with pins. Upon them rose the steep roof timbers to form a one-story dwelling with one or two rooms below and a loft above. The walls were made solid by filling the spaces between beams with wattle-and-daub, brick, or plaster; the outer sheathing was of planks or hand-split clapboards. The rooms inside were sheathed with planks, their edges plain or molded, laid horizontally or vertically.

The "fayre house" of an Endecott or a Winthrop rose above its fellows with two full stories under its thatched roof of rushes; stairs wound against its central chimney, and rooms opened on both sides of its narrow entry. Along the James stood cottages which proclaimed their medieval English origin in their timber frames, cased over with plaster, clapboarding, and shingles. John Hammond observed that they were "contrived so delightfully that your ordinary houses in England are not so handsome, for usually the rooms are large, daubed and white limed, glazed and flowered, and if not glazed windows, shutters which are made very pritty and convenient." The cabins that hugged Fort Amsterdam were likewise framed of timber with thatched roofs and sides of bark, until the schoolmaster Adam Roelantsen in the 1640's could plan a dwelling eight feet high whose walls were clapboarded.

The garrison house of the seventeenth century was not framed, but solidly built of hewn logs, piled on one another and interlocking at its corners. Scandinavia had known the log house for centuries as an ordinary dwelling, and it was doubtless the Swedes and Finns of the Delaware who built the first of them here. A fortified dwelling with a second story projecting over the first and small openings designed for muskets, it was not unfamiliar in the Dutch and English settlements, and the McIntire garrison house at Scotland, Maine, preserves the type, firm on its stone foundation, its walls under their clapboards formed of hewn logs seven and a half inches thick.

Comparatively scarce in these first decades were structures of solid brick. Stone, used much as it came from the fields, was first a foundation for wooden houses or material for a chimney and a hearth; but less than ten years after the "dorp" of New Amsterdam had been founded, five West India Company workshops, wholly constructed of stone, made their wooden neighbors look old-fashioned.

During the final quarter of the century, there was abundant proof along the eastern seaboard of the third phase of the building sequence. A structure could go higher and spread wider; the perilous wooden chimney could be discarded for one of stone or brick; the roof could be covered with shingle, slate, or tile, the windows filled by wooden or iron casements with leaded diamond-shaped glass panes. The good householder could now refine upon necessity, and his "handsom-holsome" dwelling differentiated itself from its neighbors, proclaiming his national origins and symbolizing his position in the community. Despite elaboration, his edifice proclaimed its materials and its manner of building with a terse honesty which was not to be found in the more loquacious architecture which his sons and grandsons would create.

The ideals of the colonial Englishman were summed up by Stephen Vincent Benét when he wrote in *Western Star:*

> And those who came were resolved to be Englishmen,
> Gone to the world's end, but English every one.

His fathers under Elizabeth, and under the medieval Tudors before her, had devised a language of forms which was now to become a provincial dialect. In well-remembered English towns, sharp gables seemed to jut in all directions, huddled and planless, the second story built out over the first and supported by brackets richly and often humorously carved. The long façade of the dwelling might be broken by a central gable thrust forward with an entrance porch beneath it. Walls were lively with the dark pattern of timbers contrasting with the lighter plaster between them, itself on occasion molded with intricate relief. To what was steep and irregular, a further liveliness was added by carved pendants or drops at corners, carved ornaments at the peaks of gables, and by chimneys which, instead of rising in a simple four-sided stack, went up side by side to make a clustered form. The stairway inside had pendants too, and bulbous, turned balusters; and the paneled walls, or the surfaces of chests, cupboards, and chairs, were emphatic with the scrolls, rosettes, and lozenges which Flemish and Italian carvers grafted upon English Gothic structure.

There was only a dim echo of all this in the 1640's when Joshua Hempstead of New London framed his three-roomed dwelling whose thick walls were filled with brick and eelgrass. Its cellar was of quarried stone, its roof steep of pitch with a Tudorlike gable on both sides. Against its great chimney stairs were built, and from north to south ran the summer beam with chamfered edges. Its enlargement through the next seventy-five or a hundred years was typical of countless others: the doubling of its length by a wing which made the chimney a central one; the raising of the roof to a less

"Witch House," by S. Bartol (conjectural)

Essex Institute, Salem, Mass.

steep angle, the disappearance of the gables, the lean-to built against the back of the house to give its northern roof a long slope downward, until the home of Joshua Hempstead the diarist, with its dozen chambers, lost all resemblance to its humbler beginnings.

In every settled community of New England men built plain boxlike homes with no ornament at all, while others could afford gables, overhang, carved pinnacles, and pendants. Jonathan Corwin of Salem doubtless inherited his father's Turkey-work chairs, brass andirons, and damask linen; toward the close of the century he presided at the witchcraft trial where Salem people were accused of "high and dreadful things." His remodeled house of the sixteen-seventies bristled with peaked gables, finials, and drops; it overhung at each floor, both side and end, and its plain door of thick planks studded with nails gave entrance under a projecting porch chamber. On the Connecticut River at Northampton, Judge Samuel Sewall's friend, the Reverend Solomon Stoddard, built in this fashion.

John Ward House, Salem, Mass

Wayne Andrews photo

In the cold upper bedroom of a similar house in Charlestown, Sewall himself lay one January night and meditated on "Heaven the home not made with hands, which God had richly furnished with saints," hoping that he would some day be "entertained in that Magnificent Convenient Palace."

Persistently medieval some forty years after the first Hempstead house were the "Old Ship" Church at Hingham and the home of Topsfield's Parson Capen. The former had a porch, and its roof sloped up from four sides, hip fashion, to a flat deck with a turret. Later congregations rebuilt the squarish meetinghouse for greater width, replaced the turret with a belfry, and hid with a ceiling its Gothic network of beams and braces. Nearly three hundred years before in that miracle of carpentry, the roof of London's Westminster Hall, a width of nearly seventy feet had been spanned by the builders; here in Hingham the horizontal tie beams were forty-five feet long. From their centers rose great king posts; sharing the weight from above with the roof rafters, curved struts made a pointed arch and carried the thrust down to small struts below, until the Gothic whole, which has been revealed by the removal of the old ceiling, looked indeed like the inside of a ship seen upside down.

The Reverend Joseph Capen's house of 1683 was of the better sort, thanks to a prosperous father-in-law. Brackets of pleasing profile stood beneath its projecting second story; its door was of studded planks with hinges and lock of iron, and the carved pendants from its corners were shaped like inverted tulips. From the steeply pitching roof whose gable ends had bargeboards rose a chimney so generous in proportion that one is not surprised to find its kitchen fireplace spanning one half the length of a wall. The Capen interior continually reminds one that this is a construction of framed timbers: the exposed corner posts, the summer beams with chamfered edges, the oak lintel, sixteen inches square, over the fireplace. The molded edges of horizontal and vertical sheathing in the two downstairs rooms suggested status, as did the four stout turned balusters of oak on the parson's stairway.

Boston's streets twisted as narrowly under beetling gables as those of London, although nothing but their pattern now remains. The plastered front of the old "Feather Store" in Dock Square was ornate with molded relief; on a triangular plot near by was a brick warehouse which could have stood in old Plymouth or Bristol. Boston taverns—the King's Arms and the Blue Anchor among them—were as abundant as in the home cities, and the "substantial and comely" town houses overhung the street with rows of pillars to support them. On the slope toward Beacon Hill was the brick Province House whose many gables were shaped in alternating curves and straight lines, and whose chimneys had half a dozen flues, a medievalism soon to disappear when the structure was remodeled. Across the Charles in Cambridge, the Harvard College building of wood was shaped like the letter E, and under its bell turret were studies, a kitchen, chambers for students, a library, and a great hall.

New England's sister colony on the James moved swiftly from the merely protective to the substantial and comely. Sir Thomas Gates brought his harsh "Divine, Moral and Martial Laws" to Jamestown, but he brought also blacksmiths, carpenters, and brickmakers. The fifth church there, whose ruined brick tower still stands, was finished in the 1640's, replacing earlier ones of wood; its windows had leaded diamond panes, its floor was paved with brick tiles, and its tower, entered through open arches, had a wooden spire. Both St. Luke's in Isle of Wight County, Virginia, and the second Bruton church in what was to become Williamsburg were curiously Gothic, the pointed windows of the former being the only surviving examples of their kind.

The small southern planter contented himself with a dwelling of two or three rooms and a loft; his more prosperous rival boasted as many as eight rooms. In the former class was Christopher Pearson, who died in 1698, and whose possessions are listed by Wertenbaker in *The First Americans:* three bedsteads with feather beds, pillows, bolsters, and blankets; a few pewter plates; an old warming pan, three chairs, and a table, a cheese-press, pots, and looking glass; and enough domestic

Seventeenth Century Room (based on Capen House, Topsfield, Mass.)

Metropolitan Museum of Art, New York City

odds and ends to total nearly twenty-six pounds. Only five years after he came to Virginia as an indentured servant, Adam Thoroughgood built in Princess Anne County an unassuming brick house of five rooms whose south end chimney was stepped back as it went upward; over its windows and on its end wall glazed headers were used to make patterns in the brick surfaces.

In contrast to this yeoman simplicity stood the homes of a small group of Virginians who in the closing years of the century controlled life in the colony, a class which included William Fitzhugh, Sir William Berkeley, and the first William Byrd. Fitzhugh, son of a famous English barrister, owned twenty-nine slaves and a thousand-acre plantation, and remarked that his many-winged dwelling, with its twelve or thirteen rooms, its great hall, and its study filled with books, was furnished with all that made for a comfortable and gentle living. Four of his best rooms were hung with paper or cloth, and beside the long table in his hall stood cupboards sparkling with silver plate; behind the mansion stood its dairy, kitchen, and dovecot, its stables, orchard, and garden.

Berkeley, whose arrogant struggle against the desperate followers of Nathaniel Bacon is part of the colonial story, lived at Green Spring in a brick house whose wide central hall held a copy of its owner's portrait by Sir Peter Lely. In the year 1676, Bacon's rebels seized the brick residence of Arthur Allen, built some twenty years before in lower Surrey County; and Thomas T. Waterman has called "Bacon's Castle" a "miraculous survival," the only high-Jacobean structure remaining in this country. A projecting stair tower at the rear and an entrance porch on the front gave it a cross plan; its gable ends were fashioned in alternating steps and curves, and the triple stacks of its end chimneys were set diagonally. The old English skill with brick had gone into its walls, and bricks cut and molded to various shapes made ornamental patterns over its doorway, and accented its window heads and the contours of its gables. Inside, there were crossed girders whose panel effect approximated a Tudor ceiling.

A drawing of New Amsterdam by Visscher in 1651 reveals that the Dutch, like their neighbors north and south, were not above nostalgia. The whole town was

Bacon's Castle, Surrey County, Va.

Historic American Buildings Survey, Library of Congress

vaguely Hollandish with its stepped gables, its occasional windmill, and its Broad Street ditch which would shortly serve as a canal and be named after the Heeren-Gracht in old Amsterdam, its new belfried church in the fort, its neat vegetable gardens and fruit orchards. Below the palisade on Wall Street was a rather jumbled pattern of roads whose curves the modern city has retained. The home of Adam Roelantsen had two doors, a staircase entry, a pantry, and a built-in bed; beside its portal were two benches, and its rooms were wainscoted. Men richer than Roelantsen sat on Spanish leather or Turkey-work chairs, ate from Delft china, and kept their belongings in wooden chests and wardrobes with bright flowers painted on them. Brick houses, gable-end to street as in the crowded homeland towns, were elbowed by Augustyn Heerman's tobacco warehouse, whose thick walls went up three full stories to a loft. On the eastern shore stood the City Tavern of stone which was soon to become the Stadt Huys with a cupola, bell, and weathercock.

Albany men varied their brick end-gables with the mouse-tooth pattern, laid the bricks in patterns over windows, and made visual decoration of the iron wall-anchors that held their structures together. The stone house of the Hudson Valley, whether modest town dwelling or manor farm, was plain, solid, and squat, with thick walls of irregular stone, stout window shutters, and a roof pitched steeply enough to make a loft over the single story, as in Kingston's Old Senate House, which was built during the last quarter of the century. In spite of later alterations, the Van Cortlandt manor at Croton-on-the-Hudson still keeps the long, low Dutch roof line, thick stone walls, and defensive loopholes of its first construction in the sixteen sixties.

In the middle region, brotherly love saw green lawns and gardens in William Penn's checkerboard plan for Philadelphia, but was not averse to turning an extra penny by putting four houses in a block designed for one. Robert Turner wrote to William Penn in 1685 that Philadelphians were "building to admiration," and described his own three-story home of brick, claiming that it was the first of its kind. Christopher White's brick house in New Jersey, now known through verbal descriptions and a drawing, was an odd structure thirty feet long and twenty deep, two stories high; at one end was a square tower to hold a stairway. The slope of its overhanging roof was repeated in the curious projections called "overshoots" which ran along its front at the level of the second story and were carried for a short distance around its ends. The yellow pine "breastplate" of White's fireplace was elaborately carved.

In Delaware and New Jersey the building styles of the Dutch and Swedes blended with English ones in the second half of the century. The log house sometimes went up two and a half stories, its upper half clapboarded, its roof shingled, and its stoop provided with a porch. The Swedish blockhouse at Naaman was a one-story fieldstone construction whose squat hipped roof, squarish windows, and rough-textured walls had a Dutch flavor.

Thus, gone to the world's end, did the European combine what he already knew with what the New World suggested to him or forced upon him. If William Fitzhugh's hall was bare and bleak in comparison with his father's, and if the rooms one sees in the paintings of De Hoogh, with tiled floors and high-breasted chimney pieces under their beamed ceilings, found only an approximation in New Amsterdam, it was not for lack of trying. And like house, like furnishings. The poor man built his own stools, bedsteads, and trestled tables with whatever skill in the essentials of framing and joining he had or could borrow from a carpenter; the rich man ordered his household goods from his English or Continental agent. At a time when westbound ships carried mahogany and walnut furniture to southern colonial ports, New England invoices more often listed porringers, gridirons, brass kettles, buttons, and mousetraps. As soon as the first towns took form, trained craftsmen set up shop; they invented new ways of rendering traditional designs in oak and pine and, in their effort to condense and simplify, created something new.

The American chair, chest, or cupboard, like its English ancestor, was Gothic in construction and eclectic in decoration. The Jacobean "wainscot chair" was built like its medieval prototypes, and its paneled back, topped by Flemish scrolls and Italian finials, was a hodgepodge of carved motives both geometric and floral. A specimen in the Metropolitan Museum may have been carved in England and assembled here, since few local joiners had sufficient time and skill to produce so elaborate a piece.

In homes without closets, the wooden chest, with or without drawers, became a staple piece. The simplest of its species was a plain box on legs, with a hinged lid; the finer chests were paneled and enlivened with carving—the round arch, the diamond-shaped lozenge, the rosette, the ropelike *guilloche,* the S-shaped scroll. Other pieces were enriched by applied bits of molding, split balusters and pendant drops, the relief pattern emphasized by a staining of various colors—red, yellowish-brown, and black. Similar in construction and ornament were chests of drawers standing on turned ball feet, and the still taller pieces, raised upon six turned legs with gracefully curved braces, which the next century would call highboys.

The skill of the provincial craftsman varied. Thomas Dennis was an accomplished carver and joiner; the resourceful Nicholas Disbrowe of Hartford framed his chests in the traditional manner and decorated them with his own version of the tulip-and-leaf, cutting away the surface of the wood to make his shapes stand out, and using color to accent his pattern. Up the Connecticut Valley in Hatfield, Deerfield, and Hadley, carpenters soon learned to speak Disbrowe's language with an accent of their own, and at the turn of the century produced a boxlike piece whose sides were carved, incised, and stained with the "Connecticut sunflower," the inverted heart, the lively scrolls, the curious leaf form with its ribs scratched into the wood, and the owner's initials in the center panel. Painted rather than chiseled were the fruits, flowers, and ribbons, the tulips, pinks, and parrots on the cupboards, chests, and mirrors of the Dutch colonials.

On the whole, the "serviceable carpenter" continued through these years to be more welcome in the colonies than the "curious carver." It was appropriate that a Virginia nabob who claimed the right to a coat of arms should have it cut into the top of his tomb, but many heraldic gravestones of the plantation country seem too accomplished in execution to be the work of local craftsmen. Northern communities, however, kept men like Joseph Lamson of Ipswich busy all their lives, and after him three generations of his family. Lamson cut the naked bodies of little winged men who lowered a coffin into the earth, and on the sides of his stones were borders of figs and pomegranates. Less competent carvers incised death's-heads with a few sharp curves and straight lines, and made angel faces with circles for eyes and a triangle for a nose; and the tombstone maker's repertory included skeletons, scythes, and hourglasses. Beside King's Chapel is a slab of 1678 on which nearly every emblem of the craft is displayed: a winged skull, rosettes, baroque scrolls, and a panel in which Father Time struggles to prevent Death from snuffing out Life's candle.

Such artisans could turn their skill to the cutting of wooden cherubs' heads for both sides of Sewall's gateway, and one of them earned nine pounds for carving a pew for King's Chapel in 1698. In England during these same years Grinling Gibbons carved mantels and overdoors of unbelievable complexity for Belton, Hampton Court, and Windsor. One can compare his swags and sprays of hunting horns, pheasants, rabbits, snails, carrots, and lobsters with the sober and well-considered plan of a Boston gravestone, where clustered fruits and leaves are quietly and forcefully embedded in their spaces beside the crisp and finely spaced inscription. The one is sheer exhibitionism, belying its material; the other has the "plainness, perspicacity, and gravity" of a Puritan sermon.

Carved chest, Connecticut type

Metropolitan Museum of Art, New York City

CHAPTER 2 / THE LIMNER

Baffling and obscure are the beginnings of the painter's craft in America's first century, when the struggle for a settled and secure new life allowed small margin for the luxury of the painted likeness and still less for pictured allegory or the "landskip." The professional of the Old World can have felt slight temptation to set up his easel in one of these struggling towns, or to ply his art coastwise in a day when communities were isolated from one another.

Among portraits imported rather than locally produced was the long, lean face of Governor Winthrop, whose intelligent eyes and fine gentleman's hands suggest more than a native competence, and may well have been done for him in Europe by an artist who had learned his lesson from Van Dyck. The rather astringent realism of the Dutchman Van der Spriett is to be seen in the austere *Increase Mather* (Mass. Hist. Soc.), painted during a visit to London in the sixteen eighties. Sir Richard Saltonstall's much-copied portrait was once said to have come from Rembrandt's studio, but bears no trace of the gifted hand which at the same period produced *The Man with a Falcon.* The descendants of Burgomaster Cornelis Steenwyck believed that his likeness, of which two versions exist, was painted during a visit to old Haarlem, where lived his brother-in-law, the artist Jan Van Goosen; but one cannot be sure that New Amsterdam did not already possess in the sixteen sixties a man who could render the sharply accused planes of this shrewd face, and the small view of Manhattan in its scrolled cartouche at the bottom of the larger picture.

In England, men who were close to court circles and affluent enough to patronize the more up-to-date and fashionable painters could sit to Daniel Mytens, Cornelis Johnson, or even the stylish Sir Peter Lely; if they sailed for Maryland or Virginia, they could take the originals or copies of them to grace the halls of their plantations. Johnson had acquired enough of the Van Dyck elegance to suit the poet George Sandys, and there was a courtly blend of dignity with grace in Daniel Mytens when he portrayed George Calvert. Lely was a more practiced pictorial diplomat than either, and the likenesses of several Virginians have been ascribed to him.

While these accomplished technicians were turning out "cavalier" likenesses, busy in American towns were a handful of more modest craftsmen whose work but faintly echoes that skill and that spirit, and most of whom prolong in the New World a concept which was already old-fashioned in the Old, or had become provincial. They painted as though Van Dyck, who came to England two years after the Plymouth venture, had not revolutionized the painting of his adopted country. In their minds were the forms and conventions which had gone before, that curious blend of medieval pattern-and-line which the very name of "limner" connotes, with the more sculptural approach of the Dutch and Flemish artists upon whom England of the Tudors and Jacobeans largely depended.

Wave upon wave of northerners had descended on the English coast to accommodate their Flemish method to the English temper. Holbein's sumptuous canvases, the tempered modeling of hands and faces which he knew how to combine with intricacy of dress and jewelry in the works of his English years, were a model for lesser men—for John Bettes when he portrayed Edmund Butts with some of that silken delicacy, for Lucas de Heere of Ghent and Marc Gheeraerts the Younger when they painted Queen Elizabeth or Lady Sidney and her family, stiff with brocade and lace-edged ruffs, no flower of a dress neglected, no smallest detail of necklace or stomacher unspecified. Nicholas Hilliard and Isaac Oliver, in small-scale likenesses, worked with the elegant intricacy of the medieval illuminator, the same delight in sensitive contour and colored pattern-making; and if Elizabeth favored Hilliard, there were doubtless both aesthetic and personal reasons why she approved his avoidance of shadows.

More concerned with the human exterior, to the point of unflinching realism, was Elizabeth's sergeant painter George Gower, whose self-portrait presented, not the silhouette of a man, but a plain man in three dimensions. And in the decades which followed the first Puritan migrations, there were English painters who had caught some of the refinements of Van Dyck but could record the Puritan in all his stern gravity; Robert Walker's *Oliver Cromwell* is famous, and in 1651 he is said to have done the likeness of Edward Winslow, the Governor of Plymouth Colony, who was in London at that time.

In England also labored a host of inconspicuous craftsmen who could produce a florid coat of arms for a rich man's coach or a signboard for a tavern, and for whom the making of a likeness was but one variation of their craft. It was those all-but-nameless limners, both English and Continental, who either came to the new country or were bred here and whom one calls America's first painters.

A New England limner, if he had any acquaintance with English work, could choose between the Renaissance illusion of a third dimension, for which some skill in light and shade was essential, and the more ancient concept of the flat plane and the filled-in pattern. He was more likely, being a provincial, to choose the latter. To see nature as areas bounded, and distinguishable by their colored shapes, was the simplest way of seeing and the least likely to trip him technically. In these earliest likenesses the rather remote dignity, the impersonality of English limning struggled with the sense of individual character which was always at the back of the Protestant mind. There was less temptation to stress finery in New England than in the England of the Tudors and the Stuarts; Puritan opinion frowned on such display, refusing to permit men and women of mean condition to take upon themselves the garb of gentlemen, and only reluctantly allowing the chosen few to display "gold or silver lace or buttons, or points at their knees, and to walk in boots," or their women to wear silk or tiffany.

Whether he drew a coat of arms or a head and shoulders, the limner thought of his board or canvas not as a window looking into space, but as a solid flat surface on which to trace, maplike, the shapes he saw before him. He saw light, if conscious of it at all, not as an active element breaking up his field of vision, but as something which, bathing the object, made it clear to him. Color he saw neither as drama nor as atmosphere; he saw it as a means of distinguishing one thing from another, and of giving to each object its own character in appropriate tint and texture. Our early limner set a value on the unvarnished recording of hard-bitten men, of sturdy women and of children who looked like miniature men and women. As he proceeded to paint those few colonial personalities who were important enough to have their likenesses made, he depicted not the accidents of light and shadow, but those elements which he knew to be permanent in the sitter.

Who were these first limners? A few tantalizing references to their identity are all we have; paintings without names and names without paintings. The scholarship of Alan Burroughs drew certain tentative conclusions with regard to identity and attribution; Oskar Hagen has discussed these near mysteries in the light of aesthetic-formal principles and his knowledge of European sources; most recently, James T. Flexner has provided a lively picture of the limner in his colonial environment.

One has only the name, for example, of Joseph Allen, cited in 1684 by Nathaniel Mather. No portrait can safely be attributed to Tom Child, a maker of signs and funeral hatchments, and a self-styled "painter-stainer." Child decorated gun carriages for Castle Williams and was not above painting a fence for a Boston schoolmaster; and when he died in 1706, Samuel Sewall noted the fact, adding this jingle:

> Tom Child had often painted Death,
> But never to the Life, before:
> Doing it now, he's out of Breath;
> He paints it once, and paints no more.

John Foster, who rather crudely engraved Richard Mather in wood, was evidently a painter too; but only a few formal similarities connect him with the oil portraits of John Davenport and John Wheelwright.

Was Jeremiah Dummer, the silversmith, also a painter? One no longer credits his signature on two portraits of Dummer and his wife, nor even the identity of the subjects. Who was Lawrence Brown, a limner applying in 1701 for permission to live in Boston? And one has only the dubious signature of "N. Byfield" on a presumed portrait of Richard Middlecot to suggest that a limner of that name existed.

Among the Dutch ghosts are Jacobus Strycker, a tailor who may or may not have painted, and Henri Couturier, who possessed portraits of Peter Stuyvesant and his sons when he became a burgher of New Amsterdam in 1663. In Virginia, one would like to know more about Thomas Powell, who received five hundred pounds of tobacco in 1679 for "draweing the Cherubim" for a church at Poplar Spring which has disappeared; one would like to identify the man for whom, nineteen years later, William Fitzhugh ordered six frames, some colors, and canvases to "set up a painter."

Existing works reveal the artistry of the period, if not the artists' names, and a significant contrast can be drawn between the three portraits of the Gibbs children in 1670 by an unknown limner and the self-likeness of Thomas Smith, probably done some twenty years later. Both painters were devoid of easy sophistication, of flexibility or fully rounded forms; they were either slightly trained in European ways or not at all.

Each of the Gibbs children—Robert, Henry, and Margaret—posed with dignity on the black-and-white squares of a tiled floor and was drawn with clarity, a pleasure in the contrast of bright with somber tones, and an awareness of the youngster's fragile charm. The dress of Margaret is white against a red-brown drapery, and a livelier red appears in the ribbons which bind her yellow curls, the drawstrings of her sleeves, the bows and soles of her white shoes.

There is no tenderness in the self-portrait of Thomas Smith the mariner, whose gray hair curls around a seamed and not too sensitive face, the blue eyes in their

Unknown limner, *Henry Gibbs*

Courtesy Mrs. Alexander Q. Smith

strongly marked lids hard with calculation, the crow's-feet and the double chin keenly observed and sharply recorded, the whole canvas an assembling of elements rather than an organized whole—a bit of drapery and tassel, the red corner of a brass-studded chair, the fall of lace in startling contrast to the brown-black coat, the ships joining battle beyond the window. A skull which seems to have been borrowed from a gravestone rests upon a paper where Smith's own verse has been lettered precisely: "Why why should I the World be minding, therein a World of Evils Finding," and—perhaps with reference to the smoke, the fortress, and the sinking ship over his shoulder—"Farwell thy Jarres thy Joies thy Toies thy Wiles thy Warrs."

Thus did one limner respond to youth with an eye sensitive to pattern, and the other to hard-bitten age with some power to grasp receding forms and to suggest depth and distance. Around these can be grouped other paintings. The hand which drew the Gibbs children, for example, must have traced the two Freake likenesses. The fastidious fingers of *John Freake* grasp soft white gloves and play with the pendant of his Venetian lace collar. He is an attorney and merchant of repute in Boston; and when an explosion of gunpowder aboard a ship in the harbor has ended his forty prosperous years, his tombstone will carry his coat of arms. Deep brown, black, and delicately silver are the tones of his portrait. His coat has silver braid and buttons, his frilled sleeves are puffed, his brown curls frame a young sensitive face with the slightest of mustaches. The whole man is as reticent as the color of his likeness, the face and hands against rich darkness as prudently placed as no doubt his investments were.

Freake's lady in a companion piece is Elizabeth, the daughter of merchant Thomas Clarke of North Square, and the artist has lingered over the gold and white embroidery of her red underskirt, the intricate lace at her neck, the small red-and-black bows which gather her sleeves. Her hair is blonde above a thin pale face; her hands, though not "correctly" drawn, are drawn with expressive tenderness, holding the six-months-old baby whose dress of creamy yellow completes a harmony which must have been instinctively felt by its author.

One can distinguish between this "Freake limner" and the man who saw two-year-old Alice Mason against a tiled background (Adams Mem. Soc.) and who put three other Mason children in one canvas in 1670, lining them up across the picture space in the manner of English group likenesses. *Elizabeth Paddy Wensley* (Pilgrim Hall), with her wooden arms and her stiffly drawn puffed sleeves, is somewhat differently limned from any of this group; closer to the Freake limner are Edward Rawson and his daughter Rebecca (N. E. Hist. Gen. Soc.). Rawson, the tailor's son from Newbury who became Suffolk County Recorder because he was "a good yeoman and eloquent inditer," grasps his brocaded glove, and the eyes above his plain starched collar are both steady and intelligent; the rather weak chin and startled eyes of Rebecca remind us that she married

Capt. Thomas Smith, *Self-Portrait*

American Antiquarian Society, Worcester, Mass.

"Sir Thomas Hale" only to discover that he was plain Thomas Rumsey with a wife and two children in England, where he abandoned Rebecca, taking her wardrobe with him.

Captain Smith's mannerisms are to be found in a smaller group of canvases. If he painted *Maria Catherine Smith,* presumed to be his daughter, it was with a smoother handling of his pigment; and Maria does her New England best with charms which Lely would have made more provocative—the rounding lip, the brown curl on one shoulder, the breasts whose fullness here is only suggested. Miss Smith's relationship to the court hussies of Charles the Second is as noticeable as it is distant (Am. Antiq. Soc.).

The sterner side of Puritan life is reflected in the likenesses of *Captain George Curwen* (Essex Inst.) and *Major Thomas Savage.* Both of them grasp a stout cane and look boldly and a little contemptuously from their canvases; their hard features are presented with a confident accentuation which one associates with Thomas Smith. Close to the Savage painting are the strong forms of *Mrs. Patteshall and Her Child,* the firm planes and rounded bodies, the plodding thoroughness with which a space has been created.

If the Gibbs boys and girls, the Freakes, Smith, and Savage embody the superior status of a few lay persons, there is a series of reverend gentlemen which symbolizes theocracy in New England. *William Stoughton* (Harvard Univ.) is starched with self-righteousness to his fingertips. *John Davenport* (Yale Univ.), *John Wheelwright* (State House, Boston), and the so-called *John Cotton* (Conn. Hist. Soc.) may well have come from one easel, since a bleak austerity is common to all three. It was Davenport who explained his reluctance to leave New Haven by the remark that "it is ill transplanting a tree that thrives in the soyl"; it was Wheelwright who preached, he said, that "fire of the word that burneth up all unbelievers," and as a sympathizer with Anne Hutchinson raised what Winthrop called "doubtful disputations."

A limner with a lively sense of character made a mask of the so-called *Reverend Thomas Thacher* (Old North Church, Boston). Whether by deliberate or instinctive exaggeration, he drew the shadows wire-taut, edged the white stock with a ruler-straight line, and found massive shapes for the overlong nose, the long pursed lips, and the lantern jaw. One can well believe that this is the man who preached in Old South to such purpose that Sewall concluded "it was rather a privelege to dye, and therein be conformed to Christ, than remaining alive at his coming, to be changed." The same brush doubtless underscored the dim heavy-lidded eyes, the falling jowls, and skinny fingers of *Anne Pollard,* who boasted in 1721 that she had passed the century mark,

Unknown limner, *Ann Pollard*

Massachusetts Historical Society, Boston, Mass.

and recounted, between pipefuls, how she had been the first of Winthrop's band, as a girl of eight, to jump overboard and wade through the shallow water at Salem. To find, in the second decade of the eighteenth century, a painter so baldly unaware of newer styles in portraiture, and so intent on the thing seen and the character felt, is to know how tenacious was the limner's tradition in this region.

The New England fog is no thicker than that which obscures the beginnings of the painter's art in New Netherlands. Here also are several names, a group of portraits, and rather tenuous connections between them. Dutch character appears in the solid prose, the plain recording of externals in many of the portraits. The Dutch tenure of this region, however, was short-lived, and we have no such full-length character study of the founders of New Holland as of the ministers, captains, and first citizens of the English provinces.

The limners of New Amsterdam seem to have felt more at home than their colleagues to the north in that play of light and shadow which reveals structure. A clean, sure sense of planes was in the oval-framed head of testy Peter Stuyvesant, painted in the sixteen sixties by a man to whom James Flexner has given the name of Stuyvesant Limner (N. Y. Hist. Soc.). The face seems composed of angles—the powerful forward thrust of the beaked nose, the tight mouth corners, the sharp

Gerret Duyckinck (?), *Mrs. Gerret Duyckinck*

New York Historical Society

Unknown painter, *James Pierpont*

Yale University Art Gallery, New Haven, Conn.

cheek bone, the stiff collar, and the steel corselet under its shoulder drape.

Far homelier in their thin surface, their drawn rather than painted quality, their cautious handling of the brush, are two portraits of Gerret Duyckinck and his wife, painted at the end of the century, possibly by Gerret himself. The first Duyckinck was Evert, who came to the New World in the sixteen thirties as a limner and a craftsman who made and engraved glass; his son, the above Gerret, was a glazier, and the limner's trade was continued until nearly a century after Evert's arrival by Gerret's son, grandson, and nephew. Gerret and his lady, to judge by their likenesses, were the stolid, plain people whose unimaginative spirits were to be caricatured by Washington Irving: the man's plump face is only slightly rounded under its perfunctory wig; his unconvincing hand rises from the weakly rendered folds of his garment. The wife is unsparingly revealed as a homely person with turned-up nose and incipient double chin, one nerveless hand resting on a table, the other not quite grasping a stiff and awkwardly drawn cloak.

Assigned at present to an unknown limner with a character of his own are the so-called Provoost portraits of about 1700. The husband's head is more convincingly modeled as a whole than that of Gerret Duyckinck, and its features are delineated with more finality. The nose of Mrs. Provoost protrudes from her face, rather than being an outlined form within an area; her double chin actually doubles, and the light scarf which binds her head and is tied at her neck is substantial material with a texture of its own and a tactile salience in its folds.

When these likenesses were made, New Amsterdam had been New York for more than thirty years. Dutch plainness here, like Puritan rigidity in Massachusetts, was being modified by new ways of seeing and by more relaxed and versatile techniques as the colonial world began to catch up with elegances which Europe had known for some generations.

In England after the Commonwealth interlude, the florid and handsome tradition set by Van Dyck and by Lely had been resumed in the work of Sir Godfrey Kneller. This Anglo-German was capable of manufacturing an endless series of handsome portraits, with the help of his pupils and assistants, under the Restoration kings, the reigns of William and Mary, Queen Anne, and the first two Georges; after him Thomas Hudson and Thomas Highmore would maintain the Knelleresque conventions. Addison's poem salutes this arbiter of English portraiture:

> Thou, Kneller, long with noble pride,
> The foremost of thy art, hast vied
> With nature in a generous strife,
> And touched the canvas into life.
>
> Thy pencil has, by monarchs sought,
> From reign to reign in ermine wrought,
> And, in the robes of state arrayed,
> The kings of half an age displayed.

Unknown painter, *Caleb Heathcote*

New York Historical Society

Portrait by a limner of the N.Y. region

Col. and Mrs. Edgar W. Garbisch coll.

Not only monarchs but their subjects posed for the stately Kneller, whose "delusive hand" and whose "force of light and shade" won fulsome praise from the author of the *Spectator*. They posed with one hand on the hip or thrust into the waistcoat, the other holding a book, a sword, or any other appropriate object; behind them a pilaster or a classical temple could be seen through the trees. The features under cascading wigs were part of the general handsomeness and no more emphatic than the brittle conventions of highlights upon satin. Sir Godfrey kept, to be sure, his skill in modeling a man's face and hands, suggesting the glisten of his skin and the salience of his principal features; but in his portrait of Robert Hunter, Governor of New York and New Jersey, he took an equal pleasure in the hard glint of armor and in the plushy texture of a leopard skin which lined the governor's coat (N. Y. Hist. Soc.).

Thanks to the presence of a few paintings like this in colonial cities, and many engravings made from them, the limner's art after the turn of the century increasingly concerned itself with the note of impressiveness; the pattern-making sense of the Freake master, the stark simplifications of Thomas Smith, and the literal prose of the Dutchmen gave way to a more fused and limpid quality. *James Pierpont* of 1711 is no ruthless expounder of theology but a grave and thoughtful personality with a hint of tenderness and of melancholy in his eyes; his wife, despite an awkward rigor in the shadows which define her face, has an implied feminine graciousness.

Caleb Heathcote, probably from the same brush, has worldly ostentation and a bland self-assurance. When it was done, Heathcote was about to become the Mayor of New York; his great estate was the lordship and manor of Scarsdale and he himself was the first vestryman of Trinity Church. The brush that painted this fastidious gentleman, who looked upon New Yorkers as rude heathens, not only sculptured the face with a sure touch, but lingered, varying its touch and movement, on the crisp curls of his long wig and the deft and simple indication of his gown. Even more Knelleresque in pose and handling is the suave and ruddy canvas which has been insecurely titled *Richard Middlecot.*

By the first quarter of the century important centers of colonial life gave patronage to artists with known names and personalities; the comfortable houses with their newfangled furnishings contained pictures whose authorship is no longer ambiguous. By the year 1725, Henrietta Johnston had produced a series of delicate, wan, pastel heads in Charleston, using a method which she probably learned in England. The Scotsman John Watson had been practicing his sketchy and unsubstantial version of the Kneller style for a decade in New Jersey and New York. The Swede Gustavus Hesselius had arrived at Wilmington a dozen years before,

Unknown limner, *Thomas Van Alstyne*

New York Historical Society

Peter Pelham was on his way to Boston. And in Boston, Sewall's diary noted the activity of Nathaniel Emmons, who in the twenties made small likenesses in blacks, whites, and grays, frankly translating the hand-on-hip, the sheen on silk, the steady gaze of English engravings of the Kneller type.

After some twenty years of activity in Maryland the German-born Justus Engelhardt Kühn died in 1717, leaving evidence of his limner's sense of pattern, his simple ways of achieving balance, his quiet color, and his delicacy in detail. His *Eleanor Darnall* does not quite detach herself from the balustrade behind her, and she forms an obvious pyramid with the dog beside her; but Kühn has placed her head effectively in an area of sky between draperies and a huge pot of flowers whose soft pinks, purples, and orange-reds are in muted contrast with the blue-and-white tiled floor on which the child stands. Kühn's love for accessories was nourished by engravings; hence the poplar groves, formal basins, prancing cupids, parrots, and luscious cherries which he painted with such relish in his backgrounds.

Kühn was not the only man of his time who thus combined old rigors with new sophistications. A kindred New York spirit, working in the twenties and thirties, gave charming airs and graces to the three children of Abraham and Margareta De Peyster (N. Y. Hist. Soc.). One boy gestures with a kind of miniature grandiloquence, while a dog looks up at him; another, dressed in a long red coat, strokes the head of a pet deer which has strayed into the picture from the park beyond. A rather implausible lamb observes small Miss De Peyster, who holds out a neat bouquet of flowers, standing on a terrace whose balustrade and urn look toward trees and river. The fine earlier directness, the conscientious draughtsmanship, the close relation of painter and subject are still here; and all three paintings derive much of their charm from the odd way in which the limner has solved his own problems of perspective, of folded drapery, of indoor-outdoor relationships.

More rugged are the presentments of Hudson Valley burghers and their wives, dressed for the most part in sober browns and reds, who posed with unshakable dignity for a group of limners, some of whom worked in the second and third decades of the eighteenth century. One does not know precisely how many painters are represented in surviving works, or the identity of their makers. Only further study can strengthen or diminish, for example, the claim that Pieter Vanderlyn was the limner whose brush painted *Grootje Vas* in 1723, as his grandson John Vanderlyn believed. Mrs. Vas is rather majestic, her long face modeled with a degree of subtlety inside the larger oval of her kerchief; and the artist ignored no parallelism of shape, no counterthrusting movement of sleeve or arm in his instinctive effort to create a structural design.

That architectural solidity is in a portrait of *Lavinia Van Vechten.* Her pose, with an apple in one hand and a rose in the other, could be found in numerous engravings; but she has been given the monumentality of a temple upon columns: a slanting tree branch parallels the edge of a skirt, a table edge prolongs the direction of an arm, the vertical folds of an underdress are powerfully scored. A more sensitive brush traced the silken lights in a portrait of an unknown woman whose beauty is charmingly recorded, despite occasional stiffness. She too holds a rose, but more easily, and the rhythm of her garments is more relaxed than Lavinia Van Vechten's. In the face of *Thomas Van Alstyne* there were subtleties of plane and contour which the painter of his likeness either missed or preferred to ignore; but his wiry drawing of the puffed eyes and the hard black shadows along the nose and upper lip and beneath the full mouth and chin is as powerful a statement of character as one can find in the colonial world.

The limners knew that world, and because they deeply felt what was common to themselves and their sitters in land, customs, language, class, and religion, they possessed the simplest and strongest of tongues to say what was essential about it. They could turn the dapper John Freake into a flat pattern of elegance, or chisel the dour Captain Smith as life itself had done. They found appropriate distortions for the horselike and self-righteous head of the Reverend Thacher and for the Dutch stolidity of the Duyckincks and Van Vechtens. They provided impressive settings for a Darnall child or a young De Peyster. Like the people who sat before them, they could imitate and adapt, but they could also originate.

Justus E. Kühn, *Eleanor Darnall*

Maryland Historical Society, Baltimore, Md.

Capital from Isaac Royall mansion, Medford, Mass. ▶

Courtesy Royall House Association

PART TWO

MARGIN FOR CULTURE

INTRODUCTION / NICETIES AND CURIOSITIES

A map of cultural progress in the first decades of eighteenth-century America would include not only the eastern tidewater where Englishmen tried to be as English as possible under the circumstances, but also the southwestern region where Spaniards built presidios, missions, and ranch houses, and the French communities along the Gulf Coast and up the valley of the Mississippi.

By 1730, there were a dozen missions in Texas. At San Antonio, the Alamo church was a fusion of the plateresque and the churrigueresque, and the shell-shaped niche of its façade was a foil to the rugged plainness of its walls. San José was nervous with carved ornament; San Juan Capistrano had a double tier of pierced openings in which bells hung. The walls and roof of the governor's house were thick for insulation, forming a rigorously plain adobe block whose only decoration was the floridly carved door, the carved coat of arms above its portal, and the row of protruding dark beams which cast a changing pattern of shadows along its front. Inigo Jones, that apostle of decorum, would have recoiled before the baroque extravagance of San José, but would perhaps have admired the clean and spacious interiors of the governor's residence, with tiled floors below, the rhythm of repeated ceiling beams above, and a stairway as "modern" as the twentieth century can offer.

Near Tucson, Arizona, San Xavier del Bac was founded in 1700. The present church, much restored, has plain façades of stucco-covered adobe brick enlivened by rich plaster ornament which glitters in the hard sun—shells, canopied niches, and scrolling pediments; the light from its dome accents the restless elaboration of its interior spaces. In New Mexico, the balance of the foreign with the indigenous shifted further toward the latter; on the governor's palace at Santa Fe, round wooden columns with carved brackets underlined a long horizontality which was Indian. As late as the last quarter of the century, the pueblo shapes and surfaces were in Ranchos de Taos church, with odd curving buttresses below its two towers, rather like the forepaws of a crouching animal, and the absolute simplicity of apsidal walls whose beauty was the beauty of hand-smoothed clay molded by light and defined by shadow.

In the mission shops, Indians learned from Spanish

San Xavier del Bac, near Tucson, Ariz.

Historic American Buildings Survey, Library of Congress

Mission Church, Ranchos de Taos, N. Mex.

Historic American Buildings Survey, Library of Congress

craftsmen and from priests how to carve architectural ornament, to paint altarpieces in tempera on wooden panels covered with gesso in the European manner, and to sculpture small figures of the saints and other votive objects. This was a folk art in its own limited sense; its iconography did not arise from the Indian's own past, but was accepted from his Catholic mentors, whose illustrated books provided the appropriate shapes and attributes. A painted reredos in New Mexico was sure to proclaim the origins of its imagery, but also the linear strength, the simplifying mind, and the bold color sense of the Indian limner. A mild Saint Francis or a bleeding Christ, cut from cottonwood and covered with gesso before it was painted with indigo blue and earth reds and yellows, bore the insistent realism, the thrust at the emotions which were Spanish and Catholic in tradition; but its lean economies, its eloquent elongations, and its appeal through form were in the minds and fingers which shaped it.

Primitive indeed, compared with the Spanish sophistications, were the French villages at Kaskaskia in the Illinois country and New Orleans on the Gulf. The walls of the first houses were made of upright cedar logs in palisade fashion, or framed with timbers and filled with clay and rubble; roofs of thatch or bark projected to form a porch or gallery. In larger homes, a hall ran from front to back; gilt mirrors from France and religious pictures hung on the walls, and the owner had silver on his table. Kaskaskia, before the waters of the great river swallowed it, had a *place,* a fortress, a few stone dwellings, and a crude Jesuit church; a lone survivor is the home of Pierre Ménard the trader, whose fireplaces came from the home country. Near Baton Rouge in Louisiana, Magnolia Mound preserves the general type.

Only a few similar structures have survived the fires in New Orleans, which Charlevoix called a "wild, lovely place" a few years after Bienville in 1718 laid out a *place d'armes,* the site for a cathedral, and a gridiron plan for streets. At each crossing stood four cottages of split cypress logs, their floors raised above the ground level, their steep roofs swinging outward to make a porch, and the gardens behind their picket fences planted with oleanders and orange trees. The pattern was well filled by the 1760's, when New Orleans had nearly five hundred houses. Some of these had graceful and delicate wrought-iron balconies, the work of imported French artisans and their local imitators, among whom were skillful Negro craftsmen.

In motivation and in form the English colonial arts were the antithesis of the French and Spanish. French habits of mind did not adapt themselves to frontier realities; Spaniards assimilated the native peoples into their own race, religion, and economy; Englishmen thrust them aside. The Spanish enterprise was geographically diffuse and to that extent precarious; the English was concentrated in a shallow north-south strip of the New World. The mass of Spanish subjects could never hope to achieve that self-improvement which was possible for the meanest indentured servant in the coastal provinces. History had reserved the future for men and women who could become individuals and who could mold their own lives and institutions.

Along the Atlantic and its tributary rivers the centers of cultural life took shape in the first half of the century. Boston, New York, and Albany had no marked degree of visual coherence but there was a rationalism in the broad main streets of New England villages with their accent on the meetinghouse and their home lots ranged in orderly fashion with no man crowding his neighbor. Wallingford, Connecticut, developed where a Long High Way branched from the Old Colony Road from Hartford to New Haven, each house spaced for privacy, the common pasture close at hand, the logical places allotted for grazing cattle, for raising vegetables, and even for burying the dead.

Magnolia Mound, near Baton Rouge, La.

F. S. Lincoln photo

The checkerboard regularity of Philadelphia was both mechanical and tiresome, and its squares were rapidly filling up when Samuel Powel raised his deceptively plain brick dwelling, while other well-to-do Philadelphians built wider and handsomer along the Schuylkill. Anne Arundel Town in Maryland became Annapolis, where the streets radiated from two circular spaces, a larger for the capitol, a smaller for the church, and where brick residences showed the designing hand of William Buckland. English formalism without compromise was to be found in the Virginian capital of Williamsburg, whose Duke of Gloucester Street ran broad and straight; a member of his Majesty's Assembly, looking eastward from the steps of William and Mary College, could see the new capitol building three quarters of a mile away and know that the governor's palace marked the terminus of the town's cross-axis. Widely spaced on the James and the Rappahannock stood the brick homes of planters whose fathers had built in wood; to the south the houses of Savannah stood within the rectangles which Oglethorpe had planned for them on a bluff over the river.

In the year 1719 a New England pamphleteer gloomily surveyed the "Melancholy Circumstances of the Province" and concluded that his country was not yet of that age to require that many—if any—should be employed in "niceties and curiosities." During the first half of the eighteenth century, however, at least a minority among the colonial peoples achieved what they considered the arts of cultured living. There was relative peace in the settled coastal regions; there were roads to diminish former isolation; a Boston man's letter would eventually be delivered to his friend in Charleston, and he could read his newspaper in his own tavern. Thanks to the merchant, silk stockings, broadcloths, periwigs, china ware, cane chairs, and ribbons came from abroad in such quantities that some of the less favored reminded their fellows that the good of the whole country should be preferred to that of a part.

Nathaniel Ames informed the readers of his *Almanac* in 1758 that the provincial horizon was not closed by the mountain barrier beyond the long coastal plain of the Atlantic. To the west of the Appalachians lay a region larger than all of France, Germany, and Poland, "and all well provided with Rivers, a very fine wholesome Air, a rich Soil, capable of producing Food and Physick, and all Things necessary for the Conveniency and Delight of Life: In fine, the Garden of the World!" Two mighty kings, said Ames, now contended for this inestimable prize, and their respective claims would be measured by the length of their swords.

Those swords were clashing while Ames wrote, providing themes for painters: Fort Louisburg was taken by British vessels and New England soldiers in 1758, and the figure of William Pepperell rode his horse to victory on the painted walls of the Warner house in Portsmouth; Benjamin West, a Quaker of twenty-one and a veteran of Braddock's campaign before General Wolfe took Quebec and died on the Heights of Abraham, noted that scene for future use on canvas. By the year 1763, Englishmen held the "Garden of the World" west to the great river; Canada was theirs, and Spanish Florida. The garden was ready for seeding, and the crop would not be wholly an English one.

Migrations from Europe in the first decades of the century poured new blood into colonial veins: the West German Protestants, the poverty-ridden Scotch of North Ireland, the Huguenots of France, and other peoples swelled the country's population to seven times what it had been at the end of the seventeenth century, until by 1763 two thirds of the Americans were new men and not the sons or grandsons of earlier settlers. The Scotch-Irishman had his indenture to work out before he could move to the frontier as a freeman; the German lived the frugal life of his peasant forebears, in Pennsylvania and the foothills of Maryland, in the Blue Ridge and the Carolina piedmont. Johann Konrad Beissel and his Seventh Day Baptists built the medieval cloisters at Ephrata in Lancaster County, Pennsylvania. The Moravians created in the seventeen forties the German symmetry of Bethlehem in the same colony, and later impressed their character on Salem, North Carolina.

The difference between the coastal patrician and the man whose hands and back were his main asset widened during these years. Even in the English colonies, it could not be said in 1763 that the life of the latter had become more leisurely, more polished than it had been two generations before. A New Englander with a taste for reading in that year could buy the plays of Shakespeare and Congreve, the satires of Molière and Smollett, the poems of Dryden and of Pope; yet the life of Joshua Hempstead, which had closed five years before in New London, was far more typical of the majority in its sheer drudgery, its manifold concern with the life of the well-planned community, and its prolongation of the Puritan attitude.

Joshua's famous diary reveals him as a farmer, lawyer, juryman, stonecutter, tailor, and guardian of the village morals. One January day he makes thirteen pounds of candles; on another he carts a maple log to the sawmill for a "bedstid." In June 1748, Ruth Shapley makes him two pairs of breeches, but it is Joshua who helps the Widow Smith to change her will, who on Sunday hears Mr. Adams preach all day, who spends an occasional day at "engraving," who sees a Negro whipped for striking a neighbor with the handle of an iron fryingpan, and cuts his back door wider to take in a hogshead of molasses.

While the Joshua Hempsteads thus worked in Connecticut pastures, on Hudson Valley farms, in the small homesteads of Delaware and Pennsylvania, and in the back country of the South to keep themselves in dwelling, food, and raiment, a leisure class took form in colonial America. Among its ranks were the Boston or Portsmouth merchant, the lord of the New York patroonship or the Maryland manor, the canny Philadelphia Quaker, the colonial governor and his clique, the Virginia slaveowner, and the Charleston nabob. American land was American wealth, and these gentlemen knew how to turn the one into the other. The second William Byrd inherited nearly thirty thousand acres along the James, while Governor Benning Wentworth's hundred thousand were a rich slice of New Hampshire. New fortunes were made in royally encouraged real-estate speculation, others in quickly raised tobacco crops which slaves planted and harvested; still others were the profits of the devious three-cornered traffic by sea in American fish, lumber, and grain, British manufactures, and the West Indian sugar and molasses indispensable to rum.

This group could never become, in the historic European sense, a full-fledged aristocracy while empty land stretched westward, forests stood virgin thick, and the need for men's physical toil exceeded the supply. There was no barrier of status here which a man could not break down. He became a gentleman when he could buy the work of others, and when his dress, his house, and his furniture proclaimed that he possessed not only the means to be an Englishman transplanted, but sufficient knowledge of English fashions to know what was expected of him. He was no idler, since much of his time must be spent in the direction of his growing enterprises, and much of his intellectual life be given to what Louis Wright has called "purposeful reading." In the small margin of his leisure he danced and took French lessons, collected his library, ordered decorations for his mansion, saw *Richard the Third* in a remodeled warehouse, and subscribed to local concerts.

This gentleman was no longer content in the mid-century to build a town house with overhanging gables or a country seat with Jacobean turrets and chimney stacks. Fashion had changed in England, and he did his best to keep step with it. The London of Shakespeare had become the London of Hogarth, and many a tobacco aristocrat from Virginia or a mercantile New Englander knew London at first hand or had evidence of the new modes in building, painting, furnishings, and dress upon his library shelves.

John Gay's *Trivia* described London streets where the visitor from Boston or Williamsburg dodged swinging signs, watched his pocket against the ballad singer's diving hand, and saw the tricking gamester ride past with *Loves* and *Graces* on his chariot's sides. In the Strand shops china from Delft was to be bought, and the finest Bohee tea. A promenade in Saint James's Park or a night visit to Vauxhall or Ranelagh Gardens, sparkling with hundreds of colored lanterns, kept the provincial abreast of modes in bobwig, sacque, and stomacher. The town gossip was in the newspaper which one read at the coffeehouse, and also at the card tables and in the boudoir where a lady held her morning levee. One could cultivate one's taste by viewing the paintings at the Royal Academy in Pall Mall; or one could stroll on the bank of the Thames and watch a prince and princess moving down to Kew in a Chinese barge.

London façades were proof that the age of Queen Anne and the first Georges was an age of controlled symmetry. What Englishmen called classical were the shapes and details which they had borrowed from Italian Palladio, who had borrowed them from the borrowing Romans. One could thank Palladio for conceiving a great house as a central block with adjoining wings and for domesticating the Pantheon in the form of a villa. The royal Banqueting House of Inigo Jones had stood in Whitehall since 1622 as evidence of the heavy regularity, the nice adjustment of the parts to the whole, the dignified pillaging of the antique repertory, which its designer practiced as well as preached. The baroque overabundance, the clashing and broken forms which Jones credited to the followers of Michelangelo, he believed unsuited to serious architecture; one must first design the ground plan for usefulness, according to this architect, and then adorn and compose it with decorum.

With something less than Jones's fine sense of proportion, mass, and accent, the professional architects and amateur dabblers who came after him built the English mansions of the eighteenth century with rusticated ground-floor stories, corner blocks or quoins along the edges of buildings, balustrades upon their roofs, a stately parade of pilasters along their façades, and alternating curved and triangular pediments over their windows.

This rigid control of space, this reliance on precedent, and this geometry which enlarged the proportions of plans to magnify their impressiveness, could not fail to become the architecture of the gentleman. Its snob appeal was not lost on the Shaftesburys and the Burlingtons; on the other hand, its ponderous smugness inspired Pope's comment that the great Palladian house was a "laboured quarry above ground." In his fourth *Epistle,* Pope warned Burlington:

> Yet shall (my Lord) your just, your noble rules,
> Fill half the land with imitating fools;
> Who random drawings from your sheets shall take,
> And of one beauty many blunders make;
> Load some vain church with old theatric state,
> Turn arcs of triumph to a garden-gate;
> Reverse your ornaments, and hang them all
> On some patched dog-hole eked with ends of wall;
> Then clap four slices of pilaster on't,
> That, laced with bits of rustic, makes a front.

Even the English garden, on the Italian-French model, had suffered a Palladian frost. Its endless straight vistas, Euclidean flower beds, fountains, urns, and canals annoyed Pope to the point of writing:

> Grove nods at grove, each alley has a brother,
> And half the platform just reflects the other.
> The suffering eye inverted Nature sees,
> Trees cut to statues, statues thick as trees;
> With here a fountain, never to be played;
> And there a summer-house, that knows no shade;
> Here Amphitrite sails through myrtle bowers;
> There gladiators fight, or die, in flowers.

English literature cultivated an Augustan solemnity, but it also broke out into fantasy, shrewd satire, and gusty humor; and so it was in the arts of three-dimensional form. There were alternatives to the Palladian rules. Inspired by the remnants of medievalism in English towns and villages, some men built Gothic mansions; the ceiling of Horace Walpole's Strawberry Hill was an adaptation of Henry VII's at Westminster, and a Canterbury tomb became a Walpole chimney piece. In other mansions, the brittle and graceful nonsense of the French rococo enlivened moldings, paneling, and painted ceilings. Britain's traffic with the far ports of the world stirred the imagination, and Orientalism found expression in Chinese wallpapers and garden temples, in the painted calicoes of India. The ultra-formal garden was challenged by the so-called "natural" one, whose deliberate irregularity appealed to sentiment; such expert designers as Bridgman, Kent, and "Capability" Brown produced an effect which before long would be called the "picturesque," and which often involved the building of perfectly new ruins.

It would have been difficult to say which of these conflicting ideas was dominant in the taste of Englishmen in the seventeen fifties. Even in furniture, a heavy-handed extravagance put satyrs' masks on table legs and lions' heads on buffets; but when Chippendale designed his chairs and tables, some were "Chinese," some were Gothic, some had the interlacing curves of the rococo, and some managed to combine all three. Men who wished to surround themselves with the evidence of their cosmopolitanism, and their capacity to spend money for non-useful ends, were bound to become eclectics.

The huge Palladian block was too monumental in scale for literal imitation by Englishmen in America. Tryon's Palace in North Carolina was one of the few provincial structures which even approximated the type, and colonial builders were content to apply classical principles of design and classical details of ornament to more modest dwellings and public edifices. The normal-sized house of England, however, was within the colonist's power to imitate. The Queen Anne or early Georgian house of stone or brick with a flat or hipped roof presented a neat regularity with the door in the middle of its face and orderly ranges of sash windows beside and above it. The central portion of the front might project a little, but not enough to break the smoothness of the whole. Ornament was concentrated over windows, along corners, under the roof, and on the doorway with its straight-lined or scrolled pediment.

The interior plan was simple: a hallway which ran from front to back, opening on two rooms at either side. Its stairway balusters were richly carved, and the walls of its chambers were divided into rectangular panels more severely plain than the lively subdivisions of Jacobean wainscoting. Over the doors a simple entablature was placed, or a pedimented form, and there was carved ornament, often florid and intricate, around the sides and above the chimney piece. These and a molded cornice were likely to be the room's chief decoration, with the ceiling of unbroken plaster or, at the most, divided into compartments which only faintly suggested the elaborate coffering of the earlier styles.

In such a room, the graceful card table with cabriole legs found itself near cabinets and highboys lacquered in the "Chinese" fashion, or tip-top one-legged tables with "piecrust" edges which showed their rococo inspiration. The wing chair by the fire was covered with velvet, with needlework, or with printed cotton. Rooms which were not wholly paneled were lively with painted birds and bamboo in the Oriental manner above the low dado. There was a muted elegance in the contrast between polished mahogany and flowered chintz, between the carved chimney piece and the suave panel above it, between the niched "beaufaitt" set into the wall and the brilliantly colored chinaware on its shelves. Such a room suggested a degree of affluence without forgetting Pope's admonition:

> Something there is more needful than expense,
> And something previous ev'n to taste—'tis *sense.*

England's painting, like her architecture, betrayed her cultural dualisms, her conflict between the settled aristocratic way of life and the expansive new forces of a powerful middle class. There was an aesthetics for the gentleman, a fixed hierarchy among the types of pictorial expression which had its analogy in the leveled grades of society itself. The safe appeal to precedent was in Jonathan Richardson's guidebook to art; and Charles Alphonse Dufresnoy's poem on the art of painting, several times translated for English readers, opened with this admonition:

> 'Tis painting's first chief business to explore,
> What lovelier forms in nature's boundless store
> Are best to Art and ancient Taste allied,
> For ancient Taste those forms has best applied.

Let no artist, the poem continued, disdain theoretic truth and blunder on under the illusion that he can come to full artistic expression through the "purblind practice" of his own experimenting.

Not all of English painting was artfully snobbish, however. At least some landscape makers preferred to see nature through their own eyes, not through a theory; some patrons preferred that their portraits look like what they were, not what they ought to be. The spirit of Knapton, Devis, Ramsay, Zoffany, and Wright of Derby was close to the life of eighteenth-century England. When James Thornhill painted his *Landing of George the First,* he borrowed the graces of Rubens to make an elaborate allegory; but his son-in-law William Hogarth lived for the most part in the present tense, and in his narrative pictures Georgian England came to turbulent life and the vulgarisms of common existence lost none of their harsh reality.

Although engravings of *The Rake's Progress* and *Marriage à la Mode* hung in colonial parlors while their creator was still living, there was no American Hogarth to apply his humor, his robust sense of the actual, his underlying contempt for the precious to the local scene. When the provincial painter turned to England it was to observe the fashions in likenesses. He discovered that when Godfrey Kneller died in 1723 the long subjection of England to the styles of Holland and Flanders came to an end and pompous showmanship gave place to a more English sense of affluence and grace. The Knelleresque pose lingered nonetheless in the portraits of his successors, Joseph Highmore and Thomas Hudson; the latter was a pupil of Jonathan Richardson and the teacher of Reynolds, and the fused solidity in his work contrasted with the broad and daring brushwork of Hogarth and the sketchlike dash of Gainsborough. Highmore and Hudson, not their more venturesome contemporaries, became the models for a generation of colonial face painters.

The American in search of "niceties and curiosities" discovered that among the provincial populations lived artisans of far greater competence than in former years. When a citizen died a painter was on hand to stain his coat of arms on cloth or wood to be carried in his cortege, or to carve it in wood, as the Fayerweather hatchment was done. When white labor was scarce, well-trained Negroes worked at the construction and carved the decorations of a Portsmouth mansion or a synagogue at Newport. When Poplar Spring Church was rebuilt in Virginia in 1738, Mr. Samuel Peacock was engaged to "handsomely paint the Aulter peace."

Skilled craftsmen in brass and copper hammered and cut the weathercocks which turned on steeples, and Philadelphia cabinetmakers made superb adaptations of the designs of Chippendale. Between 1756 and 1774 Baron Henry William Stiegel from Cologne operated Elizabeth Furnace in Lancaster County, Pennsylvania, whose glassware was colored, etched, and enameled by imported workmen and their local imitators. From this shop and from others came the cast-iron plates which could be assembled to make a stove on legs against the chimney flue, their surfaces rich with reliefs of heraldic motives, tulips, human figures under round arches, and the doings of the Protestant saints.

Pennsylvania German dish, 1786, by George Hübener

Philadelphia Museum of Art

Out of the red clay of Pennsylvania the German potters shaped vessels of daily use; their slip ware was enlivened by designs poured through quills, their sgraffito patterns were scratched through the slip into the brown substance underneath. The tulips, paired birds, unicorns, and flowering vases of these dishes and painted tinware were as old as medieval Europe, and so was the art of *fractur,* a species of illumination for birth certificates, religious music, and family registers. The *fractur* scribe considered his rectangle of paper a field to be subdivided and thoroughly enlivened; the quill pen drew the heavy Gothic lettering and the crisp outlines of flowers, animals, and people; the brush filled the page with earthy reds, yellows, greens, and blues. The same decorative sense adapted the German motives to the circle of a plate, the rectangle of a painted chest, or the shield form of an iron trivet; the horses and parrots of *fractur* were given a third dimension in whittled toys.

A silversmith in colonial towns was a man who not only made tankards and teapots but on occasion engraved pictures in copper. An ancient coffin, unearthed more than a century after its burial in Trinity Churchyard, New York, bore the arms of the deceased which one of these artisans had emblazoned in silver with a "pompous display of heraldic pride." Thomas Johnston engraved topographical views in the forties in New

England, and Henry Dawkins a few years later in New York and Philadelphia. The seal of Harvard College was cut by John Coney, brother-in-law of the silversmith Jeremiah Dummer and teacher of Paul Revere; a print of Joseph Sewall was the work of Nathaniel Hurd in 1768, when Peter Pelham had already produced a series of Massachusetts clergymen in black and white. If the customer preferred the imported mezzotint or engraving, the Boston picture store of William Price was only one of several where one could buy McArdell's and John Smith's versions of Kneller, Highmore, and Hudson.

It was architecture, rather than the lesser arts, which first and most forcibly established the visual character of the colonial environment. One looked for no Strawberry Hill Gothicisms or Chinese garden pagodas in the new towns, for the provincial Englishman preferred to imitate and adapt what was most securely established in the taste of a country of which he considered himself a citizen-at-a-distance.

How was that distance crossed in order that the Queen Anne house, the Burlingtonian palace, or the Stowe gardens could find a diminished reflection in the provincial mirror? Sir Christopher Wren himself was said to have designed the College of William and Mary. John Hawks crossed the ocean with Lieutenant-Governor Tryon to make the drawings for the Palace at New Bern, North Carolina, and Thomas McBean, architect of Saint Paul's Chapel in New York, had been a Gibbs pupil in England. But these were exceptions to the rule that local carpenters and local amateur designers must rely on the directions and the plates in architectural books.

On colonial shelves were the published accounts of great men's houses, with handsome illustrations: Kip's *Britannia Illustrata,* Badeslade's thirty-six famous views, and others published before 1730. The first edition of *Vitruvius Britannicus* contained superb engravings of public and private English buildings: Duncombe Park and Horseheath Hall were Palladian winged mansions; a house in Epsom, Surrey, suggested the later forms of Westover in Virginia, and Sir Robert Worsley's seat on the Isle of Wight had coupled chimneys that would reappear at Stratford near the Potomac.

For one colonial mansion which came out of James Gibbs's *Book of Architecture* there were dozens inspired by less pretentious sources; and even Gibbs emphasized that he wrote for the country builder who had no architect to follow. Gibbs cautioned his reader not to allow his designs to be altered "by the Forwardness of Unskilful Workmen, or the Caprice of ignorant, assuming Pretenders"; but altered they were when British stone had to become provincial wood, and exuberance of detail was tempered to the abilities of the local craftsmen.

The parish that wanted its church built in the style which Wren had devised, and Gibbs had popularized, could find suitable elevations in William Halfpenny's *Art of Sound Building* in 1725, which included construction details. *The Builder's Jewel,* by the Langleys, provided window patterns and gave instruction in how to frame a dome. Abraham Swan was useful to colonials because he had been a carpenter himself; in Isaac Ware's *A Complete Body of Architecture,* one found ceiling designs, paneling, and chimney pieces.

Armed with these and similar pattern books, the Massachusetts or the Virginia man set about his task of giving Palladio a new life at the world's end. After all, had not Sir Horace Walpole predicted that the next Augustan Age would dawn in America?

CHAPTER 3 / TIDEWATER CLASSICISM

The architecture called "Georgian" or by other names was the result of men's efforts in the first three quarters of the eighteenth century to give dignified and appropriate form to their needs as worshipers, as heads of families, and as citizens. Its churches, homes, and public buildings derive their interest from an interplay between norm and variation, between the stereotype and the invention bred by necessity, between European inheritance and American experience.

The spires of chapels and churches prick the sky in the old engraved views of Boston, New York, Philadelphia, and Charleston. When they were built no strict correspondence existed between a denomination and an architectural form; local habit, craft methods, and materials shaped the structure, whether Anglican or Quaker—these and the social status of the parishioners. Catholics were a tiny minority, and most of the Protestant churches were still modest, square-built, and spare of ornament when the Spaniards of Arizona created the dramatic elaborations of San Xavier del Bac.

Among Protestant communities the Anglicans set most store by outward pomp and elaborate ritual; among the Baptists, Methodists, and German Pietists the flame of the individual free conscience burned most fiercely. Between these extremes stood the Quakers and Presbyterians, the Dutch Reformed churchmen, the Lutherans, and the Congregationalists, in whom the aristocratic and the democratic ideals met and clashed, the outcome frequently depending on whether the parish was predominantly upper middle class or lower. Inevitably these conflicts determined not only the size, shape, and degree of luxury of a given church edifice but also the extent to which it felt constrained to imitate its London betters.

One would expect the Anglicans of the southern tidewater to build more lavishly than their northern brethren, but this was seldom the case. These parishes were too widely scattered, and their churchgoing was too often interrupted by weather and the claims of hospitality to require large structures. St. James at Goose Creek, South Carolina, was small, with scarcely any external ornament but quoins and a pedimented doorway; sixty years later, the pediment, entablature, and Ionic pilasters at the entrance to Pohick Church were of local freestone, and there was nothing inside to distract the pewholders except a plain pulpit and uncompromising round-headed windows in thick walls. There was neither tower nor spire on St. Thomas' Church at Bath in North Carolina in 1734; two years later at Edenton, St. Paul's was planned with a circular apse at one end; when its first service was held in 1760 it had a tower of brick and an octagonal spire covered with shingles.

Equally plain was the New England meetinghouse of the century's first two decades, a square or rectangular hall with a pulpit on one of its longer sides, the boxlike pews facing it, a gallery above and an entrance on the end or side. St. Paul's in the Narragansett country, on its present site at Wickford, Rhode Island, has lost its tower and looks no more ecclesiastical than a large clapboarded dwelling house with a doorway on its long side whose curved pediment breaks at the center in carved rosettes. Under the rounded plaster ceiling of its galleried interior the beams and braces of its construction are visible, and the stair to its five-sided pulpit has the plain newels and balusters of New England houses. As late as 1789 the builders of Alna Meeting House in Maine made no greater effort to "dress up divine and glorious truths"; its interior had the same plan as Wickford, its pews were not solid but were fenced in with rows of balusters, and its balcony supports were given a slightly curving profile.

Goose Creek Church, St. James Parish, S.C.

F. S. Lincoln photo

Anglicans and prosperous Congregationalists meanwhile became familiar with Wren's thoroughly Protestant versions of the Catholic baroque, much smaller than the vast Roman basilicas and much better adapted to the needs of worshipers who wished to see and hear the preacher. To Boston in the seventeen twenties came the gospel of Sir Christopher Wren and of his assistants and imitators: Vanbrugh, Hawksmoor, and James Gibbs. Queen Anne's Act of 1708 had offered them the task of building fifty parish churches in the city of London to replace those which the great fire had destroyed.

Most of these English churches had long naves, aisles, and crossings; some had flat ceilings with curving sides rising to meet them, others had domes, and some were barrel-vaulted. Wren struggled with the problem of supports for galleries and ceilings, at St. Bride's with coupled columns which the gallery front awkwardly interrupted, at St. Clement Dane's more successfully with rectangular piers under the balcony and Corinthian columns for the arcade above it. The tower and spire were the glory of the Wren exteriors,

Interior, St. Paul's Church, Wickford, R.I.

Historic American Buildings Survey, Library of Congress

St. Michael's Church, Charleston, S.C.

Historic American Buildings Survey, Library of Congress

rising above flattish balustraded roofs in a plain square story which was topped by round or octagonal stages one upon another, growing more richly ornamented as its design became more visible over close-crowding neighbors.

William Price, who dispensed engravings at Boston, was said to have studied London churches at firsthand before designing Christ Church, or "Old North" as it was called. Although its contemporary, "Old South," was a meetinghouse rather than an aisled church, both had much in common, and both of them reappeared on countless New England commons before the Revolution. Price translated stone into brick and wood. His church was a rectangular affair with a pitched roof, the simplest of tall windows, and a square western tower with a plain and rather stubby spire which was later replaced by a loftier one designed by Bulfinch. Robert Twelve's steeple for Old South, with one stage consisting of an open-arcaded octagon of wood, inspired others from Portland, Maine, to Worcester, including the one whose bell summoned Northampton people to hear Jonathan Edwards' Great Awakening.

The interior of Old North was lofty and harmonious, with four bays on each side, a balcony carried by paneled square pillars, and a barrel-vaulted ceiling upon fluted square ones. Price created fine spatial rhythms and simple clean planes; the curved ceiling was repeated in the heads of the round-topped windows and the arcades of the aisle, and varied in the three arches which led under the choir loft into the nave, their crisp brackets cut by the Yankee ship carver's chisel. The six-sided sounding board was as exquisitely simple as the pulpit whose stair rail curved boldly upward, and a New England reticence allowed space, proportions, and surfaces to speak for themselves.

Other provincial builders either copied Wren and Gibbs from the guidebooks, or copied the copyists. Nearly fifty years after Gibbs published his *Book of Architecture,* one of his plates was literally borrowed for the steeple of the First Baptist Meeting House in Providence. Bruton Parish Church at Williamsburg acquired a steeple although it had almost no trace of the Wren-Gibbs details. The groined ceiling of Newport's Trinity caught some of the elegance of St. Bride's in London. Wren's huge Palladian window appeared in the Chapel Royal of St. Philip's in North Carolina, where the governor sat in a higher pew than his fellows; but one found it also in the Zion Church of the Lutherans at Philadelphia and in the Bridgeton house of worship of the New Jersey Presbyterians. By the year 1766 Philadelphia possessed Christ Church, designed by Dr. John Kearsley; Peter Harrison, that "gentleman of good judgment in architecture," had built King's Chapel in Boston and the Newport synagogue; Charleston had St. Michael's and New York the Chapel of St. Paul.

Christ Church was first in point of time, its lively crisp exterior walls of brick and stone topped by a forest of balustraded urns, its flat roof concealed by a western pediment flanked with graceful consoles, its steeple a more direct imitation of London models than most cities had attempted. The dignity of its interior was not diminished by the amateurisms of its designer: galleries pass behind columns which could have supported them, and the overemphatic fragments of entablature resemble wide-brimmed Quaker hats on top of the capitals.

The Charleston Church is of brick covered with glistening white stucco; its cornerstone is dated 1752. Its rather squat round-headed windows are edged with rustication and a burly steeple rises from its roof behind a pedimented colonnade. The silhouette and a

Peter Harrison, Synagogue, Newport, R.I.
Historic American Buildings Survey, Library of Congress

few details are those of Gibbs, and a printed reference to a "Mr. Gibson" as its designer has given rise to the hopeful but uncertain theory that the great Englishman himself was responsible for the planning of this church.

King's Chapel would have been as externally impressive as St. Michael's if its projected spire had been built. There was no lack of impressiveness inside, where the paired Corinthian columns were intricately carved and where the Reverend Henry Caner climbed the lacelike pulpit stair to read Anglican prayers against the light from a high Palladian window in the rounded apse.

Harrison built his synagogue at Newport in 1762,

The Klosters, Ephrata, Pa.

Historic American Buildings Survey, Library of Congress

and its bare walls gave no hint of the exquisite room inside whose details were borrowed from Inigo Jones, Gibbs, Kent, and Langley: the Ark of the Covenant enclosed in a graceful balustrade, Ionic columns under the gallery, and more slender Corinthian shafts rising from the balcony to the cornice of the coved ceiling.

Thomas McBean was a pupil of Gibbs before he designed St. Paul's, and what Gibbs had built of white stone was here wrought in two contrasting materials: the rough, freely laid walls of Manhattan mica schist, and the decorative trim of brownstone. There was no nave in a colonial church which could equal the fourteen chandeliers of Waterford cut glass, the superbly proportioned columns with gilded Corinthian tops, the light spring of vaulting curves, the majestic outlines of the great window in the chancel. It was England in America, and when the bells tolled for its dedication in 1766 few could have believed that they were announcing the last decade of provincial society.

It is difficult to believe that the Lutheran Church at Trappe in Pennsylvania was begun when the main body of Christ Church at Philadelphia was nearly done and that the Moravians had almost completed their group at Bethlehem when the cornerstone of St. Michael's was placed. Since the turn of the century, Trinity Church at Wilmington had proven that Swedes had different notions of devotional architecture from those of Englishmen; "Old Swede's" was a massive and rather ungainly bulk of granite and brick whose tower seems to have been an afterthought, and there were no ornamental graces in its bare walls, its round-topped altar window, and the plain round columns under its gallery.

The Trappe meetinghouse of 1743 was constructed like a fine barn with thick walls of red sandstone, a gambrel roof which became a hip-gambrel in order to cover a three-sided apse at one end, and entrance porches with sturdy round-arched openings and no ornament except a dedicatory stone panel. The wealthier Lutherans sat in paneled pews with high backs; the pulpit, although imported, was of equal severity; the square-sectioned oaken supports of its gallery were hewn to tapering contour and a few moldings as they went up, and the beams under the gallery floor were exposed.

The Society of Friends met in structures as plain and solid as their own homes but slightly larger, whose only beauty was that of texture and clean shapes. Double-hipped roofs with dormers marked the communal buildings of the Moravians, whose Gemeinhaus, Bell House, Chapel and Sisters' House at Bethlehem were disposed with precise symmetry to form the letter U, and their pattern was repeated somewhat later at Bethabara, Bethania, and Winston-Salem in North Carolina. As late as 1800, the Moravian home church at Salem retained the odd cupola with its arcaded base and ogival contour.

Led by Johann Beissel, a group of German mystics brought to Pennsylvania their doctrines of total immersion and the seventh-day Sabbath, and their monastic community at Ephrata was a fragment of the Rhineland set down among Pennsylvania hills and pastures, its stone-sheathed walls as plain as the lives of its occupants: the Saal of 1740 with a steep roof, where the Brothers sang their beautiful chorales; the Sister House of 1743 where lived the Roses of Sharon, vowed to chastity, in narrow cells as Gothic as the rich painted illuminations on the white Kloster walls.

In contrast with this asceticism, the well-favored colonial of the worldly majority not only worshiped among Palladian forms, but slept, dined, and received guests in domestic versions of the Gentleman's Classic. Within the first ten or fifteen years of the century, that classicism made its appearance. Among the gables and leaded casements near the Boston waterfront, the trim brick town house of the merchant Thomas Savage, three and a half stories high, was wedged among its still Jacobean neighbors, its sash windows spaced between richly molded string courses, its doorway surmounted by a kind of pavilion with a pediment. At the same time in Philadelphia the new symmetry was to be found on Letitia Street, where a brick house two rooms deep had a low roof, sash windows, a coved cornice of plaster, and scrolling brackets of Renaissance character beneath its doorway hood.

A traveler from Portsmouth to Charleston at the mid-century would have found this building manner no longer the exception but the rule. Despite distances and the difference in materials, he would have discovered houses which had much in common, because they imitated common prototypes and because prosperous men were connected by bonds of common interest and often of family relationship.

Each region gave a local tang to a language of forms which it shared with others. The New England vernacular was crisp and emphatic; the merchant built oftener with wood than with brick, and his home of two and a half or three stories was as neatly robust as his wife's portrait by Feke or Copley. Its roof was flattish, or took the useful form of a gambrel of which the upper slopes were almost level. The ornament of its central hall, running from his front door to the entrance into his garden, was a staircase with balusters elaborately turned. He boasted four rooms to a floor, as often as not with a fireplace in each chamber, and his walls were paneled to the extent of his means, all four if possible, and if not, then at least one, with paper hung above the dado on the other three. His chairs had the cane back of the Restoration period, with fluent carvings on their crests and sides, or, if he kept up with the modes, the softer and more delicate curves of the Queen Anne, or even, by mid-century, the elegance of Chippendale.

This luxury within was suggested by the façade, whose corners had quoins of wood or stone, or slim pilasters to accent its height, whose cornice reproduced somewhat coarsely the correct members of a classic molding, and whose doors and windows, symmetrically placed, received what elaboration an entablature or pediment could give them. This was the type of Governor Shirley's house in Roxbury and those of Hutchinson in Boston, of Royall on the Mystic River, of the Lees and Hoopers in Marblehead, the Pickmans and Derbys in Salem, the Pepperells and Wentworths in New Hampshire, the "river gods" of the Connecticut valley, the captains and shipowners of Bristol and Newport, Rhode Island.

The Medford house of Isaac Royall grew from a two-story, six-room brick dwelling on Governor Winthrop's Ten Hill Farm to a more commodious lean-to, and thence to a three-story mansion with twelve rooms, a fireplace in each one, a large formal garden with alleys, "mount" and summerhouse, and brick slave quarters. Since the southern end of the house was never sheathed, its evolution can be read directly from its wall, and it is the story of a fortune slowly built and magnificently expended. The first Royall had been a cooper, the second a carpenter; the third, whose name was Isaac, lived forty years or more in Antigua, where a brisk trade in rum and Negroes became his passport to the New England aristocracy, a title which, shortly after his purchase of the estate, fell to Isaac, Junior.

It was the younger Isaac who remodeled the mansion, and who as a councilor for over twenty years never swerved in his devotion to the king. On these paneled walls hung his family portraits by Feke and Copley. From this cobbled courtyard his coach took him on Sundays to King's Chapel, and on one ominous day in April, 1775, to Boston on the way to Halifax and exile; here lived Plato, Hagar, and the rest of his dozen slaves.

East front, Royall mansion, Medford, Mass.

Courtesy Royall House Association

Oddly enough, the two sides of the Royall mansion received different treatment from their builder. Facing the Mystic was a superb façade with rusticated corners, a doorway with an entablature, and plain white panels of wood connecting each window with the one above it in a vertical rhythm. The garden side had fluted pilasters at its edges, and instead of clapboards its wooden surface was notched to suggest stonework. This door had a curved or "segmental" pediment, and fluted Ionic pilasters, and looked across the courtyard to an octagonal "gazebo" which was a delicious compound of classicism with invention. Inside the mansion, the woodcarver lavished his skill on the newel and balusters of Isaac's fine stairway and on the nervously cut Corinthian capitals of the pilasters. The colonel's upper bedroom, whose walls were hung with Spanish leather, had recessed windows under graceful arches, and the fireplaces of the house were lined with Dutch tiles.

Each of these New England mansions had its special sign of elegance, its own variation on the current norm. Governor William Shirley had a tiled entrance hall in Roxbury; Lieutenant-Governor Hutchinson's country place, Unkity Hill on the Neponset River, had crimson damask bed curtains, Turkey carpets, an engraved set of Hogarth's *Marriage à la Mode,* and thirty-five dozen of old Madeira belowstairs. His neighbor in the fashionable North End of Boston was the merchant William Clark, and there was no parlor west of London that could rival Clark's, with its inlaid floor bearing the owner's escutcheon. From London probably came the decorator whose eleven painted panels filled the spaces between white-and-gold pilasters — precipitous castles, formal French gardens,

Room from Samuel Powel house, Philadelphia, Pa.

Philadelphia Museum of Art

forest scenes and mountain vistas, with coats of arms at the top. Over Clark's fireplace a less accomplished brush limned the stolid brick exterior of the house itself behind its white picket fence.

From England came the tulip bulbs, the yew and plum trees for Thomas Hancock's house on Beacon Hill; from Braintree his granite, from Connecticut the freestone for his door and window trim. Hancock's front door, with its balcony above and a scrolled pediment window above that, was the model for many others in the colony; during the ten years which the building required for its completion, the carver William More executed what his bill refers to as "pelasters," "dubel cornich," caps for doors, and "belection Wainskit." At Marblehead, Jeremiah Lee's elaborate chimney piece was lifted from a page in Swan's handbook; John B. Jackson of London, who specialized in landscape paper "newly invented" and printed in oils by a roller, supplied the Lee house with Piranesi ruins within rococo borders of scrolls, shells, and parrots. Madam Mark Hunking Wentworth's wedding gift to her son at Portsmouth was a house whose doorway bore a carved pineapple and whose staircase could not have been matched elsewhere than in this town of ship carvers.

The Philipses, Van Cortlandts, and Van Rensselaers of New York maintained their earlier preference for stone, but covered the homely Dutch mannerisms with an English veneer. Frederick Van Cortlandt built his New York house only two years after Hancock had completed his in Boston, and upon the same Georgian principles. Mr. Lee of Marblehead would have been at home among the painted mythology of the great hall in Rensselaer Manor, for these panels had come from the same source as his own, done to order in accordance with plans and measurements which the owner had sent to England. The Rensselaer house at Albany, finished in 1765, was a central block with one-story wings, a four-columned portico, balustrades, and balconies; at Albany also stood Philip Schuyler's mansion on its seven hundred acres overlooking the Hudson.

For his wife Mary Philipse, Robert Morris built a

home in the sixties which is called the Jumel Mansion because that wealthy French merchant lived there for a time with the lady who, as a widow of seventy-seven, married Aaron Burr. The plan is two-part: a square structure much of whose space is given to a great entrance hall, and a connecting octagonal portion where George Washington had his study when the house was a military headquarters for a hard-pressed army. Crowded by drab apartment houses, the Jumel home looks from its bluff southward to the Harlem River, a monument to the late colonial splendor of New York.

The narrow brick town house of Philadelphia, continuous with its neighbors, was Quakerish in the sobriety of its exterior, but its rooms were bright with mahogany, damask, silver, and gay wall hangings. The local counterpart of the Royalls and the Van Rensselaers was Samuel Powel, whose father had been a prosperous Quaker. Thanks to Samuel's wealth, Benjamin West made the grand tour and Powel went along, sufficiently supplied with letters of introduction to meet the King of Sardinia, the Pope, and King George III. In Naples he bought statues and paintings; from Geneva he journeyed to Fernay to shake the hand of old Voltaire, drink coffee, and discuss whether dogs have souls.

Nothing was too fine or too expensive for the house which Powel furnished in 1768, two years before he became Philadelphia's mayor. Its exterior was primly deceptive with plain sash windows and wooden shutters against brick, a side door, and small dormers; for its rooms the best craftsmen of Philadelphia carved and joined the Chippendale chairs and magnificent highboy; from Europe came the painted wallpaper of Chinese design, the sleek cut-glass chandeliers, and the statuettes which were the rage in London. Across the width of the house ran the second floor parlor, whose details owed something to Swan, the cream-white woodwork fastidiously proportioned, with two exotic gilded Chinese Chippendale mirrors against plain panels, a fireplace of brittle and fine-scaled ornamentation, and a ceiling whose rococo plaster arabesques were the work of some local virtuoso with a French touch.

In the more ample spaces of what is now Fairmount Park stood country homes which looked as though they had been lifted from a page of *Vitruvius Britannicus*. There was a relaxed elegance at Cedar Grove; and no provincial residence could equal the French gracefulness of the plaster arabesques in the drawing room and stairhall ceilings of Belmont. Mount Pleasant was the most superbly English of them all, and its steep hip roof and detached side offices looked southward, stylistically speaking. Its central mass was repeated in the shapes of its smaller adjuncts; a pedimented pavilion slightly protruded from the house; its door, under a heavy pediment, had a graceful semicircular fanlight; and on its roof, between chimneys with arched openings in their tops, was a sturdy balustrade. The rococo touch was on the scrolls of its overmantel between the "beaufaitts" with their broken pediments. The cornice of its entrance hall was more burly in detail than one could have found in New England, and its upper hall was lighted by a Palladian window only a little less massive than those of Philadelphia churches.

In Lebanon County, some sixty miles away from Mount Pleasant and more distant still in its inspiration, the House of the Miller at Millbach stolidly proclaimed its kinship with baroque Germany. The date on its stone panel is 1752, and stone was used in the rough for its walls, more smoothly for its quoins and the arches over its windows. The slopes of its gambrel curved slightly as they went down, with a cornice at each pitch. Mount Pleasant contained rooms for every purpose; the great hall at Millbach was both a kitchen and a living room, the mantel of its ten-foot fireplace hewn from a single log of oak. Germanic were the contours of its flattened stair balusters and the curves of the raised carving within the many panels of its broadly proportioned doors.

Annapolis bore the stamp of William Buckland, who came to Virginia in 1755 from England, where he had helped to build for English gentlemen. Buckland's American career was of nineteen years' duration: first,

Wm. Buckland, Hammond-Harwood house, Annapolis, Md.

Wayne Andrews photo

his skill was to be seen in Mount Airy and at Gunston Hall, both Virginian mansions; at Annapolis in the decade after 1765, at least six buildings were designed by him. The Buckland masterpiece was the Hammond-Harwood house of the seventies in his favorite three-

Westover, Charles City County, Va.

Historic American Buildings Survey, Library of Congress

part style, the semi-octagonal wings joined to the central block by lower structures, the whole as exquisite in proportion as it was suave in detail. The garlands over its doorhead and the enframement of the bull's-eye window in its pediment were designed and carved with the dexterity of a minor Grinling Gibbons, and the virtuosity of Buckland expended itself on the acanthus friezes of its mantels, the *rinceaux* over the tall recessed windows of its dining room, the rich modillions of its interior cornices, the dentils, frets, and egg-and-dart in exquisite small scale to be found everywhere in the Hammond-Harwood mansion.

The great estate of Virginia and the Carolinas was rather a small village than a single house. Beside the master's dwelling were kitchens and offices; behind it ranged the stables and storehouses, the sheds for smoking ham or curing tobacco, the vegetable gardens, and the hovels in which the slaves lived. A northern visitor would have found nothing unfamiliar in the design, ornament, and furnishings of such a house, except the greater amplitude of stairways, the higher rooms, and the bolder scale of carved decoration. This plantation Palladian along the Rappahannock, the York, and the James rivers included Marmion, Stratford, Mount Airy, Rosewell, Tuckahoe, Carter's Grove, Nomini Hall, Brandon, Shirley, Berkeley, and Westover.

William Byrd of Westover lived the gentleman's life which his forebears had made possible. The first William, son of a London goldsmith, had inherited James River property from his uncle, and had increased his fortune by trade with the Indians, sending his men into the western lands with rum, hatchets, guns, and kettles to be exchanged for furs, skins, and minerals; his vessels, tobacco-laden on their eastward voyages, brought back slaves and rich English furnishings for tidewater customers. The second William was educated in England, knew Congreve and Wycherley, and tasted the social and intellectual life of London at the turn of the century.

Back at Westover, which he thoroughly remodeled, Byrd led the balanced life of his class: political service on the Council; enormously varied reading; constant supervision of life on his plantation; attendance upon Anglican services each Sunday; and, by way of relaxation, hunting and dancing, fencing and polite conversation, music and the theater. As head of the Virginia Boundary Commission, he wrote *The Dividing Line,* and his descriptive essays of the 1730's—*A Journey to the Land of Eden* and *A Progress to the Mines*—were models not only of keen observation but of English prose. Among the four thousand volumes at Westover were Erasmus, Plutarch, Bacon, Cicero, Machiavelli, and Thomas More, together with books on law, the scriptures, science, farming, painting, and architecture. In lighter moments the colonel read the sly verses of *The Beggar's Opera* to Widow Fleming; and his comment on a girl who had married her uncle's overseer could have been spoken from a stage in London:

Had she run away with a Gentleman or a pretty Fellow, there might have been some Excuse for her, tho' he were of inferior Fortune: but to stoop to a dirty Plebian, without any kind of merit, is the lowest Prostitution.

Westover on the bank of the James was not unlike Mount Pleasant—a symmetrical brick mansion with steps leading up to its pedimented doorway, chimneys at both ends of its steep hipped roof, and lower buildings at each side which were smaller editions of the main block, but plainer as befitted their meaner functions. The mahogany stair balustrades of Westover were carved in delicate spiral forms, and the floridly graceful stucco work on the ceiling above them was as French as the arabesques in Fairmount Park.

The coast of North Carolina took its architectural fashions from colonies to the north. "The Grove" at Halifax owed something to Robert Morris' *Select Architecture,* a book which had already provided details for a house at Williamsburg. Tryon's Palace at New Bern, the most luxuriant flowering of the English seed, was similar to a plate in the Morris volume. This capitol of 1767, destroyed by fire in 1798 and now rebuilt to approximate its former dignity and elegance, was costly enough to provoke an armed rebellion by overtaxed yeomen. The king's arms were in the pediment of its central block, and the two pavilions which served as kitchen and stables were joined to the palace by curving colonnades. Tryon's great hall held niches for statues, and on the "Ionic" marble chimney piece in his council chamber were medallions of the king and queen. From England came marble, hinges, and locks, window sash, and the skilled workmen who installed its unique plumbing system. From far and near in the colonies came admiring travelers to delight in its majestic orderliness and the beauty of its formal gardens.

The varied population which made Charleston society a blend of English, French, Dutch, Swiss, and West Indian elements also accounts for the diversity of its houses. To Charleston came the planters of the Ashley and Cooper rivers to market their rice, indigo, and cotton, to see the latest comedy from London at the Dock Street Theater, to attend concerts by the St. Cecilia Society, or to perfect themselves in fencing and dancing. Climate here conditioned the art of building. A general dampness pushed the ground-floor story several feet above ground, inviting the ironmaster to forge curving stair rails and elaborate gates. Sultry days and nights determined the high spacious rooms, with a corresponding coarseness of scale in their woodwork. Long porches and piazzas hinted at the tropical ways of the Caribbean Islands and had a vaguely Spanish flavor, and many a Charleston house stood endwise to the street in order that its galleries might face its gardens as they did in Haiti and Santo Domingo.

House, Meeting St., Charleston, S.C.

F. S. Lincoln photo

The Palladian touch, however, was seen in Ralph Izard's house, which was said to be the work of Thomas Hope from England. The Heyward-Washington house looked as though it had strayed from Philadelphia, and

Peter Harrison, Brick Market, Newport, R.I.

Wayne Andrews photo

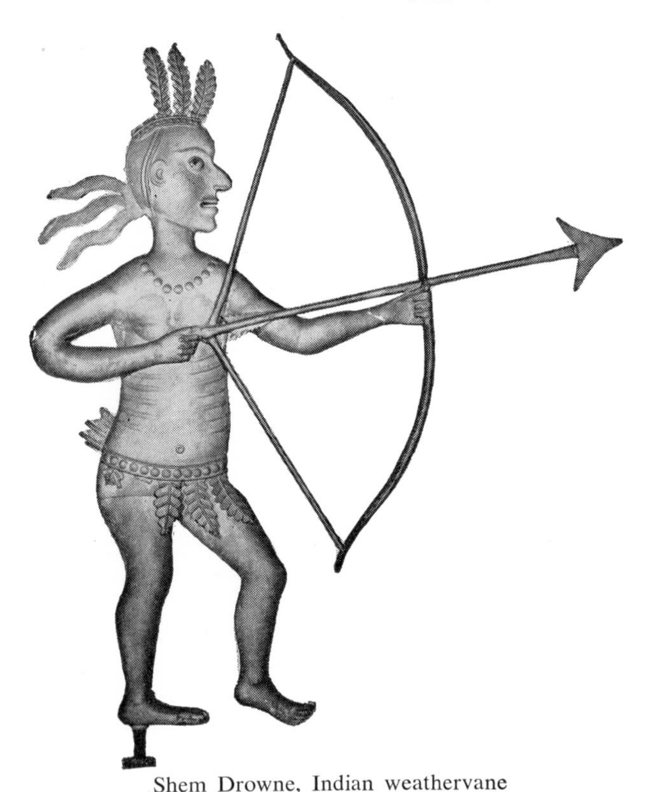

Shem Drowne, Indian weathervane

Massachusetts Historical Society, Boston, Mass.

the classic pediment and portico of Miles Brewton's brick mansion would have made a New Englander feel at home.

To think of colonial towns in terms of the Royall mansion or Mount Pleasant, or of the more countrified provinces in terms of the Carters, the Lees, and the Byrds, would be to distort the total picture. How much of this sprucely English formalism was reflected in the homes of the middle class, the Pennsylvania farms, the small holdings of the piedmont yeomen? Very little indeed, except in the greater regularity of plan, the symmetry of doors and windows, the lowered roof line, and other classical efforts of the more modest home.

In Newport, Rhode Island, in Portsmouth, New Hampshire, and in other communities whose earlier character has not yet been obliterated, one can find whole streets whose small dwellings caught some of the robust, square-built quality which was part of the English inheritance. On an occasional clapboarded front which is otherwise plain, one finds rusticated corners; on a roof, dormers with pediments which alternate between round-topped and triangular. A stout and bulky gambreled home on the Connecticut River will have ingeniously broken pediment forms over its otherwise plain windows. A man in Newport will rusticate his wooden front in the manner of Isaac Royall. A builder who knows his manuals will construct a doorway which has no more than a simple entablature above and two pilaster slabs at the sides. Hancock's scrolled doorway, whose stone came from Middletown, was copied in wood up and down the valley by men who gave it a special character at Hadley, Deerfield, Westfield, and Longmeadow. No two of these doorways are particularly alike, and each of them reveals the craftsman's capacity to play delightful variations on a given theme. For one full Palladian residence, one must suppose hundreds of plain boxes whose owners borrowed what they could afford, and no more, from the classical vocabulary.

Throughout the colonial period, men were content to transact the public business, to do their marketing, and to secure their education in structures whose main lines and ornamental details were similar to the domestic. The scale of Boston's old State House, the cupola, and the carved lion and unicorn upon its stepped gable, proclaimed an official function. The scrolled window pediment on the west front of the Colony House at Newport, its dormers, balustrade, and the rusticated border of its windows were features to be found on people's houses, but the bulk was greater, the entrance more impressive, the brick ornament more emphatic. The pilasters of Peter Harrison's Newport market went up two floors and its arched first story was open for the convenience of the purchaser. Chowan County Courthouse in Edenton, North Carolina, imitated the brick regularity and the finely proportioned cupolas at Williamsburg; the paneling of its assembly room merely adapted itself to loftier proportions than were to be found in private homes.

It was in buildings like these that one found the work of men who could not be called sculptors in the full sense of the word, since they were as yet dependent on more utilitarian crafts. One looked for evidence of the carver's talent on the legs and crests of chairs, bureaus, and highboys which Goddard, Savery, and Townsend designed as exquisitely as any Londoner. One found it in the convolutions of carved heraldry, perhaps the most splendid example being the Holden coat of arms which filled the pediment of the Harvard College Chapel, given in memory of the Bank of England's governor. The gravestone cutter still plied his craft; William Clark's tablet on Copps Hill was as richly garlanded with flowers as his mantelpiece had been; many tombs bore incised portraits of the men beneath them; the Charlestown apprentices of Joseph Lamson cut gravestones throughout the century. When William Davenport of Newburyport turned his home into a tavern in 1762, he carved the profile of General Wolfe for its signboard.

As early as 1720 Sir William Pepperell commissioned a carved lion for one of his vessels, and it was probably the Senior Simeon Skillin, referred to as a ship's carver in 1741, who cut the figurehead of *Minerva* for the privateer *Hazard* during the Revolution. On the roof of Isaac Royall's summerhouse a homely wooden version of Giovanni da Bologna's *Mercury* served as a weathervane. Between the scrolls of doorway pediments stood polychromed pineapples and even small figures like the semiclassical *Hope* which once graced a Salem portal. Before the Admiral Vernon tavern in State Street, Boston, was a painted wooden seaman whose outstretched hand was equipped with a sextant when he moved to another location to advertise an instrument maker's wares.

Whole companies of men worked months at a time on the rich capitals for the aisles of St. Paul's and similar churches, or on the Prince of Wales feathers over pulpits. And on rare occasions, sculptured figures were produced which had their own excuse for being. In Boston, Henry Christian Geyer specialized in tombs and "frontispieces" for fireplaces; but in the year 1768 he announced that he had perfected the art of "Fuser Simulacrorum," or the casting in plaster of cats, dogs, "and all other sorts of curious Animals"; from his shop near the South Fish Market came busts of Homer and Milton, King George and Queen Charlotte, together with lions, parrots, and sheep. More enterprising than Geyer was Ben Franklin's friend Patience Wright, whom Abigail Adams called the "Queen of Sluts," and who modeled famous Englishmen here and abroad in colored wax, dressing her life-sized figures in real clothing.

For his tale, *Shem Drowne's Wooden Image,* Nathaniel Hawthorne borrowed the name of a well-known Boston craftsman. There were four sons of Leonard Drowne, three of whom followed their father's craft as shipwrights—Solomon, Samuel, and Simeon. Shem had a knack for turning copper kettles into weathervanes, most of them in the traditional English form of a pennant or a rooster; his grasshopper still turns on Faneuil Market. His masterpiece, however, was the copper Indian, potbellied and adorned with curious stiff feathers, whose eye gleamed in the sun because it was made of glass, and who was always about to shoot an arrow into the wind from the turret of the Province House. His flashing gyrations above a residence where royal governors came and went in their task of building a second England may perhaps be taken as a symbol and a reminder that there was something in America which could not be hammered into English forms. Shem's glass eye looked down on Hutchinson's orchard and saw Colonel Royall's coach roll up to King's Chapel. When the wind turned, it could also see Sam Adams on his way to a meeting of the Sons of Liberty, and Paul Revere glancing at Christ Church steeple as though he already knew that it would be a good place to hang a lantern.

CHAPTER 4 / LIKENESSES IN A PROPER MANNER

In December 1735 the painter Charles Bridges waited upon Alexander Spotswood at the latter's palace, carrying with him a note of introduction from Colonel William Byrd:

> The person, who has had the honour to wait upon you, with this letter, is a man, of a Good Family, but either by the Frowns of Fortune, or his own mismanagement, is obliged to seek his Bread, a little of the latest in a Strange Land. His name is Bridges, & His Profession, is Painting, and if you have any Employment for him in that way, he will be proud of obeying your commands. He has drawn my children, & several others in the neighborhood; & 'tho he have not the Masterly Hand of a Lilly, or a Kneller, yet, had he lived so long ago, as when places were given to the most Deserving, he might have pretended to be serjeant Painter of Virginia.

When that note was written, there were at least several painters who, like Bridges, could call themselves professionals, and who in a strange land commended themselves to the families of the top colonial clique because they came as close to the Knelleresque as could reasonably be expected. The American portrait of these years has lost its earlier low-toned austerity. Rigidity of pose has given place to a kind of businesslike alertness, a self-assured tension, and, at rare moments, an affable relaxation. Sober blacks and browns have been changed for scarlet coats and for waistcoats of flowered satin brocade, as much the evidence of status as the personality in the face, or the imperious gesture. Behind the gentleman or his lady appears the sturdy column and the looped curtain which has become the accepted symbol of wealth and distinction, or now and then a ship under sail to hint that the sitter's aristocracy is of the codfish rather than the tobacco kind.

Although Kneller had been dead two years when Byrd wrote his letter of introduction, Joseph Highmore and Thomas Hudson kept Knellerism alive in England

John Smibert, *Sir William Pepperell*

Essex Institute, Salem, Mass.

until well after the middle of the century. Highmore painted the Knights of the Bath with something less than his master's "god-like form," but he had seen Rubens in Antwerp, and there was at least a faint echo of that experience in the round, full forms of his women's faces, the deft indication of the crimson satin sleeves, the gracefully curved arm playing with a necklace or holding a bouquet or a single flower, the muted sheen of a man's velvet. Hudson lacked even Highmore's degree of fluency, and could only itemize the gold buttons, the brocaded cuff, the glint of the sword hilt, and the lace-ruffled sleeve in canvases whose over-all effect was dull, despite the obvious effort of his subject to hold the correct pose. Governor William Shirley of Massachusetts sat, or rather anxiously stood, to Hudson; but the majority of patrons, as Byrd suggested, were content with the work of men who had left Europe to seek provincial bread, and who settled down in northern cities or moved from one commission to another in the less concentrated south.

In the year Byrd wrote his letter, the city of Charleston was supporting Jeremiah Theüs of Switzerland; John Watson, who had come to Perth Amboy twenty years before, was in mid-career; Henrietta Johnston and Justus Engelhardt Kühn had worked in South Carolina and in Maryland. Gustavus Hesselius from Stockholm had established his reputation in the middle provinces, and had taken up his twenty-year residence in High Street, Philadelphia. Boston had the cosmopolitan John Smibert, the plodding Englishman Peter Pelham, and the rather crude Nathaniel Emmons. Men of so diverse national origins suggest the growing diversity of the colonial peoples; the work they did is proof that the long tradition from Van Dyck through Lely to Kneller and the Knelleresques was still tenacious.

None of these mid-century face painters could match the skill and the urbanity of Scottish Smibert, though more than one attempted his fluency and his bland impressiveness. If his brush was less heavy than that of his rivals here, and his color slightly mellower, it was because James Thornhill had instructed him, and because copying old masters in Italy under the eye of Cosimo the Third had relaxed his hand and suggested how to be firm and fresh at the same time. When Smibert set up his easel in Boston in 1730 and assembled what was probably the first art exhibition in colonial America, he had produced the group portrait of *Bishop Berkeley and His Family,* as a member of which the painter had come to Newport a year before (Yale Univ.). There was a competence in the smooth and solid representation of the individual figures, and an almost graceful manner of grouping the bishop's family, the like of which New England had not seen—the drawing firm but not hard, the colors tempered to an all-embracing harmony, the personalities vigorously if not subtly realized.

No colonial painter could so firmly construct a head as it rounded off into shadow and so superbly render soft velvet, crisp linen, and the glint of light on the silken curls of a wig; and his men impress the observer with their intense aliveness, their almost arrogant forcefulness. *Nathaniel Byfield* (Met. Mus.) is a resourceful study of imperious old age by a brush that followed the pinched lines of the small mouth and the folds of jowls which had begun to be flabby; and *William Browne* (Johns Hopkins Univ.) stands full length before a background which reveals Smibert's skill with rocks, trees, waterfalls, and blue mountain distances.

Around the corner from the Boston State House in Court Street, Smibert showed in 1730 not only his portraits but copies of Italian masterpieces, and "young" Mather Byles was inspired by the novelty of the exhibition to salute the painter with homemade verses. Before the coming of this master,

> No heav'nly Pencil the free Stroke could give,
> Nor the warm Canvas felt its Colors live.
> Solid and grave, and plain the Country stood,
> Inelegant, and rigorously good.

But now, in the Scotsman's painting room, fairy scenes and gay "landskips" delight the fancy, the "breathing Statue and the living Bust":

> In hoary majesty, see *Sewall* here;
> Fixt strong in thought there *Byfield's* Lines appear.
> Here in full Beauty blooms the charming maid,
> Here Roman ruins nod their awful Head:
> Here gloting monks their am'rous rights debate,
> Th' *Italian* master sits in easy state,
> *Vandike* and *Rubens* show their Rival Forms,
> And studious *Mascarene* asserts his Arms.

Boston's opportunity to remind itself that face painting was not the whole of art was almost but not quite unique. For nearly a decade the pewholders of Saint Barnabas Church in Prince Georges County, Maryland, had taken pride in a *Last Supper* by Gustavus Hesselius. This Smibert of the South was not less famous for his portraits than for his religious and classical canvases, doubtless inspired by engravings. If either Smibert or Hesselius hoped to win commissions for landscape or mythology, they quickly discovered the error. In Delaware, in Maryland, and in Pennsylvania the Swede, who had preceded the Scotsman by eighteen years, displayed little of Smibert's robust vigor. The Hesselius pose is, comparatively speaking, nerveless, the brush inert. His portrait of *Mrs. Henry Darnall III* (Md. Hist. Soc.) is moderately solid and presents that homely person without flattery and without tact. Occasionally form slipped from beneath his brush, and his uncertain draughtsmanship produced impossibly tapering fingers with double joints; at other times he painted freely and broadly, without fussiness. In *Tishcohan* and in *Lapowinsa,* Hesselius anticipated the documentary thoroughness of George Catlin's Indians a century later (Pa. Hist. Soc.).

Both Smibert and Hesselius applied a mature Old World craftsmanship to the new commissions; the mysterious Robert Feke, by contrast, was largely self-formed and only twenty-five when Berkeley's friend was enlightening Boston, and the Swede painted a Maryland *Crucifixion.* Why was Feke called a "mariner," and did he travel in Spain and Italy during the 1730's? And was the silken finesse of his forties learned abroad from Highmore or Hudson and their like or inspired at secondhand by paintings and prints seen at home? How is it that he can be called by Burroughs a camp follower of the British school, and by Hagen an artist "in search of the human being," a search conducted with a large degree of independence?

Robert Feke, *Unknown Woman*

Brooklyn Museum

Of Robert Feke's responsiveness to suggestion there are proofs in abundance. His group portrait of twenty-two-year-old Isaac Royall and his family is a stilted effort in the direction of Smibert's Berkeley piece (Harvard Univ.); and in the four Bowdoin portraits Feke has acquired from the Knelleresques a new deftness in the sleek folds of a creamy satin waistcoat and the play of light over oil-slick satin dresses which are not to be found in the thin and unvaried textures of his youthful canvases. Yet largely through innate power and an almost feminine sensitiveness came Feke's capacity to transmute borrowings and to make every observed nicety peculiarly his own. He was born and lived in a society which was in transition, a generation still half Puritan even though its wives read Fielding and Smollett and its husbands were appraised in terms of prosperity, not piety. Smibert almost convinces us that they wear their velvet and finger their nosegays with English assurance; Feke knows they are charming amateurs who remain themselves, and goes to the heart of the self with a directness as different from the insensitiveness of Hesselius as from the aggressive masculinity and the pictorial swagger of Smibert. Youthful and handsome, Isaac Royall stands beside a table and looks straight into the eyes of the observer. The colonel's wife, his sister, and his sister-in-law are posed with the rigidity of dolls, and the year-old baby seems thrust into the group, perhaps born too late to have had provision made for her in the original scheme.

Peter Pelham, *Rev. Benjamin Colman,* mezzotint

Museum of Fine Arts, Boston, Mass.

John Wollaston, *Philip Philipse*

Museum of the City of New York

Yet even Royall's womenfolk have a grave and modest charm, a freshness and a simple grace to be found more often in Feke's than in Smibert's ladies. In comparison with the latter's *James MacSparren* (Bowdoin Coll.), Feke's sharp-featured *Thomas Hiscox* rebukes the world with an intensity that is not so much physical as psychological. Perhaps Feke had a healthy balance of personal vision and craftsmanship which made him say no more than could be said with quiet conviction and a sure economy. When Feke portrayed himself, as he did twice, his face was scarcely more than a shaded oval, its arched eyebrows, penetrating eyes, sharp nose, and thin lips set down in expressive shorthand; the painter found a contour line from the brow to the straight neck and down the coat front to convey the nervous alertness of the whole man. The self-likeness of the older Feke is heavier fleshed, the features grown sharper within a rounder head, but the same incorruptible bright eyes prove that he missed nothing that was significant in his world. Feke's ladies of the 1740's were elegantly dressed in satin whose dark folds and shimmering lights he broadly simplified in his own fashion; there is a generalization in their hands and faces but not enough to obscure their intelligence and their self-possession. The innately fastidious Feke and the integrity of his vision give a more than worldly grace to his Bowdoin family portraits.

To compare Smibert and Feke in terms of "realism" is to juggle with a slippery word which can mean the skillful assembling of surface details or an identification of the artist with the personality before him. Smibert left a superbly convincing picture of the men who captured Fort Louisburg; Feke suggests what went on in their minds when they were neither fighting nor bargaining.

The strenuous Smibert, the rugged Hesselius, and the intimate Feke had their competitors. The career of Peter Pelham had nearly run its course when Smibert died in 1751, leaving his landscapes, portraits, and history pieces to be inventoried by John Greenwood; when aging Gustavus Hesselius passed commissions to his son John; and when Feke disappeared from the New England scene. John Watson worked for nearly two decades more and died in 1768; Charles Bridges had found patrons among the Byrds and other Virginian aristocrats before he left the colonies about 1740; Jeremiah Theüs had worked as long in Charleston as Bridges in Virginia.

Pelham was skilled in the making of mezzotints, a procedure which trained his eye and hand in the separation of planes, the clear definitions, the sheen of highlights upon forehead, nose, and chin which gives his Massachusetts divines the forcefulness, if not the floridity, of Smibert's likenesses. He had preceded the latter

John Hesselius, *Elizabeth Calvert*

Baltimore Museum of Art

by three or four years in Boston, where he was prepared to teach dancing, reading, writing, and the art of painting on glass, and where some ten years after his arrival he married a widow whose nine-year-old son was John Singleton Copley. New England had possessed no such engraved likenesses of its governors and preachers as Pelham made from his own and Smibert's paintings. Peter's oil of *Cotton Mather* (Am. Antiq. Soc.) suggests not only the "keeper of the Puritan conscience" but the man of intellect who corresponded on scientific matters with the Royal Society of London; when Pelham painted a New England divine, the zigzag folds in a robe and the crests in a curled wig were accented as a mezzotint scraper would have accented them.

During the second quarter of the century Charles Bridges had no rival for the title of Sergeant Painter of Virginia. Was he responsible for the dry and perfunctory half-length of *Alexander Spotswood* (Va. Capitol)? It has been hopefully assumed that he painted Maria Byrd, the colonel's second wife (Met. Mus.). Maria sat for an artist who was obviously impressed by her beauty, sensitively recording her large dark eyes, her full lips, and young rounded cheeks, and crisply rendering the cream-and-silver gray of her satin gown. Nothing more substantial, however, than family tradition links Bridges with any portrait.

With no trace of the Virginian flattery Theüs limned society in Charleston, and his rather prim precision may have been learned at home from Liotard. The execution of his portraits of middle-aged Gabriel Manigault and his wife (Met. Mus.) is neat and forceless; Madame is given her small, buttonlike eyes, long nose, and firm, fat chin; her chunky body strains at its satin bodice, whose ribboned bow is so sharply and meticulously modeled that it springs from its plane.

The noteworthy provincial of the 1750's called on a second generation for his likeness. Bridges had left Virginia, and the New England trio of Smibert, Feke, and Pelham was no more. John Hesselius inherited his father's patronage; John Wollaston of London had learned something of Feke's skill in posing a sitter. Lawrence Kilburn, who had been born as Lorenz Kielbrunn in Denmark, announced to New Yorkers in 1754 his competence in "taking a true likeness" and "finishing the Drapery in a proper Manner." In Philadelphia William Williams turned from the painting of stage scenery to the painting of faces; and Boston knew three portrait makers, two of whom were born within sight of Beacon Hill.

William Williams, *Deborah Hall*

Brooklyn Museum

Joseph Badger, *Jeremiah Belknap*

Cleveland Museum of Art

Wollaston was in many ways the most skillful of these latter-day colonials, and covered the distances from New York to Annapolis and from Williamsburg to Charleston in twenty industrious years. When he first came, there was more than a hint of Hogarth's rugged quality in what he did, though he missed the rich, broad handling and the shrewd personalization of Hogarth. For a society which no doubt considered such frankness vulgar, and which knew the master of the *Rake's Progress* only through engravings, Wollaston tempered his American style to a less brutal vitality; and there was a ramrod stiffness in his women's bodices which became a Wollaston signature. Philip Philipse, lord of the manor, and his mother-in-law Mary Marston are quite obviously persons of importance vigorously drawn and competently painted in appropriate attitudes from the outside in, their rather fleshy forms recorded without flattery and without penetration. Wollaston's gentlemen are in mute-colored garments which set off their shiny glowing faces; for his women, he often combines gold-colored satins with delicious blue ones.

An oily smoothness seems to have marked the younger Hesselius from the start, though contact with the work of Wollaston may have furthered it. His *Elizabeth Calvert,* eight years old, was done with fluent and firmly three-dimensional modeling in a lustrous cream-colored satin dress and a red cape against dark sky and trees. Her brother Charles is only five, yet his rose-pink clothes, his cloak of luminous green-blue, and his plumed velvet hat are the Maryland nobility in miniature; and while young Charles's left hand attempts the gesture of superiority, his Negro body-servant kneels in subordination beside him in yellow-buff livery (Baltimore Mus.). Although John Hesselius even attempted infants, whom he drew inadequately in ungainly poses, his sure sense of form did not desert him, and no doubt Maryland found his overpolish to its taste, as the critic of today finds pleasure in his color schemes.

The obviously pretty delighted another painter of these years, the William Williams who made *Deborah Hall* so sprightly and so mincingly elegant in pink satin, fine lace frills, and flower-trimmed bodice, posing her in what seems a stage setting for a scene from Goldsmith or Sheridan. Williams had learned as a Philadelphia scene painter how to provide his background with statues in niched walls, with formal clipped trees sprouting from urns on pedestals. The brush with which he placed Deborah among these beauties was sharp and fine, his edges knife-clear, and every hair upon the tame chipmunk, every petal on the rose tree she fingers, was precisely itemized. He painted a *Gentleman and His Wife* as though they were playing in a scene from a London comedy, with wings in the shape of cutout trees, illumination that suggests footlights, and on the backdrop an oddly theatric view of mills, church towers, and castles which seems to have made an impression on Williams' young acquaintance, Benjamin West. One could read in a Philadelphia journal of 1763 that, at the sign of Hogarth's Head in Loxley Court, Williams carried on his business of "Painting in General" but was also qualified to instruct polite youth in drawing and to sound the hautboy and the German flute.

There was not the slightest hint, in New England during these years, of this delightful artifice. Boston still frowned, officially at least, upon the playhouse. Its people may have regretted the passing of Smibert and Pelham, and even winced slightly as Badger and Greenwood replaced them; yet these two, and a few years later Blackburn, were all that Boston had until Copley came of age. The parents of the small Calverts could delight in John Hesselius; the Belknaps and the Ornes entrusted their boys and girls to a poverty-stricken tailor's son from Charlestown who painted and glazed houses, and struggled to support his own six children.

Joseph Badger could achieve only a tenth part of Hesselius' rotundity; his forms were flaccid, his colors muddy, his flesh tones inertly dull, and there is scarcely a nose in all his work that stands at right angles to its face; the features are defined, limner-fashion, as on a map, and the hands and lace ruffles are shapes without being forms. *Captain John Larrabee* (Worcester Art

John S. Copley, *Ann Tyng*

Museum of Fine Arts, Boston, Mass.

Joseph Blackburn, *The Isaac Winslow Family*

Museum of Fine Arts, Boston, Mass.

Mus.), done full length before a seascape, seems modeled in colored wax, his telescope resting impossibly on the nose of a cannon which is behind him; the bold stance seems a parody of Smibert. When Badger turned to children, their half-formed faces and rather startled movements proved a more rewarding subject. Once at least, in his likeness of young *Rebecca Orne,* he achieved a clean and lively color in the blue gown, and his drawing was both delicate and sure (Addison Gall.). In some thirty juvenile portraits, Badger caught the innocence, the odd self-sufficiency, and even at times the pathos of childhood, as more competent craftsmen would have failed to do. His own naïveté responded to that of boys and girls who, though they wore the clothes of their elders, came from his brush not small-scale men and women but distinctly appealing creatures with a strange life of their own. Small *Jeremiah Belknap,* overdressed and solemn beside his eager dog, is but one of many canvases by the humble Badger in which, despite all too obvious shortcomings, he wrought perhaps better than he or his patrons knew.

Humility was not the word for Joseph Blackburn, whose notion of the handsome was derived from English sources. There was time enough between 1754 and 1763 for him to set a precedent for shimmering dress and rather simpering faces, as he did with his group portrait, *The Isaac Winslow Family.* Winslow at sixty-five would command the talent of Copley; now he points rather pointlessly at his young wife and two children, and Madame Winslow presents her small eyes, her thinly closed lips, full chins, and sloping shoulders above a gown whose gleaming texture has been artfully rendered. The rather smug faces are undermodeled in relation to his sharp drawing of their features, producing a somewhat vacuous effect, and the slight upturning at the corners of tight lips becomes a mannerism. The Winslow piece fails to achieve the linked unity of Smibert's and becomes a mere assembling of three main figures side by side; it was an underdeveloped sense of color which allowed Blackburn to place the brown-yellow suit of Isaac near his wife's red satin, whose highlights are pinkish-purple and whose shadows a warm orange-red.

Blackburn was at his best in the single figure of *Colonel Theodore Atkinson* (Worcester Art Mus.), with its strongly channeled features and fine hands, the body disposed in angular lines to suggest a controlled strength beneath dignity.

John Greenwood was born in Boston where he served an apprenticeship to Thomas Johnston. While other artisans gave wooden panelling the look of grained marble, decorated plaster walls with painted mandarins, peacocks and bamboo thickets, or represented a man's house on his overmantel, Johnston japanned furniture and made prints. Badger drew the Yale College building for a Johnston engraving before he established himself as a portrait painter; Greenwood's literal mind enabled him to evoke the sitter, defects of physiognomy included, and although his tones were as dull as Badger's, he somehow avoided Badger's pasty complexions.

There was no trace of liveliness in the way Greenwood described a lace ruching, nor any but the most subdued gleam in his stuffs; he painted with the steel sharpness of his earlier occupation, and it may have been his hand, as Alan Burroughs suggested, which drew the intrusive addition to the Royall family portrait. Mrs. Nathaniel Cunningham sat for him in a creamy gray satin gown and dark green-blue drapery of which Greenwood made a mildly pleasant color scheme, though his modeling of its folds was flaccid and the woman's long and too tapering fingers were wiry in outline and weak in substance (Boston Mus. Fine Arts).

Greenwood quit Boston in 1752. Within the next ten years young Copley was to prove that he could outdistance the pale Badger, improve upon his stepfather Pelham, and temper the acid sharpnes of Greenwood. For his *Ann Tyng* in 1756 Copley used the lamb and shepherd's crook which are also to be found in Blackburn; although Ann's finery was drily done, Copley proved at eighteen that he could compete with Blackburn, and make his elders seem mere gropers for illusion.

Joseph Blackburn, *Col. Theodore Atkinson* (detail)

Worcester Art Museum

General Putnam, by an unknown painter ▶

Courtesy Harry Shaw Newman

PART THREE

THE REVOLUTIONARY GENERATION

INTRODUCTION / EMERGENCE OF THE YANKEE

At Fort Louisburg and Quebec, Englishmen from England and Englishmen from New York, Boston, and points south fought side by side to preserve an empire; few of these men returned to their shops, their farms, and their countinghouses with any premonition that, within a dozen years, the imperial cord would snap. Yet already the cord was tense, and presently it became the task of the local governors to enforce new laws which made it clear that British theory and American practice were covertly at war. The Stamp Act, the Sugar Act, the Mutiny Act, the Tea Act were proofs of impasse which could not be ignored by men who would never truly be English again.

> They would try, they would swear they were,
> they would drink the toast,
> They would loyally petition and humbly pray,

yet soon realize that "the country is where the life is, not elsewhere." And the country, a few miles from the great coastal centers, was filled with humble men and women whose loyalties were those which link a man to his own plough and hammer, to plain Congregational piety, and the give-and-take of the town meeting. The mob, as Gouverneur Morris warned the gentry, was beginning to think and reason.

The colonial townsman cut his political teeth on resistance to royal officials; the mechanic borrowed from public libraries books which contained dangerously new ideas; the farmer's almanac taught him more things than he needed to plan crops and predict weather. If his faith quarreled with his common sense, he discovered that the Deists preferred Reason to Revelation. After the drone of the Puritan divine his sense of emotional self was quickened by Jonathan Edwards and by the flashing tongue of Whitefield. College-bred men still scattered Ciceronian phrases through what they said and wrote; but among the colleges of pre-Revolutionary America there were three where a man could learn geography and mathematics, and glimpse a world which behaved in accordance with provable laws of its own.

Locke had suggested that people read what sharpens the mind, develops the argumentative capacities, and serves for diversion and delight; and some colonials now took pleasure in Sterne's *Sentimental Journey,* Goldsmith's *Vicar of Wakefield,* and even Molière and Rabelais. Others read Rousseau's description of the natural man and proceeded to create an American version of that admirable creature which was to astonish and please Europe in the person of Benjamin West. From Locke, Montesquieu, and the rest of the Enlighteners was derived much confidence in the mind freed from superstition and from tyranny. One could read in the essay "Of Civil Government," and note for future use, the remark that men unite for the mutual preservation of their lives, liberties, and estates; one could even play with Locke's notion that "shaking off a power which force and not right hath set over any one, though it hath the name of rebellion, yet is no offence before God."

In economic behavior, religion, politics, and philosophy, the Yankee had emerged. This was what John Adams meant at eighty when he wrote to Jefferson: "The War? That was no part of the revolution; it was only an effect and consequence of it. The revolution was in the minds of the people . . . ."

The old gentleman might have added that, forty years before, he had been of the right wing when Gage's men marched on Lexington to provoke a war which was a civil war, a struggle between the colonials and England, but also a struggle of divided American loyalties. For the Adamses and the Carrolls, the Livingstons and the Bowdoins, the Hamiltons and the Browns, new English ideas were less a justification for rebellion than an affirmation that the state exists for the protection of a man's wealth and property. If American business enterprise conflicted with England's, let England be more generous. If seventeen million pounds of tea threatened to put Hancock and his fellows out of business, then politely refuse to drink it. And if the conservative resigned himself to an armed conflict, he hoped that those who were accustomed to manage the American affairs would still be managers when it was over.

The left wing looked forward too, but not to the resumption of the *status quo.* For one John Adams there were a thousand farmers who had read the prophecies in Nathaniel Ames's Almanac. Nathaniel believed that the movement of civilization follows the sun from east to west, and foresaw that "the Residence of Wild Beasts will be broken up, and their obscene Howl cease forever; — Instead of which the Stones and Trees will dance together at the Music of *Orpheus,* — the Rocks will disclose their hidden Gems." But while the Yankee dreamed, he must also reflect and act: "Let us, then, my countrymen, study not only religion but politicks . . . take upon us to examine every thing, and think for ourselves."

Thus urged, the democracy had not been idle before Lexington. The Ames almanac came to an end that year with a recipe for homemade gunpowder. Already the artisans, mechanics, and farmers had organized the Sons of Liberty; their Sam Adams had inspired the first constitutional convention, and with it the first gesture of intercolonial solidarity. Putnam and Stark, Allen and Marion would now outwit and outendure the British regulars along rivers and through pastures while protest became rebellion and insubordination gave way to the claim of independence. When the fighting was over came years of debate and dissension. Was the Constitution to be a charter of human freedom or a device for protecting this world's goods? Ten years after Washington bade farewell to his officers in the Fraunces Tavern, John Adams was the champion of the conservatives, while the Democratic clubs had become the Republican party of Thomas Jefferson.

Out of these years of struggle came a literature and an art in some degree conscious of its American peculiarity. Out of Addison, Ben Franklin wrought his uniquely personal style. Tom Paine moved less self-consciously, and his magnificent clarity, his fierce drive were qualities of the man called forth by the occasion. No one better than Paine characterized the Tory group: "Interested men, who are not to be trusted; weak men, who *cannot* see; prejudiced men, who *will not* see; and a certain set of moderate men, who think better of the European world than it deserves." No one was quite as close as Paine to the mind of the Revolution when Washington's men tracked blood in the snow as they fell back through Jersey, and Paine wrote with numbed fingers:

> These are the times that try men's souls. The summer soldier and the sunshine patriot will, in this crisis, shrink from the service of their country; but he that stands it now, deserves the love and thanks of man and woman . . .

While victory was still fresh in American minds, poets and playwrights "let it be told" with much verbal energy, but with something less than Tom Paine's common-sense conviction. A cause so divergently viewed was bound to have divergent spokesmen. Freneau, Brackenridge, and Trumbull were setting patriotism to the meters of Addison and Pope. The first two contrived *The Rising Glory of America;* the third was of the

Connecticut Trumbulls who upheld the patriot cause with a cool blend of loyalty and shrewdness and, in the postwar years, shared Federalist dislike for Jefferson. John Trumbull the painter defied his father, the old Governor of Connecticut, in his choice of a profession; John the writer embraced the American cause but not the "mob" on whom its success depended. Five years before blood was shed in Massachusetts he received his master's degree at Yale with an oration on the Uses and Advantages of the Fine Arts, in which he accused British authors of servility to classic models and prophesied that America would one day rule in arts and arms because she loved liberty and educated her own people. At this point young Trumbull took to verse with a "Prospect of the Future Glory of America":

> Behold some new Apelles, skill'd to trace
> The varied features of the virgin's face . . .

The poet counseled the painter in words he had filched from Addison,

> Bid art with nature hold a pleasing strife,
> And warm the pictured canvas into life.

In 1776 this Hartford Wit turned from the stilted to the extravagantly funny in "M'Fingal," uproarious satire of the British Tory. The poem, as revolutionary propaganda, was perhaps less effective than Paine and Freneau or the jingling rhymes of Francis Hopkinson's "Battle of the Kegs." There were lines in Trumbull's poem in which the Whig rabble, though ostensibly seen through M'Fingal's eyes, were described with a scorn, an underlying revulsion which betrayed the author's own fear of the democracy:

> From dunghills deep of blackest hue,
> Your dirt-bred patriots spring to view,
> To wealth and power and honors rise,
> Like new-wing'd maggots changed to flies . . .
> For in this ferment of the stream
> The dregs have work'd up to the brim,
> And by the rule of topsy-turvies,
> The scum stands foaming on the surface.

Trumbull had summoned a new Apelles; a larger group than had ever painted before was busy as he spoke in America. The generation who worked in the thirty years between the Stamp Act Congress of 1765 and the second term of Washington were for the most part native-born. In their lives, and in their art, directly or by implication, they revealed the impact of the divided loyalties which made the first American literature. A good many, like the leaders in politics and fighting, worked from the bottom to the brim, rising, if not to wealth and power, at least to honor. Had not the simple Quaker West, one year after Trumbull's youthful oration, astonished London with his *Death of General Wolfe,* and within another year become Historical Painter to the King of England?

The shadowy nameless limner is gone, and the tolerable craftsman, to be given board and keep while he daubs the family; in their place stands the independent, the quietly or blatantly self-advertised, the self-confident Yankee who makes portraits of people, not types. He paints, as Franklin writes, with an eye backward cast toward useful Old World models, but with the deliberate aim of putting old models to new uses; and, in this sense, Charles Willson Peale is the Franklin of painting. Peale begins with sign-decorating, and through his own effort becomes the artist for whom Washington poses. Copley goes from his mother's small tobacco shop on Boston's Long Wharf to a three-thousand-dollar estate on Beacon Hill with three houses and a retinue of slaves. The American success story is now enacted by a group of professional artists as it had been played before by the dynasties of Byrd and Royall. One scarcely knows where Richard Jennys was born, but only that his work spans these thirty years, and that his Connecticut Valley likenesses have a chiseled forcefulness. A hard factualism dominates the period, in pictures as in politics. It is drily firm in Abraham Delanoy; ridged and knifelike in McKay. It is sturdy and careful in John Durand's likenesses of New England, New York, and Virginia people, and in the portraits John Mare was painting in the seventeen sixties in New York.

There were suaver painters than these: Christian Gullager; Matthew Pratt, who had four London years with West; Lawrence Kilburn, claiming that he had given agreeable satisfaction to English gentlemen and ladies. Was it because his patrons had less desire to be London ladies and gentlemen than had their mothers and fathers that Kilburn found himself the manager of a paint store in 1772? Certain it is that many painters of this revolutionary generation took upon them, as Nathaniel Ames had counseled, to examine everything and think for themselves. In aesthetic matters, as in political ones, they seem to have placed a higher value on the natural truth than upon the legalistic one, on Reason rather than on Revelation. And their independence of the English manner was the greater since they had in Copley an American-born master to serve as model.

Turning from the painter to the engraver, one finds in cruder form that same love for the concrete and the authentic; for the crisis of the 1760's had stimulated American efforts in the graphic arts, and their tone was thoroughly popular on the pages of magazines, on broadsides hawked through the streets, or on prints exposed in booksellers' windows. In this people's imagery, Paul Revere was more the executant than

B. Romans engraving, *An Exact View of the Late Battle at Charlestown*

Courtesy New York Public Library

the creator, and his engraving of the British troops landing at Boston depended in part upon the drawing by Christian Remick; his *Boston Massacre,* according to Pelham, was borrowed from that indignant worthy. For the *Royal American Magazine* Revere produced an allegory of tea being forced down the colonial throat, and a view of Boston Harbor bristling with hostile men-of-war. The approach was documentary: Revere's view was provided with a key to identify each and every vessel. Bernard Romans is supposed to have made campaign maps for the Continental army, and his *Exact View of the Late Battle at Charlestown,* which appeared in Philadelphia only a few weeks after the smoke had cleared from Breed's Hill, was maplike in specifying how the provincials lined up behind their breastwork and the English broke under their fire while frigates poured shells into the flaming village at the river's edge.

That master mariner from Cape Cod, Christian Remick, sailed on Revolutionary privateers and was prepared, as he advertised, to do "Sea Pieces, Perspective Views, Geographical Plans of Harbours, Sea Coasts, &ct." Most of his stiffly delicate water colors are marines, and there are at least five versions of his Blockade pictures.

Most ambitious of all was Amos Doolittle, who engraved four episodes which, he later claimed, he had based on Ralph Earl paintings: *The Battle of Lexington, A View of the Town of Concord, The Engagement at the North Bridge,* and a *View of the South Part of Lexington.* In these four line-engravings which the *Connecticut Journal* announced on December 13, 1775, as having been "this day published," it was obvious that Amos neither possessed the skill nor harbored the intention to glorify history. Yet there was an eyewitness fidelity and conviction in these scenes. Just in this way, one believes, did the solid ranks of the British move; just so did the scattered village men snipe from behind tree and wall as flames curled tongue-like from burning houses and tawny columns of smoke darkened the blue April sky.

Working in a like spirit, more than one painter of these years discards the abstract red drapery and the vague marble pillar from his background and presents his subject where he lives and works. Copley can pose Epes Sargent leaning on a column, but he can also put one of Paul Revere's silver teapots in that master craftsman's fingers. Ralph Earl shows the Reverend Nathaniel Taylor, pulpit and all, in the act of preaching, and locates Elijah Boardman in his dry-goods shop.

Here—to use the phrase of Constance Rourke—were "fresh configurations," nor was their freshness lost on Europe. For this was the day of the first Americans abroad: young West delighting the connoisseurs of Rome when the Apollo Belvedere reminded him of a Pennsylvania Indian; Copley daring to paint recent history; Ralph Earl portraying an English gentleman as though he were a Connecticut farmer.

It seems not to have greatly mattered in the London of the sixties and seventies whether the American visitor was an ardently or only a moderately rebellious subject of His Majesty. It mattered, however, to the man himself. Charles Willson Peale was twenty-six when he saw London, Copley ten years older when he caught sight of Dover Cliffs, John Trumbull twenty-four when he sought Benjamin West. All of them had known the times that tried men's souls, and each in his own way had made his choice, with consequences for his life and for his art—whether to join the Tory flight, or hold a precarious neutrality, or follow Tom Paine's urging and lay his shoulder to the wheel. The most complete American among them was Paine's own friend Peale. While Paine was writing his *Crisis* papers, Peale was in command of troops who fought at Trenton and Germantown, at White Plains and along the Brandywine; and when Paine called a Philadelphia meeting to rally the left against sunshine patriots who were also profiteers, Charles was there, the "furious Whig" whose mind had been nourished on Milton, Pope, Montesquieu, and the love poetry of Ovid, and whose ingenious hand could engrave, make silver, stuff birds, and fashion a barrel organ or a machine for enemas—since, as he said, he loved the mechanic arts, and would much rather practice the use of his tools than ride in a coach drawn by six horses. His patriotism rather more attended, he ruefully remarked, to make his country than himself independent; but when he turned from politics to "persue the brush" in 1780, that independence was as evident in his painting as it had been in his partisanship.

There was no such simple-mindedness in the Copley whose wife was the daughter of tea merchant Richard Clarke, and who signed his name to the Loyalist apology when that tea lay in the mud of Boston Harbor. He was among those moderate men who thought better, as Paine said, of the European world than it deserved. Copley had already given hostages to fortune when he heard the breaking of Boston windowpanes and saw the Sons of Liberty marching and meeting. In the year of the Tea Party he was still desirous, as he said, of "avoiding every imputation of party spirit, political contests being neither pleasing to an artist or advantageous to the Art itself." But Boston mobs were out of hand. In the month of November 1773, Copley's half brother Henry Pelham described the turmoil:

> The various and discordant Noises with which my Ears are continually assaild in the day, [the] passing of Carts and a constant throng of People, the shouting of an undisciplined Rabble the ringing of bells and sounding of Horns in the night . . . and the infernal yell of those who are fighting for the possessions of the Devill. . . .

Five months later Copley heard that yell in his own dooryard; six months later he prepared to sail alone for England and the Continent. This was both flight and fulfillment, since the painter had long ago resolved to better himself by foreign study; yet his choice had more finality than he reckoned.

John Trumbull's view of events and issues was somewhere between Peale's passionate self-identification with the Revolution and Copley's precarious above-the-battle stand. The Federalist coolness was in his family's veins, to be revealed in the years ahead by those chilled versions of great national events on which he based his claim to the title of Painter of the Revolution. At least some of those events Trumbull had seen at firsthand. He was within eyesight, he claimed, of the battle of Bunker Hill. He joined Washington's forces on the eve of Trenton; and two months later, at the bleak moment when it seemed to Paine that nothing but hope and virtue could survive, he resigned because his commission had been wrongly dated, and went back to Lebanon to paint portraits of his family. History did catch up with him a few years later when he spent a short time in a London prison as reprisal for the capture of Major André, but there was enough friendly pressure to release him; and while the great Constitutional quarrels racked America, Trumbull worked in West's studio and met David in Paris.

Temperament, to be sure, plays its part in the contrasts among these three leaders of the Revolutionary generation. Peale was as heartily sympathetic, as warmly responsive to the sitter as Copley was detached, and Trumbull austere. But even the artist who wills not to shape events will find that events have shaped him. This was the seed time of Continental union, faith, and honor, as Paine wrote. By the critical winter of 1776-1777 Peale had joined the army, Trumbull had resigned from it, and Copley had escaped "these frozen regions." These are not the only reasons, but they are important ones, why Peale's Washington portraits are so convincing, why Trumbull's are not, and why Copley's London people seem to live in a different world from his Boston Hancocks and Boylstons.

CHAPTER 5 / FAIR FRAUD AND VULGAR IMITATION

Benjamin West and John Singleton Copley were born within a few months of each other and neither man would ever lose all traces of his provincial beginnings. The young Quaker had marched with General Forbes to Braddock's aid and was too familiar at firsthand with red uniforms and war-painted Indians to visualize the conquerors of Quebec in Roman helmets and breastplates; the Boston man never quite forgot that concern with visual fact which, he once wrote, was the main excellence of portrait in the minds of New England connoisseurs. Both had to rest content for a time with such meager technical help as their towns offered in the 1750's. West's acquaintance with William Williams the scene painter is reflected in the strange castles and prim trees of his *Landscape Composition* (Pa. Hospital, Phila.). He was scarcely twenty when he painted *Thomas Mifflin* (Pa. Hist. Soc.), modeling the boy's face not vigorously but conscientiously and using the young huntsman's fowling piece as a means for composition, the coloring safely confined to blues, greens, olive browns, and a few whites.

Copley was also in his teens when his imagination soared above his powers in *Galatea* (Boston Mus. Fine Arts), whose dolphins, flying cherubs, and seagoing horses are a dim Boston echo of Poussin. His stepfather had died when he was thirteen, too soon to be effective in his training, although Copley's painted and engraved portrait of the Reverend Welsteed had Pelham's cold solidity. John Greenwood's ramrod stiffness would scarcely satisfy a young man seeking models, nor would Badger's wan shapes of children; but he could usefully observe the bulky impressiveness of Blackburn.

West's *Mifflin* and Copley's *Ann Tyng,* done within two years of each other, were signs of promise quickly noted in Philadelphia and Boston; not so soon observed was the fact that they promised very different things. There was in the former a plodding competence, an unimaginative thoroughness, which showed little concern for the "accidents" of nature. Copley had proven that he owned the sharpest pair of eyes in colonial America, a brush that could search out the particular, and a visual excitability which would never wholly desert him.

The two men were equally discontented with the taste and patronage of their communities. West's ambition fed itself on books of artistic theory; Copley had prints and alleged old masters close at hand to remind him that art can do more than grasp appearances. In Richardson and in Dufresnoy, West could read that art's function is not to tickle the senses but to elevate the mind with what is broadly representative and universal, and that invention concerns itself with the great themes of religion and mythology. The learned painter, he discovered, was one who knew history and could give a correct account of it. The laws of beauty, his authors reassured him, had long since found perfect expression in ancient sculpture, in Raphael's celestial forms, and in Titian's color. By copying and adapting these separate excellences, according to Dufresnoy, one could achieve excellence:

> O'er the fair fraud so close a veil is thrown,
> That every borrow'd grace becomes his own.

It was a long way in time and money, from Philadelphia to Rome, where the student could

> Approach with awful step the Grecian school,

but he could meanwhile see with his mind's eye Titian's hounds "snuff the game-tainted gales of the morning," and the joyous countenances of sublime Correggio in the cupola at Parma.

Two notions among these rhapsodies and sermonizings lodged permanently in West's and Copley's minds: first, since fiction is the essence of poetry and therefore of painting, the maker of portraits stood among the least of artists, the history painter at the summit; second, the artist who could not study the great models of art at firsthand was condemned to sterility. West sought those models in 1760, hobnobbed with the first connoisseurs, and became a member of the academies in Rome, Florence, Parma, and Bologna. The Boston man still had fourteen years of life in provincial America.

Copley's self-education was dual. As a would-be English stylist he borrowed the pose, dress, background, and lap dog—everything but the face—of Reynolds' *Duchess of Marlborough* for his likeness of *Mrs. Jerathmiel Bowers* (Met. Mus.), and like his London contemporaries set the plumed hat of Rubens' *Helen Fourment* on the head of *Mrs. Samuel Quincy,* as John Hill Morgan once observed. The other Copley was a man in search of visual truth, who once remarked that there is a kind of luxury in seeing. This Copley was minutely concerned with what makes one visual ex-

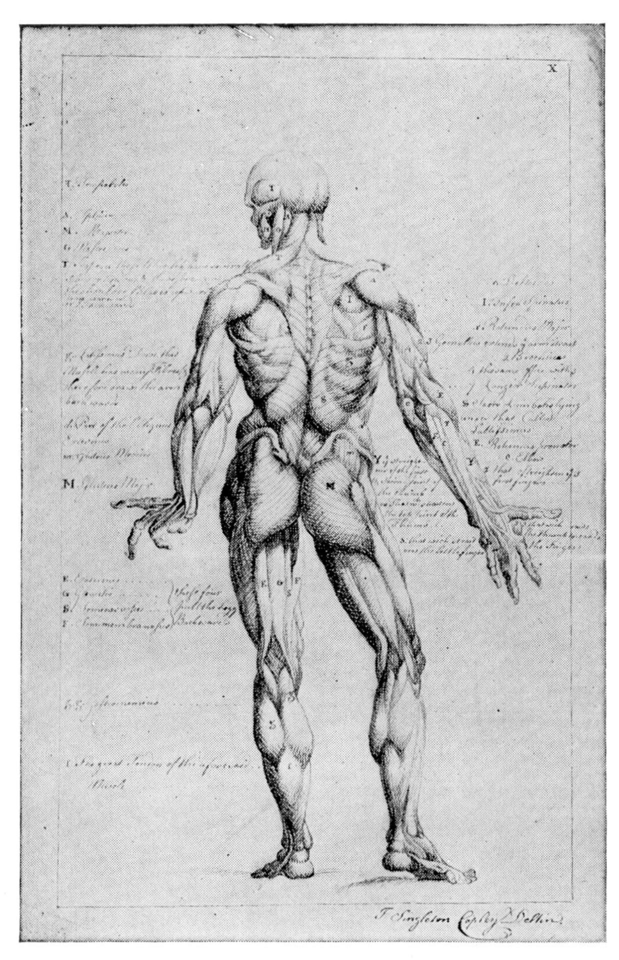

Anatomical drawing from Copley's sketchbook, 1756

Courtesy British Museum, London

perience wholly unlike another, and with those variations of form and color, quite beyond the palette of a Badger or a Blackburn, which could reproduce the experience in all its luxury of fact and of character. It was this eyesight which observed in Philadelphia that there were no gray tints to be found anywhere in a Titian Venus, even when West copied it, and filled Copley's sketchbooks with studies of human bones and muscles at a time when Boston morality forbade the nude model, "except that you may try the attitude before a glass."

There was scarcely a member of New England's upper class who did not sit for him, and there were trips to Portsmouth and New York which found more patrons than he had time to paint. From his studio on Beacon Hill came likenesses of a brilliant and startling actuality of New Hampshire Wentworths, Massachusetts Barrells, Sargents, Winslows, and Royalls, Philadelphia Mifflins, and the Verplancks and Coopers of New York. Copley could sneer that New Englanders prized likeness as the main excellence of his portraits, yet every canvas proved his own relish for three-dimensional fact.

On other occasions the artist ignored formula and presented a man surprised in the act of rising from a chair, or leaning back to compose a letter, or chatting with his lady. His immediacy owed less to precedent than to his power of detaching a person or an object from surrounding space; and his colonial rebels came as vigorously to life as did his Tories, as though the pictorial Copley was no more willing than the political man to reveal his sympathies: *Sam Adams* holds one document in his iron grip and points to another as he lashes Hutchinson on the day after the Boston Massacre, "peremptorily demanding," as he said, "the redress of grievances." One can read the character of these colonial years in Copley's hands alone, from the gnarled stubby digits of his men to the self-conscious fingers of spoiled young women and the overplump ones of elderly housewives who in less prosperous days must have known dishwater. (See color plate 1.)

Copley's progress was incredibly rapid. In 1756 he was cautious with the satin of Ann Tyng; two or three years later he made satin glitter as it never had before on *Mary and Elizabeth Royall,* young daughters of Isaac (Boston Mus. Fine Arts). One of them wore gray-green against greenish blue, the other cerise beside orange-yellow, and Copley transferred these shrill color discords to his canvas, knowing as yet no method for resolving them into a total harmony. When Mrs. Jeremiah Lee threw an ermine-lined blue cloak over

John S. Copley, *Samuel Adams*

Museum of Fine Arts, Boston, Mass.

John S. Copley, *Mr. and Mrs. Isaac Winslow*

Museum of Fine Arts, Boston, Mass. (*Karolik coll.*)

an orange dress, red petticoat, and sash of plum color, he painted the gaudy and tasteless whole; and when Mrs. Theodore Atkinson, Jr., wore pearls and a blue cloak over her gray satin dress, his color was cool and delicious (N. Y. Public Lib.). In 1766 Copley did seventy-year-old *Mrs. Thomas Boylston,* a magnificent dame in olive-brown satin against a yellow brocaded chair back, her white kerchief seen through a miraculously painted black shawl, her face and mittened hands the very peak of Copley's skill (Harvard Univ.). In 1769 Mrs. Alexander McWhorter posed for him, perhaps in a room whose walls reflected little light from windows which at this period were comparatively small; the painter here exploited a range of light and shade which was uniquely his, allowing the contours of her face to be lost in shadow (Yale Univ.).

Copley had become a master of illusion when he made his two double portraits, the Isaac Winslows and the Thomas Mifflins. Isaac Winslow sits beside a table and his wife leans easily upon it. The two heads are larger than their bodies call for, and the latter were sometimes painted from a dummy when the patron was too busy to sit for more than face and hands; but the artist surpassed himself in the aging face of Isaac with its fine wrinkles and gray shaven jowls. He did not ignore the mole beside Madame's nose, and with the virtuosity of a New England Vermeer he caused the husband's and the wife's arms to be reflected in the polished mahogany of the table top. His Mifflins were even more casually posed and in a stronger light; for sheer actualism, this canvas was unique in American painting until the time of Eakins (Pa. Hist. Soc.).

When Copley painted the Mifflins his life as a colonial was nearly done. For ten years he had been exchanging letters with Benjamin West, a correspondence which only sharpened his impatience to get disengaged, as he said, from this frozen region and to be "heated with the light of the enchanting works of a Raphael, a Rubens, Coregio *[sic]* and Veronese." The Pennsylvanian had by this time spent three years absorbing more light than heat from the masters, copying Correggio's *Saint Jerome* and attempting to combine the drawing of Raphael and the coloring of Titian in a portrait of the Countess of Northampton with her baby daughter. In Rome he had consorted with the school of Raphael Mengs in 1760, a small group of painters and cultured theorists whose heads were filled with a new rationalism and whose sensibilities responded to the moral improving note, often confusing the "sublime" with the merely sentimental. They had all convinced themselves that the painter's noblest theme was neither florid allegory nor a dangerous attachment to living persons, but the re-creation of perfect beauty as it had revealed itself to the Greeks. The artist was not, however, to discover this perfection as it walked the streets, crudely particular and distractingly concrete; rather must he recapture it from its noblest interpreters, the sculptors of the ancient world.

This confusion of the arts was fully shared by West. His first efforts in the neoclassical style achieved an archaeological correctness no less dry than that of Sir Gavin Hamilton; and, in the role of preacher, this Quaker met German idealists more than halfway. If his first efforts were hailed by Roman connoisseurs as proofs of genius, let no one be surprised; he was at least as good as Battoni or Mengs, or rather he achieved the same kind of badness with his soapy modeling, his huddled postures, and his colorless colors. There was a deep humanity in West, and the wonder is that even a little of it survived the Roman doctrines. He and his companions were looking for the "secret" of Titian's color, of Raphael's composition, of classic proportion, and of the light-and-shadow of Correggio; but the greatest secret eluded them all: an artist's power to assimilate, to build a present art on the foundations of the past, is in proportion to the depth of his own feeling, the range of his own imagination, the force of his will to give meaning to his own present experience. Since the eclectics ignored that truth, their "principles" were mere short cuts to an abstract, ideal beauty.

Sir Joshua Reynolds, as President of the Royal Academy, delivered his lectures on the grand style from 1769 to 1780, giving a less dogmatic form to theories which West had known as a boy in Philadelphia. Reynolds observed that nobility of conception was more important than sheer perfection of form, and he placed the cockneys of Hogarth, the lovers of Watteau, and the peasants of Teniers on the lowest level. Even in portraiture he insisted that excellence consists more in taking "the general air" than in observing the exact similitude of every feature. In history painting, the clothing should be neither woolen, nor linen, nor silk, satin, or velvet; it should be nothing more nor less than drapery. This meant, of course, limiting one's subject to those offered by the poet or the historian, which could be thus generalized without becoming absurd. It meant, for the painter, a discreet avoidance of the present tense.

In the very year when Sir Joshua announced these precepts, West showed a canvas on which nearly every one of them was ignored. His *Regulus* had shown his pioneering mind, for it was neoclassical fifteen or twenty years before the Frenchmen Vien and David. Now, his *Death of General Wolfe* flustered the doctrinaries. It relied, to be sure, on hallowed practice for its grouping, light, and color. Charles Mitchell has shown how its central figures were lifted from a stiffer version of the same subject by Edward Penny, done eight years before; how the flag motive resembles a relief by Robert Adam on the Townshend monument; how West adapted the theme of a dozen *Lamentations* and *Depositions* and got what he believed "expression" from the engraved grimaces of Le Brun's *Passions*. The painter had obeyed Dufresnoy's injunction to set the principal figure "fair in the front in all the blaze of light," to group the inferior train around him, to balance the whole, to "forbid two hostile colors close to meet," and to blur his distance in a general tone. West's challenge to authority was his choice of a subject remote in place but not in time, a battle fought only twelve years before, described with that "minute circumstantial particularity" which Reynolds believed injurious to grandeur. Its dying hero was dressed in the crimson and buff of His Majesty's army, and the indispensable seated figure was, of all things, an Indian.

West was not the first painter to dress history in correct modern costume; scholars have destroyed that legend by discovering that at least three other *Wolfes* preceded West's. If none of these had the profound effect of the Philadelphian's piece, it was because West's scene was more lifelike and convincing. He had taken more than one liberty with ascertainable fact, but his skill with detail, his clever translation of the *Deposition* motive, and his appeal to patriotism found their mark. When Boydell, alive to its popular appeal, hired Woollett to engrave the *Wolfe,* its image multiplied a thousandfold in England, France, and Austria.

West showed his *Penn's Treaty with the Indians* in 1772 (Ind. Hall, Phila.), explaining that its theme was the conquest of native people without sword or dagger —a significant remark at a moment when England was preparing to crush colonial rebellion. No one dared question the veracity of this first picture of the American scene to be viewed in Europe; every button was correct, and the painter's own collection of Indian costumes had supplied its documentation. West's fame was made; his portrait commissions multiplied and his murals were spread on the ceilings of Somerset House, Windsor

Benjamin West, *Death of General Wolfe*

By permission of National Gallery of Canada, Ottawa

Castle, and Greenwich Hospital. The long record of his welcome and helpfulness to other Americans had begun, and a procession of them passed through his painting room, the first of whom were Pratt and Peale, the last of whom died the same year which saw Mark Twain's *Connecticut Yankee* and the sixth edition of *Leaves of Grass.*

Fortunately for Copley's ambitious mind but not, as it turned out, for his art, there was a continuous exchange of ideas across the Atlantic in these years between himself and West. Through Copley's friend Captain Bruce, the *Boy with the Squirrel* had sailed from Boston in time to be seen in 1766 at the Society of Artists of Great Britain. It was a profile portrait of Copley's half-brother Henry Pelham, realized with all of Copley's brilliance, the boy's hand a masterpiece of illusion as it held the chain of the pet squirrel, a glass of water standing on a polished table top, the color pleasant and the light firm without being forced. Captain Bruce reported the great Reynolds' reaction in words which would have turned an older head than Copley's at twenty-seven—"It was a very wonderful Performance . . . he did not know one Painter at home, who had all the Advantages that Europe could give them, that could equal it . . . You would be a valuable Acquisition to the Art and one of the first Painters in the World, provided you could receive these Aids before it was too late in Life, and before your Manner and Taste were corrupted or fixed by working in your little way at Boston."

For seven years more Copley worked in his little way, unconscious that what he did would some day be his claim to glory. In May of 1774 he arrived at Dover without his family. He saw students of the Royal Academy drawing the nude model, met Hutchinson and Gage, Sheridan and Mrs. Siddons, and wrote from France: "It is very genteel company one meets with and no other, as there is a subordination of People in this Country unknown in America."

In June of 1775, when Bostonians climbed to their roofs to see Charlestown burning, Copley was making a replica of a Correggio at Parma for a British nobleman. He had predicted the civil conflict and he believed the colonies would never be subdued by King George. Back in London in the fall of 1775, where his family had safely arrived, he began to show the effects of West's and Reynolds' theories. In his thirteenth talk Reynolds said that painting ought perhaps to be as far removed from the vulgar idea of imitation as the refined state in which Englishmen lived was removed from a gross state of nature. The majority of mankind would always prefer imitation to that excellence which is addressed to another faculty that they do not possess; but these were not the persons to whom a painter was to look, any more than a judge of morals and manners ought to refer controverted points upon those subjects to the opinions of people from the banks of the Ohio or from New Holland.

Copley's present patrons were from the banks of the Thames, and in the portraits of his first English years there was a masterly synthesis of what West, Reynolds, and the grand tour had taught him with that "vulgar idea of imitation" which happily persisted in his mind. His *Family Picture* was a complicated problem since it included the artist himself, his dignified old father-in-law, his wife, and the four children. To it he brought new powers of color harmony, new skill in "subordination." The figures were cleverly linked in space, the movements and gestures unforced and charming, the color repetitions more sophisticated than was Copley's wont.

In the year 1778 Copley painted *Watson and the Shark,* a thoroughly contemporary subject (Boston Mus. Fine Arts). More skillfully than West he charged his canvas with grays, greens, and warm browns for unity and ingeniously disposed the boatmen struggling to save Watson, whose nude body, half under water, he managed surprisingly well. The boatman's hook and the boat's oar served him well as compositional devices, and the Negro's head and the twisted features of the old sailor whose hands stretch down toward Watson were done with splendid force. *Watson* was frankly a news picture, appealing to that sense of terror which, more than forty years later, Géricault would assault with *The Raft of the Medusa* and Delacroix with *The Barque of Dante.*

John S. Copley, *The Copley Family*

National Gallery of Art, Washington, D. C. (on Loan)

Copley tackled the more strictly historical piece with the same ambitious energy, and for a time it seemed that his grip on reality would make England forget West. The *Death of Major Pierson* had a driving unity, a compelling rhythm, an unforced drama of color which were at that moment beyond the Quaker's range (London, Tate Gall.). For this picture Copley made numerous rapid studies with black-and-white chalk on gray-blue paper in which the human figure moves with a nervous freedom and is superbly caught in the most momentary of attitudes: an officer racing ahead of his troops, coat flying, hat waved above head; a fleeing woman with her baby caught to her breast, her boy gripping her hand—a group for which his wife and children posed.

The full measure of Copley's talent was in the first London portraits, the *Pierson* and a few delightful conversation pieces. When he painted *Mrs. Daniel Denison Rogers* in 1789, posed à la Rubens against a sky whose clouds were as modishly unsubstantial as the lady herself, he proved that he had learned only too well to take what Reynolds called "the general air." Four years earlier, Londoners turned away from Hoppner's portraits of the three royal princesses to greet Copley's version of the same subject, which was a pictorial nosegay of vines, parrots, puppies, and human cherubs. Copley worked now too soft and now too hard; sometimes the hair and cheeks of his subject were generalized nearly out of existence; at other times his forced highlights and oversmooth finish were Westian.

The story of Copley's stimulus to painting in England and of his own disintegration is not an American story. Both West and Copley faced the sneers of rival practitioners in a highly competitive profession, and discovered that patronage could become as elusive as it had once been ardent. The Quaker's serene nature could better absorb these reversals than Copley's temperament. The Revolution was over; time, as the Bostonian had predicted, had settled his native country "into some permanent form of government." In the effort to regain his property on Beacon Hill, Copley shipped his son across the Atlantic with a letter of introduction to Sam Adams in which he wondered "if you still retain any rememberance of Mr. Copley, who once had the honour of your acquaintance."

It was twenty-odd years since that acquaintance had produced the iron-hard portrait of Boston's top rebel, whom Copley now addressed as "a gentleman who has borne so distinguished a part in promoting the happiness and true dignity of his Country; and who now enjoys under the calm Sunshine of its prosperity, the applause and gratitude of a brave, wise, and enlightened people . . . ." Did the painter finally regret that he had been a sunshine patriot, as the applause and gratitude of London slipped away from him? He had lost his Boston farm. He may have wondered if that other transaction had been a net gain for him, by which he exchanged his incredible eyesight for the veiled "fair fraud," the literal for the literary, and his own trenchant prose for the dubious poetry of the grand style.

CHAPTER 6 / SONS OF LIBERTY

Both West and Copley moved from the simple to the complicated, from the cruder to the more smoothly competent; and as their skill developed, there was some loss of so-called "primitive" qualities—directness, naïveté, and independence. It would be a mistake, however, to lament that loss unless one is prepared to maintain that excellence in art is in direct proportion to a man's isolation from inherited forms. Copley and West advanced not merely in technical prowess; their ideas and purposes developed, requiring new techniques for expression. Where there is growth in the artist's outlook, there must be growth in his means and methods; to deny this is to condemn him to perpetual childhood.

It is not a catastrophe when such a man becomes aware of how others managed to convey their meaning, but only when his borrowings are greater than his capacity to repay them. If that capacity is great, he assimilates without loss of integrity, and his growth is healthy. If it is meager, no amount of sophistication or acquired skill will save him from mediocrity. The tragedy of Benjamin West was not that he swallowed eclecticism, but that he could not digest it, and that his imagination soared above his power to create forms for his imaginings. Copley never perceived the undersurface character of his sitters, was seldom stirred by them, and never made that deep identification of himself with others which produces the great portraits. Such balance as he could achieve between human con-

Charles W. Peale, *The Peale Family*

New York Historical Society

tent and artistic form he reached in Boston in the seventeen seventies and in his first years in London. With his technical maturing there was no corresponding growth of understanding, love, and penetration.

Charles Willson Peale and Ralph Earl maintained that balance, although neither of them acquired the dexterity of the Londoners. The strength and the deep charm of Peale are those of a rich personality deeply concerned with the life around him, biased toward what was alive and forward-moving in his world and therefore capable of taking from others what he needed for full expression, and no more. Ralph Earl managed his own synthesis within a more modest range and failed only when his hand was too unsteady to obey his mind. The Connecticut limner claimed no more than he could do, and the Philadelphia coach painter who turned artist was sanely humble when he confessed his lack of certain painterly talents, and concluded, "as I have variety of characters to paint I must as Rembrandt did make these my Anticks and improve myself as well as I can while I am providing for my support." Charles Peale had more than himself to support, as the father of a growing family whom he christened with great names —Raphaelle, Rembrandt, Rubens, Titian, Angelica Kauffman, Franklin, Linnaeus — yet money and the customer never determined his actions. The artist's future in America was in his mind linked with her progress toward democracy, and while Copley coldly appraised American taste, Peale worked to develop it, declaring that "the people here have a growing taste for the arts, and are becoming more and more fond of encouraging their progress amongst them."

This minor Leonardo was a painter among other things, his development frequently interrupted but not less steady and sturdily integrated. Some rudiments he learned from John Hesselius, and on a journey to New England in the year 1765 he met Copley, talked with him in the painting room on Beacon Hill, and borrowed a small canvas to copy. Peale resolved to discover for himself the Boston master's light upon forms, the conviction of his poses, the solidity which fills space. The next year found him in Virginia, the next two with West in London, where he taught himself the principles of perspective — a subject which must have stirred the scientific in his mind. It was during these months in England that West painted his alert, sharp-featured pupil with an odd blend of sympathy and harshness. From 1769 to 1776 he worked in Philadelphia and Annapolis, in Baltimore and Williamsburg, and on the ninth of August in the latter year wrote in his diary, "enlisted as a common soldier in Captain Peter's company of the Militia."

Peale believed that the artist "must know the original cause of beauty in all he sees." His portraits of the

Ralph Earl, *Elijah Boardman* (Cornelius B. Tyler coll.)

Courtesy Frick Art Reference Library, New York City

Arbuckles in 1766, stiff and primly drawn, gave small hint either of that knowledge or of beauty; but a few years later he proved that West had taught him a surer draughtsmanship and a bolder approach to light. That progress was in the portrait of *William Buckland* (Yale Univ.): the architect of the Hammond-Harwood House at Annapolis was placed in strong light, smiling directly at the observer, a draughting instrument in his sure fingers; on the table before him are the plans of the house, a compass and an inkwell painted with exquisite precision. The still life of the Buckland piece is not Peale's only reminder of his debt to Copley. His rendering of dress and jewelry caught something of the Bostonian's zest for sheer texture, but they have under Peale's brush a restrained and finely tempered richness which yields the first importance to character.

A few years before Copley composed his family picture with such a graceful arabesque and with obvious mastery of the draughtsman's problems, Charles Willson Peale gathered his numerous household around a table. At one end sits the fine-featured mother; at the other end, Saint George Peale is drawing her portrait, while James smiles at him and the third brother, who is Charles himself, looks over his shoulder. There are three young women and two children around the table, and Nurse Peggy Durgan looks on with clasped hands. Peale's group derives a warm unity from their mutual affection and their quiet absorption in the work that is going forward. The painter could not have rendered so skillfully the doll which lies in a corner of Copley's picture, nor did he dare to place any but himself in a foreshortened pose; yet one can sense the exchange of thought between James and Saint George and feel the depth of Charles's concern as he bends over the drawing. The plate of apples on the table is painted with sturdy Dutchlike literalness, and the family dog is as full of life and character as any of the family.

In the first years of the republic, Peale's mind turned from the building of a triumphal arch to the making of moving transparencies for his small museum after the fashion of de Loutherbourg's London *Eidophusicon,* which he had never seen. There were specimens for his collection to be classified according to Buffon and Linnaeus, and landscape backgrounds to be painted as habitats for the birds and reptiles in his glass cases; among his projects was a panorama to be made by pasting together the separate views he had taken from the eight sides of a cupola. Men called him "the ingenious Mr. Peale," and his response to people, when he painted them, was quick and warmhearted, though his brother James and Robert Edge Pine now helped him to complete his portraits. In an oval picture of flaxen-haired *John Custis Wilson* there was a dog so knowingly done that it made Copley's spaniels look like toys; Gilbert Stuart disliked the vigorous head which Charles and his son Rembrandt made of him, perhaps because it had the Peale frankness.

The life and mind of Charles Willson Peale are an open book; by contrast, one can only grasp the essential Ralph Earl by reading between the lines of what he did with his brush and pencil. Historian Dunlap missed the point of Earl in his sarcastic comment on two full-length portraits of the Timothy Dwights, painted, "as Earl thought, in the manner of Copley" with "shadows black as charcoal," and Dunlap wrote that the man's skill had been stunted by habitual intemperance. In the formative years of Peale one can feel the hand of Hesselius and of West; one can only conjecture whose help, if any, was given to young Ralph in western Massachusetts just before the Revolution, or how many Fekes and Copleys he had seen. Scholars have reconstructed his "periods": the wandering years which produced the iron-hard *Roger Sherman* (Yale Univ.); the seven years abroad from 1778 which tempered his Puritan harshness and released a love for color; what William Sawitzky calls the "second American period" to 1798, his best and most productive; and, if one likes, the wretched postscript of the century's last two years when a fumbling painter caricatured his own best. One knows at least—and this by the evidence of one's eyes—that Earl was thoroughly of the Revolutionary generation in New England, whose unflinching strength, whose spare and wiry toughness, whose almost unwilling response to sheer beauty are in everything he did. Beneath this in the man's troubled and unhappy spirit must have lurked contradictions unresolved, emotional conflicts of an intensity which perhaps called for the false release of liquor. Earl could penetrate to the mind of a sitter, and he could also reduce that sitter to a harshly painted mask. His color could be lively and it could be drab. His sense of posture and of space was sometimes cramped and awkward, but on a few occasions he worked with the breath-taking majesty of a minor Piero della Francesca. Earl could be relentlessly literal with the buttons of a man's coat and as tender as a poet with a mother who clasps her baby's toes. To pass before his portraits is to understand how the colonies wrested their independence from England; to study his view of Worcester from Denny Hill is to see one of the first signs of pride and affection for American hills and trees.

A hard-shelled Connecticut patriotism is in the *Roger Sherman,* the piercing eyes, the thin lips pressed together, the whole tense figure in its plain Windsor chair, the bare walls beyond, the brown-red scheme whose only relief is in the white of the neckcloth and the sleeve. Some three years later, the artist proves in England that he can manage carefully but with confidence the sequence of a brilliant red-orange costume from light into shadow; the head of *William Carpenter* (Worcester Art Mus.) is as solidly three-dimensional as a sculpture, and his chair and table are as harshly substantial as they would have been in Copley. Beneath the rigid contours and the stonelike weight of young Carpenter is a suggestion that the boy's alert charm was not lost upon the artist, and in the face of his sister Mary is a sadness out of proportion to her years. In a few likenesses of Earl's years abroad his edginess succumbed to softer brushing and cool Gainsborough harmonies; Earl was more English than he would ever be again.

Earl's two portraits of the Boardman brothers belong to the fruitful decade after his return to America. The painting of Daniel is so composed that man and nature divide the interest, but not nature in the abstract, for this view of New Milford is a small landscape masterpiece in itself, its fenced-off houses and its spire gleaming in the sun which plays over Connecticut hills and sparkles on the Housatonic. Elijah Boardman was a dry-goods merchant, and Earl produced something unique and splendid by placing him in his own shop: a tall, dignified, and handsome man with his arm resting on a desk before a paneled wall whose half-opened door reveals the shelves beyond and the many-colored stripes and flowered patterns of their bolts of cloth. Earl's use of space in this canvas is superbly simple: the desk cutting across the picture exactly parallel to its plane to define the space where Boardman stands; the verticals of the moldings, desk, and door enforcing the man's own poise; the varied slanting of books to break monotony, and the backward thrusting diagonal of the shelves and door; the man's arm which is the quiet link among these movements.

It was a mastery of broad fields, tree-lined rivers, and low rolling hills, of moist greens and distant blue-grays which made the background of Earl's *Moseley* picture open so majestically and with so broad and deep an atmosphere. The scheme is of the simplest: Mrs. Moseley standing as solid as a rock with her small Charles beside her, and rising beyond and above them a view which would remind the observer of a theater backdrop were it less spatially convincing and had not the painter disposed its shaded fields, its sun-warmed meadows as countertones to the dark and light of the two figures. The power of the *Moseley* picture derives also from its color—the deep blue tone of the woman's habit, the pervasive greens, the tempered red of the boy.

One year before this, Earl used a more daring palette for the companion portraits of the *Benjamin Tallmadge* pair, in both of which the color green-blue was chosen for magnificent variation—dark and luminous in the boy's suit, a delicate robin's egg in his father's coat, breeches, and stockings, lustrous and powerful in the satin dress of Mrs. Tallmadge, pale in the sky beyond her. As intensification and as balance for this odd scheme, Earl provided variants on orange-red in the book labels and chair of the man's portrait, in the sunset glow through the window in his companion's picture and in the vermilions of the carpet which moves so solidly backward under the feet of both sitters and which is only one of the devices Earl used to relate the two canvases in terms of likeness and of difference (Litchfield Hist. Soc.).

In the year 1794 there were signs of retrogression in the disagreeably hot tones of his *John Davenport* (Yale Univ.). Earl never learned Copley's skill with hands, and relied on a crisp abbreviation of his own which sometimes convinces, sometimes not. There are other abbreviations in his best and in his poorest work; he could simplify a sleeve by rendering it in two or three tones, or he could reduce the form of an arm to a mere glimmer of light on a shapeless form beneath. When he

Ralph Earl, *Mrs. William Moseley and Her Son Charles*

Yale University Art Gallery, New Haven, Conn.

painted the feathers in Mrs. Moseley's hat, or the buttons of her coat, or the warmth of Mrs. Tallmadge's throat seen through a filmy kerchief, it was as though he asked himself how a few deft strokes of the brush could do the work of many. He found the answer here, but elsewhere lost it, and the splendid simplifications which in his best work spoke sharply of character quickly became lumpy shapes which said only the obvious. Here and there in the Connecticut Valley are Ralph Earl likenesses of 1799 and 1800, painted with

John Durand, *The Rapalje Children*

New York Historical Society

Winthrop Chandler, *Rev. Ebenezer Devotion*

Brookline Historical Society

a kind of heavy desperation on coarse cloth by a man who seems trying to remember how he once drew a hand or brought a landscape to life. There is no longer any invention; the man sits cross-kneed with one hand on a table, and an overflushed sky gleams through a window. Tree forms grow ambiguous and contours harden.

This is the rather shabby ghost of the Ralph Earl who had caught the sweep of the hills above Worcester, matched Peale's originality upon occasion, revealed a color sense far subtler than Copley's, and brought a generation to intense life in the rockbound Connecticut *Sherman,* the gracious self-confidence of the Ellsworths and Boardmans, the impregnable dignity of Mrs. Moseley and her son Charles walking near Hartford. The tensions of Ralph Earl and his inhibitions were perhaps more appropriate to the time, the place, and the patrons than he realized.

Among the Revolutionary generation were artists who stood still, others who moved forward, and still others who belied their early promise. The Huguenot John Durand was one of the steadiest; he seems to have studied Copley, and his way of painting drapery suggests an imitation of the mezzotint scraper. Dunlap conceded that his paintings must be good likenesses and bore "less vulgarity of style than artists of his *calibre* generally possess." Durand was modest enough when he advertised in New York that, although he lacked ample fund of knowledge in geometry, geography, perspective, anatomy, expression of the passions, ancient and modern history, he yet hoped that his humble attempts would meet with acceptance, and proposed to work at as cheap rates as any person in America. He need not have apologized for the delicate and proud authority of *Adriaan* and *Anna Bancker* (N. Y. Hist. Soc.); in his group likeness, *The Rapalje Children,* a response to youthful charm overcame the harshness of his details and the stiffness of his drawing, and he achieved a delightful color pattern.

Something of that wiry quality was in Winthrop Chandler of Woodstock, Massachusetts, whose wooden overmantels were among America's first landscapes. For the Elisha Hurlbut House at Scotland, Connecticut, probably in the late 1760's, Chandler limned a New England valley with a delightful blend of topography and imagination. In a portrait of *Mrs. Levi Willard* (Boston Mus. Fine Arts), he softened for once before the gentle old face and quiet eyes, but he was both hard and literal when he represented *Doctor William Glysson* taking a patient's pulse, and he explored the lined countenance of the *Reverend Ebenezer Devotion* with thoroughness and assurance (Brookline Hist. Soc.). The pose of Devotion may be Copleyesque, but Chandler outspecified his model in the bookshelves which nearly fill the canvas, and one can read their titles as easily as if one stood in Devotion's library—the works of Locke,

Christian Gullager, *Col. John May*
American Antiquarian Society, Worcester, Mass.

Edward Savage, *Abraham Whipple*
Courtesy M. Knoedler & Co., New York City

Watts's *Sermons* and several volumes of the *Spectator,* Rapin's *History of England,* and Sir Isaac Newton's *Opticks.*

As mercilessly clear was McKay of New York, who was active during Ralph Earl's best years and who itemized every stripe in the vest of John Bush, every lace thread in his wife's cap and kerchief, without diminishing the force of his presentation. McKay's crispness was wholly absent from Edward Savage, as conscientious and as dull a painter as the period offered. His *Commander Abraham Whipple* stands as nerveless as the column beside him, toes turned out, hand thrust in waistcoat, a telescope under one impossible arm, and a cocked hat precarious on his head; a kind of oily smoothness is in the face, the dress, the pillar, and the floor. Christian Gullager was of Danish origin, and Paris training may have helped him, in the likeness of *Colonel John May,* to achieve a firm solidity and a painterly richness in the buff collar, gold braids, sash, and sword blade.

Among these men were artists who had known Benjamin West, like Abraham Delanoy and Matthew Pratt. Both of them showed the fact in a kind of smoky smoothness, a dry and forceless drawing, the former in his portrait of West, the latter in *The American School* (Met. Mus.), a stilted conversation piece in which the twenty-seven-year-old West criticizes the work of his Yankee protégés.

The Yankee rigor is in the paintings of *Bradford Hubbard* (New Haven Col. Hist. Soc.), old *Abraham Redwood* (Redwood Lib.), and *John Eliot* (Mass. Hist. Soc.). Whoever limned Hubbard—it may have been Reuben Moulthrop—built the upright body and the arms as one would build a house, and with less than Earl's skill matched his directness. Equally forceful is the *Redwood,* the alert eyes under heavy brows, the firm mouth and aging chin, the whole man suggestive of Copley's elderly people and quite as convincing in its less accomplished way. The *Eliot* is a well-drawn, firmly shaped, and quietly forceful study of a young man, its sensitiveness hinting at acquired skill; there is no trace of crudity in it but more than a suggestion that its author admired Feke.

There is far more of the time, the country, and the person in these likenesses, in the careful and Copleyesque Benjamin Blyth pastels and in the neat precision of Richard Jennys than in either Robert Edge Pine or Henry Benbridge. Pine as a young man in London had won a first prize for a history painting at the Society of Arts, but had come to America to regain a lost reputation, bringing with him a cast of the Venus de Medici which Philadelphia prudery forced him to keep in a locked chest. He was a nerveless, dry, and uninspired practitioner whose brush lacked the assurance of

Peale's, and his portrait of *Molly Harris,* with its warm pink shadows, seems an attempt to engraft on a Baltimore child the sentimental appeal of a Romney. The attempt failed, and so did Pine's effort to transform *Mrs. Reid* into a voluptuous Sultana (Met. Mus.). Benbridge, Philadelphia-born, was nearly as out of place with the slippery smoothness he had learned in Italy from Mengs and Battoni and applied in Norfolk and Charleston after his return in 1770 with letters of commendation from West and Franklin. His group portrait of three generations of Charleston nabobs, *Mrs. James Hartley and Family,* was a stolid and stiffly composed ensemble with nothing to recommend it save a high satin finish in the dresses.

In short, the native touch was more incisive, the native flair for character was more keen, the Yankee rigors were more appropriate to their subject. The country had declared her independence, and although the long story of lending and borrowing was by no means ended, the best among American artists would no longer be governed by English forms but seek their own. Artistic dependence was like the political, of which Tom Paine had said, "There was a time when it was proper, and there is a proper time for it to cease."

Winthrop Chandler, *Capt. Samuel Chandler* (detail)

Courtesy Mrs. Robt. Child Paine

BOOK TWO

SELF-CONSCIOUS REPUBLIC

c. 1790 — c. 1830

Detail from Lacour-Doolittle engraving of Washington's inauguration, Federal Hall, New York City ▶

Courtesy New York Public Library

PART ONE

THE JEFFERSONIAN PROMISE

INTRODUCTION / CHRISTIANS, MOHAWKS, DEMOCRATS

Tom Paine wrote his last *Crisis* paper when the peace treaty was signed. The old firebrand exulted: "The times that tried men's souls are over, and the greatest and completest revolution the world ever knew gloriously and happily accomplished." He believed and was never tired of saying that in a world of monarchies the first democratic republic in the world's history had been launched. Six years later, what had been a temporary alliance of states became in fact a nation, with fewer than four million citizens whose modes of living contrasted as widely as the settled towns contrasted with enormous regions scarcely inhabited at all. America as a whole was far from making sense. Yet in the forty-odd years between the adoption of the Constitution and Channing's eloquent "Remarks on National Literature"—years of bitter sectional conflict, of rival parties and programs, of peaceful planning, and of wars of defense against foreign powers—the national idea moved steadily forward in men's minds.

The Revolution had done more than win political independence for a country which soon sprawled from the Atlantic to the Mississippi River. The American merchant was now free to seek new markets in the Old World, the small producer, the new industrialist, and the financier to dream of banks in all the new American cities. The estates of a landed gentry were breaking up and with them the feudal notions of tenure; vast new lands were to be had for the taking. The caste distinctions of a provincial society had lost their meaning, and more worldly concerns replaced the Puritan's rigid code in a republic which had been born, as one historian has said, in a spirit as secular as that of the later French one, whose political philosophers cited Plutarch oftener than Moses, and whose Articles of

Federation were as tersely rational as the bylaws of a modern insurance company.

American politics, Janus-headed, faced both east and west, both backward to provincial notions and forward to the realization of the national promise. To the Hamiltonian merchants and speculators who called themselves Federalists, "progress" meant direction of the national economy and of the nation's political life in the interest of a few, with the far greater number of farmers, small businessmen, and manufacturers reduced to a suitably subordinate position. Such men opposed Jefferson's dream of westward growth both openly and by covert treason, denouncing his purchase of Louisiana from France, and conspiring with Aaron Burr to dismember the new American federation at the moment when Meriwether Lewis and William Clark were pushing up western rivers and crossing mountains to reach the Pacific.

Undermined from within, the national existence faced other threats: England's refusal to recognize the Louisiana Purchase; her effort, aided by the Indians, to provoke war in the lands between the Alleghenies and the Mississippi and in Florida; her interference with American commerce on the seas. When Mr. Madison's war was over these foreign threats were ended, Burr stood disgraced, and the makers of the Hartford Convention had been driven from public life.

Federalist notions, however, continued to color the life and thought and to shape the cultural standards of a group which, because of its wealth and education, played a controlling part in matters artistic. The Federalists of the eastern seaboard lived a pseudo-English life with formal dinners, levees, and dances. To that society, whose portrait the unctuous Rufus Griswold drew in his book, *The Republican Court,* the inauguration of George Washington was a coronation. They gathered around the first President when New York was the capital and later in Philadelphia—a contracted, negative, ritualistic, and imitative cultural group.

Timothy Dwight was another champion of the refined old order, believing all pioneers to be rough anarchists not fit to live in polished society, and writing "Greenfield Hill" in praise of contentment and pious habits. The Federalists of Philadelphia had talked with the English poet Tom Moore before he visited Buffalo in 1804 and described the American people as "Christians, Mohawks, democrats" engaged in

> . . . one dull chaos, one unfertile strife
> Betwixt half-polish'd and half-barbarous life. . . .

Buffalo was but one of the many towns where Timothy Dwight's anarchists were building a democracy to challenge the staid East. Daniel Boone had crossed through the Cumberland Gap, and Kentucky and Tennessee were filling with settlers by the thousands when Moore made his visit. Families from Connecticut had taken the Genesee Road to Albany, Buffalo, and Lake Erie to build neat New England homes in the Western Reserve. Men from Philadelphia and Baltimore sailed down the Ohio where Audubon, more responsive to the frontier than was Tom Moore, recorded his amazement to see new towns on "la belle Rivière"—Wheeling, Marietta, Cincinnati, the Falls of the Ohio. Audubon remembered the cattle with tinkling bells, "the hooting of the great owl or the noise of its wings as it sailed smoothly over the stream," the flatboats heavy with immigrants, the lonely cabin of the squatter. Now he heard the noise of hammers and the whir of machinery, saw fields and farms where woods had been, and "hundreds of steamboats gliding to and fro over the whole majestic river."

This was the great new "agricultural interest" so deeply feared by Federalists, so nobly championed by Jefferson, a West rather conscious of its difference from the older centers, with a more diversified population tenacious of its small holdings, mistrustful of Washington politicians, and inclined to abolish tax and property restrictions on a man's right to vote. To Federalist ideas of progress these men who forded rivers, cleared forests, and raised sawmills opposed their different idea, building democracy on a broader and more solid foundation. The concept of the European gentleman could have little meaning here, but the sense of nationality could and did flourish.

That sense grew sharper with time in the country as a whole. Crèvecoeur in 1782 saw the American as a new man who acted upon new principles and must therefore entertain new ideas and form new opinions. Those opinions took shape in the many new magazines of the first republican decades—among them the *North American Review,* the *Analectic,* the *Portfolio,* and the *Atheneum*—whose articles on art and literature fostered the idea of cultural nationalism. By 1830 it was possible for Channing to define literature as the expression of a nation's mind in writing.

But if the philosophers, writers, and designers of these republican years were conscious of new values, they were also mindful of old forms of expression which in the previous age had become the medium of artistic exchange among men. The form was frequently older than the content. The least democratic among poets and builders clung to the urbanities of the eighteenth century, and the Hartford Wits cast their New World thoughts in an Old World mold. Even Joel Barlow, the only one of the Wits who remained a radical after the Revolution, measured his vision of America's future in Pope's heroic couplets. Royall Tyler created the stage Yankee, to be sure, in Brother Jonathan, but *The Con-*

trast was written in the style of Sheridan and Goldsmith:

> Exult each patriot heart!—this night is shown
> A piece, which we may fairly call our own;
> Where the proud titles of "My Lord! Your Grace!"
> To humble Mr. and plain Sir give place.

Timothy Dwight's dull poem on Greenfield Hill was inspired by his deep pride in his country's progress, yet English writers had determined its expression, even though this meant that shadows became "shrouding umbrage" and the brooks and hills of Connecticut "glassy rills" and "cerulean mountains."

In the paganism of Greece and Rome the republicans found, as their colonial fathers had, the richest source of borrowed forms. Hercules rode the prow of the *Constitution,* and was painted by Morse as he struggled with the shirt of Nessus. Vanderheyden's ferry became Troy, New York, and on the Mississippi River Brackenridge found a village of twenty houses which called itself Herculaneum. Yet the classicism of the century's turn was no longer the provincial classicism which had tried to keep pace with Palladian England in order to be stylish. In the interplay between political independence and aesthetic dependence, the former was a new and living force, and it transformed the latter by giving the power of symbols to the old temples, gods, and heroes.

It was the analogy between their own new state and the republic of antiquity which gave point to the work of the American classicists. Pope had ridiculed the English for turning "Arcs of triumph to a Garden-gate;" Charles Willson Peale turned them into symbols of victory, and Freneau saluted his effort in the *Freeman's Journal.*

> Toward the skies
> What columns rise
> In Roman style, profusely great!
> What lamps ascend,
> What arches bend
> And swell with more than Roman state!

When those self-made architectural designers, Charles Bulfinch and Thomas Jefferson, traveled in England and on the Continent, each found in the forms of ancient buildings or their European adaptations what he was looking for. The Bostonian acquired a repertory of plans, elevations, and details with which to house a Federal generation. The Virginian, seeking shapes for republican dignity and strength, discovered a Roman temple nobly simple enough for the Virginia Senate. Both of them learned that a new kind of classicism was sweeping Europe in the eighteenth century's latter half, no longer the burly Palladianism which saw Greece through Renaissance Italian eyes, but a more authentic version based on discovery and excavation. Herculaneum and Pompeii had been unearthed, and Stuart and Revett were publishing their *Antiquities of Athens.* By 1790 English taste was thoroughly "antique," and the delicate ornament which Robert Adam sketched in his travels reappeared on the buildings and furniture designed by the Adam brothers—the spindly Pompeian, the domestic Roman with a Raphaelesque accent, the late Roman decoration of Diocletian's palace at Spalatro.

Bulfinch in London knew the neat squares, the rows of houses with austere façades in Adelphi Terrace and Berkeley Square. On fireplaces, on doorways, on iron fences, on the backs of chairs, he saw the Greek honeysuckle or acanthus leaf; around the edges of ceilings ran the toothlike moldings which, at the hands of the new designers, lost their overemphatic and heavy quality, and merely added a grace to good proportion. The ceilings themselves which John Soane and the Adam brothers, on classical precedent, divided into squares and ovals, were miracles of lightness enlivened by painted panels where the nymphs and goddesses of Angelica Kauffmann sported. Full-time architects, gentlemen of taste, and the makers of fine furniture united to impose this new delicacy, part Greek, part Roman, and part French, upon the generation of Britishers who first saw the Elgin marbles and bought the *Antiquities of Athens.*

The man from Boston noted how the heavy ancient swag of fruits and flowers acquired a more slender grace in the festoons of Robert and James Adam; he walked past the iron lampposts which flanked the doorway of Sir Watkin William Wynn's house in Saint James's Square, and which would soon be seen in American streets. At Bath he could admire John Wood's long procession of pilasters and engaged columns above a rusticated base in Queen Square, and the suave curvature of the façades in the Crescent, with balustrades above and two-story columns for vertical accent. On the South Parade he could observe how individual dwellings were assimilated to a continuous block. This Adamesque blend of elegance with restraint would please the Boston and Salem nabobs and their imitators in the smaller American towns.

Jefferson's approach to architecture was more scholarly than that of Bulfinch, and more dogmatic. America, he foresaw, would double its habitations in the next twenty years and would need capitols, banks, and city halls. Colonial forms did not please him, and he said that the genius of architecture had shed maledictions over his native country. English buildings, Jefferson decided, were even less distinguished than American. To adapt the Georgian forms to public edifices by enlarging their plans and crowning them with cupolas was, in his opinion, an inadequate method of creating a public architecture of national proportions. His mind, like those of all his educated contemporaries, was obsessed by the culture of antiquity, whose authors he had read as a college student. That self-educated rebel Tom Paine was a lone exception when he cried that mankind had lived to very little purpose if, at this period of the world, they must go two or three thousand years back for lessons and examples. Could the mist of antiquity be cleared away, Paine wrote, and the Greeks and Romans be viewed as they really were, it is more probable that they would admire us, rather than we them; and he concluded, "I have no notion of yielding the palm of the United States to any Grecians or Romans that were ever born."

There was no such heresy in the mind of Jefferson, whose classicism took many forms. He never deserted his earlier love, Palladio, whose work inspired the designs he made for the governor's house at Richmond, which was never built, and for his own Monticello. His mind delighted in the Palladian theory that the proportions of good building are derived from the laws of nature, and his own drawings were as carefully calculated as the Italian's. His domestic work, like Monticello and Bremo and the other homes in Virginia and Maryland which embodied his ideas if not his designing hand, is simple, stately, and dignified. But there was more than Palladian rectitude in what he did. He could adapt with freedom to local needs and materials; and this son of the Enlightenment planned for Monticello pavilions, gardens, and cascades which were both romantic in style and "picturesque" in intention.

As for the more recent versions of Greek and Roman forms, Jefferson believed that Frenchmen managed them better than Englishmen. It was a Frenchman who, at Jefferson's request, planned the capital city on the Potomac, and it was another Frenchman whom he chose to model George Washington for the state of Virginia. In the Paris which Jefferson knew and loved, the same purification which had banished the cherubs of Boucher, straightened the legs of chairs, and reduced hoops and high wigs to dresses and coiffures of "antique" simplicity was active upon architecture. The American visitor walked under the triumphal arch of the new Hôtel de Salm and admired the rather frigidly classical mansion with its rows of busts in circular niches; his eye delighted in Gabriel's spacious Place de la Concorde flanked on the north by two great façades which matched each other; he noted for future use the Panthéon of Soufflot with its columned drum and dome.

Such buildings were impressive not by weight alone or by exuberance of ornament, but by proportion, surface, and well-spaced detail; yet none of them satisfied Jefferson. He was looking for a designer whose taste had been formed on ancient models, most architecture in Paris being "far from chaste." The search ended when he found Clérisseau, who had measured ancient buildings and published beautiful engravings of the *Antiquities of France*—temples which, the Virginian believed, embodied that noble simplicity, that fusion of the rational with the beautiful, which the Roman republic shared with France and his own country.

Once in a thousand times, Jefferson supposed, a new architectural idea might be profitably exploited, but it was sounder practice on the whole to use models which, standing for centuries, had won the suffrage of the world. He had never seen those models when he wrote, save in engravings; but his letter from Nîmes to Madame Tessé in 1787 reveals their later impact on his mind: "Here I am, Madame, gazing whole hours at the Maison Quarree [*sic*] like a lover at his mistress." In this temple at Nîmes he had found what seemed to him the most perfect example of the "cubic" style which had obtained the approbation of fifteen or sixteen centuries and was therefore preferable, he said, to any design newly contrived.

Virginia had snubbed his first idea for the capitol, which was to raise three separate buildings for the three functions of the state administration. Now he worked against time in Paris on new plans, knowing that construction had already begun at Richmond. He and Clérisseau worked together, the French professional aided by his students, the Virginian as an amateur who decided how the temple form was to be modified, how its spaces ought to be divided for logical use and its details simplified for American builders.

The Roman temple was given a Palladian accent: its Corinthian order was changed to the simpler Ionic, and panels appeared between the rows of windows. As Samuel Dobie, a builder who also took pride in being a draughtsman, proceeded with his task, he gave the structure a homelier and more robust appearance, made pilasters on the sides where there had been none in the original model, and cut a semicircular window in the pediment. A century and a quarter afterward, two wings disfigured what had been the first truly monumental public building in America; but meanwhile Jefferson's temple had inspired dozens of designs by other men.

When Jefferson turned his mind to the arts of painting and sculpture there was a cautious optimism in his attitude, as there was in that of Franklin. Hardheaded Benjamin believed that the invention of a machine or the improvement of a tool was more important to Americans than a masterpiece of Raphael, though he added hopefully that "the Arts have always traveled westward, and there is no doubt of their flourishing hereafter on our side of the Atlantic." Although Jefferson shared that confidence he considered painting and

Maison Carrée, Nîmes (from Clérisseau, *Antiquités de la France*)

Courtesy New York Public Library

Thomas Jefferson's Virginia Capitol, Richmond, Va.

Wayne Andrews photo

Jean Antoine Houdon, *George Washington*

Metropolitan Museum of Art, New York City

statuary too expensive for the state of wealth in his time and declared that it was preposterous that Americans should try to make themselves connoisseurs in those arts, even though his own collection included works by Italian, French, Dutch, and Flemish masters. As for the native carver, it seemed that he had neither the experience nor the skill to create monuments for the republic.

When Franklin arrived in France in 1776 he bore a commission from Congress to find a sculptor who should carve the memorial tablet to General Richard Montgomery, who had fallen at Quebec the year before. It was Jean-Jacques Caffieri whom he selected, and in the Paris Salon of 1777 were shown Caffieri's bust of Franklin and the design for the Montgomery piece: a broken column topped by a funeral urn and surrounded by the conventional symbols briskly cut into the stone—palms, liberty cap, and military trophies. Twelve years later this florid marble, admired by Franklin for its "elegant antique simplicity," was embedded in the east wall of St. Paul's Church on Broadway.

Jefferson's taste in marble embraced an insipid *Diana and Endymion* by Michael Angelo Slodtz, which he saw in France in 1787 and which he thought a "superior morsel." But Jefferson's deepest admiration went not to the rococo extravagance of Slodtz but to the sober realism of Slodtz's pupil, Jean-Antoine Houdon, "without rivalship the first statuary of this age." Houdon's bust of Jefferson is dated 1789, and in his early forties he had already modeled Franklin and John Paul Jones; in the years to come he was to portray more American celebrities. His rival Caffieri called his work mean and passionless, but Houdon was a man sturdily in search of truth. His knowledge of anatomy was profound, and in the great series of Frenchmen at which he toiled, in order, he said, to leave for posterity a faithful record of just how they looked, his psychological penetration was supported by a technique which included the taking of measurements and the casting of masks from the living or the dead face of his subject.

It was obvious to Jefferson and Franklin that Houdon was the man to model America's first citizen. They had been requested by Patrick Henry to choose the sculptor who should make Washington's portrait for the state capitol, and Houdon's eagerness so matched their own that he was willing to "leave the statues of Kings unfinished" and travel to Virginia.

In the mind of Jefferson, this Washington was to be no vague approximation but a realistic portrait of life size based on "inspection and mensuration." In one of his letters he remarked that "a statue is not made, like a mountain, to be seen at a great distance. To perceive those minute circumstances which constitute its beauty you must be near it, and in that case, it should be so little above the size of life, as to appear actually of that size from your point of view." He added, with an eye to the shrewd Virginia legislators, that a work of these dimensions would be cheaper.

The problem of costume was not easily solved. Many Europeans agreed with Sir Joshua Reynolds that contemporary dress was inconsistent with the gravity of durable stone, which ought not to be used to preserve for posterity a fashion "of which the longest existence scarce exceeds a year." But Houdon wanted to portray the great American as a farmer-citizen who had sheathed his sword and retired to the peace of Mount Vernon; and his conception was approved not only by Jefferson but by Washington himself, who wrote that "a little deviation in favour of the modern costume would be more expedient than a servile adherence to the garb of antiquity."

Houdon spent a fortnight at Mount Vernon. Back in his Paris studio, he composed his statue, aided by the life mask which he had made from Washington's features, by his own pencil sketches and careful measurements, and by a Charles Willson Peale painting of the hero in Continental uniform which the Virginia legislature had ordered for this purpose. The Frenchman's initial conception of Washington in a farmer's dress and long cape grasping a plough was modified to suit the Virginians. The Richmond statue stands with unforced dignity holding a cane; his sword rests on the fasces beside him, and the blade of the plough is tactfully behind him. The planes of his head are magnificent, and beneath his soldier's dress is felt the body of the man, visible proof that "modern" costume can be as sculpturally expressive as any cloak or toga.

It is well that George Washington died twenty years before his marble effigy for the state capitol of North Carolina was completed, with its "servile adherence" to the costume of a Roman general. Yet Jefferson himself had recommended the sculptor when he wrote to the governor that, in the absence of Americans who could carve stone and of good native quarries, "old Canove of Rome" was the man for the commission. A few years before fire destroyed the Raleigh *Washington,* Massachusetts followed Virginia's example, and Sir Francis Chantrey's version of the first President was placed in its recess in the Boston State House. The English sculptor had avoided both Canova's military classicism and Houdon's contemporaneous dress; only Washington's collar and shoes could be seen under a voluminous cloak. New Englanders believed that Chantrey had found the correct solution of a vexing problem, while Rembrandt Peale exulted that

> . . . sculpture, tending to its noblest end,
> Confined to one immortal object still,
> Bestows Canova's, Houdon's, Chantrey's skill. . . .

Fortunately, it was Houdon's skill that the emergent native sculptors most admired and imitated. Jefferson's foresight was vindicated when Solomon Willard, and after him Greenough, Ward, and many others, studied the Richmond figure. And men came to the temple which housed it in search of a republican model for building. The edifice gave travelers a specimen of the republic's taste in its infancy, and, in Jefferson's words, "promised much for its maturer age." Both statue and edifice owed their existence to a mind more responsible than any other for the growth by which, in forty years, the provincial mind became the national mind.

CHAPTER 7 / THE ADAMESQUES

The Philadelphian who wrote in 1790 that brick houses were to be preferred to wooden ones must have been of the Federalist persuasion, because he felt that wood expressed that haste, sense of the temporary, and incentive to change "which it particularly interests us to repress in our citizens." The neat brick homes which began to line the streets of American towns while Jefferson was President, and the more modest white clapboarded ones with slender porticoes for their only decoration, were the work of men already something more than carpenters, skilled artisans with a fine sense of what brick and wood can do, but not yet in the full sense architects.

Most nearly professional was Charles Bulfinch, who followed Jefferson's trail from London to Rome and came back to Boston with full sketchbooks and without Jefferson's scorn for English buildings. Lest he forget the Adamesque repertory, there was a growing collection of books in his library to be consulted and adapted to American situations. Out of Crunden's *Convenient and Ornamental Architecture,* for example, had come a sketch by Bulfinch with a central pedimented portico and a rusticated basement. The Crunden original was for a "building calculated for a large family and a country situation"; with the hand of an amateur draughtsman the Boston man simplified its details and omitted the small wings at either end. Thus adapted, the design was at hand when Bulfinch had a state capitol to plan. The Adam brothers had published two volumes of engravings of their work, including the elevation of the church at Mistley with plain round towers like the one on Bulfinch's Lancaster Church. The Boston architect owned a French edition of Vignola, and several works whose illustrations had been made in the new aquatint process, so much better adapted than engraving to render the velvet-smooth textures of the Adamesque: John Soane's *Sketches of Architecture* and Plaw's *Rural Architecture.*

The Bulfinch patrons in New England were men who had fought the Revolution and who found the War of 1812 an impediment to their fortunes. Within a stone's

Benj. F. Nutting (?) *Tontine Crescent* (C.F. Rowley coll.)

Courtesy Antiques Magazine

Charles Bulfinch, State House, Boston, Pendleton lithograph

Courtesy Boston Athenaeum

throw of the sturdy Hancock House on Beacon Hill were larger and more cubelike mansions; on its western slope in 1796 rose the first Harrison Gray Otis residence, almost certainly designed by Bulfinch. It was three and one half stories high with a flat roof; its nearly square façade of brick was divided by unemphatic and well-spaced windows, two horizontal strips of white marble, and a door with fan- and sidelights. Its plan made no radical departure from those of the mid-century; but within, the rooms were high and spacious, the moldings elaborate, the fireplaces and door frames rich with white Adamesque forms on a pale green background; the wide hallway above was reached by a richly carved stairway and lighted by Palladian windows from both front and back. In the Otis drawing room, dining room, and music room John Quincy Adams and most of the other notables of the time found suave hospitality and uncramped elegance.

Before Bulfinch journeyed to Washington to direct the completion of the national Capitol in 1817, he had given Boston streets something of the charm and dignity of London. His experiment with the continuous residential block produced Colonnade Row, whose nineteen joined façades faced Boston Common. In Franklin Crescent, his sixteen houses formed a curve as graceful as those of Bath, their fronts shaded by elms in a semioval park. His versatility embraced the tactful enlargement of Faneuil Hall and the designing of a new theater; his range included the plain front of a waterside warehouse and the monumental portico of the Massachusetts General Hospital.

In Boston, Hartford, and Augusta, the Bulfinch capitols were no slavish imitations of English precedent but sturdy and well-composed structures of American scale; as symbols of the new state consciousness, they were perhaps more appropriate than Virginia's temple. Thanks to his initiative, the term "Bulfinchian" belongs to New England's oval parlors, its smooth façades where flush boarding replaced clapboards, its spiraling staircases, its ellipse-topped doorways.

Both Samuel McIntire and Asher Benjamin took their cue from Bulfinch; carpenters who would never see Europe could find details of construction and ornament in Benjamin's *The Country Builder's Assistant,* one of many books which carried the Adam-Bulfinch forms into the back country. In his own practice, Benjamin reduced the forms of church steeples to a simplicity more in keeping with the newer taste—in the Charles Street Church, the West Church, and in a series of meetinghouses which, together with the homes he planned, made him the Bulfinch of the Connecticut Valley. There were fewer cubes-upon-cubes or cubes-upon-octagons in the new churches than in those which Wren had inspired in an earlier day; the tapering colonial spire gave place to the small cupola, the tall windows marched in solemn procession along the plain sides, the tower retreated until in some instances it rose from the main roof, while a temple portico took its place. Year after year the guidebooks of Benjamin came off the press, and from them lesser builders learned precisely how to diminish the diameter of their fluted or plain columns, how to build spiral stairs which had no visible support, and how to carve the leaves and volutes of the Corinthian order, so much more stylish than the primitive Doric cushion or even the scrolled Ionic.

If any one city was transformed by a single mind, it was the Salem of McIntire. Architecturally speaking, its ancient streets were history embodied. There were shabby steep-roofed houses with beetling gables that had been raised not long after stiff-necked Governor Endecott christened the town in 1630; they reminded Salem people that Quakers had been persecuted here and witches hanged. There was visual evidence of the growing preoccupation with fishing and shipping in a few sturdy houses of the colonial type with robust gambrels and bonnet-topped doorways considered the last word in the seventeen fifties and sixties. When the Revolution came, Salem was luckily the one port which the British did not seize, and half a hundred privateers went out of Salem Harbor with no cargo save guns and a fighting crew on the lookout for British ships to sink or capture as prizes. In this hazardous business and in the task of keeping far-off ports open to Salem commerce, no family was more active or more successful than the Derbys, with whose rising fortune the career of Samuel McIntire ran parallel.

Henry Sargent painted Richard Derby with a telescope in his hand, papers and inkwell on his table, and a seaport beyond red draperies; for Richard had sailed his own ships to Spain, Portugal, and the West Indies before he returned to become a great merchant and the owner of a fleet. He had been a staunch supporter of the Revolution and his small schooner *Quero* had raced General Gage's *Sukey* to England with the news of Lexington and reached London Port two weeks before its rival. Richard's father had been a soapmaker; Richard's son Elias was to become one of the most successful American merchants; and as the dynasty progressed, McIntire built Derby houses to mirror their magnificence, houses at first as bulky as the Derby schooners,

Daniel Bancroft, elevation of the Derby Mansion, Salem, Mass.

Courtesy Essex Institute, Salem, Mass.

Room from Hersey Derby house, Salem, Mass.

Philadelphia Museum of Art

then increasingly elegant with the tall grace and exquisite lightness of Elias' *Grand Turk*. The rather plain brick house which the elder Derby had given Elias in the years when British restrictions still bound Salem's maritime progress had the tight, snug comforts, the dark paneled walls, the low ceilings, and plain mantels which were to be soon outgrown; and from its windows one saw Richard Derby's straight wharf, lined with warehouses, thrust into Salem Harbor. Elias' luck was rising. He never went to sea, but his *Grand Turk*, Salem-built, took sixteen British vessels, and the *Astrea* crossed the Atlantic in eighteen days. The ports of Mauritius, Madras, Bombay, Calcutta, and Cathay saw Derby ships riding at anchor, with fancy carvings and figureheads by McIntire and the Skillins, and Salem parlors began to fill up with trophies of the East—china and sandalwood, silk scarves and laces, painted wallpapers with Oriental birds among bamboo branches.

Elias Hasket Derby was not long content with the small house his father had given him; he ordered another from McIntire in 1780, his "House by the Wharf"; but before it was completed he had moved to the Pickman home on Washington Street, to which McIntire's remodeling gave a new dignity, and for whose cupola the painter Corné, arriving from Naples on the Derbys' *Mt. Vernon,* painted a fresco with still more Derby vessels sailing their confined spaces.

In 1795, when Elias and his wife determined to build the most magnificent of all New England mansions, neutral ships were playing the dangerous game of trading with both sides in Napoleon's war with England. Elias was nearly sixty, and Salem at the height of her prosperity. The detail drawings for the mansion were the work of McIntire, but more than one architect submitted sketches, and Fiske Kimball has reproduced their plans and elevations in his masterly study of McIntire. Bulfinch was mainly responsible for the street front; he leafed his *Malton's Views* and came up with a design based on the Palladian façade which Lord Burlington had made for General Wade's house in London and which had been repeated in the Dublin provost's house. He refined his prototypes in the Adamesque direction for a mansion three stories high with pilasters rising from second floor to cornice, a fanlighted doorway surmounted by an iron balcony and a Palladian window, a flattish roof with a balustrade, and, on the house as built, an elaborate cupola. The side wings of the mansion were similar to those of Chesterfield House in London.

The interior was spacious and handsome with a wide hall running back from the north front on Essex Street, two large rooms on either side, a winding stairway, and beyond the hall a magnificent oval room whose tall windows faced the harbor. Out of Pain's *British Palladio* and his *Practical House Carpenter* came the designs for the paneling, doors, and fireplaces, designs which McIntire drew with all four walls of a room shown in one sketch—as though a cardboard room had been flattened. The ovals and garlands on the Derby ceilings, the fluted door jambs, and the mantel decorations were drawn and executed with an attenuated grace which made the white-and-green decoration of the Otis house seem florid and overemphatic.

Elias went far afield for ideas for his garden, having in mind the new notions of informal planting. One of the designs he received had serpentine walks and irregularly "natural" planting of trees and shrubs; another, which may have been sent from England by a specialist who had never been to Salem, surrounded the garden front of the house with a "thicket," and had straight formal walks and a central basin. Its author wrote on the margin, "If there is any prospect that is agreeable can be seen from the House, make a Ha Ha instead of a thicket."

As Derby's mansion rose, bills poured in for the ornaments outside and the rich furnishings within: from Philadelphia for his two dozen oval-backed chairs, his stone steps and iron "bannistrades"; from London for carvings in the oval room; from John Doggett of Roxbury for a carved bed and window cornices; from the Boston Skillins for four wooden figures in the garden. Two years after this mansion-to-end-mansions had been begun, young Robert Gilmor of Baltimore journeyed from Boston to Salem by coach, and noted in his journal that "Mr. Derby has just built a most superb house, more like a palace than the dwelling of an American merchant." He was sufficiently impressed to make a pen sketch from a position near the wharf.

Secure on its terrace above the masts and sails of the waterfront, the mansion dominates the town in Gilmor's drawing, its oval parlor looking seaward; above the parlor a columned portico rises to the cornice to provide a porch from which the merchant could look down on his summerhouse and garden and beyond to where his vessels rode at anchor. A few years after Gilmor's visit, Eliza Southgate was received there by Hasket Derby, "a fine majestic-looking man." With him she saw the spacious hall with large white marble images on either side, the drawing room, dining room, and parlor with their gilded girandole mirrors, their Hepplewhite chairs and inlaid tables, their sideboards rich with Sheffield plate, their tall chests-on-chests with small carved figures and urns upon their pediments. Eliza admired the exquisite tracery of a ceiling in the oval room and passed into the moonlit garden, laid out, she said, with "airy irregularity." Inside and outside, everything had for her an air of enchantment: the exquisite summerhouse, the walks lined with tall poplars, the graveled terrace edged with a white balustrade. She stood on the porch above the oval room with magnificent pillars and railing, and sat down to play the grand piano in a drawing room whose only light was moonlight.

The mansion's life was as brief as it was splendid. Elias and his wife died only a few months after its completion, and their son followed them after a ten-year residence in the home he inherited. In 1815 this masterpiece of the Adamesque, as fine a residence as one could find in the republic, was torn down to make way for a market, and Salem people carried away the carved urns, the bits of molding, the mantelpieces, and the pilasters.

McIntire had been dead four years when the Derby mansion was demolished, yet every street in Salem bore his signature. On Federal Street was the Peirce-Nichols house of his beginnings, when the pictures of Batty

Asher Benjamin, First Church, Northampton, Mass.

David Howland photo

Langley had been his guide—square built and heavily ornamented, its clapboard face sharply broken by the bold overwindow moldings, burly cornice, fat corner pilasters, and sturdy rectangular porch. Before it ran a fence whose posts bore the garlanded and flame-topped urns which the Adam brothers had first placed in the niches of English houses, and which McIntire delighted to carve. A few doors down the street was Federal Hall. On other streets were the homes of Crowninshields, Olivers, Boardmans, Littles, and Kimballs, designed, built, and carved by Samuel, his son, and their assistants. On Essex Street stood the Gardner-Pingree house, with suave brick and delicate roof-balustrade over the flattened elliptical porch—a house all grace and dignity outside, and within a place of tall, pale-tinted walls, damask-draped windows from floor to ceiling, parlor opening into parlor, and exquisite moldings and fluted pilasters everywhere. McIntire in these culminating years had learned the same restraint which made Gore Place in Waltham look so English, with its oval rooms, its gracefully spiraling staircase, and its smoothly graded park sloping to the Charles River.

Other men than McIntire had observed and imitated, and soon the Bulfinch-Adam severity transformed New England commons and made streets an orderly procession of houses more primly self-conscious than their predecessors. At Orford, New Hampshire, and Bristol, Rhode Island, groups of glistening white mansions struck the Boston note. At Portsmouth, most of whose great houses had been built in the late years of the eighteenth century, the Peirce house was elegant with shallow-arcaded windows and cupola, and its stairway sprang from ground floor to attic. At Portland, Alexander Parris designed several homes in the new manner, including the Sweat mansion with its elliptical porch and spiral stairs.

In Hancock and Washington counties in Maine, a carpenter named Thomas Lord of Bluehill was said to have built eighty-four houses, eighty-three ships, five stores, and fourteen taverns; and there were fanlights, porches, and balustrades at Wiscasset and Machias which revealed how diligently Thomas Lord and others consulted their Benjamin books, their Pain, and their Adam, and how freshly those precepts and patterns were applied. To western Massachusetts Isaac Damon carried the Bulfinch idea as Asher Benjamin understood it, and quickly rose from carpenter to self-styled "architect."

Damon already knew Benjamin's Charles Street Church in Boston when, as a craftsman of twenty-nine, he found in Northampton his first opportunity. The simple white meetinghouse with its tapered spire where Jonathan Edwards had preached with such hysterical results for his listeners, and such disastrous effects upon his own career, was about to be replaced by a larger and more worldly edifice which Benjamin had designed; Isaac Damon was probably among the skilled artisans whom the contractor, Peleg Kingsley, had engaged. But Kingsley died or disappeared within six months, and the ambitious Damon was hired by the parish committee to complete the structure. Its slender columns divided the façade without too brusque an interruption, its roof angle was masked by fanlike curves, its tower of three stories was a suave combination of Adamesque themes; an elegant gilded weather vane held the place from which a rooster had once looked down on the sprawling town, flat meadows, and winding Connecticut.

This was the first of many churches Damon built between Worcester and New Haven. There were Damon houses, too, like the one he made for himself in 1812, a country version of the Adamesque, complete with low hipped roof, balustrade, and columned porch, from which thirteen years later a rather prosperous Damon set forth in a four-horse coach with his wife and children to hear Daniel Webster's oration at the laying of the cornerstone of Bunker Hill monument.

Both Thomas Lord and Isaac Damon built from the designs of others, Lord from the drawings of Deane, and Damon after Benjamin; both on occasion worked directly from their own schemes, as often as not sketching on brown paper with a minimum of draughtsman's skill. They could both reproduce the bookishly correct details which others supplied them, but they could also simplify and adapt cornices, entablatures, and capitals into forms of construction which, as carpenter-builders, they best understood, giving a regional accent to the form-language of the city men. In New England, and also to the south and west, one can watch the movement of an architectural scheme or motive as it passes from the page of an English manual to the working drawings of some semiprofessional in America and thence to the skilled hands of the local builder—to the academic mind a process of gradual dilution, but for the rest of us a "fresh configuration" through which architecture restores its vitality in response to men's needs.

As the Adamesque moved westward it was less a self-contained style to replace colonial forms and more a general approach to form, one influence among many. As such, it graced Ithiel Town's Center Church on New Haven Green without changing what was essentially a colonial structure in the Gibbs tradition; and as such it affected the work of New York City planners. There was, after all, no real conflict between this new mode and the reticent dignity, the rather French elegance, with

Homewood, Baltimore, Md., south portico

Historic American Buildings Survey, Library of Congress

Overdoor, James Watson house, N.Y.

Historic American Buildings Survey, Library of Congress

which John McComb, Jr., designed New York City Hall in association with Joseph F. Mangin, whose father had worked with Gabriel at Versailles.

Blocks of houses not very different from those of Bulfinch rose in New York between 1790 and 1820—the work of McComb, Stanton, and Josiah Brady, who knew the Adamesque repertory. In the James Watson house on State Street there is a luxurious ceiling in relief stucco, and there are overdoors rich with garlands of leaves and berries, urns, paired griffons, and classical ladies with lapfuls of fruit and flowers, probably designed by John McComb. Duncan Phyfe's New York shop and storeroom from which went out chairs, sofas, and dining tables of slender elegance in the manner of Adam, Hepplewhite, and Sheraton, was thoroughly Adamesque; so was Alling's more modest shop across the river in Newark. In Philadelphia and Baltimore were streets where a man who had walked London's Adelphi Terrace would feel vaguely at home, as he recognized details of Thornton's Library Company in the former city, and in the latter whole rows of smooth brick accented with white marble, the work of Robert Mills.

Charles Carroll of Carrollton, who had signed the Declaration of Independence, was living out his years at Homewood House, whose exquisite portico could as well have looked down upon a New England river valley as upon the city of Baltimore, since its designer had found his slender-columned portico and the spidery pattern of his window tracery in the same books used to the northward. When Mills designed the Valentine home in Richmond, McIntire had been one year dead, but a flying staircase worthy of the Salem builder graced its interior; and the details of Montmorenci near Warrenton in North Carolina had the Salem delicacy. There

Robert Mills, Wickham-Valentine house, Richmond, Va.

Historic American Buildings Survey, Library of Congress

were homes in Charleston with oval rooms as elegant as those of Gore Place, although more spacious, like the large mansion of James Manigault with its formal gardens and templed summerhouse, or the home of Nathaniel Russell, which seemed to have strayed from Beacon Hill. Savannah felt no need to depend on northern example, since in the days of prosperity which came during the early eighteen hundreds the architect William Jay brought English regency details from Bath, creating one-story central porches with double flights of steps and enlivening bay windows with the iron balconies which soon were to run riot over southern façades. Savannah's Independent Presbyterian Church carried a steeple which was in the Wren-Gibbs tradition, but in its pediment was the shell design of the brothers Adam. At Clinton in Georgia, Lowther Hall confessed similar origins with an oval fanlight and a twisting stairway.

On the banks of the Ohio River and in Kentucky and Tennessee, towns were springing up overnight as Southerners pushed into the area of the Ohio Land Company and New Englanders settled the Western Reserve. Some newcomers, like General Tupper from Providence, built houses in the style of the 1750's; in the homes of others appeared the more delicate new accent of Boston and Salem—the fanlights, the blind arcades, the flattened roof line, the copybook Adamesque doorways which bespoke their owners' affection for the more settled East. Into New Connecticut went Colonel Lemuel Porter of Waterbury in old Connecticut to supervise the building of a Congregational Church at Tallmadge as slenderly white, as crisp in details of portico, pediment, and tower as any meetinghouse back home. The Taft house in Cincinnati, with its smooth white surfaces, its high portico, and the oval windows above its tall windows, reminded visitors of Hoban's White House. There was Adamesque in Kentucky, too: Homewood of Baltimore rose again when Judge Humphrey built at St. Matthews; Henry Clay's Ashland was planned by Latrobe, and Major L'Enfant designed its formal gardens after the fiasco on the Potomac. The Benjamin Gratz house in Lexington, where the brother of the famous Rebecca lived, had an oval-topped front door whose lights were divided by exquisite fanlike tracery. Even Shaker Town had its own severe variant on the spiral staircase in its Guest House. Over the border in Tennessee, Thomas Baker designed Foxland Hall and Fairview in the Adamesque spirit.

Charles Bulfinch had launched the Adamesque. When he left Washington in 1830 there were young men who applied the term "old-fashioned" to this gentleman of sixty-seven who had watched the battle of Bunker Hill from the roof of his father's house in Bowdoin Square. One of them was Ithiel Town, who had already built a state house at New Haven which was a Parthenon. Asher Benjamin was planning new editions of his first aids to the aspiring builder which would have a more purely Grecian flavor. Square-built Salem was soon to be an anachronism, and every man's home his temple.

CHAPTER 8 / FROM GOOSE CREEK TO TIBER

When Jefferson came home in 1789, New York City was the capital of the republic. A few months before, Major L'Enfant had remodeled the old town hall for the inauguration of George Washington. The original structure had stood for nearly a century in Wall Street; now the first President swore his oath on the balcony of Federal Hall under the canopy and the red-and-white curtains. Bulfinch had come from Boston to see the ceremony, and he sketched the façade for future use—a steep roof, a portico-balcony, a second-story pediment and cupola facing Broad Street, where crowds pressed against housefronts smooth in the new style and rough in the old one, among them the last stepped gables of Dutch New Amsterdam.

Before the year was out, the Government House was building on Bowling Green from a design by John McComb, Jr., its simple rectangular form dignified by a portico which rose from basement to attic; but by the time it was completed as a President's home, both capital and President had moved to Philadelphia. Hoban's State House for South Carolina had been finished before Federal Hall with something of the new largeness of scale, and the Girard National Bank in Philadelphia was soon to raise its stately columns, white against brick-red.

None of these structures had the proud severity of the temple on the hill at Richmond, and Jefferson wished the new monumentality to take form as soon as a permanent capital city could be built. What should be its location? The poet Freneau poked fun at rival claims in a dialogue between two housekeepers who argued the merits of Philadelphia, New York, and the junction of the Potomac River with its Eastern Branch, an area which then bore an Indian name tempting to any rhymester. Said one:

> My master would rather saw timber or dig,
> Than see them removing to Conegocheague,—
> Where the houses and kitchens are yet to be framed,
> The trees to be felled, and the streets to be named. . . .

Yet Conegocheague was chosen in 1791 and President Washington asked Major Pierre Charles L'Enfant, who had served under him as engineer in the Revolution, to survey the tangled swamps along Goose Creek where a classical-minded farmer named Pope had christened his property Rome. L'Enfant tramped the area in a storm of rain and within a few weeks was able to submit a progress map with paper streets and avenues. Jefferson contributed his plans of European towns and sketches of his own to indicate where he thought the chief buildings should be placed; a rival surveyor named Ellicott redrew L'Enfant's design before the latter quarreled with Jefferson, Washington, and the commissioners and was dismissed.

L'Enfant's conception was both handsome and farsighted, although generations of politicians were to betray its logic by putting buildings in the wrong places and allowing swift growth to smother its original layout. The Capitol stood at one end of the proposed city, the monument at the other, and between them was the "great walk." This was to be the main axis of the town, crossed by the lesser one which extended southward from the President's house. The new streets would be plotted checkerboard fashion and upon their pattern would be imposed radiating avenues which opened into circular plazas. Goose Creek was to become a stately canal.

Five years after L'Enfant's dismissal this federal city was largely a vision on paper, and Tom Moore wrote with his usual condescension:

> And what was Goose-Creek once is Tiber now:
> This embryo capital, where Fancy sees
> Squares in morasses, obelisks in trees;
> Which second-sighted seers, ev'n now, adorn
> With shrines unbuilt and heroes yet unborn,
> Though naught but woods and Jefferson they see,
> Where streets should run and sages *ought* to be.

Moore was too busy watching the "showy smile of young presumption" on Columbia's rising brow to note that one wing of the embryo Capitol was already complete. Its long and tangled history had begun—the jealousies, the compromises, the building up and tearing down which paralleled the nation's life. The competition for its design had produced drawings which ranged from the competent to the crude. Samuel McIntire had leafed his Gibbs and produced a façade in the manner of Sir William Chambers, weighty and dignified, with rows of statues on its balustraded roof; Charles Bulfinch saw the Capitol as a big brother of his Boston State House. Turner's sketch had a dome which pleased Washington; Jefferson, who must have realized that the functions of government could scarcely be contained in a temple, wondered if some variant of the rotunda could be used, like Soufflot's Panthéon in Paris.

No one felt too sure of himself, yet it was clear that

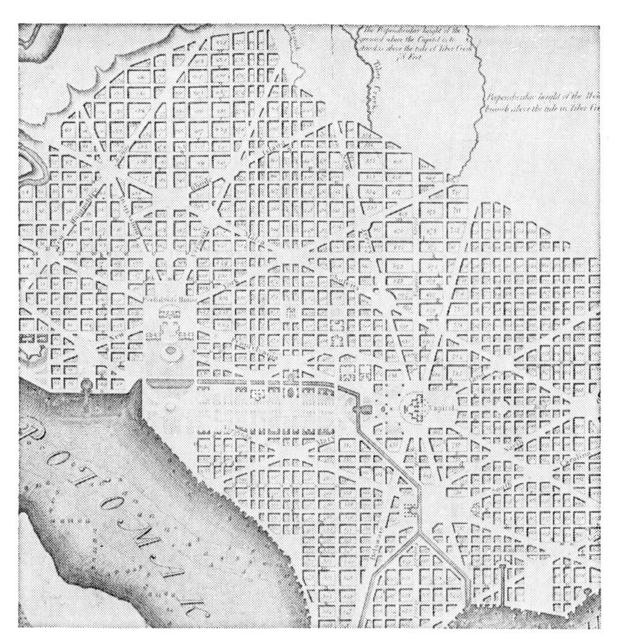

L'Enfant plan, Thackera & Vallance engraving (detail)

Library of Congress photo

Stephen Hallet and William Thornton were moving toward a plan which reconciled form with function. In the fall of 1792 Thornton turned up in Philadelphia with a plan which he had borrowed from *Vitruvius Britannicus.* This genial Quaker, whose conversation Dunlap found an antidote to boredom, wrote novels, painted miniatures, bred race horses, and composed a treatise on the education of the deaf and dumb. In architecture he was confessedly an amateur, and more than one builder had to correct the practical shortcomings of his plans for the Capitol amid a shower of angry pamphlets from Thornton. Yet his second design was virtually accepted. It resembled one of Hallet's drawings: a central mass with a rotunda topped by a dome; wings for the House and Senate; a high basement the length of the building; the main entrance through an eastern portico with a driveway underneath it.

After much wrangling, Hallet became director of construction, laying the foundations in accordance with his own plans. A year later, Thornton superimposed his own conception on these foundations, and planned a second, lower dome to the west of Hallet's. For a time the Englishman Hadfield struggled with these contradictions; two years after Jefferson became President, the firm hand of his friend Latrobe resolved them, and the Capitol gained some measure of coherence. Latrobe scrapped the extra dome, kept the delicately proportioned outer walls of Thornton's wings, and designed a handsome oval chamber for the House.

When the war with England came, the two wings stood complete with a gap between them; when the British troops left Washington there stood only a smoke-stained shell—as Freneau wrote, "they left our congress naked walls." It was Latrobe's task to complete the damaged wings, to design a new Hall of Representatives, to modify earlier schemes for the central western and eastern fronts, and to plan the great domed rotunda. The subsequent work of Bulfinch was one of completion rather than invention, but his sagacity and his taste were to be seen in his modifications of the western front, in the fence posts and gate lodges he devised for the Capitol grounds, and in a Library of Congress which was to be almost literally copied by Robert Mills some twenty years later for the University of South Carolina at Columbus.

In his work on the Capitol Benjamin Henry Latrobe had scarcely shown the full measure of his designer's skill, nor the range of his experimental mind. He was an English-born architect who had worked with Cockerell in London before he came to Virginia as an engineer in

Latrobe design, Hall of Representatives, U.S. Capitol

Library of Congress

1796. There was no slavish archaeology in the public and private work he did in Virginia, in Washington, in Lexington, Kentucky, and in New Orleans; and as for Philadelphia, he could boast with some reason that he had changed the taste of a whole city. Only his nimble mind or that of Jefferson could have conceived a new architectural order substituting the corncob and the tobacco leaf for the sacred acanthus; and his buildings, whether Greek or Gothic, had a way of being the first of their kind in America.

Five years before his thankless job in Washington Latrobe designed the Bank of Pennsylvania. Through Stuart and Revett's *Antiquities of Athens* he knew his Acropolis as thoroughly as other men their Roman Forum; and he came to Philadelphia in 1798 with a full realization that banks were modern institutions. He regretted the directors' insistence that their structure imitate a temple; and although his porticoes at both ends of the bank were carried by the Ionic columns of the Erechtheum, his interior combined use with beauty: a great circular banking hall with a vestibule in front

U.S. Capitol in 1824, T. Sutherland aquatint (detail)

Courtesy Old Print Shop, New York City

and counting rooms behind it; a square attic and a lanterned dome above for lighting, bold vaulted masonry in its construction, and offices which were fireproof. Its form proclaimed its purpose, and its creator heard a French visitor, pausing in Second Street, murmur, "Si beau, et si simple!"

As Superintendent of Water Supply, Latrobe replaced the old sidewalk pumps and noxious gutters of Philadelphia with a system which was the first in America to use steam pumps. One was in the Square, and from its reservoir the water flowed in wooden pipes through the city. Because the ancient world offered small precedent for such a structure, the Center Square Pump House became a delightful synthesis of classicism with engineering. There were offices around its sides, a pump chamber below and a tank above, and its proportions and divisions said as much. Many years later Latrobe made drawings of it as a record for his son; meanwhile its charm had been recorded by Krimmel and other artists as it stood white among the poplars with the *Nymph* of William Rush spouting before it.

In 1805 one of Latrobe's competitive designs for the Catholic Cathedral in Baltimore was classical, the other medieval. Six years later his sketch for a western approach to the national Capitol proved that the Greek simplicity was in his consciousness; his drawing freely adapted the Athenian Propylaea with its descent by several levels and its plain Doric portico.

Less than a month after Latrobe signed this design, he explained in a speech to the Society of Artists in Philadelphia the reason for his Attic preference. Greece demonstrated, he said, that art and democracy are compatible, for the Greece of Pericles was free, and only from the time of Alexander lost that freedom and with it her perfection in the arts. The monuments of the Roman Empire were coarse in taste, the Arch of Constantine a "crowded patchwork of parts." Why ignore the earlier simplicity to copy in America the corrupt style of Diocletian's palaces? A country where talents do not depend on the favor of the great is a soil as congenial to their growth as Sparta, Thebes, or Delphi. Once the new nation learns that the home of the fine arts is in the bosom of a republic, then "indeed the days of Greece may be revived in the woods of America, and Philadelphia become the Athens of the western world."

This is the philosophy of the Greek Revival, yet Latrobe used the word "revived" in a deeper sense than many who came after him. Seven years later the directors of the Bank of the United States advertised for designs which would chastely imitate the Greek "in its simplest and least expensive form"; they received from Latrobe no literal replica of the Parthenon. As he explained in his memorandum, the "necessary arrangement of a house of business,—requiring a multitude of apartments and abundant light,—is so contrary to that of a Temple . . . that nothing but the general character and style of the best Grecian Architecture can ever be preserved in such a design." The colonnade in Latrobe's drawing was confined to porticoes on either end; its door was flanked by windows, and rows of windows ran along its sides. Above its roof rose a high attic with four lunette-shaped openings to light the great banking room beneath. Its interior was both practical and spacious, with a dome on pendentives, flanked by barrel vaults

Latrobe's design for Bank of the U.S.A., Philadelphia, Pa.

Library of Congress

over the main hall. Its designer could claim with truth that he was "no bigoted Greek."

It was fortunate that two of Latrobe's pupils learned his mastery of essentials. Both William Strickland and Robert Mills were his apprentices during four or five years; both started their careers at a time when, as Brackenridge observed, "we bethought ourselves of building noble bridges, of making vast turnpike roads, of digging canals and effecting other national works." To these works the two men gave not only their draughtsman's skill but their constructive ingenuity.

Strickland had painted stage scenery, portraits, and landscapes and had made aquatints before he built the bank which Latrobe had designed, departing in many ways from the original conception. His range included a single-spanned wooden bridge over the Schuylkill and large church auditoriums. New religious sects were challenging the older ones and asked for greater interior spaces. Peter Banner's Park Street Church in Boston looked as though Wren and Gibbs had said the last word on the subject, and so did David Hoadley's United Church in New Haven and McComb's St. John's in New York; but meanwhile Strickland and Mills adapted the rotunda principle to the needs of less conservative congregations.

While Strickland built the bank on Chestnut Street, Robert Mills watched his Washington monument rise in Baltimore, a stout Doric shaft with the hero standing on its top like a modern Saint Simeon. He claimed to be the first professional architect trained in America; he had known Jefferson and worked with Hoban and Bulfinch. As a young man, he lined the streets of Baltimore with houses of Adamesque gentility; in his maturity he built state capitols and obelisks, jails, and customhouses with a taste less refined than Strickland's, and designed canals, rotary engines, reaping machines, railroads, and lighthouses. When the Philadelphia water system proved inadequate, he worked with the engineer Frederick Graff in designing and building the Fairmount Water Works.

That ensemble owed much of its grace and dignity to Mills. A dam across the Schuylkill diverted water into

Fairmount Water Works, lithograph after Geo. Lehman (detail)

Historical Society of Pennsylvania, Philadelphia, Pa.

a forebay from which hydraulic turbines forced it up to a reservoir on near-by Mount Morris; on the terrace between the river and the forebay stood the engine house, two templelike pavilions and a pair of entrance gates for which William Rush carved allegorical figures; and on the top of the hill stood a columned summer-house. It was this group that pleased Philip Hone in later years when he noted in his diary that "the grounds, gardens, fountains, pavilions, etc. . . . are all in beautiful order, and appeared at this season, when Nature is clothed in all her loveliest attire and the day unusually bright, to greater advantage than I have ever seen it. The walks were filled with well behaved people who appeared to be of the better sort of Bourgeoisie . . . and the whole scene reminded me of a French city on a fine Sunday afternoon."

The sons of the better sort of "Bourgeoisie" went to colleges and universities whose architecture remained faithful to the previous century. The Union College of Joseph Jacques Ramée, however, was at least a planned ensemble with its separate buildings symmetrically grouped alongside the circular main structure; and in 1818 a site was chosen near Charlottesville for the University of Virginia, to be built from Thomas Jefferson's designs. With the help of Thornton and Latrobe, Jefferson devised what he called an "academical village" whose terraced green quadrangle was dominated by a miniature rotunda inspired by the Roman Pantheon. On either side ranged the two-story pavilions, each with its lodgings above for the professor and its classroom below, and each in its details an illustration of some famous classical structure "to serve as specimens for the architectural lecturer." Between the pavilions were the lower dormitories for students, and a covered colonnade linked all these "schools," a scheme as useful as it was handsome.

Jefferson here proved himself the noblest Roman of them all. He had shown rather more independence of precedent in his politics than in his buildings; but his ghost would scarcely condone the obsequious borrowings of later revivalists who used his name as justification. Their imposition of past styles on present needs was to become one of those forms of "tyranny over the mind of man" to which he had sworn eternal hostility.

Much of the work done in the second decade of the century was by younger men than Jefferson, Latrobe, Strickland, and Mills. Some of it still relied on forms to be found in handbooks and on craft traditions which local carpenters best understood. Before the eyes of this generation stood the structures of the republican pioneers: the Richmond and Washington Capitols; the Center Square Pump House; the Bank of the United States; the austere Massachusetts General Hospital in Boston; the University of Virginia; the Chestnut Street Theater in Philadelphia; at Columbia in South Carolina an insane asylum whose finely proportioned portico was reached by two circular stairways and crowned by the simplest of round lanterns.

There were new names among builders, names which would become more familiar in the age of Jackson. Three New Englanders began their careers without formal training as architects: Solomon Willard was a car-

Thomas Jefferson, University of Virginia, lithograph by E. Sachse & Co.

Courtesy Old Print Shop, New York City

penter and a stone carver who in the twenties designed granite banks and courthouses; Alexander Parris from Hebron in Maine built Bulfinch-like houses in Boston and Portland, and at the age of forty-five put the Doric temple to a new use in his Quincy Market. The father of Isaiah Rogers had built ships; the son worked with Willard before he opened his own office in 1825 and became a specialist in designing large hotels.

Ithiel Town of Thompson, Connecticut, was by all standards a more "refined" spirit than the Boston builders. He traveled in Europe collecting an enormous library, and his friends were Dr. Hosack, Bryant, Irving, Morse, and Trumbull. After a few years in Boston, where he probably went to school to Asher Benjamin, he designed New Haven's Center Church in the Gibbs manner, patented a lattice truss for bridges, and in 1824 designed the never-to-be-completed Eagle Bank at New Haven. In 1825 Town's future partner, Martin Thompson, built the Merchant's Exchange in New York, one of the most impressive structures of its time, with a recessed porch in its center whose Ionic shafts were exquisitely related to the proportions of the whole, and whose massive lantern and domed cupola rode the flat roof. In the same year Strickland's pupil Gideon Shryock used the Ionic in his state capitol at Frankfort in Kentucky and Jonathan Goldsmith supported his national bank at Painesville, Ohio, on Doric columns which were incorrectly slim.

It was obvious in 1825 that Jefferson's unswerving devotion to the Roman was giving place to an exploration of the Grecian vein. As the postwar republicans enlarged their scale of domestic living, the Greek idiom appeared in houses, but rather as an accent than a full language of forms. During the war Robert Mills designed a Doric portico from ground to roof level for a house in Richmond, and there were Attic details on Parris' Appleton and Parker houses on Beacon Hill in 1818. In this age, as in all others, the great majority of American homes had no pure stylistic character. American streets were not lined with temples but with old family structures remodeled and enlarged by successive generations. When Stephen Salisbury, son of a rich Boston merchant, established a branch of his hardware business in Worcester in the seventeen sixties, he lived for a time in a small one-story shop. His later house was based on sketches by Abraham Savage of Boston—a rather plain Georgian structure with a hipped roof and a pedimented doorway. In the nineties his south façade acquired a pediment and a fanlighted door in the Adamesque mode. Shortly after the War of 1812 a Grecian portico ran the length of the Salisbury mansion, which stands today as a record of the family fortunes and a summary of taste for sixty years.

That summary would be incomplete, however, if it concerned itself only with ancient forms, for the same men who worshiped the Roman and the Greek also dabbled with the Gothic. In the same year which saw Latrobe's design for the Bank of the United States, James Wyatt died in England after building many a "castellated" country house. Even Sir Christopher Wren and Robert Adam had produced Gothic churches and interiors. Sir Horace Walpole had his Strawberry Hill and Beckford his Fonthill Abbey, and the latter was still building when in Philadelphia Latrobe designed Sedgeley in the Gothic manner. Not until a generation of Americans would tremble over the pages of *The Castle of Otranto* or relive the Middle Ages with Sir Walter Scott would Greek meet Goth fully and the battle of the styles be joined; in the meantime there were handbooks like Batty Langley's *Gothic Architecture Improved* which tempted the Yankee builder to turn on occasion from the Doric to the pointed arch and the imitation vault.

Latrobe's Christ Church in Washington and his St. Paul's in Alexandria were pseudo-Gothic in detail. Ithiel Town's Trinity Church stands on New Haven Green beside its two Adamesque companions, a barnlike structure of the local rock trimmed with sandstone, with rows of plain pointed windows along its sides and a tower which was originally of wood and stone and of a Gothic which owed as much to Town's invention as to historic precedent. The interior of Trinity makes an effort to catch the spirit of medieval vaulting in lath and plaster, with ribs springing to intersect one another in the liveliest fashion. New York's second Trinity Church, attributed by Davis to Josiah Brady, was a similar effort, and Mangin's designs for St. Patrick's included a vast nave and two towers. There were details from Batty Langley in John Holden Greene's St. John's in Providence, and Strickland's Masonic Hall in Philadelphia was quasi-medieval.

Rather more authentic was St. Mary's Catholic Chapel in Baltimore, the work of Maximilian Godefroy. The Frenchman arrived in Baltimore in 1805 after adventures which the "Gothic" novelists would have envied; hostile to both the Revolution and the Republic, he had been a prisoner at Bellegarde, had escaped, and had been tracked by bloodhounds through the Catalonian mountains before finally being permitted to sail for America. In Baltimore he taught architecture and the fine arts at St. Mary's, worked and quarreled with Latrobe, designed the strange Battle Monument, and made his delightfully literary water-color sketch of the proposed chapel, with saints standing in their niches across its façade for the first time in the New World and a tower whose form owed more to Godefroy's imagination than to any historic model. The tower was never built but the lower walls and curious

Godefroy's drawing for St. Mary's Chapel, Baltimore, Md.

Historic American Buildings Survey, Library of Congress

Lippitt Mill, Lippitt, West Warwick, R.I.

William Pierson photo

buttresses remain, with vaguely Gothic ornament approximated in brick.

Builders far less sophisticated than Godefroy built churches in what has been called "carpenter's Gothic." Stripped of their finials, pointed windows, and battlemented boards, they would reveal a boxlike eighteenth-century structure. Like the odd small library with eight sides, lancet windows, and fanciful detail which adjoins the thoroughly Georgian Linden Place in Bristol, Rhode Island, such work is a naïve Gothic frosting of the classical cake.

The story of architecture in the new republic is not fully told in terms of survival and revival, of Roman symbolism, and of Greek and Gothic fumblings. The new statecraft found what it believed to be its appropriate housing in state capitols, the religious interest in churches, the financial system in templed banks, the family needs in more stately mansions; but manufacture and commerce also outgrew the spaces and shapes which earlier had contained them. At eighteenth-century Hope Furnace in Rhode Island, the Browns of Providence had forged cannon for the Revolution; at Peace Dale and at Hazard after the victory were the makers of woolen textiles. In such communities stood the small factory, with rows of workmen's cottages beside it. At Lippitt there remain a few houses of what was once such an ensemble where Christopher Lippitt, a veteran of the war, began to make cotton in 1809. Seventeen years later, the first power looms were spinning at Peace Dale.

The architectural sequence of the mill was from the wooden box, with little to differentiate it from a house except its belfry to call workers, to structures of stone and brick whose size and plainness hinted their function and whose fine proportions reveal the professional designer's hand. The Slater Mill of 1793 at Pawtucket is of the earlier type; the stone woolen mill at Woonsocket a generation later was probably the work of James C. Bucklin, whose partner Russell Warren worked in Fall River, New Bedford, and Charleston.

There were sections in the American cities whose commercial activities called for replanning and redesigning in the early years of the century; and here too the development moved from quasi-domestic brick and wood to the stone façade with many windows. Between the old State House and the wharves in Boston, Charles Bulfinch helped to plan a business district, and for it he designed the India Wharf Stores, a severe structure in three parts whose grim façade was accented with lighter stone over its windows. The fronts which lined the market area in Boston a few years later were plain granite, their only variation a series of roundheaded windows, their skeletons built with posts and lintels of the solid stone; and John Holden Greene's Bristol Hotel in Providence was inspired by Boston's Alexander Parris.

When in the eighteen twenties a whole factory community was planned and built by the Merrimac Company at Lowell in Massachusetts, the bend of the river and the straight lines of canals determined the pattern

Shaker Barn, Hancock, Mass.

Index of American Design, Natl. Gallery of Art

Shaker cupboards, New Lebanon, N.Y.

Index of American Design, Natl. Gallery of Art

within which the separate brick structures were to be placed, with an eye to function and to the order of importance of those who would live or work in them: the large mills were lined up next the river, the buildings for skilled laborers down one side, those for the unskilled opposite them; the offices of the executives closed the rectangle. The symmetry at Lowell bore a curious resemblance to that of Jefferson's academic village at Charlottesville, but its formalism had been shaped by hard necessity.

Finally, there were necessities of quite another sort in the minds of the men who built New Harmony and the superb constructions of the Shakers. These were no modifications of existing models but genuine creations where the need directly shaped the form. When the stolid, practical followers of Rapp came to Indiana in 1814 they planned "Harmonie" without help from any outsider. About forty Rappite dwellings still stand in New Harmony, as the settlement was rechristened when Robert Owen and his followers took it over in 1824—plain houses with their doors turned away from the street, an old fort and a granary whose thick sandstone walls have loopholes; the fanlighted door of its steeple house over which Frederick Rapp carved a golden rose surrounded by a wreath; the old tavern with its double staircase.

The Shakers had lived in America since 1776, obedient to their founder's charge, "Put your hands to work and your heart to God." It was not aesthetic purism but the law of their society which forbade "odd or fanciful styles" or "beadings, moldings and cornishings," and prescribed that meetinghouses be painted white, dwellings a light cream color, and barns lead-gray or dark red-brown.

To the Shaker craftsman, for the most part nameless, "every force has its form," and he wrought in that belief with a fine sense of materials, a deft workmanship which never hurried, and no effort whatever to please the "world's people."

There were Shaker meetinghouses, schools, and mathematically grouped dwelling houses at New Lebanon and Watervliet in New York, at Harvard, Hancock, and Shirley in Massachusetts, at Gorham, Alfred, and New Gloucester in Maine, at Union Village in Ohio, and in the neighborhood of Lexington, Kentucky; and here and there, as they made converts in the years before the Civil War, in Tennessee and Indiana. The Shaker church was a simple rectangular building of two stories with a gambrel or a "boiler" roof, dormers, and on the side two doors for the sisters and brothers. The Shaker barn was built on a side hill to be entered on more than one level; the most remarkable one was at Hancock with ground stories of stone in circular form, a twelve-sided wooden superstructure, and a hexagonal cupola above that—a barn where a hay wagon could drive in, unload, and drive out the way it entered. The walls of Shaker houses were sometimes two or three feet thick with folding wooden shutters; their rooms were reduced to final essentials, the walls and beamed ceilings whitened, the woodwork painted blue. There was no elaboration of the rhythm which doors and windows made except the low wainscot, the perfect planes and proportions of built-in shelves and cupboards, the sequence of peg boards from door to door, the slim and exquisite chairs, benches, and tables of cherry, maple, or butternut.

The Shakers raised their Shirley meetinghouse at night to avoid trouble with worldly neighbors, in the same year which saw Hallet and Thornton quarreling over the national Capitol. Within a few months of each other the Hancock farmers built their round barn, and Thompson his Merchant's Exchange in New York with a majestic lantern and a domed cupola above its recessed Ionic portico. In the age of Duncan Phyfe and the cumbrous later Victorian, the brethren made their exquisitely plain chairs and tables. The "world's people" could adapt forms; the Shakers could create them. More than one generation would pass in America before this conception of logic with beauty would come into its own.

CHAPTER 9 / SCULPTURE'S WOODEN AGE

The great parade which wound through the streets of Boston in 1788 to celebrate the ratification of the Constitution saw proofs of the carver's and metalworker's skill on every hand. Shem Drowne was dead, but his grasshopper still "discharged his office" from the top of Faneuil Hall. In the graveyards on Tremont Street, Henry Christian Geyer's death's-heads and angel faces grinned at passers-by, and on the mantelpieces of Boston houses stood his plaster cats, dogs, and parrots. In the processions at Boston, as in New York and Philadelphia, the carvers walked in a body—the chairmakers, the cabinetmakers, the engravers—or stood on "cars" which they had made and decorated, like the guildsmen of the Middle Ages.

They looked upon themselves, and were looked upon, as artisans with a useful skill; yet already more than one of them had glimpsed the distinction between artisan and artist. By the time young Americans rushed to Europe in the 1830's for training in the art, America had produced McIntire, the Skillins, Rush, Frazee, and Augur, men with some right to the title of sculptor, not one of whom ever left this country.

Samuel McIntire of Salem never mastered, to be sure, the freely cut full figure, but remained to the end a decorative relief carver in wood with a fine sense of what wood could do, and with an exquisite feeling for proportions, whether of the buildings he designed or of the doors and window cornices he made for them. His ship carving for the Derbys and the Crowninshields from the close of the Revolution to the early years of the nineteenth century was more architectural than sculptural — cabin interiors, billet heads with drum and flags on them, great screaming eagles, scrolls, and swags for the stems of vessels, his preliminary drawings for which are anything but fluent, and suggest that the chisel was more at home in Samuel's

Samuel McIntire, *Governor Winthrop*

American Antiquarian Society, Worcester, Mass.

Hope, architectural carving

Index of American Design, Natl. Gallery of Art

hand than the pencil or the pen except when he could use a ruler in designing the façades and plans of houses. But when there were slenderly fluted pilasters, delicate sheaves of wheat, and baskets of fruit and flowers to be cut in pine for the rooms in Salem homes, McIntire proved his mastery.

In the seventeen nineties when, perhaps in emulation of the Boston Skillins, he turned his hand upon occasion to the making of free-standing figures, he showed neither the confidence nor the flexibility of his rivals. Among the McIntire carvings at the Essex Institute in Salem is a lunette-shaped panel rich with the emblems of war and industry: cannons, muskets, flags, lances, and harpoons disposed around the coat of arms of Massachusetts and ringed by thirteen stars. When Salem Common became Washington Square, McIntire designed its gateways and for the western one he carved a large profile medallion of the first President which had its own stiff austerity. It was his friend William Bentley who commissioned a wooden bust of John Winthrop, less than a foot high, based on a copy of an old miniature; and McIntire chiseled the starched collar and the long locks with the minuteness, the delight in repetition with which he grooved the flutings of pilasters. The patron voiced his disappointment with the egg-shaped smoothness of the head, the staring eyes, the ridged hair, when he wrote, "I cannot say that he has expressed in the bust anything which agrees with the Governour."

Identical in size and in the shape of its pedestal is the *Voltaire* which Bentley owned, so much more sensitively carved than the *Winthrop* that it may be either proof of Samuel's progress or a work by one of the Skillins. Too small to be a figurehead, but braced like a figurehead against an imaginary gale, is a small lady holding a portrait medallion to whom McIntire gave a tense movement out of all proportion to her diminutive size (Peabody Mus.).

Figures like these were the fruit of McIntire's later years, and his tombstone recorded: "He was distinguished for Genius in Architecture, Sculpture, and Musick: Modest and Sweet Manners rendered him pleasing: Industry and Integrity respectable . . . ." Bentley recalled that all the improvements of Salem for nearly thirty years past had been made under McIntire's eye. On a previous occasion the diarist had observed that "he cuts smoother than Skillings but he has not his genius."

Bentley referred to Simeon Skillin, Jr., one of the four carving Skillins, as Leroy Thwing has called them. When Simeon, Sr., died in 1778, he had been famous as a woodcarver for forty years up and down the coast, and three of his ten children were trained to continue the name and improve the quality of Skillin figureheads. Samuel was the youngest and his work is least known today, but hundreds of bills and receipts attest the industry and importance of John and Simeon, Jr., partners for twenty years. From their shop on Lee's wharf in the 1790's came brackets, trailboards, catfaces, and a long procession of figures—mythological, historical, and fanciful—to stare from the prows of American ships at the harbors of Canton and St. Petersburg. They cut the eleven-foot *Grand Turk* for the second Derby vessel of that name. For the Boston State House in 1798 the brothers itemized their "carve work": 32 Corinthian capitals, 133 modillions for the council chamber, 482 for the outside cornice, 337 feet of ovolo molding, and a pine cone for the top of the dome. A few years before they had supplied similar ornaments for the Derby summerhouse and garden—a hermit, a shepherdess, a gardener, and a goddess of Plenty.

The younger Simeon probably carved the *Mercury* which once stood on the Boston Post Office, a small wooden offspring of Giovanni da Bologna's statue, his plump legs imitating the flight of the original, his winged helmet suggesting a bowler hat; and similar in style is *Hope,* a female between four and five feet high, who rests one arm on an anchor and points skyward with the other, her hair and classic gown fashioned with a graceful assurance. Mabel Swan has convincingly shown that three small pediment figures—thoroughly feminine with their delicately rounded cheeks and breasts, their well-drawn features and flowing hair—on a chest-on-chest in the Garvan Collection at Yale were done by the Skillins.

If these home-grown craftsmen hoped for commissions in the rising national capital, they were disappointed. The Washington statues and ornaments were to be cut in stone, and Jefferson determined to employ foreign artisans, not the makers of ships' heads and tavern signs; he wrote to Mazzei to find and to send over competent men.

The Italian invasion began in 1806 with Giuseppe Franzoni and Giovanni Andrei. To the former was entrusted the bald-headed eagle over the Speaker's chair, not a Roman but an American bird for whose details he had to rely on the knowledge of Charles Willson Peale. Andrei worked on the twenty-four capitals for the House of Representatives which Jefferson insisted must be Corinthian. After the destruction of 1814 a second immigration brought Franzoni's brother Carlo

Corn cob columns, U.S. Capitol

Library of Congress photo

to carve a chariot of History with a Canova-smooth goddess riding it and a clock in one wheel. Giuseppe Valaperta replaced the lost eagle; Luigi Persico designed an eastern pediment whose "heathen mythology" was modified in deference to the taste of President John Quincy Adams; other Capitol details were cut by Peter Cardelli and by Canova's pupil, Antonio Capellano.

The only Capitol sculptures which seemed to later visitors above the level of stilted competence were the capitals in the Senate wing rotunda and in the Supreme Court wing. The latter were cut by Jardella from designs by Latrobe, and one can share Jefferson's admiration, for although the Corinthian principle was their basis, the forms were those of the leaf and blossom of the American tobacco plant. Even more original were Giuseppe Franzoni's corncob columns, which had been carved earlier and survived the fire of 1814; their capitals bore ears of corn and the flutings of their shafts were cornstalks.

Some of these foreigners worked elsewhere than in the federal city. Enrico Causici, after replacing in plaster the *Liberty* of the Hall of Representatives, carved a huge Washington for Mills' Doric column in Baltimore

William Rush, *Comedy*

Philadelphia Museum of Art

and modeled an equestrian first President without receiving the coveted commission. Capellano's statue of Victory was placed on the top of Godefroy's Battle Monument at Baltimore; Giuseppe Ceracchi modeled heads in Philadelphia and New York.

When Valaperta died he left in America several miniature profile portraits in red wax, and there were others who worked in this medium; the most proficient among them was a Dane named John Christian Rauschner, whose reliefs were duplicated in molds. Rauschner's small heads were lifelike in flesh-colored wax with features and costume details added in pigment, and after his work in Salem he was kept busy in New York and Philadelphia and in Delaware, Maryland, and Virginia. His Philadelphia rival was George M. Miller; in Boston, Daniel Bowen specialized in wax. A few years before old Patience Wright died in England her son Joseph arrived to paint bust portraits, but also to practice the art of encaustic. Another visitor was John Dixey from Dublin, whose copy of Ceracchi's bust of Hamilton was seen in 1814 at the joint exhibition of the Columbian Society and the Pennsylvania Academy. In the same show were half a dozen works by Miller, including copies of Houdon's *Washington* and the head of the Medici Venus. The exhibition also showed two bust portraits by William Rush, the most prolific and accomplished of all the native carvers.

Rush was taught his craft by the Englishman Edward Cutbush and learned also from Ceracchi when the Italian visited Philadelphia in 1791. His iconography owed something to such books as *Taylor's Repertory or Encyclopedia of the Fine Arts,* but Rush studied the human figure itself. He once remarked to Dunlap, "When I see my boys bungling in the carving of a hand, I tell them, Look at your own hands, . . . imitate them and you must be right."

Philadelphian prudery forced Robert Pine to keep his cast of the Medici *Venus* under lock and key; Rush braved that prudery, it is said, when he carved his *Water Nymph and Bittern* from a local miss willing to pose in the presence of a chaperone. Before the wooden original had disintegrated, a bronze cast was made which preserved the sculptor's full-bodied conception of the human figure, his ability to suggest the rounded torso and swelling breasts beneath draperies (Phila. Mus.).

His head crammed with the neoclassic repertory, William Rush had elaborate ideas of republican symbolism when he described to Naval Officer Humphreys how the figureheads should be designed for six frigates authorized by Congress to fight the Barbary pirates. The Revolution, he said, called for an elegant figure with fasces and liberty cap, standing on the rock of Independence. Congress should be the Goddess of Wisdom on a pedestal supported by the Cardinal Virtues, with the volumes of the law beside her, reading the Constitution as she sped over the waters. The ship *Constitution,* since she was the product of union, and union makes for strength, required a Hercules, and Rush made a sketch which he believed John Skillin was capable of cutting. For six dangerous years, until the bombs of the Tripoli engagement crippled *Hercules* beyond repair, this eight-foot bearded creature with his lion's skin and club, no doubt painted in natural colors, rode the gilded trailboards of *Old Ironsides.*

Allegory was not the only language Rush could speak. When the swifter and smaller vessels left the ways they carried portrait busts of French or American notables which set an example to other carvers. As the perceptive Latrobe told an audience, "Commerce has called for beauty in the forms and decorations of her ships, and where in Europe is there a Rush?" To which an editorial hand has added, "The constrained attitude of a figure on the prow of a ship would appear an insuperable difficulty. With him it is nothing. There is a motion in his figures that is inconceivable. They seem rather to draw the ship after them than to be impelled by the vessel."

A roomful of carved figures in the Philadelphia Museum of Art reveals Rush as America's most skillful classicist in wood. His *Water Nymph and Bittern* stood in Center Square beside Latrobe's Pump House to disprove an earlier critic's remark that ashore his figures lacked repose. There was poise, albeit jaunty, in the pair, *Comedy* and *Tragedy,* which stood in their niches on the Chestnut Street Theater. Larger than life, the two muses had a sprightliness and grace no American could match, with a hint of the rococo in their linear and intricate draperies and with underlying forms which were robustly sculptural. Everywhere in Philadelphia his clean and vigorous art was to be seen: his crucifixes stood in the churches; his cherubim smiled from the organ of St. Paul's. His *Justice* and *Wisdom* graced the arch for General Lafayette; his emblem decorated the Masons' Lodge; his eagle perched on the fire engine of the Hibernia Company with a ferocity lacking in the anemic bird which hovered over the Speaker of the House in Washington. Professors of anatomy taught from the large models of human organs he had carved in wood; and over the doorways to the wheelhouses of the new Water Works were his *Schuylkill Chained* and *Schuylkill Freed,* the former cribbed from ancient Nile. At the Pennsylvania Academy exhibitions were seen his portrait busts of a searching naturalism, a blend of subtlety and strength worthy of Houdon; and it was the Houdon inspiration which produced his full-length *Washington* (Ind. Hall, Phila.) and the bust of *Lafayette* for which the patient Frenchman sat in 1824 to a sculptor on the verge of seventy.

William Rush, *Lafayette*

Pennsylvania Academy of the Fine Arts, Philadelphia, Pa.

Before the old marquis went back to France at least two Americans — Frazee and Augur — had dared to carve heads in stone. John Frazee of New Jersey was literally what Horatio Greenough called himself, a "Yankee stonecutter." When he composed his homely autobiography in 1834 for Dunlap's *History* he had come a long way from farm hand to the owner of a thriving New York business, and his manuscript clearly marked the milestones in the progression from self-taught craftsman to self-conscious practitioner of the fine arts—in some degree the progression of McIntire, of the Skillins, and of William Rush.

The tenth child of a Scottish carpenter in Rahway, young Frazee worked on his grandmother's farm and in a sunny corner of the barn whittled boats, weather vanes, and windmills from old shingles. He was eighteen when he volunteered to carve a stone tablet for a bridge over the Rahway River at Bridgeton. At twenty, he worked after hours in New Brunswick to learn stonecraft from Ward Baldwin, who had cut details for the New York City Hall; at twenty-one, he made a tablet for a house at Haverstraw, but this time he ventured an ornamental border.

During the war years Frazee said, "I began my career among the tombstones," carving all day and at night lifting his voice at singing school in the "Song of Zion." He scorned the stiffly carved borders of his rival gravestone cutters, for none of them "possessed anything like genius or the power of invention as applied to Fine Arts"; all of them repeated themes from English books a century old which had "neither germ nor root in nature." Real ivy leaves and the flowers of New Jersey fields began to appear on Frazee's tombstones, though he confessed himself utterly ignorant of every rule of art and of those symbols, images, and attributes that had their origin in the classic ages. Nothing daunted, he carved in 1815 what may have been the first native stone figure—a "Grief" leaning upon an urn over the grave of his first son at New Brunswick.

When the peace of 1815 brought prosperity and new commissions, this restless and ambitious artisan, whose puritanical fear of drinking and dancing had not prevented him from devouring the life of Cellini with as much delight as the maxims of Poor Richard, was prepared to work in stone, wood, or metal. He was in business for himself and could supply lion's feet for chairs or gilded wooden doves for the pulpits of churches; for the Adamesque mansions of New York and Savannah he could produce ornate marble mantelpieces. On a trip

John Frazee, *Thomas H. Perkins*

Courtesy Boston Athenaeum

Hezekiah Augur, *Daughter of Jephtha*

Yale University Art Gallery, New Haven, Conn.

to New York, whose "pomp and worthlessness" had so disgusted him in earlier years, there was the work of Italian carvers to be studied and imitated by a man who never missed such opportunities. Frazee could have seen Causici's model for an equestrian Washington in the Italian's New York studio, or in City Hall Park, where it was set up for the Fourth of July in 1826. On the west front of St. Paul's Chapel was the glistening and impeccable tablet of General Montgomery by Caffieri to inspire Frazee's monuments and cenotaphs for Trinity and other churches. Another revelation was the Academy of Fine Arts with its imported casts, where John Trumbull warned Frazee that sculpture would find no popular support in America for a century to come.

Never discouraged, Frazee proceeded to execute what was his first marble bust, and what he believed was the first of its kind made by a native carver—the monument of John Wells in Grace Church (1825), for whose likeness the sculptor had to rely on a Waldo portrait. A series of busts followed—seven of them commissioned by the Boston Athenaeum. These heads are vigorously cut and bear witness rather to Frazee's sharp eye than to his possession of that idealizing faculty with which others of his profession would soon woo the marble in search of intangibles, while he attacked it as something resistant to be conquered. Frazee's concern was with the specific. His *Bowditch* and his *Perkins* are grim Boston Romans; above the folds of their togas he spared his sitters no tiniest wrinkle, no swelling vein, no incipient dewlap, and every lock of hair was counted, measured, and rendered with minute precision and with a relentless finish no Italian could have surpassed.

The future looked promising to John Frazee at forty-three. Dunlap's *History* reported him "full of employment." He had belied Trumbull's pessimism and was ready to attempt the full-length figure. Closing the story of his early life, he hoped soon, he wrote, to exhibit something of greater interest and merit than mere heads and shoulders of men, and he felt no need for European study to accomplish it: "Some say it cannot be done without a visit first to Europe, to Rome and her Vatican. . . . For myself I believe not a word of this." He was immune to the corrupt Roman and to the modern Italians, but the Greek fever had infected this New Jersey stonecutter and he resorted to block letters on the subject: "IT IS TO THE CLASSIC SCHOOLS OF THE GRECIAN alone that I adhere,—and am determined to follow their example,—sink or swim."

In New Haven a morose young man whose father, a carpenter-joiner, rejoiced in the appropriate name of Augur duplicated Frazee's progress. The boy devised ingenious toys and odd-looking bird cages; the young man piled up debts and disappointments in the dry goods business and in a fruit shop where, after hours, he indulged his love for carving. In his twenties Hezekiah Augur made chair legs for a local cabinetmaker, invented an "improved" wooden leg, and when his father's death freed him to cheat thought, as he told Dunlap, by chiseling, as others drowned the memory of misfortune by the glass and bottle, Augur set up shop for himself, hired assistants, and became a full-fledged carver. The turning point for him was the work and advice of Samuel Morse, who suggested that he attempt stone. Morse had acquired a cast of Apollo and it was perhaps this head which Augur copied, cutting his *Apollo* directly in marble and showing it at the Academy of Arts in New York in 1825.

The painting and sculpture of Morse's *Dying Hercules* which were shipped home from London to New Haven may have been Augur's inspiration when he carved two statuettes of *Jephtha and His Daughter*. The king's bearded face and the gesture with which he veils

Samuel F. B. Morse, *The Dying Hercules*

Yale University Art Gallery, New Haven, Conn.

John H. I. Browere, Life mask of Thomas Jefferson
N.Y. State Historical Association, Cooperstown, N.Y.

it as the girl moves to meet him "with timbrels and with dances" suggest the *Hercules;* his armor is elaborately carved, and his only child has the profile of a Greco-Roman Venus. Her every detail, from the flowers in her hair through the complicated drapery of her gown to the sandal on her foot, is minutely chiselled. Before he died the melancholy Augur saw his *Jephtha* statuettes installed in the Trumbull Gallery. He owned the New England Wood Carving Company, held an honorary degree from Yale, and was content, like Frazee, to dispense with an Italian tour which his friends had been willing to finance.

When William Rush died in the year 1833 a craft had become an art. Samuel McIntire's chance to carve a self-sufficient piece of sculpture had come through his patron Bentley's desire to encourage home talent. The Skillins owed a similar freedom to the merchant Derby, Frazee to the Boston Athenaeum, Augur to the sympathy of Morse, and Rush to the neoclassic vogue which Latrobe had fostered in Philadelphia. A handful of men had overcome obstacles to free sculpturing: the prudery which had held them from a study of the nude; the utilitarianism which saw carving as an adjunct to building; the philosophy which exalted the foreign over the native artist; the prevailing ignorance of techniques and processes.

Yet whatever was strong in the work of these sculptors came from the old craft tradition. With expanding commerce in the days of peace which followed 1812 there were ships enough to be carved and houses to be adorned to keep workshops busy, while the proliferation of heroes after the war provided a wide choice of subjects. From Kittery in Maine to Charleston, South Carolina, more than a hundred individuals or firms carved ships, eagles for pulpits, and goddesses for gardens. The craft descended from father to son, and in Newburyport there were two Wilsons to continue the work of Joseph, whose most ambitious effort had been the nearly forty full-length figures he cut in wood for Timothy Dexter. The mansion of that eccentric man was approached through triumphal arches and rows of pedestals upon which stood Wilson's *Washington,* his *Bonaparte* and his *Nelson,* his lions and unicorns, his *Adam* and *Eve* and *Timothy Dexter.*

From Massachusetts Solomon Willard went south in 1817 to study Houdon's masterpiece before he cut his own *Washington* figurehead and became a carver of architectural ornaments in stone for Boston houses and churches. The ingenious Willard invented a hot-air furnace, constructed small-scale models of the Parthenon and the Washington Capitol, refused the invitation of Bulfinch to make interior decorations for that building, designed buildings of his own, and devised methods of quarrying and transporting Quincy granite for the Bunker Hill monument, for whose construction he was responsible. Meanwhile a thousand nameless Yankees continued to carve weather vanes and toys with a chunk of pine, a jackknife, and a vivid imagination—makers of a people's sculpture which waited for a century to be recognized as art.

When Dunlap wrote his *History,* another generation was turning its back on the native tradition to seek finesse in Europe, where Houdon's objectivity had been dethroned by the flaccid neoclassicism of Canova and Thorwaldsen. Hiram Powers and Thomas Crawford were preparing in 1833 to make the Italian journey, and Horatio Greenough was at work in Florence on the first important sculptural commission received by an American. The earlier spirit, however, was in John Henri Isaac Browere's protest that "ideal likenesses ought not to be palmed off on a generous public for real ones." Browere had lived in Paris before Houdon died. Like Houdon, he visualized a gallery of national celebrities for his own country, and it was perhaps from the French master that he had learned how to make life masks. Lafayette permitted Browere to cast his features in 1825 but, in the years that followed, it needed persuasion to get sitters, especially after rumor spread that the eighty-two-year-old Jefferson had nearly suffocated under Browere's hands.

Unimpressed by the astonishing reality of these heads, or repelled by it as Houdon's countrymen had been repelled by the smallpox scars of his *Gluck,* the arbiters of taste in America denied their validity as works of art, and scorned them as the result of a merely mechanical process. Browere had spent all his money, and President Madison refused funds for casting this national portrait gallery in bronze. Dunlap's readers found no mention of Browere in the *History*, and it was Charles Henry Hart who unearthed the busts half a century or more after they were stored away on a New York farm. Again, one could debate the question: were they sculpture? They were character in three dimensions, at any rate, and they proved that a love for the concrete and the specific was as much a part of the country's sculptural tradition as the cult of classical abstraction. They belonged with McIntire's *Winthrop,* the *Bowditch* of Frazee, and the *Lafayette* of William Rush.

Chest on chest (detail)

Museum of Fine Arts, Boston, Mass. (Karo'ik coll.)

Vanderlyn's Rotunda, drawn by A. J. Davis ▶

New York Historical Society

PART TWO

REPUBLICAN PAINTING

INTRODUCTION / MUSEUMS, ACADEMIES, AND PANORAMAS

Between Jefferson and Jackson lived a generation of Americans whose artists ranged from the Paris- or London-trained professional to the modest self-disciplined itinerant, men whose artistic speech was grandiloquent and men who were taciturn. Among the nation's sprawling people new forms of patronage emerged, new national themes asked to be illustrated, new ways of multiplying imagery were quickly seized upon.

The merchants and men of industry who weathered the first stormy years of national life were not content, as their provincial fathers had been, with a few family portraits and engravings; by 1830 many of them had become systematic and shrewd collectors. The taste of Philip Hone was a blend of admiration for vaguely felt artistic qualities with the smart investor's sense which he applied successfully to real-estate transactions. When Boston gentlemen contributed sums for the completion of Allston's *Belshazzar,* Hone observed that money spent does not excite to execution so much as money expected.

That "liberal gentleman" Robert Gilmor was the eldest son of the Gilmor who had come from Paisley in Scotland in the seventeen sixties and built the family fortunes as a Baltimore merchant. Robert Junior's taste embraced Poussin and Hals, Ruysdael, Holbein, and Velasquez; but the partial list of his collection which he made for Dunlap also included the names of Gilbert Stuart, the Peales, Sully, Allston, Cole, and Doughty—evidence of pride in American accomplishment and a willingness to help the living while they were still alive.

In 1827 the enterprising Colonel Stevens of Hoboken hired Sully, Vanderlyn, Morse, Doughty, and Cole to paint pictures for his steamboat *Albany,* which plied the Hudson River. And when young painters could not afford foreign travel, there were often merchants and

John J. Audubon, *Brown Pelican,* water color

New York Historical Society

bankers who financed the grand tour by commissioning copies of the old masters; and young men and women like those in Morse's picture of the Louvre toiled at replicas of Titian and Raphael for some dry goods merchant back home.

In New York City the aspiring connoisseur bought dubious old masters from old Paff, who called himself a "restorer," or bid for them at the weekly auctions of Gourlay and of Levy and Harrison. Mr. L. P. Clover opened a looking-glass and picture-frame store on Fulton Street in 1816 where American canvases were to be seen and purchased; men like Hone and Hosack got into the habit of dropping in at Parker and Clover's, and more than one young painter was there introduced to his future patron.

To the new private patronage was added the public commissioning of works of art. The Capitol was rising from the Potomac swamps; why should not the federal government become a patron of artists? Congressmen, however, were slow to spend money and quick to resent artistic behavior. More rewarding were the municipalities which demanded portraits of the commodores and generals of the War of 1812 whom every city council sought to wine, dine, and perpetuate. As the "Croaker" jingled in the *New York Evening Post:*

> The board is met,—the names are read;
> Elate of heart, the glad committee
> Declare the mighty man had said
> He'll take the "freedom of the city."
> He thanks the council, and the mayor,
> Presents 'em all his humble service;
> And thinks he's time enough to spare
> To sit an hour or so with Jarvis.

The horizons of 1820 were wide enough to include much more than the well-to-do collector, the aesthetic builder of steamboats, the alderman in search of a national lion, or a semiliterate Congress. A vast new public could be sensed among the American middle class and in the fresh-painted villages of the West—a public too easily satisfied with mere competence but stirring with civic pride, with a curiosity to know what the rivers and villages looked like, with a desire to get not only its face painted but its daily occupations and its specific environment recorded. There were twenty-three states in the Union by 1820, and America's center of gravity was shifting both culturally and politically westward. More and more politicians went in these years "from the rude wigwam to the Congress Hall"; more and more painters journeyed westward until scarcely a town of any size from Maine to Florida and from the Atlantic to the Mississippi was beyond the reach of a traveling artist, and many a town had raised artists of its own.

No man watched with more delight the growth of the infant Hercules than John James Audubon from France. Toward the end of his amazingly busy life an artist painted his long gray locks and his chop whiskers, the firm ruddy features, the stubborn mouth, and the clear eyes of a man who at sixty was still young. More than forty years before, those eyes had probed the secrets of American fields, woods, and swamplands whose wild life this self-made naturalist had determined to record. Back and forth between America and Europe went Audubon as he added new species to his collection and supervised their engraving and publication in England. The first volume of his elephant-size *Birds of America* was ready in 1827; the last of its plates appeared in 1838.

It was said that Audubon learned from David the firm drawing with which he attempted to make every feather and crest correct; it was a superb designer who planned the *Brown Pelican* and his forest setting to fill the page, who made a brilliant pattern of yellows, greens, and vermilions in his *Carolina Paroquets,* and who found a foil for his grays and whites in oak leaves turning from green to crimson. An almost inconceivable strength and patience sustained this man who tramped the country in all seasons and weathers, who traveled up and down Europe and America to find subscribers to his volumes, and whose careful brush created the more than four hundred large water colors of the *Birds of America.* His skill was matched by Robert Havell, Jr., who engraved all but a few of the drawings with only a slight loss of vigor and a hardening of contours, and with respect for their brilliance of draughtsmanship, color, and design. (See color plate 2.)

Audubon was not the only artist who explored the new regions, and in the eighteen twenties a traveler to the west or south could marvel at the artistic bustle he found. Charles Balthazar Julien Févret de Saint-Mémin had gone back to France leaving his delicate and sure profile drawings in most of the cities between New York and Charleston. He had drawn Indians from the upper Missouri River—chieftains with scalp locks, pigtails, carmine spots on cheeks and eyelids, blue-and-white stripes on faces, with headdresses of brilliant feathers and blue beads in their ears.

When Morse went to Charleston in 1820 he found "a fresh line of adventurers in the brush line" fairly swarming. William Edward West settled in Nashville, Tennessee, and turned out Sullyesque likenesses, which he provided also for his native Kentucky and for Cincinnati. Jouett and Neagle were helping Lexington, Kentucky, to earn the title of Athens of the West. Chester Harding had set up his easel in Paris, Kentucky, for a few months. Cincinnati had its Academy of Drawing and Painting in 1812, and Nicholas Longworth was soon to become the local Maecenas. Audubon sailed down from Natchez between the levees over which the smell of orange blossoms blew from on shore, and when he reached New Orleans he found Vanderlyn and Jarvis there.

On these frontiers the distinction between professional and amateur, between sophisticated and self-taught tended to break down. In all the new towns were young men, self-made artists who had only the briefest touch with men of greater skill. In contact with the new West, hardheadedly realistic, loving the concrete, the prosaic, and the local, the most urbane Easterner found his work grow more solid and more direct; on the other hand, native limners as often mellowed under the mutual impact.

While the arts thus traveled westward American writers and painters in ever-growing numbers made the grand tour to Europe. They no longer went as provincials hoping to reflect Old World glories, but as Americans conscious of their nationality; some of them studied Raphael and Michelangelo quite without the idolatry of earlier visitors, and without the excessive rapture of later ones. Rembrandt Peale could even look with some contempt upon works which Copley and West would have considered faultless, and did not hesitate to remark that the smoke-darkened *Last Judgment* was as complete a ruin as the Baths of Caracalla

C. B. J. F. de Saint-Mémin, *Cachasunghia, Osage Warrior*

New York Historical Society

and would not arrest attention if it had not already become famous.

These Americans were always meeting one another in Paris, Florence, Rome, or Naples. In London, Washington Irving knew Charles R. Leslie, whose genre paintings were so much like his own literary ones. In Paris, where Rembrandt Peale had watched the coronation of Napoleon, Cooper and Morse met Lafayette and Béranger, and Cooper realized how deeply he preferred his own republic to the Bourbon Monarchy. On the Italian shore at Baia artists lunched on a stone fallen from the ceiling of the Temple of Venus, with oysters from Fusaro, boiled crabs caught in the shadows of Mercury's temple, and bottles of Lachryma Christi from Vesuvius.

The Americans soon discovered that in Europe the old rigid canons and practices were breaking down. Sir Joshua had ended his discourse in 1790 by kissing the hem of the garment of Michelangelo and he had championed to the end the superiority of the ideal over the particular. Yet already in the work of English poets nature was freshly seen, not through formula, and the abstract devices of Claude and Poussin were losing their power. In their place one saw a new "picturesque" both genteel and literary, but also an affectionate recording of known times and places. Englishmen continued to make portraits which were visible proofs of style and status, but Reynolds' *Lord Heathfield* was a statement of a man's character; Gainsborough painted *Mrs. Graham* with a sketchlike fluency and directness; Lawrence mingled sensibility and sentiment in his languishing beauties and his moist-eyed children.

An even more drastic revolution had taken place in French art, as Trumbull discovered and after him Vanderlyn, Fulton, Allston, Rembrandt Peale, and Samuel Morse. Trumbull was Jefferson's guest in Paris four years before the Bastille fell, and the Virginian "thought him superior to any historical painter of the time except David." The Frenchman had just completed his tribute to those Spartan virtues which his friend Robespierre was soon to embody, *The Oath of the Horatii.* A recent critic has compared the *Horatii* with the *Declaration of the Rights of Man and of the Citizen:* "Not a comma to change in the latter, and in the former not a fold of cloth without its reason for being." David's portraits of the martyrs Marat, Bara, and Saint-Fargeau were, as Milton Brown has said, "direct expressions of the power and realism which established the Revolution and for a brief time ruled its course."

Neither Trumbull nor Vanderlyn shared Jefferson's enthusiasm for that Revolution, and their obligation to David was a technical one. Trumbull could find a cool ordering of people in David's interiors to suggest compositions on subjects which had already become American history. Vanderlyn arrived in Paris three years after the *Marat* had been painted; before he left, he had seen the *Madame Récamier,* and his own work had acquired some of that cool objectivity and incredible smoothness. When Vanderlyn made his second visit, the France which he and Fulton knew was the France of the Empire, and David was fabricating huge machines in which the poses of noble Romans reappeared but only as stilted postures.

Vanderlyn left the capital when David did, the former to try his fortunes at home, the latter for Brussels and exile as a man who had voted the death of a king. Had the American lingered he would have seen in *The Raft of the Medusa* and in *The Barque of Dante* that new power, that blend of the documentary with the exotic, which marked the transformation of history painting. In the meantime more than one picture of Vanderlyn, Trumbull, Fulton, and Rembrandt Peale confessed its debt to the sharp finalities of David.

The American, whether a returning traveler with new notions of form and content or a man who had never left home, knew that his country had outgrown the provincial categories. Stuart's patrons were satisfied with a stylish head and shoulders against conventional drapery, but landscape invaded the background of the large commemorative likenesses which Inman painted. History painters enlarged mythology to alarming proportions, but the spirit and scale of Charles Willson Peale's *Mastodon* picture were those of genre painting. As a rule, landscapes were portraits of places or they were generalized with an eye for allegory and genteel moralizing; some of them were responses to nature's beauty itself, and others were inspired by pride in the majesty of America's scenic wonders.

Thanks largely to the Peales there were native paintings of still life in American collections, a subject rarely attempted in prerepublican days, when a few men of importance owned Dutch examples. There had been still-life canvases by William Birch, Copley, and James Peale in the Columbianum show of 1795, but it was James and Raphaelle Peale who studied the European way of placing a bowl or basket of fruit on a table and rendering its textures and rounded forms with a neat thoroughness. Raphaelle's *Peaches and Grapes* was shown in Philadelphia in the year 1814, and the *Portfolio* admired "the correct manner in which he represents each individual object," adding that "if he displayed more judgment in the *arrangement* and *grouping* of his pictures, they would rival the best productions of the Flemish or Dutch School." (See color plate 3.)

While Raphaelle Peale worked on the intimate scale of Chardin, his brother Rembrandt experimented with the huge picture intended to be sent on tour and shown in tents or rented halls for a small admission fee. Copley had once built special rooms for exhibiting his work, and now Peale, Vanderlyn, and Morse used this means of appealing to the public's curiosity or its sense of the marvelous.

Another experiment in group patronage was the American panorama. A Scottish painter and teacher of perspective named Robert Barker had once stood on a hill above Edinburgh and wondered why the artist must limit his painted view to that segment of the horizon which can be seen by a man standing in one spot without turning his head. Charles Peale, at almost the same time, made drawings from the eight sides of a cupola at Annapolis to be combined in a continuous print. The final result of Barker's experiments was a complete circular painting for which, about 1792, he built a "rotunda" in Leicester Square.

Spectators entered Barker's Rotunda from below and came out on a small platform in the center designed like the deck of a frigate. Above them were the concentric rows of windows which lighted the panorama from above and which were hidden from the observers by a canopy. Between the "deck" and the painting Barker had set up pieces of canvas painted to imitate waves. Standing there with no real objects to challenge the reality of the great canvas around them, spectators

Raphaelle Peale, *Still Life with Cake*

Brooklyn Museum

had the illusion of being out of doors in the very thick of the fight between the British and Russian fleets at Spithead. Other sensations followed—*The Battle of the Nile, The Battle of Copenhagen, Athens*—as Barker and his son traveled far to make sketches; while a German named Breysig had devised, either independently or through reports of Barker's progress, a panorama of *The Emperor's Palace in Rome* for which he had made on-the-spot studies and which he opened in Berlin during the summer of 1800.

Americans quickly realized the popular appeal of the new device. One of them said to Dunlap that "panoramic exhibitions possess so much of the magic deceptions of the art, as irresistibly to captivate all classes of spectators, . . . for no study or cultivated taste is required fully to appreciate the merits of such representations. They have the further power of conveying much practical and topographical information."

New York saw the "magic deceptions" as early as 1795, when William Winstanley opened what Dunlap called the first of its kind, a view of London, in Greenwich Street. *Rome* was to be seen in 1810, and the battle of the *Constitution* and the *Guerrière* was shown on Broadway in 1813. John Trumbull had doubtless seen the London and Paris rotundas, and his long and narrow paintings of Niagara Falls are panoramas in miniature. John Vanderlyn was in Paris when Fulton's show opened and in the year 1815, just before he ended his second French visit, he made careful drawings of the palace and gardens of Versailles, which he was later to enlarge and exhibit in the ill-starred Rotunda.

Another form of landscape which multiplied in this period was the engraved or lithographed "view" which showed Americans the topography of their country. There were soon shops in most of the cities where prints could be bought: Henry J. Megarey and the firm of Parker and Clover published them in New York, H. S. Tanner and T. W. Freeman in Philadelphia, John Coles in Boston. Sometimes these views were sold separately or in portfolios; sometimes they illustrated the magazines which so enormously increased in the early years of the republic.

The makers of views could now employ techniques more subtle and more direct than line engraving on metal. England in the late years of the eighteenth century saw the vogue of aquatint, so exquisitely adapted to the reproduction of water color; and it was Englishmen like John Hill and W. J. Bennett who applied their skill to American subjects. In 1798 an obscure Bavarian named Senefelder perfected a process by which the artist could draw on stone as freely as on paper. Eighteen years afterward, Bass Otis made the first American lithograph for the *Analectic Magazine;* in 1825 the Pendleton brothers set up their lithographic press in Boston, and young Alexander Jackson Davis drew the most impressive buildings he could find for reproduction in the new medium.

During the period of revolution Yankee humor had expressed itself in occasional rude engravings issued as broadsides or as magazine illustrations. As the pantheon of national heroes grew, and political tensions sought release, the cartoon multiplied in America. James Akin made burlesque portraits; William Charles aped Gillray and Rowlandson in his lampooning of John Bull during the War of 1812; David Claypoole Johnston etched in the manner of Cruikshank; Jarvis designed perhaps the first newspaper illustration on the death of the embargo; Elkanah Tisdale made drawings for "M'Fingal."

It was through the medium of illustration that many artists of the time established that contact with the authors of a rising American literature which had so many mutual consequences, not the least of them the discovery of the American landscape. New York by the eighteen twenties had become the literary hub of America, and the association of writers like Bryant, Irving, and Cooper with painters became intimate. They had their Bread and Cheese Club; Allston and Leslie and Inman drew illustrations for the *Knickerbocker History* and the *Sketch Book.*

Sooner or later the nation's curiosity and its thirst for information would require permanent and public collections of art. The first museum was the work of Charles Willson Peale, whose collection of Revolutionary portraits was shown in his own house in 1784 and later moved to Independence Hall. When Flint saw Peale's museum in 1818 it had acquired insects, stuffed birds, and the tools of primitive man. Its upper walls were lined with portraits, to which a few years later were added those of French celebrities which

Rembrandt Peale painted on his Paris journey: Houdon, David, Cuvier, and others. Faux noted in his journal that he had seen the great skeleton of the mammoth there, viewed the dried bodies of Indian chiefs and Hawaiians, and crept down the throat of an alligator. In Baltimore from 1814 to 1830 Rembrandt and Rubens Peale's Museum and Gallery of Fine Arts was an "elegant rendezvous of taste, curiosity and leisure" where visitors could wonder at the mastodon, the stuffed animals, the portraits and the *Court of Death* or hear Rembrandt Peale lecture and see him demonstrate the use of gaslight.

In the midst of so much diversity and so many challenges to ingenuity it was natural that the artists of the older centers should seek methods for drawing more closely together as men associated in a common enterprise, eager to provide training for the younger men and to raise the level of American taste. The nation's first academies owed more to the persistence of the elder Peale than to any other man. He tried in 1791 to establish what would have been the first art school in America, and three years later his Columbianum exhibition, the first of its kind, opened at the State House. By 1805 it was possible to found the Pennsylvania Academy of Fine Arts, despite the narrow ideas of Philadelphians, many of whom, like the anonymous author of an article in the *American Museum,* believed that to make education cheap would hurt the learned professions and create a dangerous independence among the common people: "If their heads become crowded with learned lumber, and a passion for study occupies their minds, farewell to industry and sweet content."

Devoid of such Federalist fears, Peale stated the aims of his academy:

> To promote the cultivation of the Fine Arts in the U. S. A., by introducing correct and elegant copies from works of the first Masters in Sculpture and Painting, and by thus facilitating the access to such standards, and also by occasionally conferring moderate but honorable premiums, and otherwise assisting the Studies and exciting the efforts of the Artists, gradually to unfold, enlighten and invigorate the talents of our Countrymen.

By the month of March in 1806 the academy was ready to open. Nicholas Biddle, then secretary of the American legation in Paris, had shipped over plaster casts of the *Laocoön* and other "correct and elegant copies." Modesty was preserved by providing for separate visiting days for ladies; and the whole experience cost twenty-five cents. Meanwhile, businesslike New York had formed its own academy of fine arts as a corporation with officers and shareholders; Robert Livingston had sent casts from Paris, and John Trumbull was president.

The conflict between the ideas of laymen and of artists began as soon as the academies of New York and Philadelphia opened. The layman made money, the artist defended the dignity of his profession. In Philadelphia the traveler Svinin observed that the founders of the academy, while eager for the glory of their country, had not neglected their private interests; and one artist resigned rather than truckle, as he said, to these aristocratic gentlemen. Before long, rival institutions had appeared in both cities: The Society of the Arts in Philadelphia, and in New York Morse's Drawing Association, which soon became the National Academy of the Arts of Design.

When Morse addressed the "young gentlemen" of his academy on May 3, 1827, to celebrate the institution's first year of existence, he reported that the National Academy had given free instruction to thirty students, had offered two courses of anatomical lectures, and was now about to confer prizes on successful beginners. He warned his young hearers that a healthy public taste must grow gradually, "urged onward by the constant action and reaction of the artists and the public upon each other."

When Morse said that young artists returning from study in Europe would find themselves sadly in advance of native taste he was perhaps remembering with some bitterness the heads he had painted in New Hampshire for fifteen dollars each, or the public's indifference to his *Hercules.* Yet his tone was confident: "Our own soil must warm into life the seeds of native talent." It was rather better, he implied, to stand here and face discouragement than to plant one's artistic seeds in the more genial climate of Europe and then seek to transplant them to colder American earth. The implicit democracy of Morse lay, despite his assumption of the superior "refinement" of the Old World, in his emphasis on the task of tilling native ground.

The pompous old president of the Academy of Fine Arts viewed matters differently. John Trumbull foresaw, to be sure, a future of the arts in America which would redeem them from "being as in Europe, only the base and flattering instruments of royal and aristocratic luxury and vice." But in the absence of patronage by the church or by Congress in the new nation Trumbull declared that artists were "necessarily dependent upon the protection of the rich and the great"; and he justified the fact that his board of directors had three lawyers, two doctors, one hardware merchant, one professor of mathematics, one drawing teacher, and two portrait painters. Morse replied that an institution with two hundred stockholders, nine tenths of whom were laymen profiting by the works they "permitted" artists to show, was no true republican academy.

Beneath this acrid war of words two ideas faced each

other; Trumbull at seventy-seven looked backward to the eighteenth century, forty-two-year-old Morse looked forward to the nineteenth. The present triumphed over the past, and when Dunlap wrote his *History* in 1834 the National Academy held the field alone; Charleston and Cincinnati had formed similar institutions, and the Boston Athenaeum had its plaster casts, its exhibitions of paintings and sculptures and its galleries where students could paint.

As exhibitions became more frequent, more than one lady or gentleman took pen in hand to comment upon them in the magazines and newspapers—America's first art critics. Along with biographical notes and florid description there were efforts to evaluate. How closely those efforts followed the growth of an articulate nationalism becomes clear when one compares Eliza Godefroy's contributions to the Baltimore *Observer* in 1806 with John Neal's articles eighteen years later in *Blackwood's Edinburgh Magazine*.

Eliza, that "fierce Fury," was no more happy than her architect husband in republican America, where she found the works of Byron and Scott in roadside inns whose food not even pigs would have eaten. The wealthy merchants of the cities evinced more haughtiness than all the nobility of Europe, and the people as a whole were worshipers of Mammon, perfidious, vulgar, ignorant, and vain. Extolling the merit of the painter Groombridge against the crudity of his rival Guy, Eliza accused the latter of making mosaics out of other men's compositions, and implied that he could have developed his talent but for the necessity of making coats and pantaloons. To which Guy replied that the greatest liability of Groombridge was the friendship of the *Observer*.

John Neal had been a haberdasher's clerk, a soldier in the War of 1812, a student of law, and a novelist before he began, as he said, to scribble in the papers about art and to belabor artists for their own good. Neal's confidence in the American future never failed him, nor did his eagerness to discover new talent falter. He chose *Blackwood's* for many of his articles because it was "the cleverest, the sauciest, and the most unprincipled of our calumniators." There was chauvinism and much florid exaggeration in what Neal wrote, but also shrewd appraisal. He pointed out the superiority of West's studies to his finished paintings and classed Trumbull's Capitol paintings among the greatest and most unaccountable failures of the age. He characterized John Vanderlyn neatly as a man "a little Frenchified in his notions of painting" and found in Washington Allston a sort of artificial heat and not "that sort of inward fervor which flashes into spontaneous combustion."

On the whole it was a healthy omen for American artists that, when pictures like *The Court of Death* and *Christ Healing the Sick* appeared on the walls of our galleries, John Neal walked among them with his tongue in his cheek and a notebook in his hand.

CHAPTER 10/PORTRAITS

Out of the provincial aristocracy came a new one: Tories who had avoided exile; planters and merchants of inherited wealth; the newly rich by privateering, by speculation with paper currency, by shrewd real-estate transactions, and by profiteering in a time of crisis. There was a degree less of stiffness in the way the republican worthy sat for his portrait than in Copley's time, and his wife's ostrich plumes were the finishing touch to an accustomed dressiness, not ornaments worn obviously for the occasion. Americans like these found their appropriate painters in the suave Gilbert Stuart and the limpid Sully.

This urbanity, however, did not suddenly replace the earlier plainness. A Tory cattle dealer named John Bush hired Matthew Pratt about 1785 to smooth his own ugliness and transpose his young wife into a Romneyesque beauty with a curl on her shoulder and piled-up hair with white plumes; but six years later Bush had married again, and the painter McKay specified his homeliness as on a map and gave a harsh precision to every ribbon and lace edging of Abigail Bush. Some of the finest portraits of the early republic were done by Ralph Earl and the Peales, who seldom took short cuts to flattery. Earl painted his Ellsworths, his Tallmadge pair, and his *Mrs. Moseley* in these years, and his son Ralph acquired some of that wiry strength for the time when he would multiply the image of Andrew Jackson.

The nineties left Charles Peale small margin of time for painting his Gallery of Illustrious Personages. The Columbianum in 1795 showed his remarkable *Staircase Picture* in which two of his sons were seen on a staircase,

Matthew Pratt, *John Bush*

American Antiquarian Society, Worcester, Mass.

Charles W. Peale, *John De Peyster*

New York Historical Society

as though the picture frame were a doorway. If, as has been said, the artist added a real step at the base of the picture to complete the illusion of his painted ones, the notion was typical of the man.

No other artist of the time could have produced this illusion of people moving in light and space-depth, these chunky small bodies, this delicate study of cast shadow, this beauty of drawing, or this charm, which is the charm of young people being young. Others could make children into cherubs; in Peale's mind and in his art, they remained superbly themselves. With no precedent whatsoever the painter made a splendid organization with the movement of the stairs, the slanting line of the older boy's body and his stick, the counter-direction of the palettes and brushes and a shadow on the wall. Peale set out to deceive the eye and succeeded down to the last knot in the wooden stairs, the card which someone had dropped, the shine on a boy's nose, the seam in a stocking.

Three years later Charles portrayed his second wife's uncle, John De Peyster. The artist was fifty-seven, the sitter sixty-seven, and there was in both a ripe wisdom, a sane maturity which made the occasion memorable. Peale discarded the hard shadows of Copley, preferring a bland light which revealed the sitter in his sober completeness. With infinite patience he searched the face for every sign of age and character; with infinite delicacy he gives us first the whole head with its half-severe, half-benign authority, then the thin white hair, the wide mouth, the finely wrinkled eyes, the folds of jaw settling into the neckcloth. Every slightest plane of the fine old face is suggested; yet the person, like the painting, remains integral.

James Monroe was President when the tireless Peale journeyed to Washington in 1818 to make nineteen portraits for his gallery. The artist was seventy-seven and had given to the Peale brood something more precious than the rudiments of drawing and the cuisine of the brush; to the end of their days they kept his interest in the most ordinary things and something of his originality. When George Washington granted three sittings at Philadelphia in 1795, no less than four of the painting Peales had set up their easels around him: Charles, brother James, and sons Rembrandt and Raphaelle. James, who was eight years younger than Charles, took over his brother's commissions for miniatures in the 1790's, and his delightful conversation piece of this period shows him walking with his wife in a wooded park, surrounded by five children (Pa. Acad.). Of those five, four became painters in the republican years: James Junior did seascapes in water color, while Anna, Sarah, and Margaretta made portraits and miniatures and inherited their father's skill in still life. Charles Peale Polk, nephew of the older Charles, was welcomed to that crowded household as a child, and learned painting from his uncle.

Rembrandt proved himself the most talented son of the founder of this family. Even the venerated Washington had failed to embarrass him at seventeen, although his father worked at his side by way of assurance

Charles W. Peale, *Staircase Group* (George W. Elkins coll., Courtesy Commissioners of Fairmount Park)

Philadelphia Museum of Art

while he drew what he called that "dismal countenance." During the eighteen busy years when the younger Peale was making portraits from New York to Savannah or recording Paris notables for his father's museum, there is an enormous variety in his work; some canvases have the all-over mellow tone of Reynolds; other heads are done with an almost brutal forcefulness and with sketchlike breadth; in still others, he seems to be trying to outpolish David with silky-smooth, unpleasantly pink

Rembrandt Peale, *Thomas Jefferson*

New York Historical Society

flesh and tones that are overfused. He was at his superb best when he painted Jefferson from life in 1805.

The sixty-two-year-old Jefferson is here not only seen but felt and understood, neither drily as West would have painted him nor with the suave oversimplifications of a Stuart. The man's humanity and his intellect are expressed by an artist who shared his scientific interest, his innate dignity, and his democracy; no happier combination of sitter and painter could have been found.

The Peales, however numerous, could not meet the demand for likenesses. The small profile portraits of Pierre Eugène Du Simitière in the eighties were harshly incisive; a few years later a flock of miniature painters on ivory, of whom Edward Malbone was the most brilliant, found ample patronage. Other customers paid fifteen dollars for the forceful if rather insensitive small pastel portraits of James Sharples, his wife and two sons, or twenty-five for an original profile by Saint-Mémin and a dozen smaller engravings made from it by the exiled marquis who thus boiled the pot while he waited for the kings of France to be restored.

Saint-Mémin used a mechanical device called a "physionotrace" to reproduce the sitter's profile on pink paper; this drawing he enlivened with crayon and water color, accenting the outline, filling in the hair, features, and clothes, and tinting the flesh with an accomplished hand. By another device, the pantograph, he then reduced his likeness to a two-inch oval space on copper and engraved it with a fine delicacy. Between 1793

John Trumbull, *John Vernet and His Family*

Yale University Art Gallery, New Haven, Conn.

and 1814, more than eight hundred Americans sat before Saint-Mémin's tracing machine; and although the Peales, Isaac Hawkins, and others used it also, his were the most charming results.

The black-and-white profile could be carved in ivory, as Valaperta carved the McVickars a few years after the War of 1812, or cut from paper in the manner of eighteenth-century Étienne de Silhouette. Charles Peale turned out silhouettes at his museum, and William James Hubard arrived in New York in 1824 to demonstrate his virtuosity with scissors, often adding details of figure and setting with India ink.

The cold definitions of John Trumbull's portrait of his brother's family (Yale Univ.) seemed rather the product of a pair of shears than of a brush. Trumbull had been copying engravings when he made this painting in 1777 in which three pairs of sharp eyes look straight toward the observer. Twenty-nine years later, in his *Family of John Vernet,* the generalizing of West has been attempted. The arms and faces are modeled more delicately but more timidly, and the compact vigor of the early group has given place to a more studied rhythm which leaves each member isolated mentally from the others. One regrets that a man who seldom responded warmly to people was further chilled by London and Paris.

John Vanderlyn was more thoroughly "Frenchified" than any American. When only twenty, John impressed Aaron Burr with his talent—Burr called it genius which he purposed to "rescue from obscurity and develop to its highest point of perfection." John had already made portraits of his own family, technically clumsy work but honest, direct, and solid, and had studied at the drawing school of Archibald Robertson in New York.

Here and in Philadelphia for a few months Vanderlyn also worked with the great Gilbert Stuart, copying some of the suave Stuart portraits, freshening his palette, and lightening his touch. Burr financed his five-year trip to Paris in 1796, and it was not long before the

James Sharples, *Isaiah Thomas,* pastel

American Antiquarian Society, Worcester, Mass.

John Vanderlyn, *Severyn Bruyn*

Senate House Museum, Kingston

relentless contours of the Davidians appeared in his work, as well as the marble-hard modeling with its glassy reflected lights. On this and on the second French journey of 1803, which lasted twelve years, the genius from Kingston developed indeed to the highest point of perfection as it was then conceived by David and his followers.

With some of the French neoclassicist's solemn clarity, he painted Robert Livingston, minister to France. The artist placed under the hand of his subject a sheet of paper with the inscription: *Plan for establishing an Academy of Fine Arts in New York,* much as David had placed near his dead *Marat* the letter of Charlotte Corday. The long nose, the tight lips, the watchful eyes of the ex-Federalist are here rendered with superb assurance by a man who never surpassed this effort.

Vanderlyn at home kept himself alive with portraits of New York merchants and Washington politicians—mature, solid, and rather sleek performances. In his teens at Kingston he had limned the child Severyn Bruyn, the wide mouth, firm small nose, and intent eyes delicately suggested in thin pigment; nearly forty years later the middle-aged Severyn is again recorded by a Vanderlyn whose polish and hard assurance match his own (Senate House Mus., Kingston, N. Y.).

John Vanderlyn, *Robert R. Livingston*

New York Historical Society

Closer than Trumbull or Vanderlyn to the roots of national character were those artists of the people who, with little or no help from the professionals, worked humbly and sometimes namelessly in these years. The old Puritan austerities retained their power, for example, in Reverend Jonathan Fisher, who went to Blue

Jonathan Fisher, *Self-Portrait*

Courtesy Samuel Fisher

J. William Jennys, *Mabel Billings*

Courtesy Louisa Billings

Hill, Maine, in 1796 after spending his Harvard vacations in drawing and painting. Jonathan summoned his reluctant flock to service in words crackling with brimstone, but he also designed and built his own home, painted it with the ochre that was in Maine earth, invented a clock which ran perfectly for fifty years, printed his own Hebrew lexicon with handmade type, and walked the Maine winters without overcoat or flannels. Jonathan's small apples on a pewter plate are patiently rounded in the light and securely placed in space; his water color of a pea vine has something of Audubon's sense of pattern. His *Self-Portrait* reveals the whole man: the shading of the head gives it a startling reality against its dark background, and on this firm structure Fisher has traced every wrinkle and crease which age and character produce.

The Blue Hill preacher was but one of thousands of plain Yankees who were as much a part of America in the republican years as the merchants, the authors, and the urbane gentry of the "cultured" cities. Some of the men who limned them had just enough skill to plot a face and a figure, set down its most arresting shapes, and leave it at that. In Newburyport Charles Octavius Cole drew the North Shore captains. At Hampden, Maine, Jeremiah Hardy's first portrait of his sister Mary, done when he was sixteen, was as primly drawn as any likeness of colonial days; the second, a few years later, had a fused and self-conscious quality which proved that in the brief interval he had seen Gilbert Stuart.

Through Connecticut and western Massachusetts went three painters whose name was Jennys, leaving a trail of likenesses in New Haven, New Milford, Westfield, Hatfield, and Bennington. The likenesses of Elisha Bostwick and his wife in the New Milford Historical Society are dated 1799 and presumably are the work of Richard Jennys; they have a firm and conscientious modeling, precise draughtsmanship, and no little skill in casting shadows. William Jennys, the most elusive of the trio, may have done the *Asa Benjamins* in 1795; and in the year 1801 Doctor William Stoddard Williams of Deerfield wrote in his account book that he paid twelve dollars apiece to J. William Jennys for two portraits of himself and his wife. The same hand drew the faces of *David* and *Mabel Billings* of Hatfield with an assurance which suggests an engraver's skill, and cleanly modeled them with a few tones and well-placed highlights. Deerfield neighborhood knew other face painters—Nathan Negus before 1825 and after him his nephew Augustus Fuller.

One multiplies Deerfield by hundreds of towns as far south as New Orleans and west to the Mississippi to grasp the richness of popular portraiture. One notes that William Clarke of Baltimore painted *Ann Purnell* in the 1790's with the ramrod stiffness of a southern Ralph Earl and that when Maryland people could choose between Rembrandt Peale and Sully, Neagle and Vanderlyn, a Negro named Joshua Johnston painted small *Letitia McCurdy* with a charming directness but with no trace of Baltimore elegance.

The making of portraits was for the Peales and for Trumbull and Vanderlyn one among several modes of painting; Gilbert Stuart was a portrait man and nothing else. His ruddiness was more appropriate to the national complexion than the pallor of John Vanderlyn, and when Stuart described the latter's flesh tones as "like putrid veal a little blown with green flies" he had become the supreme specialist in this field, with a more decisive influence than any other upon the making of American likenesses.

It was Stuart's many George Washingtons which established the image of that gentleman in the mind of his contemporaries. Charles Willson Peale, John Trumbull, and Gilbert Stuart multiplied the Washington image throughout Federal America. A Washington by Peale is posed none too gracefully with his hand on a cannon and one long leg stiffly crossed over the other, his homely features recorded by a man who shared with him the dark days of 1776. Trumbull poses the general self-consciously at the battle of Trenton, the gesture perfunctory, the color inert and conventional. A horse competes for attention by rearing behind him, and the distant soldiers firing a cannon seem an ill-placed afterthought. The Stuart *Washington* stands with handsome authority, superbly brushed in color and texture; he is a Federal icon, elegant in dress and gesture among imposing columns, sweeping draperies, and expensive furniture.

Aloof from the Revolution and from the issues which stirred the young republic, the Stuart who opened his New York and Philadelphia studios in 1792 had spent seventeen of his thirty-seven years in England and Ireland. Neither of the artists he had known in his early years had much to teach him: the Scotsman Cosmo Alexander of Newport who took Stuart abroad when the lad was in his teens was conscientious but uninspired, and Samuel King's likenesses were stiffly old-fashioned. When Stuart, newly arrived in London, painted *Dr. Benjamin Waterhouse* (Redwood Lib.) he was a sober naturalist who firmly and a little drily defined the lean young face, slighting no detail of feature or dress.

During Stuart's twelve English years, Reynolds achieved two of his most accomplished portraits, *Jane Countess of Harrington* and *Lord Heathfield,* both symbolic of the current concept of social and accepted elegance. Before Stuart crossed to Ireland, Gainsborough painted *Mrs. Graham* and *The Morning Walk* with a deft craftsmanship which was not concealed or smoothed away, but allowed itself to be seen in the brush stroke left as it was first swiftly applied to the canvas. Not lost upon Stuart was the clean painting of

Joshua Johnston, *Letitia McCurdy* (Mrs. J. E. Moore coll.)

Courtesy Frick Art Reference Library, New York City

Romney, with its dewy fresh color and its economy of method, nor Raeburn's swiftly brushed heads. Stuart's enormous success in London proved how completely his sharp eye and accomplished hand could assimilate this charm and this surface "reality."

The Stuart recipe, once mastered, was simple, systematic, and dependable. He scorned preliminary drawing with pencil or chalk and first set down the essential shapes of his subject with the brush, blocking in the large masses with no detail. His palette had few colors, and they were mixed methodically: so much vermilion, white, and lake for ruddy complexions, a special mixture for reflections, and another for shadows. These colors Stuart applied with round blunt strokes and avoided that blending of tones into one uniform color which, in his opinion, gave flesh the consistency of buckskin. As his painting proceeded, the first blurred study acquired details and more delicate transitions from light to dark, until a few crisp accents and a glaze or two of transparent color completed the last stage and left his work fresh and untroubled. (See color plate 4.)

The incredible number of Stuart's American commissions—Lawrence Park has listed nearly a thousand exclusive of the *Washingtons*—proves that his was the manner in which the prosperous republicans wished to be regarded. Before his vogue got under way he painted a few portraits which had Copley's actuality with an ease and economy of execution which Copley never

Gilbert Stuart, *Mathilde de Jaudenes y Nebot*

Metropolitan Museum of Art, New York City

achieved in America. The companion portraits of *Josef* and *Mathilde de Jaudenes y Nebot* can scarcely be matched in the nation's painting for their synthesis of reality with style: the unforced richness of satin and velvet and the sense of the body beneath them, the masterly construction of the heads, the brilliant rendering

Gilbert Stuart, *John Adams* (Hon. Chas. F. Adams coll.)

Courtesy Frick Art Reference Library, New York City

Chester Harding, *Isaac Bates*

Courtesy Forbes Library, Northampton, Mass.

of gold lace and brocaded flowers, the play of cream yellows against vermilion and dark blue.

The English lesson was soon more fully applied. From the 1790's to the 1820's the balance between matter and manner shifted toward the latter as the artist moved from the painting of personalities toward the production of Gilbert Stuarts. His later years were spent among the Bostonians, whose Bulfinch houses with their pale tinted walls were an excellent background for his delicate flesh tones and pleasant accents of red and blue. When he did sixty-three-year-old John Adams his eye shrewdly seized upon essentials; twenty-five years later that pinched old countenance was tactfully presented as through a mellowing haze by a painter who was on the verge of seventy and whom Paul Svinin described as "an old man hunched, gouty, but with flaming, penetrating eyes, such as I have never beheld in any one." And Svinin's estimate was just: "He has a remarkable gift for conveying resemblance . . . and his portraits are more like excellent sketches than like completed paintings."

John Hill Morgan has named twenty-two younger men who directly or indirectly learned the Stuart touch, and there were many others in whom his influence is to be seen. Mather Brown of Boston learned from him, as he did from Reynolds and West, and applied those lessons when he painted young Jefferson and John Adams in London in 1786. James Frothingham of Charlestown was a Stuartesque, and Charles Osgood in Salem. Francis Alexander met Stuart in Boston where the master encouraged him to open a studio. Jacob Eichholtz of Pennsylvania German origin had observed Stuart's tricks, but his solid and literal manner was largely his own. Ezra Ames was a coach painter whose first great success was the majestic *George Clinton* of 1812 (N. Y. Hist. Soc.). Here the artist chose for Clinton the parchment-grasping gesture of convention against sturdy columns and swelling crimson draperies, and the firmly molded nose and jowls, the steady eyes beneath the jutting brow, the ruddy cheeks and thinning white hair owe something to Stuart but more to the vigorous realism of Ames himself.

When aging Stuart asked a friend in Boston, "How goes the Harding fever?" he paid sarcastic tribute to a rival whose career was the antithesis of his own and whose sense of American realities went far deeper. Stuart prolonged the eighteenth century into the nineteenth; Chester Harding was of the new age, and although his records of New England men and women were being painted when Monroe was President, he continued to live and work through the days of Andrew Jackson and of Abraham Lincoln, painting up to the day of his death when he was seventy-four—a large-framed, muscular man who had been a farmhand in Conway, Massachusetts, a chairmaker, a woodsman, a saloonkeeper, and a peddler.

Ezra Ames, *George Clinton* (detail)

New York Historical Society

Samuel F. B. Morse, *Lafayette,* N.Y. City Hall (detail)

Bogart Studio photo

At twenty-four Harding traveled down the Allegheny River with his family in a flatboat and opened a sign painter's shop in Pittsburgh. Dunlap tells how the tough-minded Chester engaged an itinerant portraitist named Nelson to paint his own wife and child, watched Nelson at work, and immediately turned the lesson to his profit by making a dozen likenesses himself. In Paris, Kentucky, and in St. Louis Harding's fee rose to forty dollars and in 1821 he went to Washington for commissions to paint congressmen. The next year he made what he called his "pilgrimage" to Stuart in Boston, quickly borrowing enough of the master's method to modify his own harsher style.

Having opened a studio in the small town of Northampton only a few miles from his boyhood home, he produced a series of heads of influential persons which, shown at the annual cattle fair, divided honors with the prize poultry and the Connecticut Valley farm horses.

Harding's portraits commended themselves to their sitters because it was less difficult and less expensive to sit for him in Northampton, Pittsfield, or Springfield than to be painted by Stuart in Boston. They commend themselves to us by their sane balance of the sensuous qualities Harding had observed in Stuart with an interest in solid facts which remained with the artist through every later contact with suaver painting here and abroad. His canvas of *Mrs. John Ball Brown* has a color scheme far more original than most of Stuart's; the lemon-yellow ribbons and the olive-gray dress with its ermine trimmings handsomely set off the warm flesh tones of a face which is as finely characterized as it is deftly painted (Boston Mus. Fine Arts).

It was work like this which diverted eighty sitters from Stuart in six months before Harding went abroad at thirty-one. In England, where he earned twelve thousand dollars in three years, the chairmaker from Conway remained unimpressed by masterpieces which left others of his countrymen breathless. He considered Raphael a poor colorist in the cartoons, and heartily disliked Rubens' dashing *Chapeau de Paille.* His three weeks' experience of high life as guest of the Duke of Hamilton evoked this simple and democratic comment in his *Egotistography:* "As I walk about the grounds, the laborers, old and young, lift their hats as I pass them. This respect and reverence sit but ill on me, who have been all the early part of my life in as humble a sphere as those who pay it."

Boston and London warmed to this man, not in spite of his backwoods origin but because of it. As the years went on, the unpretentious dignity, the sober factualism of his work increased rather than diminished, and the men and women of his later paintings could have lived in no other age than that of Andrew Jackson.

Thomas Sully reminds us that neither the engaging Stuart nor the bluff Harding could take the full measure of the national character. Statesmen posed grandly in the new Hall of Representatives but they also wept when Fanny Kemble played Juliet. Sully had shared the hardships and the unreality of strolling actors' lives with his parents in the South. He had studied for a time with Stuart in 1806 and four years later settled in Philadelphia, where he painted a full length of the actor George Frederick Cooke with the "heroic scowl" and the coarse features which, Dunlap wrote, "could give form to the poet's airiest creations and were capable of expressing the widest range of passion." Sully's *Cooke as Richard the Third* is the never-quite-sober hero of Dunlap's temperance novel, *Memoirs of a Water Drinker,* and the artist portrayed him with a force and firmness he was soon to lose (Pa. Acad.).

It was in England that Sully learned from Lawrence how to suppress those elements of form which did not yield a lush femininity, how to draw loosely and carelessly, how to destroy the shape of chin and cheeks in order to emphasize the glowing eyes, how to contrast pearly skin with soft shadow accents of a pinkish orange and reduce modish curls to a few silken highlights. When Sully painted *Robert Erwin Gray* (Minn. Institute of Arts) soon after his return to America, his gradual liquefaction had begun. His influence is noticeable in the portraits done by William Edward West in Natchez; it helped Philip Tilyard in Baltimore to give a moist luster to his dark-skinned *"Envoy"* from Santo Domingo.

The English fluency also impressed Samuel Morse, and a painterly breadth was in the small New Hampshire heads of his itinerant years. But Morse retained a sense of bulk and a respect for character, and his New Haven likenesses of David De Forest and his wife had Stuart's breadth but a richer variety of textures and a firmer grasp on the form which reveals personality. Two years later, he portrayed the majestic old Lafayette full length with an easy grace and a monumentality which no other painter of the time could have achieved: the sensitive yet powerful sculpturing of the head, the broadly handled yellow trousers, the dark cloak enlivened by a touch of orange-red. The setting was equally handsome, with busts of Washington and Franklin and light-touched clouds to suggest the warm sunset of the hero's life.

Heavy-handed beside the Morse canvas seem its neighbors in New York City Hall whose subjects had time "to sit an hour or so with Jarvis." English-born and apprenticed to the engraver Edward Savage in New York when he was twenty, John Wesley Jarvis advertised ten years later that his rates were three hundred dollars for full lengths, sixty for half lengths which included hands, and forty for those which did not; and he warned those who wanted likenesses of their deceased friends that they must apply to Jarvis "time enough before they inter them."

John W. Jarvis, *Oliver H. Perry,* N.Y. City Hall (detail)

Bogart Studio photo

The temperate Dunlap loathed this extravagant wastrel who met his own unlawful offspring on the street without recognizing them and whose guests ate venison with one-pronged forks and knives without handles. To Dunlap, the career of Jarvis was "a chaos hastening to destruction," and he was in mid-career when Audubon met him at New Orleans in 1821, a burly, bare-necked figure in a flapping straw hat, green coat, yellow trousers, and pink waistcoat, with a magnolia blossom and a baby alligator among the folds of his lawn shirt-collar, in one hand a cage of birds and in the other a silk umbrella labeled STOLEN FROM I.

When Jarvis copied a Stuart, he remarked to Dunlap that he would give its face the color of nature; pointing to the original, he said, "That's not nature." At his best he could make delicate and skillfully drawn faces like that of Mrs. Robert Gilmor I, with the color of her own aging skin, and with a lively sense of individual character; but many of Jarvis' portraits in the New York Historical Society and elsewhere suggest that nature for him came to mean unpleasantly smooth textures, pinkish-purple complexions upon faces too large for their bodies, and heads devoid of charm whose coarse and prosy features curiously repeated some of the ruggedness of the painter's own countenance.

The War of 1812 gave Jarvis his opportunity to paint

John Neagle, *Pat Lyon at the Forge*

Museum of Fine Arts, Boston, Mass.

heroes fresh from Plattsburg and Lake Erie. For the Governor's Room in City Hall, New York, the Common Council ordered half a dozen commodores and generals on huge canvases whose subjects stand unshakably on both feet, clasp their sword hilts, and glare upon the public. Oliver Hazard Perry had been given the keys of the city, and Jarvis chose to represent him in a small boat with three sailors about to board the *Niagara* in a shower of bullets and turn defeat to victory with his "We have met the enemy, and they are ours."

Among the republican portrait makers were Matthew Harris Jouett, who adapted Stuart's manner to Lexington, Kentucky, in the 1820's, and William Edward West, who left Kentucky for Philadelphia to study with Sully. Young Samuel Lovett Waldo could blend Sully's theatricalisms with the sobriety he had learned in London from West and Copley; his self-portrait had the sketchlike Sully dash and his *Andrew Jackson* was a bluff and strongly lighted characterization.

John Neagle's constitution was robust enough to assimilate a double dose of manner: the stylisms of Stuart and the graceful evasions of Sully. His father was from County Cork, his mother a New Jersey yeoman's daughter, and he worked mainly in Philadelphia, now and then taking the road to southern and western regions. He had married Sully's stepdaughter before his brief contact with Stuart resulted in the famous Neagle portrait of the blear-eyed and gouty old master (Boston Mus. Fine Arts). Neagle, like so many others, never quite decided whether he preferred Stuart's velvet or Sully's satin. He used the former's pose and general formula in 1823 when he painted *Mrs. George Repold* in Baltimore, but not Stuart's suave and thin-grained style. The planes of the old face are strongly accused, almost sculptured in paint, and rather brusquely executed as though in a hurry to set down a vivid impression. The picture, a forceful presentation of old age, is blunt rather than bland (Md. Hist. Soc.).

Three years later, Neagle's rather sleek portrait of the blacksmith *Pat Lyon* was as much like a scene from a play as his father-in-law could have wished. Pat, who insisted that he was not to be painted as a gentleman, is like a stage Irishman in the warm light from his forge, and seems about to deliver a humorous line while a charming super works at the rear and a view of Philadelphia hangs like a backdrop behind them. Pat was one of the first manual workers to be painted as he worked; and Neagle's huge canvas belongs in the line of American genre. Neagle could paint staid Philadelphians in the style which they preferred; he could also rival Sully in likenesses of Kean and Forrest; but he was at his most irresistibly sentimental in painting children, and his limpid small studies of papooses are the lovable creatures of Romney and Hoppner whom Neagle has discovered among the forests of Lake Huron.

Stuart died in 1828. Charles Willson Peale had gone one year before, after painting himself as a benevolent old man lifting the curtain of his museum to show its glass cases, its ranks of painted celebrities, and the skeleton of the famous mastodon (Pa. Acad.). The maturity of Stuart and Peale had seen the republic made secure and the artificial bond, as Brackenridge said, become a natural one. The Dutch painters of the seventeenth century and the Englishmen of the eighteenth had mirrored a class more homogeneous and a life more conventionally stable than those of the American people. Tight-lipped or pouting, ramrod-stiff or gracefully urbane, dowdy or stylish, richly born or newly enriched, the new nation had found its appropriate interpreters.

The age which produced Jonathan Fisher's stern self-revelation and Morse's superb *Lafayette,* Rembrandt Peale's *Jefferson* and Neagle's *Pat Lyon,* Stuart's *Nebots,* and Vanderlyn's *Livingston* deserves to be called the Golden Age of American portrait painting.

CHAPTER 11 / THE DYING HERCULES

"Where does Jupiter come in as against the lightning rod?" A political economist asked the question when Samuel Morse was sixty-six years old and had learned that his own *Judgment of Jupiter* did not come in, as against his telegraph. He had been one of those who believed that his young country could not find complete artistic expression through portraiture alone. With Trumbull, Allston, and Vanderlyn he had essayed the epic style as Reynolds defined it, with subjects from the scriptures and from ancient history which were not "degraded by the vulgarism of ordinary life." In his fourth "Discourse" the Englishman had warned that works which depended upon particular customs and habits could only be coeval with that which first raised

John Trumbull, *Death of Gen. Montgomery at Quebec* (study)

Yale University Art Gallery, New Haven, Conn.

them from obscurity. "Present time and future may be considered as rivals; and he who solicits the one must expect to be discountenanced by the other."

At the very moment of Reynolds' speech, however, Benjamin West painted his *Death of Wolfe*. Edgar Wind has observed that, by substituting remoteness of place for that of time, and by emphasizing the exotic in his foreground Indian, the Pennsylvanian could risk being discountenanced by Sir Joshua and the future. Copley took the next logical step in 1781 by painting the *Death of Lord Chatham,* which was remote neither in time nor in place, and by dressing his characters in the clothes they wore on that occasion. In 1789 his son and two daughters were old enough to assume the stilted poses of Faith, Hope, and the Red Cross Knight from Spenser's *Faerie Queen* in a canvas which has nothing to recommend it. "The vulgarism of ordinary life" no longer interested Copley.

While John Trumbull was copying Correggios and Raphaels in West's studio it occurred to him that the great episodes of his country's revolution were potential themes for epic paintings. He had not, like Peale, thrown himself completely into the making of that revolution, and while its outcome was uncertain had resigned, piqued by a technical slight, from the Continental army. In London he was reminded of realities by being jailed in reprisal for the arrest of André; released on the surety of West and Copley, he came home; but 1784 saw him with West again, and in 1785 he was in Paris as the guest of Jefferson. He seems always to have stepped around history in the making and was in New York when the Bastille fell, painting from life the heads he would introduce into his canvases and sketching the scenes where battles had been fought such a brief time before. Thirty-six figures in the *Declaration of Independence* were done from life, another nine from portraits, one from memory, and one from a verbal description. It was under West's eye that his compositions were sketched, and much of the painting was done in London and at Jefferson's Paris home.

Trumbull's small oil studies in the Yale University Art Gallery are of two types, battles and ceremonies—men clashing and men standing or sitting. He was more successful in the former; his *Death of General Montgomery* had a controlled variety of dramatic movement, powerful diagonals, a tonal scheme which reinforced the story, and a pigment which was both thick and thin. The heads were superbly drawn, especially the foreshortened features of Montgomery, and crisply painted. The swirling folds of a flag and a snow-laden wintry branch were suggested by the broadest and most fluid touch, and the small canvas glowed with warm and brilliant color There was some of that force in the *Bunker's Hill* where flags and moving masses of men developed a rhythm; but the figures at the right eluded that dynamism. In representing the battle of Princeton, Trumbull found himself at the mercy of an unmanageable horse who insisted on holding the center of the stage.

In the *Declaration* and in the *Resignation of General Washington,* the artist faced episodes whose drama was psychological rather than physiological, and the best he could do was to play dull variations on symmetrical balance or poise a large near group against a small distant one. The *Declaration* did not try to reconstruct that episode but rather to group significant Americans some of whom had not been present, and the grouping remained inert after eight years of labor. In the *Surrender of Burgoyne* the troops had the look of over-rehearsed and badly directed supers in a third-rate pageant. The *Resignation* was located in a large room whose bare walls formed a relentless void in spite of the shadows which the artist threw across them. As though to underscore his shortcomings, Trumbull painted most of these compositions with a hard Davidian finish, a dry and ugly color which emphasized the stilted gestures, the banal grouping, and the airless spaces. There was at least a nervous vigor and a painterly solidity in the separate portrait heads which were part of his laborious preparation for the series.

While Trumbull wrestled with his national project, two younger men were attempting lofty subjects. Old Benjamin West now warned his listeners that they could not live by historical painting, and that only fashionable painters of vacant faces could expect to be successful; perhaps Morse and Allston should have heeded the remark and saved themselves much heartbreak. But Samuel Morse was only twenty-three in 1814 and scarcely aware of the realistic element in his character which would find its best expression in portraits and scientific invention; Allston, with a temperament less robust than that of Morse, never wholly recovered from the spell of West.

Morse in London read Spenser, Dante, and Chaucer, and resisted his parents' efforts to persuade him to come home, his mother's insistence that he learn how to make portraits in the best style. The son replied that he was happy only when practicing what he called the intellectual branch of art, and he added that "portraits have none of it; landscape has some of it, but history

Washington Allston, *Belshazzar's Feast* (study, Dana coll.)

Museum of Fine Arts, Boston, Mass.

John Vanderlyn, *Ariadne*

Pennsylvania Academy of the Fine Arts, Philadelphia, Pa.

has it wholly." His purpose was to "elevate and refine public feeling by turning the thoughts of his countrymen from sensuality and luxury to intellectual pleasures." Thus spoke the Congregational minister's son from Charlestown, Massachusetts, while his friend Allston wrote the elder Morses how tragic it would be if Samuel should "raise no higher superstructure than the fame of a portrait painter."

To justify his mentor's faith, Morse exhibited in 1813 two versions of his *Dying Hercules,* a small sculpture and a huge painting (Yale Univ.), in which the hero struggled with the poisoned shirt of Nessus. The former was nervously alive, its muscular tensions proving how well young Morse had observed the ancient torsos and perhaps the living model. The latter was forty-eight square feet of tiresome borrowing from the *Laocoön* and the *Drunken Faun* of the Naples Museum, its ribs and flanks precisely drawn and then obscured by a smoky darkness, its unpleasantly warm brown flesh tones overfused in what then was taken to be the manner of the Italian masters. A London critic, however, placed the painting among the first dozen in the Royal Academy's two thousand pictures, and the sculpture won Morse a gold medal before he shipped both statue and canvas home and regretfully returned to paint heads for fifteen dollars in New Hampshire.

When Morse manufactured the *Hercules,* Washington Allston was in his early thirties. This South Carolinian had studied at Harvard and lived at Newport. In Europe he shared Vanderlyn's experience of Paris and Rome, became an intimate of Washington Irving and Coleridge, and toiled away at a long series of oversized and underimagined paintings. In 1817 he made his first sketches for a *Belshazzar's Feast.*

This was the year when West exhibited *Death on the Pale Horse,* proving that he could break new ground at eighty, as he had once done with the cold perfection of his *Regulus* and with his *Wolfe* in modern dress. In 1802, a study for the *Death* picture had taken Paris by storm, twenty years before the French Romantics essayed that kind of dynamics. Now his pale horse plunged among thunderheads, lightning bolts, and writhing figures with a turbulence and an assault on the emotions which were something new in painting (Pa. Acad.).

Allston's landscapes were proof that he, too, could command the stormy, the desolate, and the wild. His first sepia study for the *Belshazzar* had a colonnaded background similar to that of West's *Regulus,* and the general grouping of his figures recalled those of West's own *Belshazzar,* though in reverse; its light was evenly distributed and gave due prominence to Daniel. A second sketch in colors threw the king and his throne glaringly off balance, and submerged the prophet's gesture. The painter's troubles with an ill-fated picture had just begun, but he wrote to Irving that he knew no subject which so happily united the magnificent and the awful.

While London gaped at West's *Death on the Pale Horse* in 1817, New York saw three efforts of John Vanderlyn to transcend portraiture: a panorama, a nude *Ariadne,* and a "classical" *Marius Amid the Ruins of Carthage.* Paris and Rome rather than London had inspired him. From a ceiling by LeMoyne at Versailles he had copied a group of figures which no Kingston citizen would have thought fit to look upon; traveling in Italy with Allston, he had sketched Roman ruins and copied a female figure from Raphael's *Transfiguration.* The attitude of the heroine in his *Death of Jane McCrea* recalls David's *Sabines,* and the postures of his Indians are like those of the Frenchman's Roman warriors. On a page of Vanderlyn's European sketchbook at Kingston is a seated figure drawn "from the antique" which may be the origin of his *Marius;* but that brooding person also resembles the Ludovisi *Ares* and both the *Leonidas* and the *Brutus* of David. The large *Marius* (De Young Mus.) and a small version which Vanderlyn made many years afterward (Albany Inst.) are wiry-hard in drawing. The ivory flesh tones of the Roman contrast with the brilliant deep red of his cloak, and the distant ruins are precisely painted in a sunset light. (See color plate 6.)

Vanderlyn's *Ariadne,* which Paris saw in 1812, revealed a draughtsmanship of which no other young American was capable, and the delicate cool flesh tones were more Parisian than Venetian (Pa. Acad.). Had the artist seen, at the Park Theater in 1797, the melodrama of *Ariadne Abandoned by Theseus?* The attitude of his nude figure suggests that he knew the Hellenistic marble of that title in the Vatican, at least through an engraving, and perhaps the *Cymon and Iphigenia* of Sir Joshua Reynolds in a print by Francis Hayward. He need not have expected that his own *Ariadne's* nakedness would be welcome in America.

John Vanderlyn, detail from *Versailles* panorama

Metropolitan Museum of Art, N. Y.

When he brought her home in 1815, writers were protesting Wertmüller's *Danaë* as an offence against decency, and Rembrandt Peale's *Jupiter and Io* was thought unfit for public showing. In the *Portfolio* a "Lover of the Arts" condemned their nakedness, and the Columbian Society adopted resolutions against the display of painted indecency. The city of Charleston was more responsive to *Ariadne* in 1822. Its *Courier* described her crimson lips, teeth of pearl, and pure white skin as "subjects of eager attraction and awakening interest" to southern connoisseurs of graceful form. But when Vanderlyn painted a second version of *Ariadne* for a New York patron, he gave her an extra garment against the northern chill.

Both the *Marius* and the *Ariadne* hung in the vestibule of Vanderlyn's New York Rotunda, which he had built on a plot in the corner of City Hall Park leased to him by the corporation. On its round walls he had placed the panorama of Versailles, three thousand square feet of canvas. With his customary precision, the artist had drawn the great palace itself, correcting its horizontal lines to overcome the distortion of the circular shape. He had represented its basins with their fountains, the formal walks where dapper men and women strolled, the dark clipped hedges and white statues; and he prepared an illustrated guidebook as a key to identify the points of interest. The *Versailles* was a *tour de force* by a man who at forty had become a superb draughtsman.

What was the American response to these efforts to elevate its taste? Boston had praise for the Morse *Hercules* but no potential buyers, and his plaster figurine soon reposed in the damp cellars of the national Capitol. Vanderlyn's panorama lost money for its creator, who quickly learned that his countrymen had little appetite for the frozen posture of his *Marius.* Long out of touch with his own country, he could not have

Charles W. Peale, *Exhuming the Mastodon* (Mrs. Harry White coll.)

Courtesy Municipal Museum, Baltimore, Md.

known that a Tory horror of Jacobin excesses had combined with a reviving religious movement to reject everything that was French, especially the details of anatomy and the "images of voluptuousness" in French authors.

An even greater frustration awaited Trumbull at the hands of Congress. When the Capitol was about to be rebuilt in 1814 he took six of his historical paintings to Washington with the proposal that they become the nucleus of a national gallery, and Jefferson wrote that Trumbull's pictures should be retained in America as "monuments of the taste as well as of the great revolutionary scenes of our country." Of Trumbull's twelve proposed subjects, however, a cautious Congress ordered only four, to be placed in the rotunda: the *Burgoyne,* the *Cornwallis,* the *Declaration,* and the *Resignation.*

The sixty-year-old painter had now to compose two new pictures and then enlarge all four from his two-by-four-foot studies to six times those dimensions. Whatever warmth was in his sketches became thoroughly chilled in the nine hundred square feet of the finished works. When John Quincy Adams saw the nearly completed *Declaration,* he wrote in his diary that he was not disappointed because his expectations had been very low. As soon as the four canvases were installed, Senator Holmes pronounced the *Resignation* the most solemn daubing he had ever seen, and when Trumbull sought four more commissions to complete the rotunda, John Randolph labeled the *Declaration* a "shin piece," explaining that "never was there before such a collection of legs submitted to the eyes of man." The government refused to buy a collection on which the painter had worked for more than forty years; Congress doled out its fees reluctantly to him; dampness was already coating the backs of his rotunda pictures with mildew; and in the *National Advertiser* Halleck and Drake lampooned his *Declaration:*

> How bright their buttons shine! how straight
> Their coat-flaps fall in plaited grace;
> How smooth the hair on every pate;
> How vacant each immortal face!

To Trumbull's frozen history Charles Willson Peale preferred history in the making. He wrote to his old teacher West in 1807 that he had begun the previous summer to do a picture of getting up the bones of the mammoth, an episode in which he had been the chief actor. He said there were about fifty figures in the painting, of whom eighteen were portraits, for the most part of his own family; and he wished that he had used a larger canvas.

News of an odd discovery had come to Peale in 1801. Near Newburgh on the Hudson a farmhand had uncovered a thigh bone which was thirty-nine inches long. Peale lost no time in reaching Newburgh, where he directed a three months' campaign to excavate a complete skeleton of what Rembrandt later described as "a nondescript carnivorous animal of immense size" which could be neither an elephant nor a hippopotamus but the fossil of an extinct monster.

Peale engaged a small army of helpers, supplied them with grog, and designed a huge wheel with buckets on it to drain the swamps while the watchful scientist stood by with a sketch of what he hoped to find. The search went on until Peale had exhumed the complete under jaw of his mammoth and shipped the bones to Philadelphia, where the task of reconstruction began. By sheer perseverance the Peales managed to piece together the frames of two animals, eleven feet high and thirty-one from tusk to tail. One skeleton was to be seen in Peale's Philadelphia Museum, the other went with Rubens and Rembrandt to London in 1802, where visitors to its Pall Mall exhibition room could read the brochure which Rembrandt published. The text explained that almost no part of the ancient animal was missing. "What we do not unquestionably know, we leave deficient."

The same honesty had made the painting. A keenly remembered event, not any hallowed formula, had determined its cross-rhythms and its well-managed sequences and oppositions. Its "composition" did not demonstrate a principle but explained an action. It is one of the first as it is surely one of the best of American genre paintings, so intimate and faithful a record of a significant event that Rembrandt's narrative can serve as a description of the painting: "Every farmer with his wife and children, for twenty miles round in every direction with waggons, carriages and horses, flocked to see the operation; and a swamp always noted for being the solitary and dismal abode of snakes and frogs, became an active scene of curiosity and bustle; the greater part astonished at the whim of an old man traveling two hundred miles from his home to dig up as a treasure, at incredible risk, labor and expense, a pile of bones which, although all were astonished to see, many believed fit for nothing better than to rot and serve as manure."

Fifteen years after the *Mastodon* picture Samuel Morse also produced a painting whose organization was determined by the facts of the case. No doubt he

Rembrandt Peale, *The Court of Death* (study, Charles C. Sellers coll.)

Courtesy Frick Art Reference Library, New York City

still agreed with Reynolds that works built on general nature would live forever; but after five years in America he must have decided that works of a less lofty nature might enable the artist to live today. His countrymen paid twenty-five cents to see Granet's large interior of the *Capucin Chapel at Rome,* and Morse decided to show them the Senate and the Hall of Representatives in tents or rented exhibition rooms. The former view was never made; the latter was thoroughly documented, his purpose being "a faithful representation of the national hall, with its furniture and business." He improvised a basement studio at the Capitol and sketched from life the eighty-six politicians who appeared in the finished work and who could be identified by a diagram which he provided. The members are assembling for the evening session and the general tone is as richly somber as the oratory of the day: the scarlet curtains fringed with gold, the ornate Brussels carpet on the floor, the legislators' faces emerging from the general gloom as the great Argand chandelier is lighted.

Morse was preparing this appeal to patriotism when Rembrandt Peale completed his pictorial attack on the public's emotions, *The Court of Death* (Detroit Inst. of Arts). Its evolution in his mind began with a poem by Bishop Porteus:

> . . . Deep in a murky cave's recess,
> Laved by Oblivion's listless stream, and fenced
> By shelving rocks and intermingled horrors,
> . . . the Monarch sits
> In unsubstantial majesty.

Peale had no mind to personify death by outworn symbols, by mythology, or by vague allegory. He wanted to show the forms of death which man brings upon himself by his own follies. He hoped to produce "pure figurative" work of a new kind which by its colors and forms would "strike the heart at once as with an electric glance"—a primitive expressionism, so to speak.

Peale considered Roubillac's sculptured skeleton in Westminster Abbey and the withered rider of West's pale horse, and rejected both. His Death, sketched roughly in London, was a hooded figure not unlike the one West had painted in *Saul and the Witch of Endor.* In Baltimore he had to build a special studio for a canvas of twenty-four by thirteen feet. His venerable father posed for Old Age, who stands, supported by Virtue, and faces the judgment. At the feet of Death is a young man struck down, for whom the artist combined sketches made from his brother Raphaelle with studies from a corpse in the medical college. His wife, his three children, and his friends appeared in the group at the right where the widow, the orphan, Want, Dread, and Desolation expressed the death-before-its-time which War brings; and among the left-hand figures were Gout, Dropsy, Hypochondria, and Intemperance bearing witness to human ignorance and self-destruction.

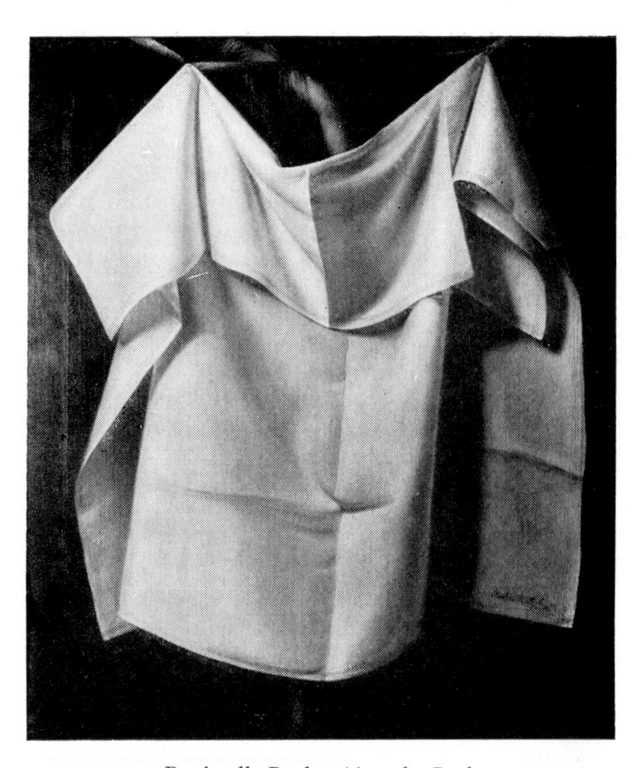

Raphaelle Peale, *After the Bath*

William R. Nelson Gallery of Art, Kansas City, Mo.

Rembrandt showed his *Court of Death* in 1820 at the opening of the Baltimore Museum, where its lurid grays and greens among the wax figures and stuffed snakes must have been horrid enough under the new gas lamps. He felt his purpose had been accomplished when his old Negro cook Aunt Hannah understood the painting at first glance. Under his shrewd promotion the canvas toured the seaboard cities, where over thirty thousand Americans paid nine thousand dollars to see it and to read his explanatory pamphlet, which included Aunt Hannah's testimonial. Ministers preached sermons on it; the Common Council of New York solemnly viewed it in a body; a hundred thousand colored engravings of it were made to be sold for a dollar each. At Albany a senator fell dead as he entered its exhibition room, and Peale took care to explain that this was a mere coincidence.

If none of the history painters, as West had prophesied, could live by that "intellectual branch" of art, it was perhaps because their pioneer efforts reckoned too seldom with the realities of public taste. Scenes from the national past, more vigorously rendered than by Trumbull, would soon find a warmer reception than did his. The panorama which failed to interest Vanderlyn's public would flourish once it became a symbol of the western expansiveness. Americans of 1817 were offended by naked *Ariadne;* thirty years later they would find a genteel sublimation of that prudery. In the meantime Raphaelle Peale eluded censure in his witty painting, *After the Bath,* where only the arms and feet of a nude girl appear, and the main space of the canvas is occupied by a sheet whose realistic execution a Dali might envy. If the painting Peales often succeeded where others failed, it was because they did not scorn what Reynolds had called "the vulgarism of ordinary life." They had no mind to struggle like Hercules with the shirt of theory, and they knew that even Hercules was at the mercy of Antaeus so long as that giant's feet kept contact with the earth.

CHAPTER 12 / THE RISE OF LANDSCAPE

Who painted the first landscape in America? Some visitor who had seen Poussin and Claude in the original, or some nameless yeoman who enjoyed the way a river coiled through his pasture and sat down to record his pleasure on a slab of wood? There are more important questions: How did Americans see and feel nature? And to what extent did observation form their pictures of her, to what extent the ready formula?

Formulas had existed in Europe since the time of the first colonial settlements, together with philosophies which justified their use. Poussin had naturalized himself in antiquity, as Reynolds said, and painted his *Funeral of Phocion* at Rome in 1648, ordering nature with the logic of a Descartes in his effort to equate a noble subject with the nobility of its setting. Every detail of its architecture was as correct as the archaeology of his time could make it, and its rocks, trees, and clouds were no mere background but functional parts of a solid intellectual structure. Some twenty years later, and with the same austerity, Poussin made landscapes in which men and gods had conceded a larger place to nature.

The eyes of Claude Lorrain were less steadily fixed on the sublime, in Reynolds' phrase, than were those of Poussin. He had been dazzled by the Italian sun and found ways of irradiating his pictures with it; sunset glowed from the center of his harbor scenes; morning light slanted across his temples or fell upon a clearing in his forest.

Both of these Frenchmen, painting in the studio from notes they had made out of doors, found devices of color and design by which the accidental could be firmly generalized; and through engravings these methods became the conventions of lesser men. Poussin showed how two cupids, placed in the center of the foreground, would stabilize the nonsymmetry beyond them, or how a large tree would subdivide the rectangle from top to bottom. His dark near rocks and bushes were used to enframe a village in the middle distance; or a winding stream could bind the near, the middle, and the far. Poussin's light could be studied to find how arbitrarily it struck the necessary and the important and left the rest in gloom; his color showed not how trees and houses looked but how each could sound its note in a majestic orchestration. Claude was equally resourceful with his primary near tree and his secondary one in the middle distance, his zigzag road, his alternation of dark and light planes to lead one into the scene, the bland simplifications of color which steeped his groves and seaports in half-mythical light.

The temperament of Salvator Rosa was neither intellectual nor bland. He had tramped the mountains of Calabria and the Abruzzi, where ancient villages perched on the edge of frightful cliffs, and on the storm-beaten coast he had seen weird caverns which his imagination peopled with sea-gods. His *Banditti in a Desert* carried emotional conviction because he had himself been captured by bandits. Rosa had found the subject of his *Purgatorio,* one admirer said, "amidst earthquakes and volcanic flames, in an atmosphere of lightning, and the perpetual crash of falling thunderbolts."

For the eighteenth-century aesthete exploring the causes of artistic pleasure, Poussin, Claude, and Rosa were supreme masters of the Beautiful, the Sublime, and the Picturesque. Edmund Burke, author at twenty-seven of a famous essay, would have found in Poussin the awe-inspiring vastness which he associated with sublimity, and in Claude the smooth continuities and the clean colors he called beautiful. Nearly forty years later Uvedale Price carefully located the picturesque midway between the other two attributes and defined it as variety, intricacy, and freedom from constraint, with rough and sudden imperfections; not the perfect

Grecian palace but its moss-grown discolored ruin.

The reign of this triumvirate was long indeed; but even in France there were those who challenged the formalized brown trees and the glow of eternal afternoon. Louis Gabriel Moreau dared to paint what was called the *paysage-portrait.* Rousseau's personalized descriptions of nature put a touch of green, as Sainte-Beuve wrote, into French literature, and Fragonard's drawings had that freshness. From his prison window, David painted the Luxembourg gardens with sober truthfulness. In England, Reynolds condescended to the "little" Dutchmen but included their landscapes in his own collection; other connoisseurs bought views of the Thames whose neat, precise draughtsmanship and sturdy literalism could be traced to the Dutch and their local imitators.

Sir Joshua accused "the late ingenious Wilson" of introducing gods and goddesses into scenes which were unfit to receive such ideal beings. Richard Wilson's early work was heavy with recollections of Poussin, Claude, and Joseph Vernet, but gradually his delight in times of day and the play of wind and sun over the ponds and hillsides of England produced a thoroughly outdoor Wilson. Gainsborough, who preferred the countryside to London, drew the forms of trees with a swift freedom which Reynolds could not wholly approve.

When Claude painted his Roman views and Poussin his myths, Americans were battling the first winters at Plymouth and Salem, and a century passed before Boston caught a glimpse of Smibert's collection, among which were "landskips." The river scenes which Nathaniel Emmons was said to have painted have disappeared, and nature remained, with few exceptions, a formalized fragment for portrait backgrounds, as it was in Justus Kühn. Before the Revolution a colonial town was occasionally sketched and sent to England to be engraved; with characteristic enterprise, Charles Peale made views of his friends' estates and a few landscapes which he said would do credit to Claude or Rosa. Winthrop Chandler spread nature on his overmantel scenes; the green hills beyond Ralph Earl's *Mrs. Moseley* were more than a stock background, and his view of Worcester was landscape pure and simple. But these were exceptional efforts, and to specialize in this mode was to gamble for patronage.

That risk was taken, however, by four English-born and English-trained artists who came to America between 1790 and 1795: William Winstanley, William Groombridge, Thomas Beck, and Francis Guy. Winstanley knew the reliable tricks — the indispensable foreground tree, the winding Claudian stream, the nicely calculated spatial sequences; Guy stole judiciously from Claude, as John Neal said. The names of European landscape masters rolled off the tongue of Groombridge when Dunlap talked with him, and his *English Landscape* was all mellow browns, with a thatched cottage and a bridge where cattle crossed as they did in Claude; his swift notation of foliage masses had the Gainsborough touch.

In the outskirts of Philadelphia and Baltimore lived a merchant and shipowning aristocracy whose lawns looked down over valleys and towns which their industry had populated. The prospect was sufficiently English to call for academic treatment—the near grove, the Adamesque mansion, the smooth park where deer grazed. Mr. Hamilton of Woodlands hired Beck to paint views of his elegant villa near Philadelphia; Robert Gilmor collected Groombridge drawings in Baltimore, and in that city Guy made views of gentlemen's estates.

In the England these men had left, Wilson and Gainsborough had broken the grip of conventions with landscapes where fishermen and shepherds were more at home than the deities of Claude and Poussin; soon Crome and Constable, with their power to catch the fleeting outdoor instant, would further revolutionize landscape painting on both sides of the Channel. American patrons had more literal tastes than the British nobility. As these four men worked thousands of miles from home, what was local and specific gradually sharpened the edge of generalization. Winstanley was self-conscious when he painted the falls of the Potomac, balancing the two cascades with a slanting rock at either side (Natl. Mus.); but Beck's Niagara landscapes were sufficiently topographical to be engraved for a series of American views.

Guy, some ten years younger than Beck and Groombridge, was the most independent of the four. He scarcely bothered to compose his *Perry Hall* but simply strung his main theme of hills, driveway, and house along the canvas, planted a tree at either edge, and in the center grouped several of his oddly paired figures. In the downstream and upstream views of *Pennington Mills* he was at his most delightfully specific (Peabody Inst.). The former painting has a five-horse Conestoga wagon and a river which Guy uptilted in perspective as though its winding curves delighted him; the latter is rich in details and evokes a place—the gambreled house above the stream, the mill buildings in action, the dam where dead tree limbs are caught.

More "atmospheric" is Guy's *Tontine Coffee House* with its bustling harborside activity, its mellow red-orange brick against a blue sky where summer clouds gather, its ingenious perspective of one street crossing the picture plane and two others meeting at a point in the center, its crowds moving two-by-two, a phenomenon which is the Guy signature. For greater accuracy, Guy used to trace the outlines of his subject on a

Francis Guy, *The Tontine Coffee House*

New York Historical Society

stretched gauge before transferring them to his canvas, finding no contradiction between mechanical aid and inspiration. The three last years of this dyer-tailor-painter's life were spent in Brooklyn, of whose quiet streets he painted one summer and at least two winter scenes, the latter inevitably reminding one of Brueghel with their small dark animated figures moving against the whites and grays of snow. His one-man show of landscapes at the Shakespeare Gallery near Park Theater in New York, probably the first of its kind held in America, coincided with his death in 1820.

None of the four Englishmen wholly succeeded in turning trees and mountains, as Eliza Godefroy said, into bread and wine. Winstanley opened a panorama in New York; Groombridge painted portraits; Beck made chemical experiments and translated the Odes of Anacreon; Guy dipped into marine painting, frescoed the walls of a Baltimore tavern, wrote essays on Deism, and announced a cure for toothache. He had caught something of the American enterprise, even though, in what was perhaps his last letter, he railed at the "sly, say-nothing, smiling, deep speculating, money-hunting Jonathans of this all-men-are-born-equal-free-and-independent, negro-driving, cow-skin republic."

The citizens of that republic evidently preferred nature when it was given a local habitation and a name, and the landscapes of Saint-Mémin, the Robertsons, and the Birches in the 1790's were topographical views intended to circulate as prints. In Saint-Mémin's water-color view of New York Harbor from Mount Pitt, a large tree threw its shadow across a winding road to darken the foreground, and the town with its steeples and small houses lay on a low horizon beneath a sky which filled much of the frame, as it does in Dutch landscapes.

The Robertson brothers arrived from Scotland, Archibald in 1790 and Alexander the next year; at their Columbian Academy in New York they taught the drawing of heads, figures, historical subjects, flowers, patterns, and landscapes in water color, India ink, chalk, or any other medium. As a study for an engraving, Archibald shortly painted a delicious water color in which the town from Trinity Church to the Battery was seen from the Hudson River, the indispensable foreground motive a moored vessel with its sails furled. Samuel Scott, the "Canaletto of London," had managed the Thames with the same firm delicacy and sense of outdoor light which Robertson gave to the Hudson.

On the heels of the Scotsmen came William Birch and his son Thomas to do for Philadelphia what the Robertsons had done for New York. The father soon produced twenty-eight views which ministered to civic

Archibald Robertson, *View of New York City from North River*

New York Historical Society

pride and the curiosity of rival towns by presenting the Arch Street Ferry and the new bank with accurate and charming dignity. The son in his twenties drew the straight wharves and clustered masts from beneath William Penn's treaty elm, with men building boats in its shade and three classical young ladies in white who look as though they had stepped down from the pedestals of William Rush. When Dunlap saw the quiet Schuylkill views of Thomas, he briefly observed, "Birch could design."

The War of 1812 was an auspicious moment for the rise of marine painting, for it made Americans sea-conscious. From Naples Michele Felice Corné had sailed on a Derby vessel to work in many genres in Salem, Boston, Providence, and Newport. He could paint shepherds à la Claude in unpleasantly warm sunsets and assemble the façades and groves of that master on a fireboard over a mantel. In a hallway at Providence his entire repertory was spread—a strange island with a ruined castle, bristling rocks like those of Rosa, tropical palms, winter snow, tumbling waterfalls, and a sailing boat dark against moonlight.

The triumphs of the American Navy demanded a dramatic rendering and in the postwar years received it from both amateurs and professionals, from Thomas Ruckle's naïve eyewitness record of the defense of Baltimore to the suave canvases of England's most accomplished marine painter, Nicholas Pocock. Corné and Birch were somewhere between these two, and both men adopted the device of narrating a battle in a series of views. Corné thus represented the fight of the *Constitution* and the *Guerrière*—the preparation, the closing in, and the surrender—and his record was faithfully documented, the ships expertly drawn, the large sky thinly painted, the waves stiffly conventional (New Haven Col. Hist. Soc.). Thomas Birch had doubtless seen the livelier harbor pictures of Joseph Vernet, and although the tempests of Turner were beyond him he managed a saltier sea than did Corné. With his sober color and his hard touch, Birch could paint battling ships with greater conviction than any of his competitors except Robert Salmon. The latter came to Boston in 1828 with nearly thirty years of experience in this mode. His naval scenes in distemper were almost as large as the drop curtain he painted for the Boston Theater and his panoramic view of the city and harbor from Pem-

Thomas Birch, *The Constitution and the Guerrière* (Addison Gallery)

Courtesy Mrs. Francis P. Garvan

berton Hill (Otis House, Boston). Boston admired his solid composition, his meticulous draughtsmanship, and his agreeable colors.

The landscapist of the 1790's could not be sure that the stiff engraved line or the wiry etching would do justice to his original. The views of Birch and son, of Saint-Mémin, and of Archibald Robertson were mostly etched or engraved, although Saint-Mémin lithographed his own *West Point* with the *Clermont* on its way to Albany. A few years later there were aquatinters in England who could superbly translate the delicate tint and the graduated wash. From England to America between 1816 and 1818 came a group of men who were both accomplished water colorists and trained aquatinters. They could practice the stylized charm of Cotman and what one critic called Girtin's "castigated purity," but they also dared the deeper plunges into space, the play of clouds over great mountains, and the drama of distance which were called "picturesque."

Most American cities by this time had shops where people who could not afford paintings bought views of native scenery or urban street scenes. At Clover's in New York were nineteen prints of cities from Boston and Buffalo to Richmond, Charleston, Mobile, and New Orleans. They were the work of William J. Bennett, who drew Fulton Market with precise perspective lines and clear-cut lighting, and the prim housefronts of Broadway curving gracefully northward along Bowling Green, a quiet, tree-shaded Broadway which Philip Hone remembered after it had passed.

Joshua Shaw had challenged Turner's *Deluge* with one of his own before he toured nearly every state to make *Picturesque Views of American Scenery,* comprehending, the announcement said, "all the varieties of the sublime, the beautiful, the picturesque in nature." They were aquatinted by John Hill, who had made prints in London from Turner's work and whose own *Landscape Album* appeared in the same year as Shaw's. Hill's son was to become a prolific viewmaker; it was the father, however, who matched his technical skill with the superb talent of William Guy Wall in the *Hudson River Portfolio.*

Wall was not the first to tramp the valley with his sketchbook, for Dunlap had made water colors along the river and as far north as Niagara, and John Vanderlyn had painted the Hudson from his own town of

View Near Fishkill, by W. G. Wall, engraved by J. Hill, from *Hudson River Portfolio*

Courtesy New York Public Library

Kingston in a small and modest oil at the very beginning of his career. Writers had peopled the river's caves with Indians and its bluffs with the ghosts of Dutchmen: Washington Irving had begun his "companionship with this glorious river" as a boy, and his *Sketch Book* fixed its image in the minds of Americans in the year Wall made his drawings. The small island between two cataracts at Glens Falls, which is one of the plates in the *Hudson River Portfolio,* had been a hiding place for Cooper's Chingachgook and for his Hawkeye, who described its wild beauty in *The Last of the Mohicans.*

The Hudson was in everyone's mind when the *Portfolio* appeared; Clinton's canal was done in 1825, and the *Seneca Chief* made her triumphal nine-day passage from Lake Erie to the Atlantic. The memoir which described these celebrations used the new process of lithography to reproduce a Robertson drawing and a copy was sent to the King of Bavaria, where lithography had been born, modestly noting that "the new method is in its infancy with us, and in its crudest form."

There was no crudity in Hill's aquatints for the *Hudson River Portfolio* nor in the original water colors. Wall had sketched the river southward from Luzerne, where mountain brooks tumbled over rocks into the wide stream from the Schroon and the Sacandaga, down to Troy, to the town of Hudson, which had been Claverack Landing, before Nantucket whalers had taken it over; down to Newburgh, which Germans from the Rhine had settled in the days of Queen Anne, and where Washington had pitched his camp in the darkest moment of the Revolution; down to West Point, part of the "garden of Dutch aristocracy," as Willis described the eastern shore; down past the sheer basalt precipices called the Palisades to New York Harbor.

Wall struck the picturesque note in the plunging stream and the dim hills at Luzerne; at Fishkill the light shimmered on water, nature was vast and majestic, man was small, and from the clouds came shafts of sunlight. The complex topography of hills, of winding roads, and of the river now narrowly bending and now flowing broad and straight was all within the painter's compass—the lazy summer haze, the sky over Castle Garden heavy with a squall, and the clarity after storms. The publisher called attention to the fact that Wall had not worked up his pictures in the studio from hasty sketches as others did, but had completed them on the spot "with a faithful attention to nature."

Thanks to the multiplication of landscape imagery through prints, the amateurs worked for their own satisfaction during these years. Few of them were as

John Neagle, *View on the Schuylkill*

Art Institute of Chicago

accomplished as Benjamin Latrobe when he made his charming small water colors; many of them adapted the plates in Shaw's *Picturesque Views* or the lithographs of Birch and Strickland; and for the more systematic there were such manuals of instruction as Hill's *Drawing Book of Landscape Scenery* and Fielding Lucas' *Baltimore Drawing Book*.

On the professional level, a glance at the occasional landscapes by Allston and Vanderlyn, Morse and Neagle suggests that the art had come of age in America by the 1820's. From the topographical it had moved to the lyrical, the grand, the allegorical; and nature in this decade could mean a variety of things to a variety of people. Both national pride and response to the marvelous welcomed pictures in which the wonders of nature were celebrated, while the writers reminded one that a pushing civilization had not yet destroyed those wonders. John Vanderlyn was one of many, though perhaps the first, to sketch "sublime" Niagara; he was there in 1802 to make one of his several versions which suggest preparation for a panorama, competent and sober records which would inform but not stir the observer to a sense of grandeur.

That objectivity could scarcely satisfy a generation whose favorite authors had sharpened their enjoyment of natural beauty for its own sensuous sake. The lyricism of Bryant and Wordsworth found an echo in the Morse landscapes at Cooperstown in 1827 and 1828; two or three years later, Morse in Switzerland caught the play of light and shadow over snowy peaks, green slopes, cottage, and roadway in his *Wetterhorn and the Falls of the Reichenbach.* The same sunniness was in John Neagle's *View on the Schuylkill,* bathing the tree stump and burdock and the doll-like small girl with her dog, and falling aslant trees which were real trees and not generalized types. This landscape had an easier and less formal rhythm than that of Morse, and its handling was bolder.

But Americans would not yet surrender themselves completely to sheer pleasure in rocks and forests. The religious and the moral fibers were still tough in them, and both the sublime and the picturesque were more acceptable when in the service of the elevating thought. Bryant was descended from Mayflower Puritans and never forgot that

> the groves were God's first temples.

His "Thanatopsis" has been called a "great Puritan dirge"; and although he could make his readers see and feel the glitter of the mighty Hudson with Sunday bells

Washington Allston, *Italian Landscape*

Addison Gallery of American Art, Andover, Mass.

ringing across the water, he could also describe Time as a river whose flood swept mankind into eternity.

This moral overtone was in the landscapes of Washington Allston, one of which he painted in his college days. This favored child of Charleston and Newport devoured the *Mysteries of Udolpho* and painted the episode of Damon and Musidora from Thomson's *Seasons*—a passage which must equally have appealed to the sensuous and the priggishly moral in the Harvard student. In Rome, Allston retraced the steps of Nicolas Poussin, who dreamed among those ruins how to bring the ancient world to life. His *Italian Landscape* had the mellowness of a Golden Age which had haunted the Bostonian ever since, as an undergraduate at Harvard, he had read in the *Seasons* of

> . . . . stupendous rocks,
> That from the sun-redoubling valley lift,
> Cool to the middle air, their tawny tops;
> Where palaces and fanes and villas rise;
> And gardens smile around, and cultured fields,
> And fountains gush, and careless herds and flocks
> Securely stray . . . .

Allston's picture, like the one drawn by Thomson, is "a world within itself, disdaining all assault"; yet it has neither the breadth nor the majesty of Poussin, even though Poussin's well-placed trees grow in it, his temples catch the warm light and his figures move in the somber foreground, his bridge repeats itself in mirror-smooth water. The Poussin words are there, but not the sonorous phrasing.

Allston proved that he could create rocky valleys, gnarled oaks, and storm-filled skies with a power of their own which must have delighted his friend and fellow traveler Coleridge. His *Elijah in the Desert* was a thoroughly "picturesque" achievement hinting at the admired Salvator Rosa in its great gnarled tree, a stark metaphor of desolation (Boston Mus. Fine Arts). (See color plate 5.) Vanderlyn borrowed that tree for one of his Niagaras, but not its impact on one's feelings; and it was Allston's "early turn for the wild, the marvelous, the terrible"—a phrase of Mrs. Jameson's—which made possible his awesome *Deluge* with its livid sea-washed bodies under a terrible sky.

Landscape became not a side line but an art in the

ten years between Guy's show of 1820 and Joshua Shaw's exhibition at Sully's Gallery in Philadelphia. In Thomas Doughty and Thomas Cole—soon to be joined by Asher Durand—America now had painters for whom landscape was to be a lifelong occupation. Doughty gave up the leather business in 1820 to be a professional painter in Philadelphia with no more preparation than some advice by Sully and a few lessons in drawing with India ink. By the next year he had eight canvases for the Academy show, revealing his sensitiveness to the play of light over near forms and the loveliness of far distance, though his tones were brownish and his brushwork was dry.

Durand did not give up engraving for the palette until the mid-thirties. Meanwhile, Americans could admire his reproductions of Trumbull's *Declaration* and Vanderlyn's *Ariadne,* or the six small but exquisite plates for a series called *The American Landscape* of which only one number appeared in 1830.

As a youth in frontier Steubenville, Ohio, Thomas Cole was stirred by the wilderness around him, and his introspective mind nourished itself on the romantic poets. In the late 1820's he painted with Doughty in the White Mountains and swung his cloud forms, trailing blue mists, and glittering crags into a rhythm of his own. He was becoming what Goethe called an Imaginant, a man with the power to create worlds. Comparing the serene Claude with the tormented Rosa, Cole once said, "I believe I am best in the stormy and wild."

The painter's friends agreed with him, and Bryant once compared the impact of his early work to the excitement of some great discovery. Cole's pictures, he said, "carried the eye over scenes of wild grandeur peculiar to our country, over our aerial mountain tops with their mighty growth of forests never touched by the axe, along the bank of streams never deformed by culture and into the depth of skies bright with the hues of our own climate."

When Cole departed for Europe in 1829, Bryant wrote him a sonnet. The painter, he said, had fixed the living image of America on his canvas, the lone lakes and the solemn streams, the desert and the rock. Everywhere in Europe Cole would find paths, graves, and ruins which marked the trace of men. The poem ended with a warning:

> Gaze on them, till the tears shall dim thy sight,
> But keep that earlier, wilder image bright.

Washington Allston, *The Deluge* (detail)

Metropolitan Museum of Art, New York City

COLOR SECTION

1. John S. Copley, *Nathaniel Hurd* (detail), ca. 1765–1770

Cleveland Museum of Art

Copley was largely a self-taught provincial in his late twenties when he made the likeness of this local silversmith, yet here is proof that he could draw with great precision and give a startling reality to his subject in three dimensions by his strong, sure handling of lights and shadows. At first his application of pigment was dry and smoothly uniform, but already in this portrait he could render contrasts of material and texture—the soft white shirt cuffs, the silken luster of the gown, the glittering buttons, the sheen of leather bindings—and do so with a directness of touch which marks the painter in command of his medium. The hands, with warm reflections in their deep shadows, are as individual as the face. As Virgil Barker has said, they are a portrait in themselves.

2. John James Audubon, *Purple Grackle*

New York Historical Society

As a naturalist, Audubon wished in Plate VII of his *Birds of America* to show this species of blackbird "in the exercise of their wicked ways"; as an artist trained in the firm draftsmanship of Jacques-Louis David and possessed of a fine feeling for decorative design on the large white page, he created a delightful pattern with the dark shapes of the birds against the lighter corn, drew every detail of feather and of corn silk with exquisite precision, and in delicate washes of water color contrasted the blue-black iridescence of the grackles with the tawny yellows and soft greens of their natural setting.

3. Raphaelle Peale, *Still Life,* ca. 1820

Toledo Museum of Art

Peale's arrangement of his subject on a table top against a shadowed wall and his meticulous rendering of detail remind us of the work of the Dutch painters, some of which the American must have seen. One can imagine with what relish for the tangible the artist worked to suggest the density and the weight of each object, the characteristic texture of an orange or a grape, the gleam of a wineglass in half-light. But Peale goes beyond mere transcription to create a pleasant harmony of colors, to build his elements into a satisfyingly balanced whole which is centered on the bowl and the peeled orange but is saved from a rigid and obvious symmetry by the lighting of the wall and by the seemingly casual placing of the fruit. His intensity of observation gives extraordinary life to these inert things, communicates his own affection for the common forms of matter, and renews our response to the often ignored beauty of the familiar.

4. Gilbert Stuart, *Mrs. Perez Morton* (detail), ca. 1802

Worcester Art Museum

Because it was never completed, this canvas tells us how Stuart, basing his technique on that of the contemporary British painters, proceeded from the rough sketch to the finished likeness in a series of orderly stages: first, the drawing of the principal shapes with a brush; then the preliminary blocking in of the lights and shades to suggest the volumes, and the rubbing of colors into this brownish underpainting to suggest the particular hues of dress, scarf, and sky. Only in the head has Stuart carried the process further by defining the features, creating the flesh tones, and adding those crisp accents which bring the subject vividly to life. Stuart's use of few colors, his avoidance of complex and muddy mixtures, his sketchlike handling, established a new standard of freshness and of painterly directness for the American artists who observed his work.

5. Washington Allston, *Elijah in the Desert,* 1818

Boston Museum of Fine Arts

Allston had studied Poussin and the Venetian masters with their "gorgeous concert of color." Out of similar motifs—the gnarled tree, the small foreground figure, the brown crags of the near distance, the blue peaks of the far, the scudding clouds against a bright sky—and by using the process of underpainting and glazing, by contrasting warm and cool tones, and by washes of pigment which unified the whole, he achieved a poetry of his own, a sense of vast and lonely space, which made him the American pioneer in the use of color for expressive ends.

6. John Vanderlyn, *Marius amidst the Ruins of Carthage* (detail), 1807

M. H. de Young Memorial Museum, San Francisco

Under the spell of antiquity in Rome and inspired by the neoclassical art of Jacques-Louis David in Paris, young Vanderlyn obeyed every precept of the school in this ambitious canvas: the heroic theme from ancient history, the pose of his Marius which follows that of antique statues, the head based on a Roman portrait bust, the background ruins which were done from a small studio model, the cold precision of the drawing, the careful modeling of the ivory-smooth body and its scarlet drapery. The great man broods in exile, a colored statue rather than a living person, in a work of disciplined craftsmanship where color is subordinated to the sculpturesque rendering of form by a man who, in the words of a contemporary critic, was "a little Frenchified" in his notions of painting.

7. Thomas Cole, *Expulsion from the Garden of Eden,* 1827–1828

Boston Museum of Fine Arts, Karolik Collection

The rocky gateway of Eden, centered in Cole's design, separates two worlds: the lush green fields, bright flowers, and clean sunshine of the garden, and the outer world of dark violence, of writhing trees, storm-laden clouds, and crashing torrent into which the two small figures have fled, pursued by shafts of angry light. Cole's handling of details was overprecise, his colors turgid; but one recognizes his skill in melodramatic contrast, his masterly control of light, and the powerful handling of masses which give this early work its lurid unity.

8. William S. Mount, *The Power of Music* (detail), 1847

Century Association, N.Y.

This figure is divided from the others in the painting by Mount's favorite device, a barn door, whose shadows repeat the directions of the Negro's arm and leg. The fine head, the patched and faded work clothes, the jug and axe beside him, are fully characterized by meticulous drawing. With the aid of several books on the technique of painting, Mount worked out his own palette with a limited range of pigments, preferring the durable earth colors. Establishing his main darks and lights with brownish tones, he varied them by adding brighter passages without disturbing the warm unity of his picture. Details and the contrasting textures of workworn fabric and weather-beaten wood are indicated with a sleek touch which has the glisten of sunlight.

9. Edward Hicks, *The Residence of David Twining, 1787,* 1845–1848

Abby Aldrich Rockefeller Folk Art Collection, Williamsburg, Va.

This is the farm of the "primitive" artist's boyhood in Bucks County as he remembered it in his sixties, a faithful and loving inventory which includes the farm buildings, ten people, and over thirty animals. On the uptilted plane of the ground he distributes these in an orderly and coherent pattern. There are odd discrepancies of scale and of perspective, but the precise drawing, the warm browns and tempered greens, the neatly and simply stated relationships of people and work, are symbols of the thrift and peaceful competence of Quakers.

10. William M. Hunt, *Chief Justice Lemuel Shaw* (detail), ca. 1860

Court House, Salem, Mass.

The artist wished Shaw "to look as he did in court while giving his charge to the jury." His work with Millet in France had taught him to think of the whole before the parts, to reveal essentials and ignore details. Hunt concentrated on the massive head with its powerfully modeled features, and on the monumental dark silhouette of Shaw's rumpled and baggy figure against a plain yellowish-brown wall. Every contour and every shadowed form speak of the massive strength, the stern New England conscience of the Justice.

11. George Inness, *The Coming Storm,* ca. 1880

Addison Gallery of American Art, Andover, Mass.

Inness once said that his aim was not to instruct or to edify but to awaken an emotion, to convey his own highly individual sense of the wonder and mystery of nature in her shifting moods. He had freed himself from the niggling details, the hot brown tones and the compositional clichés of the earlier landscape painters when he caught this fleeting moment before the storm blots out a sunny countryside. His colors—the lush green of meadows, the momentary glint of treetops touched by the sun, the turbulent sky—are those of nature keenly observed and brilliantly summarized with a brush which suggests rather than literally describes. As his contemporary, James Jarves, said, "We can breathe in his atmosphere and travel far and wide in his landscape."

12. Thomas Eakins, *William Rush Carving the Allegorical Figure of the Schuylkill River* (detail), 1877

Philadelphia Museum of Art

To illustrate the legend of the girl who consented to pose for the Philadelphia sculptor, Eakins recreated a dim workshop where a shaft of warm light throws into powerful relief the central figure of the model, the glow of whose flesh reminds one of the nudes of Rembrandt. All the artist's profound knowledge of the body, its bony framework, its muscular action, its subtle variations of color, went into the painting of this figure, but also a Whitmanesque reverence for its youthful grace.

13. Albert Ryder, *Constance,* completed 1896

Boston Museum of Fine Arts

In Chaucer's *Man of Law's Tale* an emperor's daughter was cast adrift with her baby son and, after years of wandering, miraculously reached Rome. The theme haunted Ryder's imagination—the small boat in an immense sea under a sky heavy with the threat of storm. In the long and patient process of painting and repainting, he reduced the scene to its essential shapes—the dimly seen bulk of the boat, the endless horizon, the ominous cloud forms—and his strangely glowing greens and yellows create an unforgettable image of perilous isolation.

14. John Sargent, *Daughters of Edward D. Boit* (detail), 1882

Boston Museum of Fine Arts

Four children, informally posed in the shadowed hall of their home, are given a startling bodily existence by a magician of the brush, whose palette ranged from a dazzling white to the black of stockings. Having developed his own version of the Impressionist techniques, Sargent constructs each figure and renders the impact of strong light upon it with bold strokes of the brush which are meaningless when closely observed but skillfully calculated to produce an illusion when seen from a distance. At twenty-six, Sargent already is a master of surface "realism," of charm without penetration.

15. Maurice Prendergast, *Central Park,* ca. 1900–1902

Whitney Museum of American Art

This mild and sensitive artist, whose manner was influenced by Cézanne, Bonnard, Signac, and other experimentalists, worked out his own personal style to convey his pleasure in holiday occasions when many people make intricate arabesques of gay colors. Central Park was so planned that people on foot, horseback riders, and carriages could move in separate areas, and Prendergast has taken advantage of that scheme to create a pattern in horizontal bands. Within this basic plan he orders his bright shapes and hues: the blue dresses and red umbrellas, the varying browns of horses, the darker accents of carriages against the mild green foliage, the long band of seated people stabilizing the design. He manages to reconcile space-depth with two-dimensional painted surface, and his thin washes of water color characterize the place and the people without sacrificing the over-all beauty of a charming and exquisite mosaic.

Homer's water colors in Nassau have a wider range of color and a more brilliant light than his northern scenes. No artist has better understood the peculiar capacity of this medium for direct, fresh, and vivid suggestion by the most economical of means—thin washes which allow the white paper to give them luminosity, and swift indications of solid form made with a minimum of brush strokes. By such deft means Homer gives us the receding sandy beach under a hot sun, the battered dory, the glistening body of the Negro; he sends the black clouds scudding across the sky in the aftermath of the storm, and makes the untouched white paper suggest the white crests of surf. A few deft touches are enough to evoke wind-tossed palms on a distant headland, the texture of shattered wood, the sharp spikes of beach grass. On such occasions as this the hardheaded realist gives us, almost in spite of himself, a hint of tragedy.

16. Winslow Homer, *After the Tornado* (detail), 1898–1899

Art Institute of Chicago

17. John Marin, *Tunk Mountains, Autumn, Maine,* 1945

Phillips Memorial Gallery, Washington, D.C.

Using a shorthand of his own invention, not to describe space by means of "correct" perspective and atmospheric gradations, but rather to convey the visual excitement of a crisp fall day, Marin creates a riotous clash of autumnal browns, the yellow and crimson of foliage, and the brilliant blue of an October sky. All is in movement—the heave and roll of hills, the restlessness of the nearby trees, and the rapid march of clouds; yet all elements in this controlled and intricate pattern are kept on the two-dimensional plane of the canvas without losing their power to suggest the generously modeled forms of earth and a vast sweep of countryside. Marin gives us not only the things seen but the exhilaration of seeing.

18. John Sloan, *Three A.M.* (detail), 1909

Philadelphia Museum of Art

Like his fellow artists of the "ash can school," Sloan found homely urban subjects and rendered them with a rugged simplicity. This girl, seen in "night vigils at the back window of a Twenty-third Street studio," is a vigorous and sketch-like study, her warm flesh and white nightgown indicated with a broad, direct brush against the contrasting green wall of a cheap kitchen. There are no subtleties, no probing of character, but a sympathetic and unpretentious response to the ordinary, in the tradition of American genre painting.

19. Irene R. Pereira, *Undulating Arrangement,* 1947

Wadsworth Atheneum, Hartford, Conn.

Pereira is at once a philosopher, a scientist, and a poet in her effort to explore the nature of space and to embody in objective forms the unity behind all experience. She has given new dimensions, literally and figuratively, to abstract art by exploiting the visual possibilities of glass, sand, mica, marble dust, parchment, gold leaf, plastic, and other materials, and by painting, as in this instance, on several transparent planes which project from the background and through which light and color are transmitted in complex and ever-changing ways.

20. Edward Hopper, *Pennsylvania Coal Town,* 1947

Butler Institute of American Art, Youngstown, Ohio

No self-conscious regionalist but an artist of classical restraint, Hopper has suppressed every detail which could diminish the strength of his statement, in order to convey not only the nature of a place but his feeling for it. The stolid cornices, the mustard-colored shingles, the vulgar urn, the man in shirt sleeves in hard sunlight, powerfully summarize all such streets and people we have seen; but these are ordered in a design whose visual rightness and whose underlying intensity go far beyond the merely picturesque.

21. Charles Burchfield, *An April Mood,* 1955

Whitney Museum of American Art

In his early works the artist employed a rather obvious expressionism in which childhood terrors were conveyed by frightening shapes; later, he used his characteristically drab palette to comment on the ugliness of mining towns and Midwestern cities. In this recent work he uses water color on a scale usually reserved for oils to suggest the death of nature and her annual rebirth with a muted palette of blue-greys and browns, his rain-heavy clouds pressing down upon soggy fields, his dead trees gesturing grotesquely, the whole scene a powerful synthesis of the previous phases of his art.

22. Morris Graves, *Guardian,* 1952

University of Illinois, Urbana, Ill.

This creature of Graves' imagination, superbly drawn and delicately colored, poised on a tawny yellow ground, with its ghostlike white head, piercing black eyes, and crown of antlers, with a hint of blood-red in its plumage, has the monumental grace of the birds that Oriental artists evoke on gold screens. Its power as a symbol is enhanced by dual and contradictory suggestions: on the one hand a gentle and serene wisdom, on the other a fierce capacity to rend and to destroy.

23. Loren MacIver, *Venice,* 1949

Whitney Museum of American Art

This is not the Venice of the postcards, nor has it the descriptive savors of Guardi and Canaletto. This Venice exists in the mind and is a figment of memory, whose essence has been recaptured: a string of palaces turned golden by the sun, a pale blue sky and a wide expanse of deeper blue water, the dip and toss of a patched nearby sail. Here, as elsewhere, MacIver gives us not the place itself but the magical reverberation of its shimmer and movement in the traveler's recollection.

24. Hyman Bloom, *The Anatomist* (detail), 1953

Whitney Museum of American Art

Bloom's colors, applied in many layers of thick and of transparent pigment, are violently insistent, with something of the glowing radiance of stained glass. Presenting the cadaver on an uptilted slab as though to spare us nothing, the painter exposes the torn flesh under the blood-stained hands of the surgeon in seering crimsons, burning yellows, and in the greens and purples of corruption. It is a reminder of death, of the nightmarish brutalities of war and racial persecutions; but it is also a work of art whose writhing pattern of twisted forms and whose livid hues have a terrible beauty.

25. Charles Sheeler, *Architectural Cadences,* 1954

Whitney Museum of American Art

Sheeler has always delighted in the sharply defined complexities of our mechanical environment. He has recently abandoned the photographic detail of his middle years, and draws upon the cubist experiments of his early period in order to define architectural continuities and blocks of contrasting sun and shadow in a counterpoint of overlapping and intersecting walls and roofs. Using a restricted palette of clean blues, purples, and browns, and reducing his industrial objects to semiabstract shapes, he gives each element its necessary place in a design which functions as smoothly as a machine but has the rhythm of a musical composition.

26. Mark Tobey, *Broadway,* 1936

Metropolitan Museum of Art, N.Y., Arthur H. Hearn Fund, 1942

A journey to the Far East revealed to Tobey the intricate and allusive beauty of Oriental calligraphy. Here he employs his "white writing" to convey his enchantment with what Dorothy Miller has aptly called "the electric night of cities"; against a dark background his threadlike lines of white tempera weave a synthesis of crowded sidewalks, jammed traffic, densely packed buildings, and flashing signs. Tobey has written a poem on the infinite complexity of an American city, its glittering density, and its reduction of man to a nameless atom.

27. Arshile Gorky, *The Liver Is the Cock's Comb,* 1944

Albright Art Gallery, Buffalo, N.Y.

As a surrealist, Gorky knew that what we see is shaped and colored by the subconscious. His forms, although based on study of natural objects, take on a tantalizing, hybrid quality in this flashing improvisation, with its disturbing hints, its rich variations on a few basic hues. This explosive phantasy whose shapes and colors swing into a feverish and mocking dance is the work of an elegant draftsman whose seeming spontaneity conceals a long and careful preparation, a skillfully conceived design.

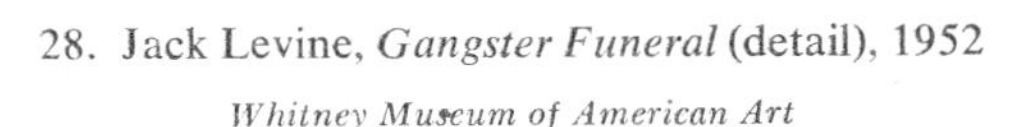

28. Jack Levine, *Gangster Funeral* (detail), 1952

Whitney Museum of American Art

Critics have traced the influence of Rouault and Soutine in Levine's earlier handling of pigment, but his irony and his seemingly mild but often bitter sarcasm are his own. His touch is more delicate and more suggestive in this recent work, where the gently caricatured faces of the gangster's friends seem to float in the yellow atmosphere, the contrived murkiness of an official place of mourning, and where the humorous and the macabre, the respectable and the sinister, are oddly mingled in an atmosphere of expensive flowers and simulated grief.

29. Jackson Pollock, *Convergence,* 1952

Albright Art Gallery, Buffalo, N.Y.

Pollock placed his canvas on the studio floor and with no preconceived plan dripped pigment from a brush, stick, or trowel in large rhythm[illegible]. As he proceeded, the emerging complex suggested its own development through more intricate involvements of varied colors which were the visual trace of the painter's own gestures, until he felt that the work "existed on its own," not as a centered composition adapted to its rectangle, but as an ever-expanding image intense in every part and capable, one feels, of infinite extension. For some observers, a Pollock painting presents a fascinating pattern, a richly decorative one; others find here "a visualization of that remorseless consolation—in the end is the beginning," a metamorphosis of the phenomena of our present world into the energy, the infinite complexity, the continuity which is common to them all.

30. Ben Shahn, *The Blind Botanist,* 1954

Wichita Art Museum, Roland P. Murdock Collection

Shahn's painting plays subtle variations on a few colors, mainly a red-orange and a greenish blue, and there is a visual counterpoint between the stark, monumental bulk of the man and the twisting, spiky shapes of the plant. The artist is as economical as he is expressive in the drawing of the sensitive blind face and the strong hands which replace sight by touch. As a symbol, Shahn's botanist is less obvious and more susceptible of varying interpretations than his earlier images of humanity, and suggests rather than baldly states the artist's deep sympathy for man's groping effort to understand his present world.

BOOK THREE

DEMOCRATIC VISTAS

c. 1830 – c. 1870

John Rogers group, *Checkers Up at the Farm* ▶

New York Historical Society

PART ONE

JACKSONIAN FERMENT

INTRODUCTION / SHAPES OF DEMOCRACY

That fastidious gentleman, Thomas Hamilton, no sooner stepped on shore in New York than he saw a huge placard:

> Jackson Forever,
> Go The Whole Hog!

His subsequent travels only confirmed the rudeness of this first impression. *Men and Manners in America* described a nation where the mob was dictator, where people pitchforked food into themselves, built country houses with three-story columns which supported nothing, and laid out Euclidean towns which were a "mathematical infringement on the rights of individual eccentricity." The citizens who shouldered one another at Presidential receptions were sooty artificers begriming the furniture, millers who left flour tracks on the White House carpets, Irish canal diggers who smelled of sweat.

The domestic manners of Jacksonian America likewise shocked that cultural missionary, Frances Trollope. Cincinnati men in their shirt sleeves, reeking of onions and whisky, thumped their feet in theater boxes; even that stately Hall of Representatives which Morse had painted a few years before was filled when she saw it with men who sat in the most unseemly of attitudes with their hats on and spat with a fluency which decency forbade her to describe. Yet Fanny discovered occasional signs of taste: there were splendid exhibitions of natural science in the Peales' Baltimore Museum, and in the Philadelphia Water Works a charming *jet d'eau* which fell upon the head of a marble naiad of snowy whiteness—a chaste if inaccurate reference to the Rush fountain. Her eye found pleasure in the handsome green blinds and the well-carpeted floors of the upper-class town houses and in the "pretty coxcomalities" of their parlors. One year before Andrew Jackson became President she made her own contribution to architectural chaos by building her Bazaar in Cincinnati, a composite of Gothic, Classic, Moorish, and Venetian which was known as "Trollope's Folly."

That other Fanny who was an actress and the daughter of Charles Kemble found time between playing Violante in draughty theaters to appraise the land and the people with greater shrewdness and a deeper sympathy. In Philadelphia she sat for Thomas Sully and found the cool clear marble of the Chestnut Street bank in harmony with the brilliant American sky and the clean atmosphere. New England reminded her of home and it was there she met Doctor Parkman and Doctor Channing in Bulfinch drawing rooms whose mantels held marble statuettes by Canova. Those plebeian pits and galleries which had so offended Mrs. Trollope were evidence for Fanny that the mass of people had not, like the sophisticated classes, lost their power of imagination, but still retained their sympathy for the loves of Juliet and the sorrows of Ophelia.

Fanny was a spoiled, perverse, and unreal creature to the tough-minded Harriet Martineau, who saw the last wild buffalo herd in Kentucky, played hostess to Daniel Webster and seven Supreme Court judges, and called Mrs. Trollope's Bazaar the great deformity of Cincinnati. A Jacksonian reception from which Thomas Hamilton recoiled seemed to Harriet a "very fine spectacle," and Margaret Fuller was set down as a pedantic woman in a pedantic town and a pedantic age.

It was the aristocrat Alexis de Tocqueville who saw the essential America beneath these crudities and contradictions in 1831 and 1832. Seven years after his visit, the American edition of his *Democracy in America* recorded his belief that the people of the northern states were the most enlightened under the sun. "America, then, exhibits in her social state a most extraordinary phenomenon. Men are there seen on a greater equality in point of fortune and intellect, or, in other words more equal in their strength, than in any other country of the world or in any age of which history has preserved the remembrance." And after Tocqueville the English geologist Charles Lyell responded to the freshness and hopefulness of a country where, as he said, instead of dwelling on the past and on the signs of pomp and grandeur which have vanished, the mind was filled with images of coming power and splendor.

Jacksonian America, in short, was furiously at work, her independence won and her quarrels with Europe at an end, building a democracy. Her leaders were, in Arthur Schlesinger's phrase, the keepers of the Jeffersonian conscience; her task was nothing less than the rounding out of a continent; and Bancroft proclaimed as her mission the culture and happiness of the mass of her people.

No wonder the observant foreigner and the nation-proud American were stunned by the speed and violence with which the experiment went forward. Thirteen colonies had become twenty-four states and in the two decades which followed Jackson's inauguration Texas and California and Oregon swelled the nation's size. Ambitious men thrust into the new territories, taking their local notions and habits with them: the pioneering woodsman, the exploring scientist, the surveyor, the buyer and seller of land, the migrant Yankee in his thousands with all his possessions in a wagon or on a flatboat, climbing mountain passes and pushing up rivers, his cabin in a few months giving place to his farmhouse, his first rough clearing to a village.

Steadily the human tide advanced to fill the great middle basin which William Gallagher described as the most stupendous inland valley upon which the sun shone, scooped out for man's use by the hand of Omnipotence. Year by year the Indian receded, Gallagher said, into the recesses of the wilderness "as the dusky shadows of a dark and unblest age recede and disappear before the light of a high, Christian civilization." Destiny, he wrote, had decreed that the red heathen give place to his betters and that America should look upon two oceans.

Destiny moved along the waters, up rivers and down canals, and within the first Jacksonian decade the steamboats multiplied on midwestern streams; there were bridges of iron to shorten distances, and at least the beginnings of a railroad network which by the end of the Civil War would cross a continent, pushing through prairies and over mountain passes which had known only the covered wagon, the mail coach, and the pony express.

Thanks to water, steam, and iron there were nearly twice as many people in the United States in 1850 as in 1830—English and Welsh, Scotch and Irish, Germans and Dutchmen, Swedes and Belgians—and all were welcome in the expanding West and in the urban centers of the North whose factories and shops drew young men and women from the small agricultural villages. Much that seemed "picturesque" in the westward settling derived from the odd folkways of the immigrant; much of the struggle for equality was waged by the city workers who stood from sunrise to sunset before the machines at Lowell and held their first trade-union meetings in the opening years of Jackson's presidency.

To organize the sprawling nation was a task which called for more than the accustomed American ingenuity. Out of the tensions of political life came the fierce party spirit of the local caucus, the barbecue, and the stump speaker's rally; out of the needs of expanding capitalism came the chartered corporation and the new moneyed class, the Biddles and the Wards. Men discussed liberty and self-realization no longer in terms of Jeffersonian philosophy but on the political-economic level of Jackson the realist. If the bank war of the eighteen thirties embroiled a whole continent it was because here the issue was most sharply joined: on the one hand Nicholas Biddle's private monopoly on the national money and on the other an administration determined, as Jackson said, that laws be not used to make the rich richer and the potent more powerful.

While the bank war educated a whole people in the nature of democracy's new problems, tensions of another sort kept life in unstable equilibrium. Each of the three great regions had its own version of the national good: the industrial North with its great cities where, because inequality was so painfully obvious, the spokesmen of reaction and of reform were most active and eloquent; the spacious West where every man was the equal of his fellow on the economic level and insisted on translating this frontier democracy into politics; the southern empire of King Cotton where slavery was essential to the survival of the great plantation and where, as one man prophesied in 1840, "in a few years owing to the operation of this institution upon our unparalleled natural advantages, we shall be the richest people beneath the bend of the rainbow."

And there were tensions within tensions in this turbulent America: the Southerner hesitating between the enmity of northern radicals and the friendship of northern business; the Know-Nothings rising against the foreign-born in the fifties; conservative Democrats fighting their own left-wing Locofocos; the force of Jacksonianism checked by the coming of Polk one year before Old Hickory died; the Conscience Whigs joining Free-Soil Democrats as the Republican party in 1856 became the party of Lincoln; the great civil conflict which broke out five years later.

These were the "peculiar, original and creative circumstances" of which Channing had once spoken, and never before had they found such vigorous expression in the verbal and visual arts. There was a fresh consciousness of the national past in Bancroft's *History,* whose first volume appeared in the years of the bank war to be followed by the works of Parkman and Prescott, none of them a mere assembling of legends but rather a scholarly re-creation of achievement. And the historians, poets, and essay writers of the day to a surprising degree took sides with the Democrats in a strife which, as Theodore Sedgwick said, urged forward the whole American mind: Hawthorne and Whittier in the *Democratic Review,* Irving until he drew back from the roughness of the Locofocos, Hiram Powers from his sculptor's studio in Florence, Bryant in the New York *Evening Post,* and Bancroft in the *North American Review.*

The more sedate publications were in the hands of Whigs, but Orestes Brownson issued his fiery paper on "The Laboring Classes" in his own *Boston Quarterly Review.* To the intelligentsia, Coleridge and Byron were geniuses; to the anonymous author of "Poetry for the People," which appeared in the *United States Magazine* in 1843, the former seemed a tiresome conservative glorifying the good old times and the latter a melodramatic egotist. Among Emerson's "heretics with seething brains" were Garrison of the *Liberator,* Brisbane the disciple of Fourier, and the blacksmith Elihu Burritt traveling from Connecticut to Brussels in the cause of peace. Industrial America bred its own critics and reformers, and the contrast between Nicholas Biddle's white Parthenon and the dingy slums along the Delaware was not lost on Matthew Carey. Utopian Frances Wright planned the colony of "Nashoba" and Robert Owen his "New Harmony," while the Sons of Temperance organized their lodges in the forties, each with its "worthy patriarch."

Not all these voices spoke unreservedly for the Jacksonian idea. The notion of cultural equality implied a leveling downward as one man sought to prove his taste as good as another's; and more than one intellectual asked himself, as Cooper did, whether young Hercules was not passing too rapidly from the gristle into the bone. Samuel Morse warned Cooper in 1833 that he would return to an America whose tastes and manners had profoundly changed; and Cooper in turn wrote in 1836 to Horatio Greenough, "You are in a country in which every man swaggers and talks, knowledge or no knowledge; brains or no brains; taste or no taste. They are all *ex nato* connoisseurs . . ."

Despite his fear of numbers, however, Cooper maintained in *The Sea Lions* that the gravitating toward a common center was more to be desired than the mutual repulsion between the extremes of society which had angered him in Europe. The great republic was laying the foundation for the enjoyment of generations to come. Despite mediocrity, "the direction is onward, and when the task shall be achieved, the work will stand on a base so broad as to secure its upright attitude for ages." And friend Greenough responded with even more warmth to America's hopeful mood, declaring England had failed to understand the new democracy:

> She taunted us because there were no statues or frescoes in our log-cabins; she pronounced us unmusical because we did not sit down in the swamp with an Indian on one side, and a rattlesnake on the other, to play the violin.

Greenough believed that the art of a young people must develop slowly, not by the morbid growth which had produced the "royal mushroom at Versailles." In the long run "the monuments, the pictures, the statues of the Republic will represent what the people love and wish for—not what they can be made to accept."

It was a new thing in America, this willingness to see in the awkward and the unfinished not signs of inferiority but signs of health. It moved Dunlap to salute "that thrice happy country where the man of virtue and talents is the only acknowledged superior, where the artist needs no protector and acknowledges no patron." Twenty-two years later it inspired Walt Whitman's "Song of the Broad-Axe":

> The main shapes arise!
> Shapes of Democracy total, result of centuries . . . .

Ralph Waldo Emerson, like his friend Thoreau, stood aloof on most occasions from literary politics; they were "unsocial worshippers, talkers who talked the sun and moon away, speaking for thoughts and principles not marketable or perishable." Yet Emerson offered in the *Dial* a definition of art within which the fierce loyalties and the expanding self-concern of creative minds could find complete expression. Art, he said, is the conscious utterance of thought by speech or action to any end. From the tattooing of the Owyhees to the Vatican Gallery, it is the spirit's voluntary use and combination of things to serve its end. Enthusiasms like love, patriotism, or religion have bred the arts, never dilettantism or holidays; and the deeper sources of art are as indigenous to Massachusetts as to Tuscany or the Isles of Greece. Too many poets, Emerson said on another occasion, are content to write only from the fancy, at a safe distance from their own experience.

> We do not, with sufficient plainness, or sufficient profoundness, address ourselves to life, nor dare we chant our own times and social circumstance. . . . We have yet had no genius in America, with tyrannous eye, which knew the value of our incomparable materials, and saw, in the barbarism and materialism of the times, another carnival of the same gods whose picture he so much admires in Homer. . . . Banks and tariffs, the newspaper and caucus, Methodism and Unitarianism, are flat and dull to dull people, but rest on the same foundations of wonder as the town of Troy, and the temple of Delphos, and are as swiftly passing away. . . . Our log-rolling, our stumps and their politics, our fisheries, our Negroes, and Indians, our boats and our repudiations, the wrath of rogues and the pusillanimity of honest men, the Northern trade, the Southern planting, the Western clearing, Oregon and Texas are yet unsung.

Emerson lived to see his challenge accepted by poets, novelists, and painters, many of whom were deaf to his transcendental overtones. Whitman, the young editor of the Brooklyn *Daily Eagle,* already knew the value of our incomparable materials and would come as close as any man to being the genius with tyrannous eye. Homeric legends of her own were forming in the West —gaunt Johnny Appleseed wandering in Ohio with his sack of seed, a Bible in hand and a stewpan on his head; the lumberjack Paul Bunyan who was ninety-seven axe handles tall and the smokestacks of whose sawmill had to be lowered on hinges to let the clouds go by; Mike Fink, last of the boatmen, a brown Hercules in moccasins, red flannel shirt, and blue stocking cap whom Morton Neville described as the Rob Roy of the Mississippi. Our stumps and their politics were in the pages of Longstreet's *Georgia Scenes* and Baldwin's *Flush Times of Alabama and Mississippi;* our Indians inspired the *Algic Researches* of that ethnologist with an imagination, Henry Schoolcraft, and likewise Cooper's novels and the *Yemassee* of William Gilmore Simms. Our boats were in Benjamin Drake's *Tales and Sketches from the Queen City* with its oddly assembled passengers aboard the "Sea Serpent"—the courtly southern major, the cheesemaker from the Western Reserve, the ladies napping in their cabins. As for the southern planting and the western clearing, John P. Kennedy's *Swallow Barn* was a mellow-toned picture of life in the Old Dominion, and Caroline Kirkland of Michigan described in *A New Home—Who'll Follow?* how Tinkerville rose in three years from a plan drawn with chalk on a barroom floor to a town whose cottages had chintz-covered sofas, pianos, and well-filled bookcases.

The writers were not alone in their effort to record the American times and social circumstances; the visual arts as well caught the excitement and the novelty of these years. The national capital was a symbol of rapid growth and hopeful confusion: a few scattered temples, a canal filled with sewage, a prancing bronze of Andrew Jackson, and the stump of an obelisk. The Capitol building itself acquired two sprawling wings and congressmen stumbled over blocks of stone and lumber on their way to the new chambers while above them rose the naked iron skeleton of the great dome. In the country as a whole the Greek fever gave way to the Gothic mania in building and the Gothic to the Tuscan, the Norman, the Indescribable as swiftly as the Americans changed their politics, their tastes in reading, their modes of travel, and their methods of getting ahead.

The square-shouldered individualism of the age spoke from her painted portraits and her daguerreotypes. A thirst for self-improvement drove crowds to Lyceum lectures; it filled the theaters and town halls where Jenny Lind sang arias from the *Messiah* with *Home Sweet Home* for an encore; it sent those who had earned leisure to the southern spas or up and down the Mississippi on thick-carpeted and bedizened steamboats. The scientific curiosity of these years was nourished by artists who painted the dress and customs of the Indian, the orchids of South America, and the icebergs of Labrador. The spectacle of a people's westward expansion enlarged both the subject matter and the actual scale of landscape painting. Still life flourished because the Jacksonian found, as Whitman did, "ever the most precious in the common"; the genre painters peopled their canvases with a variety of human types and with new forms of local color.

Never before had so warm an encouragement supported painters and sculptors; and, for a time at least, many patrons spent more freely on native work and were content with old masters at second hand in the copies they hired their fellow countrymen to make in London, Paris, and Rome. Robert Gilmor financed the European study of Alfred J. Miller, and William Thompson Walters ordered copies of Miller's Indian paintings for his Baltimore collection. That Whig of Whigs, Philip Hone of New York, who looked upon Abolitionists, strikers, "low Irish" immigrants, and the proponents of universal suffrage with equal scorn, wrote in 1845 that the Goths were in possession of the Capitol; yet the querulous ex-mayor had done much for his country's artists.

Hone was proud of Catlin's courage and the patience of Audubon in their American documentations and he believed every Yankee was bound to prove his love of country by admiring the "solid, massy and umbrageous" landscapes of Thomas Cole. When Cole came to New York, poor, friendless, and "worse than all, modest," as Hone said, he brought two Catskill scenes which he had offered in vain to Philadelphians at ten dollars apiece. These pictures, Hone added in 1848, were now installed in his back parlor for one hundred and twenty-five dollars, a sixth of what the Philadelphia dilettanti would be glad to pay for them.

This willingness to support the living as well as to preserve the dead was to be seen in other rich men's houses. Sam Ward commissioned Cole to paint *The Voyage of Life* series; Joseph Harrison, Jr., wealthy from the sale of railroad equipment to the Russian government, brought home *Penn's Treaty* for the gallery of his mansion on Rittenhouse Square; David Hosack owned a dozen Trumbulls; Luman Reed's pictures were almost all by Americans. When James Jackson Jarves offered a group of Italian paintings worth sixty thousand dollars to any city which would pay him twenty thousand, the *Crayon* declared that the sum asked would be better spent on native works. Harding's Gallery in Boston announced that its paintings were "fresh from the studio of the American artist, not smoke-dried old masters."

The civic-minded collector opened his galleries upon occasion to the public, and not all collections were in private hands. Both the National Academy and the Academy of Fine Arts in New York held exhibitions, the former on an annual basis. Receipts from three years of shows at the Boston Athenaeum totaled ten thousand dollars and from them a Doughty landscape was purchased for three hundred and fifty, two Hardings for seven hundred and fifty, Neagle's *Pat Lyon* for four hundred, and a Trumbull *Gibraltar* for two thousand. Cincinnati's Fine Arts Academy moved one rhymester to proclaim that city "home of the arts and literati," and soon there were similar institutions in Buffalo and in San Francisco.

Even with these forms of encouragement, however, the native artist found himself in competition with foreigners, since the most patriotic collector craved a few old masters, real or synthetic. Uneasily, the American painter watched the profits of Leeds and Company, picture dealers, rise from seventy-five thousand to three hundred thousand dollars in one decade, and the New York branch of Goupil, Vibert and Co. challenge the best of native anecdotists with the work of Frenchmen, while German paintings filled the Düsseldorf Gallery. It was rumored that some dealers had agents who dogged the Yankee abroad, helping him to "discover" lost masterpieces with faked signatures; and one writer from Florence claimed to have seen a shop where a "Salvator Rosa" was being manufactured for a Fifth Avenue merchant prince. A contributor to the *Crayon* in 1860 thus described the middleman:

> He studies the nature of public impressibility; he knows how to work the mine of crude sentiment and turn it to account. With a small outlay of capital and muscular energy he is able, through the press and business agents, to create an excitement in behalf of very ordinary material; he can concentrate public attention upon any one work or man so as to make the public see them in magnified proportions and really believe both to be marvelous productions.

Thus challenged, the artists found means of acting on their own behalf. In such groups as the Lunch Club and the Sketch Club they made friends among connoisseurs and literary men; and in the expansive forties they developed the Art Union as a device for eliminating the dealer's profit, for joining the aesthetic with the acquisitive, and national pride with national zest for a bargain. The Union was an organization for distributing prints to a membership of subscribers and original paintings by lottery to the lucky ones. There were slightly more than eight hundred members in 1839, its first year; in its tenth and last, nearly nineteen thousand. The Union's managers were chosen each year by the members and served without pay; and there were local secretaries all over the country whose job was to secure new subscriptions.

The art-minded hardware merchant in Concord, New Hampshire, or the lumber dealer in San Francisco paid

Distribution of the American Art-Union Prizes, Sarony & Major lithograph
Courtesy Old Print Shop, New York City

his annual five-dollar fee; he received an engraving of Bingham's *Flatboatmen* or Huntington's *Sibyl,* and a lottery ticket. The managers in the meantime purchased landscapes, figure paintings, and genre directly from the artists, who had to be Americans, and put them on exhibition at the Union's gallery in New York until the yearly meeting in December, when the originals went to the holders of a few lucky numbers. From receipts which at the end climbed to ninety-six thousand dollars, nearly five hundred paintings were thus handled, for there were Union members by then in every state, in Canada and England, in Bavaria, and in the West Indies.

Painters had no reason to complain of the prices they received from the Union. A landscape was seldom bought for more than five hundred dollars, but the Union paid two thousand for Gray's *Wages of War.* Boston, Philadelphia, and other cities soon had Art Unions of their own, and Philadelphia varied the procedure by awarding cash prizes each year with which the member could buy a work of art of his own choosing. There is a lithograph of 1847 in which silk-hatted gentlemen and ladies in crinolines crowd the Tabernacle on Broadway while two small misses in pantalettes draw tickets from the lottery under the flaring gas jets.

As might have been expected, this enterprise made its friends and its enemies among the artists. Some painters—usually the favored ones—insisted that its directors, who were respectable gentlemen, should choose works of art with the same taste and judgment which had formed their own collections; others complained that they bought up trash by third-rate men in order to swell the number of pictures to be distributed, and either haggled with men of established reputation or ignored them altogether. Thomas Doughty, for example, sold fifty landscapes to the Union gentlemen, yet denounced the body for its "impudent assumption to dictate in matters it knows nothing about." He urged his colleagues to stop prating about the dignity of art and to act as men should when they see others usurping the place that legitimately is theirs. These attacks were followed by a relentless campaign by the New York *Herald* to put the Union out of business as a violator of the state lottery laws. In the fall of 1852, the Supreme Court dissolved the organization.

Seven years later the artists made a concerted bid for public support, assembling in Washington to demand "that consideration and encouragement to which they conceived it [art] to be entitled at the hands of the general government." Their memorial proposed an Art Commission whose members would be artists and chosen by artists, to direct all expenditures for art in public places. A Congress which at that moment was only too conscious of the foreign daubs and statuary which disfigured Washington allowed a three-man committee of Kensett, Lambdin, and the sculptor Brown to be appointed, but a year or two later it had disbanded.

Thanks to the Art Union, thousands of small-town Americans had been given their first real experience of art. That experience was molded to a great extent by what people read. The year 1834 saw William Dunlap's *History of the Rise and Development of the Arts of Design in the United States,* the first effort to record two centuries of progress in painting, architecture, sculpture, and the graphic arts. From interviews and letters, from his own recollections, and from the biographical data the artists and their descendants provided, Dunlap produced a series of essays which earned him the title of the American Vasari and the gratitude of subsequent scholars. The author believed that the personal character of an artist must be considered in judging his achievement, and the early men came vigorously to life on his pages. His definition of the art of design was "form displayed in space," and in its light he shrewdly appraised the "defeats" of Trumbull, anticipating the modern preference for that painter's small studies.

Dunlap's information was no more accurate than his varied and not always reliable sources, but his record was amazingly inclusive; he gave a lively account of the quarrel between the two Academies and listed the works in several private collections. When he spoke favorably of Joshua Shaw, whom he had set down in his diary as a conceited English blockhead, he tempered his own bias; but he made no effort to conceal his firm Jacksonian principles, contrasting the self-reliant Yankee with the painter of England who was an "appendage to my lord's tailor when Raphael flourished in Italy."

Art history and criticism in these years was not a specialized profession but one interest among many. Charles Lanman, author of *Letters from a Landscape Painter,* was an amateur explorer who had been a pupil of Durand and whose uncritical eye found "glowing colors" and "fine offhand drawing" in third-rate pictures. Charles Edwards Lester was a Presbyterian minister who wrote on labor conditions in England before he published *The Artist, the Merchant and the Statesman of the Age of the Medici and of Our Time;* his *Artists of America* borrowed heavily from Dunlap and was illustrated with steel engravings. Adam Badeau, a soldier, diplomat, and writer of romances, had heard "the stammering of the infant Muses" in America when he gathered his pieces on music, drama, sculpture, and painting into *The Vagabond.* Henry T. Tuckerman made art exciting and intelligible to his generation. His pages glowed with a lofty, pious, and sweet sentiment, and his overestimates recall the remark of Cooper that genius was getting to be quite a drug in America; yet there were shrewd observations in Tuckerman, who called attention to the honest work of the colonial limner and who understood the breadth of Horatio Greenough's mind.

A few years after Tuckerman's *Artist Life* of 1847, Americans could read more scholarly essays. Extracts from Ruskin were published in the *Crayon,* a sixteen-page weekly founded in 1855 by John Durand and William J. Silliman and published until 1861. *Art Hints* was written by James Jackson Jarves because he saw Yankee tourists "doing" a Venetian church in five minutes; Jarves declared that we needed men who would go down on their knees in the dust to read the soul-language of the mightiest minds in Europe, and his own works included *The Art Idea, Art Thoughts,* and an investigation of the Renaissance which he called *Art Studies.*

Charles Eliot Norton's Italian notes appeared first in the *Crayon,* and Norton was a fastidious liberal who once defended John Brown and who could discuss the theories of the socialists quite calmly despite his belief that it was the will of God that progress should be gradual. In Whitman's *Leaves of Grass,* that "rough and ragged thicket," Norton found genius and an epic vastness of conception, although he wrote that no woman should read past the title page. He knew Rome as well as he knew Boston, and Carlyle and Ruskin as intimately as his guests at Shady Hill or Newport; he translated Dante and wrote frequently for the *Nation.*

In *Tuscan Sculptors* and other books, Charles Callahan Perkins explained the greatness of Renaissance sculpture to Americans. He gave lectures at Trinity College, Hartford, in the fifties and used his own skill as an etcher and wood engraver to illustrate his earlier essays. The plates in his *Italian Sculptors* of 1868 could only suggest the forms of Verrocchio and Donatello, but they helped those masters to emerge from a long neglect in America.

This age, which fed its youthful imagination on "Thanatopsis" and its mature mind on *Democratic Vistas,* has been called the age of Romanticism. That troublesome term has been applied narrowly to the revolt of European groups against the frozen formulas of their "classical" predecessors, and broadly to the timeless and endless war of Imagination against Reason; and a word thus burdened with contradictory meanings often breaks down beneath its load. If one's purpose is not to fit experience into categories but to understand one of the most complex periods in American art, one recognizes that life in both Europe and America in the late eighteenth and the early nineteenth centuries made necessary and possible a vigorous assertion of the individual and with it a changed attitude toward the world around him. If the poems and paintings of the American romanticists resembled those of their foreign contemporaries it was because this attitude was common to both. It impelled both to seek the same models in the art of the past or to invent similar new forms of expression.

Yet the differences were as significant as the parallels. The European was more burdened with religious, political, and aesthetic absolutes which must be overthrown; in the sharp American air the movement could take more positive and more varied shapes. It could embrace the fierce optimism and fact-facing of the western democrat, the fastidious conservatism or the toplofty idealism of the North, the self-coddling of the nostalgic Southerner.

Here, as in Europe, the aesthete must free himself from the restraints of the past as Margaret Fuller rebelled against the cold common sense of her Roman father and tasted the more "soulful" charm of Ovid. Yet minds like hers retained the Puritan's grip on moral values and a mistrust of outward forms which blinded them to the difference between Titian and Washington Allston. The modesty which spoke of "bosoms" was like Puritanism's second wind, and profoundly affected the Yankee sculptor.

In America, as in the Old World, man's perceptions of nature became more intense and his mind dwelt on the supernatural; as early as the eighteen twenties, the *Wieland* of Charles Brockden Brown had found images of impending horror in the murmur of a waterfall and the wind among pine trees. But although the painted landscapes of Cole seemed the projections of a tormented mind, other men made them as symbols of regional pride or of beauty soon to be defiled by progress, and still others drew them with a surveyor's eye for scale and a scientist's respect for detail.

These contradictions were at the heart of American romanticism. Bingham claimed that the powers of the artist are limited to representing what the eye sees, while Tuckerman urged him to stir his fellows mainly by his soul. Whitman praised Mount for his effort to copy nature with truth and soberness; Elizabeth Peabody adored Allston because he had pictured those states of the spirit which hovered near the unconscious. The national mood in the years between Jackson's election and the second term of General Grant ranged from the boisterous in Whitman to the genteel in Longfellow and the melancholy in Poe and Hawthorne. In these "peculiar, original and creative" circumstances, the United States of Emerson and Barnum was more thoroughly romantic than it had ever been before or would ever be again.

CHAPTER 13 / TEMPLED HILLS

To think of Jacksonian builders as what Latrobe had called "bigoted Greeks" would be to oversimplify the national mind. "The whole picture one gathers of architecture in the late twenties and early thirties," Talbot Hamlin has written, "reveals a situation chaotic but violently alive"; and young Alexander Jackson Davis, walking the streets of New York to make sketches of its principal buildings, found a mingling of classical and Gothic flavors. A glance at the New York *Mirror* of 1829, where six of Davis' drawings were engraved on a single page, dispels all notion of the period as one of pure classical revivalism.

At the upper left of the page is Vanderlyn's Rotunda, solidly classical with its pilastered pediment and saucer dome. Next comes the Merchant's Exchange whose Ionic portico was twenty-seven feet high and whose oval exchange room had a dome forty-five feet high above the floor—one of the most spacious interiors in the country. Next is Brady's Second Unitarian Church with Roman niches at either side of its unfluted Doric porch. Below are three buildings which it seems difficult to believe are contemporary. The B'Nai Jeshurun Synagogue in Elm Street has a Gothic square tower on the roof of a Greek temple. In the center is Thompson's Branch Bank of the United States, which is neither Greek nor Roman but has the dignified phrasing of Hoban's White House, with rusticated piers below and fluted Ionic above. Finally there is the Masonic Hall on Broadway which the *American Magazine of Useful Knowledge* attributed to Hugh Reinagle and described

Plate from the New York *Mirror,* Sept. 26, 1829

Library of Congress photo

as "purely Gothic" and "copied from the most approved models." In spite of the great diversity of styles here represented, all of these buildings were finished within a period of ten years.

Why, in the chaotic twenties and thirties, did the Greek so often hold the field? Some historians of the Attic revival have explained it as a fad; others have called it a national expression. It is traced to the revulsion after the Revolution against English taste in general and it is hailed as one of the distinctive contributions of America to architectural style.

Clearly there were both practical and ideological reasons why older homes acquired Grecian porticoes and why templed façades lined village streets, why banks and customhouses were Parthenons, why country churches had square cupolas instead of octagonal spires, why in the South a plantation Greek developed which was something new in the world. These were the work of professional designers and of back-country builders; all of them lived in a country which grew fast and therefore built fast; and they worked for patrons who wished a maximum of impressiveness with a minimum of cost. What the average builder needed was a vocabulary simple enough to be spoken by the unlearned, flexible enough to take a character from the local dialect, and, above all, translatable into wood. Given these, the remotest Michigan settlement could pass in a few months from the log house to the framed dwelling and Tinkerville could have its Astor House. It could have its temples, too, and Mrs. Mary Clavers, walking its streets when the town, having risen like a rocket, had fallen like a stick, noted the mournful shuttered windows of its "porticoed edifices."

The men who built the Tinkervilles lacked the skill to achieve proportion on their own or to fuse ornament with structure; for a time the Greek relieved them of their embarrassment while it challenged their ingenuity. Few of them were conscious of creating a national style, and for one philosopher who identified the age of Pericles with his own there were hundreds of carpenters and householders who missed the connection. When the citizens of Possum Trot and Brandy Gulch discussed a permanent name for their community, the musical Indian words contended with the Grecian;

Root's Landing became Chattanooga and Summit was renamed Akron.

Even among the few for whom the new mode was a symbol, the meaning of the symbol varied. Greece for Hawthorne was a land of beautiful myths to be twice told; for Emerson, a nation whose people so loved art that they made a political issue of the merits of Phidias. Other Americans were stirred by the Greek war of liberation as the struggle of a free people against despots and fought the good cause by proxy with Byron and with Bryant. If Margaret Fuller preferred the Attic law of life which was beauty to the Roman which was stern composure, it was because the Greek, she said, let nature play freely through him, while the Roman had no divinity, no demon, no unfulfilled aim.

For more conservative minds the Attic had snob appeal and seemed to justify their hatred of change; one of them wrote that Grecian elegance would check the nation's taste for a mongrel Gothic whose only appeal was its novelty, whim, and caprice. The banker Nicholas Biddle who had once visited Sicily and Greece was editor of the *Portfolio,* where his friend George Tucker refuted those "licentious spirits" who questioned the value of a classical education, and set forth the Grecian as a supreme standard of excellence. We are satisfied with these forms, he asserted, because we venerate antiquity and authority and because knowledge of the ancient manner is an accomplishment which sets its possessor apart from the common mass. There is no reason to suppose that classicism will not continue to rule our taste "until some moral convulsion shall sweep away in one common ruin civilized man and the works he has created"—among them doubtless the new temple on Chestnut Street from behind whose Doric façade Biddle waged war against the "frontier Catiline" in the White House.

Perhaps the strength of the temple style derived from just this ability to mean one thing to a banker, another to a sugar planter, and still another to a Boston transcendentalist. Yet the columned hotels and the pedimented farmhouses of the Jacksonian years far outnumbered the Biddles, the Fullers, and the Emersons. They were built this way because they looked good and were inexpensive. If Michigan's porticoed edifices resembled one another it was in part because the equality-minded frontiersman approved no luxury which could not be his neighbor's also. If those of the townsman varied it was because democracy leveled upward as well as downward and the difference between one man and another might be the difference between a round column and a square pilaster, between the graceful Ionic and the blunter Doric. Here at least was a symbolism which all could understand.

The actual forms of this Greek Revival were as varied as their motivations, and one hesitates to give a style name to a way of building whose very ubiquity depended on its being in some respects no style at all, but Greek only in the sense that it was more Greek than anything else. When the Attic vein began to be explored in earnest in the twenties, Latrobe was dead but his pupils Strickland and Mills had his sense of the monumental and his capacity for innovation, and would turn out state capitols, marine hospitals, and courthouses into the mid-fifties as inspiration to younger men. The fastidious scholarship of Ithiel Town would play an important part in the movement, and A. J. Davis was a superb draughtsman whose sketches of other men's work came to the public through lithographs. Davis was a pupil of Brady, for whom he made renderings as he did for Martin Thompson; and in 1829 he joined Town as a partner.

Boston had its Grecians in Alexander Parris and Ammi B. Young, who translated ancient marble into modern granite. Russell Warren worked in Providence, Thompson and Calvin Pollard in New York; and in Baltimore the Junior Robert Carey Long built brick rows not unlike those of the larger city. With Gideon Shryock, whose father had sent him from Kentucky to be Strickland's apprentice, the Ionic crossed the Alleghenies. Jonathan Goldsmith took the Doric to Lake County, Ohio, in the twenties and John Ames took it to the Western Reserve; Francis Costigan had learned the refinements of Latrobe and Mills in Baltimore before he worked in Indiana. Richard Lathers and Thomas Carmichael were Town pupils who became his missionaries in the Carolinas. Detroit saw the work of Henry Leroy; St. Louis, that of Joseph C. Laveille, Gabriel Paul, and George Morton; the Galliers and the Dakins in New Orleans had known Town's discipline.

These men were in a sense professionals; but what Talbot Hamlin calls "the quick and universal flowering" of the Greek can only be understood as the work of a thousand carpenters, many of them nameless, who worked with a saw in one hand and a book of instructions in the other. They might derive their notions of correct Greek orders from John Haviland's *The Builder's Assistant* from 1818 to 1821, but it was Asher Benjamin, Minard Lafever, and Edward Shaw who supplied what was practically needed. Books like these poured from the press in the next decades, Benjamin's *Practical House Carpenter* achieving fourteen editions between 1830 and 1857, Lafever's *Beauties of Modern Architecture* five issues before 1855, and Shaw's *Civil Architecture* no less than eleven, the first of which was dated 1830, the last 1876.

The earlier manuals provided details and working diagrams to show how Greek-inspired forms could be made into mantelpieces, windows, doors, and cornices. Benjamin moved with the times and wrote in his 1830 preface that since his former publications the Roman school had been entirely changed for the Grecian. The reason, he said, was that Greek details are bolder, more visible from a distance, and cheaper to execute. With these sixty-four copper engravings before him, any carpenter of ordinary capacity, he claimed, could master the orders by himself, and here were diagrams explaining how to glue up the shaft of a column and how to lay out the complicated curves of a spiraling stair rail. Here were ideas for front doors and fence posts; here was a fireplace whose lintel carried no spidery Adamesque but rather a bold meander, and whose supports were miniature Doric columns. Later editions offered plans for whole dwellings and churches, and the historian of today can set the published plate beside the finished building to demonstrate the synthesis of the borrowed with the originated in the work of men whose names are beginning to emerge as the American regions discover their own past.

Visiting the new public buildings, would a ghost from Pericles' Athens have felt at home? In 1827, he would have recognized in Town's New Haven capitol and in the New York Custom House the most literal efforts to reproduce his Parthenon made by Americans. The latter building—now the Sub-Treasury—was the work of many hands, among them Town and Davis, Ross and Frazee. Eight Doric columns formed its portico beneath a bare pediment, and its interior centered upon a rotunda with Corinthian capitals. Today its granite shafts seem stubby and its details overgenerous in scale, yet its Jacksonian self-assertion, its massive and sturdy bulk make the near-by Stock Exchange seem foppishly anemic. Girard College, commissioned in 1833, was a temple because Nicholas Biddle insisted that it should be one—a two-million-dollar marble temple whose designer was Strickland's pupil Thomas Ustick Walter. The trustees and committeemen tried in vain to "get these ideas of Greek architecture out of Biddle's head," and Walter was still further bound by Girard's will, which specified the dimensions, the number and placing of rooms and stairs, and ordered fireproof construction throughout.

Structures like these in scale and function required no great departure from prototype in their exteriors; but the contemporary of Phidias would have been shocked in the forties to find the Indiana capitol a pulled-out Parthenon of extreme length with a drum and dome riding its back. No true Greek ever valued size or impressiveness for its own sake; for him there had been a true relationship between height, breadth, and length, between that which supports and that which is supported. Gideon Shryock's capitol at Frankfort,

Thomas U. Walter, Girard College, lithograph (detail)

Library of Congress photo

Gideon Shryock, Old State House, Frankfort, Ky.

Historic American Buildings Survey, Library of Congress

Kentucky, still retained that sense of fitness in the late eighteen twenties; the Philadelphia Exchange of Strickland in the thirties, delicate in scale and detail, was well adapted to its triangular site. Between 1848 and 1860 the Ohio state capitol at Columbus, in whose fashioning Alexander Davis and Henry Walters seem to have been most decisive among seven advisers and competitors, became a huge rectangle with a recessed Doric porch on each of its four sides, topped by an incomplete cupola which looks like an oversized bandbox. And seeing the Nashville capitol of Strickland in 1854 riding high on its rustic base, with templed ends and pavilioned sides, the Greek ghost might well have asked why the choragic monument of Lysicrates perched on its roof.

The rational mind of the ancients would perhaps have appreciated the interiors of such edifices, which made no effort to reproduce old forms—the fine vaults beneath the Sub-Treasury, and Walter's ingenuity in accommodating classrooms to the Girard temple. The endless colonnades of Mills suggested that Washington would become a city of multiplication-table Grecian; but Mills and Strickland knew how to provide for the work to be carried on behind the gigantic façades of state legislatures, post offices, and governmental departments. And there was scarcely a trace of archaeology in the commercial structures of the time.

Russell Warren, Providence Arcade, lithograph (detail)

Rhode Island Historical Society photo

One saw no Attic ornament, for example, but only a severe and honest reticence, in Davis' rendering of Town's granite front for the Tappan store on Pearl Street in 1831, perhaps the first of its kind. The business block of the eighteen forties presented its plain brick walls to the street with row upon row of identical windows and perhaps a jutting pavilion of granite to break the monotony, like that of the Washington Buildings at Providence. No Greek had done his shopping in a glass-covered arcade like those of Stonington, Philadelphia, and Providence, the latter duly provided with a Doric porch but also with iron stairways which led to a second floor of shops.

An occasional Greek detail was to be found even on the blank façades of mills and factories; a Harris mill in Rhode Island bore on its roof a belfry no different from those of churches; Lowell's railway depot in the thirties was a temple under whose colonnade passed the trains. No Greek mansions of the period were more stately than those of the mill owners, and the twelve identical double houses for the workers at White Rock in Westerly, Rhode Island, had their own simple versions of their employer's classic porches.

The land of Pericles contributed nothing but decorative themes to that triumph of the thirties, the American hotel. Isaiah Rogers, whose great coffered dome of brick for the Merchant's Exchange was to be a marvel of New York in 1842, became a specialist in hotels. The old taverns, with their twenty rooms, ballroom, and bar, had become an anachronism when Rogers designed the Tremont House in Boston where Tocqueville and Beaumont were so "magnificently served." It was built of stone from Quincy and Cape Ann; its cornerstone was laid on the Fourth of July in 1828 and its doors were opened in October, 1829. The Tremont had more galleries, colonnades, and passages than Charles Dickens could remember, and it was typical of Boston that William Havard Eliot published a description of this first of its kind which cited classical authority for every detail and remarked that Doric simplicity and New England granite were made for each other.

The site was a problem in itself, since Beacon Street climbed steeply at less than a right angle from Tremont, forcing a parallelogram on Rogers which must cover nearly thirteen thousand square feet and provide one hundred rooms. By rounding the ends of his main block on Tremont Street the architect minimized the awkward site. Guests entered a portico which, Eliot said, had been adapted from a plate in Stuart and Revett, and climbed to a rotunda whose circular skylight was brilliant with stained glass "inspired" by frescoes in the Baths of Titus. To the right and left of the main entrance were the ladies' and gentlemen's drawing rooms and along Beacon Street was the huge dining room with Ionic columns and a coffered ceiling. In an opposite wing the private parlors and chambers opened on both sides of a long corridor, and completing the fourth side of an inner courtyard was a block with eight indoor water closets in a row. The second and third floors contained rooms for guests, who paid two dollars a day for food and lodging.

The Tremont House, in its clever adaptation to a sloping site and its corridors branching from a rotunda, was a masterpiece of thoughtful planning, though Eliot's plates suggest that its gilt and color were as overrich as the thirty-seven dishes of its opening dinner. Eight years later the Astor House in New York was built from Rogers' design with an ample portico where "the whiskered dandy and the blushing belle would lounge and flutter," and a great salon which resembled the Chapel of Henry VII. In far-off New Orleans his St. Charles Hotel, with rooms for more than seven hundred people, fronted on three streets; on sofas under its vast domed rotunda sat the beauties of Cincinnati and Nashville; and Abraham Oakey Hall from Manhattan called it "a palace for creature comforts; a college for the study of human nature; and an exchange for money and appetite."

Far more conservative than the merchants and hotelkeepers were the religious congregations. A few churches, like Parris' granite St. Paul's in Boston, were Greek temples and nothing more; hundreds were plain white boxes somewhat larger than a house but with scarcely more decoration: a few anta-like pilasters, a bare pediment, and no tower. If the parish insisted on a portico, one designed the two entrance doors and

Isaiah Rogers, The Tremont House, Boston (water color by George Harvey)

Courtesy Boston Athenaeum

central window with a dignified sense of the whole. If one retained the steeple habit, the tower rose in simple diminishing squares to where the tapering spire began. There was no spire on the church near Exeter, Rhode Island, with its steep pediment and boxlike cupola, and the meander pattern over its doorway. There were infinite degrees of orthodoxy in the style of country churches, and the village of Bluehill in Maine had both the correct Congregational meetinghouse planned by Colonel Benjamin Deane and the more naïve Baptist Church whose carpenter-designer was Thomas Lord.

It was in a man's own home that the greatest mutual adaptations had to be made between pure style and the demands of living, and here the question arose: Who conceded more, the ancient Greek or the American householder? As land values increased in the cities, a few men were wealthy enough to own whole blocks, and their free-standing residences were cube-shaped and spacious, like the "palace" which Davis designed in 1845 for James Cox Stevens in New York, the low dome in its flat roof a sign of the great central hall beneath, the semicircular portico rising two stories, the ornamentation on capital, pilaster, and cornice of an Attic elegance which only Davis could supply.

For New Yorkers who could not achieve this amplitude Colonnade Row and Washington Square were built in the eighteen thirties. The first of these was more elaborate in Davis' drawing than in its realization—a continuous group of nine homes behind a portico of nineteen columns with entrances through a rusticated basement, an iron balcony above them, and a roof garden on its top. Much plainer was the continuous row, probably by Martin Thompson, on the north side of Washington Square in which a type is clearly established: a narrow unit wide enough for one room and a hallway and deep enough for two rooms; the front door at the side and reached by a "stoop"; the basement partly above ground; the windows vertical in proportion and the height two and one half or three and one half stories.

Intricate posts and railings of wrought iron, and later of cast iron, graced the front steps of the narrow city house; its doorway was either round-topped or rectangular with two columns spaced to allow window lights on either side. Of this type was the house which

Alexander J. Davis, Colonnade Row, New York City

Wayne Andrews photo

John V. Gridley House, New York City

Historic American Buildings Survey, Library of Congress

Church near Exeter, R.I.

Harvey A. Weber photo

the hardware merchant Seabury Tredwell bought from Joseph Brewster on East Fourth Street in 1835: its thin vertical façade is pierced by severe tall windows; its only elaboration is the tracery of its doorway, which has both Greek severity and a lingering trace of Adamesque floridity, and the complicated pattern of its iron porch railings. From the narrow side hall the stairs rise in two straight stages to the second floor where two large bedrooms open at the side, and a small one at the front which after 1830 became a bathroom, replacing the primitive outdoor convenience behind the house. By placing one's kitchen in the basement one could have a double parlor on the main floor, and when the Tredwells opened the mahogany sliding doors between their two parlors, daylight from front and back revealed the heavy grace of a Duncan Phyfe sofa, the gloomy richness of black marble fireplaces, the pale tinted walls, and the buff carpet severely divided into panels of crimson and blue. From the ceiling, fourteen feet high, with its richly molded rosette, hung bronze chandeliers which were lowered on pulleys to supplement the meager daylight filtering through lace curtains.

With scarcely more than thirty feet of width, life in these houses adjusted itself as best it could to vertical

Parlor, Old Merchants House, New York City

Wurts Bros. photo, courtesy Historic Landmark Society, N.Y.

Ithiel Town, Joseph Bowers House, Northampton, Mass.

***A. J.** Davis drawing, **engraved by** Fenner Sears **&** Co.*

compression; but in the more spacious communities one could keep the old balance of neighborliness and detachment; and here the temple form with its variations was ubiquitous. As early as 1825 Town designed two such houses for Northampton, Massachusetts. His Bowers House had a great Ionic portico flanked by wings whose smaller porches were formed by square pillars. No house in New England could rival its magnificence; and not far away on the main street stood the Judge Dewey House, a simple rectangular box set endwise to the street with an Ionic portico before it. At New Haven Town played variations on the house-with-wings in his own home and in the Hillhouse villa, Sachem's Wood. Others enlarged the rectangular temple plan with ells which gave a T or an L shape to the dwelling.

Soon there was scarcely a community of average size from the Maine village to the Michigan settlement, from Georgia to Louisiana, which did not possess temples, complete or approximated. Isaac Damon of Northampton, who had helped to plan the Amherst Chapel, improved on his old partner when he spaced the great Doric columns superbly under the plain pediment of the Adams residence. Others who could not afford a projecting portico got the general effect by placing the gable end of the house toward the street with pilasters embedded in it. Plainest of all was the house whose cornices projected to make a pseudo pediment, and whose corners bore vertical projections without orders and without capitals, suggesting the ancient antae in either wood or brick.

Instead of the pediment the Greek mansion could have a plain entablature above its columns or a parapet broken into steps and topped by an anthemion. This was the type which Russell Warren designed in 1833 for the wealthy whaling merchant, William Rodman of New Bedford. Its main block was granite and its six fluted columns with elaborate Corinthian capitals were of wood; a full entablature ran along its four sides. It was said that Rodman paid seventy-five thousand dollars for his twenty-two-room edifice, whose long main hall of gray and white marble mosaic led to a stately double staircase with elegantly curving rails.

On similar principles the Simon Perkins house was built at Akron, Ohio, in 1830, and the James Lanier residence at Madison, Indiana, fourteen years later. Perkins' father had come from Connecticut to explore the Western Reserve for the Erie Land Company and had founded the town of Akron; his son's home was a cube-shaped structure with a low hip roof, a cupola, and pillars unequally spaced in an apparent effort to secure light for its windows. The fifty-thousand-dollar mansion for Lanier was crisply and suavely designed by Francis Costigan, and looked down terraced lawns

Damon-Adams House, Northampton, Mass.

W. E. Corbin photo

to the Ohio. Its slim fluted columns were widely spaced before a wall whose smooth whiteness was broken only by the simplest of window and door openings. Three small circular windows pierced its entablature, and in the center of its slightly sloping parapet was a graceful ornamental device which came to Costigan, via the handbooks, from the reliefs which ran along the gutters of ancient temples. From the ground level the octagonal cupola was scarcely visible, and from the Lanier hallway a staircase spiraled gracefully upward.

Many a house of this period was Grecian by afterthought. One could achieve the Attic flavor by adding a two-story portico to the plain, flat-roofed home of one's forebears; Nicholas Biddle commissioned Walter to dignify his country home Andalusia in this fashion and Jackson's Hermitage acquired its portico many years after its original construction. One could make other revisions: the porch could be of one story; an old square cupola could become a temple in miniature; one could deepen one's cornice and ornament it with wreath motives or set small windows in the frieze with pierced grilles of anthemion pattern.

The severity of these façades was contradicted by their interiors, where one no longer found the old unity between house and furnishings which the Salem Derbys had known, and before them the Hutchinsons of Boston. The Rodman house at New Bedford, to be sure, had classical scenes on painted panels in its music room; the frescoes by foreign workmen in the Alsop house at Middletown, Connecticut, accented the elegance of the mansion; and a water color of about 1830 by the re-

Francis Costigan, Lanier House, Madison, Ind.

Courtesy Indiana Department of Conservation

sourceful Davis shows a room of Spartan austerity whose tinted walls harmonize with its white columns, whose well-proportioned mirrors and picture spaces are surrounded by delicate borders, and whose furniture is derived from classic sources. More frequently, however, the owner displayed his fondness for gaudy flowered carpets reaching from wall to wall, heavy ornate gilded mirrors, and shapeless sofas of plush and horsehair. Greek might be the name for his piazza, but Jacksonian was the style of his bookcases and his bedsteads.

While northern rooms were often cramped in space and the high parlors chilly and dark, the Southerner could expand his floor plan and raise his ceilings in the interest of coolness and circulation; master of many servants, he could multiply his rooms. The great two-storied colonnades which were to be the conspicuous feature of the "southern Greek" made their appearance at Land's End and Orton plantation in the tidewater of North Carolina; they were less often found in the piedmont region, although Belo House at Winston-Salem was a handsome exception. The Georgia mansion retained a plan which was of the eighteenth century, deriving a new impressiveness from a central portico with a pediment or a row of two-story columns along the façade with an entablature above them and iron balconies or porches at the second-floor level. But the Greek seed flowered most luxuriantly in the lower Mississippi Valley, for reasons both practical and literary.

That region, save for a brief Spanish interlude, had been deeply French for more than a century. New Orleans streets, after two disastrous fires, were lined at the turn of the century with two- and three-story façades of colored stucco whose carriage passageways led into paved courts where tropical flowers bloomed underneath tiers of galleries. Thirty years later one found the fret and the honeysuckle in the local ironwork, proof that the Greek was busy here, too. There were Attic shapes in the stair railings which rose in double curves to the Beauregard house with its slim Doric pillars; and a Yankee was at home in the Grima house and among the columned porches of Lawyer's Row in near-by Clinton, which could have bordered some New Hampshire common.

Across from southeastern states and down the river came men in search of the quick and easy fortunes promised by the cotton gin, by new ways of granulating sugar, and by what seemed an inexhaustible supply of black labor. The creoles still heard *Robert le Diable* from the latticed boxes of the French Opera House which the younger Gallier had built, and there was a French elegance in the domed lobby of Jacques de Pouilly's St. Louis Hotel. In the creole capital still lived Bernard de Marigny, at whose estate on Lake Pontchartrain King Louis Philippe had once dined on snipe and terrapin; now old Bernard was a curiosity. "I ignore," he said, "the destiny that awaits me"; and the world he represented was destined to survive only in the romantic reconstruction of the novelist.

From the new Garden District the pushing Northerner made war across that "Rubicon of creole prejudice," Canal Street, against the Vieux Carré; his home was likely to be a two- or three-story structure entirely surrounded by a columned porch whose second-floor balcony was ornate with cast iron. From both northern and southern foundries came ironwork of such luxuriant detail that, by the 1850's, houses in New Orleans, Mobile, and other cities possessed balconies which were façades in themselves. The passengers on Mississippi steamboats sailed between a double row of sugar and cotton palaces of even greater size and magnificence from Memphis down to the port; while plantation houses rose along the Natchez trace southeast from Nashville, beside the Tombigbee in Mississippi, in Alabama, and among the bayous to the west of the big river. Their very names suggest both creole sensibility and Yankee push: Asphodel, Belle Grove, and Rosedown; Rattle and Snap, and Uncle Sam.

The basic form of the "Plantation Greek" was not the temple; even at the height of its elaboration, as at Dunleith in Natchez, built in 1849, it confessed its relationship to the old French houses of the river valley. Magnolia Mound was of this type, with a gallery around three sides and a music room with an arched ceiling.

Detail of iron grille, Conti St., Mobile, Ala.

F. S. Lincoln photo

Parlange on the banks of False River had galleries on four sides and five tall doors along its front; in its good days, which were the 1840's, skilled Negro hands carved the paneled ceilings of its porches, the medallions for its chandeliers, and the delicate moldings of its chimney pieces.

As the sugar and cotton fortunes swelled, the plantation enlarged its scale and enriched its decorations. It went up two full stories with an attic, and in place of the brick piers below and the thinner wooden columns above, white stuccoed-brick pillars rose from ground level to cornice. Uncle Sam at Convent, Louisiana, halfway between Baton Rouge and New Orleans, remained until the encroaching river condemned it—the most complete reminder of what its type had been in the heyday of King Cotton, a small village sufficient to itself, with seven large buildings and forty lesser ones. Seen from the levee, its main house of yellow stucco dominated the group, one hundred feet square in plan with a more or less Doric portico on all four sides. Smaller temple buildings stood beside and behind it—two guest houses or garçonnières, an office, a kitchen, and a pigeon cote. Along the "street," which ran back at a right angle toward the sugarhouse, were the cabins which housed Samuel Fagot's Negroes—his cooks, gardeners, carriage men, dairy workers, nurses, weavers and blacksmiths, and the field slaves who labored in the mill and in the sugar cane beyond.

More sumptuous than Uncle Sam in the last decade before the civil conflict were Nottoway and Belle Grove, both of them a few miles north of the Fagot estate. John Randolph considered a dozen designs by New Orleans men before he decided that an oval ballroom was to be the heart of his plan for Nottoway. Corinthian columns bordered his hallway, his porcelain doorknobs were hand-decorated, and tons of cast iron made the railings of his gallery. Two years before, in 1857, John Andrews had surpassed him with seventy-five rooms at Belle Grove, whose florid Corinthian shafts went up two stories, their solid cypress capitals a man's height. The brackets of its gallery, the great winding stairway, the pink stucco walls above its tall basement, were as graceful and as expensive as anything in America.

To match external splendor the plantation owners ransacked Europe for their bronze and crystal chandeliers, French wallpaper, Empire sofas, carved rosewood chairs, and enormous gilded mirrors. Their mantelpieces were carved in green-and-red Italian stone, and satin canopies draped their bedsteads. A French designer had planned the Rosedown garden, with its statues of the four seasons and the six continents in white Carrara marble. Korean camphor trees and palms from Central America grew in Valcour Aime's garden, tropical fruits in his hothouse; and there were Chinese pagodas with stained glass and tinkling bells on his artificial lake. The pink Doric portico of Bon Sejour was framed by an alley of twenty-eight gigantic oaks.

King Cotton's reign was short. In Claiborne County, Mississippi, twenty-four naked columns and a few strands of iron tracery are all that is left of Windsor Castle today; Belle Grove and many another handsome plantation have lost their battle with neglect and weather, as their masters lost theirs to the armies of the North.

In the last year of the civil conflict, Brady's photograph of Richmond showed the old templed Capitol standing unharmed above the ruined city; and one could measure its fine Jeffersonian scale against the Jacksonian sprawl of Mills's Post Office, the Treasury, and the Patent Office in Washington. The first of these was masonry-vaulted and revealed Mills's gift for functional planning. It is possible that drawings by Town and Davis helped him to decide the final form of the Treasury, which sat athwart the vista from Capitol to White House which L'Enfant had planned. Sixteen oxen raised the thirty-four monoliths of its colonnade, each thirty-six feet high and of the best Ionic. Its five hundred feet was a tiresome length, but the construction of its innumerable rooms was a triumph for the engineer in

Uncle Sam Plantation, near Convent, La.

F. S. Lincoln photo

Belle Grove Plantation, near White Castle, La.

F. S. Lincoln photo

Robert Mills, General Post Office, Washington, D. C., Köllner lithograph (detail)

Library of Congress photo

Mills, who made their vaults and partitions thin, strong, and fire-resistant with hydraulic cement.

The Patent Office façade was built with freestone blocks which had been quarried on a Maine island, and its construction over thirty years was the work of many minds. The long row of exterior pilasters and the central portico gave no hint of the structural experiments inside: the iron tie-rods which Thomas U. Walter used in one wing; the brick vaulting of Mills and Walter in the south and east wings, which withstood the fire of 1877 when iron trusses and ceilings buckled and collapsed.

Only in the superficial sense could Mills, Walter, and Strickland be called Greeks; under their colonnades and pediments they had created something which the Greeks never knew. In an essay which was never completed Mills explained that servile imitation of antiquity had never been his aim. Go back, he said, as the Greeks themselves did, to the source of all art forms in nature; "study your country's tastes and requirements and make classic ground *here* for your art."

A younger man than Mills more boldly proclaimed the organic principle toward which the builder of the Treasury was here groping. Revivalism, Greek or otherwise, had no more trenchant critic than Horatio Greenough. The external form of Walter's Girard College had shocked him, and he could scarcely believe his eyes when he saw so stupendous a display of material and workmanship covering a few Quaker-looking rooms: "It was like seeing the Pitt diamond on an Indian squaw." Greenough declared that a column used as a monument—and Mills had done this at Baltimore—belonged to "the numerous and respectable family of makeshifts"; and in his essay on "Aesthetics at Washington" he ridiculed the oval temple which Mills had designed for the obelisk. Only the Patent Office pleased Greenough because it had no makeshift and no afterthought. Perhaps he knew that the iron girders, the vaulting, and the cement behind its façade were making architectural history. At any rate, he would have seconded Mills's advice to American builders:

> We have entered a new era in the history of the world; it is our destiny to lead, not to be led. Our vast country is before us and our motto, Excelsior.

CHAPTER 14 / A FEW CROCKETS AND FINIALS

It is probable that few Americans were disturbed by Thomas Hamilton's ridicule of their "Grecian" buildings. He preferred the dinners at the Tremont House to its decorations and observed that the Providence Arcade had Doric shafts beneath an Ionic entablature. If the Greek proved wanting in America, however, it was not because of its incorrectness but because it no longer answered the American needs, both practical and moral, no longer expressed personal aspirations and the national enterprise.

There were still minds in the eighteen thirties like those of Biddle and Tucker, which looked contemptuously with Gibbon on the "stately monuments of superstition" and identified the Gothic with the barbarous. With the possible exception of the unhappy Godefroy, no designer in America had yet specialized in the arched style, nor had we a medieval past, as England had, to which we could turn in search of models. Latrobe's Sedgeley had been mildly and pleasantly medieval; the Gothic had tempted Strickland on a few occasions, as it had Town when he designed the somber Trinity Church for the New Haven green. Tocqueville admired the functional ingenuity of Haviland's Eastern State Penitentiary at Philadelphia, where all the cell blocks radiated like spokes from an observation chamber and every prisoner had his own walled garden; but the Frenchman questioned its "castellated" rectangular enclosure which cost two hundred thousand dollars and was "intentionally picturesque." Gothicism of this sort was no more organic in the historical sense than Walpole's Strawberry Hill had been or James Wyatt's queer Fonthill Abbey.

But attitudes had changed in the England of the eighteen thirties, where no self-respecting architect would have attempted, as Batty Langley had done in 1742, to improve the medieval by reducing it to orders. Not visual pleasure nor general picturesqueness but an archaeological rectitude was the order of the day when Augustus Charles Pugin published his meticulous detailed drawings and sober water colors of Lincoln, Wells, and Oxford. He had been a draughtsman for John Nash, and the two volumes of *Specimens of Gothic Architecture* began to appear in 1821. For twenty years after Pugin's death his son preached the same gospel but with deeper conviction; for Augustus Welby Northmore Pugin turned Catholic and, since he saw the outward form and the sacred content as one thing, he understood the relation between the organic basis of the Gothic and its decorative elaborations. He drew the details for Barry's Parliament Houses and one year after their completion issued his *True Principles of Pointed or Christian Architecture.*

These religious and historic motivations were reinforced by emotional ones when Samuel Coleridge lectured in 1818 at Flower-de-Luce Court in London. The Greeks, he declared, were remarkable for complacency and completion; but "if I wish my feelings to be affected, if I wish my heart to be touched, if I wish to melt into sentiment and tenderness, I must turn to the heroic songs of the Goths, to the poetry of the middle ages." When Coleridge entered a Greek temple his eye was charmed and his mind elated; when he stood in a cathedral he was filled with awe, his whole being expanded toward the infinite, and he knew that the Gothic was sublime.

Greek met Goth in America under somewhat different circumstances. There was no Anglican revival here; and although the Yankee readers of Pugin might have agreed that faith, zeal, and unity built the great churches, how many of them could share his conviction that Protestantism had meant the decay of morals, and that the revived pagan architecture of the Renaissance had been a symbol of that decay? Studying the plates where Pugin put his contrasts in pictorial form, a Jacksonian might concede that the Catholic town of 1440 had more grace than the same town in 1840 with its jail, gas works, iron factories, and lunatic asylum; yet he would have accepted these as inevitable to human progress.

Nor would the local designer pay much attention to Pugin's functional explanations of the Gothic in *True Principles.* That essay contained diagrams to show how Gothic moldings took their shape from the need to shed rain water, and how the bargeboards along the gable ends of medieval houses had been put there to protect the beam ends of the roof and not for sheer decoration. Pugin warned the American, but in vain, that a "castellated" mansion was but a caricature of a true fortress; and as for furniture, he confessed that he had perpetrated enormities at Windsor Castle before he learned first principles, putting flying buttresses on armchairs, and crockets and mitres in places where they would inflict discomfort on the householder.

The American Gothic of the thirties often consisted,

as it had more than a generation before in England, in the addition of medieval details to structures square-built in a manner not in the least medieval. When James Fenimore Cooper returned from Europe in 1833 he found the republican sun harsh after the mellow light of Italy. Using fictional names in *Home As Found,* he described his own journey up the Hudson between rows of "mushroom temples" which were the offspring of Mammon. Arriving at Templeton, Mr. Effingham (who was Cooper himself) proceeded to remodel his ancestral home by stringing battlements along its roof, changing its Georgian sash to trefoil shapes, and creating what Cooper frankly called a mongrel of the Grecian and Gothic orders. His architect (in reality Professor Morse) defends himself in the novel by asking, "Is architecture so pure in America, that you think I have committed the unpardonable sin?" Cooper indeed can have felt no discomfort in his Wigwam, since he knew so little about architecture that he wrote *medallion* when he meant *modillion.*

More aggressive than Morse were the writers of essays in the forties who attacked the Grecian on grounds both practical and aesthetic. An ingenious Chicago man had contrived a "balloon frame" for houses which used thin plates and studs nailed together instead of the heavy joinery which had been a limitation on construction since colonial days. The American builder could now find release from what Robert Dale Owen called the "Procrustean regularity" of the Attic forms. Owen's father had founded New Harmony as an experiment in human cooperation, and the son no more believed that buildings should cramp life by rigid externals than that society should do so. In *Hints on Public Architecture* Owen condemned peristyles which darkened rooms, and ridiculed the colonnade of Girard College, fifty-five feet high, which could not protect its corridor from the rain. A medieval structure, he claimed, would have cost less per cubic foot of construction. Moreover, "Arch Architecture" lacked monotony and was bold, candid, and lofty. Were not these the American qualities?

Four years before Owen, Horatio Greenough maintained in the *United States Magazine and Democratic Review* that the sheer beauty of the Roman temple had not justified its reappearance at Richmond: "The want of an illustrious ancestry may be compensated, but the purloining of a coat of arms of a defunct family is intolerable." And in 1844 the *North American Review* published an attack by Arthur Gilman on those old-fashioned five-order men who merely discarded Vitruvius for Asher Benjamin, and who made of the Greek in America one long misquotation, of Stuart and Revett an inexhaustible quarry of bad taste. The Custom House at Boston contained enough masonry, he said, for three buildings of its size; and as for the Doric cottage, he compared it with the skin of a lion on the body of an ass.

While comments like these prepared Americans for a new freedom in architecture, the Gothic multiplied in the land. For designers of the thirties the appeal of the "pointed style" lay chiefly in its flexibility and its vitality, which matched their own. The novels of Scott were peopling the American imagination with armored knights and tournaments. The aquatint and the lithograph were training people to see more atmospherically with their velvet textures, blurred definitions, and sketchlike suggestiveness. Seated at his drawing table, the architect saw Scott's cavaliers and ladies walking the terraces or standing beneath the chimney pieces of Nash's *Mansions of England in the Olden Time.* The dry "carpenter's Gothic" of Rogers' Unitarian Church at Cambridge, Massachusetts, would not have satisfied the eye of Davis, who found the new cusps, quatrefoils, and oriels a greater challenge to his pencil than the triglyph and the anthemion had been; and Davis saw no reason why patrons should be "foolishly frightened by a few crockets and finials."

The wealthy Gilmors of Baltimore had no such fear, and Davis had become a partner of Town when he drew Glenellen for them in 1832. One entered its grounds through the arches of a make-believe ruin which served as gatehouse, and the façade of the villa was sprightly with eight-sided towers and lacelike oriel windows carefully placed to avoid any trace of symmetry. The floors inside were of marble, and the ceilings had pseudo vaults whose details were picked out in pleasing colors. For sheer delicacy and forthright honesty it remained for half a century, in the opinion of Roger Hale Newton, a "triumph of perfection."

If Cooper's Effingham had sailed up the river again in the forties he would have observed that real estate had proved a tempting investment there, and that the Hudson looked vaguely like the Rhine. Near Tarrytown in 1841 Philip Hone examined William Paulding's villa, in process of remodeling, whose details Town and Davis had cribbed from Pugin's *Examples.* Hone wrote in his diary that it was an immense thing of white or gray marble like a baronial castle or a monastery with towers, turrets and trellises, minarets, mosaics and mouse holes, peaked windows, pinnacled roofs, and many other fantastics too tedious to mention; "an edifice of gigantic size with no room in it; great cost and little comfort." When Anne Sophie Winterbotham Stephens wrote her lushly romantic novel, *Fashion and Famine,* she placed her characters in the castellated home which Davis had designed for William Waddell on Fifth Avenue, the first of its type in Manhattan when it was built in 1844. The next two years saw Davis' cottage for William Rotch in New Bedford and his Harral house in Bridgeport.

Alexander J. Davis, Wm. G. Rotch house, New Bedford, Mass.

Wayne Andrews photo

Stairway detail, Afton Villa, Bains, La.

F. S. Lincoln photo

Richard Upjohn from England, another pioneer in residential Gothic, built Oaklands, a stone country house for the Gardiner family in Maine, in the years 1835 and 1836. Its buttresses, medieval window moldings, and clustered chimney stacks were applied to an architectural mass which suggested classical plainness rather than Gothic informality. Soon, however, the expansiveness of the age and its intolerance of restraint broke through the old symmetries. House plans acquired semicircular features, five-sided bay windows, L-shaped masses which provided an area for a porch, and other irregularities on which the "picturesqueness" of the whole depended.

The halls of such houses were long and narrow; doors opened from them in all directions, and stairs were crowded into their back regions or wound upward in round or polygonal turrets. Rooms were darkened by thin diamond-paned windows and by doors with patterned frosted glass; they were restless with flowered or Gothic wallpaper; floors were intricately tiled, inlaid, or hidden beneath flowery carpets. The mantelpieces had flattened Tudor arches of unlovely marble.

Joseph Byrnes was one of several cabinetmakers of the day who designed rosewood beds, tables, and armchairs of pseudomedieval character, and the Harral house has kept its bedroom sets in which the pinnacles of cathedrals came to roost on bedposts and supported the mirrors of bureaus despite Pugin's reminder that the furnishings of the Middle Ages had functional forms of their own and never resembled anything like a cathedral-to-sit-on.

As the public lost its fear of a few crockets and finials, the domestic Gothic spread. A most unscholarly medievalism invaded Gambier, Ohio, in the late thirties and later attacked Kentucky. Even the South, that stronghold of the Grecian, saw more than one castellated plantation. In Powhatan County in Virginia stood Tudoresque Belmeade, designed by Davis. At Columbus, Mississippi, a planter made the pillars of his house octagonal and filled the space above and between them with vaguely Gothic tracery, a gesture repeated by his neighbors. Malmaison on the Natchez trace was brittle with wooden fretwork, and there was a Gothic stairway at Afton Villa in West Feliciana Parish, Louisiana.

New York University, Henry Hoff lithograph, drawn by Charles Authenreith

Courtesy Old Print Shop, New York City

Mark Twain was to recall these towers and ivy-mantled porches when he wrote in *Life on the Mississippi* that *Don Quixote* had destroyed the age of chivalry only to have it restored by *Ivanhoe.*

Town and Davis demonstrated that public buildings as well as private ones could be built in the new fashion. Their design for the Astor Library on Lafayette Place was Gothic, although its detail as actually built by others was mildly "Romanesque," and there is little trace of the Town refinement in this hearty architectural pudding of red brick and rusticated brownstone. The partners applied what they called "English Collegiate Gothic" to a series of large educational buildings. New York University faced Washington Square in 1837, the chief wonder of its façade a huge window of stone tracery inspired by the one in King's College Chapel at Cambridge, England. Other men—Dakin, Weeks, and Douglas—had a share in its planning; and it is possible, as Roger Hale Newton suggests, that Hezekiah Augur carved its bosses, pendants, and grotesques. Town and Davis also made designs for the University of Michigan, and in the early eighteen forties for a library at Yale which translated the towers of Henry VII's Westminster Chapel into Connecticut sandstone. Thus were the planners of American colleges made conscious of Educational Gothic, with consequences still to be reckoned in our time.

The Wadsworth Atheneum in Hartford, commissioned in 1842, was the work of Town, Davis, and Town's pupil Henry Austin, and had Tudor casement windows and rugged square towers. Five years later in Boston, George M. Dexter's station for the Fitchburg Railway crouched over its tracks, each corner bristling with a rough granite turret. But the greatest feudal stronghold of them all in 1852 was the Smithsonian Institution on Washington Mall, which Robert Dale Owen described as "the first edifice in the style of the twelfth century and of a character not ecclesiastical ever erected in this country." Owen's brother and Robert Mills made drawings for it, but James Renwick was finally responsible for its red sandstone eccentricities, which people called "Anglo-Norman." The Smithsonian façade is nearly five hundred feet long with a bewildering variety of heights and thicknesses in its gables, towers, and turrets; an edifice which manages to be a unit because of a certain sturdy crispness in its piers, moldings, and corbels and the controlled vitality of its many parts. Its ugliness is masculine and its self-

Richard Upjohn, Trinity Church, New York City, drawn by Upjohn, lithographed by Forsyth & Mimée (detail)

Library of Congress photo

assertion mocks the discreet classicism of its neighbors.

It was James Renwick and Richard Upjohn who built the most spirited churches of the period. Christ Church at Raleigh, North Carolina, with its sturdy compact shapes and its detached tower, showed what Upjohn could do with stone, and at Wilmington in the same state, Thomas U. Walter's St. James's in 1839 was as straightforward as Upjohn's Trinity seven years later. Upjohn revealed, in St. John's at Bangor, Maine, the essential grace of Gothic, even though plaster and lath were the materials of his vaulting. In Maine, as elsewhere, carpenter-builders produced a medieval which was less correct than his; they changed the curves of lancet windows into straight lines; and the detail which Upjohn derived from Pugin was translated by them into homelier wooden shapes at Christ Church in Gardiner and Grace Church at Bath.

The year 1846 saw three impressive New York churches; Upjohn's Trinity, Renwick's Grace Church, and Joseph C. Wells's First Presbyterian. Even Arthur

Christ Church, Gardiner, Me.

J. C. Smith photo, Courtesy Samuel Green

Gilman conceded that Trinity was magnificently simple and thoroughly consistent. In a small workshop behind the church, Upjohn, like any master builder of the thirteenth century, had planned the ornament and directed the making of the stained glass windows and the carving of the statues. The result expressed his sense of mass and proportion with quiet conviction; on its plain surfaces his laconic detail was placed with originality and force.

The masterpiece of Renwick was St. Patrick's Cathedral; he became its architect in 1853, and its immense bulk was not completed until more than thirty years later. When St. Patrick's got its spires in 1887, men with less imagination and greater scholarship were planning more literal re-creations of Old World models. Thanks to the earlier pioneers, some form of the medieval has determined the design of most religious buildings in America.

Even as the Gothic contended with the Greek there were Americans who had read architectural history and knew that the past offered other stylistic possibilities. The Greek revivalist limited himself to an approximation of one historic type; but when Owen said that the medieval lent itself to the "free play of anachronism," he tempted his countrymen to take greater liberties with forms in the interest of human living than they had ever taken before. Thomas Hope complained as early as 1835 in his *Historical Essay on Architecture:*

> No one seems yet to have conceived the smallest wish or idea of only borrowing of every style of architecture whatever it might present of useful or ornamental, of scientific or tasteful; of adding thereto whatever other new dispositions or forms might afford conveniences or elegances not yet possessed; of making the new discoveries, the new conquests, of natural productions unknown to former ages, the models of new imitations more beautiful and more varied; and thus of composing an architecture which, born in our country, grown on our soil and in harmony with our climate, institutions and habits, at once elegant, appropriate and original, should truly deserve the appellation of "Our Own."

This was the notion of eclecticism, and Hope's words were read in America by a generation only too glad to separate forms from their historical contexts and to play freely with them. The architect, James Britton said, was like a bee extracting honey from every source for plagiarisms which were not only excusable but glorious.

Alexander Jackson Davis' portfolio bulged with glorious plagiarisms. Many of these were Gothic, to be sure; and his "Design for a Villa in the Pointed Style" was a concoction of Tudor chimney stacks, bargeboarded gables, dripstone moldings, oriel windows, and Tudoresque porches brought into harmony by a sense of over-all symmetry and a knack for placing accents where they were pictorially needed. But Davis' watercolor rendering of a farmhouse was vaguely Swiss; and his sketch for Blythewood's gatehouse included a small balcony supported by rustic columns which were simply the trunks of trees. The Salisbury villa near New Haven was his effort, aided by Town, to achieve what was called the "Tuscan" manner, suggested by the country houses of the Italian hills with their square, tile-topped towers and rather plain walls, to which the American designer added piazzas and which he accented with detail left over, so to speak, from the Greek Revival.

At New Rochelle in 1835 the Codwise villa was called Tuscan, designed by Town and Davis as a rectangular mass with a low hip roof, delicate corner pilasters, and a porch whose uprights were decorated by Greek meanders. As Henry Austin and others planned them in the forties, Italian houses had deeply projecting roofs, towers, and flat-roofed porches, and their smooth wooden walls were painted in a variety of colors from ochre-yellow to brown-purple. The Stebbins villa at Springfield by Henry A. Sikes, a pupil of Town and Davis, was characteristic of a dwelling type whose clean lines and lively hues were not the least attractive sights on the lawns of American towns.

These villas and cottages, so ingeniously invented by Davis, the self-styled "architectural composer," im-

An Italian Villa

Samuel Sloan, Homestead Architecture

plied a new philosophy of the domestic; to explain and illustrate that philosophy was the mission of Andrew Jackson Downing. Davis illustrated Downing's "rural" volumes and worked with him in what amounted to a partnership after Town died in 1844.

Downing of Newburgh-on-the-Hudson was twelve years younger than his friend. After establishing himself as a nurseryman he had become the country's authority on landscape gardening. His sandstone villa was like himself with its impeccably smooth lawn, its carefully groomed rock garden, and its tall rooms where the sun fell slantwise through trefoil tracery upon Gothic bookcases with busts on brackets above them.

Downing believed that certain men were "unextinguishably" superior to others in spite of what the Jacksonian politicians said; yet the democratic ferment was working even in this "Hudson River aesthete," as Carl Carmer has called him. He insisted that New York's half million souls needed a green oasis; he believed that love of nature made men healthier members of society and that fine houses made fine people. It was true, as one of Downing's friends remarked, that the workman, author, and artist in him were subjugated to the gentleman; but it was also no exaggeration for Fredrika Bremer to write that he was more responsible than any other man for the new conception of beauty in all realms of life which she found in the United States.

From many sources Downing drew the materials for his crusade. His insistence on the harmony, as in a charming water color, between the dwelling and its grass and trees found reinforcement in the plates of Peter Frederick Robinson's book, *Rural Architecture;* his campaign against white paint was inspired by what Uvedale Price had said about its clash with the harmonies of nature in *The Beautiful and the Sublime.* And he may also have owned that ingenious work by Thomas L. Meason, *On the Landscape Architecture of the Great Painters of Italy,* in which over fifty paintings by Claude, Poussin, Veronese, Giorgione, and others were reproduced with the suggestion that the houses in these pictures be used as models for new ones of the same charming irregularity and the same intimate relation to their sites.

Downing's whole principle of landscape gardening, inspired by the Englishmen Repton and Loudon, was nature "refined and softened by art." This meant taking advantage of what was peculiar to one's own place and pointing it up, so to speak, with judicious transplanting, with seemingly informal groupings of trees, with pleasant contrasts of rugged growth and close-shaven lawn, with contrasts of dark and light foliage, with gracefully curving roads and parks. As for the house itself, its "style" would come from a creative adaptation of past forms, since no new way of building had ever

A. J. Davis, Wm. H. Drake cottage, Hartford, Conn.

Metropolitan Museum of Art, New York City

been invented outright. Whether the mansion of a country gentleman, the vacation villa of the middle class, or the cottage of the rural American, each edifice should express its owner's individuality. Its design should suggest its purpose, and Downing approved the principle of Loudon that there should be no feature "at variance with propriety, comfort or sound workmanship." All ornament should consist of enrichment of the building's essential construction; so conceived, the American home would have important moral effects on its owner, and hence on society as a whole.

Downing assured his readers that he had no patience with mere showiness or eccentricity, and he quoted Lowell's satirical poem on *The Rural Cot of Mr. Knott.* That worthy man "from business snug withdrawn," being middle-aged himself, resolved to build a medieval mansion of wood, to be "petrified" by the painter; his clothes would be dried in a donjon, and his pigs kept in a porter's lodge.

> And so the greenest of antiques
> Was reared for Knott to dwell in;
> The architect worked hard for weeks
> Inventing all his private peaks
> Upon the roof, whose crop of leaks
> Had satisfied Fluellen.

One fears that the Knotts of America took some encouragement from Downing's essays and editorials in the *Horticulturalist* and often ignored his more practical counsels — his observation, for example, that America's favorite poison was the combination of hot stoves with inadequate ventilation. Yet if life in the small villas and "cottages ornées" which he inspired was more pleasant and more diversified than it had been in temples and castles, more comfortable and healthy, the credit was largely his.

The last ten years of Downing's short life were busy ones. In 1841 he published *A Treatise on the Theory and Practice of Landscape Gardening Applied to North America,* and in the next year his *Cottage Residences.* His *Architecture of Country Houses* appeared in 1850, at the time when Downing, discovering the talented Calvert Vaux in Europe, brought him home as a partner. The following year he submitted to President Fillmore his plan for laying out the public grounds at Washington, in which every formal device of Major L'Enfant was ignored, and the White House enclosure and the long axis from the Capitol to the Washington Monument were elaborated with serpentine walks, informally planned "pleasance gardens," mazes, and fountains—all in the best "natural" manner.

Downing's Washington scheme would help later men to plan the Central Park for New York which had been his dream; his design for suburban Llewellyn Park in New Jersey, for which Davis drew cottages, was the germ of the modern garden city. This man of thirty-seven had influenced the lives of thousands when, on a July day in 1852, the Hudson steamboat *Henry Clay* caught fire from its own overtaxed boilers and ran aground at Riverdale, where Downing drowned in shallow water a few feet from the shore.

The denouement was worthy of Edgar Allan Poe, and there is evidence on more than one of the poet's pages that he had absorbed the Downingesque influence. His young Ellison in *The Landscape Gardener,* like the philosopher of Newburgh, had spent his fortune creating "novel moods of purely physical loveliness." And Poe must have known the Downing volumes when he described Landor's cottage: it stood on a lawn smooth as Genoese velvet and Poe moved toward it along a carriage road whose every bordering stone had been arranged "with a kind of half-precise, half-negligent and wholly picturesque definition."

Such "tasteful simplicity" was beyond the range of millions in America, whose self-appointed spokesman was Orson S. Fowler, the author of *A Home for All.* It was Fowler who condemned Downing for having designed only for the upper classes; and this phrenologist and dabbler in socialism presented his own invention, the domestic octagon, as a cheap and practical dwelling for ordinary people.

Among the advantages of the polygonal plan, as he presented them, were its elimination of ill-lighted corners, the steps it saved between room and room, the space economy of its furnace. Odd triangular spaces were made into closets and water tanks. As for the exterior, Fowler preferred that it tell its own story without those "finified carvings and cornicings" which he disliked in the cottage style. His own octagon of 1850-1853 at Fishkill had scarcely more elaboration than the balustraded balconies around its second and third floors and on its roof below the eight-sided cupola. As *A Home*

John Richards Octagon, Watertown, Wis.

Historic American Buildings Survey, Library of Congress

Leopold Eidlitz "Iranistan," Sarony & Major lithograph

Courtesy Old Print Shop, New York City

for All went toward its seventh printing in the fifties, men built octagons both plain and fancy, like the one designed by John Richards of Watertown, Wisconsin.

Neither the Downing cottage, however, nor the Fowler octagon could satisfy the thirst for elaboration of the fifties, a decade of stylistic anarchy in the United States. The gentle Downing would have winced before the "wedding cake" house at Kennebunk in Maine, whose owner had incased his solid old brick dwelling in a wooden filigree of vaguely Gothic character. The owners of plain cottages along the Mississippi stepped aboard steamboats which were called floating palaces; Mark Twain described the white wooden lace on their pilot houses, the gaudy symbolic paintings on their paddle boxes, the intricate vaults, brackets, and pendants of their gold-and-white saloons with skylights of colored glass through which the sun fell in rainbows on Wilton carpets soft as mush.

Thomas Cole had painted in 1840 *The Architect's Dream:* among cushions on the top of a huge column reclines the visionary, and before him spreads a vista of Roman colonnades, Greek temples, Egyptian pyramids, and Gothic steeples. The canvas was intended for Ithiel Town, who rejected it. Four years later Town was dead, but his partner lived on for nearly half a century, rendering his visions with a smooth skill which a modern architect can envy. When Davis was sixty-four, he listed in his diary the various items in his repertory of suburban and country dwellings:

> American Log Cabin, Farm House, English cottage, Collegiate Gothic, Manor house, French suburban, Switz cottage, Lombard Italian, Tuscan from Pliny's villa at Ostia, Ancient Etruscan, Suburban Greek, Oriental, Moorish, and Castellated.

When Davis wrote this list in 1867, the architect's dream had become a nightmare. At Bridgeport stood Iranistan, a domed and minareted mansion by Leopold Eidlitz which looked like the palace of a Shah but was the home of P. T. Barnum. The wooden Egyptian gateway to Mount Auburn cemetery, where Pierce Butler had courted Fanny Kemble, had been rebuilt in stone. The red bulk of the Smithsonian clashed with the white wings which sprouted from both ends of the near-by Capitol, whose new dome, three hundred feet high, was veneered with cast-iron plates which simulated stone. At Natchez, Samuel Sloan designed Longwood for Thomas Nutt in the "Byzantine" manner, and its thirty-two rooms held niches for the marble statues which, sent from Italy, never reached port. When Lincoln proclaimed a state of war, the carpenters threw down their tools and the painters their brushes; and only one of the master's children lived on for seventy-odd years in the basement of "Nutt's Folly."

The rooms within such houses matched their exteriors in meaningless elaboration. No square foot of the Morse-Libby music room in Portland, Maine, was spared its bulging reliefs of fruits and flowers, its frescoed arabesques. In the same decade of the 1850's Richard Upjohn designed a Brooklyn home for Henry Evelyn Pierrepont whose parlor was confusion itself. A carpet with a pink ground bloomed with huge roses and conch shells; a frescoed ceiling tried to combine garlands of flowers with vaguely Moorish arabesques. Its windows were ceiling high, swathed with heavy lace and heavier blue brocade under a gilded lambrequin whose sharp angles competed with its curving scrolls. No inch of floor or wall was free of visual torment, thanks to the jigsawed *étagère* on which china imitated lace, the console table with its soapy statuette, the rosewood cabinet with tapestry panel, the flamboyantly Gothic chairs, the innumerable small pictures hung in random fashion, the chandelier with crystal pendants and engraved glass globes.

To defend their profession against stylistic barbarism,

Music Room, Morse-Libby House, Portland, Me.

Historic American Buildings Survey, Library of Congress

the designers organized the American Institute of Architects in the late fifties. It soon had branches in most of the larger cities, and sponsored lectures, discussions, and competitions. Richard Upjohn, replying to a toast at Delmonico's in 1858, contrasted his earlier years of lonely effort with this new solidarity. The majority of architects, builders, and manufacturers, however, ignored the reproof which the Institute implied, and continued to plunder the past as Sherman plundered Georgia. Their motives were summarized by Gervase

Wheeler: "All we can do is to combine, using bits here and there, as our education affords more or less acquaintance with the models from which we steal our material." And Wheeler's remark that out of this Babel an American speech might emerge expressed more hope than expectation.

CHAPTER 15 / THE WHITE MARMOREAN FLOCK

Had Benjamin Latrobe lived a decade beyond 1820 he might have said less complimentary things of the new carved figureheads than he had said of William Rush. The new clippers were sleeker and swifter than the broad-beamed *Constitution,* and the men who cut the portraits and allegorical figures for their prows lost in vigor what they gained in slickness of detail.

On the slaver *Creole* rode a stylish young woman in a blue dress holding a flower in one hand, her face, hair, and costume as thoroughly carved behind as before and painted with lifelike colors. An Isaac Fowle figurehead in the old Boston State House has the traditional forward-bending pose, but the carved details of her petticoat hem, the bodice buttons, the flowers in her hair, and the fine features are more appropriate to a beauty admired at close distance than to one who must contend with wind and salt spray. White-and-gold figures replaced colored ones as the old heroes and gods gradually lost their sea legs. Many ship carvers continued in the forties and fifties to work with the earlier ruggedness, but it was clear that new ways of seeing and of shaping three-dimensional volume were at work even in this conservative craft.

In sculpture meant to be looked at closely on land, a polished perfection had been the unquestioned aim since Jefferson's imported band arrived from Italy to decorate the Capitol; Jefferson had declared that "old Canove of Rome" was without a rival in the art, and for nearly half a century that opinion was accepted by Americans.

Modern writers on sculpture have pointed out that a full-rounded figure of stone or clay provokes by its tangibility the response we give to actual human figures; as Richard Guggenheimer says, this condition tempts one sculptor merely to reproduce human forms while another finds it difficult to "inject intimations of infinity into so finite a medium." Yet intimations of one kind or another were what the sculptor most desired in the days of Margaret Fuller. He might concede that when a Hiram Powers chiseled the mane, the eye sockets, and the toothless mouth of Andrew Jackson there was nothing to do but translate flesh into marble. But when he turned from portrait busts to the "ideal," he sought a moral and physical perfection never to be found in one mortal creature.

The transcendentalists, as Van Wyck Brooks has written, saw works of art not through the eye but through the mind. In sculpture, Miss Fuller said, "the heights to which our being comes are represented; and its nature is such as to allow us to leave out all that vulgarizes,—all that bridges over the actual from the ideal . . . The man who could not write his thought of beauty in his life, wrote it in stone." Fanny Kemble had seen Canova statuettes on Beacon Hill mantelpieces, and Bostonians knew by heart the lines which Byron had written on the sculptor's *Helen:*

> In this beloved marble view,
> Above the works and thoughts of man,
> What Nature *could,* but *would not* do,
> And beauty and Canova can.

Reverently, in the *Dial* of 1843, Margaret Fuller quoted the Italian master's remarks on sculpture, which she had found in his biography: "As poetic diction should be pure, lucid, elegant, dignified, even so statuary should not make use of a coarse and porous stone, but of the finest and hardest marble . . . You ought to know anatomy well, but not to make others observe this," for nature "does not draw attention to the anatomy, but covers it admirably, by a well contrived veil of flesh and skin, presenting to the eyes only a gentle surface, which modulates and curves itself with ease over every projection."

The work of American sculptors before the Civil War is proof that Canova's skin-deep aesthetics ruled most of them. Had more Yankee carvers stayed at home, there might have been homelier sculptural speech and less elegantly poetic diction. As it was, a Powers or a Crawford could feel somewhat more secure than a Rush or a Frazee. There was plenty of work to be had by a young man whose hands could model wax into speaking likenesses for the museums, as Powers did in Cincinnati; and American graveyards were becoming

Figurehead from the ship *Creole*

Museum of Fine Arts, Boston, Mass.

vast areas of "natural" scenery which called for glistening tombs, urns, garlands, and weeping women. Bankers and merchants sought permanence, if not immortality, in busts. Legislators up and down the land were in a mood to commission stone reminders of those who had made the republic.

In the matter of form and style there were two native traits which reinforced the Canovan theory. Only a few Americans understood the philosophy behind his polished curvatures, but there were many who admired polish for its own sake. Americans enjoyed a difficult feat well done, and a finished statue represented a long, patient, and intricate process of chipping and polishing, a triumph of ingenuity and skill over an unyielding material.

The second trait was a moralism of long standing, a mistrust of the merely physical. This prudery of the middle class was a furtive and self-contradicting modesty which seemed none too sure of its own premises. Joel Hart's nude female was first called *Venus,* then *Purity,* then *The Triumph of Chastity;* breasts were called bosoms, and a Mr. Fazzi of Cincinnati was hired to make fig leaves for the statues which the Ladies' Academy of Art in that progressive city had imported from Europe. Canova had said that the sculptor need not fear to copy God's work, but "always in purity and with that veil of modesty which indeed nature did not need in the innocence of first creation, but does so now in her perverted estate." Puerilities like these—and the American writings are full of them—were the genteel verbal equivalents of the fig leaf, the mincing hands of the Medici *Venus,* and the chain of the *Greek Slave.*

Scarcely a stone figure of these years, from the *Chanting Cherubs* of Greenough which Boston saw in 1831 to the *Endymion* of William Henry Rinehart, which was made in Rome in the eighteen seventies, but entered the American perception with a literary-moral passport of some kind. Akers' *Pearl Fisher* was praised because it had a soul which made its nudity poetic, and Hiram Powers preferred his own *Proserpine* to the Medici *Venus* because the spirit of his statue shone through her eyes, while *Venus* had the stare of an idiot. The statues of Henry Kirke Brown were executed, the New York *Mirror* said, in the spirit of the antique, but with the feeling of a Christian.

Their minds inspired by these lofty if ambiguous ideals and their notebooks filled with commissions, the "white marmorean flock" (a phrase which Henry James applied to Harriet Hosmer and her sculptress friends) established themselves in Italy. In that witty book, *Yankee Stonecutters,* Albert Ten Eyck Gardner has listed over a hundred of them who were born between 1800 and 1830. William Cullen Bryant counted thirty expatriates in Rome in 1859, and Horatio Greenough's brother Henry contrived a half-fictional novel, *Ernest Carroll or Artist Life in Italy,* describing how Powers and his friends gathered to discuss art in the Caffè Doney in Florence. William Wetmore Story watched brilliant cardinals climbing a Roman staircase by the light of torches, heard Allegri's *Miserere* while the mighty

Tomkins H. Matteson, *A Sculptor's Studio* (the Albany studio of E. D. Palmer)

Albany Institute of History and Art

figures of Michelangelo looked down from the Sistine ceiling, and picnicked with the Brownings at Bagni di Lucca. What a relief after bleak New England, Story thought, for he remembered the advertisements in Yankee horsecars of "Reversible Food" and "Overstrung Pianos," and decided that the latter were typical of an overstrung country.

The search for a mellow atmosphere was not the only motive for this emigration. Models, materials, and living were cheaper in Italy than at home, and marble cutters worked for four dollars a day. One could make clay portrait studies in New York and take them abroad to be turned into stone; and Bryant shrewdly observed that Rome was a better place to obtain orders from one's own countrymen than any American city: "The rich man who, at home, is contented with mirrors and rosewood, is here initiated into a new set of ideas, gets a taste, and orders a bust, a little statue of Eve, a Ruth, or a Rebecca . . . for his luxurious rooms in the United States." White marble invaded the American villa, hotel, and public hall as commissions went eastward and the all-too-finished product came west in seagoing crates; the various art associations began to distribute sculpture as well as pictures to their members; and the American cemetery became an outdoor statuary show.

Among the Yankees abroad were Shobal Clevenger, William H. Rinehart, Chauncey B. Ives, Joel T. Hart, Harriet Hosmer, Randolph Rogers, Hiram Powers, Thomas Crawford, and Horatio Greenough; most of them had known no other training than apprenticeship to a maker of gravestones, window sills, and mantelpieces. When they were not chipping away at the "ideal" they busied themselves with more mundane subjects, and in their workrooms the long shelves of portrait busts kept company with the *Clyties*, the *Zenobias*, and the *Cleopatras*. Bryant observed seven replicas of *Proserpine* in Powers' studio; but she had frock-coated companions—Webster, Calhoun, Marshall, Van Buren, and over a hundred others—before Powers died. Miss Hosmer produced a bronze statue of Thomas Hart

Benton for St. Louis; in Crawford's studio *Orpheus* was jostled by *Patrick Henry*. The *Ruth* of Henry Kirke Brown, gleaning "in tears amid the alien corn," was inspired by Keats, but Brown is remembered for his Union Square *Washington;* and Connecticut praised Chauncey Ives for his bust of Ithiel Town, polished and lean-featured, with his chest resting on a copy of *The Antiquities of Athens*.

The *Zenobias* and the *Nydias* deserve no extended comment in our time. Nearly devoid of personal style, alike in size, shape, and proportion, plagiarisms from inferior ancient models, they represent an empty victory of "mind" over matter. In their capacity to see what was not there, and to ignore what was, the people who called them masterpieces were like those who admired the emperor's new clothes. The men who made them were caught in an aesthetic dilemma which they were powerless to resolve.

That dilemma is between the lines of Hawthorne's tales and travel notes. The sculptor's art obsessed Hawthorne, and several of his tales played variations on the Pygmalion idea: "The miracle of imbuing an inanimate substance with thought, feeling, and all the intangible attributes of the soul." The conversations of Kenyon and Miriam in *The Marble Faun* reflected the author's own doubts about sculpture. Kenyon was a man of contradictions, feverishly working the facile clay as though guided by an unseen helper and tormented meanwhile by the doubt whether marble was ever anything but cold limestone with a beauty merely physical.

The problem of nudity also troubled the Puritan in Hawthorne. As Miriam pointed out, the human body had been a familiar experience for the Greeks, but nowadays "people are as good as born in their clothes"; the artist cannot therefore sculpture nudity without guilty glimpses at hired models. Yet Hawthorne wrote more shrewdly when he saw Powers' statue of *America*, "warmed out of the cold allegorical sisterhood who have generally no merit in chastity, being really without sex."

Marble and bronze clothing, on the other hand, were dangerous in sculpture because fashions changed with history; and Hawthorne once counseled Powers to use cloaks and other half-abstract garments. Perhaps, as Kenyon hoped, mankind would consent to wear something more sculpturable than the hoop petticoat and the cutaway; at least the man of the chisel must do his best to "idealize the tailor."

Untroubled by these misgivings, most of the Yankee stonecutters continued to turn out busts which Hawthorne said were the petrifications of a vain self-estimate, and allegories in which he saw only the skill of "some nameless machine in human shape." And when he spoke of those complacent and clever men "who on the strength of some knack in handling clay . . . are bold to call themselves sculptors," one thinks of Hiram Powers.

That sharp-featured Vermonter, whom the novelist found so "racy and oracular," had clerked in a Cincinnati store before he produced the wax figures in Dorfeuille's Museum which Mrs. Trollope described—"dwarfs that by machinery grow into giants before the eyes of the spectator; imps of ebony with eyes of flame; monstrous reptiles devouring youth and beauty." Hiram's talent with wax, paint, and springs, and his proficiency at bust-making under Frederick Eckstein's instruction, moved Nicholas Longworth to finance his journeys to Washington and Europe. Powers went to Italy in 1837 to spend his life, a man who was called a genius, who made the most publicized statue of a generation, and whose yearly income Albert Gardner estimates at over five thousand dollars.

As Hawthorne remarked, no mysteries of the sculptor's art perplexed the Vermont man. In odd moments Powers invented a machine for curing colds, a two-tongued jew's-harp, and a scheme for laying the Atlantic cable; but there was small leisure in a life which produced, according to his son, some one hundred and fifty portrait busts (for which his fee was a thousand dollars each), a half dozen full-length portrait statues, and a long parade of *Eves, Clyties, Hopes, Ginevras,* and *Evangelines*. He was paid four hundred dollars apiece for his fifty replicas of *Proserpine;* and the New Orleans merchant or the New York banker who wanted one of his six versions of the *Greek Slave* had to pay four thousand dollars for it.

Although the Greek War had ended a decade before Powers modeled his *Slave* in 1843 it was still vivid in men's minds; and Powers read that the female prisoners of the Turks had been sold in slave markets. "As there should be a moral in every work of art," the sculptor explained, "I have given to the expression of the Greek slave what trust there could still be in a Divine Providence for a future state of existence, with utter despair for the present, mingled somewhat of scorn for all around her . . . It is not her person but her spirit that stands exposed."

No sooner had the statue been approved by a committee of Cincinnati clergymen, and shown at the Crystal Palace in London, than thousands proved that they too could see what Powers claimed was there, and not the characterless pseudo-Grecian face, the slippery and boneless body, the discreetly modulated forms, the chained hands coyly placed. Even Philip Hone melted before her and wrote: "I have no personal acquaintance with Powers, nor had I with Praxiteles, but I am not willing to undervaluate my countryman

The *Greek Slave* at the Düsseldorf Gallery, New York City, R. Thew engraving (detail)

New York Public Library photo

because he was not born so soon as the other gentleman of the chisel." Henceforth for half a century, parlors from Boston to San Francisco held miniature copies of the *Greek Slave,* as Henry James recalled, "so undressed, yet so refined, even so pensive, in sugar-white alabaster, exposed under little glass covers in such American homes as could bring themselves to think such things right."

One other statue of the period became as famous as the *Greek Slave,* but for different reasons — the Capitoline George Washington of Horatio Greenough. It was largely through the effort of Washington Allston that Greenough received this government commission in 1832; its price was to be five thousand dollars and its destination the Capitol rotunda. The sculptor was twenty-seven and had had several years in Italy. Behind that were his Boston and Cambridge days—the sketches in the Athenaeum when he was twelve, the lessons in clay modeling from Solomon Willard, Doctor Parkman's help with human anatomy, the steeping in New England gentility at Cambridge, where Greenough succumbed to Allston's charm, "so adapted," as he later said, "to kindle and enlighten me, making me no longer myself, but as it were, an emanation of his own soul." Before joining the expatriates, Horatio was asked by Robert Gilmor to model a portrait bust, and worked in the Gothic library at Glenellen with its stained glass and its Flemish and Italian paintings, in his ears the "frolic fingering of the young ladies' waltzes."

Greenough in Italy was thoroughly content with what he called "dear, compact, bird's-eye, cheap, quiet, mind-your-own-business, beautiful Florence." Out of his shop came Cooper's *Chanting Cherubs* and other "shapes etherial." On a delicious evening in 1835 Henry Tuckerman found Greenough in his studio; it had once been a chapel, and "the softened effulgence of an Italian twilight glimmered through the high windows." Tuckerman thought of the long and soothing days which his companion would devote to his statue of the first President. "May the benignant countenance of Washington beam with life-like vividness in the visions of the artist, and its image emerge nobly from its marble sleep . . ."

The story of the *Washington* was long but scarcely soothing. As the clay took shape it became a modernization of the great seated Zeus which Phidias had once carved for Olympia. Greenough had doubtless seen in a niche at the end of the Gallery of Statues in the Vatican a distant cousin of the lost Phidias work, seated on his marble throne, nude to the waist with drapery thrown over his legs and sandals on his feet, his right arm in his lap and his left grasping a spearlike scepter. This was to be the general pose, and the head was to be the head of Houdon's famous statue.

A year and a half passed and the small clay model was complete. The letters of the next three years recounted the sculptor's difficulties: the problem of a chair which would be grand rather than "Frenchy," the trouble in finding a cast of the Houdon bust, the ignorance and trickery of his hired mechanics. By 1836, the full-scale clay figure was ready to be cast in plaster. After three years more, the sculptor professed himself pleased with the likeness but added, "What will be its reception as a work of art I know not."

Washington crossed the Atlantic on a sloop of war and reached the nation's capital in July, 1841. The marble was ten and a half feet high and weighed twenty tons; to the captain's bill of seventy-seven hundred dollars was added five thousand to move it from the Navy Yard to the rotunda. Greenough was on hand in 1842 to present his own bill; and by the time *Washington* sat down in the Capitol, he had cost the government some twenty-one thousand dollars.

Horatio Greenough, *George Washington*

Hillyer Art Library photo

The sculptor's troubles were not yet over. The rotunda lighting was a failure and in 1843 he petitioned Congress to move the figure to the grounds of the western front of the Capitol and to protect it with a building of some sort. Congress moved it instead to the eastern front with a makeshift shelter above it; and by 1847 the shelter was torn down and the Jovian George exposed to rain and frost. But nature was less unkind than man to this "noble enterprise." The statue became at once the "butt of wiseacres and witlings," as the sculptor said, and waves of outraged purity and patriotism broke over its bare shoulders. When Philip Hone saw the colossus under its octagonal canopy, he wrote in his diary:

> . . . it looks like a great herculean Warrior-like *Venus of the bath,* a grand Martial Magog—undraped, with a huge napkin lying on his lap and covering his lower extremities, and he preparing to perform his ablutions is in the act of consigning his sword to the care of the attendant. . . . Washington was too prudent, and careful of his health, to expose himself thus in a climate so uncertain as ours, to say nothing of the indecency of such an exposure, a subject on which he was known to be exceedingly fastidious.

Greenough was back in Florence when Hone wrote,

but he had left behind a tart rejoinder to his critics. He had outlived, he said, the sneers which had greeted this first effort to represent a great man without a shirt; perhaps the American sculptor of the future would be allowed to show that the writer of the Scriptures meant more than the face when he declared that God had made men after His own image. And in a letter of 1847 to R. C. Winthrop, he declared that the general mind alone could judge his work. "When . . . the true sculptors of America shall have filled the metropolis with beauty and grandeur, will it not be worth $30,000 to be able to point to the figure and say — 'there was the first struggle of our infant art'?"

After more than half a century in the open air, the *Washington* was moved again, this time to gather dust in a dim alcove at the Smithsonian. The imperious head stares across the cluttered room, one sandaled foot thrusts forward, the left arm extends a sheathed sword, and the right hand points to Heaven. No American had dared to be so monumental in scale or so majestic in pose and gesture. The conventions of the time are in the silky-smooth surfaces and the minute perfection of every lock of hair, every fingernail, and every fold in the general's robe, yet these formal inconsistencies do not wholly destroy the power of the conception.

Greenough failed, as most of his contemporaries did, to resolve the conflict between Ideality and Substance, but his effort was mightier than any other. His intellect towered above those of the expatriate flock as his colossal *George* towered above their *Clyties* and *Endymions*. To reverse Margaret Fuller's phrase, this man who could not write his thought of beauty in stone, wrote it in words. His notions of art, published in magazines or jotted down for future use, ranged far beyond his time, and his analysis of the art he saw around him was brilliantly perceptive. Emerson talked with him in Concord in the year 1852, which would be Greenough's last, and noted in his journal:

> He makes many of my accustomed stars pale by his clear light. His magnanimity, his idea of a great man, his courage, and cheer, and self-reliance, and depth, and self-derived knowledge, charmed and invigorated me, as none has, who has gone by, these many months. . . .

In that year, a group of the sculptor's friends suggested a professorship of art for him in a university, and Greenough published a collection of essays and lectures under the pseudonym of Horace Bender, *The Travels, Observations and Experiences of a Yankee Stonecutter*. As a democrat he declared that full economic and social equality were the first condition for the development of his country's art; as a believer in the organic principle—nearly half a century before Sullivan and Wright—he gave his highest praise to the works of man which this principle had shaped:

Thomas Crawford, *Indian Chief* (for Senate pediment)

New York Historical Society

> Observe a ship at sea! Mark the majestic form of her hull as she rushes through the water, observe the graceful bend of her body, the gentle transition from round to flat, the grasp of her keel, the leap of her bows, the symmetry and rich tracery of her spars and rigging, and those grand wind muscles, her sails. . . . What Academy of Design, what research of connoisseurship, what imitation of the Greeks produced this marvel of construction? . . . God's world has a distinct formula for every function, and . . . we shall seek in vain to borrow shapes; we must make the shapes, and can only effect this by mastering the principles.

On December 18, 1852, Greenough died of brain fever. Emerson had just asked him his age. " 'Forty-seven years of joy I have lived' was his answer." Would the later years have seen the fulfillment of his philosophy in his sculpture? Perhaps he would have come to know that he had condemned his own master work in advance when he wrote to Allston in 1831 that "no model of past times . . . has a prescriptive right to cramp our convenience or to repress our invention." Too many years of Greenough's life had been spent in isolation from the democratic ferment of his own country.

That ferment had produced many verbal comments on the sculptural habits of America. Emerson found no passion for form in the statues of his time, which had "a paltriness as of toys and the trumpery of the theater"; the sculptor Thomas Crawford wrote that "the darkness of allegory must give way to common sense."

Crawford had studied in his youth with John Frazee, and Hawthorne visited his Roman studio in the Piazza di Termini. From Thorwaldsen the American learned

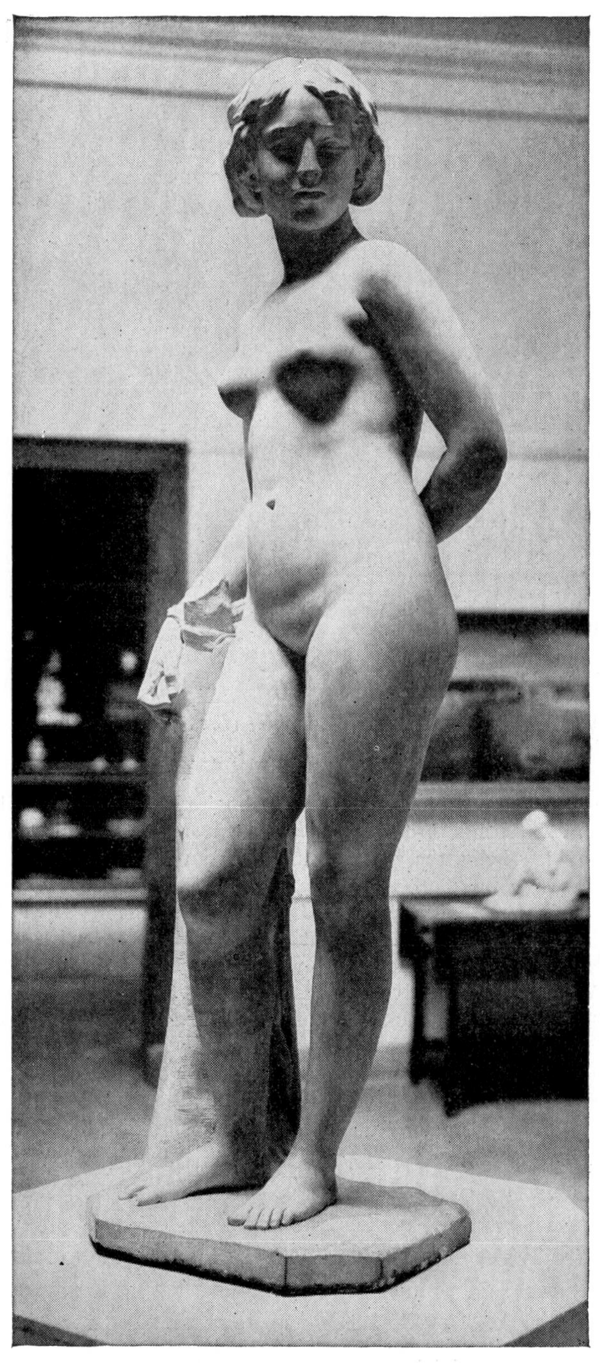

Erastus D. Palmer, *The White Captive*

Albany Institute of History and Art

that the plastic vitality of a sculpture as a whole was more important than the slick perfection of its parts; yet his *Orpheus* was a cold, classical paraphrase, and so was the Senate pediment which Italians cut from his designs, although there was a degree of vigor in some of its individual figures. In his bronze doors for the Senate portico, Crawford avoided the complex movement and the clever perspective illusion of Ghiberti's reliefs for the Florence baptistery, and his episodes from American history were soberly composed within their rectangular panels.

Before Crawford died he had completed the plaster model, nineteen feet high, of a bronze *Freedom* for the Capitol dome, a formless, bulky female whose liberty cap, at the suggestion of Jefferson Davis, had become a plumed helmet, and whose every fold and fringe was cut with a minuteness forever invisible to all but the Washington sparrows. After a year's voyage the statue reached Washington in sections and was cast by Clark Mills. At noon of December 1, 1863, guns roared from the field batteries which ringed the wartime capital, a flag went up, and Thomas Walter gave the signal for *Freedom's* bronze head to rise and complete her body. She was not the last of her kind, but perhaps the worst, the questionable plumes and odd silhouette rather suggestive of a pregnant squaw three hundred feet in the air.

In the eighteen fifties, Americans could compare Crawford's equestrian *Washington* at Richmond with the work of more independent spirits, many of whom had learned their craft in America. Clark Mills had adapted for his *Jackson,* as Professor Valentiner has observed, the rearing horse which Bernini once modeled, and Falconet in the statue of Peter the Great at Leningrad. It was the first of its kind in America, a great metal bulk balanced on the hind feet of Andrew's mount, and had more spirit than sophistication. Henry K. Brown modeled his *Washington* for Union Square, New York, in plaster, and entrusted it for casting to the Ames Company in Chicopee, Massachusetts. The Brown statue may derive from the Marcus Aurelius on the Capitoline, but has its own sturdy sense of volume and controlled dignity of movement; and Brown himself declared that he saw no reason for young sculptors to flock to Italy.

Robert Ball Hughes was another who never saw the Vatican, though he once made an Apollo Belvedere in bas-relief. He was a Londoner who worked in Boston and New York, and who learned to "idealize the tailor." His original model of Alexander Hamilton for the New York Merchant's Exchange represented that gentleman in the dress of his period; a woodcut in the *Mirror* two months before *Hamilton* was destroyed by the fire of 1835 provides him with a vaguely classical chiton, draped around him and hanging down behind. But Hughes's seated bronze of Nathaniel Bowditch for Mount Auburn cemetery froze that eminent author of *The New Practical Navigator* in his own clothes and his own chair at Salem.

Among the genteel there were still demands for ideality. Rinehart, Rogers, Akers, Ives, and Story continued to export it from Rome and Florence, but men who stayed at home could move more freely with the popular current. Europe never saw Edward Brackett or James MacDonald, and Erastus Dow Palmer of Albany

John Q. A. Ward, *Indian Hunter,* Central Park, New York City

Hillyer Art Library photo

worked on his own at cameos, cabinetmaking, and wood carving before he showed his marbles in the fifties. Badeau preferred Palmer's *Indian Girl,* which he called American in conception, type, idea, and execution, to the spiritless *Slave* of Powers; and Palmer's *White Captive,* despite its smoothness, has a lithe grace, a sense of bodily articulation, and a fullness of volumes which the Grecian girl had lacked; her head was vigorously and freshly modeled from the sculptor's own daughter.

Thomas Ball fashioned his plaster model for an equestrian *Washington,* not in the effulgent light of an Italian studio but in a cold barn on Tremont Street in Boston. He had struggled, in company with George Fuller, to equal the color of Washington Allston in painting, and then turned to making small portrait busts of celebrities to be cast in plaster, and this rugged Yankee found his own way of solving technical problems. For two years Ball joined the colony in Florence, but the force of the *Washington* was his own, and in *My Threescore Years and Ten* he described his months of struggle with the huge figure as he built up its forms piecemeal on his armature with bits of plaster, walking to and fro in the freezing studio to gauge its effect. When the bronze was unveiled in Boston's Public Gardens in 1869, ten years after Ball's first sketch of it, he had triumphantly solved the most difficult problems of the sculptor's art, and produced a horse and rider worthy of comparison with Brown's in Union Square.

Neither John Rogers nor John Quincy Adams Ward conformed to the pattern of the idealizers. Rogers was a sharp Salem man who spent less than a year abroad, and his Centre Street studio in New York was a small factory where twenty workmen—then sixty as his business grew—helped him to fashion the plaster groups which, with the aid of his flexible molds, were reproduced in their thousands from his clay or bronze master models. His circulars came out year after year, each listing his subjects and giving its dimensions and its price. Rogers quoted the testimonials of Garrison and Whittier, who knew that his *Fugitive's Story* was

Henry K. Brown, *George Washington,* Union Square, New York City

Bogart Studio photo

as useful in its way as *Uncle Tom's Cabin,* and he boasted that his figures of the Abolitionists had been conscientiously modeled on measured studies and photographs.

From the first commonplace pieces in which one or two figures were placed awkwardly together, Rogers moved toward more complicated works whose composition was determined by the story which they told and whose details he rendered with extraordinary skill. His *Checker Players, Village Schoolmaster,* and *Town Pump* were the three-dimensional counterpart of the genre which Bingham, Mount, and Woodville painted.

It was a similar documentary spirit which sent Ward to the West to study his subject at first hand before he made the *Indian Hunter* for Central Park. There was a hint of Grecian handsomeness in the face of his first study for this work, but the intent and scowling head of the completed statue was rather magnificent in its knotted forms, and there was a lithe unity between the postures of man and dog. American sculptors had not yet learned how different bronze is from marble, but Ward made something of the contrast between the lean muscles of the Indian, the broken and shaggy forms of his fur garment, and the animal's coat. A true sculptor's sense of form and texture was in his fingers.

The vigor which Ward achieved at his best was in everything that William Rimmer said, wrote, painted, or carved. In the Boston of the eighteen forties this odd and contradictory Englishman dissected corpses at the Massachusetts Medical College. Doctor Rimmer soon knew human and animal anatomy as few others did, and during the war years his lectures in Boston and New York delighted not only medical men but artists. Standing at his blackboard, he drew men's bodies whirling through space or locked in battle with every bone, tendon, and muscle doing its appointed work, yet with no loss of dramatic expressiveness or grace.

With clay or in stone Rimmer shaped his material on

Greenough's organic principle as Greenough himself failed to do. Even *Despair,* a figure less than a foot high which he cut from chalk when he was in his teens, had an emotional intensity out of proportion to its size and a masterly design in its contracted legs and arms (Boston Mus. Fine Arts). Thirty years later he carved a head of *Saint Stephen* directly in granite; making no effort to force his medium to a degree of detail beyond its range, he achieved a noble study of human suffering devoid of the mawkish. Rimmer never saw the torsions of his *Falling Gladiator* rendered into bronze but his plaster of 1861 was shown in the Paris salon of the next year. French critics asked whether it had been cast mechanically from a human body, but under its realistic surfaces was a thrusting sense of forms in space which was art, not science.

Rimmer had just begun to carve granite when Jarves wrote in *Art Hints* that "the only sure source of power for the artist is from within himself," a sentence which can be applied to the Doctor. Jarves knew that the scale, finish, and design of a statue derive from its location, material, and function, and his chapter on American sculpture in *The Art Idea* was the most thoughtful evaluation yet made in the United States. He dismissed the *Greek Slave* as the work of a mere technician and wrote that Crawford's Capitol pediment was hastily conceived, crude, and puerile. He perceived that Greenough had been a true artist ahead of his time, though his conception surpassed his execution; in Ward's *African Freedman* he saw the hint of great work to come and in the Rogers groups "not high art, but genuine art." And Jarves' conclusion was phrased in the optative mood:

> . . . a people whose school of sculpture, commencing in a Greenough, in less than one generation gives birth to artists of the varied calibre of Ward, John Rogers and Story, has no occasion to envy the progress of other nations in the same space of time.

William Rimmer, *Despair*

Museum of Fine Arts, Boston, Mass.

William S. Mount, *The Painter's Triumph* (detail) ▶

Pennsylvania Academy of Fine Arts

PART TWO

AT THE FEET OF THE FAMILIAR

INTRODUCTION / PAINT FOR THE MANY

The forty-odd years between Morse's intimate landscape of Cooperstown and the huge panoramas of Bierstadt were as productive as any in our history. When they began, men still lived who had seen the first President and who read Channing's remarks on the literary future of the republic. When they closed, Winslow Homer had done his *New England Country School* and Ryder the first of his moonstruck seas. Channing's essay had become a classic to a generation which heard the fierce affirmations and thunderous prophecies of Whitman's *Democratic Vistas.*

The pioneers of republican painting lived into the age of Jackson, in whose atmosphere many of them found frustration. The Peales had sold their Baltimore Museum in 1830 for a city hall, and Rembrandt Peale at fifty-two had outlived the public sensation of the *Court of Death;* the thirty years before him would be spent in preparing his *Graphics* for publication, in traveling to Europe, in teaching the Philadelphia High School children to draw, and in an occasional portrait done with the Peale vigor. His shrewd and ripe recollections appeared in the *Crayon* and his replicas of the Washington portrait were everywhere.

In Cambridgeport, James Russell Lowell saw Washington Allston mounting the omnibus for Boston, a beautiful old man fastidiously neat, with a cloud of white hair and a face like pale flame, whose nature had been so steeped in Italian sunshine that the east winds of Boston assailed it in vain. Yet this Titian of Cambridgeport could not breathe life into the great cold *Belshazzar* which stood unfinished, year after year, in his painting room. Ten enlightened Bostonians had once subscribed one thousand dollars each for its purchase, and this moral obligation weighed heavily on the artist as he struggled to achieve the breadth and the all-compassing rhythm he so admired in the Venetians.

At one moment Allston painted out the figure of the king, at another he enlarged the figures on the right; he revised the gesture of Daniel and multiplied the background courtiers. His larger-than-life charcoal drawings of hands and his mechanical perspective diagrams for the "barbaric" columns prove how meticulously he went about a task beyond his powers. Margaret Fuller observed that the beautiful was Allston's domain, and that "the Prophets and Sibyls are for the Michael Angelos." It was Allston's tragedy that he could not leave the prophets and sibyls alone. Lowell called him "a man all soul"; and as the huge canvas darkened at Cambridgeport, its creator may have realized that more than soul was involved in being a Michelangelo.

Just before Allston died in 1843 Elizabeth Peabody visited his studio, and the kindred spirits discussed how a scene from the *Faerie Queen* should be painted. Britomartis, Miss Peabody thought, should be buoyed up into the lightness of a vision by her joyous and spirituelle maidenhood, and Sir Artegal should be given a pale face through which his intellect would shine like a light through an alabaster vase. Having risen to that electric sphere which needs no words, Elizabeth departed. Within three weeks Harvard students were carrying Allston's body by torchlight to Christ Church graveyard and Richard Henry Dana stood looking at the unfinished *Belshazzar* with its murky shadows, its unconvincing spaces and its static forms; a solemn awe stole over him in the presence of that sacred relic. Sixty years later Henry James recalled the dim Allstons he had seen in the parlors of Boston houses; he summed up the *Belshazzar,* in which an occasional passage of melody leaped from a troubled symphony, as the mask of some impenetrable strain in Allston.

Only a little more successful were the experiments of Morse in what he called the intellectual branch of art. His mind was already busy with a new use for electricity when he wrote from Paris in 1832, "Will my country employ me on works which will do it honor?" His country had ignored the *Dying Hercules,* and he discovered one cast of it in the dust and rubbish of the Capitol cellar years later when he was stringing wires to demonstrate his telegraph. And in spite of a pamphlet signed by distinguished friends which urged Congress to buy his *Old House of Representatives,* an Englishman finally possessed the painting; it was twenty-five years old when someone discovered it, stretcherless, cracked, and dusty, nailed to a board partition in a New York warehouse.

Morse went abroad in 1829 with commissions to copy Rubens, Rembrandt, and the *School of Athens.* The Paris which delighted him was not the city where Tom Paine had watched mobs gather, but one which had seen the amiable and stupid Louis Philippe crowned king. Fifteen years of the Restoration, with their disillusions, had broken the classicism of David, whose pupils now repeated the master's stage effects but omitted the plot. Ingres, along with his splendidly solid portraits of the new bourgeois, pieced together several classical stereotypes—but what was Hecuba to a grocer? In France, as in Morse's America, men were forgetting that the ghosts of Brutus and the Gracchi had watched over the birth of their new society; and the classical weapons had become the shabby props of a tiresome charade. Morse arrived in time to see Delacroix's *Liberty Guiding the People,* young, vigorous, and shapely, with bared breasts, striding the barricade with something of Michelangelo in her movement and something of Rubens' breadth and boldness in the artist's brushing.

Neither by birth nor by temperament was Morse prepared to adopt the French Romantics' contempt for the "vain pasturage" of common men, their hatred of the bourgeois; but he could and did profit by the new freedoms of color and form. Even his Charleston portraits had been done with a delicacy and a delight in fresh tones which his dead-surfaced *Hercules* had lacked. Here in Paris, while Cooper looked over his shoulder, Morse reproduced the Salon Carré of the Louvre with its Rembrandts, Titians, and over thirty other masterpieces on a canvas nine feet wide and slightly over six feet high. His picture was intended to tour the American towns whose people had never seen the *Mona Lisa* or the *Wedding Feast* of Veronese; yet the painter made no effort to be more specific than his scale warranted. The great hall is filled with light and its contents are summarized with a free brush which somehow conveys in a space fifteen inches long the drama of Poussin's *Diogenes,* the radiance of Claude, and the tragedy of Titian's *Entombment.*

The *Louvre* was a tour de force of which no other American was capable, but it sold for a little more than one half of what he asked for it to finance his telegraph. The Morse who explored photography and taught the arts of design at New York University had little time for painting. He tried and failed to secure a commission for four historical pictures for the Capitol, and wrote in the year 1864, when he was seventy-three, that he had sacrificed a profession in order to benefit mankind through science. And Morse confessed that he had never possessed the skill to work in the grand style.

The face of John Trumbull in the portrait by Waldo and Jewett in 1832 (Yale Univ.) is that of a patrician with a hint of aloof resentment. He had dreamed of a great National Gallery, and his project for twelve history paintings had shrunk to the four which his government finally installed in the Capitol rotunda when the artist was sixty-eight. When Yale College offered in 1831 to provide him a small annuity and a gallery for

Samuel F. B. Morse, *The Louvre* (Syracuse University, Syracuse, N. Y.)

Photo courtesy Metropolitan Museum of Art, New York City

his collection, he knew there was no better choice for him. Twelve years later this man who had scorned the French Revolution and had recorded his own with a Davidian coolness was buried beneath the Trumbull Gallery with the epitaph:

Patriot and Artist.
To his Country he gave
his Sword and his Pencil.

Out of the scramble for the rotunda spaces John Vanderlyn secured one through the efforts of his friend Allston and went off to Paris in his sixty-fifth year to complete a thoroughly dull *Landing of Columbus*. The erstwhile friend of Aaron Burr was no lover of the new ways in America, a state which he believed more favorable to impudent quacks and impostors than to modest and unassuming merit. To the young Benjamin Champney, who saw Vanderlyn in Paris in the year 1841, he was a decrepit old-school gentleman who had once heard Gilbert Stuart tell racy stories to George Washington.

It was Champney who climbed a ladder to paint the sky in the Columbus picture and who helped finish a *Niagara Falls* from sketches Vanderlyn had made forty years before. "I dared say but little in praise of my country," the assistant recalled later, "it so stirred his ire." The vast *Columbus* came home, and Philip Hone, after an oyster-and-champagne dinner at the National Academy, pronounced it a spiritless huddle of costumed studio models. The *Niagara* was rejected by the Art Union. There seemed nothing more for Vanderlyn than to die inconspicuously, which he did alone in a hotel room at Kingston.

The remaining three rotunda spaces went to far younger men—John G. Chapman, Robert W. Weir, and William H. Powell—whose sprawling failures made the Trumbulls look almost distinguished. The last garrulous word had not been said, however, until Emmanuel Leutze covered six hundred square feet of Capitol wall with his *Westward the Course of Empire Takes Its Way*. Jarves' comment upon it — "Confusion reigns paramount"—applies to most of the history pictures of the time. From Allston to Leutze, forty years of such painting had demonstrated that Americans had neither the controlled dynamism of Rubens nor the architectonics of Raphael. The first in their hands became chaos, the second a rigid formalism. It was from humbler material that the finest compositions of the age were made—the barn doors and haylofts of William Sidney Mount, the tavern porch of Woodville, and the decks of George Caleb Bingham's riverboats.

An age which looked with no great enthusiasm on

Rubens Peale, *Still Life,* 1860 (Robert Graham coll.)

Courtesy Victor D. Spark

vague allegory and diluted history took pleasure in bowls of fruit and the assorted products of the kitchen garden. The Peales were among the pioneers of still life. Raphaelle Peale died in 1825, old Charles two years later, and James in 1831; but Rubens worked with the Peale solidity in the 1850's, and the daughters of James produced dishes of strawberries, apples, and quinces—Anna Claypoole Peale, Margaretta Angelica, and Sarah. Similar in design and handling were the groups of Abraham Woodside. The flower pieces of Adele Evans were assembled in the Dutch manner and painted with a lighter touch than that of the Peales. Linear conventions and a decorative flatness were to be found in bouquets by L. Babcock, and in the still life of John F. Francis was a painterly suggestion of textures which recalls Chardin.

America of the thirties and forties supported a small army of portrait painters, and there was an enormous variety of style among them, as tough-minded men got themselves represented with a waxen hardness, and languishing women with a misty charm. Andrew Jackson himself, with his bristling hair, his horselike face, and his sharply cut features, was one of the most paintable of men, and Hawthorne wished, as he stood before the likeness of Pope Julius, that Raphael were alive to do Old Hickory justice. The victor of New Orleans sat many times to many men as though to demonstrate not only his own individuality but that of the artists. The son of Ralph Earl married a niece of Jackson's wife, went to live at the Hermitage in Nashville, and became known as "the King's painter" as he portrayed his hero sitting, walking, and standing, with a dry astringency of forms and a spindly honesty which were almost primitive. Waldo and Sully gave Jackson a bluff and handsome mask, and Asher B. Durand penetrated his character more deeply when he was sixty-eight. Tired John Vanderlyn worked from him in Washington before going back to die in Kingston; George Peter Alexander Healy painted the gaunt, pain-ravaged face of the seventy-eight-year-old ex-President a few hours before it relaxed in death.

This variety suggests that an older tradition was being modified by new conceptions of character and painterly form as the belated Stuartesques and Sullyesques surrendered to younger men who had been born within the new century. The Stuart heritage was in the hands of such men as Charles Osgood, Henry C. Pratt, and James Frothingham; John Neagle was nearing fifty when he gave to his portrait of *Henry Clay* (Union League, Phila.) the bluff instantaneity and the theatric

Ralph E. W. Earl, *Andrew Jackson* (detail)

Yale University Art Gallery (Mabel B. Garvan coll.), New Haven, Conn.

Thomas Sully, *Frances Kemble,* sketch (detail)

Museum of Fine Arts, Boston, Mass.

dash of his earlier paintings of Kean and Forrest; and Thomas Sully's women in the thirties had the moist eyes and limpid grace which had been his specialty twenty years before in Philadelphia.

Aided by study of Romney and Lawrence, Sully had mastered a simple and systematic method, drawing his sitter with charcoal and white chalk on a gray background and establishing his tones and colors from memory in a free and sketchlike manner, using few pigments and freshening the whole with glazes. His *Fanny Kemble* of 1832 was one of several studies of the actress. One catches a glimpse here of the intelligent Fanny who read Goethe, Dante, and Racine in the original and who rebelled against the trashy lines of *The Wonder* as she tried in dilapidated hotel rooms to batter its pointless prose into her head; but Sully's accent is on the exquisite heroine of a long line of potboilers in which she drew tears from two Chief Justices of the Supreme Court.

Sully lived to be eighty-nine, and his liquefying influence was to be seen in many others. It gave a florid and blowzy quality to the Eichholtz portrait of *Mrs. John Diffenderffer*. Henry Inman's self-portrait of 1834 borrowed Sully's translucent shadows and he was at his light-fingered best with a sitter of such charm and wit as *Fitz-Greene Halleck* (N. Y. Hist. Soc.). Like his teacher Jarvis, he made large official canvases, and in his *Martin Van Buren* (N. Y. City Hall) a delightfully painted house shares interest with the statesman. A portrait of *Grace Ingersoll* which may have been painted by Nathaniel Jocelyn of New Haven has Sully's tricks: a young girl plays a harp ecstatically, her moist eyes cast upward, her hands pink-tipped but anatomically impossible (New Haven Col. Hist. Soc.). As a pupil of Sully, James Reed Lambdin of Kentucky preferred the bland to the characteristic. The work of Charles Ingham, whose early study of Lafayette was dark, solid, and real to a startling degree, became pretty and chic, earning him Dunlap's title of "a ladies' portrait painter." And William Powell of Ohio succumbed to Sully in a weak and carelessly drawn likeness of *Mrs. Graham,* whose pinkish-orange reflections almost annihilate the forms of her face (N. Y. Hist. Soc.).

In contrast with the directness of Neagle and the limpidity of Sully one finds in many a portrait of the forties and fifties an oily smoothness of execution which reminds one of what Hiram Powers did to marble. Even the Morse portrait of his daughter as *The Muse,* painted ten years after the *Lafayette,* had the solidity but not the breadth of that earlier work. Jocelyn was no longer

Henry Inman, *Georgianna Buckham and Her Mother* (detail)

Museum of Fine Arts, Boston, Mass.

Mrs. Vincent, Southworth & Hawes daguerreotype (detail)

Society for Preservation of New England Antiquities

Sullyesque when he gave the sheen of ebony to the African *Cinque* (New Haven Col. Hist. Soc.). The *Nathaniel Bowditch* of Osgood was as smoothly forceless as the bust of Laplace at his side (Peabody Mus.).

Chester Harding in his maturity and Rembrandt Peale in his old age both concealed their workmanship with carefully fused gradations. There was an almost slippery finesse in Jacques Amans of New Orleans and a viscous quality in the *Henry Clay* of Theodore Moïse (Met. Mus.); Poe condemned the false *tournure* of Inman because it left nothing to the imagination. Inman's *Georgianna Buckham and Her Mother* confirmed Poe's judgment by its sleekness and simper, and Ingham's *Flower Girl* was glazed to a tiresome polish (Met. Mus.).

This emphasis on the objective detail owed something to foreign methods and something to native thinking. It reinforced itself by the example of the Düsseldorf school, where meticulous drawing and impeccable modeling were taught and where Emmanuel Leutze in 1841 learned to be visually impartial. Long before the great New York exhibition of Düsseldorf pictures in 1863, Leutze had earned extravagant praise for a *Washington Crossing the Delaware,* which he painted in the German city, each block of ice as carefully defined as the features of the general (Met. Mus.). The Düsseldorf precision was bound to appeal to the patron who wished his likeness to specify what distinguished him from others. He wanted a record, not an interpretation; and Mrs. Trollope remarked that close resemblance and careful finish were what Americans most admired in painting. Certainly the glassy sheen of many Jacksonian portraits harmonized with the glazed wallpapers, the polished marble table tops, and the horsehair upholstery of Jacksonian parlors. Finally, the painter of the forties found himself in competition with a new medium which men praised for its impartiality—the "sun picture" of Daguerre.

In the year 1837 the Frenchman made a silvered copper plate light-sensitive by fuming it with iodine, exposed it to a still life in his studio, and developed the image with mercury vapor. To be sure, one had to hold the silvered plate in a certain way to the light in order to see the picture, and there was only one picture for the one exposure; yet Samuel Morse in Paris saw the Daguerre interiors and pronounced them "Rembrandt perfected," noting that every house, every tree, and every chimney pot in a boulevard view was faithfully reproduced.

The first printed account of the invention had no sooner crossed the Atlantic by steam packet than alert Yankees managed to produce sun pictures of their own, while Morse and Draper explained the process. When Daguerre's pupil Gouraud showed his daguerreotypes in December, 1839, Philip Hone called them one of the marvels of the world, and soon the Americans were coloring their silver plates by hand and attempting to reduce the long and paralyzing exposure time. John

Plumbe advertised his "Plumbeotypes," which were lithographs made from daguerreotypes, and others used wood engraving as a means of reproduction. Before 1840 the Englishman Talbot succeeded in making paper positives from a single negative, and photographers soon made their exposures on wet collodion plates which had to be developed immediately.

The Boston notables sat to Southworth and Hawes for their daguerreotype portraits; in New York, a young Irishman named Mathew B. Brady set up a gallery at the corner of Broadway and Fulton Street. His ambition was to record the appearance of every famous person of his time, and he had made measurable progress toward his goal when the Civil War began, offering him new subject matter.

"A spirit in my feet said go, and I went." The bold Brady in a linen duster and a straw hat set forth with three assistants in the general direction of McClellan's Peninsula Army to photograph the advance on Richmond. Stray shots whistled around the black-curtained buggy to which Brady rushed his wet plates, and he got lost in the woods near Bull Run; but when the war ended, Brady and his assistants had made several thousand visual documents. Here bloated death stares at the sky from trenches; here is Centerville, Virginia, bleak and bare in March; here Lincoln in a stovepipe hat towers above his generals.

Hone and his contemporaries admired the camera for its rendering of textures and its inability to omit any detail which had been before it; Brady had an artist's sense of character and composition. He had taken lessons in painting from William Page and often chose his place and moment with a flair for what makes a picture more than a random collection of facts. Into his gallery with its florid rugs, green-and-gold furnishings, and ponderous gas chandeliers came the great of the American earth—Lincoln and Whitman, Webster and Calhoun, Jenny Lind and Barnum; and Brady posed them hand in vest or hand on table as a portrait painter would have posed them against a draped curtain, a mantelpiece, or a bit of column. The best of Brady's outdoor pictures, despite the inevitable opportunism of his craft, are superbly composed; his gutted Richmond buildings are the very silhouette of ruin. And A. Gardner, his assistant for a time, must have been familiar with painted landscapes when he made *Burnside's Bridge across the Antietam:* a picket fence establishes its foreground, a zigzag road defines its space, and every tree, house, and

A. T. Gardner photograph, *Burnside's Bridge Across the Antietam*

Courtesy Museum of Modern Art, New York City

wagon plays an indispensable part in the balance of the whole.

The painters themselves watched the camera's progress with mixed feelings. Delaroche said the instrument was a challenge to the artist because of its correctness of line, its precision of form, and its broad, energetic modeling. In America one critic poured contempt on a medium which, because it registered all light areas without distinction, "attached no more importance to expression than a politician does to truth"; but the attitude of old Rembrandt Peale was less defensive. He had himself "taken" in the late eighteen fifties by his nephew, posing in profile before one of his innumerable *George Washingtons;* and in the *Crayon* he discussed the relation of painting and photography. This sturdy realist pooh-poohed the notion that the superiority of the painter to the photographer lay in the former's ability to see with the "soul." He emphasized the more material limitations of the camera: its inferiority to the brush in the gradation of shadows, the rigid pose made necessary by an iron head-clamp, and the vacuous expression which usually resulted.

The proper sphere of the camera, Peale said, was still life, architecture, and the recording of explorations and scientific experiments. The painter had a task of his own which required many sittings and a sound knowledge of form if a permanent characterization was to be made. Let him take courage; the vogue of photography would for a time diminish his customers, but in the long run it would whet people's appetite for painted likenesses.

The critic Charles E. Lester was more cordial to what, he observed, had progressed in a dozen years from an "accidental discovery" to one of the "exquisite embellishments of life." With the painter, as Lester said, everything depends on the genius that guides the hand; in photography the invisible hand of Nature herself is allowed to "trace the forms of creation in all their delicacy, witchery and power." In *M. B. Brady and the Photographic Art* Lester saluted the man whose skill had given dignity and beauty to the new medium and had placed the daguerreotype permanently among "the arts of taste and utility."

The camera in the meantime influenced painting both directly and indirectly. Morse said that his purpose in making daguerreotypes was "to accumulate for my studio, models for my canvas," and before Neagle painted Daniel Webster he had watched Brady photographing him. The painted mountain landscapes of the fifties and sixties owed some of their sharp details to the fact that painters strapped a camera to their backs along with a paintbox and an easel. William H. Jackson made a photograph of Thomas Moran painting the Yellowstone River, and Thomas' brother was a photographer.

It was inevitable that the camera's characteristics should modify the vision of the painter. That influence was most obvious in the work of such men as Francis B. Carpenter, whose *Lincoln Family* was done in tones of gray and black with a stiffness of pose, a scheme of lighting, and a contrived background which suggest a sitting in Brady's studio (N. Y. Hist. Soc.). Perhaps the daguerreotype stimulated the painter to a greater consciousness of light and its behavior; certainly the sullen impressiveness of some daguerrean portraits appears in more than one canvas of the period. In several instances the painter copied the photograph; on other occasions the brush seemed to become as impersonal as the lens, and to seek the glossy smoothness of the metal plate.

This "finish," common to both media, was not simply the result of mutual interaction but derived from the response of both the camera and the brush to the preferences of the customer. The men of means in the middle years of the century wished to have life-sized presentments of themselves. Their houses were higher, wider, and handsomer than those of their fathers, their chairs and tables of more burly proportions, their mirrors and chandeliers more stridently gilded. To match this opulence the portrait grew, and with it the temptation to sheer enumeration.

As the imitators of Stuart and the followers of Sully died their places were taken by men whose busiest years would lie in the second half of the century: Charles Loring Elliott, Henry Peters Gray, George P. A. Healy, Daniel Huntington, William Page, Thomas Buchanan Read, Thomas Hicks, and Joseph Oriel Eaton. The average of their ages was twenty-three in the year 1839, when Delaroche praised the camera, and their productivity almost rivaled that of the photographers. Gray turned out more than two hundred and fifty portraits, Healy six hundred, and Elliott over seven hundred.

Gray had passed thirty when he painted the dignified and handsome *William Cullen Bryant* with firmness and delicacy (N. Y. Hist. Soc.). Preoccupied with the color methods of the Venetians, he seldom equaled this effort, though his more diffused manner found popularity. Elliott became a pupil of John Trumbull despite that bitter man's advice to follow the safer profession of architecture which Elliott's father practiced. In *Mrs. Thomas Goulding* he found a hundred minor incidents of light and form, of textual variation, to define what age had done to her face, and proved that the artist's years had enlarged his vocabulary without deepening his power to penetrate beneath surfaces.

When Daniel Huntington was thirty the New York *Mirror* announced that his name, like those of Raphael and Buonarotti, was "destined to descend, growing brighter and brighter in its descent, to the last generation." He had begun his career with Inman, and his

Charles L. Elliott, *Mrs. Thomas Goulding* (National Academy)

Courtesy Frick Art Reference Library, New York City

Mercy's Dream (Corcoran Gall.) was one of several fabrications in which he failed to achieve the color of Titian and Correggio but succeeded only too well in avoiding their sensuality. As a portraitist he acquired a smoky, coal-black shadow tone which disguised his weak drawing and which he manipulated to produce an expression of benevolent dignity in the face of the hardest merchant. In the great hall of the New York Chamber of Commerce where the likenesses of the successful hang from floor to ceiling are forty-three canvases by Huntington. Some of these were done from life and some were not, but one can scarcely distinguish the former from the latter; the conscientious dullness of his *Richard Lathers* in 1869 was in his *Morris K. Jesup* of 1896.

William Page spent his foreign years in research for the laws of color. One no longer finds in his work, as his contemporaries did, "color in all its glory as the minister of light, in all its significance as the sign and expression of the plenitude of life." Rather, one concedes to Page a presentation of character which is always steady and dignified, and occasionally forceful.

Eaton was a plodding naturalist whose reputation rested on his likenesses of children, on such excursions into genre as his *Little Nell and Her Grandfather,* and on a profile portrait of Lincoln which seems to have been done from a well-known Brady photograph.

Thomas Read had been a cigar maker, a grocer's clerk, and a female impersonator before Nicholas Longworth of Cincinnati financed his study of art. Read's high spirits were undiminished when his patron reproached him for his behavior in New York: "You have let ignorant friends induce you to believe yourself a Painter before you have learn'd the Rudiments of the art and instead of devoting your leisure hours to close study you've Been Parading the streets with the followers of the Play House Without a Dollar." Both fame and dollars came to this rather flashy cosmopolitan as he wrote *Sheridan's Ride* at Longfellow's urging, and painted the poet's children. Attributed to him is the eight-by-seven-foot canvas of the *Children of Marcus L. Ward* (Newark Mus.), brittle in its rendering of every last detail of parrot's feather or lace pantalette, and posed with a staring rigidity that suggests the daguerreotypist's clamp.

Healy's career was more dramatic than his art, for this Boston urchin who earned pennies by holding gentlemen's horses became the painter of the world's most famous people. Before he was twenty he had taken lessons from Gros in Paris. At twenty-one he portrayed Delacroix with a conspicuous absence of the Frenchman's nervous intensity; at twenty-nine, the fierceness of old Daniel Webster broke through his smooth handling of the hawklike face. Healy was at his best in sober and solid portraits of impressive men, and his seated Lincoln of 1864 had the factual honesty of a Brady daguerreotype. A year after Lincoln's death he was again in Europe, where the example of accomplished Frenchmen would modify but not fundamentally change his art.

Quaker-bred Thomas Hicks had learned coach painting from his father's cousin, the Edward Hicks of the *Peaceable Kingdoms,* before he saw Italy and France in the forties. Back at home in the Springfield office where Lincoln the presidential nominee received his neighbors' congratulations, Hicks made a homely and penetrating study of the fine eyes, untidy hair, and sensitive mouth—the first painting, Hicks claimed, for which Lincoln sat. That unassuming strength was in everything Hicks did, and no man of the age more vigorously characterized its representative men. He showed them in their surroundings in portraits whose furniture and accessories gave them the flavor of genre.

Hicks posed *Hamilton Fish* against a light wall to bring out the aggressive elbow of this "safe man and true Whig of good blood" whom Hone admired. Here as in other canvases the painter introduced an elaborate background and accessories and the *Crayon* poked fun at Hicks by describing an imaginary portrait of the "Honorable Jefferson Keggs of Mobile" sitting among

Thomas Hicks, *Hamilton Fish,* New York City Hall

Bogart Studio photo

his offspring in an immense red plush chair against Doric columns with a view of wharves and cotton fields beyond. Yet this emphasis on man in his daily surroundings was characteristic of the age.

There was but one cure for the hardening of the arteries which afflicted the majority of portraits in the years before the Civil War and for a short time afterward: a new selectiveness inspired by a deeper notion of the painter's work as painting. Now and then in the work of Hicks one sees the result of his brief contact with Thomas Couture in Paris, and it was fortunate for American portraiture and figure painting that several young men worked with that independent Frenchman.

Couture scorned all the schools of painting—Romantic, Angelic, Turkish, Realistic—and called Ingres an embalmer. He showed his pupils how to establish the dominant light and the principal shadow in a swift monochrome study of the masses; he warned them never to use more than three colors, loosely blended, to make a mixture; he explained how a thin, transparent shadow tone avoided the flabby, viscous tonality of the academic men. Under the influence of this bold technician, William Morris Hunt and Eastman Johnson relaxed their Düsseldorf tensions in the early 1850's. Before the Civil War, both Robert Loftin Newman and John La Farge were for a short time pupils of Couture.

Newman and Hunt, however, were in search of values which the worldly Couture could not provide; they found them in the work and the companionship of Millet, who had settled down to a life of "sublime monotony" in the Forest of Fontainebleau. Millet was a mild-tempered and utterly self-contained individual with the austerity of a Biblical patriarch, whose purpose was to make a synthesis of the peasant and the earth which nourished him. When his *Sower* appeared at the Salon of 1851, it was as though a gross and bestial clod were tracking manure through artistic drawing rooms; among the seductive nudes of the day his small, luminous sketches of bathing women found no welcome. Hunt was among the few men who understood him; he bought *The Sower* and went to live at Barbizon, along with Newman and Wyatt Eaton.

When Hunt came home in 1855 he brought the gospel of Millet and the painterly vigor he had learned from Couture. Petty detail, he said, was fit only to confuse a child, deceive a fly, or amuse an idiot. "Simplify your masses," he insisted, "look for the big things first." Hunt's genre pictures challenged the overfinish of his contemporaries and Boston had no precedent for the

William M. Hunt, *Self-Portrait*
Museum of Fine Arts, Boston, Mass.

bold handling of his *Jewess* (Boston Mus. Fine Arts). His self-portrait of 1866 reveals the man whom Henry James described—the lean body, all muscular spareness and absence of waste, with a great forehead, a boldly arched nose, and a spreading beard which suggested Don Quixote.

The critic Tuckerman, in spite of his romantic overtones, had no more use than Hunt for the superficial and the obvious when in 1867 he surveyed his country's achievements in *Book of the Artists*. There were mediocrities in the land, he said, portraits which were caricatures and wooden villas of anomalous character; and artistic reputations were often made on the principle of the stock market. "What we especially need, is to bring Art within the scope of popular associations on the one hand, and, on the other, to have it consecrated by the highest individuality of purpose, truth to nature, human sentiment, and patient self-devotion."

When Tuckerman thus phrased the American needs his "truth to nature" had found a place in landscape. Art had been brought "within the scope of popular associations" by the genre painters. And there were both "individuality of purpose" and "patient self-devotion" among those nameless Yankees who continued and enriched a people's art in the United States.

CHAPTER 16 / WESTWARD THE COURSE OF LANDSCAPE

Sydney Kellner has called Thomas Doughty, Thomas Cole, and Asher Durand the founding fathers of the Hudson River school. There were other rivers, and other mountains than the Catskills which inspired them, and if they painted that lordly stream more often than other subjects in their beginnings it was because the Hudson held a special interest in the thirties.

From New York to Albany the traveler of that day knew every bend in the river and every new prospect the steamboat's course provided. Everyone had read Irving's *Sketch Book* and could see ghostly Dutchmen and legendary Yankees in its mist-hidden valleys. Drake, Halleck, and Cooper had nourished their wit and their imagination on this region's past; Charles Fenno Hoffman wrote his *Lays* after recalling how he had strolled through mazy thickets and climbed to Fort Putnam to look down on the "burnished bosom" of the Hudson and see

> The sloop, slow-drooping down the placid bay,
> Her form reflected in its glassy sheet.

One scarcely distinguished between the literary and the pictorial in the Hudson River enchantment as poet and painter exchanged imagery. Robert Havell in the forties pictured sloops on the Hudson at West Point; Doughty painted Bryant's "cool shades and dews," his "silence of the early day," and Durand the deep sunless glens

> Where brawl o'er shallow beds the streams unseen.

Bryant in turn wrote the prospectus for a proposed series of Durand's landscape engravings in 1830.

What did Bryant and his contemporaries mean when they called the Hudson "picturesque"? For a century or more, writers had been rigidly dogmatic with this word and "sublime." Philosophers of nature were now less concerned with aesthetic categories and more emotionally alive to cliffs, chasms, and torrents. In his essay on *Art,* Emerson bade the landscape painter omit the details, the prose of nature, and give us only the spirit and the splendor, the suggestion of a fairer creation than we know. Here as in Europe the artist claimed imaginative freedom; but America modified that freedom with the old moral and pious obligations of her own Puritan past.

Beneath Emerson's counsel was the notion of a nature uncorrupted by man. That grandeur and tranquillity were now to be found only in a few eastern valleys and on the frontier where Cole had begun his painter's career. Hoffman assured his reader that one day and two dollars would take him to West Point, "far from town, its dust and busy strife." When Cooper saw lovely old villages despoiled by fiery trains he decided that a country on the decline was in many ways more enjoyable than one on the advance.

But if man could corrupt Nature he could also, if one believed the landscape gardener, perfect her crudities and play God to her waywardness. When Downing clipped here and transplanted there, when he changed the straight to the gracefully winding, and when he composed the controllable foreground as a framework for the far and unalterable distance he achieved the same pruned informality, the blending of house with setting, the tactful underlining of the beautiful which were in the painted landscapes of his time.

When the painters of our first river and mountain school began to give form to these ideas of scenic beauty they knew that landscape had never supported its practitioners in the past. But they knew also that they could build on the groundwork laid by the literary men. They could rely on the townsman's affection for the rural when they painted the country lane and the cows in the meadow. They could appeal to the nation's preoccupation with its dwindling frontier by scenes of wild grandeur which attacked the sensibilities. And they could count on middle-class moralism to find "tongues in trees, books in the running brooks, sermons in stones."

Clearly the pastoral was to be the sphere of Thomas Doughty. He had spent a year in Europe when he settled down at Newburgh to join the Hudson River men. His work was engraved and lithographed in a dozen publications, his *Solitude* hung in the Astor House, and the Art Union paid five hundred dollars apiece for his landscapes. On a few occasions his piled clouds, straining trees, and light-struck rocks caught something of Cole's dynamism; his customary mood, however, was tranquil, and he preferred the slowly curving horizontals of meadows and low hills, the large bland skies of the Dutch masters, the great elm near at hand, and the smaller foliage group in the middle distance.

Gradually the forms of earth grew more solid and continuous under Doughty's brush, and his feathery elms began to grow convincingly where they belonged and not where Claude would have placed them. One can believe that Melville had Doughty in his mind when he

Thomas Doughty, *In the Catskills*

Addison Gallery of American Art, Andover, Mass.

described a Saco Valley landscape in the opening pages of *Moby Dick:* "Here sleeps his meadow, and there sleep his cattle. . . . Deep into distant woodlands winds a mazy way, reaching to overlapping spurs of mountains bathed in their hillside-blue." Thomas Hofland in 1839 called Doughty the master of a new school which combined the best of Claude and Rosa. Within a few years, however, people asked for bluer skies and greener foliage, for more form and less formula, and Charles Fenno Hoffman called Doughty's meticulous manner a "tea-tray style." By 1850 the Art Union was refusing to buy his pictures and the impoverished painter complained in the *Herald* of "an effort to put me down that some of the younger aspirants may rise on my ruin."

Alvin Fisher of Boston was painting New England mountain streams with something of Doughty's carefulness in the thirties, finding a fallen tree trunk to make a parallel with the shadow aslant a bluff. In Portland, Maine, the former sign painter Charles Codman surrounded his inlets with heavily drooping trees of his own devising. Robert W. Weir, appointed instructor in drawing at West Point in 1834, studied the rock and cloud forms along the Hudson in preparation for his precise and charming landscapes. And Asher Durand was exhibiting a more masterful grasp of nature's light and color than any of these men.

Two large Durand paintings of 1840 struck the philosophical note, *The Morning of Life* and *The Evening of Life* (Natl. Acad.). They proved that Durand knew trees, meadows, and mountains well enough to compose them freely out of his own fancy as Cole did, using shadows to punctuate his moral message and light to contrast the spring freshness of youth with the sunset ripeness of age.

Both Doughty and Durand would have admitted that their friend Cole did such things much better. Having returned from Europe in 1832, Cole painted the Catskills in a few large swinging masses, hill and mountain steeped in the wine-reds and purples of autumn. He pushed antithesis to its limits in *Crawford Notch,* one side of the pass deep in shadow, the other brilliant with crimson and yellows, the great mountain bulk here swathed in purple storm-clouds, there cleanly outlined against a serene blue. In 1836 he looked down from

Thomas Cole, *The Oxbow*

Metropolitan Museum of Art, New York City

Mount Holyoke to the oxbow of the lazy Connecticut at Northampton, and re-created its rich and sunny fertility.

Europe had made Cole more American, and in that same year he read his Lyceum essay on American scenery. Men in Europe, he said, had molded and tamed nature, but here she was still undefiled. He described a landscape he had seen here which is much like his *Oxbow:* enameled meadows and lingering stream, rural dwellings shaded by elms and garlanded by flowers, the village spire above the dark mass of foliage. "You see no ruined tower to tell of outrage, no gorgeous temple to speak of ostentation," but only "the abodes of plenty, virtue and refinement."

The moral Cole was bound in the end to submerge the naturalistic Cole. Did he study on one of his trips abroad the works of Caspar David Friedrich at Dresden—the turbid and blood-colored clouds, the tormented oak trees, and the cliffs like a giant's decayed teeth? Certainly he knew John Martin's theatrical paintings; and in the years between 1836 and 1848, when Cole's mind was turning to mysticism, he created strange worlds of his own in *The Course of Empire, The Voyage of Life,* and *The Cross and the World.* Luman Reed commissioned the *Empire* series, and Cole worked at the five large canvases for four years after his return from abroad. Sitting among the ruins of Rome he had conceived the idea of recording the cycle of civilization. He was probably familiar with Volney's *Ruins,* whose author had meditated like himself among the ashes of a great age:

> These walls where now a mournful stillness reigns, once echoed to the fame of artists and the gay shouts of festivals. These fragments of marble once formed noble palaces, these prone columns were once the ornaments of majestic temples. And now . . . The palaces of Kings are the lair of wild animals; and lizards usurp the holy places of the gods! Thus perish the works of mankind, thus vanish empires and nations!

Cole believed that colors affected the mind like sound, and he intended the color atmosphere of each picture to yield the appropriate emotion. He put to work the hours of the day, the seasons, and the weather to tell man's history, inventing a topography and maintaining it throughout the series with expressive variations—a harbor surrounded by forests with an oddly shaped cliff rising beyond it. In the first painting purple mists rise from somber thickets where primitive man hunts and builds shelters around a fire. The pastoral age is clear and calm, with fresh green meadows where sheep graze

Thomas Cole, *Consummation,* from *The Course of Empire*

New York Historical Society

beneath a great stone temple; girls dance under the trees and a philosopher traces a theorem with his stick in the earth. In the third and central picture of the series, somewhat larger than the others, Cole renders imperial glory with a "gaud and glitter" of crimson, gold, creamy marble, and pale noon sky; a great terrace is supported by maidens from the Erechtheum; temples rise upon temples; a gigantic fountain shaped like a dolphin spouts water; galleys crowd the harbor as the emperor's parade crosses a great bridge. For the fourth canvas, as Wolfgang Born has observed, Cole borrowed elements from a panorama of *Paradise Lost* which was shown in London when he was there. The barbarian has descended on the capital; tall statues fall from their pedestals; the sun is dimmed by the smoke and flame of pillage; the serene lines of the previous picture are broken into tortured and writhing curves. Finally nature reasserts itself and the sun is setting. No human life remains, and the heron has built his nest on the lone column which rises from heaps of rubble, mantled with ivy. "The gorgeous pageant has passed; the roar of battle has ceased; the multitude has sunk into the dust; the empire is extinct."

One reads Cole's lesson today less earnestly than his generation did; but one marvels at the plastic resources he displayed, at the colors, lines, forms, and spaces which give each canvas its own unity both as organism and as expression. (See color plate 7.) The four paintings of his *Voyage of Life* were more emotionally conceived; half a million visitors saw them at the Art Union and thousands bought James Smillie's engraved versions (Proctor Inst.).

Ezra Ames of Albany seems to have anticipated Cole's *Voyage* with a rather crudely painted allegory; perhaps both artists made use of Bryant's poem in which time was described as a river. Out of a mysterious canyon sails the infant, his guardian angel at the helm. Now Youth takes the tiller, steering toward cloudlike domes and minarets. Now, with rudder gone and the demons of Suicide, Intemperance, and Murder over him, Manhood rushes toward the sea. He reaches the ocean at last, an old man with immortality before him.

Before Cole's cloud temple faded, it seems to have inspired a page of Poe's *Domain of Arnheim,* whose traveler sails into a somber gorge. The fairy bark propels itself toward gates of burnished gold, and as they open at its approach the whole Paradise of Arnheim bursts upon the view, with tall slender Eastern trees, flocks of golden and crimson birds, meadows of violets and poppies, "and upspringing confusedly from amid all, a mass of semi-Gothic, semi-Saracenic architecture, sustaining itself as if by miracle in mid-air; glittering in the red sunlight with a hundred oriels, minarets, and pinnacles; and seeming the phantom handiwork, conjointly, of the Sylphs, of the Fairies, of the Genii, and of the Gnomes."

There were really two Thomas Coles. One of them pictured the *Oxbow* very much as it looked, knowing that the "dollar-godded" patron preferred it so; the other Cole succumbed to what Willis called "the poetry of decay" in Europe and painted crumbling towers stark against the sun. Religion obsessed his inward-turning mind when in his forty-seventh and last year he groped with the banal symbols of his never-finished *Cross and the World.*

A few artists and laymen, even while Cole lived, preferred his topography to his theology; after his death a nameless critic in the *Crayon* declared that art should not become the slave of ethics and that Cole had "grounded on both rocks and quicksand." The comment suggests that in painting as in sculpture the darkness of allegory was vanishing before common sense. The middle-class American now went touring up and down the world admiring its more obvious externals or bought them in printed form. William J. Bennett drew many of the American localities in water color to be aquatinted in the thirties, and more than a hundred scenes by W. H. Bartlett were engraved in the fine-spun steel manner for N. P. Willis' *American Scenery*. There was a Düsseldorf accuracy in August Köllner's sketches of American cities which were issued as colored lithographs in the late forties.

A generation with a concern for sheer facts grew impatient with men who painted things as they were not. Americans were reading Ruskin, who scolded the art lover for admiring "glosses, veils and decorative lies" and who praised Turner for combining the naturalistic with the idealistic. His *Modern Painters* was published by the *Crayon* in installments, and in 1855 Asher Durand wrote his *Letters on Landscape Painting* for that journal, of which his son John was editor. When Durand said that the artist should use his imagination not to create another world but to reveal the beauty and meaning of this one, he turned his back on Cole. That pioneer was dead and Doughty was about to die; Durand was fifty-nine and had freed himself from stereotype and melodrama.

In 1844, Durand's Catskill scene had been composed around the conventional middle tree, but his *First Harvest* of 1858 was a masterly rendering of outdoor light (Brooklyn Mus.). The stones and fallen trees in his foregrounds were patiently studied and then painted with a truthfulness of detail which would have delighted Ruskin. He could show the drift of cloud shadows over hillsides, and the cross play of light through dense foliage; he could flood an immense valley with sunshine and he could concentrate his skill on nothing more dramatic than a single rock and the uprooted bole of a tree.

As Durand said in his *Letters,* he disliked the substitution of an easily expressed falsehood for a difficult truth: "Stop muddling the fresh green of summer with brown," and paint out of doors, not in the studio. Begin modestly, he urged, with accurate drawings of small things, and frankly imitate as a step toward representing. "Let us away then with these false alarms" concerning the Real and the Ideal. The painter who selects the time and place where Nature displays her chief perfections will have "no occasion to idealize the portrait." And Durand practiced what he preached in *Kindred Spirits* of 1849, where Cole and Bryant stood on a ledge deep in the Catskill forest, whose delicate tree forms were drawn by the same careful hand which spent three years engraving the Trumbull *Declaration.* Ten years later, Durand found a woodland brook, bending trees, and distant hill which satisfied his sense of wholeness and perfection, and painted them as they stood, with every nuance of form and distance in plausible relationship.

Younger artists than Durand were also seeking "difficult truth." James M. Hart's *View on the Hudson* was fresh and limpid, with clean blue-greens in water, sky, and horizon, and no tightening of detail (N. Y. State Hist. Assoc.). His brother William studied the smooth shapes of *Mount Chocurua* with something of a geologist's eye, and one had the sense of being inside the space he represented, not looking into it from a distance (Univ. So. Calif.). Under the influence of Ruskin's books John William Hill abandoned the restraints he had learned from his father and painted from Halifax to Havana with a clear palette, working directly from nature. Benjamin Champney claimed that he and John Kensett discovered the beauty of the White Mountains at North Conway, and others came shortly—Russell Smith, Jasper Cropsey, Thomas Hill, and Albert Bierstadt—until "the meadows and banks of the Saco were dotted all about with white umbrellas."

Kensett was the most subtle colorist of them all, building his grave and quiet compositions with simple broad areas of sky, sea, and mountain. He was the poet of the hushed moment when one feels rain in the air. In his *Chocorua* there is majestic space, and in his studies of rocks, their colors best seen against the light, there are exquisite variations of gray-greens, blues, and purples. The headlands in his Newport scenes of the late fifties are a threefold contrast of pale sky, deep green water, and orange-brown rock.

That quiet strength was beyond Cropsey, whose deli-

Asher B. Durand, *Kindred Spirits*

New York Public Library

cate pen-and-sepia studies said all he had to say, and whose paintings, spotty and discontinuous, had a pretty pink-and-orange glow suitable to the chromolithographs which were made from them. There was a finicky touch and a dark, narrow color range in the early work of John Casilear, and in his later canvases a quality both impersonal and commonplace, with a preference for the orthodox cows wading in streams. Handsomely obvious

John F. Kensett, *Newport Harbor* (Frederick Sturges, Jr., coll.)

Photo courtesy Art Institute of Chicago

George H. Durrie, *Returning to the Farm*

New York Historical Society

were the New Hampshire scenes of Russell Smith, whose shoddy way with trees perhaps reflected his work as a scene painter in Philadelphia.

Thanks to a new interest in seasonal variations, American landscape was no longer a land of perpetual summer. When Robert Havell had completed his great Audubon prints he came to live on the Hudson, and his autumn hills were brilliant with reds and yellows. Régis François Gignoux rendered snow with a competence he had learned from Delaroche, and FitzHugh Lane painted ships locked in the ice of New England harbors. Lane lived close to his subjects at Gloucester and in the Penobscot region. From the Dutch marine artists he borrowed his low horizons and his large skies; there was a bland enveloping light in his canvases, and a suggestion of down-East reticence in his firm drawing of vessels and their rigging.

It was George Durrie whom the prints of Currier and Ives made the Whittier of American painting. He had studied with Nathaniel Jocelyn before he turned from portraits, still life, and genre to small and exquisite studies of the East Rock at New Haven (New Haven Col. Hist. Soc.). His early version of the rock had traces of the primitive in the tight conventional foliage, the prevalent browns, and the uncertain planes; ten years later, his touch was livelier and the forms of earth and cliff were as firmly set as they were deftly brushed. When Durrie used a large canvas, as he did for his *Cider Making in the Country,* he recorded a hundred incidents of farm life which he failed to pull together by line or by mass and which had to be read like a book (Farmers' Mus., Cooperstown). But he was a master without peers in the small winter farmyards which hung in so many Civil War parlors.

The lithographer somewhat hardened Durrie's forms and simplified his colors, but in the main his quiet browns, cool grays, and near whites came admirably through the translation. A farm scene by Durrie is a simple and steady relationship of cottage, barn, fence, and trees, making much of repeated horizontals. His winters have the white-and-gray silence of *Snowbound:* oxen draw a great log before a gambreled house under heavy purplish clouds, and on the outer branches of elm and oak, so crisply painted by Durrie, are the small pockets of snow which are like a signature of the artist. He understood how the color of snow changes with the time of day, and his drifts are now glaringly sunlit, now tempered with warm afternoon light. Having chosen his theme he played endless variations on it to the delight of a generation for whom the word "rural" had poignant meanings.

While the makers of eastern landscapes revealed the quiet beauties of river, mountain, and farmyard, more venturesome painters seemed bent on proving the truth of Ben Franklin's observation that the arts had always traveled westward.

George Catlin had painted vigorous but rather harsh portraits in Albany and Washington before he caught sight of his first Indians in Philadelphia and hastened westward in 1832 to record their life before they disappeared "to the shades of their fathers, toward the setting sun." His description took two forms: his *Letters and Notes,* and hundreds of drawings and paintings which lost none of their liveliness for being documented down to the last detail of bead and feather. Among Catlin's sketches in pen and pencil in the New York Historical Society there is one in which he represents himself calmly painting a portrait of the Mandan chieftain Mah-To-Toh-Pa while the whole tribe looks on.

There is a staccato quality in these studies and a sometimes garish but wholly original color in his canvases. He knew how to grasp the dramatic essence of his subject, and the dark forms of his men and animals were firmly placed in landscapes whose trees, hills, and plains were indicated in broad summary fashion. If he glorified the Indian he seldom did so at the cost of specific truth; and he was self-reliant enough to attempt anything from a prairie fire to a buffalo hunt on snow shoes. Catlin came east in 1837 to show his Indian Gallery—a collection of his work with real wigwams and Indians for atmosphere—and the ubiquitous Hone was there to sit down to a collation of buffalo tongues and venison, and smoke the calumet of peace under a tent. Two years later, Hone noted Catlin's departure to exhibit "the raw material of America" to the crowned heads of Europe.

That raw material was refined by the superb plates which Ackermann made from paintings of Karl Bodmer, who traveled farther west than Catlin in 1833 with Prince Maximilian of Wied to draw the Yellowstone River, the Mandan villages, and the Little Rockies for Maximilian's *Travels.*

Alfred J. Miller, who was in Oregon before that region became an American state, caught some of its untamed beauty. This pupil of Sully, who could make lush Infant Samuels of Baltimore children, joined the expedition of Captain William Stewart and recorded Sioux camp scenes and trappers' weddings in crisp water colors, with a slight tendency to languish over some of their details. On a paper seven by twelve inches he managed to suggest the loneliness and chill of that last frontier, the Wind River Mountains, with a bold and shaggy method appropriate to his subject.

Seth Eastman, who was at Fort Snelling, Minnesota, in 1830, learned his draughtsmanship at West Point. His drawings of the Sioux and the Chippewas were offered to any distinguished college which would give free tuition to his children; and he later used his sketches to

George Catlin, *Buffalo Hunt on Snow Shoes,* Ackerman lithograph

Courtesy Old Print Shop, New York City

John M. Stanley, *Western Landscape*

Detroit Institute of Arts

make illustrations for Schoolcraft's six volumes on the tribes. Eastman's painting, *The Rice Gatherers,* was one of a series of nine made for the Indian Affairs Committee of the House of Representatives—a drily explanatory picture with the look of having been worked up painfully from studies made long before.

Emerson had no sooner said that Oregon and Texas were yet unsung than John Mix Stanley made drawings at Santa Fe and was nearly massacred by the Indians of the Willamette. The former house painter of Detroit had gone as far as Arkansas and New Mexico by 1842, painting Choctaws and Cherokees, Seminoles and Creeks. When General Kearny marched on San Diego four years later Stanley was on hand as military draughtsman; when a band of explorers worked their way up the Columbia River he was there to paint Mount Hood. And when Governor Isaac Stevens left St. Paul in 1853 to find the best route for a northern railway, Stanley with his paint box and camera was one of the party.

Fire at the Smithsonian destroyed most of Stanley's labors, along with those of Catlin and James Lewis, but he began a new series from his old sketches for an *Indian Portfolio* which never was published. They reveal a man who, though his imagery was to some extent dependent on his photographs, composed with an eye for what makes a picture. He made a pyramid of Blackfeet Indians huddled on a cliff top, and the Apache who waves a torch in *Indian Telegraph* takes some of his power from the paralleling shapes of the boulder below him (Detroit Inst. of Arts). When Stanley grouped hundreds of figures in *The Trial of Red Jacket* (Buffalo Hist. Soc.) he scarcely more than itemized them. His small *Western Landscape,* however, is nature well observed and delicately rendered; the mountain forms are broadly painted in clean blue-greens, and on a raft in the middle of the river are tiny figures which Stanley suggested with a few broad accents like those of Guardi.

In the two decades which followed Catlin's pioneering there was scarcely a village or a natural wonder of the West which had not been pictured in one medium or another. That documentary record included Indian portraits by Charles Bird King for a three-volume work on the tribes of North America; the paintings of Michigan aborigines which James Otto Lewis made for the government, whose quality can now be judged only by lithographs and a portfolio of sketches; the work of a self-trained ex-tinsmith, Jacob Cox, who "made Fall Creek as classic to the lovers of Indianapolis as Irving did the hills and valleys of the Hudson"; the rather dry fruits of George Winter's years among the redmen of the Wabash, where he painted Kick-Ke-Se-Quah and O-Shaw-Se-Quah before their fathers folded their tents and disappeared; the minutely detailed scenes of the Mississippi, which John Casper Wild painted and lithographed from St. Louis and Davenport.

The content of these pictures varied with their purpose. George Harvey's forty "atmospheric landscapes," of which four were aquatinted as *The Seasons,* were intended to promote good will between his native England and America, and his original water colors were the basis of huge paintings by Harvey to illustrate his London lectures on the primitive wonders of the frontier. When Edwin Whitefield went into Minnesota it was to chart towns and cities as an artistic publicity agent for the Whitefield Exploration Association; and his water-color views were made into lithographs whose function was openly that of advertisement. J. H. Fitzgibbon was one of many daguerreotypists whose work persuaded Easterners to tour the inland valley; and the prints of Henry Lewis, issued in Düsseldorf as *Das Illustrierte Mississippithal,* were perhaps intended to lure Germans into that region.

For Lewis the spectacle of empire's westward course asked for dimensions beyond those of the normal picture, and he applied his scene painter's technique to the production of a panorama. Having sketched that "sublime immensity," the upper Mississippi River, and having made careful studies in oil of such subjects as the Dalles of the St. Croix River and the Falls of St. Anthony, Lewis combined them on a canvas twelve feet high and over twelve hundred yards long. In 1837, Frederick Catherwood had built a permanent rotunda in New York for his panoramas, advertising a *Jerusalem* for which he had made on-the-spot sketches; and John Banvard's three-mile painting, seen in Boston in 1846, perhaps inspired Whittier's poem, *The Panorama,* a long sequence of word pictures in which he surveyed the beauty of his country.

In the spirit of the panoramists a group of painters enlarged their canvases and intensified their palettes. On a May day in 1869, the ties of the Union Pacific and of the Central Pacific were joined at Promontory Point in Utah; but the mighty rivers and canyons which could now be seen by the passengers had already been painted for them in staggering dimensions.

Kensett was one of the few who did not succumb to grandomania. He was with General Pope in Colorado in 1866 and in New Mexico, a man too close in spirit to the Hudson River masters to indulge in histrionics. The early work of Albert Bierstadt was of normal scale, and his European tour with Worthington Whittredge yielded delightful views of Italian hill towns which suggest those of Corot. For the modest-sized *Bombardment of Fort Sumter* (Union League, Phila.), Bierstadt found an exquisite white curve of beach to swing his picture; there was a latent theatricalism, however, in the startling contrast of yellow sand and dark green-blue water. He was among the corps of artists who sketched and made photographs on General Lander's surveying expedition over the South Pass in 1859; this journey and subsequent ones bore fruit in such western scenes as *Mount Corcoran,* which became grandiose in scale and wiry-small in detail. From time to time the freshness and immediacy of his early work reappeared in small-scaled landscapes which now seem the true measure of his talent.

Bierstadt's friend Whittredge could also be both intimate and spectacular: his charming and original painting of deer at Mount Storm Park in Cincinnati (Worcester Art Mus.) was of the former type, and so was his unhackneyed and plausible New England scene, *Home by the Sea;* but *Crossing the Ford,* which he painted in Colorado, was overlarge and overtight (Century Assoc., N. Y.). The Turneresque harbor scenes of Thomas Moran were steady and restrained in contrast with his Yellowstone bombast in the sixties, and some of the vivid details of crags, waterfalls, and thunderclouds which prevent his pictures from becoming wholes may have been supplied by the photographs of his brother John.

In his White Mountain days Sanford R. Gifford was content with a small panel for a fresh and luminous study of *Mount Mansfield* and its valley irradiated by late afternoon sun (Smith Mus., Springfield); in 1871 he attempted the dramatics of Cole and the brilliance of Turner in his effort to interpret Alaska. Thomas Hill, who went to San Francisco in that same year, was as fond of New Hampshire peaks as of giant redwood forests. For his *Crawford Notch* he borrowed a sweeping curve of shadow from Cole to bind his composition, freed himself from the safe olive-browns of the earlier men, and worked with a freshness of autumn coloring and a breadth of pigment which he had seen in Corot's work and in Barbizon forest (N. H. Hist. Soc.). Before long, Americans would learn from the French impressionists how to achieve in broken color the equivalent of nature's light; Hill moved a step in that direction here.

William Keith was Hill's rival in exploiting the lakes and peaks of Oregon, of California, and of the Grand Canyon and the Yellowstone. He remarked once, "I'd be satisfied if I could reach the power and success of Tom Hill," and Keith tried hard enough, with a rather messy touch and a sense of the obvious. The best of Keith was in small paintings with dark, mysterious foregrounds, scarlet sunsets, and brilliant autumnal masses which owed something to Inness but could not reach his depth of feeling for nature.

The work of Frederick Edwin Church, despite his accomplished draughtsmanship and his gift for binding a thousand details into a kind of flamboyant unity, also ministered to the current confusion between quality and quantity. One admires him today for other reasons than his contemporaries, and one prefers his *New England Scenery* of 1851 to his *Chimborazo* some twenty years later. Church was twenty-five and had been the only pupil of Cole when, in the first of these two paintings, he found a balance between Cole's willful distribution of light and his own gift for constructing the solid planes of nature. His near bridge and covered wagon anchored the design firmly, and the receding spaces, despite intricate detail, convincingly explained themselves (Smith Mus., Springfield).

Church was not satisfied for long with such familiar themes. Before Alexander Humboldt died in 1859 his writings had aroused the interest of Northerners in the landscape and archaeology of Central and South America. The English artist Frederick Catherwood published in 1844 his twenty-five lithographed *Views of Ancient Monuments in Central America;* and when Conrad Wise Chapman drew small studies in 1865 for a panoramic view, *Valley of Mexico,* Church had already made two trips to the southern continent. Among the results of those expeditions was his *Cotopaxi,* whose scale and exoticism caused one critic to exclaim, "This is art's noblest, truest function; not to imitate nature but to rival it." The roving Church also painted Jamaica and Jerusalem, the Bavarian Alps and the Aegean Sea. In 1863 London saw the icebergs he had sketched off Labrador, and two years later the New York *World* described them as "frozen white and mute with horror at the dread secrets of ages."

Too often in the larger Church canvases the firm plane and the receding space were submerged by purplish plumes of smoke, rainbows, and Turneresque sunsets reflected in turbid water, or sacrificed to an overprecise enumeration of details, betraying in the latter case the artist's reliance on his photographs of icebergs and tropical foliage. Such paintings were made for the same public which crowded the concerts of Louis Gottschalk, hearing the sound of rippling brooks and seeing the moonlight on Mount Olive in his piano fantasia, *Jerusalem.* Church exploited a combination of the spectacular and specific for people who loved to wander "among the tangled luxuriance of the *Heart of the Andes*" and to contemplate its "shining or shadowy sublimities." The painter's Labrador companion, the Reverend Louis Noble, explained that Church had combined the observation of a geologist and a physicist of light with "a revelation of almighty power so wondrously apparalled with the silvery, the dim and unsubstantial" that shadow and cloud seemed to flit and change before the observer.

Thus in a single picture could Church appeal simultaneously to this generation's pleasure in the exotic and

Albert Bierstadt, *Merced River, Yosemite Valley*

Metropolitan Museum of Art, New York City

Frederick E. Church, *The Iceberg*

Courtesy Mrs. Theodore W. Church

Martin J. Heade, *Orchids and Hummingbirds* (Henry Schnakenberg coll.)

Courtesy Harry Shaw Newman

its respect for science. Yet even when Noble wrote, a reaction was evident against the windy painted acre and the niggling fact. One found it in the small canvases of Martin Johnson Heade and in the work of Hunt and Inness.

Heade's tropical birds were intended as illustrations for a book on the hummingbirds of South America, and his orchids would have satisfied the most literal botanist. Imagination carried the artist beyond mere documentation, however: a spray of exquisitely drawn apple blossoms was placed in a spring landscape; an orchid glowed brilliantly against rain clouds, tropical palms, and drooping moss. And Heade was a dramatist of unusual power when he painted white sails livid against a thunderous sky in *Storm over Narragansett Bay* in 1868.

In landscape as in figure, Hunt "looked for the big things first," whether his subject was Niagara with its prismatic bow or an apple tree on a foggy morning at Magnolia on the North Shore of Massachusetts. Millet was not the only exile from boulevard aesthetics in France, as Hunt well knew. Rousseau and Diaz had penetrated the forest of Fontainebleau, painting it as though one were lost in its sunshot depths. At Isle-Adam, Jules Dupré patiently studied and ruggedly constructed a single oak tree; Constant Troyon painted sheep with a breadth and play of light not found in the Dutch masters; Daubigny tramped the banks of the Oise to record every change of spring or autumn foliage in canvases too strong and too "coarse" for the Parisian appetite. The wind moved through Corot's trees and the light filtered through his woodland clearings.

Like the Barbizon men, Hunt was more interested in the brief play of light over natural forms than in the permanent look of the forms themselves. Under his influence at Newport, John La Farge painted *Paradise Valley* in the late sixties. The younger man had already admired at first hand the clean intensities of the Pre-Raphaelite palette in England, and in France the penetrant studies of the Barbizon men. Before he was thirty he made flower pieces of exquisite color modulations and at Newport set himself the task of suggesting bleak meadow and distant sea without using the stock devices of the landscape painter. There was no tree to establish the foreground in *Paradise Valley,* no focus of interest, no alternation of light and dark planes to lead the eye backward, but only a sequence of subtle variations in muted browns and greens—an almost scientific experiment, as remarkable as it was prophetic, to discover what color alone could do.

The new vision of Rousseau and Daubigny, of Millet and Corot was not lost upon George Inness, who made two trips to Europe before his four-year visit of 1870

George Inness, *Harvest Scene in the Delaware Valley*
Walker Art Center, Minneapolis, Minn.

to Italy and France. He had been in his teens a map engraver and briefly a pupil of Gignoux. If his landscapes of the fifties looked backward toward Cole and Doughty he was nonetheless steadily seeking his own forms of expression. He gradually freed his palette from the Hudson River browns and broke with the conventional devices for receding planes of distance; he was completely unhackneyed with the stump-scattered pastures of *Lackawanna Valley* (Natl. Gall.), where a train moved on tracks drawn with a masterly skill in perspective, and the far town with its roundhouse was vague in the heat and haze of a summer day. In Italy he learned to make clouds move swiftly; in Delaware he became the master of quiet greens, firmly blocked earth forms, and densely massed foliage.

The Inness landscape of the 1860's refused to become a type. The dynamics of storm were in *Passing Shower*—the zigzagging road, the wind-tossed trees, the rainbow aslant the sky. The clouds of *On the Delaware* (Brooklyn Mus.) were majestic and full, the hills heavy with moisture-charged blues and purples.

Inness achieved a sturdy balance of truth and poetry in his *Delaware Meadows* of 1867, and this painting suggests much that had happened during thirty-odd years of American landscape. It has Doughty's quietude but a bolder draughtsmanship than his; it has the spacious breadth of Bierstadt without his pompous dimensions, the patient knowledge of Durand, but less explicit. Landscape had been epic during these years, pastoral, rustic, and exotic. The painting of Inness at forty-two implied a new lyricism which was at once more personal and more intense.

CHAPTER 17 / ART FOR THE PEOPLE

Although that branch of art which is called "genre" eludes final definition, its underlying motives and its spirit are unmistakable. The portrait isolates man from his cluttered environment, while genre finds him among his fellows in a moment of action. Nature in landscape painting has her own justification, but in genre becomes the stage for human comedy, tragedy, or melodrama. History painting comes closer to genre than either portrait or landscape since it presents a group enterprise, but it comes closest when the episode is so nearly of one's time that men feel themselves personally involved in the outcome and not coolly detached from it by elapsed time. Genre, despite the many occasions when it mingles with other modes, has for its essential purpose nothing more heroic than to interpret man to himself by showing how he behaves on simple and present occasions.

This was the motive of those calendar pictures of the Middle Ages where the farmer ploughs his field under the high walls of his lord's castle and in winter guides his cattle through snow while his womenfolk warm their shins at the hearth. This was the origin of the swarming fat couples whose reds, greens, and whites weave such a lively pattern in Pieter Brueghel's *Wedding Dance* and of the oblivious ploughman who occupies the foreground of Brueghel's *Fall of Icarus.* It crowds the smoky taverns of Ostade, Dou, and Brouwer in seventeenth-century Holland, and links the knitting, chatting, and housekeeping women of Metsu, Vermeer, and De Hoogh intimately with their bedrooms and back gardens. In Rembrandt the genre spirit gives a new applicability to Biblical episodes; in the next century it announces the new middle class in the kitchens of Chardin, the cottage sentimentalities of Greuze, the raucous intimacies of Hogarth's *Gin Lane,* and the tittle-tattle of his *Marriage à la Mode.* As the farmer, the grocer, and the small professional found his place in the nineteenth-century world there were solemn artists like Millet to dignify his commonest moment, and humorous ones like Daumier to mock his pretensions.

Even in colonial America John Greenwood produced a spirited if somewhat explosive genre composition, *Sea Captains Carousing at Surinam.* The pewterers of 1788 represented themselves at work in their shop, and Elijah Boardman in the next year was painted by Ralph Earl among the shelves of his dry goods store. Both the *Staircase Picture* and the Museum portrait of Charles Willson Peale were in the genre mood; Copley's *Watson and the Shark* was literal reportage. The emphasis in John Krimmel's *Fourth of July* was on Philadelphians taking the air in Center Square; and William Dunlap recalled in paint the moment when he had shown one of his landscapes to his father and mother.

The America of Jackson furnished more varied themes for genre than that of Jefferson. Literary subjects were even more popular than in the early republican days, and no novelist lacked for illustrators. But the Jacksonian was more responsive to the ordinary and the nonfictional. Concrete differences of environment, rustic and urban, were more curiously viewed, and an eager sectionalism was not limited to the political sphere. The moralist was sure to find an audience for his homilies on family virtue, the patriot painter was welcome provided he reduced great events to human scale and presented heroes as normal fellows. "Give me insight into today," said Emerson in *The American Scholar,* "and you may have the antique and future worlds." The poet believed it a sign of new vigor when the currents of warm life ran into the extremities of society: "I embrace the common . . . and sit at the feet of the familiar." In *Poets of the People* Margaret Fuller contrasted two conceptions of literature: the small garden where a few masterpieces could be created, and the ruder cultivation of the broad soil where all men communicate with one another; and she conceded that the "genial and generous tendency" was the predominant one in 1845.

An art for the people must possess a means of propagation, and more than one artist specialized in the multiplied imagery of the cartoon, or engraved illustrations for the gilt-bound *Galaxies, Keepsakes,* and *Treasures* which loaded parlor tables. Andrew Jackson was the hero or the villain of lithographs in the late twenties and early thirties, and graphic artists invented log cabins and hard cider jugs to transform the aristocratic Harrison into a man of the people. David Claypoole Johnston was called the "American Cruikshank" because he drew little men with the comic, wiry lines of the English master. When replicas of Cole and Bingham had to be made, one could rely on James Smillie and John Sartain to render pigment into crosshatched metal lines with astonishing fidelity not only to the letter but to the spirit of the originals.

If the illustrations of Felix Octavius Carr Darley

John Quidor, *Ichabod Crane Pursued by the Headless Horseman*

Yale University Art Gallery (Mabel B. Garvan coll.), New Haven, Conn.

were sprightlier than most others, one thanked his actor father, and his own resourcefulness in wash drawings to which the engraver did only partial justice. Darley's invention was adequate for a long line of picture books which included Cooper, Dickens, Simms, Longfellow, Poe, and Trowbridge. One must seek the full flavor of his drollery in rapid pencil studies and water color. His *Sketch Book* of 1848 was done on wood, but in the same year the Art Union subscribers received his *Illustrations of Rip Van Winkle* whose plates were drawn and lithographed by him with humorous charm and a delightful linear clarity. Ten years later, Augustus Hoppin's illustrations for *Tricks and Traps of New York City* were stiffly engraved on wood as part of a series of small books exposing vice and folly in "perfectly unexceptionable language and sentiment."

From 1857 dates the formal partnership between Nathaniel Currier and his former bookkeeper James M. Ives, whose thousands of lithographs were a pictorial invasion of American homes. The drawings, water colors, and oils from which their prints were made employed a small regiment of specialists. Louis Maurer was adroit with horses and horse racing, and James E. Butterworth with trim yachts; Fanny F. Palmer pictured transcontinental trains in hard, prim water color while William T. Ranney drew *The Trapper's Last Shot* to preserve the memory of a frontier which the railway would soon annihilate. Arthur F. Tait re-created the pleasures of hunting and fishing; George H. Durrie made city men homesick for the sound of sleigh bells on a frosty morning in New England.

Currier and Ives had their competitors in J. Baillie and the Kelloggs, in Thomas Kelly and Sarony and Major. The American agents of foreign print makers issued handsome subjects which were sometimes the work of Americans, like Goupil's hand-colored lithograph of 1856, *My Birthday Present,* a lustrous and delicate translation of the little-girl-with-doll theme in a painting by Lily Martin Spencer of Newark, New Jersey. If Currier and Ives led the field, however, it was because the shrewd partners exploited every tender domestic moment, every sign of national progress, every regional oddity, every private or public disaster from a cut finger to a forest fire.

One found both naïveté and sophistication among the genre painters. A down-Easter named Jeremiah

David G. Blythe, *Whoa, Emma!* (Mrs. James Hailman coll.)

Courtesy University of Pittsburgh, Department of Fine Arts

Hardy was largely self-developed and had established himself as a portraitist in Bangor, Waterville, Skowhegan, and near-by towns when he essayed the domestic tableau in *Picnic in the Maine Woods.* In other instances the precise prose touch appropriate to genre was learned at Düsseldorf or at second hand from Leutze and other Düsseldorfers in America. Browere and Blythe borrowed the tricks of seventeenth-century Dutch and Flemish masters; for younger men—John W. Ehninger among them — a fresher palette and a broader brush were suggested by Couture and Millet.

No models need be cited for the knock-kneed antics and lightning illumination of John Quidor, although the baroque men would have been at home with his swirling spaces and playhouse gestures, and Pieter Brueghel would have approved the grotesque and prickly blasted trees which framed his *Voyage to Hell Gate.* He was less the genrist than the illustrator of other men's fancies; born at Tappan, he resurrected the legendary figures of Irving and Cooper. One could scarcely call Quidor a success in his generation, and Dunlap found little to say about him except that he painted fire buckets and fire engines to keep himself alive. Jarvis had evidently taught him very little, for his bonfire chiaroscuro was wholly original, his compositions were held together by his own hysterical intensity, and his Rip Van Winkle scenes told their story with the ramshackle amiability of Rip himself. Sixteen of the thirty-five known works of Quidor, assembled in 1942 by John I. H. Baur, revealed a delightful and unique American talent.

The anecdotes of Albertis D. O. Browere lacked Quidor's fire; he was born at Tarrytown and died at Catskill, the son of the John who had made the life masks of the republican heroes. His mining scenes were painted in the California of the gold fever and his painting of 1844, *Mrs. McCormick's General Store, Catskill,* is a Hogarthian anecdote solidly if soberly painted by a man who had neither the dynamics of Quidor nor the comic pointedness of David G. Blythe.

The latter deserves to be called the Ostade of Pittsburgh, for the shadowy rafters of the Dutchman's taverns throw into relief Blythe's gesticulating citizens; and seventeenth-century burghers with bullet heads, spindly shanks, and monstrous buttocks are strangely naturalized as Pittsburgh horse traders and Irish coal miners. Blythe possessed the skill to make a diagonal board emphasize an upraised arm by its parallel direction in a trial scene and to frame his characters in the archway of a post office. In *January Bills* (Yale Univ.) the outline of a desk, the shadow behind an open door, and the shape of a wall map were the means of telling a crisp and ludicrous anecdote; and shortly before his death Blythe showed that he could construct a landscape and steep it in June warmth, in a picture where long lines of Union troops cross the Potomac and wind over the far hills under the eye of General Doubleday.

The artful exaggerations of Quidor and the strange tricks of Blythe with the scale of his manikins were in the spirit of caricature; more reasonable from the visual point of view and more temperately humorous was the genre of William Sidney Mount, George Caleb Bingham, and Richard Caton Woodville.

Mount, who rejected three offers of aid for European travel to chronicle the life of the Long Island villages, was the complete embodiment of Margaret Fuller's "genial and generous tendency." Charles Lanman gave three cheers in 1845 for "the laughter-loving and incomparable genius of Stony Brook, whom I know to be a first-rate fisherman and a most pathetic player of the violin." Mount was thirty-seven when this was written, and had found his subject and his style. He had been apprentice to his brother Henry, who painted signs and an occasional still life; he had known the discipline of the National Academy and had made a brief contact with Inman's genial talent. A third brother, Shepard Alonzo, specialized in smoothly rendered portraits, and William Sidney could produce likenesses of equal firmness and precision but with a livelier sense of personality and charm. In 1831, however, his *Dancing on the Barn*

William S. Mount, *The Power of Music,* Goupil, Vibert & Co. lithograph

Library of Congress photo

Floor was evidence that an original artist, as Lanman said, was tasking his own mind for subjects, and proof that he grasped the picture-making possibilities of Long Island farmyards.

Mount's purpose was simply stated: "Paint pictures that will take with the public—never paint for the few, but the many." His *Power of Music* (Century Assoc., N. Y.) took with the many, and so did his *Raffling for a Goose* (Met. Mus.). A genteel critic of 1835 wished that his superior talent would find subjects "of a higher grade in the social scale" than tavern revelers, but the wealthy Jonathan Sturges ordered an interior from Mount four years later with the assurance that he would not object to a kitchen.

When Mount painted *The Truant Gamblers* he put geometry to work: the verticals of the barn door break the large surface into usable units and its diagonal brace points to the pivotal figure of a boy. Mount has seen the dark rectangle of the barn's interior not only as a counterweight to the lighter areas of ground and shingled wall but as an indispensable element for his story, and he has slanted a hoe handle and silhouetted the shape of his vengeful farmer as a master anecdotist marshals his words and phrases. In dozens of small pencil sketches one sees the schemes of Mount develop toward a formal and psychological rightness. In *The Power of Music,* one could not remove a stone from under his barn or change the shadow of his listening Negro; one could not alter the reflected angles of his oar and spear handle in *Eel Spearing at Setauket* (N. Y. State Hist. Assoc.). (See color plate 8.)

The Stony Creek painter had never seen Teniers and Ostade in European museums, but he had read in Frank Howard's book, *Color as a Means of Art,* how they had thrown the greater part of their pictures into brownish and gray tones, and balanced them with small sparks of bright color. Howard had explained the warmth of shadows and reflections and had observed, "The light of noonday sun is so vivid that it diffuses its color over all the illumined parts of the objects under its influence,"[15] which then assume a rich golden hue. In Mount's thin and lustrous pigment, in his transparent shadows, and in his delicately brushed highlights there is a bland, pervasive, and sunny warmth. His modeling of a Negress' head in *Eel Spearing* and his study of a shingled Long Island farmhouse with the pattern of tree branches on it (Met. Mus.), are patient and minute but never forced.

Mount's sunniness was not only of the weather, for his countrymen were well-liked neighbors and his Negroes were people, not stereotypes. He lived in the days of Ethiopian minstrels when Philip Hone complained that Italian opera was less popular than the black banjo players with their worn-out conundrums and when George Washington Dixon sang "Coal Black Rose," "Zip Coon," and "Push-a-long, Keep Moving." But Mount painted *The Banjo Player* as a man who shared his own delight in music, and did so without a trace of condescension. Walt Whitman, writing about art in the New York *Evening Post* in 1851, praised him for his picture of a Negro who has won a goose in a raffle, because it was an American portrait and not a minstrel show caricature.

Bingham's rowdy boatmen and sweating politicians were of a stouter breed than Mount's Long Islanders, yet the two men had similar purposes. Mount wrote that he had heard enough of ideality and the grand style; Bingham at the close of his life attacked the notion of an ideal beauty to be discovered by closing one's eyes to the objective world and looking within. He discovered no mere symmetry of form in the men and women of the Dutch masters, and decided that the powers of the artist are limited to representing what the eye sees. Bingham labored, in his own words, to "assure us that our social and political characteristics . . . will not be lost in the lapse of time for want of an Art record rendering them full justice"; and one must consult his record to know life on the great western rivers.

Bingham was a child when his Virginia parents moved to Franklin, Missouri, and both child and town grew up together. When a writer on the *Missouri Intelligencer* welcomed his talent in 1835 with more local pride than critical insight the young man had opened a studio at Columbia and was producing hard-grained likenesses for twenty dollars. His skill, the *Intelligencer* said, was more fortunately displayed in the design, delineation, and coloring than in "chiaroscure," and Bingham combined the virtues of the Leontine and Venetian rather than the Lombard school. Let his gifts be excited and drawn out by liberality of encouragement at home, and the whole country would hail a Western Meteor of Art.

The Missouri meteor never lacked encouragement and as the years went on, his portrait commissions multiplied, his genre scenes brought substantial prices, and their engraved reproductions sold by thousands. For a few months in Philadelphia between 1837 and 1838 he observed the work of more sophisticated men, and a few years later made the first of his genre paintings. No one can say what part the work of other men played, and what part his own senses and intelligence, in the fine color orchestration which these early works revealed, the muscular draughtsmanship, response to outdoor light, and firm ordering of space.

Each of the figures in these river paintings had been first sketched individually from life, the supple and incisive brush uniquely characterizing each man, sculpturing the clothes on the rounded body, and casting the deep shadows and the hard lights; these swift-action drawings of slouching drunkards, top-hatted politicians, and smiling gamblers are among the finest drawings in American art.

The tanned fur trader in his scarlet shirt and tasseled stocking cap would soon be legendary, but not before Bingham had placed him in the stern of a dugout in *Fur Traders Descending the Missouri,* his young companion lounging against the cargo, and a chained fox mirrored in the water. These and a mist-hidden clump of island trees under clouds touched by a warm afternoon light are all that Bingham needed for his memorable image. The dark animal and the brilliant blue-green and red of the men's shirts are his major notes; his minor, the pale green water, the darker green of trees, and the sun-charged sky.

Equally simple was the balanced grouping of six figures on the deck in *Raftsmen Playing Cards* and the placing of this motive between receding river banks (City Art Mus., St. Louis). The poetry of the earlier painting here gives way to prose but one can imagine the boatman singing, as he thrusts his pole into shallow water:

> Hard upon the beach oar
> She moves too slow
> All the way to Shawneetown
> Long while ago.

In both these paintings nature divides the interest with people; in other works it is man, and particularly political man who most concerns him. True to his declared purpose he documents the life which Fredrika Bremer described, "the gambling and rival parties," the flags and the abusive newspapers, the great placards *Beware of the Whigs!* and *The Democrats Are Incendiaries!* One of the campaign banners which Bingham painted, with Henry Clay as a mill boy riding a pony, has survived to indicate his activity as an artist-politician and his progress in the thirties toward a more fluent

George C. Bingham, *Fur Traders Descending the Missouri*

Metropolitan Museum of Art, New York City

style. Before he painted his *Stump Orator* he had himself stumped as a Whig and an anti-Locofoco, had run for the state legislature unsuccessfully, and on a second try had been elected.

His Whiggery and his art culminated in two canvases painted while the Free-Soilers, Bingham among them, fought their critical battle with the Secessionists in the early fifties. Both *County Election* and *Verdict of the People,* as Professor Arthur Pope has remarked, suggest the Venetian masters of space composition. His ground plans could be plotted by an architect: the middle ground half occupied by a porticoed building; the street receding at right angles to the picture plane; the foreground motives swinging the eyes upward and backward toward the chief actors; the crowds of less importance massed across the street vista; the seemingly casual play of light and shadow giving each individual his rightful place in a scene which numbers hundreds. Here and there an acrid blue or a hot vermilion cries out like a heckler at a rally, but Bingham holds his crowd like an oratorical spellbinder. For two years, while the artist traveled in search of ten-dollar subscribers, John Sartain worked at his engraving of *County Election,* reducing it to twenty-two by thirty inches with no sacrifice of its vigorous characterization and its sturdy wholeness.

Bingham's *Order No. 11,* with its wiry drawing and hot color, was a consequence of his three years in Düsseldorf. From that German city also came the dull costume pieces which Richard Caton Woodville sent to the Art Union. The Woodville genre, much of it lithographed, became more familiar to Americans than the Baltimore man himself, for Woodville spent most of his painting years abroad and died at thirty-one. New York saw two of his pictures in 1848 which assembled small groups in a confined setting with something of Bingham's and Mount's skill. The disputant and the listener of his *Politics in an Oyster House* are framed by their curtained booth, the accessories cleverly placed, and the figures painted with a relish for personality

George C. Bingham, *The County Election*

City Art Museum, St. Louis, Mo.

which redeems the sleek handling. *War News from Mexico* (Natl. Acad.) builds its climax on the steps and porch of a tavern through a sequence of massed figures which the Missouri Whig would have admired; and four years before he died, Woodville enlarged his space to room-size for *The Sailor's Wedding,* disposed his neatly characterized party against shadowed wall-paper in the side light from a tall window, and painted homespun and silk with the deft clarity of a Terborch.

Few if any of the genre men deserve to be placed alongside Mount, Bingham, and Woodville. When Henry Inman's works were sold at his death in 1846, there were a few genre canvases among his portraits which, like *Mumble the Peg* (Pa. Acad.), were gracefully composed and exquisitely painted. The forced humor of Durand's *Wrath of Peter Stuyvesant* (N. Y. Hist. Soc.) proved that his forte was landscape. Beside the false emphasis of Daniel Huntington's genre and the dry, platitudinous sermons of Henry P. Gray, the work of John F. Weir was both honest and forceful. In the sixties Weir made sketches of the gun foundry at West Point, and the dim rafters of *Forging the Shaft,* the straining workmen, the gun barrel emerging white-hot from the furnace, were his record of what Whitman called an "original and really picturesque occasion" (Met. Mus.). Charles Deas was a painter who understood that genre is most convincing when its scale is intimate, and his small *Turkey Shoot* had the drollery of Blythe in the contours of its sportsmen against snow and in the dwarfish proportions of its children; his *Devil and Tom Walker* suggests Quidor but is more firmly brushed.

The nature of genre tempts mediocre artists to capitalize the event and evade the more difficult problems of form. When Frank Blackwell Mayer attempted a barn door anecdote in the Mount manner without Mount's humor or his architectonics, his *Leisure and Labor* (Corcoran Gall.) was spotty and uncoordinated. When John Blake White revived a Revolutionary theme his mock heroics carried no conviction; when D. Malone Carter composed his Molly Pitcher scenes he imitated Trumbull's weaknesses and repeated his trite methods. Compared with Mount's touch, the sleek and monotonous brushwork of Francis W. Edmonds in *The Bashful Cousin* denoted the second-rater. There was an echo of Woodville's charm in the rustic interiors of Enoch Wood Perry, who worked in Düsseldorf in 1852, but he lacked Woodville's sense of space

Richard C. Woodville, *The Sailor's Wedding*

Walters Art Gallery, Baltimore, Md.

depth and the play of light on people and furniture.

The figures in Lily Spencer's *War Spirit at Home—Celebrating the Victory at Vicksburg* were held together only by their enthusiasm (Newark Mus.). E. L. Henry piled detail on detail until the interest of his *9:45 Accommodation* became the mild one of amused enumeration (Met. Mus.). It was the content, not the form, of William T. Ranney's scouts and covered wagons that made his reputation, for he lacked Bingham's gift for phrasing; and when Thomas Satterwhite Noble painted his *John Brown's Blessing,* the near-life size of his people only emphasized his banality as the dramatist of a tragic event (N. Y. Hist. Soc.).

Noble's painterly quality, however, was a welcome relief from the niceties of Düsseldorf, and could be credited to his study with Couture. John Whetton Ehninger was another who managed to combine the explicitness he had learned in the German city with the Couture generalizations. Some of his episodes were from Irving's *Knickerbocker History,* and in 1858 he made illustrations for "The Courtship of Miles Standish" which were "copied by the photographic process"; but his *Yankee Peddler* was genre of a contemporary sort, the women grouped near the cart with an artful plausibility, the figure of the peddler and his customer strongly modeled in the clear light, the colors fresh and unforced.

Another American who refused to be garrulous about the unimportant was Eastman Johnson of Lovell, Maine, whose career as a portraitist had been well begun when he was the companion of Leutze in 1849 in the German city and, a few years later, the pupil of Couture. His draughtsmanship was learned at seventeen in Bufford's lithographic shop in Boston, and most of the likenesses he made in Augusta, Portland, and the national capital were not painted but drawn with crayon on toned paper—his sketches of the eighty-nine-year-old widow of Alexander Hamilton, Dolly Madison, John Quincy Adams, and Daniel Webster. Johnson came home in 1855 with something more than the undifferentiated "realism" of Leutze and the power of Couture to block out general forms in solid pigment, for he had seen the Vermeers and the Rembrandts at The Hague and had admired the luminous interiors of the former, the latter's conquest of detail and form in near shadows.

Johnson's first essays in genre have a Dutch solidity. His *Old Kentucky Home* of 1859, to be sure, was a

John W. Ehninger, *The Yankee Peddler*

Newark Museum

rather aimless anecdote whose ramshackle tenement and Negro families were not firmly composed in space (N. Y. Hist. Soc.); but his *Corn Husking* of 1860, in spite of its Düsseldorf hardness, was a firm integration of the farm people with their barn setting (Syracuse Mus. Fine Arts). His *Lilies* of 1865 was superbly designed by a man who could be architectural with the reflection of a gesture in water and who could ignore the incidental. Johnson's flesh tones in the sixties were those of living matter, and his painting of costume had breadth and a delight in textures.

One other Yankee could match this pictorial integrity and this freedom with a medium which others tortured. The *High Tide* of Winslow Homer (Met. Mus.) took almost the same elements Johnson used in *The Conversation* (Addison Gall.)—three women and a small dog on a beach—and organized them with equal steadiness though with a livelier sense of wind, wave, and sunlight. Homer, twelve years younger than Johnson, was a strongheaded person whose mother came from Bucksport, Maine, and whose father was a hardware merchant. He, too, worked at Bufford's in Boston, where he produced pictorial covers for sheet music and was taught by a French expert how to draw on wood for the engraver.

A reader of *Ballou's Pictorial* in 1857 or of *Harper's Weekly* in the following years would have found in Homer's illustrations of life in Boston and New York one more competent picture maker; but Homer had seen a genre painting and had made up his mind to do the same thing "a damned sight better." When he joined McClellan's army in 1861 as special artist for *Harper's* he had established a studio in New York and had studied nights at the National Academy. What Homer brought back from the Peninsular campaign was not military histrionics but a record of unheroic discomforts and quietly humorous situations. There was battle smoke in Homer's six lithographed *Campaign Sketches,* but even his *Sharpshooter* is less the medium of death than a young man perched in the half light

Winslow Homer, *The Bridle Path, White Mountains* (detail)
Sterling and Francine Clark Art Institute, Williamstown, Mass.

of a pine tree's foliage, and a skillful exercise in pictorial dynamics.

Almost at once Homer's brush moved with a decisiveness and a laconic strength which came slowly to Eastman Johnson. In his *Prisoners from the Front* he balanced the figure of Colonel Barlow with monumental simplicity against the group of captives in a field scarcely more than indicated, delicately suggesting a mental interchange between victor and vanquished (Met. Mus.). The artist was exploring the variations of brown and gray in war-shabby clothing and the intensity of a blue uniform against a lighter blue sky, achieving quiet sonorities with no loss of specific character.

Homer's *Croquet* was painted one year before he saw Europe and *The Bridle Path* a year after his return. In the first of these, his dusty browns and tempered blues gave place to the glaring brilliance of white satin, strong green-blue, and flaming orange in the bell-shaped dresses of two women who stood on the greenest of lawns with shadowed green woods beyond them, in a composition like a seesaw with the straw hat of a kneeling man as fulcrum. Light in *The Bridle Path* was more tempered and pervasive, veiling the White Mountain ranges with a golden haze and reflecting itself from the rocky foreground to modify the shadowed arm and body of the riding woman and the forms of her white horse.

Homer was thirty-two with his master work still before him, but these paintings demonstrated his continuity with the genre tradition. The words of Horatio Greenough applied to him, as to the earlier painters of man in his environment: "I love the concrete, my brother!"

CHAPTER 18 / ART BY THE PEOPLE

Although she's all my fancy paints her, I could wish she were painted a great deal better." With these words in 1847 a self-taught limner, who had made a *Magdalene* with housepaint on a board provided by his sympathetic landlady, sent his work to the Art Union. This modesty is perhaps the common trait among thousands of painters and carvers whose lives enriched the texture of art in the middle years of the century.

That richness evades the terms which have been used by its recent discoverers. The name "Sunday painter" applies to those for whom a still life or a portrait was marginal to their chief occupation. "Self-taught" suggests the nonprofessional character of this art; "popular" recognizes its deep social roots; and "pioneer" its self-reliance and courage to invent. "Folk art" has been made the designation of useful craft objects which were fashioned by small isolated groups into shapes inherited and tenaciously conserved. The modernist uses the word "primitive" to express his admiration for that creative state of mind which reproduces the mind's image of things with small concern for conventions or so-called "real" appearances.

The art of the common man cannot be confined in any one of these categories: the Sunday painter often finds that response to his efforts which will keep him busy on his weekdays; the amateur, under certain circumstances, exchanges his naïveté for more sophisticated methods, and shades off into the professional. The pioneer turns out as often as not to have found his imagery in a magazine, a book illustration, or a print, and to have disciplined his pencil, as Carl Drepperd has shown, through study of the instruction books so numerous in the early years of the nineteenth century. Behind the admiration of the modern aesthete for the primitive there lurks an unsound assumption that learning is a dangerous thing, and that the child is wiser than the man; much of this art is heavy-handed and without interest either as design or as expression.

As for the concept of folk art, one could make better use of it in Herder's Europe than in Jackson's America. Herder believed in the inherent capacity of a nation as a whole to express its group character and thus offer a distinctive contribution to human culture. But there were no established over-all forms in sectionally minded America which could perform Herder's function. In a country of many racial origins, of enormously varied geography, of rampant individualism, of railways, cameras, and cheap manufactured articles, only a few folk islands could for a time resist the flood of industrialism.

Such islands had existed here since colonial days. Before the Russians withdrew to the north in the days of the Monroe Doctrine they built barns and churches in California which had the character of their own land. In North Dakota, where Russians drank tea out of tumblers and Finns steamed themselves clean in "saunas," the farmers made the floors of their houses bright with orange paint, and covered their barns with diagonal stripings of red, white, and blue.

In New Mexico the ritual of the flagellation was reduced to its essentials by the weaver of a bedspread; at Lebanon the Shakers bound their rugs with braid in severely geometric patterns. Wherever the Swedes went there were stiffly conventional stags on their lace borders and human figures reduced to triangles on their boldly colored weavings. The odd dragons and serpents on the chair backs and bridal benches of American Norwegians were a part of their viking ancestry.

No transplanted folk was more tenacious of its figurative habits than the Germanic, whose greatest concentration was in eastern Pennsylvania. In contrast to the Amana Society, whose seven communal villages were established in Iowa in the fifties, the Pennsylvania Germans had lived in America since the seventeenth century, and the richest fields and broadest barns of the region were owned by descendants of the Rhineland Pietists who had come west at William Penn's invitation. The Amana crafts were laconic and austere; those of the Pennsylvania "Dutch" were exuberant in shape and color. By the mid-century more than a hundred years of delightful German handicraft succumbed to the slicker products of the crockery store and the printing press, but not before the craftsman had given old shapes a new meaning and even invented new shapes. The ancient eagle often became the bird of the republic. Not only did he spread his wings and grasp his shield on the coverlets and wallpapers of New England but on the broad-bottomed dishes of the Pennsylvania potters. George Washington rode his horse; Samuel Troxel in 1846 retained an old German maxim on the edge of an earthenware plate, but in its center he coupled the word *Liberty* with the name of President Polk. The *fractur* scribe who celebrated the baptism of James David Musser in 1852 evidently had neither the skill nor the desire to practice the rich decorative

Birth certificate of James David Musser

Courtesy Harry Shaw Newman

elaborations of the earlier penmen, but his bouquet is in the old tradition.

The Negro folk artist was more conscious of the world around him than of his distant African heritage. The monstrous grinning faces on the so-called "slave pottery" recall the ancient idols, and a Missouri Negro of the 1860's carved a lizard, a turtle, a snake, and a human figure climbing toward the beautifully whorled handle of a hardwood cane with a tense vigor one finds in the past of this people. But the hen and chicken which Jean Lafitte's slave cut in wood had no specifically racial quality; and when the Negro painted portraits they differed in no way from the hard effigies of his white contemporaries.

While the folk islands resisted the modern tide, the American mainland was fertile in portraits, still life, genre, landscape, and allegory which had the common touch. The fruit of leisure hours, it was intended for the pleasure of its makers and their families, or to record events of family importance. When a loved one died, a water colorist or a needlewoman produced a monument under weeping willows, grouped the mourners around it, and carefully lettered the inscription.

In order to identify what she has called the "native abstract tradition," Jean Lipman contrasts a primitive portrait with a Gilbert Stuart, a "funeral piece" with a professional view of Washington's tomb, an anonymous

Theorem painting of still life (water color)

Courtesy Harry Shaw Newman

still life with the solid and illusory grapes and apples of James Peale. One accepts the antithesis although the "abstract" qualities in a people's art are often involuntary, the humblest limner wishing to improve his technique by any means he can find. For example, the still lifes of the period, often on silk or velvet, derived their neat outlines and their decorative disposal of shapes and colors as much from the stencils or "theorems" which could be purchased by the young ladies in seminaries as from the aesthetic instinct of the young ladies themselves. And the wandering portrait painter was quick to learn a few tricks whenever his wandering brought him into touch with more competent work than his own.

The portraitists were the most ubiquitous artisan-artists in the first decades of the century, and Mrs. Lipman has listed more than twenty men thus active in Maine during the thirties and forties. Having set up his easel in a town or village, the face maker advertised, as J. Atwood did in a printed handbill, that he guaranteed "correct likenesses of the originals." The result was often a stiff and unprepossessing map of the customer whose explicit flatness linked the New England of Daniel Webster with that of Miles Standish. These "primitive" simplifications were not always the mask of ignorance, however; in the work of William Matthew Prior they were an adaptation to the customer's pocketbook. This New England itinerant announced his willingness to supply a flat portrait for one fourth the price of a shaded one, and was competent on both levels.

Captain Greeley of Ellsworth, Maine, was limned in the flat manner by Joseph Greenleaf Cole, son of the Moses Cole who plied the same trade in Newburyport;

Erastus S. Field, *Portrait of a Woman*

Colonial Williamsburg, Inc.

George and Jane Bigelow (Mrs. Dwight Hughes coll.)

Henry Elkan photo

and Charles Octavius Cole was another seaport artist who placed telescopes in the firm grip of his sitters. In Augustus Fuller's *Lady with a Red Pompon* there are rudimentary shadings under the eyes and around the nose and chin of a head which seems to have been planted on a neck and shoulders both sharply contoured and flatly painted. Contemporary with Fuller was the octoroon painter Julien Hudson of Louisiana, who employed shadow to emphasize his own beaked nose in a self-portrait, but in *Colonel Fortier* had learned a more delicate use of tonal contrasts. Philip Hewins did not long remain a primitive. He began crudely in the Maine villages near his native Bluehill and by 1834 he had a studio at Hartford, Connecticut, near enough to the work of men like Jocelyn and Morse to assimilate their lively flesh tones, their sleek touch with the curls and ringlets of women's hair, their deft indications of the highlights in puffed taffeta sleeves.

As the printing press destroyed the art of the German *fractur* writer, so the daguerreotype diminished the need for painted likenesses among that large element of the population who could not afford the life-sized presentment of a modish professional. The work of nameless limners in their thousands was consigned to attics until the day when a new generation could admire their mannerisms.

The man who painted landscapes for his own pleasure seldom had the generalizing faculty of the sophisticated workman. Literally unable to see the woods for the trees, he was likely to enumerate the latter with precision. Unable to place a house or a horse in space, he made the near thing as clearly emphatic as the far, producing an effect that has been called "decorative" or—quite unintentionally on his part—work that a century later would be hailed as "abstract." Unsure of perspective, he diminished the people in the street more rapidly than the street itself, giving rise to a charming syncopation. No scientist of light, he caused shadows to fall toward the sun without losing a sense of sunshine. His delight in people and their occupations often produced a picture which is both landscape and genre at the same time.

More than one householder of recent years, peeling the wallpaper from his parlor or hallway, has found the painted landscapes of the itinerant mural artists—panoramas of lake, village, and hill broadly indicated in brownish or greenish pigment. There are many decorations of this sort in the neighborhood of Dedham, Massachusetts, and another group near Reading and Groton. The hallway painting of the Knowlton house at Winthrop, Maine, was signed by E. J. Gilbert in the eighteen thirties, but in most instances one can only guess at the authorship of prim square-rigged ships in harbors with box-shaped houses on their headlands, bald hills with

Wall painting, Howe House, Westwood, Mass.

Courtesy Antiques Magazine

their network of stone walls, and huge elms whose feathered masses were laid in with a sponge. There are scenes which must have been lifted from travel books, and scenes with a reference to the local topography; at Ithaca, New York, a venturesome brush covered the parlor walls of the Hibbard house from floor to ceiling with a continuous pattern in which Niagara Falls and the Erie Canal keep company with Mount Vesuvius.

The prudent New England muralist was likely to follow Rufus Porter, a Boxford man who signed his name in the Colburn house at Westwood, Massachusetts. The Porter formulas are to be found on many walls, in shrubs and trees which fill the spaces between windows, in high rolling hills and important looking edifices reserved for the overmantel, in the long continuities of white fences and the umbrella shapes of elms which frame a doorway.

Now and then, a householder sat down and proudly drew his house, or a townsman his street corner. In Louisiana, A. Persac recorded both the front and back views of that delightful plantation, Shadows-on-the-Teche. An unknown Cape Codder painted Barnstable in the fifties with no sense of how earth was to be made solid, but with an obvious and communicable feeling for the one-horse chaise drawn up in the shade, and the church spire on the windy hill (Addison Gall.). Another hand drew a street in Brooklyn with a prim and literal brush, lining up the blank façades of brick and brownstone before whose stoops the carriages waited.

Such views had the actuality of firsthand observation, but it is obvious that a black-and-white scene of Washington's tomb done on sandpaper in 1850 was a homemade translation of Bartlett's famous print, and Susan Whitcomb relied on Alexander Robertson's *Mount Vernon* when she made her water color at the Literary Scientific Institute of Brandon, Vermont, in the year 1842. Susan, however, not the sober Scotsman, perched Washington's mansion on violently heaving hills, bordered the Potomac with mountainous headlands, and framed the prospect between a tropical palm tree and one whose foliage masses borrowed the technique of embroidery.

Thomas Chambers was not above lifting a Hudson River theme from a Bartlett print of 1840, and his foliage, rocks, and small houses had the conscientious primness of the nonprofessional. But his draughtsmanship was equal to the problem of a winding and descending foreground road in a view of Kingston, New York.

Thomas Chambers, *View of Kingston, N.Y.* (detail)

Smith College Museum of Art, Northampton, Mass.

A. Persac water color, *Shadows-on-the-Teche*

E. R. Courrege photo

Edward Hicks, *The Peaceable Kingdom*

Brooklyn Museum

Chambers could swing luminous cloud forms, bulging headlands, and sweeping shore lines into a pictorial rhythm of his own, and the brilliance of a June morning is in many of his landscapes.

Both work and that amity between men which makes work possible were the lifelong themes of the pious Quaker Edward Hicks. He believed that farming was a more Christian occupation than painting and even in his sixty-ninth and last year declared that the latter appeared to be "one of those trifling, insignificant arts which has never been of substantial advantage to mankind." But Hicks failed as a farmer, and consoled himself with the Quaker admonition to mind one's calling, avoid idleness, and do the work of which one's mind was capable; he used his brush "within the bounds of innocence and usefulness."

In middle age he recalled every detail of the farm where he once lived as an adopted child of David Twining. It was here that Twining's daughter Beulah read novels in bed by moonlight, fell from grace, and ran away to marry a worthless Presbyterian; it was here that she returned as a penitent prodigal to achieve her own salvation and her peace of mind. Hicks drew the plain house, barns, and fences, the cattle in the yard, and the farmer at the gate with Quaker neatness and a faultless distribution of his material. (See color plate 9.)

In 1821 the Hicks dwelling at Newtown, Pennsylvania, with its studio shed, was next door to a Friends' meetinghouse where he preached and whence he set forth on horseback through the lanes and highways "to gather the halt and the blind to the marriage supper of the lamb." He lettered mileposts for the country roads, made a sign for the Niagara Temperance House in his own village, and painted a *Washington Crossing the Delaware* for a covered bridge at McKonkey's Ferry. Hicks sat before his easel in a portrait which his young cousin Thomas made in 1838, a ramrod figure with probing eyes, a stubborn mouth, and a high forehead with spectacles riding on it; and beside him was one of the canvases by which he is best known, *The Peaceable Kingdom.*

Peacefulness haunted Edward Hicks. From Isaiah he drew his theme, translating the Biblical speech:

> The wolf shall with the lambkin dwell in peace,
> His grim carnivorous thirst for blood shall cease,
> The beauteous leopard with his restless eye,
> Shall by the kid in perfect stillness lie;
> The calf, the fatling, and young lion wild,
> Shall all be led by one sweet little child.

The lion which lies down beside the lamb in these *Kingdoms*—of which it is said that nearly eighty were

Erastus S. Field, *Historical Monument of the American Republic*

Springfield Museum of Art, Springfield, Mass.

painted—is of the same species that swung on boards above taverns throughout the country; and the lettered bands which frame Hicks's allegories are the device of the sign maker's craft. But no other could have grouped the beasts with such monumental gravity, nor rendered their character with such intense conviction and such a scrupulous workmanship. To reinforce his point the artist on occasion combined Quaker history with Isaiah by placing a small version of *Penn's Treaty,* borrowed from West, in the open space beyond his kids and fatlings.

Biblical scenes absorbed another "primitive" who lived in Massachusetts: Erastus Salisbury Field dramatized Exodus in a series on the plagues of Egypt, in one of which the mourners carry coffins through streets lined with his own notions of Nile Valley architecture. Field's *Garden of Eden* presents a curious parallel with the work of Hicks, though the Leverett man worked in ignorance of the Newtown preacher; his paired animals are as solidly drawn in a tropical landscape whose recession between twin mountain ranges is both orderly and original. Winding brooks repeat their oval shapes, and fronded trees stabilize the whole, while Adam's modesty is protected by a clump of lilies.

Except for three New York months when Field looked over the shoulder of Morse while the latter painted his *Lafayette,* the Connecticut Valley limner worked out his own pictorial schemes through a series of local portraits. The shrunken cheeks and hooded eyes of old Elizabeth Billings Ashley were rather drily indicated by Field in the 1820's, and a decade or so later the puffed sleeves and pantalettes of the child Ellen Virtue Field were drawn with a stiff and insensitive brush. That rigidity never disappeared in seventy-odd years of effort, save on those occasions when Field tempered accessories to emphasize human character and suggested color and texture by small dabs of the brush which were a kind of involuntary impressionism. His portrait masterpiece was a woman with a frilled cap and a lace fichu who may be Mrs. Pearce of 1830 or Mrs. Wiley of 1840; here for once Field modeled the face gently under the lustrous curls and the ruching of the flowered bonnet, and traced the lace figures of her collar with the pattern sense of a minor Holbein.

When Americans were talking of the Centennial Exposition in the seventies the aging Erastus set up a canvas thirteen feet long and nine feet high to celebrate one hundred years of freedom; and the *Historical Monument of the American Republic* was like nothing else in the country's art. From a strange architectural base rose stranger towers in diminishing stages, their round or polygonal sides incrusted with reliefs and statues of unbelievable complexity in which every major historic episode and every national hero was represented. Seven of these Babel towers were joined near their tops by steel bridges with steam trains puffing along them, and the eighth and central turret was given to Abraham Lincoln and the Constitution. Troops paraded the avenue below and citizens in their Sunday best entered the portals of a structure whose extravagance exceeded the "waking vision" in Whitman's "Song of the Exposition":

> Mightier than Egypt's tombs,
> Fairer than Grecia's, Roma's temples,
> Prouder than Milan's statued, spired cathedral. . . .

Long after the majority of her people either lost the leisure to shape their thoughts with a brush or a jackknife, or put that leisure to less creative purposes, America retained her people's art. The years of democratic ferment had been those of her richest achievement in these humbler forms; but women in southern hills continued to weave bedspreads as their mothers and grandmothers had done, and fishermen carved decoy ducks whose sleek perfection an old Egyptian would have envied. *The Navigator,* two feet high, had begun his service before a New Bedford shop in the 1830's; trim *Captain Jinks* was created by some exile of the forties to caricature the pompous Franz Joseph, and stood at the doors of cigar stores in New Jersey, Pennsylvania, and Michigan. That most conservative institution, the American circus, blazoned its wagons with gilded wooden beasts, goddesses, and Barnumesque rococo, the work of Swiss and German Americans. At Abilene, Kansas, and at Nashville, Tennessee, the old craft was kept alive by the makers of carnival equipment and merry-go-round horses.

One draws certain conclusions from the existence of a people's art. One knows that a vast reservoir of artistic strength is in the country, and that the urge to externalize experience is continuous and irrepressible. One learns that professional training may or may not improve a man's power of expression, depending on the strength of his conviction and his will to communicate. One realizes that the gap between artist and layman has been too often bridged to be as wide as one had supposed. A highly "civilized" people whose aesthetic life is the special privilege of a few is in no true sense a highly artistic people. When the democrats of the nineteen thirties looked backward to the age of Jackson for their inspiration, not the least of their discoveries was the richness, variety, and plastic worth of an everyday art which had been forgotten while more ambitious talents competed for patronage and fame.

The Navigator

Old Dartmouth** Historical Society, New Bedford, **Mass.

BOOK FOUR

BETWEEN TWO PANICS

c. 1870 — c. 1900

Charles Crocker Mansion, San Francisco, Calif. ▶

New York Historical Society

PART ONE

A CHROMO CIVILIZATION

INTRODUCTION / THE SPIRIT OF '76

When Jarves wrote in 1870 that the budding season of our national art was nigh at hand, this country had much of the gaud and glitter which Thomas Cole had painted into his *Consummation of Empire*. It was an Empire of Business Enterprise, worshiping its gods and parading its triumphs under a bland noonday sky whose thunderheads were just below the horizon. War had settled forever, it seemed, the question of slavery, and political union was assured, if not some other forms of unity. The North had been victorious, and the party of Lincoln was in the hands of eastern bankers and industrialists who now built what Beard has called the principalities of cotton and wheat, oil and pork, coal and iron and timber.

One golden railway spike had linked two oceans, and soon an iron network laced the continent. From Boston in the year 1870 went the first through train to the Pacific, with eight cars whose equipment included two melodions, and whose passengers at the end of the ten-day journey solemnly poured a bottle of Boston Harbor water into San Francisco Bay. American ingenuity shrank distances and changed the habits of thousands. Brokers could exchange news in seconds through the telegraph which Morse had once demonstrated to Van Buren's doubtful cabinet; city families read their *Ladies' Home Journal* by gaslight; farmers had automatic reapers; sewing machines and bathrooms were no longer curiosities; and the descendants of those fire worshipers for whom Hawthorne had spoken warmed themselves with that "cheerless and uncongenial" enormity, the airtight stove. The citizen of the larger town could put his neck into the photographer's iron clamp and emerge with his image on a card tactfully retouched and feverishly colored in imperial size; or he could buy small cabinet-sized prints for twelve dollars a dozen which showed him lolling on cardboard rocks, or his wife sporting her furs in a paper snowstorm, or his daughter swinging on a rustic gate among stuffed canaries and paper apple blossoms.

In the great inland valley which was now America's industrial heart, row upon row of ungainly wooden boxes housed the citizens of sprawling towns—Duluth, Topeka, Davenport, Wichita, and Omaha. Thanks to the Homestead and the Immigration Acts, strange peoples from a dozen countries of Europe and Asia flooded the new West and the old East—Germans, Irish, Croats, Italians, Turks, Greeks, Jews, Russians, and Poles—settling the farms in ways they had learned from their ancestors and working in mills and factories for the cheapest of wages. The folkways of the peasant lasted only as long as it took the railroad, the crop speculator, and the newspaper to destroy them; the homes of the city immigrant quickly became slums.

In this empire the cruder sectional contrasts of Jacksonian days were bound to disappear. The mansion of the lumber millionaire of California was stocked with bric-a-brac as expensive as that acquired by the member of the New York Stock Exchange. It was an empire ruled by its first-generation millionaires, its corruptible public officers, its large and petty gamblers and bribers.

Mark Hanna was eloquent in defense of the nine-man oligarchy of Standard Oil; and in the year 1870 the City of New York was managed by William Marcy Tweed and his Tammany; three years later the bankruptcy of Jay Cooke provoked a national panic which demonstrated that the remotest country man was now linked to the ups and downs of the reckless city financier. In the year 1875 Eugene Debs began his long and patient struggle to organize the trainmen into unions on the industrial principle, and James J. Hill formed the Northwestern Fuel Company and laid the foundations of a vast railway system. The conflicts of these years would be fought, not between section and section as in earlier days, but between those who had and those who had not.

Where now were the Jacksonians, the champions of the common man? Most of the old warriors were dead by the mid-seventies or had retired to the sidelines, their strength exhausted by the war. Postwar America demanded new weapons with which to carry forward democracy. It was the conservatives, as Arthur Schlesinger, Jr., remarks, who now draped the Jefferson mantle on their shoulders while democratic thought, "deprived of the social myth which had united and sustained it before the war, was left uncertain and incoherent."

No man of ideals, whether critic, artist, or philosopher, could ignore the changed atmosphere around him. He saw that the old word "competition" had acquired a more metallic ring. He discovered that inequalities of wealth and status which had once been looked upon as temporary—a moment in democratic time—were being perpetuated by every device the ruling clique could fashion. Money had once been regarded as that which gave the democrat his chance to take his place among his fellows. Now it was something to be wasted visibly by men who valued a house or a landscape in terms of how much its owner had been overcharged.

And where was the old relish with which Americans had once tasted their odd localisms and their regional flavors? Past realities had become present legends: the southern aristocrat was gone forever and his plantation life was a theme for literary reconstruction; the last Indian had been either shot or "civilized," and Buffalo Bill pranced in the arena of his Wild West Show. The carnival of the Jacksonian gods, as Emerson had foreseen, was passing away as swiftly as had Troy and Delphi. The new epic was more brittle, and the new gods were of a smaller stature. Before the centennial year the masterpieces of what Professor Matthiessen calls the American Renaissance had all been written. After Emerson and Hawthorne, Melville and Whitman and Thoreau came the half-gods—Mark Twain, Eggleston, Joaquin Miller, Jewett, Page, and Aldrich. Their localism had a milder flavor; John Stafford has observed that Joel Chandler Harris, writing *Nights with Uncle Remus,* was conscious of his southern audience but also of northern response to the idyllic and the pastoral. Bret Harte has been called by Parrington a "literary middleman who skillfully purveyed such wares as his eastern readers wanted."

What would Horatio Greenough have said of an age whose Midas fingers turned to profit every product of man's inventiveness? Of that double-entry system of mental bookkeeping which saw no relation between engineering and architecture, between private ethics and business morality? If any youth in this America aspired to be an artist he had John Frankenstein's warning in his ears:

> Young man! Would you to Art devote your life?
> Would you be minus babies and a wife,
> Resign cash, sympathy, position too,
> Have every dunce turn up his nose at you
> Who waxes rich with rise of real estate,
> Who onions, beans, pork, whiskey learns to rate,
> Who in man's lowest wants can speculate . . . ?

When the plutocrat ceased turning up his aesthetic nose and began to speculate in the higher wants of man his behavior was of a sort to provoke refined despair among the sensitive. In the days of Philip Hone and Luman Reed, five hundred dollars had been considered a generous price to pay for a work of art. The gallery which Reed had made in the top floor of his house in Greenwich Street was a place for entertaining Washington Irving, Bryant, Cole, and Durand. When he bought a landscape for its walls, the transaction was a personal one and represented his interest in the painter as a friend and an American; there were few foreign works in his collection.

An Astor or a Stewart, on the other hand, possessed far greater sums for conspicuous spending and less interest in what was native and original. He regarded a picture or a statue as a costly object with the accent upon acquisition. He raided the art market as Daniel Drew and Jim Fisk raided the stock exchange, and cornered Bouguereau and Meissonier in the manner of Jay Gould cornering the nation's gold supply.

Genre, landscape, and portraiture for this connoisseur could be of American origin provided they held their own on his wall with the size and dexterity of his French and German items. Thomas Hovenden's *Breaking Home Ties* appealed to the collector because its technique left nothing to the imagination. E. L. Henry's finical brush reduced the theme of *Capital and Labor* to an amusing domestic anecdote. Enoch Wood Perry's rustic vein was inexhaustible, and the red-cheeked and smiling newsboys of John George Brown were an American phenomenon only a little less insistent in their pathos than the urchins of Seymour Joseph Guy.

The city man delighted in Brown's *Berry Boy* climbing a stone wall, his face shaded by a torn straw hat against the June sun; and George Newel Bowers' *Newsboy* prolonged the vogue for this subject into the eighties. Such work was as skillful in its rendering of every least detail as that of Düsseldorf. It meant nothing to the postwar connoisseur that the essence of genre is its small and intimate scale: Hovenden's *John Brown* (Met. Mus.) was over six feet high; Thomas Satterwhite Noble made *John Brown's Blessing* nearly life size (N.Y. Hist. Soc.). Thoreau had written in 1859, "I foresee the time when the painter will paint that scene, no longer going to Rome for a subject"; and both versions of the martyr of Harpers Ferry appealed to men who had doubtless approved Brown's hanging a few years before.

The landscape pioneers were dead before the centennial year—Cole, Catlin, Stanley, Kensett, Miller, and Eastman. One found the spectacular in Bierstadt's *Hetch Hetchie Canyon,* which manifested, Jarves said, the superficiality of mental childhood. Had not Congress paid ten thousand dollars for Moran's *Grand Chasm of the Colorado?* Charles Crocker gave five thousand for Hill's *Yosemite Valley,* and Senator Leland Stanford eleven thousand for two Hill monstrosities, although Edward Bruce compared these stunning assaults on the eyes to the literary assaults of Bret Harte and Joaquin Miller, and asked, "Is it really impossible to express the immensity of the Great West otherwise than in feet and inches?"

That foot-and-inch master, F. E. Church, proclaimed

John G. Brown, *The Berry Boy*

George W. V. Smith Art Museum, Springfield, Mass.

superior to Turner in his power to "penetrate to the inmost soul of the physical world," was rich enough in the seventies to retire to his Moorish castle on the Hudson, where a disabled right hand soon made painting impossible; but there remained James Hart to make pastoral idyls for city men, and Jasper Cropsey and William Gedney Bunce to turn nature opalescent in the White Mountains and in Venice, while on the western edge of the continent Thomas Hill lay in wait for the moneyed tourists, his supply of Yosemites as inexhaustible as their demand.

The painted portrait of the postwar years was expected to be at least as large as life. The career of Charles Loring Elliott ended three years after the war. Thomas P. Rossiter, Thomas B. Read, Joseph Oriel Eaton, Henry Peters Gray, and William H. Powell died in the seventies and were survived for a time by Robert M. Pratt, Theodore Sydney Moïse, William Page, Samuel Osgood, Asher B. Durand, Cephas G. Thompson, and Frederick P. Vinton. The line continued into the nineties with Jacob H. Lazarus, Wyatt Eaton,

George P. A. Healy, Frederick Church and Jervis McEntee, *The Arch of Titus* (detail)

Newark Museum

Nicholas B. Kittell, Henry Alexander, Francis B. Carpenter, Daniel Huntington, Eastman Johnson, Charles Noël Flagg, and Asa W. Twitchell. The American portrait painter was competing with the French, and his patron was a cosmopolite in the making. Catherine Lorillard Wolfe, benefactress of the Metropolitan Museum, posed for Cabanel in Paris in pale lemon satin against a dull red wall, and many of her contemporaries were as likely to commission Cabanel or Bonnat as Huntington or Healy.

The industrious Healy never lacked portrait jobs; his clientele was international, and his days on ocean liners were his only respite from painting. He was the John Sargent of his generation; indeed, it was Healy in Rome in the year 1870 who advised young Sargent to become a painter. This competent, affable, and quite untemperamental man could remember how Lafayette was received at Bunker Hill in 1825; he had weathered the French revolution of 1848, the American Civil War, and the Paris Commune; his career was to end only twelve years earlier than that of Cézanne. From 1866 to 1892 he lived and worked in Paris, as gracefully at home in his white-and-gold salon in the rue de la Rochefoucauld as in the plush-lined drawing rooms of the McCormicks and the Potter Palmers.

There was an occasional sign in Healy that he would have preferred landscape and historical painting to his endless task of portraying the world's notables—Grant and Sherman, Thiers and Bismarck, Pope Pius IX, Jenny Lind and Franz Liszt—and that he was aware of new methods to catch the sun and shadow of outdoors. At Rome in 1869 Longfellow and his "Edith with golden hair" stood under the Arch of Titus while Frederick Church sketched them and Healy and Jervis McEntee looked over his shoulder. All three collaborated on a large painting of the scene, using photographs of themselves, the poet, and his daughter to complete a canvas which has unusual breadth and a sense of Italian sunshine, and whose distant view of the Coliseum has a suggestion of the warm haze which Corot so deftly rendered.

But Healy in his sixties was committed to a firm factualism, modified only to a subdued elegance and a broader rendering under the influence of the Second Empire painters. The somewhat leathery textures of his mid-century work became fresher in the seventies, as he found a delightful clarity for the creams and pinks of his women's faces, the ruddy cheeks and crisp white mustaches of his gentlemen. There was a new grace in his drawing of arms and hands, and he knew the effectiveness of a pink rose in a pale blue satin bodice when he painted *Emma Thursby* in 1879.

Healy's importance—and his fee doubled and tripled until he received two or three thousand dollars for a full length—derived from his being a mediator between Paris and Chicago, between London and New York. His friends and patrons were the better people on both sides of the Atlantic; and what was the difference in way of life, in thought and taste, between a man who had guessed well and dared boldly in the New York Stock Exchange and his French brother who had the foresight to buy property in Paris of which Haussmann's new boulevards multiplied the value? The same process by which in a Zola novel a small shop became a great department store had produced in America the iron-fronted dry goods emporium of A. T. Stewart on Broadway.

Photograph of Longfellow and His Daughter Edith

Courtesy Henry W. L. Dana

Many an American fortune was built on the same tricky and unstable foundations as those of Zola's Aristide Rougon. Zola described his mansion in the opening chapter of *La Curée:* its walls were muffled in thick red velvet and at the base of its marble staircase two naked figures of gold bronze held gas lamps with a hundred globes; its *grand salon* was upholstered in crimson silk and carpeted with purple-flowered Aubusson; and its gold-and-mosaic furniture, its great Chinese vases, and its gigantic mirrors flashed and glittered under immense crystal chandeliers.

If Zola had seen the mansarded granite fortress which Jay Cooke built during these same years in the Chelton Hills outside Philadelphia, he would have known that Rougon's taste, like his financial code, was international. Ogontz cost, it was said, two million dollars, and seventy guests could live in its half a hundred rooms, whose walls and ceilings were frescoed by a crew of forty painters, whose stair hall was lighted by a stained glass window of Indians, and in whose Italian garden stood a brand-new ruined castle.

Some three hundred paintings and prints lined Ogontz, rank upon rank from floor to ceiling as though they were the stones of which Cooke's pride was built. They conformed to the standards of what Zola called "boudoir art," when he reviewed the Paris Salon in the year which saw Ogontz completed: the Oriental spiced sauce of Fromentin, the bathed and powdered Venuses of Cabanel, the battles of Meissonier where, as one wit observed, everything was metallic except the armor. The Rougons and the Cookes had no use for the solid flesh of Courbet's peasant bathers, or for the breadth and power of Manet's *Boy with a Fife;* and out of the Salon each year came hundreds of canvases which had been done with an eye to the Yankee millionaire, and which promptly found their destinations from New York to San Francisco. An American owned Bonnat's *Roman Girl at a Fountain* with its too blue sky; another had dared to admire the sly half-nudity of Hughes Merle's *Falling Leaves;* still others had succumbed to the flutter and fireworks of Pierre Cot's *The Storm.*

Was such taste better or worse than the national average or the international? Americans had been given an opportunity to measure their artistic prowess against that of other peoples in the London and Paris expositions which were so characteristic a creation of a showy century. At London in 1851 Joseph Paxton's great "cathedral of industry" itself had more deeply impressed visitors than the goods shown inside it. Sheer practicality and the wish to get the most for the least had given Paxton, among nearly two hundred competitors, the job of building the Crystal Palace. He had designed greenhouses for the nobility, and now he covered eight hundred thousand square feet of exhibits, spanned seventy feet with a prefabricated iron skeleton and acres of plate glass, and proved the stability of his edifice to the skeptical by marching troops of soldiers along its floors. It was a revolution in building; its airy nave and transepts loomed, Edward Bruce said, like the cloud castle in Cole's *Voyage of Life.* Victorians looked upon it as a fitting shrine for the *Greek Slave,* who stood there under a curtained canopy among the Chickering pianos.

New York missed the point when two years later an American Crystal Palace rose beside Renwick's Croton Reservoir in New York. Hawthorne had criticized the London structure as an overgrown conservatory with no privacy, no mass, weight, or shadow, a structure unsusceptible to ivy, lichens, or any mellowness of age. The Forty-second Street Palace, designed by Carstensen and Gildemeister, rose from an octagon to a Greek cross to a dome, and Greenough's brother Henry directed the corps of Italian fresco painters who gilded and beflowered its iron spandrels and tracery.

Men could see use in naked metal and glass but not yet beauty. Henri Labrouste had already devised a scheme for metal-supported vaults in the Bibliothèque Ste-Geneviève when, in 1855, French engineers managed to bridge one hundred and fifty-seven feet with the circular-shaped girders of their Palais de l'Industrie; but the mighty structure was thereupon encased apologetically in a stone jacket. And an American who saw the seven concentric ellipses of the "Coliseum of Labor" at the Paris Fair of 1867 wrote that it needed a façade as badly as did a confectioner's plum cake.

America's turn to play host came in the year 1876, the hundredth anniversary of her independence. She had made a poor showing in Paris in 1867. The best an American painter could do on that occasion was to win one out of twenty second prizes, a dubious honor which fell to the Church *Niagara.* As for her manufactured objects, the American commissioners reported them inferior not in workmanship but in design. The reforming ideas of Pugin, Henry Cole, and Owen Jones had restored a degree of common sense to industrial designing in England at a time when Cooper Union in New York was alone in its effort to advance science and art together.

Five years before the Centennial Exposition, Walt Whitman had built in words a fair which should be a great monument to the common destiny of the world's people and a symbol of the unity among workmen of all nations. He must have been thinking of the Crystal Palace when he spoke of structures

> High rising tier on tier with glass and iron façades,
> Gladdening the sun and sky, enhued in cheerfullest hues. . . .

Buoyant Walt had summoned the muse to migrate from Greece to a better, fresher, busier sphere in America; on May 10, 1876, the Philadelphia Centennial opened its gates, not to Walt Whitman's tune, but to the sober words of Whittier's ode:

> Our father's God! from out whose hand
> The centuries fall like grains of sand,
> We meet today, united, free,
> And loyal to our land and Thee,
> To thank Thee for the era done,
> And trust Thee for the opening one.

The visitor passed between the two main buildings to find something less than the brood of lofty palaces Whitman had conjured. Machinery Hall covered, to be sure, four times as much ground as St. Peter's, but it

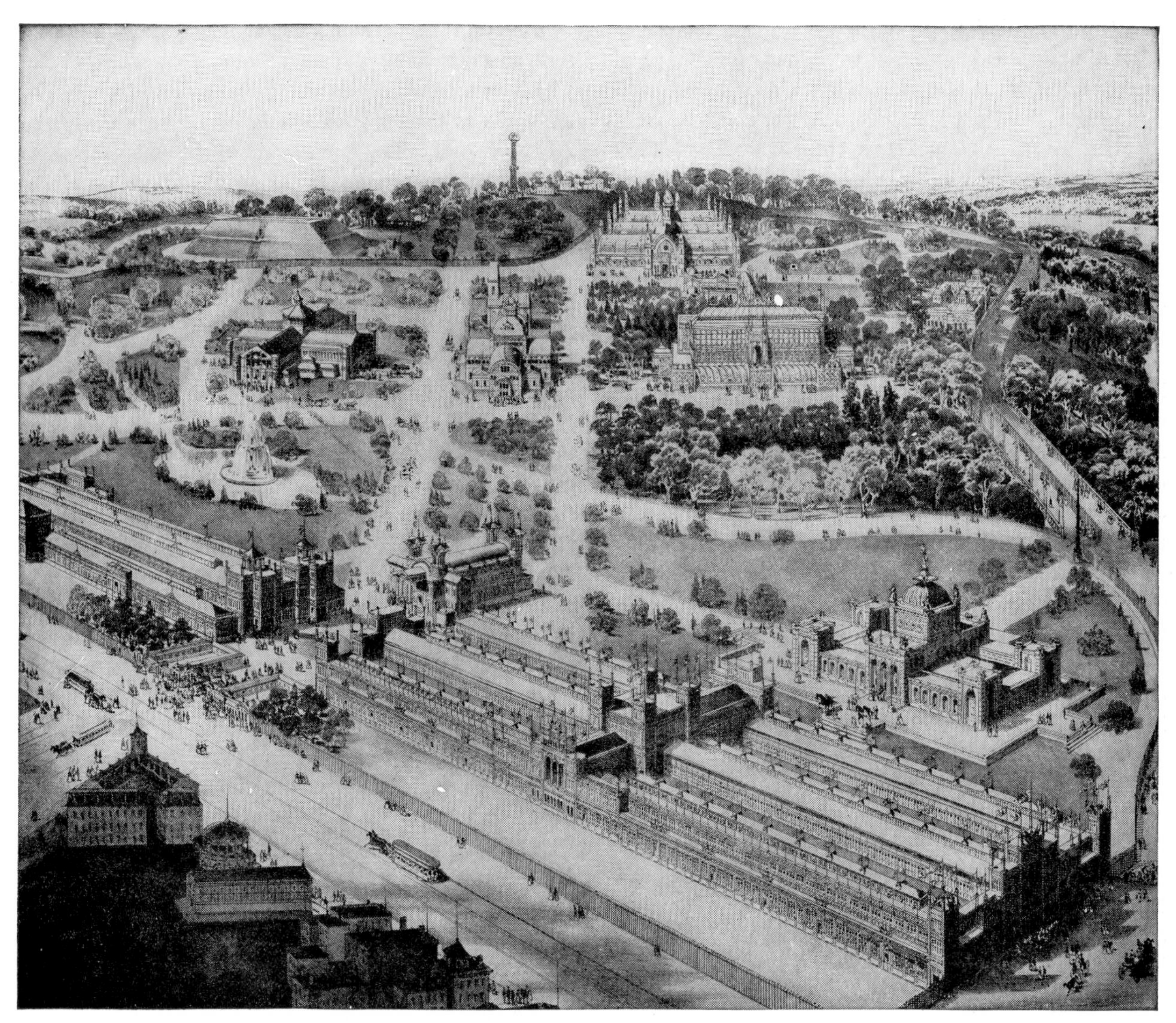

Philadelphia Centennial Exposition, A. L. Weise lithograph (detail)

Library of Congress

was a long, barnlike pavilion quite without distinction once its mighty skeleton had been covered. Not the "Nest of Titans" itself but the plunge and clatter of its machines marked American progress. Among hydraulic waterfalls and Baldwin locomotives stood the immense Corliss engine, its pistons flashing to supply power for the looms which spun silk handkerchiefs and wove carpets, for the mechanisms which drilled rock, made cigars, and turned out galoshes as one watched them.

Across the avenue in the Main Building were the products of thirty-six nations — silver from Mexico, feather flowers from Brazil, porcelains from France, mosaics from Italy, lace curtains from Switzerland, and Aztec skulls from Peru. There were a hundred buildings, and *Harper's Weekly* printed an engraving made from a balloonist's photograph. It shows the oddest collection of structures that had ever been assembled in America, and assembled in that rather careless way which was still a convention in landscape architecture, with winding paths and unexpected openings. Here a Swiss chalet rose above its shrubbery and turned out to be the New York State Building; there stood a colossal Moses on the fountain of the Catholic Total Abstinence Union with water pouring from under his feet.

What was the visitor's most memorable experience? Was it a statue which had been copied from Leutze's *Washington Crossing the Delaware,* or the Turkish Bazaar where one smoked a hookah? A cabinet of ebony and lapis lazuli in the style of Henry II, priced at $6,250, or a ruby-colored Bohemian glass vase three and a half feet high? Or perhaps the *Sleeping Iolanthe* which a certain Mrs. Brooks had modeled in good Arkansas butter in the space of one hour and fifteen minutes, and which was shown in an iced tin frame?

One approached Memorial Hall, given to the display

of art, with a mind prepared for wonders. In the center of its rotunda stood the largest work in ceramic that had ever been made, an *America* riding a bison and guided by Canada, the United States, an Aztec, and a Spanish cavalier. Even this epic terra cotta was dwarfed by Conrad's *Antietam Soldier,* twenty-one and a half feet high; and all around was the "swarm from the Carrara hive"—a colossal George Washington riding heavenward on the back of an eagle; Story's *Medea,* Rogers' *Nydia,* Pozzi's *Youth of Michael Angelo,* and a *Dying Cleopatra* by the Negro sculptress, Edmonia Lewis.

There were fifteen rooms of American painting at Fairmount Park, and over a thousand pictures. In the retrospective group were Copley's *John Adams,* West's *Death of Wolfe,* ten Stuarts, John Neagle's portrait of the old master, Vanderlyn's *Ariadne,* and the *Lafayette* of Morse. Still life was sparsely represented, but the genre display was generous, led by Eastman Johnson's *Old Kentucky Home,* which had crossed the ocean for the Paris Fair of 1867. Winslow Homer's *Snap the Whip* was there, as well as Walter Shirlaw's *Toning the Bell,* John F. Weir's *Gun Foundry,* William M. Hunt's *Bootblack,* and earlier works by Mount and Woodville. The large portraits of Huntington, Healy, and Thomas Hicks underlined the popularity of these three men.

It was landscape which stole the show, however, receiving more than one half of the Centennial prizes. Roughly one third of the canvases were by those still popular men whom a later generation was to call the Hudson River school — Cole, Kensett, and Durand among them. Sanford R. Gifford showed a dozen paintings, more than any other artist, with Worthington Whittredge a close second, and Albert Bierstadt third. Among the smaller pictures were over a hundred of Catlin's Indian scenes, three *Cross and the World* visions by Thomas Cole, and four water colors by Winslow Homer; but they were elbowed by the gigantic landscapes of Bierstadt and Moran, the *Donner Lake* of Thomas Hill, and the lurid *Chimborazo* of Frederick Church.

Turning to the English and French rooms one found the same effort to surpass one's neighbor on the wall by being bigger, more lushly sentimental, more naked, or more melodramatic. Scarcely a visitor noticed the few canvases by Millais or Holman Hunt compared to the crowds which gathered before Frith's *Marriage of the Prince of Wales* and Alma-Tadema's *Vintage Festival.* The men of Barbizon were conspicuously absent from the French show, to which Carolus-Duran sent an equestrian portrait of Mademoiselle Croisette which someone said was as large as a barn door. Grisly enough was Becker's *Rizpah Protecting the Bodies of Her Sons,* and mildly reminiscent of the great Venetians was the Austrian Makart's *Caterina Cornaro Receiving the Homage of Venus.* From Germany came Wagner's huge *Chariot Race.*

More than one visitor to Memorial Hall must have found solace in Doctor Radway's Ready Relief and Sarsaparillian Resolvent, which was advertised in the back pages of the art catalogue. Even the *Tribune's* guide to the fair summed up what the visitor saw as a "rich exhibition of international mediocrity." And while the complacent reflected that America could hold her own by the standards here displayed, a more thoughtful minority could read among all these riches a confession of artistic poverty. William Dean Howells, after a week at the fair, could only suppose that the foreign pictures he had seen with horrified interest were canvases that had not succeeded at home. As for his own country, he found her engineering superior to her art: "It is still in these things of iron and steel that the national genius most freely speaks; by and by the inspired marbles, the breathing canvases . . . for the present America is voluble in the strong metals and their infinite uses."

No one could doubt at any rate that there now existed an international standard in accordance with which a work of art must first impress by size alone, must then reveal the most polished manufacture. It must stab the eye with its novelty, enlist one's pity, or stir one's sexual curiosity. And whether it took the form of a picture or a chair, a statue or a stove, it must be a prevarication, a torturing of materials up to their limit of endurance. One could forgive amateur Mrs. Brooks for using butter instead of bronze and even believe her choice a fortunate one. But what of the professionals who treated bronze as though it were butter, who made vases of zinc and Limoges urns encrusted with water lilies and garter snakes, and mosaic table tops which imitated paintings?

If Americans could not do these things quite as well as foreigners did, they soon would learn. As the *Revue Contemporaine* had sadly observed at an earlier fair, there would soon be no greater difference between the paintings of one country and those of another than between their respective brands of calicoes.

CHAPTER 19 / FALSE FRONT

Between the boom of 1865 and the bust of 1873 America seized upon every known style of building with the predatory zeal which marked her genius for business exploitation. A. J. Davis at his most inventive had kept a sturdy sense of the structure as a whole; now ornament was applied to structure with as reckless a disregard for truth as could be found in any mining company's prospectus, and "originality" consisted in being lawless with every shape man had devised in his long history. That lively magazine, the *Crayon,* had railed at pointed-arched piggeries and battlemented hencoops, urging a return to Downingesque first principles and common sense. Horatio Greenough had tried in vain to stem the eclectic tide. He had attacked the degraded majesty of the Greek and Gothic in our towns, and he had said that "the puny cathedral of Broadway, like an elephant dwindled to the size of a dog, measures [America's] yearning for Gothic sublimity, while the roar of the Astor House, and the mammoth vase of the great reservoir, show how she works when she feels at home, and is in earnest."

It was this divided mind which kept architecture and engineering as far apart as piety and business, and left the experimenting with iron, glass, and steel to the builders of stores and factories. In the year 1858 appeared a small pamphlet with the title: *Cast Iron Buildings: Their Construction and Advantages.* It was written by John W. Thomson and sponsored by James Bogardus, who called himself an architect in iron. This material, in cast form, was as old as America's eighteenth century. Columns of it, and even roof trusses, had been made in the early eighteen hundreds and there were a few commercial buildings with fronts of iron when Bogardus put together in 1847 what he claimed was the first complete iron framework in the country for his own factory at Centre and Duane Streets in New York.

Bogardus admitted that cast iron had not the tensile strength of the wrought metal, but one cubic inch of it would bear eighty tons, as neither brick, wood, nor stone could do. His shop went up four stories, each vertical member bolted to a horizontal one until the frame was complete, its spaces filled with glass, its decorative panels and pilasters only a slight digression from the main theme. By the time Bogardus built the Harper Building on the western side of Franklin Square he had devised a scheme for iron flooring which combined thin columns with truss girders. He called attention to the "fireproof" nature of his work and to the fact that it could be taken apart, moved, and bolted together again, and could have thinner walls than masonry buildings. Indeed, Moses King's *Handbook* claimed that John Milhau's five-story drug shop on Broadway had been assembled in three days.

On the subject of ornament Bogardus was both progressive and reactionary. He suggested that iron, because of its strength, opened a field to the invention of new decorative forms based on a new proportional fitness between parts; but his own designs for the Harper Building were Renaissance and Venetian, and for his prospectus he drew a capital where three iron cupids played among the acanthus. He pointed out that from one mold an indefinite number of capitals, borders, and cornices in any style could be made cheaply and quickly, and all exactly alike. A few years later, one enthusiast prophesied in the *Crayon* that the grandeur of the Tuileries would be repeated in American streets. Even the Louvre, he said, with all its richness of carved ornament, could be reproduced in iron for a comparatively trifling cost.

America was spared a cast-iron Louvre, and it was rather the commercial districts which began in the sixties to show the Bogardus influence and to suggest what would be done when steel replaced iron and the passenger elevator was no longer a novelty to be shown at expositions. The old store of A. T. Stewart on lower Broadway had looked like several five-story buildings pushed together, with a heavy cornice and, on the ground floor, a row of Corinthian columns interspaced with plate-glass show windows. Philip Hone called it spacious and magnificent although he decried the six-by-eleven-foot glass panes which a boy's marble or snowball could shatter. Hone did not live to see the new uptown Stewart's, designed by John Kellum and built during the Civil War. It filled a whole block, its iron façade a series of flattened arcades one above another, filled with glass, with the simplest of horizontal bands between floors and a quoinlike vertical strip on each of its corners. A decade after the Stewart building, St. Louis showed business fronts which, like the Booth-Papin Building, made intelligent use of new materials with thin metal columns spacing their large windows.

The wealthy American meanwhile looked enviously at the work of Haussmann's architects along the broad straight avenues of Paris. The special brand of Renais-

A. T. Stewart Store, New York City

New York Historical Society

A. B. Mullett, Old New York Post Office

New York Historical Society

sance practiced by Garnier, Visconti, and Lefuel had at least this advantage, not lost on the Yankee: it could be squeezed for a private mansion and stretched for a hospital, a courthouse, or a railway station. Its cornices could bristle with sculptured groups, and its mansards, with flat, bulging, or concave surfaces, could be pierced with bull's-eyes and trimmed with iron lace.

In the hands of American designers, the Haussmannesque became a mode whose simplest unit—generally an arcaded window with doubled pilasters or columns on each side—could be multiplied horizontally and vertically until one had frosted the American cake with wood, brick, stone, or iron. One could follow the course of Napoleon's Second Empire westward from Boston, where A. B. Mullett's post office received sculptures by young Daniel Chester French. Mullett's New York Post Office went up stack upon stack like his State, War, and Navy Building in Washington. The city hall in Philadelphia bristled with French ornament, the mansarded Windsor Hotel in far-off Denver was vaguely Napoleonic, and so was Hotaling's wholesale liquor store in San Francisco.

The client for whom such edifices were too stately could find architects who played with medievalism in the postwar years. On Michigan Avenue in Chicago stood a roughhewn limestone water tower one hundred and eighty-six feet tall in what someone described as the "goldfish castle" style, prefiguring the feudal stronghold which Cobb and Frost would build for Potter Palmer in the eighties. If the Gothic needed new sanctions, John Ruskin's *Stones of Venice* and the essays of Charles Eastlake had supplied them for this generation, many of whom read the loving description of the Ducal Palace which Ruskin called the supreme effort of the Venetian imagination. The National Academy which Peter B. Wight designed in 1862 when he was twenty-four was itself a Ducal Palace in miniature, and every ornament of its façade was inspired by an American plant or flower.

Russell Sturgis knew the classical, but he practiced the Gothic with far greater enthusiasm in his work for Yale College in the years before he turned from practicing architecture to become its critic. The lacelike details of Hatfield's drawing for The New York Life Insurance Building were Ruskinian in spirit, and Italian Gothic was the style of Henry Austin's city hall at New Haven. Striped voussoirs and stubby columns appeared on the façades of hotels in St. Paul and Minneapolis, and from the Boston Art Museum, by Sturgis and Brigham, the terra-cotta busts which Filarete had used to decorate a Milan hospital looked down on Copley Square. Completed in 1874, the Memorial Hall of Ware and Van Brunt at Harvard made much of the striped alternation of dark with lighter material which was the most dubious feature of the Gothic in Italy. Henry James was to describe it as a great bristling brick Valhalla which "spreads and soars with the best will in the world, but succeeds in resembling rather some high-masted ship at sea."

Out of these turrets and prickly cast-iron trimmings, these bluntly pointed windows and many-colored tiles, the builders of new campuses made a collegiate Gothic. The young ladies of Smith College at Northampton, Massachusetts, went to class in a T-shaped edifice of brick and stone whose lancet windows were grouped at random in two's and three's with stained glass in their heads; a square clock-tower with small turrets was imbedded in this huddle of gables and mansards, which one entered through a portal of striped voussoirs and slender red stone colonnettes with cabbagelike capitals upon them.

While the post offices and the halls of higher learning thus played with French symmetries and English-made Gothicisms, the rich American's home became his castle or his Haussmannesque stone pile, but it also became his chalet and his Alhambra. The colored photolithographs of A. A. Turner's *Villas on the Hudson,* published in 1860, would have seemed vulgarly ostentatious to A. J. Downing, whose pupil Calvert Vaux clung with difficulty to the chaste simplicities he had learned from his master. The plates in Gervase Wheeler's *Homes for the People* were a debased and fretful Downingesque, like those in Henry Hudson Holly's *Country Seats,* where the owner of an old square-built house could learn how to convert it into a villa shaggy with the product of the jigsaw. Even in the American Institute of Architects the more professional revivalists debated the merits of one "style" as against another, avoiding more fundamental questions.

There would soon be architects whose learning and whose taste purged the art of its worst eccentricities, but in the meantime there was no restraining the wealthy American's will to build more stately mansions. The narrow city house of the seventies groaned under the load of its façade; the free-standing mansion moved uptown and filled a block; the country seat on river and seashore, once a "cottage," outgrew that designation. The Westerner of means could occupy new streets—Euclid Avenue in Cleveland, Chicago's Lake Shore Drive, and Prospect Avenue in Milwaukee — where there was room to set houses back among trees and space them widely; the eastern man often had to be content with a vertical slice in a continuous block.

The basic plan of this architectural type had been determined long before in New York by the narrowness of Manhattan Island, and in other towns by the rapid multiplication of land values. Thus confined, the city house could grow only upward and backward. For

Peter B. Wight, Natl. Academy of Design, New York City

New York Historical Society

the Greek revival brick-and-trim it substituted in the eighteen fifties and sixties a four-inch-deep veneer of brownstone, a material of which Henry James said, "even time can do nothing for it." Graceful iron railings gave way to cumbrous ramps and posts either of stone or of wood sanded and painted to imitate stone, whose rasping touch James remembered in later years. The pediments over doors and windows, the consoles which supported these, and the sheet-iron cornices along the roof line were spotty and unfunctional in character.

In the high-ceilinged parlor of such a house Eastman Johnson painted wealthy Alfrederick Hatch of Park Avenue in 1871 with his family around him. Deep-fringed crimson curtains blanket the windows. Red are the tops of tables which can hardly support their own weight of knobby ornament; red is the upholstery of sofas and armchairs which elude classification of style. In this tempered domestic light one sees only the gleam of bronze figurines on the mantel, the sheen of rosewood and mahogany on massive bookcases. The gaudiness of the prewar years has become the ponderous plush gloom of Lewis Mumford's "Brown Decades."

In Boston's narrow streets the domestic unit often carried its front steps inside its own walls; Chicago before the fire of 1871 preferred buff-colored limestone to the gloomier brown; the western house often presented a loggia to the street, and its entrance hall was

"Olana," Hudson, N.Y.

Wayne Andrews photo

Henry H. Richardson, Watts Sherman house, Newport, R.I.

Wayne Andrews photo

big enough for a reception room. The designers of the seventies and eighties adorned these basic forms with turrets and bays of copper and galvanized iron, and bricks of every color in the spectrum, as each householder strove to be more emphatic than his neighbors in the procession. James Renwick had discovered in the fifties that terra cotta weathered rain and frost more successfully than brownstone, and had used it for windows and cornices in a few New York houses; in 1878 the first factory was producing this material in two colors, buff and red. Critics who once complained of brownstone monotony were now appalled with the irresponsible look of their streets, where fronts of yellow brick joined those of red and green with projecting bay windows of every conceivable shape, loggias cut into their faces, and carved decorations of all periods stuck where they would make the greatest show.

As the American cities grew, it was only the financial princes who could build complete houses with strips of lawn about them, like John Kellum's chunky stone mansion for A. T. Stewart on Fifth Avenue, the Chicago home of Cyrus McCormick, and the Crocker show place in San Francisco. The first was Napoleonic at least by intention, with a forest of columns on its sides and an iron-crested mansard; it looked, Russell Sturgis said, like a small house seen through a magnifying glass. The McCormick pile had the same stone gravity and heavy-sharp detail, its roof broken by projecting bays, each of which was capped by its own mansard. And at the continent's opposite end where stone became wood through fear of earthquakes, Charles Crocker dominated San Francisco with one of the largest and ugliest of the mansards. The shrewd, hard-living Crocker went West at the golden moment of 1850, and by mining, real-estate, and railroad enterprises which provoked a senatorial investigation swelled his fortune in a few years to something like forty millions; one and a half million built his gaudy exhibit on Nob Hill.

For the interior of his palace the rich man re-created more often than not the salons of eighteenth-century France and the boudoirs of the Second Empire, but these were not the only alternatives. A more exotic taste than the Parisian was in evidence, a phase of that Orientalism which one saw in the private art galleries—Moorish women languishing in courtyards and Arabs strolling through bazaars. The colored plates of Owen Jones's *Details of the Alhambra* were in American libraries, and soon the horseshoe arch was competing with the lancet. Remembering Eidlitz' none-too-successful effort to domesticate the Taj Mahal for P. T. Barnum, most Americans confined their Orientalism to interiors, but F. E. Church the painter was an exception.

The "provincialized Persian" villa near Hudson, New York, to which Church retired in the early eighteen seventies was in part his own contrivance. Several schemes for it were drawn by Vaux and Withers in 1870, but Church himself seems to have taken pleasure in working out every least detail of its complicated decoration. The exterior of Olana bristled with turrets which suggested minarets, and a large square tower provided a magnificent survey of the Hudson and the Catskills beyond it. The "Persian" note was in the many colored bricks which patterned its walls, the green tiles embedded in them, the profiles of windows, the spindly Saracenic arcade along the veranda, and the pattern painted along the wooden cornice. An elaborate window on the stair landing bathed the cross-shaped hallway in amber light; in the rooms which opened on all four sides of it were inlaid tables, wrought-metal hanging lamps, tiled fireplaces, and painted friezes which proved the artist's Oriental obsession and his perseverance as a collector in Palestine and Syria.

To the Ruskinians and the Downingesques, the Napoleonists and the Turkophiles must be added the loyal followers of "Queen Anne" and the revivers of the "Colonial." The great rambling country houses of Richard Norman Shaw in England of the seventies had Jacobean peaked gables and Tudor chimney stacks, and his elevations were laced with half-timbering and casement windows. When to these forms were added the baroque details of Inigo Jones and Sir Christopher Wren, someone called the mixture the Queen Anne style. America saw it in the British Pavilion at the Centennial, but Peabody and Stearns had already tried it at Newport in a "cottage" which was a mass of interlocking forms, imitation half-timbering, hipped gables, and tall clustered chimneys. The near-by Watts Sherman house by Henry Hobson Richardson was a more compact stone-and-shingle version of the Queen Anne.

In the centennial year two young men whose names were Charles McKim and William Mead traveled up and down New England sketching and studying colonial houses with the revivalist's eye. It was only eight years since Upjohn had discussed the subject before the Institute, and a writer would soon coin the word "Georgian" to describe eighteenth-century buildings in America whose beauty had been so long neglected and whose graceful ornaments were applied by the McKim firm in the eighties to structures far too large and informal to receive them—Miss Julia Appleton's homestead in Lenox, Massachusetts; at Newport, the Taylor house and the residence of Commodore William Edgar, for which the designers borrowed the steep roofs of Williamsburg and the odd chimneys of Stratford in Virginia.

Was this reconsideration of their own past a sign that Americans were in search of one leading motive powerful enough to be the basis of a coherent national style? To the Englishman, his own Middle Ages seemed still capable of fresh permutations; the French looked to no other past than their own for precedent. There were a few designers here who could not be content with architecture as conspicuous waste, surrounded though they were by unabashed eclectics and pressed by impatient and often illiterate clients. Henry Hobson Richardson was in his late thirties when the Centennial came, and had already worked below the shallower surfaces of his time; John Wellborn Root was twenty-six, and Louis Sullivan twenty. But Richard Morris Hunt, older than the oldest of these by ten years, was far more typical of the seventies than any of them. He was no rebel questioning the validity of the historic styles but a scholarly eclectic who refined other men's barbaric treatment of them; and it was Hunt, more than any other, who determined what the house of an Astor or a Vanderbilt should be.

At twenty, Hunt established a precedent by enrolling at the Paris École des Beaux-Arts, with painting and sculpture lessons on the side with Couture and Barye. When he came home in 1855 to work for a short time with Walter in the national Capitol he had learned discipline and an elegant restraint by helping Lefuel to complete the Louvre; in his first American years his Rossiter house and his Tenth Street Studio Building in New York had a conscious restraint and a sophistication of detail which were to be Hunt's signature.

His work of the seventies proved that he could make intelligent use of new materials though he lacked the boldness to explore them fully. When the Chicago fire demonstrated the inadequacy of iron for tall structures, many designers sought new solutions with combinations of solid masonry and iron-framed floors. Hunt's Victoria Hotel and his Tribune Office in New York were pioneers among these "elevator buildings," ten or a dozen stories high. The first was an apartment house; in the second he recognized a new type to the extent of devising tall piers with connecting arches to prevent his façade from being a mere piling up of single-story windows. At Newport his earliest houses were an effort to find forms appropriate to an overgrown seaside villa; in less than ten years Hunt progressed from the lumpy and restless cottage of Professor Shields to the bungalow of J. R. Busk, all of rough stone, a three-part horizontal structure which rambled successfully, its forms adjusted to the rocky sloping ground, its long shingled roof sweeping down to form a veranda. There was an impressive monumentality even in his Scroll and Key chapter house at Yale in the Hispano-Moorish vein; and his classical pedestal for the Statue of Liberty adroitly made use of the fortress walls from which it rose.

The clients for whom Hunt designed town houses would have balked at the uniformity one found in Paris; that city seemed, as one critic said, to have been built by the state rather than by its citizens. The Vanderbilts were competing with one another for dominance of Fifth Avenue when George B. Post planned the home of Cornelius; it was a compact and sturdy mansion of red brick and gray limestone with a steep red-tiled roof, and looked like a fortress with its jutting top story and its pointed corner turrets; its details from Orléans and Blois were called "French Renaissance." William H. Vanderbilt lived in a double sandstone box by the Herter brothers and John B. Snook, who called it "Greek Renaissance"; despite the bands of intricate carving on its sides, which kept sixty foreign workmen busy for months, the mansion impressed one mainly by its bulk.

Hunt's town houses scored over their rivals by their studious reticence. He was no colorist, and after the patchy effect of his red brick Presbyterian Hospital, which was peppered with white stone trim, he began

Richard M. Hunt, William K. Vanderbilt house, New York City

Wurts Bros. photo

to prefer the monochrome stone which best revealed his proportions and his accents. Two things above all Hunt had brought back with him from France: the atelier plan of working by which the master not only employs but instructs his assistants, and an abiding love for the great châteaux of the Loire Valley. The former scheme he applied at once, and many of the country's most skillful architects called themselves his pupils—Van Brunt and William Robert Ware, Post, Furness, and Gambrill. His French historicism found expression in a house for William K. Vanderbilt, whose three years of construction ended in 1881, and whose pleasant gray limestone, severely plain walls, and well-placed openings, oriels, and angle turrets made the other Vanderbilt structures seem vulgarly clumsy.

In this one building Hunt attempted to tell what the French designers had done in a century from the late Gothic of the Rouen Palais de Justice to the Loire castles. He knew every inch of those buildings, for, like McKim, he had visited and sketched them. To remind him of details there were photographs and the handsome engraved plates of Eugène Douyer's *L'Art Architectural en France* and of César Daly's *Motifs Historiques.* Here were façades and paneled interiors which ranged from the ingenious outdoor staircase at Blois to the bold salient decorations of the Hôtel de Sully, the burly carved doors of the Sorbonne, and the elegant scrolling balconies of the Hôtel de Lauzun. Here were nude ladies in marble who could step down from the bedroom walls of Fontainebleau to hold up a millionaire's chimney piece. Every detail of the Vanderbilt house was drawn under the scholarly eye of Hunt and exquisitely carved or molded, and there was "correctness" and a superb craftsmanship in its interiors, which were far less strident, coarse, and explosive than the chambers of most rich men's houses.

Similarly, when William Astor moved thirty-one blocks north into the home which Hunt designed for him, he left clutter and a raucous ostentation for the more consistent splendor of a ballroom in the true Renaissance manner. As one of Hunt's pupils said, the architect must be historically self-conscious, but he can at least be conscientiously self-conscious. In respect to style, Hunt was conscience embodied. His clients held no such stylistic scruples; they paid the fee and enjoyed the prestige which his learning gave them. As one critic observed, a Louis more or less made little difference to them.

CHAPTER 20 / A MIGHTY HANKERING

Did the Centennial mark the end of provincialism in this country? It proved beyond doubt that on the level of what might be called "exposition art" our painters and sculptors could hold their own, it sharpened the Yankee's curiosity to see cathedrals and Alps for himself, and it suggested a thousand new ways in which the American craftsman could torment iron and terra cotta. The average citizen recovered in a few years from the crash in 1873, but what Lewis Mumford has called his "panic for aesthetic security" lasted much longer.

The world had come to Philadelphia in 1876; now a whole generation of writers found humorous or tragic material in the American who returned the visit. This pilgrim could be as naïve as one of Mark Twain's *Innocents Abroad* or as shrewdly perceptive as Christopher Newman in Henry James's *The American*. He mused at the graves in Père-Lachaise, delighted in that "fairy delusion of frostwork" which was Milan Cathedral, decided that St. Peter's was less handsome than the Capitol at Washington and that its baldachino looked like a magnified bedstead. A full-page engraving after A. B. Frost in *Harper's Weekly* represented the George Washington Jones family en route for Paris, three generations of them on the deck of a steamer in the rumpled and dowdy clothes of their native Bungtown, their faces alight with anticipation.

More subtly drawn was James's portrait of Newman bargaining for his first purchase of a work of art, a wretched copy of Murillo's Louvre *Madonna* which he liked better than the original. His life had been given to making money. "He had won at last, and carried off his earnings; and now what was he to do with them?" For the first time in his life here in Paris he felt not at all smart. He had come, as he said, "to see all the great things and to do what the clever people do: I am not cultivated . . . I know nothing about history, or art, or foreign tongues . . . But I am not a fool either, and I shall undertake to know something about Europe by the time I have done with it. I feel something under my ribs here that I can't explain,—a sort of a mighty hankering, a desire to stretch out and haul in."

The tourist who had been a provincial abroad proved often to be a cosmopolitan at home. Two months after Frost had drawn the Joneses' departure, he pictured their return to Bungtown, whose natives scarcely recognized dandified Mr. Jones with his black velvet jacket and checked trousers, his monocle, and his affected gestures, nor his wife and children muffled in sashes, lace, and ostrich feathers.

Ridicule could not divert the middle-class American from his quest for self-improvement. The life of the mind was nourished in these years by the magazines, by the novels of Mrs. Southworth, and by the traveling lecturer. James Redpath's Lyceum Bureau paid Henry Ward Beecher a thousand dollars for one lecture in Boston's Music Hall, and a few years later Mark Twain and George Cable were billed throughout the country as "twins of genius." James Whitcomb Riley read his Hoosier jingles to thousands, the explorer Stanley lectured on the topic "Through the Dark Continent," and New Yorkers paid two dollars to see, if not hear, Matthew Arnold struggle with the acoustics of Chickering Hall. Chautauqua, from being a Methodist camp meeting on the shore of a lake, became a vast educational chain, and its Literary and Scientific Circle brought the *Odyssey, Paradiso,* and *Faust* in English to small-town Americans who were either too poor or too busy to get themselves a college education.

In less sober moments the American applauded Booth and Modjeska when the old stock companies gave way to the visiting star in chains of theaters managed by businessmen. Joseph Jefferson's Rip Van Winkle was

A Simple Suburban Cottage

Calvert Vaux, Villas and Cottages

created for the playgoers of the sixties and delighted their grandchildren of the nineties. Bostonians heard their own Symphony Orchestra in 1881, New Yorkers their Metropolitan Opera two years later. The summer vacation became an American institution as the big hotels went up at Nahant, Niagara, Virginia Springs, and Saratoga and on the summit of Mount Washington. The millionaire had his Ocean Drive at Newport, but the less wealthy vacationist could do his piazza sitting, his bathing and croquet, his driving and gambling at Long Branch, inspect the yellow-and-green Aladdin's Palace of Solomon Guggenheim on Ocean Avenue, and walk the five-mile bluff hoping to catch a glimpse of Jim Fisk, Lily Langtry, or President Grant.

In architecture and furnishing one emulated one's betters, and Calvert Vaux's *Villas and Cottages* was one of the many books by which, with the aid of a local architect and builder, the man of middle station could pay his artistic way in copper and nickel instead of in gold. Vaux deplored any class-recognizing advance in art, yet he was forced to concede that the rich spent the money and dictated the taste of the nation. And there was an obvious social contrast between his first illustration, a wood-and-brick cottage on a twenty-five-foot lot for Mr. Ryan, a plumber of Newburgh, the cost of which would be sixteen hundred dollars, and the plate showing a stone-and-brick marine villa built at Newport for a trifle less than twenty thousand.

Graded in size and showiness, the architectural poor relations of the Napoleonic, the Gothic, and the Queen Anne could be seen from ocean to ocean, and still stand on innumerable Main Streets with red-and-blue striped mansards, fretted piazzas, and half-timbered gables, beetling cornices, and forests of iron finials. They were the work of men who bore the same relation to the city professional with his office and assistants as the Newburgh plumber to the Newport broker. Most of them began with a plan and elevation by a local builder and ended with wooden decorations which the planing mills supplied in appropriate quantities to be cut, combined, and nailed in place as local fancy pleased.

As guides for interior furnishment, books like Vaux's *Villas and Cottages,* along with exterior designs and estimates, offered suggestions for room decoration. With these and with notions inspired by the rooms shown at the Centennial the American could remake his parlor. He could even be amused by Mark Twain's account, in *Life on the Mississippi,* of the prewar citizen's dwelling. Twain did not so much describe as itemize The House Beautiful behind its pine Corinthian portico: the mahogany center table with its homemade yarn lamp-mat; the polished iron stove before the bricked-up fireplace; the engraved *Washington Crossing the Delaware* over the mantel; landscapes with "petrified clouds" and "anthracite precipices" committed on the premises and framed in black; family portraits "fresh, raw and red, apparently skinned"; a shell with the Lord's Prayer carved on it; a horsehair sofa which kept sliding from under you; gaudy lambrequins of gilded tin; and window shades with milkmaids and ruined castles stenciled on them.

Years before Mark Twain's gruesome inventory Catherine Beecher and her sister Harriet Beecher Stowe struck the improving note in their *American Woman's Home.* The sisters declared that beauty in the home not only had great moral value but could be secured cheaply. Eighty dollars, in fact, would furnish one room. It would buy buff wallpaper with a maroon border, straw matting, fringed lambrequins, white muslin curtains, chintz for the ottoman, and a piece of green broadcloth to hide the ugly underpinnings of the poorest table. The American woman herself could make rustic frames for the chromolithographs of Eastman Johnson and Bierstadt, could reclaim tin pans for growing plants, and fashion out of a coconut shell the hanging basket from which ivy would climb over these modest beauties.

The more ambitious reformer of the seventies looked to England for his ideas, consulted Owen Jones's *Grammar of Ornament,* and followed Charles Eastlake's *Hints on Household Taste in Furniture, Upholstery and Other Details.* The first American edition of that work appeared in 1872 with an introduction by Charles C. Perkins, who remarked that Eastlake's strictures on English popular taste applied as well to America, with her fatal craving for novelty and her failure to be original. Perkins reminded his readers that Egypt had derived a multitude of lovely forms from the lotus flower, and described a Florida lily whose forms, exploited in the same way, would make a gas burner "poetical."

Eastlake's purpose was to show the public how to acquire a sense of the picturesque which would not interfere with comfort and convenience. There must be one style throughout a man's house, not a style for every room; and Eastlake proceeded to suggest that style with colored illustrations: encaustic tiles for one's hall in geometric patterns; good Oriental rugs on a parlor floor; a wall divided by a wooden dado below, a decorative frieze above, and the surface between covered with grained blue or crimson paper enlivened with small repeat patterns in gold which were inspired by old Italian textiles; hangings at window and door which fell straight from a metal rod fashioned like a spear and were made of heavy wool with bold abstract patterns. His sideboards, tables, and bookcases were modifications of the Jacobean, heavy and straightedged; their carving was geometrical and their structure was based on the carpentry of the Middle Ages.

The American version of Eastlake frequently missed the main point and merely provided new fodder for the hungry jigsaw. At the best it reminded householders that a room can be designed consistently as one unit; at the worst, Eastlake's many-shelved cupboards and chimney pieces became roosts for the china-hunter's trophies. What American could read Major Byng Hall's *Bric-a-Brac Hunter* without wishing that he, too, could sit like the Major in the frontispiece among Sèvres cups which the lips of Du Barry might have kissed, and plates whose painted view of the Bay of Naples recalled his own first glimpse of Mount Vesuvius? The smug hero of John Hay's *Bread-winners* lived in Eastlake rooms where Chinese bowls, Limoges vases, and Barbédienne bronzes "dwelt together in the harmony of a varied perfection."

If the artistic standards of the country were to be raised above the level of gingerbread and bric-a-brac, there were at least two instruments for that purpose, the art school and the museum. A young man or woman with professional ambitions could draw from the living model at the Art Students League or similar schools, where separate hours were scheduled for the two sexes. Charles C. Perkins, one of the founders of the Massachusetts Normal Art School, believed that an age which was practical rather than poetic demanded schools of design where artisans would learn the difference between the crude and the beautiful in objects of daily use. Since 1859 the wealthy iron master, Peter Cooper, had provided free instruction for men and women of the working class at Cooper Union, which had seven rooms for a Female School of Design. There was no distinction of age, color, or sex at the Union, where respectable young women could provide themselves with a means of livelihood by learning how to engrave on wood and to color photographs. For a time in the sixties, William Rimmer challenged what seemed to him too narrowly vocational a program by organizing a series of courses at the Union whose inclusiveness a modern art school would envy.

The private colleges were beginning to list art teachers among their faculties. Before the war, Perkins lectured on the rise and progress of painting at Trinity College in Hartford; in 1871 Charles Herbert Moore was appointed at Harvard to teach freehand drawing and water color according to strict Ruskinian principles; and three years later Charles Eliot Norton became Lecturer on the History of Fine Arts, and the Cambridge undergraduate could attend his *Rise and Fall of the Arts in Venice and Athens* or his famous Fine Arts 3, *The Renaissance*. The New Haven student had the Jarves collection to document his studies in Christian art, since Yale had been the only bidder for its purchase. To Vassar College the Poughkeepsie brewer had given some five hundred paintings and prints to "illustrate the loftiest principle and refine the heart," and the emphasis at Vassar was upon the application of design principles to dress and interior decoration. Under the Gothic rafters at Smith College was a collection of plaster casts and a series of alcoves lined with photographic reproductions of great masterpieces.

Too often the visual education of this generation was based upon secondhand reproductions which only in the vaguest way suggested the qualities of the great originals; and there was much discussion of this point among the founders of the first public art museums. What was to be their function? Bryant's speech to the Union Club in 1869 suggested a moral one, and he asked why the richest city in the world could not provide an institution where the city's temptation to vice would be countered by the wholesome, ennobling, and instructive appeal of works of art.

Others believed in the historical purpose. George F. Comfort explained in 1870 that an art museum should illustrate the history of all the fine and applied arts. Sculpture could be shown in reproduction, architecture by models in cork and alabaster; as for paintings, it was now too late, in his opinion, to acquire important works by the old masters. In the same vein Perkins advised the founders of museums not to spend thousands for a single original but rather for fireproof buildings to show plaster casts, photographs, and electrotypes, which he considered adequate for educational purposes. Jarves, on the other hand, wrote that it was useless to erect buildings first and then fill them with trash. The time had come, he said, for the confusion of private collections to give way to ordered public exhibition as an aid to the careful and scholarly study of art. Only the best should be shown, and its purchase, arrangement, and cataloguing was a task for experts.

When the Metropolitan Museum was established in 1870, artists like Kensett, Church, and Ward sat on its board of trustees among men of substance, and its president was the railway and coal millionaire John Taylor Johnston. The institution advanced cautiously, relying

Frank Waller, *The Metropolitan Museum in Fourteenth St.*

Metropolitan Museum of Art, New York City

on loaned paintings and statuary to fill the rooms of the private houses in which its first decade was spent. When a connoisseur offered to give the Museum a colossal statue of a dancing girl the president warned his colleagues that "hereafter we must curb the exuberance of donors except in the article of money." Five years after its founding a visitor to the Museum's rooms in Fourteenth Street saw at least the makings of a historical collection: the Cesnola antiquities, the plaster casts, the Audubon engravings, the thirty-odd landscapes by Kensett which the artist had given, and a loan collection of armor. If one believed that American art deserved a place among these masterpieces there was a room of Modern Paintings loaned for the show of 1873 where Diaz and Couture were hung, along with Troyon, Gérôme, and Boldini, but where one could also find James M. Hart's *Connecticut River* and Daniel Huntington's *Italian Shepherd Boy.*

At the end of its first decade the Metropolitan opened its permanent home, a building in Central Park which had been designed by Jacob W. Mould and Calvert Vaux. The years ahead were ones of steady expansion, of appeals for money, and of gifts from private collections, until the new limestone façade by Hunt and Post at the turn of the century left the original brick-and-stone gallery a mere appendage. Among the "treasures" of the Museum in the nineties were Rosa Bonheur's *Horse Fair* and the banalities of Pierre Cot and Bastien-Lepage, which one commentator excused on the grounds that great art is rare; but its Marquand gallery held Van Dycks, Rembrandts, and canvases by Rubens and Hals.

For the hundreds of city people who could study art in the original or send their children to colleges, there were hundreds of thousands in America whose "art life" fed upon reproductions. If the indulgent sentiment and the easily read story of Brown, Guy, and the other makers of genre became familiar to this wider public it was because the pictorial press found cheap and speedy ways of multiplying their popular imagery. Every reader of *Harper's Weekly* had a personal acquaintance with Brown's moist-eyed bootblacks, and many of the genre painters worked directly for the makers of chromolithographs. The process by which colored cigar-box labels were produced could also turn out rather gaudy landscapes. Prang was famous for these in Boston in the 1870's and Hatch and Company in New York owned steam presses which made five thousand "chromos" in a day.

On the Eastlake shelves of the period stood the illustrated art books of Earl Shinn, George William Sheldon, and Samuel G. W. Benjamin, ranging in price and excellence from the popular handbook to the *de luxe* edition. Both Sheldon and Benjamin tempered the fierce nationalism of earlier days to a mild claim that our painters have an honorable position in the world; and after all, as Sheldon wrote, Americans were beginning to talk less of American art, or Munich art, or French art and to think more of art itself. Benjamin was a painter himself and a globe-trotting diplomat who paid calls on painters in preparation for his *Our American Artists* of 1879 in order to describe their studios crammed with bric-a-brac.

It is difficult to see how a reader could have developed his understanding of native artists from the muffled and scratchy plates in Sheldon's *American Painters* of 1879 or in Benjamin's *Art in America,* which was a superficial outline of the nation's "very creditable" artistic history; Benjamin himself was dubious whether his plates conveyed the tones or the brushwork of the originals. They had been engraved not upon metal but upon wood. The former is an "intaglio" method with lines cut patiently in copper or steel to hold the printing ink. The latter calls for even greater finesse, its printing surface consisting of lines and areas which are left in relief on the block when the rest of the wood has been cut away, with gradations which the graver's tool has made with a crisscrossing of fine white lines. Since the days of Bewick and Darley, wood engraving had found superb practitioners in Europe, where Englishmen reproduced Charles Keene's intricate pen drawings and Tenniel's *Alice* by this method; and Gustave Doré in France drew directly on the block before cutting his rich and complex illustrations of Dante, Rabelais, and Tennyson.

As early as the mid-fifties in America, *Frank Leslie's Illustrated Newspaper* and *Harper's Weekly* both used wood engravings. Every pen line of a Thomas Nast cartoon had to be rather stiffly cut on the hard block and if a large printing required a more durable surface, a metal cast was made from this block which had a rigidity of its own. A mere hack could reduce the original forms and textures to wiry contours and frozen crosshatching; and the *Nation* in 1865 warned artists to pay heed to what the engraver did to their work.

Among the commercial shops of the seventies, however, a group of young men learned from accomplished elders to become incredibly skillful. The young journeyman cut in wood the clean and hard mechanical drawings which advertised pumps, furniture, corsets, and pianos. From the near-by offices of *Harper's* and the *Tribune* came orders for blocks which were sometimes of full-page size and had to be carved in sections by several craftsmen and then bolted together. The medium was subtle enough on occasion to suggest the light which filtered through apple blossoms in a Winslow Homer illustration or glistened on the crisp white ruffles of his Long Branch ladies. Among the new men was Elbridge Kingsley from Hadley in Massachusetts, who studied at Cooper Union night class in the second year of the Civil War and worked by day for J. W. Orr in Nassau Street. Timothy Cole had learned the craft in Chicago in his teens and could work miracles with patient stippling and crisscrossing lines which suggested the very touch of the painter's brush in Hals, Vermeer, or Velasquez. Many of the engravers specialized, and it was W. B. Closson who best rendered the blurred mystery of George Fuller; Frank French, the pastel quality of a figure by Frank D. Millet; and Elbridge Kingsley, the tonal veils of Inness and Ryder. Some of the older men protested when, in the interest of greater fidelity, a

Timothy Cole, engraving after St.-Gaudens (detail)
Courtesy Forbes Library, Northampton, Mass.

photographic image of the subject was placed on the block. Kingsley, however, used the new method and worked with one eye on the painting itself, or a photographic print of it, to check the accuracy of his translation.

There were other ways in which the camera could be used to increase the truthfulness of pictorial reproduction. Thousands of prints in a special building at the Centennial revealed the progress of the camera, if not toward art, at least in the mechanical fixing of an image. Its use for reproducing works of art took various forms. A photographic image could be transferred to a stone from whose surface photolithographs were printed. The carbon print or "autotype" depended on the varying degrees of solubility of a film of bichromated gelatin when exposed to a photographic negative. In the "woodburytype" the image of a gelatin relief was pressed into a plate of lead and printed from the latter, producing a grainless and faithful reproduction of the original photograph in all its most delicate gradations. Basic to the "photogravure" was a gelatin positive whose lighter areas were thicker than its darker ones; when this was transferred to a copperplate and the latter was bitten with acid, the image could be inked and printed.

Here were devices which gave tone for tone, not the wiry approximations of the average steel and wood engraver. Writers and publishers of art books knew their superiority but knew also that they required much expert handwork, time-consuming revision, and in some instances a special kind of paper; they remained, therefore, the aristocrats of illustration in the seventies and eighties. Earl Shinn, whose pseudonym was Edward Strahan, used both wood engravings and photogravures in his three-volume *Art Treasures of America,* which claimed to reproduce the most valuable and important pictures and statues in public and private collections. His *Études in Modern Art* boasted a typographical perfection heretofore unattained in this country. There were one hundred gravures in his one-volume selection of *Art Treasures* in 1888 and its only rival was Sheldon's *Recent Ideals of American Art,* whose publisher proclaimed it sumptuous, exquisite, and matchless, the Greatest Art Book of the Age. From private collections Sheldon had chosen nearly two hundred oils and water colors whose dullness scarcely deserved the superb photogravures which Goupil made of them from photographs in Paris, setting a new standard for the costly art book in America.

At least some Americans could now have the old masters on their parlor tables, and framed images of the Coliseum and Notre Dame on their walls. The makers of the less sumptuous picture books and the magazines needed cheaper and quicker reproductive methods. One solution was Gillot's process by which a line drawing no longer had to be cut in wood but could be photographed upon a piece of zinc and its white areas etched away to make a relief plate. Mounted on wood, this block was of a proper height to be used with type when a page was printed.

The zinc cut, however, would print only lines, not tones, and for the latter purpose the half-tone came into wide use in the eighteen eighties: the subject was photographed upon a metal plate through a network of lines which reduced the visual image to a series of dots widely spaced in the lighter and more densely in the darker passages. By etching the plate these points of metal became the printing areas. The half-tone could be inserted in a newspaper column or on the printed page of a magazine. In the cheap journalistic cut it was spotty and coarse-grained. The magazine, however, with its finer screens and excellent paper, was capable of superior full-page illustrations in monochrome and later in colors.

In the early eighties one could find in the same issue of *Century* or *Harper's* wood engravings, process blocks, and even an occasional half-tone, the work of the young men who were soon to create the Golden Age of American illustration. Art editors could offer in the new reproductive methods an incentive to painters and draughtsmen who had watched the earlier engravers betray their intention. Young illustrators were not concerned with the art which interprets another's art but wished their own drawings in pen and ink, oil, or water color to be seen just as they left the drawing board or the easel. Timothy Cole, to be sure, continued to rival the half-tone by his consummate skill; but Kingsley became an artist in his own right, built a studio on wheels, and engraved the Connecticut Valley woods and mountains directly from nature on his blocks, many of them to be printed on fine Japan paper and sold as individual prints. More than one veteran engraver was now hired to touch up the murkier passages in the new half-tones.

The old volumes of *Harper's* are a record of progress where one can watch the development of Abbey, Frost, Pyle, and Reinhart as artists, together with improvement in the reproduction of their work. The *Harper's* of the Civil War years had double columns of text and no full-page illustrations; there was a noticeable improvement in its wood engravings of the seventies. The October issue of 1889 contained an article by Charles Eliot Norton on *The Building of the Church of St. Denis,* and all its line cuts of architectural detail were obviously redrawn in pen and ink from photographs; in the next month's issue, Norton's piece on the building of Chartres had four half-tones made directly from the photographs of façade and sculpture.

The art of Abbey, Frost, and Pyle developed as these artists learned to take advantage of new reproductive techniques. The great pen-and-ink masters of Europe —Daniel Vierge, Adolf Menzel, Phil May, and Fortuny —worked with a fluency and a crispness beyond the graver's power to imitate; only the metal plate, photomechanically etched, could do justice to them or to their American rivals.

Edwin Austin Abbey seldom drew a clear sharp line, and one of his friends said that the thin strokes of his pen were as soft as the hairs on a spider's leg. He had been nineteen when he went to work for *Harper's* in 1871, and three years later his first drawing for a Herrick poem appeared. Thanks to its grace, its sensitive response to the old English sweetness, Abbey re-created over the years the small Tudor village, the odd rustic characters, the sprightly women of a dozen English poets, which were published first in the magazine and later in book form as *The Quiet Life* and *Old Songs.* Alfred Parsons collaborated with Abbey in the series for *She Stoops to Conquer;* and both men settled down in the late eighties in a Worcestershire cottage at Broadway, "thatched, latticed, mottled, mended, ivied, immemorial," as Henry James described it. Here, as James said, remote things became actual to Abbey. An episode from *Sally in Our Alley* had no trace of archaeological effort, and after painstaking research Abbey could draw scenes from the comedies of Shakespeare as though he had observed them at first hand. If any man succeeded in evading time it was this neat small person with the rimless glasses and the scholarly look.

Edwin A. Abbey, pen and ink drawing

Library of Congress

The Quaker Joseph Pennell had none of Abbey's historical imagination, but he had studied the sun-filled sketches of Fortuny and in 1881 sold his first drawings to *Scribner's.* He soon proved himself the perfect illustrator for Howells' sketches of life in Venice, and his views of courtyards, cathedrals, and *cabildo* for George Cable's *Creoles of Louisiana* were brilliant pen-and-inks with a fine sense of the value of whites and a pleasant way of selecting details and of rendering them with a few brisk lines. Pennell soon turned to etching in London, and his mature years were given mainly to the making of prints, to writing about them, and to canonizing his friend Whistler.

The first illustrated book of Arthur Burdett Frost was published in 1874 under the title of *Hurly-Burly,* and its drawings were done on wood. Among his later illustrations were painted genre scenes of Yankee farmers and huntsmen, but Frost could be broadly funny with a few pen strokes and a good deal of white paper. His baseball pitcher winding himself up in a series of small sketches was essentially a comic strip; his first *Uncle Remus* illustrations were made in 1892, his last ones a quarter of a century later.

Howard Pyle, *Thomas Jefferson* (detail)

By permission of Charles Scribner's Sons

Edward W. Kemble, pen and ink drawing (detail)

Library of Congress

Howard Pyle brought to life the medieval world of the old folk tales and the world of colonial America. He was born at Wiimington not far from the scenes of Washington's campaigns and there he built the studio where his work and teaching were done. Like Pennel he was a Quaker, and like Pennell he could write as well as draw. Quickly learning the simplifications appropriate to photoengraving, he became a delightful designer of small head- and tailpieces, and by study of German printmakers an illustrator of fairy stories of whom Pennell said, "It is very hard to tell where Dürer ends and Howard Pyle begins."

With a few strokes of a fine pen Pyle could suggest the bleakness of a Caribbean shore where a dead pirate lay bleaching. In *The Wonder Clock* and *Robin Hood* he designed with a firmer line and a rich sense of pattern, the picture surrounded with decorative borders in a fashion made popular by William Morris and the Kelmscott Press. He was not alone in reconstructing American history, for Joseph Boggs Beale, a pupil of Eakins and an illustrator of *Harper's* and the *Daily Graphic,* made a reputation for competent pictures of Ben Franklin, the Boston Tea Party, and the Burr-Hamilton duel. They seem perfunctory beside the pages where Pyle set historic characters moving through the streets of seventeenth-century Salem or in bleak Georgian rooms. When Pyle used the brush he limited himself at first to grays and browns as though to help the engraver; when color reproduction became possible, he proved himself an original and powerful colorist.

Slightly behind these men trailed the other talents of the Golden Age, among them Harry Fenn with his clever black-and-white renderings of landscape, and Reginald Birch with *Little Lord Fauntleroy*. Edward Winsor Kemble gave something like Frost's crackling humor to his pen-and-inks for *Huckleberry Finn* and his innumerable "Kemble coons." Charles Dana Gibson in the eighties had not yet mastered the technique or matured the social types for which he was soon to be famous, and his stiff and rather labored *Life* drawings looked like inferior imitations of Kemble.

The West which Buffalo Bill successfully dramatized found a more authentic interpretation in Frederick Remington's *Crooked Trails* and his *Men with the Bark On*. Remington could not only draw but sometimes wrote his own texts; his sun-parched deserts, his frontier posts in the snow, his mule packs toiling up mountainsides, his galloping cowboys, and his Indians with hard shadows under their horses' feet made an instant appeal to a generation which realized that the frontier was

Frederick Remington, *The Sentinel*

Remington Art Memorial, Ogdensburg, N.Y.

closed forever and the western types were vanishing. Remington knew those types down to the last feather and saddle strap. In black and white, he practiced the incisive economy of an A. B. Frost; in color "under a burning sun," as Royal Cortissoz once said, "he worked out an impressionism of his own."

The illustrators of the Golden Age served a public whose enthusiasm for these historical and literary reconstructions confessed perhaps its own failure to imagine for itself. The appeal of Pennell was to Americans with an excessive hankering for the crumbling picturesqueness of an older, foreign world. Yet one cannot look with scorn upon a generation which visited the castles of ancient France with him, knew Herrick through Abbey, and watched Jefferson over Pyle's shoulder writing the *Declaration* by the light of a single candle. Tenniel had fixed the image of Alice for all Englishmen; Americans would always see Uncle Remus, Br'er Rabbit, and the Tar Baby as A. B. Frost had seen them.

Howard Pyle, Initial letter for *The Wonder Clock*

Courtesy Harper and Bros.

Thomas Nast, *Let Us Prey* (detail) ▶

Harper's Weekly

PART TWO

CRITICS, REBELS, AND PROPHETS

INTRODUCTION / THE AMERICAN CONSCIENCE

One could almost count on one's fingers the men and women of brains and talent who were not comfortable in the House of Have. Attacking the very foundations of that House, Wendell Phillips declared that "labor, the creator of wealth, is entitled to all it creates," and piled heresy on heresy by upholding the Paris Communards, as Edward Bellamy upheld the rebel Daniel Shays in his novel, *The Duke of Stockbridge*. The well-heeled American applauded when the state militia dispersed the Pittsburgh strikers in 1877 and the steelworkers at Homestead fifteen years later, but drained the dregs of his vocabulary to find epithets for Governor Altgeld of Illinois, who pardoned some of the Haymarket anarchists.

The reformers built utopian worlds with words, but they also attacked greed and special privilege in the here and now. If one could not reconcile what Henry George called "monstrous wealth and debasing want," one dreamed with him of a land restored to its owners by the single tax; yet George, while he shaped the philosophy of *Progress and Poverty,* waged his battle against the monopolists of California. In the Chicago *Tribune* Henry Demarest Lloyd exposed the practices of Standard Oil and the Chicago Board of Trade, and subsequently preached government ownership of railways and banks. The Nationalists and later the Populists were fortified by men who had read *Looking Backward,* Edward Bellamy's vision of a socialized commonwealth.

George William Curtis made *Harper's Weekly* the sworn enemy of graft and paternalism and toppled Boss Tweed in 1871 not so much by the written word as through "them damned pictures" of Thomas Nast. The gross Tweed, who owned the mayor of New York, the state governor, the judges, the police and election officers, had blandly asked, "What are you going to do about it?" Nast's cartoons answered that question. Readers could skim Curtis' verbal attacks on the corruption of Tweed's spoils system, but Nast's drawing of "The Brains"—a potbellied boss with a moneybag for a head—lodged in the mind. Nast had a richly developed graphic style whose lines and textures lost none of their bite in being engraved upon wood. His picture of military glory posed a livid white skeleton on a throne of cannon balls against the flame and smoke of burning cities; and when Louis Bonaparte collapsed in 1870 the artist clothed him in the rags and patches of his uncle's uniform with the caption: "Dead Men's Clothes Soon Wear Out."

Turning to Boss Tweed in that same year Nast horribly metamorphosed him into Hamlet's Queen assuming a virtue that she did not have; in "Let Us Prey" he drew the man and his three henchmen as vultures on a crag with lightning playing around them. His "Tiger Loose," a full-page composition, was credited with breaking the ring: Tweed's court sat in the imperial box like the Romans in a painting by Gérôme and watched the Tammany Tiger maul the body of the republic. Daumier would have concentrated his terrible indignation into a few lines; Nast piled up pictorial indictments with elaborate detail, and when he campaigned, after the breaking of the ring, against Greeley, Hayes, and Tilden, his crowded page began to be garrulous and his point harder to find.

Charles Stanley Reinhart drew the Tammany gang in 1871 as germs in a magnified drop of water; and Nast's elaborate parodies found an echo in Bernard Gillam's travesty in 1884 on the *Phryne* of Gérôme in which Blaine stood naked before the Chicago Convention. Joseph Keppler was at his droll best when he drew Brigham Young's widows mourning their spouse in a gigantic bed, and Frederick Burr Opper as a newspaper cartoonist was to make *Happy Hooligan* a national character.

The visiting foreigner assayed American civilization with very little humor. Carlyle, Ruskin, and Morris had ruffled British complacency with their comments on the moral and artistic ugliness of the industrial age, and from England came the liberal Edwin Lawrence Godkin to preach an enlightened laissez faire to the cultured few who read the *Nation.* James Bryce was in New York when the Tweed scandals broke, and in his *American Commonwealth* summed up his impressions of America's intellectual life: a fondness for bold and striking effects rather than delicacy of workmanship; a passion for novelty; a habit of mistaking bigness for greatness. If democracy had found a distinctive expression in American art and literature, Bryce could not discover it.

More specific were the comments of Oscar Wilde, who stepped off the boat in 1882, not the wizened aesthetic Bunthorne whom admirers of *Patience* had expected, but a huge-framed man with an enormous white face above his fur-trimmed green overcoat and with long dark hair to his shoulders. Wilde's Chicago audience smiled when he told them that the rise and fall of the great machines in its waterworks was the most beautifully rhythmic thing he had ever seen; they winced when he called its tower a castellated monstrosity with pepperboxes stuck all over it. From Boston to San Francisco Wilde ridiculed the creaking rosewood chairs, the cast-iron stove with its funeral urns, the frock-coated bronze memorials which, he said, added a new horror to death, the dinner plates decorated with sunsets, the moonlit soup plates whose bottoms seemed to vanish in the distance.

Seven years after Wilde, Matthew Arnold expounded his doctrine of the unsound majority and the saving remnant. Observing from the height of his middle-class snobbism the boastfulness, the exaggeration, and the materialism of America, its want of soul and delicacy, Arnold warned his audiences that the American remnant, which was Protestant in religion, Puritan in philosophy, and Germanic in ethnic origins, must set its mind on whatsoever things are elevated, just, amiable, and pure, if it wished to save the state.

Who were Arnold's few "highly civilized individuals" who could be counted on to make our civilization "interesting"? Doubtless they were men like John Hay, Henry Adams, and Henry James. Hay's "social" novel, *The Bread-winners,* whose theme was the conflict between property and labor, turned out to be a portrait of its author's paternalism rather than a picture of an American community at war with itself. Its hero was the polished, unimaginative, and thoroughly complacent Arthur Farnham, its villain the repulsive and murderous agitator Offitt, and most of the clichés of the labor-hating mind were in its pages.

Henry Adams seemed to have stepped from Holmes's *Autocrat of the Breakfast-Table.* The man of family, as Holmes described him, should have four or five generations of gentlemen behind him, a colonial councilor, a governor or so, one or two doctors of divinity, and a member of Congress not later than the time of long boots with tassels; family portraits by Smibert and Copley; books with the family names in them, and an old place furnished with claw-footed chairs, tall mirrors, and stately cabinets. Henry Adams was this man incarnate. His family had produced two Presidents of the United States and a minister to Great Britain, and in the mansion house at Quincy hung their portraits by Copley and Stuart and their busts by Powers and Greenough. In the garden grew the York roses Abigail Adams had brought from England in 1788; in the small granite library were the glass cases of Adams mementos and, from floor to ceiling, the books whose collection John Adams had begun before the Revolution.

Henry's lifelong quest was for a world that "sensitive and timid natures could regard without a shudder." In his novel *Democracy* he probed Washington politics with an inquisitiveness which he attributed to his heroine, "the feeling of a passenger on an ocean steamer whose mind will not give him rest until he has been in the engine room and talked with the engineer." In the Washington of Grant, Henry found men who talked about virtue or vice as one who is color blind talks about red and green; and at the end he could say with Madeleine Lee, "Democracy has shaken my nerves to pieces."

Henry James had no better luck as he searched that "poor little barren artificial deposit," the soil of American perception. Both James and Adams were looking for an eighteenth-century needle in the nineteenth-century haystack. The perfection they sought was to be found only in a few social oases or in the dream of an unrepeatable past, not in the America which Godkin called "a chromo civilization."

Walt Whitman had a conscience, too, but not of the New England variety. The "savage, wolfish" politics and the corruption depressed him, and he could see no solution of the labor question; but he knew its central importance and believed it could be solved. In *Democratic Vistas* he reproached his country not for her failure to approximate Old World culture, but for her obtuseness in not seeing that such models, "appropriate for former conditions and for European lands," were but "exiles and exotics here." Walt saluted the temples and statues of the Old World, the masterpieces of Dante and Shakespeare, but not as patterns for imitation: "On your plane, and no less, but even higher and wider, must we mete and measure for today and here . . . accepting the old, the perennial elements, and combining them into groups, unities, appropriate to the modern, the democratic, the west, and to the practical occasions and needs of our own cities, and of the agricultural regions."

The democracy of Frederick Law Olmsted was of Whitman's kind, and it was for the "needs of our own cities" that he designed Central Park. Like Whitman he had seen the woebegone rabble of soldiers straggle into besieged Washington and, indignant at the do-nothingness of the Medical Bureau, he built the Sanitary Commission into an agency for the relief of veterans, designed hospital cars with swinging stretchers, storehouses for the distribution of supplies, and hospitals to wage war on epidemics. Three years after the war he prepared his report on Central Park. That long and narrow green oasis had been the vision of Downing, and it was Downing's pupil Calvert Vaux who helped Olmsted to plan its final form.

The park was to be no formalized European affair but an enhancement of the beauty which was already there—the rough and hilly area to the north, the pastures below it, the rocks which Olmsted called its treasures. The various features of the scheme—the lower lake, the music hall, the flower garden, the casino, the tower on Vista Rock, the skating pond, the reservoir—were to be linked by informally winding roads and pathways, and the Grand Avenue was to be but a short promenade with a few well-placed statues. There would be no temptation to trotting matches along the curving carriage roads, and crosstown traffic would move in channels cut below the park's level. Thanks to its designers, Central Park was a magnificent adaptation of beauty to use, a place of infinite surprises, and the delight of all the city's people.

Walt Whitman's essay implied that art was no fanciful decoration on the surface of a civilization but the expression of man's deepest beliefs. This lesson, so badly needed in the age of bric-a-brac, was brought home to Americans by a group of writers and educators whose scholarship and whose critical penetration were something new in the land. The *Raphael and Michelangelo* of Charles C. Perkins was published in 1878 and other Italian essays appeared in the eighties. Charles Norton probed the past, using old Latin documents for his study of the Duomo at Siena, and writing college lectures in which the great Gothic churches were discussed as "a single, joint and indivisible product" of all the arts at their highest energies.

While Jarves, Norton, and Perkins explored the past in terms of first principles, a few writers criticized the architecture of the false front. The editor of the *American Architect and Building News* complained that the Institute of Architects convened to discuss the metric system and the question of sewerage "when they should be thinking of the underlying principles of design on which all good work must rest." Henry Van Brunt was capable of that thinking, and his translation of the *Discourses on Architecture* of Viollet-le-Duc was published in 1875. The Frenchman scathingly denounced eclectics for their "profitless and unsystematic gropings among a chaos of ideas and materials," their minds "closed to the reception and expression of new ideas for the sake of being correct in . . . imitation of old ones."

In the same spirit, "Where are we to look," asked Van Brunt, "for a remedy for the increasing embarrassment of our knowledge?" The remedy for him was in truth of material; it was in principles and not forms, since forms are the language, not the end of art. Primitive architecture shaped its forms out of necessity and developed them to the limit of their inherent capacities; the learned modern repeats these forms and affects impressions which he does not feel. To create, "we must know ourselves and our own distinctive capacities for the utterance of monumental history. . . . We need to design without caprice, reasonably, logically, be refined without weakness, bold without brutality, learned without pedantry. . . ."

Many and various were the contributions of Russell Sturgis to intelligent thinking about art—his manual of the Jarves Collection, his pieces in the *Nation,* his lectures at the College of the City of New York. A stimulus to the architectural conscience was in his lively articles on contemporaries in the *Architectural Record;* the books he wrote in his later years attempted to provide their readers with a critical basis for understanding art; *How to Judge Architecture, The Appreciation of Sculpture, The Appreciation of Pictures,* and several other volumes.

The most brilliant among historian-critics was Montgomery Schuyler, a descendant of Dutch aristocrats, whose conversation was the delight of his cronies at the Century Club and who could dissect the Brooklyn Bridge with the skill of an aesthetic surgeon. His versatile pieces were done for the *World,* the *Times,* and the *Sun,* his essays on building for the *American Architect* in the eighties, and in the nineties for the *Architectural Record.*

A Ruskinian and a medievalist at heart, Schuyler condemned the Queen Anne as wholly inorganic; its American followers, he wrote, had sucked the dregs of the whole English Renaissance. In New York streets he saw one vertical façade after another which had neither rhyme nor reason. This enlightened eclectic had no objection to the use of past styles; he insisted only that effects cannot precede causes. For the true architect "the point of departure is much less important than the point of arrival . . . and the historical styles of architecture will be rated according to the help they give in solving the architectural problems of our time."

Schuyler reserved his enthusiasm for those men whose point of departure had been a consciousness of function. He believed that what was most wrong in America was the estrangement between building and architecture, between its prose and its poetry. The ancient cathedrals had convinced him that engineering and art could not be disjoined, and he was quick to praise the structural courage of western architects. When other visitors from the East recoiled before the "Peorian Renaissance" of Chicago and the absurd Gothic-cum-classic porte-cochere of the Minneapolis Government Building, Schuyler maintained that such strength could be refined, whereas much of the eastern refinement could never be brought to life. Men who loved freedom, he observed, could learn to use their freedom wisely, and it was "more feasible to tame exuberances than to create a soul under the ribs of death."

While Whitman called for "more solid achievement and less windy promise," and men like Norton and Schuyler worked to make public taste more sensitive, a group of sculptors and painters were learning new disciplines of the chisel and the brush in Europe.

The smooth Canovan generalities had little appeal to a France where Rude had set his troops marching on the Arch of Triumph under a screaming head of Liberty; and an American could acquire a lively sense of three dimensions from the façades of the Second Empire and the monuments to famous men which the Third Republic multiplied. There was a superb stride in Frémiet's equestrian *Joan of Arc* in the Place des Pyramides, and Carpeaux's groups, *Music* and *Dance* at the portals of the Opera, were like the music of Offenbach in stone. Jean-Jacques Pradier had designed rather frivolous muses of Comedy for the Molière Fountain, and Pradier's pupil Jouffroy became the teacher of the American, Augustus Saint-Gaudens, who left Cooper Union to work at the École des Beaux-Arts. When the events of 1870 forced him to give up Paris for Rome and Florence he learned from Verrocchio and Donatello that naturalism need involve no loss of sculptural values. The French work, in spite of its sometimes flashy and meretricious quality, showed him that neither the sun nor the frock coat was the sculptor's worst enemy. He observed the work of men who knew how their clay figures would look in bronze; their lyricism and their crisp naturalism would reappear in his American statues.

Young painters from New York, Boston, and Cincinnati were meanwhile being given a new respect in Europe for paint itself, and a sense of organic structure in figure and landscape. Most of them preferred the discipline of the École des Beaux-Arts to the less beaten trails which Hunt, Inness, and young La Farge had explored. At the Beaux-Arts the great Taine discoursed on the laws of art history, and the student drew from casts and the living model week after week under the relentless academic eye of a Cabanel or a Gérôme.

The list of the Beaux-Arts Yankees grew longer every year. Thomas Eakins was a pupil of Gérôme and acquired some of the rocklike solidity which Léon Bonnat put into his portraits. Gérôme taught Wyatt Eaton, John Alden Weir, and Abbott Thayer in the seventies, and Bastien-Lepage took both Eaton and Weir under his guidance for a time.

The alert American in Paris could watch Manet's skirmishes with the academics and the sentimentalists and admire his austere *Street Singer,* his finely simplified *Olympia.* Here was a painter who worked with the reticent solidity of the old masters but whose directness with the brush and whose power to evoke space and volume with tones nearly devoid of the traditional light-and-shade modeling were wholly modern. Zola called him the embodiment of the positivist idea in a scientific age and wrote that his handling destroyed the glove-box imagery of the Salon: "We have here neither the plaster Cleopatras of Gérôme nor the pretty little pink-and-white ladies of Dubuffe, but just some everyday people who make the mistake of having muscles and bones like the rest of us."

Equally defiant in the seventies was James McNeill Whistler, who had been a child at Lowell and a young man at West Point before he knew Degas, Fantin-Latour, and the vigor of Manet. He was a maker of knife-edged witticisms, an assiduous collector of enemies, and a brilliant defender of the artist's right to his own way of seeing. Whistler's sharp personality oddly contrasted with the ghostliness of many of his portraits and nocturnes. He was a master of characterization in the *Carlyle,* whose shapes were delicately balanced on the two-dimensional surface; but the *Sarasate* and the *Henry Irving* were frail contraptions, the faces and bodies thinly painted against flat walls. His admired Orientals had made landscapes, as Whistler did, with scarcely more than a horizon line and the piers of a bridge, but they achieved tension and a dynamics which were only faintly echoed in *Battersea Bridge.*

Yet Whistler imposed himself on his generation. An American student with a muddy palette had much to learn from his fresh and delightful color; a man discontented with the clutter and detail of conventional painting could take courage from his ingenious simplifications; a sensitive spirit could share his view of art as "a goddess of dainty thought . . . selfishly occupied with her own perfection only." If one wished to defy the Philistines Whistler had set an example in the famous Ruskin lawsuit: the prosecutor asked, apropos of *Battersea Bridge,* "Do you think you could make *me* see the beauty of this picture?" and Whistler replied, "No! Do you know, I fear it would be as hopeless as for the musician to pour his notes into the ear of a deaf man."

If Paris proved unrewarding, the American student could join the Munich Academy, where the formless finish of Düsseldorf had no place, but rather the space-evoking tones of Velasquez and the open avowal of medium in the brushwork of Frans Hals. Inspired by the brutal vigor of Courbet, Wilhelm Leibl constructed heads in one lighter and one darker tone, underscoring the forms of the face and the texture of beard and mustache with broad directional brush strokes. The robust externalism of Munich appealed to strapping, blond-bearded Frank Duveneck from Covington, Kentucky; he enrolled as a pupil of Wilhelm von Diez and became himself a teacher of Munich methods to a group of Americans who were known as the "Duveneck boys."

Before the end of his ten German years Duveneck made a portrait of Professor Ludwig Loefftz in one day's sitting and built the skull of his *Old Professor* (Boston Mus. Fine Arts) with a few powerful planes and shadow shapes, with no niggling transitions and no disruptive light reflections—a quizzical face turned directly to the observer with a bold if momentary glimpse of character. His portrait of a fellow student in 1873 made no effort, once the essentials had been established, to assume a further finish, but remained a brilliant sketch. Duveneck's work in the seventies had the controlled opulence of Rubens, and there was a more patient search for form in the hands of his *Woman with Forget-Me-Nots* (Cincinnati Art Mus.) than in the earlier studies, a hint of Manet in his *Cobbler's Apprentice* (Cincinnati Art Mus.). Henry James even compared him with Velasquez for his "magnificent rendering of flesh and bloom, warmth and relief, pulpy, blood-tinted, carnal substance."

The course of Duveneck's fellow pupil, J. Frank Currier, ran parallel to his own. William Merritt Chase at Munich learned confidence and dash, and Walter Shirlaw freed a cramped hand which had once engraved bank notes in Chicago. John Twachtman worked there in later years with less enduring effects upon his style.

The American abroad, if he lingered beyond the mid-seventies, discovered a group of Frenchmen whose experiments with color were far more revolutionary than those of the Barbizon painters, of Manet, or of Whistler, and beside whose palette the Munich browns seemed dull and inert. In the late sixties Zola had dared to praise Monet as a "man among all these eunuchs" and to salute Pissarro as an unknown of great promise. Pissarro had made fresh clean studies of the red roofs and hilly pastures of Pontoise; Sisley's snow-covered horse pond at Marly and his poplars along the river at Moret were reduced to a few broad passages of lights and darks. Both men were struggling toward a more vibrant play of light, though neither had yet allowed his forms to lose their identity nor his local colors to merge in prismatic color. In April, 1874, thirty French painters showed the result of their experiments, among them Monet, Pissarro, Sisley, Berthe Morisot, and Cézanne. Here were the dancers and laundresses of Degas, the *Loge* of Renoir, and a Monet which he called *Impression, Sunrise.* Zola had wished that they be called "naturalists," but a critic's sarcastic reference to the word "impression" fastened this name upon them.

Ridicule and hostility gave a group character to the efforts of the French impressionists which had not been their intention. Segregated by intolerance, they were forced to define their objectives. One of these was an emphasis on pure color in preference to light-and-shade contrast in defining natural objects; another, the semi-scientific breaking down of a tone into its prismatic com-

Frank Duveneck, *Portrait of a Young Man* (Harold W. Nichols coll.)

Courtesy Victor D. Spark, New York City

ponents, relying on the observer's eye to synthesize these spots of bright separated hues. Again, the will to preserve at all costs the first luminous impression required a speed and breadth of execution, a renouncing of finalities. Concern with the direct translation of light activity into color made the subject itself relatively unimportant: a man's shirt front was as absorbing as the man himself, or a haycock glimpsed at sunset. Shocked by the absence of fixed contour and careful detail, Frenchmen failed to see that the delightful shimmer of

Monet and the handsome and vibrant fleshiness of Renoir were appropriate to a middle class which boated and picnicked in the open air and delighted in the music of Offenbach.

American students who had seen the almost brutal nakedness of Manet's *Olympia,* the nervous surfaces of Parisian sculpture, the exquisite tonal patterns of Whistler, the power of the Munich brushmen, and the shimmer of Monet's Channel cliffs could never produce the slick article which the majority of their countrymen demanded. Alden Weir, touring Holland and Belgium with his brother and with Twachtman, discovered Rembrandt, and Weir bought Manet's *Boy with a Sword.* Eakins saw the Velasquez portraits in Madrid and the terribly swift descent from light to dark in Ribera. Saint-Gaudens came home with no appetite for the banalities of the local statue makers. Walter Shirlaw and Wyatt Eaton returned in 1877, William M. Chase the following year, and Abbott Thayer in 1879, to find that the National Academy was no more responsive to new ideas than were the academies of Europe.

Meeting at Helena Gilder's house in June, 1877, a few of these malcontents formed the Society of American Artists, an informal group whose course was to run parallel with the Academy until it rejoined the larger body thirty years later. The public stayed away from the Society's early shows, and even in the liberal *Nation* a writer referred to the work of its members in 1878 as "college exercises" of a "pulpy vagueness." Four years later the same critic saw "dangerous tendencies rapidly gaining ground in what is now called our new art movement."

The group was better understood by John Ferguson Weir when he wrote in the same year an article, "American Art: Its Progress and Prospects," putting his prestige as an Academician and Director of the Yale School of Fine Arts squarely behind the innovators. He explained that American art had now two generations, those in their prime or already passing into shade, and the newcomers from Paris and Munich. The weakness of the elders lay in their choice of the milder phases of nature and human character, in a thinness of painterly procedure, a weakness in light and shade, a shallowness of coloring, and a poetry without body or force. As for our young men, Munich had taught them an attractive and brilliant directness, Paris a more thorough sense of form. If they would choose subjects relevant to American life, they might find new ways of expressing the nobility of concept, the emotional depth, and moral sense which were in the best work of the older men. We were learning now to "grasp the object with palpable truth in its expressive values and characteristic facts." Give these experimentalists, Weir urged, the benefit of the doubt. "Our art will not be overturned by this new upheaval, though it may be greatly shaken by it."

Thanks to the men Weir championed, only the complacently backward mind of an Andrew Carnegie could believe in the eighties that the French Salon was "still the highest art tribunal in the world."

CHAPTER 21 / PALPABLE TRUTH

Most Americans would have understood by Weir's term "palpable truth" the eye-deceiving "realism" of painters like J. Haberle, J. F. Peto, J. D. Chalfant, and R. L. Goodwin. An Irishman named William M. Harnett received two thousand dollars for one peep-show picture, for he could so paint the red embers in a meerschaum pipe that one felt their heat, and he could reproduce a five-dollar bill on canvas which the Treasury Department considered close to forgery. One could almost read his newspapers, or reach out to lift his revolver from its nail. What one usually ignored was the skillful engineering of his shapes and colors, and the fine organization of volumes in his space, whether deep or shallow. Chardin had possessed this ability, as had the Dutch still-life men whom Harnett so carefully studied. The critic of today knows that Harnett not only reproduced what he saw but intensified it, and suspects that some of the mysteries of the mind are behind his locked cupboards. But to a generation which knew little and cared less about its mental secrets, Harnett was the magical technician who provided nature predigested; he was praised for the quality that made him least the artist.

Weir was careful to include in his definition "expressive values and characteristic facts." That meant selection, even in the field of portraiture; and if one compares the heads of Wyatt Eaton with those of Hunt, whose pupil he had been, one learns the importance of the words "expressive" and "characteristic." *Century* maga-

William Harnett, *Old Models*

Museum of Fine Arts, Boston, Mass.

zine in the seventies published Eaton's rather stodgy crayon portraits of famous Americans through the medium of Timothy Cole's engraving; Hunt built the head of *Lemuel Shaw* with greater breadth and solidity and characterized *Francis Gardner* as much by posture, clothes, and hands as by the face. (See color plate 10.)

For ten or fifteen years Hunt had been preaching the gospel of Millet to politely deaf ears in Boston. What was Cambridge to make of this Harvard man's remark that the university had not graduated a great man for fifty years, or Boston connoisseurs of his observation that they would fail to recognize Michelangelo if he walked down Beacon Street? His *Talks on Art,* which one of his pupils had scribbled on bits of paper and canvas, appeared in 1875, and three years later came his Albany commission—two murals for the capitol, each of them forty-five feet long and sixteen feet high.

Many years before, Hunt had painted Anahita, the Persian goddess, drawn through clouds in a chariot, and he had modeled the three galloping horses in a powerful clay relief. The painting had been destroyed by fire in the artist's studio, and now he repeated the composition for his Albany mural, achieving a graceful if somewhat loose rhythm to link the gesture of the goddess with the figures of Night and the violent downward plunge of the horses. His companion piece, *The Discoverer,* lacked even this degree of unity—a man's figure in a boat propelled by one allegorical lady and surrounded by others in the water.

Hunt was given eight weeks to paint his designs in oil on the stone lunettes under Eidlitz' bold vaulted ceiling, with only a scaffold from which to judge their effect from the floor forty feet below, a task which he compared to "riding eight horses in a circus." The pigment sank into the porous stone or threatened to peel off. Feverish days and nights of work, and Hunt's anxiety lest the mural prove to be a "twin mortification," drained his courage and his strength. Within a few months his drowned body was discovered in a pool at Appledore on the Isles of Shoals. Ten years later one of his murals was nearly obliterated by dampness from a leaking roof, and Eidlitz' vaults had begun to crack. A lighter ceiling was built underneath them, sealing Hunt's work from view. Today his brave conception must be judged by fragments still visible on the dark attic walls, from old photographs, and from the artist's sketches.

Shortly before his death Hunt saw a naked boy balanced on the shoulders of a companion among the shadows of a swimming hole, and his *Bathers,* monumentally simple, had the half reality of a remembered dream; they lived in a far different world from the well-turned nudes of that day (Worcester Art Mus.).

Other men made their private worlds and centered their art on visions of their own; they were the "solitary voices" of whom Emerson once wrote. America has always had such voices: Quaker Hicks with his Peaceable Kingdoms, Thomas Cole building an empire on canvas and then destroying it, Erastus Field imagining an Eden without Eve. When Henry Adams now spoke for "sensitive and timid natures," he spoke for such men as George Fuller, Robert Loftin Newman, Ralph Blakelock, and Albert Ryder—painters of unequal talent who had in common the inward-turning habit.

Fuller began as an itinerant portrait maker in New York State, an associate of the sculptor Henry Kirke Brown and a studio mate of Thomas Ball in Boston. He was thirty-seven when he got his first glimpse of the great Venetians, and after his return his world for fifteen years was the small farm at Deerfield where he was given over, as he said, to the demon of ploughing and

William M. Hunt, *The Flight of Night* (mural photographed during its execution)

Photo Forbes Library, Northampton, Mass.

George B. Fuller, *Country Lass*

Smith College Museum of Art, Northampton, Mass.

Robert L. Newman, *The Letter*

Phillips Memorial Gallery, Washington, D.C.

Ralph Blakelock, *Moonlight, Indian Encampment*

National Collection of Fine Arts, Washington, D.C.

draining, "hoping to come out of it some day and look on a smiling landscape which I have helped to form." In a studio which had been a carriage house Fuller tried to "see nature for himself"; when the tobacco market collapsed in 1875 his canvases began to appear in exhibitions, and in the nine years before him Fuller knew that his effort had borne fruit.

His art was both prose and poetry, and his best figures were projections of his own half-religious, half-sensual image of the young woman, saved from ethereality by a sturdy sense of form. *The Romany Girl* (Addison Gall.) was almost smoothly painted, the sweet gravity of her face emerging from vaguely dark suggestions of forest; the light which falls on his *Country Lass* is the ruddy light Fuller had seen in the Venetians and in Rembrandt's *Girl with a Broom.* These children live in a world of their own, however, with only the vaguest hint of Deerfield woods and pastures. The brush gropes timidly sometimes, at other times it grasps the volume; and the mistiness of Fuller and the tempered warmth are those of Indian summer.

The self-taught Ralph Blakelock was obsessed by another image, an Indian encampment beneath trees whose mass is darkly fretted against a crimson sunset or a blue-white moon. Over and over, with variation of size and arrangement, he built upon that contrast and staked everything on the moment which had left its pattern on his mind.

Few contemporaries of Robert Newman had seen his work when, nearing seventy, he was given his first New York exhibition. Americans who admired Diaz and Monticelli could find in his *The Letter* something of their glow, and a color like that of a raveled tapestry. Today one asks whether Newman during his French years had seen Daumier's bathers and playing children. *The Good Samaritan* (Newark Mus.) has the tense solidity of Daumier, the concentration upon a few forms powerfully modeled against the dim line of hills, the contrast of a few browns and greens with a red cloak and the gleam of flesh. Newman painted what had happened only in his mind, but although he fumbled for his shapes and sometimes lost his forms in the shadows

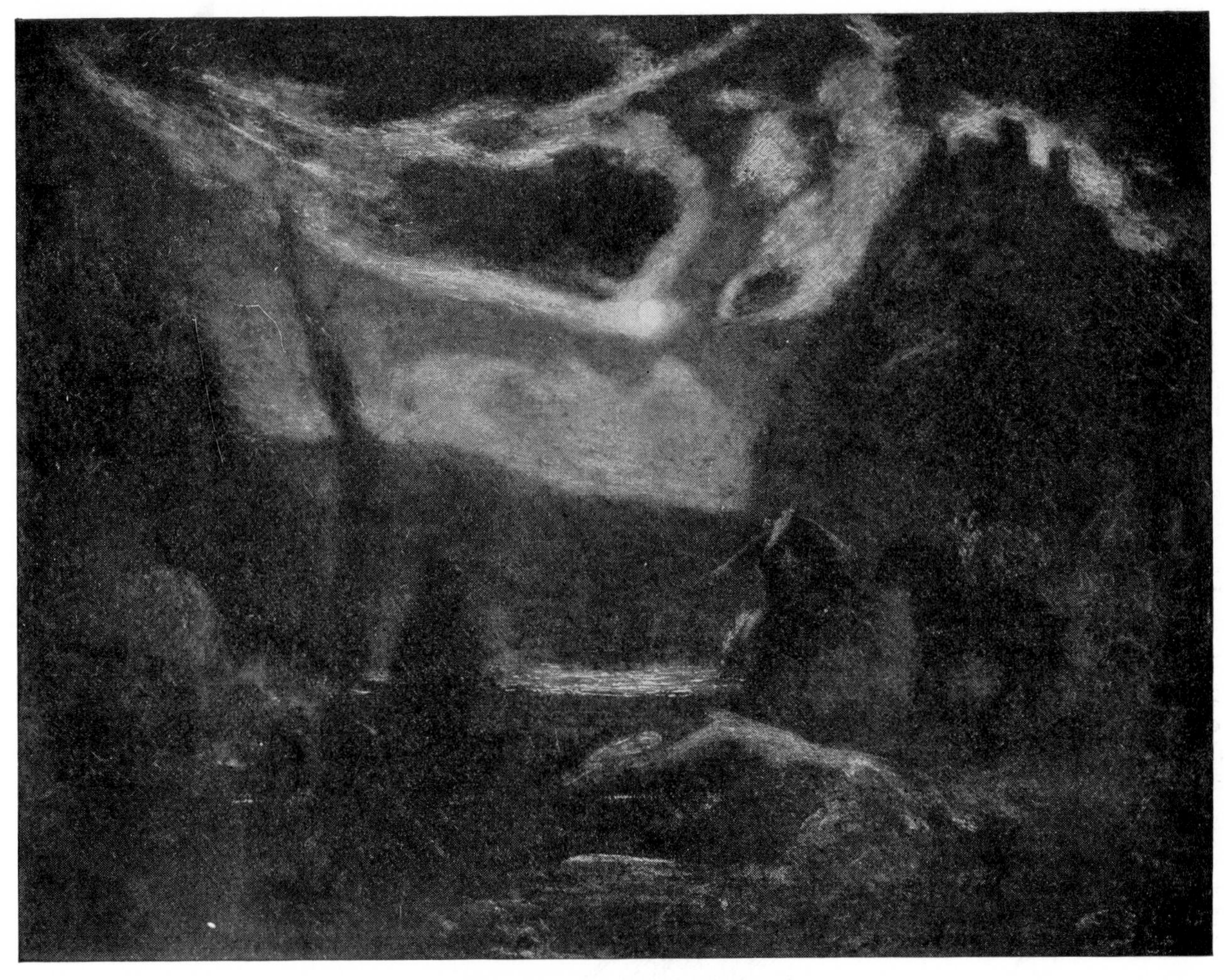

Albert Ryder, *Macbeth and the Witches*

Phillips Memorial Gallery, Washington, D.C.

he had created, the intensity of his conception found its realization.

The mind of Albert Ryder was stocked with a richer imagery than Fuller's or Blakelock's. His brush was more inventive than that of Newman, and among these solitary voices his was the most eloquent. His New Bedford ancestors had fought the storms which Ryder painted; Chaucer, Shakespeare, and the Bible had peopled his imagination. Neither the painter-engraver William Marshall nor the National Academy could show Ryder how technically to proceed. His was an untrodden path, and his indifference to his contemporaries and his rapid glance in 1882 at the European painters were signs that he knew this.

That indifference was mutual, and Ryder at forty could count on his fingers the few artists and friendly purchasers who did not scorn his "poor drawing" and his "slovenly execution." The dealer Daniel Cottier was one of these, and the painter Alden Weir; Thomas B. Clarke bought several of his paintings, and so did a few other men who were far from being millionaires. To the rest of the art world Ryder was a pitiable solitary whom one accused of the eccentricities and the crudities which the next generation would charge to the cubists. Those who called him an impressionist missed the point, for while others made pleasant dissolutions of the real world, Ryder worked with the stubbornness of a Cézanne to make solid and luminous and sharp a world that no one had ever seen. The level, shadowed eyes of his self-portrait, the straight nose, the whole mask framed by the red locks and the beard, reveal a poet whom nothing could divert from his effort.

Charles de Kay, to whom this likeness was given, called Ryder a "modern colorist" whose panels glowed like gems; he described the "humble boldness" of Ryder, his gift for causing "a string of simple-seeming words" to form "by some enchantment a great little poem." Here was the gist of Ryder; and when de Kay compared others' ways of reaching color through form with Ryder's struggle to reach form through color, he knew the source of the painter's difficulties. Color itself, whether the line of melted gold or the acrid green-blue

George Inness, *The Coming Storm*

Albright Gallery, Buffalo, N.Y.

water and the livid cloud in moonlight, was so directly and completely the language of Ryder's feeling that one is tempted to reach into the next century for the word "expressionist." For years at a time Ryder would paint and repaint a single picture in his effort to weld the "simple-seeming words" into a sentence. Layer upon layer of pigment was deposited, glaze upon opacity and opaque forms upon glazes, until chemistry itself protested and the picture buckled and cracked.

Elbridge Kingsley, commissioned to engrave several of Ryder's canvases, watched him at work on *Jonah and the Whale.* The painter's mood was like that of the old chaplain in *Moby Dick,* and his story, "billow-like and boisterously grand," was the story Melville's preacher told:

> And ever, as the white moon shows her affrighted face from the steep gullies in the blackness overhead, aghast Jonah sees the rearing bowsprit pointing high upward, but soon beat downward again towards the tormented deep. . . . He goes down in the whirling heart of such a masterless commotion that he scarce heeds the moment when he drops seething into the yawning jaws awaiting him. . . .

Ryder, that red-bearded Prospero, had called forth the mutinous winds and now struggled to control them. Kingsley marveled as he watched the changes in the picture from day to day:

> The main points of interest would move all over the canvas, according as the stimulating influences of the color accidents would appeal to Ryder's imagination for the moment. I enjoyed the jugglery myself, and never tired of the suggestions continually arising out of the transparent depths of color.

Kingsley noticed that, every night, Ryder put a light glaze over his day's work and in the morning "commenced to work out the suggestions hidden in the transparent masses of color." This was no dabbling with pigment, however; no search for lucky accidents. The intent was clear, the mental image unambiguous, and Ryder insisted on pushing that image to utter completeness of form. The moonlight in his *Temple of the Mind* was not so much described as felt, something to be absorbed by one's senses as though the painting had generated its own light (Albright Gall.). In a completely different mood Ryder flooded his *Forest of Arden* with an atmosphere that was Shakespeare's, but planted his trees, shaped his sloping meadows, and moved his clouds with the majestic economy of a Bach, creating tensions of mass and color beside which most landscapes of his day seem listless and anemic.

Ryder's vision encompassed the broad and tranquil *Constance,* the awesome *Macbeth and the Witches,* and the small marines where he wove his magic with nothing

Homer Martin, *Lake Sanford in the Adirondacks* (Century Association, New York City)

Courtesy Frick Art Reference Library, New York City

more than a wave, the shape of a boat, and a tormented cloud. As the years passed in his cluttered studio, the aging artist ignored dirt, heat, and cold as he doggedly painted and repainted, a man all conscience in an age of compromise. (See color plate 13.)

The door of George Inness' studio at Montclair as effectively shut out the world as did Ryder's garret. His *Coming Storm* was done in 1878 with a powerful massing of clouds over its darkened valley. Perhaps, as Elizabeth McCausland has suggested, only a synthetic version of nature could please a generation which was busily mutilating field and forest. Certainly Inness had given reverent study to what Durand called "the visible works of God," and they had awakened in him a response as deep as it was personal, and as strong as it was modest. (See color plate 11.)

Pictorial economy could go no further than in his *March Breezes* of 1885: a small barn, three trees, a foreground field of intense green passing without transition to the brown distance, the lone figure walking, and the dense clouds above. Within a few years the solid planes of earth became insubstantial, and the foliage and trunks of trees gleamed mysteriously. In *Home of the Heron* (Princeton Univ.) the sun neared its horizon, touching only a tree bole and a few pendent vines. In an old photograph of Inness the tense figure sits with nervous hands, strained eyes, and stringy locks and beard; behind him on the easel are dark pastures and serene distances. Nature has come to exist mainly within the painter's mind.

Through the advice of Inness and the example of Barbizon, Alexander Wyant overcame the Hudson River mannerisms he had learned from James M. Hart. A detailed and conscientious topography gave way in his Catskill scenes to a freer handling of foliage, and there was a hint of the Inness generalizations in *The Pool.* Wyant was less than forty when a paralytic stroke forced him to work with his left hand, with which he could indicate but not fully realize his intention. *Moonlight and Frost* (Brooklyn Mus.), with its silvery green tonalities and its gray-purple halo, was a brave effort by a man who died in his fifties hoping for a few more years of fulfillment.

Another visionary who inherited old landscape methods and who struggled toward new ones was Homer Dodge Martin. In England, Constable stirred his sense of form and color; his several years in France enlivened his response to space and light. As one surveys the patient explorations of this man, whose talent few of his contemporaries recognized, one finds the Barbizon touch, a hint of Corot in his *Blossoming Trees,* and in the eighties the shimmer of impressionism in *View of the Seine* (Met. Mus.). Montgomery Schuyler contrasted the work of his "prismatic and scintillating prime" with the "sober livery" of later years when Martin's eyesight failed him. Yet the essential man was in the more sober moments. He was in his thirties when he painted *Lake Sanford in the Adirondacks,* with its dark and massive middle ground and its dead trees sharp against the mist-covered mountains. *Westchester Hills* was austere in color, with a few bare slopes, a fragment of stone wall, and a patch of sky, but it had a bleak and elemental grandeur.

It was Scotch thoroughness rather than vitality of temperament which gave the Weir brothers a grip on palpable truth. Their father, Robert Weir, taught drawing in his meticulous way at West Point for nearly half a century, John Ferguson became an art professor at Yale, and Julian Alden an instructor for twenty-five years at the Art Students League and at Cooper Union. The Yale portraits by John and his study of *East Rock* were competently drawn and solidly painted. Alden's somber portrait of President Seelye at Smith College marks the beginning of his American career, after his glimpse of Spain and Holland and the discipline of Bastien-Lepage. His *Delft Plate* (Smith College) was simply and charmingly painted and completely lacked the sensuous tone of Chase; his *Oriana* (Smith College) was a rather freely brushed study in low tones of a young face to whose charm the artist responded. One would like to know more of this man who never bragged in paint and who so often seems aloof from the personality or the scene before him. When impressionism became known in America both Weir brothers made characteristically modest use of the new language.

The truth of Hunt and Fuller, of Ryder and Inness, relied upon what Weir called "expressive values"; his "characteristic facts" found a more objective record in the work of Eastman Johnson, Winslow Homer, and Thomas Eakins. In *Democratic Vistas* Whitman urged the poets to strive for a "native, first class formulation," finding "ever the most precious in the common." The year of Whitman's essay was the year of Johnson's *The Old Stage Coach* and of Eakins' *Max Schmitt in a Single Scull;* in the following year Homer painted his *New England Country School.* All of these were native, first-class formulations.

Johnson never risked his security by specializing in genre; but he had made on-the-spot notations of Civil War episodes, of maple sugaring in the Maine woods, of cranberry harvesting on the Nantucket moors. In the quiet of his studio he reduced this raw material to essentials. The cluttered rooms of the seventies were his equivalent for the neat rooms of Vermeer; in his *Not At Home,* he had the courage to place his human figure at the side in half shadow and to open his central area to a glimpse of parlor through a dark archway; the molded ceiling and the bric-a-brac were touched by a light from an unseen window, and the whole picture was a delightful evocation of space with a few broad colors and limpid highlights. Condensation of form and content went still further in *The Conversation* (Addison Gall.): two women stood on an empty beach, the details of their faces and dresses resolved in a few lights and darks against a sea and sand which were suggested by unmodulated flat tones, with only a barrel, a basket, and a tub for equipoise.

Many of Homer's war studies took form several years after the conflict, when he was an Academician and a leader in the Water Color Society with a few months in Europe behind him. No detail of his subsequent work could be credited to European artists, but his *Rainy Day in Camp* of 1871 commanded a more spacious sense of earth under a heavy sky than the first war pictures (Met. Mus.), and there was a new brilliance in his rendering of the Negroes' ragged garments under brilliant sun in *Sunday Morning in Virginia* (Cincinnati Art Mus.).

Homer's life on Ten Pound Island in Gloucester Harbor in 1880 was not his first experience of the sea; a year later that experience was deepened at Tynemouth on the east coast of England. American boys and girls had played in the mild Gloucester sun; now the impassive wives of fishermen stood on cliffs, unconscious of their dignity, watching the gray sky and the grayer ocean. In 1883 began that quarter century of intimacy with the Atlantic which links Homer's name inseparably with Prout's Neck in Maine, as Van Gogh is linked with Arles, Millet with Barbizon, and Thoreau with Walden Pond.

Both Inness and Homer made their own bargain with nature, and both kept it steady and uncorrupted; but to compare the former's *Harvest Moon* with the latter's *Eight Bells,* both done in the same year, is to understand that nature was for Homer something external to the man. He remarked that once he had selected the thing carefully he painted it exactly as it appeared. His statement needs qualifying, since the breaking wave and the storm-bent palm tree do not wait to be recorded exactly as they appear, nor the trout in mid-air, nor the canoe in the rapids. Yet the selection and the transforming activity of the artist were more completely dominated in Homer by what the man had seen than in the case of Inness; and Homer's occasional poetry seems to have been involuntary—a by-product, so to speak, of his traffic with earth, rock, and water.

This self-contained and practical New Englander knew precisely what he wanted to do and effectively shielded himself from the distractions of the socially superficial. Homer rebuffed a would-be biographer by

Eastman Johnson, *Not at Home*

Brooklyn Museum

saying that the most interesting part of his life was of no concern to the public, and his description of Prout's Neck was not calculated to lure the casual guest: "I do not keep a horse and my nearest neighbor is half a mile away—I am four miles from telegram and P. O. and under a snow bank most of the time. . . ." As for the purchaser, he was content to leave the marketing of his art to dealers in Boston and New York. A direct inquiry, if answered at all, would be answered in a businesslike way: "I can offer you only water colors. I have

Winslow Homer, *Eight Bells*

Addison Gallery of American Art, Andover, Mass.

them from Canada, Bermuda, Bahamas, Florida, and the coast of Maine. They always net me $175 each, no frames, no matter the size; they are mostly about 14 x 21. Do you think you would like any sent to you on immediate approval for cash. . . . If so what country would [you] like represented? Hurry up—as it's very cold here!"

Recognition and patronage were his from the beginning on a scale which suited his modest needs: his work was shown each year at the National Academy, the Brooklyn Art Association, and the Water Color Society. Paris saw it in 1867, Philadelphia at the Centennial, Munich in 1882. In Homer's pocket the Temple Gold Medal, one of eight which he received, kept company with a buttonhook and small change.

From his delightful small genre scenes of the seventies to the "elemental themes" of the nineties, as Lloyd Goodrich calls them, Homer developed his naturalistic talent to its limit. From the vigorous anecdote based upon drawings, Mr. Goodrich has traced his growing selectivity and the reconstructive powers of his memory as he concentrated his gifts upon water and woods rather than upon people, who never became in any deep sense his concern. The two large figures in *Eight Bells* tell us what they are doing, but tell us nothing of themselves. Rare indeed was the lyrical moment which produced *Summer Night,* where girls dance on a piazza and dark shapes watch them against a gleaming moonlit sea which Ryder might have painted; and compared with the swift terror of a Ryder shipwreck, Homer's *Gulf Stream* (Met. Mus.) is no more than a vigorous dramatic anecdote superbly told. In the large marines of his mature years he found that a foreground rock, a foaming wave crest, and a scudding cloud were sufficient to convey the immensity and power of a sea which he knew better than any man of his time.

"Composition" for Homer was the knack of holding things stable or setting them into swift movement by the simplest means—the centering figure or clump of trees, the diagonal shape crossing the space, the repeated vertical, the balancing of the small and important against the large and less important, the light against the dark mass. The strength of his *Sunlight on the Coast* was in its broad suggestive economy and its masterly simplifications of the textures, shapes, and movements of natural elements.

As a colorist Homer commanded in his later oils a harmony of greens, tempered red-browns, and subtle grays, but there was also a zest in him for the luminous and the intense. He delighted in the sonorous green reflections of a dory in shallow water, the blinding whiteness of a farmhouse porch, the blue flash of a berrypicker's ribbon. His colorism found its full expression in his water colors.

This medium had once been a preliminary to the making of a print, and the timid spreading of smooth washes down the paper, the deft blending of gradations, and the local coloration of drawn shapes were sufficient for the men who first rendered American hills and harbors. The narrow range of a color print thus limited the parent study, together with the early century's habit of seeing foliage as either brown or the dullest of greens. Few men before Homer escaped these inhibitions, and only when unprecedented subjects forced new visual methods upon them—the cold brilliance of Oregon mountains as Alfred Miller saw them, the mist and spray of Niagara Falls which Dunlap attempted, the gaudy tropical plants, and the pink snow on the cones of South American volcanoes in Church's studies. In an age whose sculptors made bronze look like flannel and whose iron-and-glass buildings apologized for not resembling a solid cliff of granite, people admired the water colorist who least respected his medium.

Homer's first steps in a wiser direction were cautious, and there was opaque color in his early efforts and a line drawing to support his forms. But when he painted the fishermen's wives at Tynemouth in 1882 he had mastered the most hazardous of techniques to the extent of achieving volume, space, and depth without obvious labor. *Sun and Cloud* (Freer Gall.) was swiftly and courageously done, the dark sea a smear across his sheet, the three central figures massed with a few movements of his brush. The range of color was narrow, but more and more was being suggested with less and less. When Homer went to Prout's Neck and thence on his trips to the Adirondacks and to Nassau and Bermuda the history of American water color truly began; and his lifetime saw the brilliance of Sargent's Venetian impressions and the beauty of John La Farge's South Sea idyls.

Homer led them all in the work of his late fifties and sixties. He knew that the white paper behind a transparent wash of color was what made it brilliant, and that every layer imposed upon another dims that brilliance; that fumbling or afterthought is forever exposed in this medium; that the pale tint is weakness and the overdarkened one is heavy without strength. There was no trick he could not perform with a broad brush to establish main forms, a wiry-thin one for accents, a thumb or a piece of blotting paper to suggest a texture, or the scratch of a knife blade to make water glisten or raise a highlight on a Negro's forehead. He could lead a blue wash down around white paper until that paper was cumulus cloud in the sky or foam on a reef, and he could twist his loaded brush once and for all across water to make it heave under the tropical sun. He could build the spiky fronds of palm tossed by the wind and catch the gleam of a felled tree in the half daylight of the Adirondack woods. His range was from the dazzling summer cloud to the deepest green of pines with the light behind them. His woodsmen stand full-rounded against the pale sky, and a pink-bellied fish jumps or a sleek deer drinks among shadows miraculously clear.

Among these pine-shaded lakes and dense autumn woods Homer's contemporaries could relive their own experiences as hunters and fishermen. The American middle class admired and purchased his work because his encounters with nature were similar to its own. What stirred his age, and pleases us, is his re-creation of the self-sufficient moment when the American responds with his senses to weather, place, and season. (See color plate 16.)

Charles Homer said of his brother as a sportsman

Winslow Homer, *The Fallen Deer,* water color (detail)

Museum of Fine Arts, Boston, Mass.

Thomas Eakins, *The Gross Clinic* (Jefferson Medical College of Philadelphia)

Photo Metropolitan Museum of Art, New York City

that he did not go in much for expensive or elaborate tackle but usually caught the biggest fish. The tackle of Eakins was more elaborate; he learned more about the human mechanism at Jefferson Medical College than any artist of his time, and when he settled down in Philadelphia for forty years of painting and about twenty-five of teaching, he was prepared to catch bigger fish in deeper waters than the New Englander.

That contrast became more obvious with time: the even, productive years at Prout's Neck, the accumulating honors, the steady if modest purchases; at Philadelphia, the growing tension between Eakins and the respectable, the meager patronage, and the long hours of teaching at the Academy. At the Centennial, where Homer's work was given a prominent place, Eakins' *Gross Clinic* had to be looked for among the medical displays. When the painter died in 1916, only three museums owned his work.

Compare the thrifty tone of Homer toward his patrons with what Thomas Eakins wrote to a discontented sitter: "I cannot bring myself to regard the affair in the light of a business transaction," but rather as "a trespass upon your complacency." Homer was accepted by his professional colleagues; Eakins severed his connection with the Society of American Artists because they rejected his *Agnew,* "a composition more important than any I have seen upon your walls." There was a terrible sarcasm in Eakins' reply to a doctor whose friends had disliked his portrait and who asked the painter to change it:

> I presume my position in art is not second to your own in medicine, and I can hardly imagine myself writing to you a letter like this: Dear Doctor, The concurrent testimony of the newspapers and of friends is that your treatment of my case has not been one of your successes. I therefore suggest that you treat me a while with Mrs. Brown's Metaphysical Discovery.

It was the fate of Eakins to become an artistic surgeon in an age of quacks, a prober of symptoms with no tolerance for patent remedies. As Hunt in Boston had urged his young pupils to look for the big things first, so Eakins cried to his class, "Get the character of things. I detest this average kind of work." For the careful preliminary drawing he substituted the directly painted study since "the outline," he said, "is not the man." How could the well-bred slaves of plaster casts face his demonstration of anatomy through the flayed stiff and the completely naked model? How understand his coupling of art with mathematics, in both of which "the complicated things are reduced to simple things. . . . You establish these, and work out from them, pushing them toward one another." (See color plate 12.)

Eakins plotted the positions and shapes of his Biglen rowing scenes on elaborate perspective diagrams; the horses in his *Fairman Rogers Four-in-hand* (Phila. Mus.) and the diving boy in *Swimming Hole* (Fort Worth Mus.) had been modeled in clay before they were painted. It was typical of Eakins that he helped Edward Muybridge in the photographic analysis of human and animal motion. Muybridge photographed galloping horses on a series of plates by setting up twenty-four cameras in a row, and by the time his

Thomas Eakins, *The Concert Singer* (detail)

Philadelphia Museum of Art

Animal Locomotion appeared in 1887 Eakins had already fixed the stages of a man in motion upon a single plate. There was much debate on the value of thus trying to broaden human vision; but meanwhile one step had been taken toward the "moving picture"; and in the Fairman horses and the spinning wheels of the coach, as in the swimmer's arc through the air, a new dynamics entered painting.

The painter of these canvases knew the difference between science and expression. When he pried out nature's secrets it was to make his own use of them, and if he knew "physiology from top to toe" he had no desire to reflect it as a mirror does. He said that one copied up to a point, and then the intellect took over; that a painter's picture of a hot day was the distillation of all the heat he could remember.

That selective process was at work in *Katherine,* a large painting which is both portrait and genre: all shadowy browns and reds, the face powerfully emerging, the cream-white dress touched by the probing light, a rich crimson in the fan, the ribbon, and the chair back. French teachers and Spanish examples had taught Eakins the quick movement from full light to mysterious shadow, but only a man with the organic

Thomas Eakins, *Mrs. Edith Mahon*

Smith College Museum of Art, Northampton, Mass.

sense and a penetrant eye for character could so have applied the lesson in those high dark rooms of the "Brown Decades."

New York saw *The Chess Players* in 1878, a very small painting in which the old men's faces, their chessboard, and the decanter and glasses at their side are all one sees at first in the dim parlor; the red-figured carpet loses itself in the background where gleam the mantel ornaments. The total scene is realized in a few fresh and vigorous touches with nothing forced beyond its plane and lighting. The personalities of the three men are revealed in a few broad planes and accents, their rumpled clothes and knotted hands set forth with relentless observation and affectionate sympathy (Met. Mus.).

The huge *Gross Clinic* of 1875 was a more courageous enterprise in subject and in form, their relationship determined by what was going forward, the noble head of Gross dominant as the light fell directly upon him and upon the patient's livid thigh. This picture drew from Benjamin an evasive comment: "As to the propriety of introducing into our art a class of subjects hitherto confined to a few of the more brutal artists and races of the Old World, the question may well be left to the decision of the public."

Brutal again to this mincing mind would probably have been *The Swimming Hole,* which reminds Professor Matthiessen of Whitman's frank imagery in *Song of Myself*. Six men, Eakins among them, had gone "to the bank by the wood and become undisguised and naked"; one of them dives from the rock, another stands upon it with the splendid corporeality of a Signorelli figure. Out of the reclining, the leaning, the swinging of the six bodies, Eakins created a rhythm in space as well as a frontal pattern upward to the crowning figure and swiftly down to the diver. Within the depth given by his water, his mass of projecting rock, and the wooded bank beyond he gave his bodies an air-surrounded solidity that had seldom been seen in America.

That power appeared again in the *Agnew Clinic* (Univ. of Pa.); and to compare Eakins' studies, fourteen years apart, for the heads of his two surgeons is to see the ripening of his mastery of form. Gross is made to emerge from the surrounding shadows with only three tones—his shaggy nimbus of hair, his bald brow, his compelling, deep-set eyes, and his tense mouth. The *Agnew* head is likewise built with a few planes and accents, but with less reliance on dramatic contrast. It is broader and firmer, and as trenchantly solid and alive as any head by Courbet.

When the popular Healy painted the concert singer Emma Thursby he found her lush sky-blue dress an easy foil for the cream-and-peaches skin; he lingered over the tricks of light with satin, and competently described a face which, in this glittering context, one scarcely notices. Eakins took two years to paint Weda Cook as *The Concert Singer*. She was his friend and Whitman's and had composed the melody for "O Captain! My Captain!" Eakins' purpose was to represent her in the act of singing. He built an extraordinary figure, her hands clasped before her, a bouquet of roses at her feet, the conductor's hand below, the light from the wings molding the young face, the muscles of her throat and the lustrous rose-pink satin of her gown, the green-gray wall behind.

The later portraits of Eakins were painted from compassionate depths and from a brooding sense of human dignity which had its democratic implications. Let the exquisite young miss and the well-turned matron go elsewhere to be flattered; Eakins would search for the play between character and experience, between physiology and thinking. He would ennoble *Edith Mahon* with every shape of illness, of sorrow, and of strain he could find in the sharpening planes of the skull, the shadows of the nose and chin, the firm lips, and the relaxing folds of the neck. Her eyes would be like those which look out from his portraits of himself and whose intensity derives from the tenacious will, the restless mind, and the profound humanity which his intellect could discipline but not defeat. His was the gift which Howells called for in the writer: "Robust enough to front the everyday world and catch the charm of its work-worn, care-worn, brave, kindly face." And Eakins' pupils never knew how painfully he had come by the philosophy which he once summed up for them:

> If America is to produce great painters and if young art students wish to assume a place in the history of the art of their country, their first desire should be to remain in America, to peer deeper into the heart of American life.

None of the painter's pupils peered as deeply as their master. The early landscapes of Henry Ossawa Tanner, and his portrait of his father, who was a bishop of the Methodist Church, had something of Eakins' keen penetration of character, and his *Banjo Lesson* was a promising attempt at genre. Tanner did not follow the master's injunction to remain in America, however, but in his thirties worked in Europe, where he could be judged as an artist, not a Negro. The discipline of the Académie Julian appeared in his Breton peasant pictures; and in his religious canvases the inspiration of Rembrandt mingled with that of his first teacher to produce moving re-creations of Biblical incidents whose backgrounds were based on firsthand study in the Holy Land.

Even as competent a pupil as Thomas Anshutz could acquire Eakins' science but not his art. He was too fastidious a southern gentleman not to recoil from his teacher's brusque methods in the life class, yet the older man's concern with present realities was in his sturdily brushed *Steel Workers, Noontime,* and his pastel portraits made few concessions to mere prettiness or charm. As an Academy instructor he transmitted Eakins' honesty to Henri, Sloan, and Glackens, who would have been luckier had they received it at first hand.

One would have assumed that the sculptor of the seventies, whose material was stubbornly three-dimensional, could scarcely escape palpable truth. The businesslike John Rogers, with his handsome Grecian nose, his tam-o'-shanter, his lustrous long hair and well-trimmed beard, was a hardy survival in this age, still manufacturing plaster groups in meticulous detail of theatrical figures like Joseph Jefferson and in the eighties elaborate tableaux from Shakespeare's plays. The *Emancipation* of Thomas Ball in 1875, despite its obvious sincerity and feeling, seemed like an enlarged Rogers group; and John Q. A. Ward alternated between robust naturalism and descents into what he once called "namby-pamby classicism." In 1878 he was busy with allegories of Law, Commerce, Science, Agriculture, Music, and Equity whose puerility, once they had been installed on the rim of the Hartford capitol's dome, no eye could see.

The work of Olin Warner in the seventies proved that his study with French masters had not overcome his neoclassical habits. Save for a few lessons with Rimmer in Boston and with Ward in New York, Daniel Chester French was a self-taught sculptor when he

Henry O. Tanner, *The Banjo Lesson* (detail)

Hampton Institute, Hampton, Va.

modeled his Concord *Minute Man* with the pose of the Apollo Belvedere and the costume of the embattled farmer. The year 1876 found him in Rome with Thomas Ball, producing a child's head in marble as impeccably smooth as one by Hiram Powers.

Boston, where Jarves saw a bronze *Webster* based on "an intense study of his last suit of clothing," and an *Everett* "bursting his coat buttons in a frantic effort to box the sky," had no standard by which to measure the greatness of Rimmer. His brilliant life drawings were published in 1877 as *Art Anatomy;* and in the following year, when Hunt was fumbling with the composition of the *Discoverer* for his Albany mural, Rimmer redrew the scheme, and his version more boldly stabilized the central figure, forcing Hunt's sea nymphs into the rhythm of the vessel.

The Doctor was dead when the Boston Museum of Fine Arts showed his work in 1880. Here were lions and gladiators with more terror in their massed shadows and fiercely sharp contours than in all the vast, dull

William Rimmer, *The Dying Centaur,* plaster

Museum of Fine Arts, Boston, Mass.

arenas of Gérôme; and the running figures in his *Flight and Pursuit* were as sinister as they were enigmatic. No draughtsman in America could match the freedom with which Rimmer had sketched a lion and a mouse with a pencil on warm pink paper, nor the consummate fusion of knowledge with poetry in his figure drawings.

Only the Frenchman Barye could model animals with the thrusting force, the play of light over sleek muscles and straining flanks, which one saw in Rimmer's *Fighting Lions.* One had to move around this piece to grasp its crescendo of interlocked forms; and the *Dying Centaur,* thrusting his torso upward from the recumbent body with one leg doubled painfully beneath it and another straining to raise it from the earth, told its full story only when experienced from all sides. Some thirty years would pass before these plaster figures were made permanent in bronze.

When Rimmer died Daniel Chester French was about to model his bust of Emerson, of which the poet said, "Yes, that is the face I shave"; and Augustus Saint-Gaudens would soon undertake his first public commission. The National Academy was unreceptive to Saint-Gaudens' work, but the veteran Ward, who had been favored for the *Farragut* commission, said, "Give the young man a chance." In 1881 the admiral rode his pedestal in Madison Square, New York, a stocky figure whose stance was not unlike that of Donatello's St. George, the feet braced as though on a rolling deck. Here the problem of sculptural handling of modern dress was triumphantly solved. Six years later, the gaunt Lincoln, whom the child Saint-Gaudens had once seen towering over Fifth Avenue crowds in a procession, stood in Chicago, a synthesis of strength and delicacy by a man who understood bronze as no American had before him and who worked for years on a single commission before he was satisfied.

Most sculpture in the eighties and nineties suggests the title which George Gray Barnard used for a work of his youth, *I Felt Two Natures Struggling within Me,*

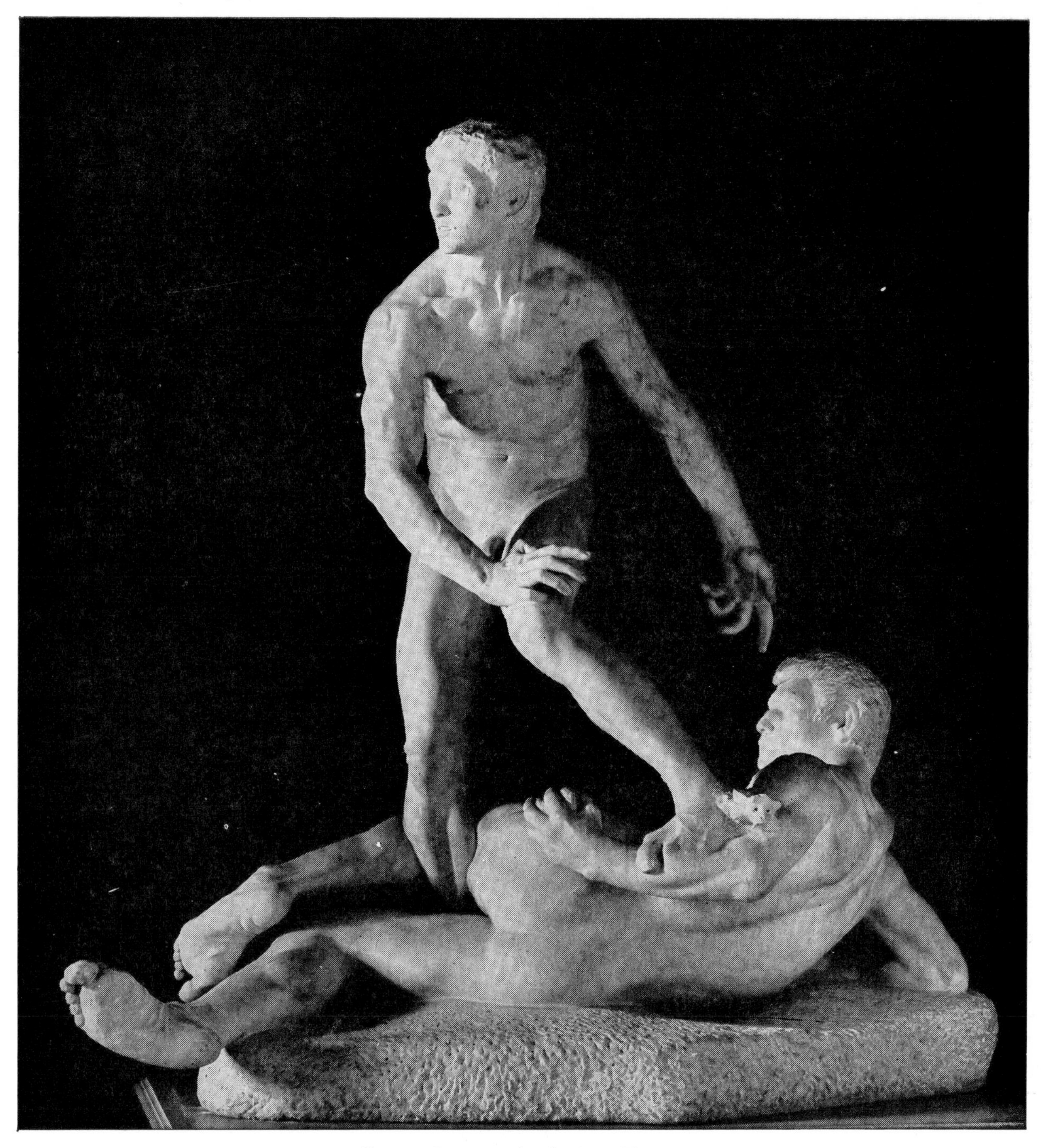

George G. Barnard, *The Two Natures*

Metropolitan Museum of Art, New York City

for naturalism contended with rather dubious idealizations in the stone and bronze of these years. Barnard's *Two Natures,* carved directly in marble after he had seen the bound slaves of Michelangelo, was a courageous and promising achievement. Thanks to Frémiet in Paris, Paul Weyland Bartlett became a consummate technician in bronze and his *Bear Tamer* was in the Salon of 1887.

The allegorical nature of Dan French produced a *War* and *Peace* for the St. Louis Custom House; in Paris, however, Antonin Mercié taught him to handle clay with boldness, and the results were to be seen in two works of the late eighties. The *Lewis Cass* stood firmly on both feet, a vigorous and sturdy characterization (Natl. Statuary Hall, Washington); *Gallaudet and His First Deaf-Mute Pupil* was conceived in the genre spirit of John Rogers, but with a far livelier sense of surface planes and textures, and the child's gesture

John Q. A. Ward, *Henry Ward Beecher*
Photo Forbes Library, Northampton, Mass.

hinted at the graceful curvatures of the feminine figures which French was yet to make.

It was characteristic of John Ward that he made dozens of research drawings for the standing *Washington* on the steps of the Sub-Treasury in Wall Street, carefully noting every button on the general's cuff. The finished statue owed some of its authority to Houdon, and Ward added a cloak and a small column to his original design, blurring its directness and simplicity. As late as the nineties the naturalism of old Ward could hold its own with that of younger men; the standing *Beecher* in Brooklyn and the seated *Greeley* in New York both stoutly asserted the personalities of their subjects.

There was palpable truth also in the equestrian statues of Grant and Lincoln for the Brooklyn Memorial Arch which Eakins and William O'Donovan made together in 1893 and 1894, using Brady photographs and their own camera analyses of horses in motion. Hamlin Garland in *McClure's* praised Edward Kemeys for his buffaloes and Indians, and Frederick Remington showed his first sculptured group, the *Bronco Buster.* Kemeys was self-instructed and had studied his subjects at first hand; Remington, in his *Fallen Rider* and twenty-odd other bronzes, taught himself how to design movement in three dimensions from the tail of a pony to the foot of a thrown cowpuncher. The Remington statuettes, in their nervous, wiry strength and the brittle play of light on broken forms, drew an admiring essay from Theodore Roosevelt, who had also encouraged Kemeys.

It can be said of Hunt, Duveneck, and Homer, Eakins and Rimmer, the aging Ward, and the young Saint-Gaudens, that in an age of surfaces their minds were three-dimensional. They willingly paid a price for having centered minds in a centrifugal America. Zola would have called them what he called the best among his contemporaries, "Makers of men and not artificers of shadows."

CHAPTER 22 / ARCHITECTS WITH AN IDEA

An original creation is more difficult for the architect than for the painter or the sculptor, for he must in some degree accommodate himself to what others expect; and the pressure of time, the marshaling of a troop of assistants, and the concern with purely practical problems leave him small margin of time for philosophizing. His delegation of work to others dilutes his own idea, and the always-present evidence of how other men have built tempts him to facile borrowing.

That borrowing in the eighteen seventies had reached a point which left the debtor's solvency in doubt. Van Brunt had said that the solution of the architect's problems lay in principles, not forms, and Schuyler saw the beginnings of a national style not in eastern scholarship but in western exuberance. But one had to penetrate many layers of habit to find principles, and it needed more than exuberance to escape misconceptions which had the prestige of centuries behind them. Young architects were now emerging from the Beaux-Arts or from its American equivalents with an eye and a hand superbly trained but with a mind which confused means with ends.

Long ago, Horatio Greenough had scorned the "cumbrous machinery and mill-horse discipline" of the academies and their "cold reception of all attempts to invent." From his deathbed in 1852 he had suggested one way out of the eclectic-academic impasse: to observe the plant, the animal, or the man-made object whose shapes and proportions had been determined by the work to be done. Architecture's initial downward step had been its introduction of the first inorganic, nonfunctional element. Was nakedness, then, the alternative to false embellishment? "In nakedness I behold the majesty of the essential instead of the trappings of pretension."

Five years after Greenough died a German-American engineer named John Roebling proposed to join New York and Brooklyn with a span half as wide again as any that had yet been built, and Greenough would have seen in the Brooklyn Bridge the majesty of the essential. Suspension bridges were no new thing when this maker of iron, wire, and cable constructed them on the Allegheny and the Monongahela, the Delaware, the Ohio, and the Niagara; but his were longer and stronger than any others. Now he promised to carry eighteen thousand tons on four bundles of steel wires slung from two stone towers and anchored in the earth at both ends. "As a great work of art, and as a successful specimen of advanced bridge engineering," he wrote, "this structure will forever testify to the energy, enterprise and wealth of that community which shall secure its erection."

Twenty-six years later, on May twenty-fourth in 1883, the guns at Castle William and the Trinity Church bells announced that President Arthur and Governor Cleveland had opened the Brooklyn Bridge. More than twenty workmen had lost their lives in its construction, and Roebling himself had crushed his foot and died of lockjaw in 1861, leaving his son Washington Augustus Roebling to complete the project. Seventy-eight feet under water, the sandhogs faced deafness, pneumonia, and the "bends," the hazards of flood, fire, and explosion, as the caisson for the New York pier went down. Both towers stood complete in the Centennial year, higher than anything in New York except Trinity's steeple, when the first wire was sent across from one anchorage to the other. Funds gave out, wires proved defective, newspapers charged the builders with fraud, and the younger Roebling himself caught the caisson disease; yet day after day, year in and year out, the steel threads were spun back and forth until the great cables, with nearly six thousand wires in each of them, were

Brooklyn Bridge, Currier and Ives lithograph

Library of Congress

ready to receive their load. Swinging in boatswains' chairs high above the river craft, riggers lashed the stays and suspenders from which the roadway would depend, while Washington Roebling, paralyzed and growing deaf and blind, watched its completion through field glasses from a window in Brooklyn.

"Sound building is beautiful building," D. B. Steinman says in his book about the Roeblings. "Between the two pierced granite towers the arching roadway slowly sweeps upward to meet the swift downward sweep of the cables. These curves and proportions were not accidents." To Montgomery Schuyler, writing in the year of its completion, that aerial bow was as perfect as an organism of nature. Only in its towers, he said, had Roebling's "artistic" sense led him to contradict or conceal what he was doing and to forget that "the function of an organism, in art as in nature, must determine its form."

One could easily oversimplify this word "function," for the work of art is no sheer mechanism. It has been shaped by man's imagination and his will, not only as an instrument for need but as a symbol of his values and beliefs. Architectural greatness lies not alone in the strict correspondence of each shape to each necessity but in the synthesis of the form and the idea which resolves their contradiction. That truth, or something like it, was working in the minds of Henry Hobson Richardson, John Wellborn Root, and Louis Henry Sullivan, each of whom meted and measured, in Whitman's phrase, for today and here. It was New World vigor, not feudalism in stone, that distinguished Richardson; John Root rolled up his sleeves in Chicago before the ashes of her great fire were cold and saw a nobler and more honest city rising from the ruins despite the "numbskulls" and "fossils" among his colleagues. And Sullivan, whose god was Whitman, spent his life in discovering "groups, unities, appropriate to the modern, the democratic, the west."

The work of these three was no more diverse than their personalities: Richardson was the child of a well-to-do Louisiana family, with a Harvard education, a membership in the exclusive Porcellian Club, and a vast appetite for good living; Root was of old Connecticut Valley stock and found as much poetry and as great a stimulus to his fantasy in the nebular hypothesis of Laplace as in the Wagner and Schubert which he played in Chicago parlors; the philosopher-mystic Sullivan was the child of a Swiss woman who loved music and an improvident Irishman who taught dancing in Boston.

All three had known the "mill-horse discipline" of which Greenough spoke—Richardson at the Beaux-Arts in the war years, Root in the engineering class at New York University, and Sullivan in William Ware's cut-and-dried course at Massachusetts Institute of Technology, where a style was a style and an order was an order.

Richardson's escape was his work for Théodore Labrouste, whose brother Henri had made architectural history with the terra-cotta vaults and metal piers of the Bibliothèque Nationale. The great hospital at Ivry was fortunately no academic project, and it taught Richardson how to plan with originality and how to think of a building as a related group of large space-enclosing solids. When Root was not busy with mathematics, he indulged his prodigious imagination and his thirst for color by sketching impossible buildings for the sheer fun of it. His quick mind absorbed in a year or so all that the Gothic Renwick or the uninspired John Snook could teach him; and by the time he was twenty he could build a complex elevation on a sheet of brown paper with amazing swiftness and accuracy. Sullivan's antidote for Ware's stylistic dosage he shortly found in the Philadelphia draughting room of Frank Furness, a recklessly eclectic designer who could swear as fluently as he could draw.

They were readier than most men to commit blunders. Richardson's Worcester High School was a mistake in brick, with its uncouth bulk and pinched-looking tower. Root's early houses "jumped and howled," in his own phrase, as noisily as did other men's Queen Anne; and Sullivan's Chicago Loop façades were garrulous with bulging bays and florid incrustations. Yet these were the evidence of the courage and originality they had in common. Richardson was once quoted as saying that, before he died, he wanted to design a grain elevator and a Mississippi steamboat; and his canary-colored vest and his monk's cowl were all of a piece with the flamboyant dandyism of Sullivan's early years and with Root's departure from the cornerstone ceremonies of his Temperance Building to get a drink. Boston had never seen anything like the trumpeting angels on the tower of Richardson's Brattle Square Church. Root's Monadnock was described by Sullivan as an "amazing cliff of brickwork" rising sheer and stark with a singleness of purpose that gave one the thrill of romance. As for Sullivan, Chicago would not believe that his Auditorium tower, which weighed thirty million pounds, could float on a metal and concrete raft.

The partners and assistants of these men complemented their own abilities. Charles Gambrill left George B. Post to join Richardson, relieving him of much administrative detail, and in their studio for a few years worked Charles McKim and Stanford White, whose fluent draughtsmanship had its effect on the details of several of the firm's buildings. Shrewd Daniel Burnham was the sturdy tree, as Harriet Monroe once said, around which played the lightning of Root's mind; and he could draw up the plan of a building as competently as he organized a *soirée* for future clients. Sullivan's co-worker was the stocky, bearded Dankmar Adler with kindly, sensitive eyes behind his spectacles, with a gift for solving the unsolvable in building problems, and with enough imagination to discern the genius of Sullivan and take the second place. When the Auditorium was being designed in 1887 an eighteen-year-old joined the firm, and it was discovered that Frank Lloyd Wright could translate Sullivan's intention more faithfully than could any other draughtsman.

There has been some misunderstanding of what these extraordinary men gave to American architecture. Richardson has been pigeonholed as a revivalist of the Romanesque, yet his inspiration and his force derived from a deeper source. He was a child of the age of masonry, and he used masonry to symbolize the strength and self-reliance which were in his grain and in the American grain. The outline of his buildings was bold against the sky; their monumentality was of the whole, and the carved decorations which he designed in the seventies, before his details had to be parceled out to others, were crisply and boldly naturalistic. He was a craftsman who responded to the texture of brick and the color of sandstone as he responded to food and drink. In Springfield he built with the near-by Longmeadow stone and Monson granite, in Hartford with brownstone, at Harvard with traditional brick, and at Newport with shingles.

Richardson cribbed as other men did—from the English magazines, from the French *Croquis d'Atelier,* from photographs of Arles, Pisa, and Ravenna, and from Revoil's treatise on the Romanesque of southern France. Only a man with enormous digestive powers could successfully have built the Palazzo Vecchio tower into the Hampden County Courthouse. Others before him had revived the round arch; English publications were full of Victorian designs with doors and windows shaped to the half circle. James Renwick's Church of the Puritans in Union Square had been "Romanesque," and both Leopold Eidlitz and Paul Schulze had spoken a Germanic-Romanesque dialect. Richardson simply found in pre-Gothic building the general qualities which reinforced his own, and he left behind him no vocabulary which any man could speak with his conviction. His life and his work were not a system but a demonstration.

The sprightly Root was no more a philosopher than Richardson, nor had he the slightest respect for the so-called historic styles. Their very names, he once declared, were obsolete, and he proposed new ones: the Victorian should be called the Cathartic; the Romanesque, the Dropsical; the Queen Anne with its wens, carbuncles, and ringworms he rechristened the Tubercular Style. Root had absorbed enough science to love problems in pure engineering, and he regretted the divorce of scientific and aesthetic thinking. Science, he believed, could teach architects how to use color, and he preferred the decorative pattern which sunshine and shadow gave a building to what the builder could design: "A broad wall surface should fairly cry out for an ornament before it gets one." But Root was no mechanist, for he maintained that "reason should lead the way . . . and imagination take wings from a height to which reason has already climbed." His virility shocked the decorous Easterner and was noticeable even in Chicago.

Aggressive was hardly the word for Sullivan, whose mind, more given to speculation than Root's or Richardson's, went back beyond the first false step in architectural history and reconsidered the whole matter. The results were to be seen in his buildings or studied in his essays, for he had the gift of words as well as of forms and colors. His ornament in terra cotta, inspired by Gray's *Botany* and his own imagination, was something new in the world, and proclaimed him a master designer. Sullivan believed that the solution of every problem was contained within itself. But he never saw a problem as structural alone or utilitarian; and his famous phrase, "Form follows function," has misled as many people as Cézanne's remark that all nature is composed of geometrical units. His biographer Hugh Morrison has come nearest to what he meant by function: "The expression of an emotional synthesis of practical conditions."

Such men as these deserve to be judged by their best; and if one's purpose is to measure their integrity and originality against the confusion and conformity of the majority of their fellows, one must survey their master works.

As early as the mid-seventies a new space conception was to be seen in the interior of Trinity Church and the Senate Room of the Albany capitol, the work of Richardson and his assistants. The squat bulk of Trinity, built with Milford granite and Longmeadow stone in bold contrasting colors, the massive central tower and the separate parish house linked to the church by a cloistered colonnade—these were the evidence of the robust ordering mind of Richardson rather than White's adaptation of the Salamanca details on the tower, or the Romanesque ornaments derived, no doubt, from Revoil's *Architecture Romane du Midi de la France,* or the perfunctory scheme for the porch which is by other hands than his.

The Trinity interior spaces which the central plan made possible still have some of the breadth and richness which he intended, despite the fact that his powerful trussed wooden ceiling became a barrel-shaped vault which concealed the roof angles and the great arches supporting the tower. John La Farge was persuaded to

Henry H. Richardson, Trinity Church, Boston, Mass.

American Architect and Building News

direct the decorations, assisted by Saint-Gaudens, Frank Millet, George Maynard, Francis Lathrop, and others. With only four months to complete their work and with no plans or measurements for the spaces to be filled, the corps achieved a magnificent design in which painted angels and splendid stained glass played their full part against the dark beams and the rich gold, orange, and green-blue of the plaster. If one ignores later intrusions, one finds this dim interior, as Professor Hitchcock has remarked, "not altogether unworthy of comparison with St. Mark's."

A year after Trinity's completion Richardson planned the Albany Senate as a harmony of pink-gray marble, mahogany, and contrasting stones of many hues—the golden-colored onyx of Mexico, the yellow Siena marble, the polished red granite. Above the embossed and gilded patterns of its upper walls was a superb oak ceiling whose beams rested upon marble corbels. The great open arches behind which the galleries were built had weight and dignity, and the two fireplaces, had their carving been completed, would have been as richly original as their stone and wooden setting.

In 1879, a year after the first design for the Albany interior, Adler and Sullivan in Chicago built their first office building on a corner lot eighty feet by ninety. Its exterior revealed the experimental nature of its construction. These were the years when commercial buildings grew from a five- to a twenty-five-story height, and the more timid designers labored to conceal that fact. On the Aristotelian principle of the beginning, the middle, and the end, or the analogy of the classical column with its base, shaft, and capital, they devised a triple horizontal phrasing for their walls; or if the cellular character of the tall structure became obvious the architect apologized by placing a trellis of pilasters and horizontal bands over the whole. Some men designed a many-storied base with colonnades, which looked like a complete building with another riding on its back. A sculptured giant seemed to be trying to carry George B. Post's St. Paul Building on his shoulders; the Washington Life Building rose bold and clean, only to have a small French château capping its summit.

The Borden Block only hinted at the three-in-one theory and paid no lip service to the masonry tradition of the continuous stone foundation and the uniformly solid wall. One saw the thicker piers rise with a minimum of interruption from sidewalk to cornice, and in the bays between them a lighter and obviously thinner wall with carved stone panels above and below the windows whose flat ornamentation preserved the continuous rising plane. Above the last window, half-round panels and a slightly projecting cornice quietly terminated this vertical rhythm. Stone and cast iron were here used with a new intelligence and a fresh visual sense of what their use implied.

In the year 1880 the designer of Trinity created three masterpieces, each a brilliant solution of a problem which was perceived to require its own forms: a library, a seashore residence, and a railway station. The Crane Memorial Library at Quincy has the same utter simplicity, the same ability to use a given material up to its maximum of weight, texture, and structural power and no more, that one finds in its ancient neighbor, the granite "Stone Temple" of Alexander Parris. Its longitudinal mass is of gray stone and its roof is unbroken except by the gable over the entrance and the curious eyebrow-shaped dormers. The sandstone trim breaks this mass and expresses the interior spaces—the long unbroken range of windows which light the stacks, the bands of reddish stone which speak of the floor and ceiling divisions within, the great vertical group of openings for the reading room, the round stair turret. These phrasings-within-the-sentence are the authentic Richardson speech, not the "Romanesque" triple windows in the gable or the yawning entrance arch below. La Farge enriched the structure with small stained-glass windows whose pattern dispensed with heavy lead tracery and was fused by a cloisonné method of his own devising.

When Quincy outgrew the original library a wing was added in the spirit of conscientious imitation. It stands as negative proof of Richardson's gift for composing and his sure touch with materials. The first library is beautifully proportioned, its seeming irregularity of windows and doors superbly under control. The modern addition, linked to the original by a short arcaded passage, is a forgery which manages to make the same granite and sandstone look flimsy. The robust parent trails anemic offspring.

Henry H. Richardson, Crane Library, Quincy, Mass.

Wayne Andrews photo

Richardson's Bryant house at Cohasset improved upon his William Watts Sherman residence at Newport, built five years earlier, and was a preparation for the more masterly Stoughton house in Cambridge. Concise and well integrated, the over-all plan of the Sherman house is Richardson's own; its stone and shingle exterior has his rugged unity, despite the traces of Queen Anne half-timbering, and its interiors display the facility of Stanford White. At Cohasset Richardson achieved a unity of scale and sloping planes, a linked continuity and a fine texture of stone and shingle. Here was a direct solution of a problem in living by a designer who had seen the old shingled American homes and who recalled the beauty which sun and rain had given them.

At Auburndale the Boston and Albany Station was the first of many which Richardson and his successors did. Earlier men had designed stations whose wooden tracery and stone machicolations were more appropriate to the age of King Arthur and Charlemagne than to the age of Huntington and Pullman. Twenty years before Richardson one sees Henry Holly groping toward a more reasonable solution with an extremely fancy drawing which includes canopies and a bridge across the tracks. The Auburndale structure had no shape or detail extraneous to the work it had to do, being a

Henry H. Richardson, Marshall Field Wholesale Store, Chicago, Ill.

Inland Architect and News Record

simple stone box with a red tile roof extending to cover a porch for passengers, a projecting bay for the station-master, and a covered carriage entrance on three-branched wooden posts. These, and the rather bleak wooden interior, are simple terms which other stations elaborated. The best of them had the terseness of which the master was capable; the rest varied a formula which his assistants understood but did not feel.

In the year of these three Richardsonian achievements, Burnham and Root's ten-story Montauk Building in Chicago began a series of what were called in those years tall buildings, among them the Rialto, the Phoenix, and the Rookery. The crispness of their ornamentation, the bold contrasts of their openings, the prevalent round arch, and the bluff stone textures confessed a debt to Richardson. The importance of the Montauk lay in the structural courage it embodied. To rid the basements of such buildings of the great masses of stone which had encumbered them on the pyramid principle of a greater mass supporting a lesser one, a new type of foundation was in order. Frederick Baumann had published in 1873 his *Theory of Isolated Pier Foundations,* in which a group of iron rails embedded in concrete formed a grillage beneath each basement pier. Peter B. Wight, in whose office Burnham and Root were trained, was their consultant for the Montauk, and Wight claimed that his experiments made possible the fireproof sheathing of tile which covered its iron frame, and the grill foundation which cleared its valuable spaces and carried Chicago one step closer to the skyscraper. The footings of the Rookery were rafts which floated in the Chicago mud, not on the bedrock a hundred feet below surface.

While Root tackled the problem of how to make a building stay upright, Richardson designed the Allegheny Court House group for Pittsburgh. "Here for

Louis Sullivan, Wainwright Building, St. Louis, Mo.

Inland Architect and News Record

once," as his biographer says, he "had the opportunity to be as massive as he desired and, at the same time, perfectly expressive of the purpose of the building." The jail, with its enormously tall and narrow openings, stands inside a blank wall whose strength and beauty depend entirely on the play of light over stone shapes, and whose round entrances are framed in voussoirs eight feet long. A chimney stack here becomes a work of art, not a plain stone cylinder. More formal is the spacing of windows on the courthouse, the sweeping arcade which frames the lesser forms in the courtyard. The square tower is Richardson's supreme achievement with this feature and as perfect a synthesis of volume with contributing forms as an American had designed.

The year 1885 was one of the most important in the country's architectural history, for in that year Chicago saw Richardson's Glessner house and Marshall Field Wholesale Store, and also the completion of Jenney's Home Insurance Building. The Glessner was a domestic variant on what people were beginning to call the "Romanesque," like the Gratwick home next year in Buffalo and the St. Louis house of W. H. Potter. Almost as fortresslike as the Pittsburgh group were the coarse granite walls and small windows of the Glessner design, and Montgomery Schuyler recoiled from a residence which raised doubt whether stone walls do not a prison make.

The Marshall Field Wholesale Store was but seven stories high, and it is said that Richardson learned some of its construction methods from John Root. It was built around a central court and, with the exception of a few metal floor beams and interior piers, was solidly of sandstone; its "ornament" consisted in the size and placing of the stones themselves and the sequence from the round arched bays of the lower to the doubling of the upper stories and the quadrupling above that. As

Burnham and Root, Monadnock Building, Chicago, Ill.

Chicago Architectural Photographing Co.

Montgomery Schuyler said, simplicity could go no further.

By the time the Field Building was completed, Richardson was dead, and Chicago, by a series of experiments and calculations, had "invented" the skyscraper. Sooner or later, it was inevitable that the use of metal in the foundations and interiors of buildings would imply the further possibility of a structure whose armature should be wholly of metal with a covering veneer literally hung upon it. The electric elevator suggested, moreover, that structures of twenty-five or more stories were feasible. No man could take all the credit for the skyscraper, although Leroy S. Buffington spent years in presenting the claim that he was first to conceive it—a claim based on drawings whose dates were inaccurate. His was certainly one of the first minds to grasp the new possibility; but in the years 1884 and 1885 William Le Baron Jenney built the almost self-sufficient skeleton of the Home Insurance Building, whose masonry sheathing could have been even thinner had Jenney been sure that the daring principle would work; and in the years 1887 and 1888 the Tacoma Building by Holabird and Roche carried its exterior wholly upon its frame.

These two buildings were the first of their kind, and within a year or two other men were building skyscrapers; Bradford Gilbert gave the Tower Building to New York, and Burnham and Root the Rand McNally to Chicago. French engineers in 1889 achieved the great fifty-meter span of the Galerie des Machines for the Paris Exposition, which carried its own weight of iron and glass without benefit of crossties or buttresses; and what Giedion has said of this great work applies no less to the American skyscraper: both are "an unprecedented conquest of matter."

Sullivan's Wainwright Building in St. Louis, begun in 1890, was the noblest among these pioneers. Jenney's crucial design had been revolutionary in structure only, and its visible details were a quotation from Richardson. The New York Life Insurance Building by McKim, Mead, and White in Kansas City, whose building coincided with the Wainwright, merely provided larger fields for the surface play of Italian Renaissance ornament. The Wainwright has no style; it *is* style. One does not read on its face of red granite, brick, and sandstone a word-for-word description of how it was constructed; rather, one finds a superb expression of the lightness and loftiness which were new qualities in experience and which asked for new forms. The corner piers spring unbroken from ground to roof, the terra-cotta panels play variations on the theme of conformity, the frieze and cornice say, "The whole stops here." Compared with such a synthesis, Burnham and Root's Woman's Temple of the same years seemed a display of surplus energy, the implications of its skeleton construction richly obscured by Queen Anne and Romanesque phrases, a French Gothic roof and dormers. Root's Monadnock, with its sixteen stories of solid masonry and its magnificent untroubled surfaces, was a worthier companion to the Wainwright.

Chicago in 1892, having produced a building type new to the world, was planning a World's Fair for Lake Michigan; Adler published his description of the mighty Auditorium; Sullivan designed the Wainwright tomb; and Frank Lloyd Wright, in his last year as their draughtsman, gave his own personal quality to the Charnley house.

The brilliant engineering of the Auditorium was Adler's, and the shape of the four splendid elliptical arches beneath which Patti sang the "Echo Song" at its dedication in 1889 had been determined by the laws of acoustics. The mechanisms of its theater were the last word in their kind, and the ornament which clothed its forms, in carved wood and molded plaster, mosaics, and wrought iron, was the flowering of Sullivan's imagination and that of his young pupil. From its tower, which rose nearly a hundred feet above the main block, the visitor Paul Bourget looked down on the city with its columns of smoke, its immense rumble, and its brick

Louis Sullivan, Wainwright Tomb, Saint Louis, Mo.

Wayne Andrews photo

and stone stacks rising like the islands of the Cyclades.

Sullivan's Wainwright tomb, the third of its kind, stood in St. Louis, a silent reproach to the garrulous commentaries upon death in all the American graveyards, and a symbol not only of death but of gracious and intelligent living. It was a block of smooth gray limestone broken only by bands of ornament along its vertical and horizontal edges and covered with a simple dome. Here and in the Getty tomb at Chicago one can take the full measure of Sullivan's decoration in its astonishing originality. It is neither the florid frosting which Stanford White provided in terra cotta, now available in many colors, nor the bleak geometrical outcropping which later men would prefer. Sullivan saw his ornament as the corollary of his structure, and said that its "organic fluency and plasticity" continued and completed the expression of his thought. The bands across the Wainwright and around the Getty arches derive, in the last analysis, from oak leaves and similar sources; seen at the proper distance, their origin dissolves in the play of light on intricate small forms, and Sullivan's poetry is enriched by metaphor.

The Charnley house has a double meaning, since it suggests how Sullivan's counterpoint had impressed itself on Wright, and at the same time hints at the younger man's coming mastery of form. It is of limestone below and yellow brick above, the smaller developing from the larger form, a superbly solid interlocking of the recessed middle block, the two ends, and the wooden projecting balcony above the doorway. Its dignity and beauty derive from the play of light and shadow over clean surfaces, and only its cornice and balcony are given decoration. Its character resumes all the best that had happened for twenty-odd years in those few architectural minds which one can call creative. Richardson's joy in the weight and tangibility of the materials is here, his decisive way with space-defining solids, and his unerring sense of where to place a window and in what proportion to its wall. In the play of its gray stone with yellow brick, of stained wood and greenish copper, there is a suggestion of the colorism which was Root's. But only the mature Sullivan and the twenty-three-year-old Wright would have dared in 1892 to imagine anything as supremely simple as the Charnley house.

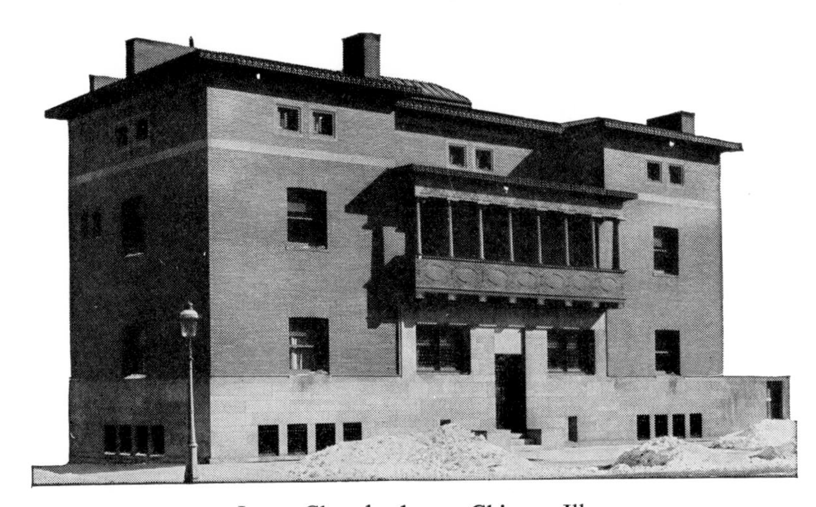

James Charnley house, Chicago, Ill.

Fuermann photo, Chicago Architectural Photographing Co.

Saint-Gaudens, *Diana* ▶

from a photo by DeWitt C. Ward

PART THREE

COSMOPOLITANS

INTRODUCTION / THE RENAISSANCE COMPLEX

In the decade which opened with the famous Vanderbilt ball of 1883 and closed with the Columbian Fair on Lake Michigan the United States grew wealthier by over twenty billions. The Goulds, the Vanderbilts, the Rockefellers, and the Carnegies moved, as Matthew Josephson has said, "upon the crest of an historic wave of 'centralization,' " and the great American fortunes, having been spectacularly made, were conspicuously spent. With the land, the railways, and the productive machinery of the nation in his control, the Yankee Croesus proceeded to the conquest of "society" and the dominance of "taste."

There were feasts at Delmonico's where seventy guests sat around a table in whose center was a thirty-foot artificial lake enclosed in a gold cage where swans sailed up and down. The picnics organized by Ward McAllister at Newport in the seventies were modest affairs in comparison with the next decades, when the budget for a single ball was one hundred thousand dollars.

Henry James protested that Newport's original sly sweetness had been "bedizened and bedevilled." James Gordon Bennett's villa, with great bronze owls on its gateposts, seemed relatively modest when Cornelius Vanderbilt remodeled The Breakers for three million dollars, Stuyvesant Fish seated two hundred guests in his "colonial" dining room, and Frederick Prince imported yellow Caen stone for his marble palace whose iron gates in the Louis XIV style kept fifty craftsmen busy for a year. The main hall of Richard Hunt's Ochre Court for Goelet went up several stories, and its gilded incrustations and painted ceiling recalled the Paris Opera. Hunt rebuilt The Breakers as a mammoth Italian villa with a loggia of mosaic and a double stairway wide enough for a railway station. And when the Vanderbilts commissioned him to design Biltmore for their estate at

Richard M. Hunt, "Biltmore," Asheville, N.C.

Wayne Andrews photo

Asheville in North Carolina, patron and architect toured the châteaux of France in search of inspiration, engaging hundreds of foreign artisans for the enterprise. In 1895 Hunt's great rambling castle faced the Great Smokies from the end of its formal lawn. It had been five years in the building, had cost three million dollars, and was the closest approximation Hunt ever achieved to his beloved models at Amboise and Chenonceaux.

While men of wealth lined Fifth Avenue with châteaux and Ocean Drive at Newport with huge structures which were "cottages" in name only, their countrymen enjoyed these glories at second hand in the de luxe picture books of Edward Strahan and George Sheldon. The former edited *Mr. Vanderbilt's Home and Collection,* a tour of that mansion in photogravures: the paintings of Bonnat and Meissonier, the more or less Pompeian atrium, the bronze replicas of Ghiberti's famous doors, a Japanese parlor where a temple gate had been metamorphosed into a chimney piece, and a gilded staircase with life-sized bronze females who wore jewels on their dresses and who supported crystal urns with gas lights.

The two handsome volumes of Sheldon's *Artistic Country Seats* reproduced one hundred achievements of the post-Centennial "Renaissance" with unctuous commentaries. Here and there among its plates could be seen an original mind working—in Richardson's Stoughton house at Cambridge, Massachusetts, for example. It was, however, the right wing of American architecture whose achievements were here celebrated: McKim's undernourished "Colonial," and his "old English" mansion for Joseph H. Choate at Stockbridge; the aggressively ugly estate of Spencer Trask at Saratoga Springs. Here was the Potter Palmer dining room in Chicago, of Santo Domingo mahogany with a frieze and ceiling which John Elliott had covered with cupids among grapevines. What eastern reader, noting Palmer's Venetian mosaic vestibule, the Cairo-inspired ebony and gold bedroom where Mrs. Palmer slept, and the Moorish sunken pool in which she bathed, could question the author's statement that, in the ten years since the Centennial, the man of wealth had consented to "act the Medicean part" in America?

The social setting for this act was an America where people waltzed to "After the Ball" and applauded Reginald de Koven's *Robin Hood* and Charles Hoyt's extravagant farces. Even pictorial satire had lost its sharp edge, and Charles Amos Mitchell founded *Life* in 1883 to domesticate, as he said, the casual cheerfulness drifting about in an unfriendly world. *Life* tried "not to be too sweet to live nor too good to be true," and its drawings were for a public which found *Puck's* humor cluttered and a little coarse. Both W. H. Hyde and Charles Dana Gibson imitated the drawing-room elegance of Du Maurier in the English *Punch,* and Gibson freed himself from the labored style of his beginnings. He mastered the economy of Phil May, his white becoming more rich and open, his pen lines more varied and supple. By 1890 he drew full-page cartoons whose old men and handsome youths were vigorously characterized, and his "Gibson girl" moved with a stately grace, complete from her sleek and heavy coiffure to the end of her lustrous satin train.

In this complacent atmosphere the middle class admired the palaces of the new Medici and easily forgot the manner in which their tenants' fortunes had been made, just as the clever portrait painters suppressed a predatory jowl and mitigated the nose of Morgan. The generals of finance and industry were described as connoisseurs; yet few of "nature's noblemen" had ever acquired more than an elementary education. They were hard-grained and tiresome people of whom Charles Francis Adams said, "Not one that I have ever known would I care to meet again in this world or the next"; and artistic sensitiveness was not among their virtues. The taste of William Vanderbilt was implied by Henry Clews' remark: "He was equal to the task of grasping all the material essentials from a common sense point of view."

It required three nights in 1887 to dispose of the two hundred or more canvases which A. T. Stewart had gathered for his Fifth Avenue palace. A *Niagara* by F. E. Church was knocked down for $7,050, a Daubigny for $7,900, a Fortuny for slightly over $10,000. Gérôme's *Chariot Race* brought more than $7,000, his *Pollice Verso* $11,000. Jay Gould was there to be outbid by Knoedler and Company on a Troyon cattle scene but to capture a worthless *Children's Party* by Knauss for $21,300. The climax came when Meissonier's *1807* was placed on the auctioneer's table and the whole audience rose to its feet. Stewart, it was said, had bought it by telegraph from the painter for a price between $60,000 and $75,000; now its thirty-six square feet of mediocrity went to Judge Hilton for $66,000. The rest was anticlimax, when a "Rembrandt" head was sold for the suspiciously low sum of $400, and a "Titian" madonna for twice that amount. After the canvases came the French and Oriental porcelains, the ruby glass, the innumerable bronze statuettes, and the replica of Powers' *Greek Slave* on a green-and-rose marble pedestal with a revolving top. Thus, to the tune of over half a million dollars, was the taste of the dead millionaire revealed.

The living plutocrat, however, was more sophisticated; and when he discarded his earlier treasures and raided Europe for old masters under the guidance of hired experts, the public forgot his artistic indiscretions as easily as his ethical ones. Morgan paid one hundred thousand dollars for a Vermeer. Frick, who had once bought two small Corots reluctantly under pressure from his friends, was heard to remark that "railroads are the Rembrandts of investment"; and soon his boudoir was paneled with Fragonards and his rooms held Rubens, Hals and Goya, Holbein and Bellini.

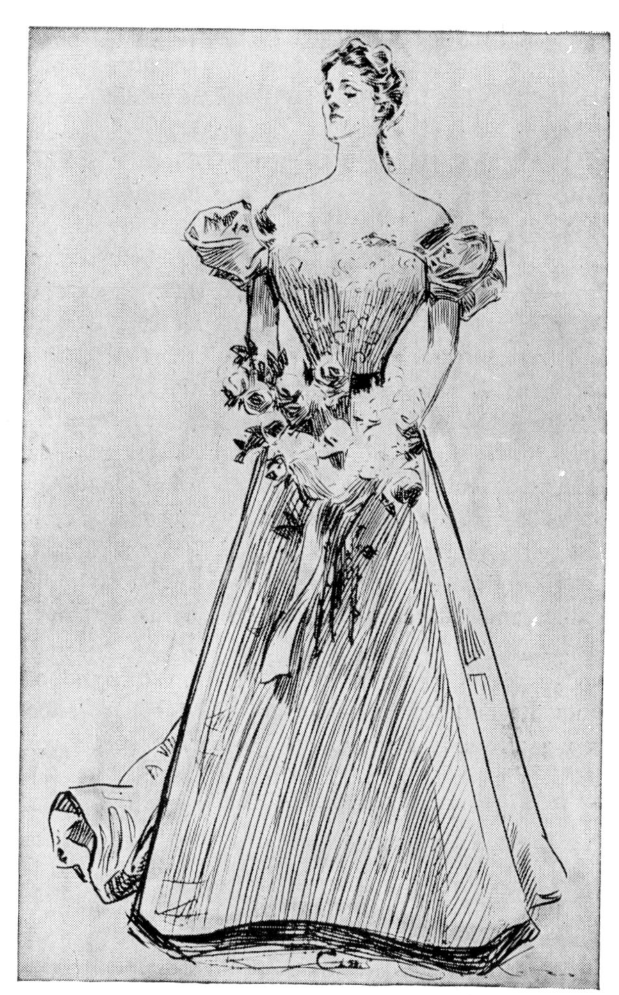

The Gibson Girl

Pen drawing by Charles Dana Gibson

Small wonder that 1880 was compared to 1480, and the Morgans to the Medici. One writer frankly declared that only the forms of patronage had changed: the artist has to live, the rich man's intellect to be nourished, and "the gratification of the latter provides for the physical needs of the former." The parallel weakened, to be sure, when one tried to imagine the picnic master Ward McAllister designing a pageant for Lorenzo the Magnificent; yet a Renaissance complex was developing in many American minds. Burckhardt's study of that age had been familiar since 1860, Pater and Symonds wrote their charming accounts of it in the seventies, and scholars like Jarves, Norton, and Perkins caused the age to live again. *Century* readers in 1890 admired Timothy Cole's engravings of Filippino Lippi and

Botticelli in W. J. Stillman's articles on the Italian masters, and before 1900 Bernhard Berenson published the first of his brilliant essays on the Renaissance painters.

Thus stimulated, several men of talent in architecture, painting, and sculpture saw in themselves a reincarnation of the grace, energy, and fertility which Rome and Florence had once known. Abbott Thayer wrote to Cortissoz, "You and I are Mantegnas and Gozzolis, not Yankees." From the Florentines, George de Forest Brush learned how to paint his American madonnas. Henry Adams described Saint-Gaudens as a child of Cellini "smothered in an American cradle." The brusque forms of quattrocento palaces rose on Madison Avenue, the Vatican murals were quoted on the walls of the better clubs, and Verrocchio's angels fluttered within a few blocks of Washington Square. American decorators marshaled Parnassus on vault and ceiling, and Thayer painted wings on his wife and children.

One useful lesson was drawn from the age of Bramante and Raphael—the notion of collaboration among artists in a group enterprise. Trinity Church had demonstrated the value of this notion, and the following years saw more frequent efforts of the kind—D. Maitland Armstrong's mosaics for the wainscot under a La Farge mural, Stanford White's pedestals for Saint-Gaudens' statues and his picture frames for Thayer, the ceiling decorations of Dewing and Abbey for McKim's Imperial Hotel.

In these delightful exchanges the firm of McKim, Mead, and White led all the rest in urbanity and sophistication. Charles Follen McKim's reticence and his austerity dominated the partnership he formed in 1879, and a Boston friend compared this gentleman, scholar, and lover of music to the famous Alberti. McKim had worked four years with Richardson, then traveled and sketched in Europe; he knew every least detail of the villas and palaces of Rome and Tuscany, and would later persuade Morgan and Walters to provide funds for establishing the American Academy in Rome. It was largely due to McKim that his firm's buildings were praised for an "air of distinguished breeding."

William Rutherford Mead, the levelheaded Vermonter, was a counterbalance to the exuberant Stanford White, whose Calvinist ancestors arrived in America in 1632. Young White, with bristling red hair and mustache, was never mistaken for a Calvinist. For six years in Richardson's office he had shown himself a prodigal designer of easygoing decoration which was complex, fluently graceful, and cleverly derivative. White's bustling figure in swallowtail and knee breeches was to be found in the newspaper cuts of all the important balls and banquets; yet he found time to design yachts and Pullman cars, a Renaissance directors' room for the New York Life Insurance Company, a dining room à la Henry II for the James Stillman house, an alphabet for Saint-Gaudens' inscriptions, and a thoroughly Renaissance cover for *Century Magazine*. If McKim was Alberti, then White's appetite for living and even his sensational murder by the jealous Harry Thaw were a Manhattan version of Cellini.

The domestic work of McKim, Mead, and White in the 1880's continued to adapt the Colonial, and there was English half-timbered charm in their Newport Casino, a touch of Richardsonian informality and ruggedness in their work at Narragansett Pier. Perhaps, as Professor Hitchcock suggests, out of such experiment might have come a national consistency of style; but the Villard houses had only the consistency of historic precedent. Joseph M. Wells, a draughtsman for the firm, had fallen in love with Bramante. In White's absence from New York in 1882 the Villard design was given to Wells, and the Cancelleria Palace became, with modifications, the home of the prince of railroads. Out of Paul Marie Létarouilly's *Édifices de Rome Moderne* came the elevation and the balconies for Villard, and White's elaborately gracious interiors contrasted with the cold elegance and dry correctness of the group, four individual homes connected in U-shape. Henceforth the McKim gods would be Bramante and Peruzzi, Alberti and San Gallo.

When architects with a Renaissance complex needed murals, reliefs, and stained glass, they called upon John La Farge and Augustus Saint-Gaudens, both of whom were familiar figures in McKim's reception room and in Century Club gatherings. The father of La Farge had been a distinguished member of the *émigré* colony in New York and his great-uncle in Paris knew every artist, writer, and politician in the Second Empire. John himself was a learned cosmopolitan as thoroughly at home in the Boulevard Saint-Germain as in Washington Square or Newport, and he had a fifteenth-century Italian's zest for experiment. Among all of Henry Adams' friends, his was the most complex mind, and his conversation, Henry said, was opaline "with infinite shades and refractions of light."

La Farge could make illustrations which, like his early *Wolf Charmer*, combined strength of drawing with imaginative invention. His head of *Saint John* had the firmness and breadth he had learned from Couture and Hunt; and his *Centauress* of 1887 evoked a Golden Age which was no pale myth in the artist's mind but a world of somber groves and iridescent fountains where luminous gods and creatures moved (Brooklyn Mus.). When it was painted La Farge was best known as a

John La Farge, *Bridle Path, Tahiti,* water color

Fogg Museum of Art, Harvard University, Cambridge, Mass.

master decorator. His were the lunettes of *Music* and *Drama* for the music room of Whitelaw Reid, the three windows, each three stories high, for the stairway of William H. Vanderbilt, the carved and inlaid panels which he designed and Saint-Gaudens wrought in mahogany, ivory, marble, silver, coral, and mother-of-pearl.

One of the solvents at work in the mural painting of the period was a fallacious notion of the "decorative," the notion that forms had to be drained of their volumes and reduced to anemic two dimensions to serve the mural painter. Ignoring the Humanist motivations of their favorite Italians, the decorators made themselves subordinate to the architects and attempted merely to add a grace to structure. The Frenchman Puvis de Chavannes was a master in this mode, and his allegories in pale delightful colors matched the cool rectitude of neoclassical buildings in Paris. Hence the windy generalizations on American walls, the whittling down of space and volume, the discreet color, and the obvious symmetries of composition.

La Farge, like so many of his contemporaries, drew upon memories of the past for what Henry James called "artful evasions of the actual"; but his visions were more concrete than most, and the figures of his *Ascension* mural in the late eighties for the church of that name in New York had a more bodily existence and a more plangent color than the bloodless nonentities of Puvis. They were assembled in the Vatican manner of Raphael, but their blue-purple mountain background had first been seen by the painter in Japan.

The colorist in La Farge found expression in the finest stained glass that America had seen. He was not the only artist to experiment with this medium; Louis Comfort Tiffany applied a sense of color learned from Inness to the products of the Tiffany Glass and Decorat-

Augustus Saint-Gaudens, Sherman Monument, New York City

Bogart Studio photo

ing Company and produced exquisite lamp shades and vases of a type known as "Favrile." La Farge was more resourceful and instead of entrusting his designs to other craftsmen as the Pre-Raphaelites did, he built his own panels, allowing the material to modify his paper plan—"a painting with glass by an artist with glass." He used not only "pot metal" glass which is colored throughout while molten, but material to which a color film had been fused with heat, and glass in several thicknesses with smooth or wrinkled surfaces. He invented a glass which was opalescent. His church windows were "magnificent gems," in the phrase of James, and in his panels for private houses white peonies gleamed against blue and peacocks spread their glittering tails against the light.

In his late fifties, La Farge looked forward with no pleasure at all to "that civilized life which is to surround my few remaining years." He had brought back from his South Sea travels with Adams the finest work of his life—a series of water colors of the "rustic and Boeotian antiquity" which he had found in Tahiti. Here were figures with the burnished nobility of ancient bronze against seas as blue as the Aegean. Here the whaler, the missionary, and the beachcomber could see beauties which the civilized would find only in Virgil and Homer. When the two pilgrims met Mataafa, chief of chiefs at Samoa, Henry Adams remarked, "La Farge, at last we have met a gentleman." It was a final commentary on the painter that his most brilliant work, his fullest form, his most splendid color, his most original groups and rhythms were inspired by a Polynesian culture which he believed would soon disappear forever.

The sculptor Saint-Gaudens, that "survival of the 1500" was also in the habit of making strategic retreats into the past. When Adams stood with him before Amiens Cathedral, its Virgin was for the former a channel of force, for the latter a channel of taste. Saint-Gaudens felt the dignity, unity, and scale of the edifice, its lights, lines, and shadows, more deeply than Gibbon or Ruskin, "but he was even less conscious than they," Adams observed, "of the force that created it all." His *Farragut* and his *Lincoln* revealed a sturdy and sensitive naturalism; his *Grief* for the grave of Adams' wife in Rock Creek Cemetery, Washington, was an inscrutable hooded figure. When laymen could find no specific meaning in the *Grief* and clergymen suspected it of atheistic denial, Adams himself wrote that it embodied the oldest idea known to human thought.

Saint-Gaudens' low reliefs had the exquisite delicacy and fluent grace if not the subtlety of his admired Florentines, but the playful angel musicians which he designed for the Morgans' tomb were less at home than in Florence, and Stanford White urged him to explain them tactfully to those "bluenosed Presbyterians." And when the sculptor sought inspiration for the angels on the reredos in St. Thomas' Church, to be cast in cement and tinted by Will H. Low, La Farge advised him that "any medieval sculpture or Renaissance (not a late one) or painting of the early time (Italian) gives the type that will be needed to be neither high nor low church." This was a far cry from the conviction and belief which created the angels of Lincoln Cathedral. It was the Saint-Gaudens of reassuring precedents who placed a Greek chair behind his Chicago Lincoln. When people criticized the flying Victory above the splendidly modeled Negro heads in the Shaw Memorial in Boston he explained that the Greeks and Romans had done that sort of thing in their monuments. If the *Sherman* bronze was gilded, so had been *Marcus Aurelius* on the Capitoline.

Sherman sat to the sculptor for a portrait bust in 1888, and Saint-Gaudens modeled his chunky head, aggressive nose, and grizzled jaw with the force of a Renaissance master. The equestrian Sherman was commissioned in 1892, and for eleven years the sculptor worked and worried over its details. Its nervous textures suggest that Rodin's *Burghers of Calais* had impressed the American; the crispness of its contrasts indicates that he knew his game was with light, although he nearly lost that game in the deep concavities of his drapery. Horse, rider, and companion unite to create a rhythm which is almost musical—the movement of Mozart rather than of Beethoven. One thinks of the great Renaissance horsemen at Venice and Padua, concluding that the *Sherman* lacks their muscular surge, their density, and their sense of the hard bronze surface.

The new collaboration — McKim's scholarly reticence, White's fluency of detail, and the lyricism of Saint-Gaudens—found complete expression in Madison Square Garden and the Boston Public Library, the former in 1890, the latter between 1887 and 1895. The Garden stood at the northeast corner of Madison Square, on the site of the old Union Station and afterward of Barnum's Hippodrome; it was an obviously festive structure at whose dedication Eduard Strauss conducted Viennese waltzes. The building contained offices, restaurants, supper rooms, a concert hall, and a great amphitheater where twelve thousand New Yorkers could see pageants, national conventions, flower and dog and horse shows.

Like the Chicago Auditorium, the Garden was a great brick block with a tower, but there the resemblance ended. Stanford White had frosted his architectural cake with overblown ornament in white terra cotta. There were eight graceful turrets on its corners at the level of the roof garden, and above them rose White's tower, a variation on the Giralda at Seville; it held seven stories of bachelor suites and a café, and on its top, three hundred and fifty feet above the sidewalk, Saint-Gaudens' twenty-foot *Diana* pointed her bow and arrow into the wind. She was a hollow copper shell and, thanks to ball bearings, responded to the least puff of the breeze. By day she seemed a golden girl poised easily with a wisp of drapery billowing from her shoulders; at night the crescent moon on her head glowed with lights inside its prisms, and hidden floodlights outlined her nakedness against the sky.

The Boston Public Library, like all McKim's work, had to have prototypes, and no drawing could be done until one had leafed through photographs and the indispensable Létarouilly. Consulting the oracles over cigars and brandy, the assembled artists designed the long front with its round-arched bays and rusticated ground story. It reminded some people of Alberti's San Francesco Palace in Rimini; others recalled the Florentine façades; and no one who had seen Labrouste's Bibliothèque Ste-Geneviève could consider the design an original or a courageous one. The great branching irons which held its lanterns had presumably come from the Strozzi Palace, and the Cancelleria inspired its courtyard.

Masaccio and Tiepolo were studied before the library designers sent measurements of its yellow marble stair hall to Puvis de Chavannes, who was to paint its murals in his Paris studio. Saint-Gaudens' brother Louis modeled the two lions for the stairway, and Augustus himself did the three seals over the main entrance. His two groups for the terrace before the building—*Ex-*

McKim, Mead, & White, The Boston Public Library

Photo Hillyer Art Library, Northampton, Mass.

ecutive Power, Law, Love, Labor, Science, and *Art*—were never completed; the small studies which survive suggest that they would have added nothing to his reputation, but would have sat rather uneasily sunning themselves and staring across Copley Square at the rugged Trinity.

In the years to come, Sargent and Abbey would provide further decorations and Daniel French three pairs of graceful bronze doors; in the meantime, literary Boston was pleased with its library. To be sure, the great barrel-vaulted reading room was not the easiest place for reading; one could see the Holy Grail murals, which were Abbey's handsome oversized illustrations, only by electric light in a delivery room whose proportions suggested the unimportance of delivering books. One could stand above the marble staircases and read the ancient story of Aeschylus and of Virgil in the pale blues, wan flesh tones, and cautious browns of Puvis de Chavannes, even though this entrance area and the courtyard beyond it had been given so generous a portion of the total space that the more practical functions of the library had to be cramped around the outside of the hollow square.

Only once did the intelligentsia protest, to banish MacMonnies' naked *Bacchante* from the McKim courtyard, that "shameless exaltation of wine, women and song," as President Eliot described her. And when John Sargent attempted to record on the new walls the development of religious thought from paganism to Christianity, Abbey wrote reassuringly from England: "The Boston people need not be afraid that he will be eccentric or impressionistic or anything that is not perfectly serious and non-experimental when it comes to work of this kind."

The notion of artistic collaboration, of the public or private edifice as a joint effort, found in Boston its most complete expression; but Boston's rejection of the *Bacchante* and her insistence upon the nonexperimental were of the nineteenth century, not the fifteenth. They revealed a society in which, as Henry Adams said, "an American Virgin would never dare command; an American Venus would never dare exist."

CHAPTER 23 / THE MORE SMILING ASPECTS

When William Dean Howells wrote *Criticism and Fiction* he had steeped himself in the New England afterglow and had known delightful Indian summer days in Venice. Only when he came face to face with the city of New York did he turn, as Parrington says, "in the mid-afternoon of life . . . to the work of spreading the gospel of social democracy in the America of the Gilded Age." In his *A Traveler from Altruria* one glimpsed a world far different from the world of capitalist America in the nineties. The slums near Chatham Square shocked Howells, as they vaguely disturbed his March in *A Hazard of New Fortunes:* "The whole at moments seemed to him lawless, godless; the absence of intelligent, comprehensive purpose in the huge disorder." Only for a moment, for in the next paragraph March wondered why artists who loved Naples had not discovered the picturesqueness of Third Avenue slums.

Howells acknowledged in *Criticism and Fiction* that much writing of his time was done by men who had formed themselves not on life but upon old masters. Much fiction, he said, was conventional, complacent, and averse to the mass of men, consenting to know them only at second hand; and he praised Henry James for his refusal to spoon-feed the "nurselings of fable." But the optimist in Howells fought with the critic, and their compromise is evident in his assurance that the sins, suffering, and shame he sees about him are in the nature of things, and not peculiarly American. Here one breathes a "rarefied and nimble air full of shining possibilities and radiant promises." Howells concedes that the relation of class to class is changing for the worse; yet peculiar to the nation is "the large, cheerful average of health and success . . ." The novelist concerns himself, therefore, with "the more smiling aspects of life, which are the more American."

Two painters whose careers had begun together—Frank Duveneck and William M. Chase—responded differently to those smiling aspects, and the difference was in their paintings. They had both belonged to the Leibl group in Munich, and the *Head of a Man* by Chase was broadly brushed with the liveliness of Duveneck, though with a thinner medium (Albright Gall.). In Venice Duveneck produced etchings which were mistaken for the work of Whistler; in Paris the cold perfection of the Salon affected him, and his rich browns and olive flesh began to seem murky against the brighter palettes of the innovators. He never fully recovered from his wife's death in 1888, and his splendid vitality had begun to ebb when he came home at forty to paint and teach for thirty more years in Cincinnati. His pupil De Camp painted him aging into a corpulent man with stubby features and a mop of gray hair. When the painter was sixty-seven he presented a hundred of his pictures to the museum in Cincinnati, and it was possible to know the soundness of his craftsmanship and the male healthiness which John Root and Henry Richardson expressed in another medium.

The Chase alternative was an accommodation to prevailing tastes, a skillful appeal to eyes which took their pleasure in the handsome, the external, and the obvious. Twenty years after his Munich days he could still paint with the Munich sobriety and direct response to personality, as he proved with a portrait of his wife, the *Woman with a Shawl* (Pa. Acad.). But this man from Franklin, Indiana, was far too cheerful and too comfortable in this world to challenge the Philistines. He had an enormous zest for pigment and fed his stylistic appetite on a rich variety of foods.

Having discovered the Spaniards in 1881, Chase painted Frank Currier with a Spanish collar in the Velasquez manner; a few years later he met Whistler, and the pattern of *Miss Alexander* reappeared in his own *Alice* (Chicago Art Inst.). He dressed his children as Infantas; he went pleasantly decorative under the guidance of Japanese prints; the flicker of Fortuny's brush was in the two pictures of his Tenth Street studio, the sheen of satin, the gleam of antique wood, the luster of brocades, the crisp highlights on the bric-a-brac he never stopped collecting.

Chase walked Fifth Avenue with a white wolfhound on a leash, a dapper and distinguished figure with bristling mustache and beard, a carnation in his lapel, and a black ribbon on his monocle. For more than thirty years his students learned from him how to see with their own eyes, but they also heard him praise "the snapshot glance" and that mode of painting in which there is "no intermission between the hand and head." "Do not imagine that I would disregard the thing that lies beneath the mask," he assured them, "but . . . when the outside is rightly seen, the thing that lies under the surface will be found upon your canvas." Chase moved within a narrowing mental circle, more concerned with the life of the artist than with the serious aspects of the life around him. His dashing and

William M. Chase, *In the Studio*

Brooklyn Museum, New York City

elegant portrait of Whistler was a tribute to a man whose flamboyant artiness he admired. In the end, what Chase could paint most brilliantly was a shining pink-white fish on a table top beside a polished copper kettle. He was the Fortuny of the Tenth Street studio and the John Sargent of the English cod.

As for Sargent, he could hold his own with those immensely popular men, Munkácsy, Boldini, Menzel, and Alfred Stevens, and his *Madame Gautreau* amazed Paris with its suave simplifications, unconventional posture, and daringly simple color. This Florence-born American entered the studio of the clever Carolus-Duran when he was eighteen, and within a year or two made his master's work look dowdy. At twenty, Sargent's swift notation in grays and blacks of the rehearsing *Pasdeloup Orchestra* (Boston Mus. Fine Arts) was a brilliant tour de force; at twenty-three, the Whistlerian pattern of *Luxembourg Gardens at Twilight* was enlivened by a play of colored dresses and a suggestion of late day much fresher than Whistler (Minneapolis Inst. of Arts). And in 1881 and 1882 three paintings swept the doubters off their feet.

Sargent's *Lady with a Rose* was no wan silhouette but a grave and solid presentation of a lovely young woman in a black satin dress. To demonstrate another kind of prowess, he showed within a year his *El Jaleo* and his *Boit Children*. The Spanish dancer whirled in white skirts, while dimmer figures played castanets, guitars, and tambourines. Neither Boldini nor any other magician of the brush could so evoke the flashing moment: the twisting movement, the flash and crackle of white silk, and the flicker of shadow against the dingy whitewash (Fenway Court, Boston). Here was the "snapshot glance" of Chase and an even nimbler brush to record it. And although the Boit picture was a quieter one—a small child playing on a great rug, the older girls standing half in deep shadow — no painter of the time could so have managed the range between black stockings and starched white pinafores, the polish of high blue-and-white Chinese vases, the corner of a red screen. No wonder Henry James found in Sargent "the slightly 'uncanny' spectacle of a talent which on the very threshold of its career has nothing more to learn." (See color plate 14.)

There was much more to learn about man and his world after twenty-six had Sargent wished to learn, but Sargent had no time for deeper discoveries. The nervousness of the age was in this athlete of the brush,

John Sargent, *The Daughters of Edward D. Boit*

Museum of Fine Arts, Boston, Mass.

who could jump the highest visual hurdles without seeming strain. Beside a Sargent portrait, an Eakins head looks tired. The latter preferred as sitters the scientist, the scholar, or simply the ordinary man or woman; the former was at his best with the polished, the well turned, the mildly distinguished, and the obviously successful. One commentator said that in his work "one is conscious of being in good company." Critics compared Sargent to Velasquez, unaware that the *Boit Children* is a brilliant collection of visual fragments without the majestic articulation of forms in enclosing space that one finds in *Las Meniñas*. He was called the modern Rubens, though there was only a well-bred hint in his corseted ladies of the fleshy beauty which Rubens gladly avowed. He was nominated the Van Dyck of the Edwardians by men who could not differentiate between unshakable dignity and a brittle self-assurance.

Sargent was a descendant of Epes Sargent, whose gnarled hands Copley had painted five generations before, and he had Copley's "luxury of seeing." James might have asked in 1882 which was to be the ultimate Sargent—the sober naturalist of the *Lady with a Rose* or the flashy executant of *El Jaleo?* The answer was provided in the nineties by a Sargent who scurried from Hunt's château at Asheville to the Boston of Peabodys and Lodges, to the Players' Club of Edwin Booth, the London of Coventry Patmore, Ellen Terry, and Lord Ribblesdale, with excursions into Greece, Morocco, and the Holy Land to document his Biblical murals in the Boston Public Library. In spare moments he made swift notations in water color of fountains playing among Italian gardens, dark gondolas moving from shadowed bridges into the Venetian glare, the scarcely tolerable brilliance of sun on a quarry at Carrara, and the chill of Canadian lakes.

The intense blues of Sargent's Italian shadows and the flashing highlights of Chase on copper kettles gave more than a hint of the new ways with color and light which were called "impressionism." In the year 1880, most Americans were as reluctant to accept the new language as Frenchmen had been six years before at the famous Exhibition, and the art critic Benjamin expressed his mistrust of what he considered an effort to "paint the soul without the body." In *Harper's* a few years later Theodore Child accused the experimentalists of blurring their ignorance of drawing: "If you proclaim Claude Monet and Renoir to be masters in the art of painting, you must have thrown overboard forever Velasquez, Rembrandt and Titian." That stubborn Ruskinian Charles H. Moore characterized the movement in the *Atlantic Monthly* as a mistake destined to be short-lived; had not the Venetians proven for all time that form, color, and light and shade were all essential to the complete work of art?

It was Hamlin Garland who championed the impressionists in his *Crumbling Idols* of 1894. This was three years after Howells' essay on *Criticism and Fiction,* and Garland's fierce belief at thirty-four in "the mighty pivotal present" was a different thing from the tentative affirmations of Howells at fifty-four. Garland's stories had been rejected by the *Century* because their language was not that of the University Club; now he saw a new spirit invigorating Europe and he welcomed impressionism as the means by which a new age could depict itself. Garland defined its method as "a complete and of course momentary concept of the sense of sight; the stayed and reproduced effect of a single section of the world of color upon the eye." Here was a radical change in attitude toward the physical universe and an advance in man's perceptive power. Its painters had taught Garland, he said, to see colors everywhere. Inness, Corot, and Millet conceived too much and saw too little; they no longer represented the sunlight and shadow Garland saw. Let the American artists abandon the dull mists of the Lowlands and the North Sea and learn from the impressionists how to paint a June day in New England.

The men who were to lead the new movement in America had to modify previous methods before they could experiment with the new disintegrations. John Twachtman, Childe Hassam, and Theodore Robinson had acquired low tones and firm drawing in Munich and Paris before Hassam studied Monet's paintings of cliff and sea at Pourville and Etretat, and Twachtman discovered he could learn more in Paris than from Loefftz. Robinson set up his easel at Giverny beside that of Monet; Abbott Thayer returned from France obsessed with the color problem. The palette of Maurice Prendergast, sober with the grays of the Normandy coast near Dinard and St. Malo, became brilliant with the whites, reds, blues, and greens of the Revere Beach crowds and the children playing in Central Park. When *Crumbling Idols* appeared, Twachtman had become the Monet of the icebound Hudson, and Hassam the Sisley of Madison Avenue in the spring.

When Hassam went abroad in 1883 he had learned wood engraving, had studied in Boston with I. M. Gaugengigl, had taught Celia Thaxter to paint in water color, and was familiar as an illustrator to the readers of *Saint Nicholas, Harper's, Scribner's,* and *Century.* His would be a compromise between the careful drawing he learned from Boulanger and Lefebvre at the Académie Julian, and the prismatic dissolutions of Monet, whom he never met. When he returned after five European years it was to continue a double career in illustration and painting. His sprightly and cosmopolitan sketches of New York, London, and Paris appeared in magazines and on canvas—wet sidewalks and umbrellas on Fifth Avenue, the shape of Madison Square's tower in a snow flurry, Westminster Palace clothed in fog, the shape of Notre Dame against the sky, and the pale yellows, pinks, and greens of spring in Union Square. His *Century* drawings of the prim brick in Washington Square, the ruffled dresses of children, the Arch tactfully posed behind an elm, are like the nostalgic images of that neighborhood in Henry James's *American Scene.*

The fishing boats and their reflections at Gloucester, the elms and white churches of Connecticut, and the surf at Appledore permitted Hassam a broader and freer rendering of light and atmosphere, as did his studies of the muted light in rooms shaded against the sun. There was a mild sunlight, not the dazzle of Monet, in his *Capri* (Addison Gall.), with its pleasant and lively pinks, lavenders, blue-greens, and vermilions. His paintings were not rigorous studies of light, but delightful evocations of well-liked places, like the rapid and tentative etchings he also made.

The eye of Twachtman could perceive subtleties in a bank of snow or an icebound river which were beyond Hassam. His meeting with Anton Mauve and his discipline at the Académie Julian rather confirmed the sober coloring he had learned with Duveneck at

Childe Hassam, *Union Square in Spring*

Smith College Museum of Art, Northampton, Mass.

Munich; but his years in France produced a transformation, the results of which were lost when his paintings went down with the ship that was carrying them. One can measure the change, however, by comparing his study of oyster boats in New York Harbor, painted in 1879, where the play of light on water is conveyed as much by dark accents as by color, with the iridescence of *The Waterfall.*

Twachtman eliminated the lower register from his palette the better to convey his sense of the unity about him, the melting snow, the harmony of brook with sky, the quietness of winter, and the interchange between a farmhouse and its trees and fields. When he began his American work at thirty-two he had only seventeen more years before him, lean years when his teaching at Newport, at Cos Cob, and in the Art Students League consumed his time and strength. The quiet probity of his friend Alden Weir was in his classwork and in the etchings of Bridgeport Harbor, the studies of Niagara, the thaws of February, and the drift of summer clouds over Greenwich pastures.

There was more in Twachtman, however, than delicately rendered snow and the play of waterfalls poetically seen. There was a dynamism, a controlled forcefulness which appeared only on few and late occasions—visions of cascading streams which no longer

John H. Twachtman, *Snow-bound*

Art Institute of Chicago

had a veiled and luminous quality but a tense and powerful thrust of dark rocks against swirling shapes of water and ice. These stark boulders and these plunging streams would reappear in the modern Marsden Hartley.

Impressionism helped Alden Weir to generalize his *Willimantic Thread Factory* (Brooklyn Mus.) until it was any white building shimmering through foliage. The quiet, unforced landscapes of his late years had gained breadth and freshness, and summer sunshine dappled the forms of the little girl and her donkey in *Visiting Neighbors*. When Weir and Renoir died in the same year the contrast between their paintings of young people was too obvious to be missed—the Frenchman's sensuous gusto, and what Duncan Phillips has called Weir's "reticent idealism."

Only in his late thirties did Theodore Robinson adopt the impressionist handling under the influence of Monet at Giverny. He had made careful crayon portraits in Wisconsin and had known the discipline of Carolus-Duran and Gérôme before Barbizon inspired a new breadth and a new sturdiness in his painting. Robinson never surrendered the strong contrasts of light and shadow which suggest Winslow Homer; they appeared in his *On the Tow Path* two or three years before he died. Millet's ruggedness was in his *Watering Pots* (Brooklyn Mus.); *Spring in Giverny* was unreservedly impressionistic; and in 1895 the statue of George Washington loomed through a Union Square snowstorm in a composition which made Hassam's similar themes look flimsy.

The cheerful average of American painting in these years is not to be measured wholly by Sargent and Chase, Hassam and Twachtman. Alongside these in the exhibitions hung genre paintings of a conscientious dullness, portraits without even the dexterity of Sargent to redeem them, landscapes in which nature was seen through no temperament, and "ideal" figure pieces where studio models personified everything from Music to Mathematics.

J. Alden Weir, *Visiting Neighbors*

Phillips Memorial Gallery, Washington, D.C.

Dwight W. Tryon was twenty-four years younger than Inness, and could paint with strength and conviction, as he did in the somber *Lighted Village* (Freer Gall.), a small picture with an Inness-like breadth of foreground slopes and pond and a moon which could have ridden one of Ryder's skies. The "successful" Tryon, however, worked on a larger scale and learned from the impressionists only how to be pleasantly unfocused. A row of thin trees against an October sky had tenuous grace, but the conviction grows that his career became the production of Tryons steadily year by year, not the creative mind's reaching for deeper experience.

And beside the best of Chase, how evasive seem the "conversations" of Thomas Wilmer Dewing, only two years younger! Like Tryon, Dewing began with more strength than he retained; his *The Mirror* (Freer Gall.) is a solid small genre with the pervasive warm tone of a room whose shades are drawn against the sunlight, and its figure and accessories are brushed with a firm delicacy. The same woman, alone or with companions, sits or stands in all the Dewings, growing less substantial until she seems a wraith; outdoors she moves against meadows which have no weight, being vague green stains. Dewing the pastelist, it seems, overcame Dewing the painter. Cortissoz praised his "breeding," but his blue blood grew thinner with every year.

As impressionists one could compare Hassam with Willard Leroy Metcalf, his senior by one year, and discover that Metcalf could charmingly break his colors and flick his brush to convey the brilliance of October in Connecticut, but that he lacked the vitality of Hassam, and conceded more to sentiment and sweetness than the Monet of the Isles of Shoals. The moonshine in Metcalf's *May Night* (Corcoran Gall.), the pale glimmering colonnade, the drifting figure are of the theater, and like the theater's effects they hold the interest only for a moment.

Abbott H. Thayer was thirty when he returned from Gérôme's classes in 1879, and fifty-two when he turned hermit under Mount Monadnock. His research on the protective coloration of animals and the resulting "Thayer's law" were much discussed; his paintings reveal that there was something of protective coloration in his relation to a world whose "monkeyfied" individualism he detested.

Abbott H. Thayer, *The Stillman Sisters*
Brooklyn Museum, New York City

George de F. Brush, *Mother and Child*
Museum of Fine Arts, Boston, Mass.

Thayer was at his best in broad impressionist renderings of Monadnock with deep blues, intense purples, and warm orange-reds, at his most dubiously "ideal" in the numerous canvases like *Caritas* where his wife and children were transformed into a cheesecloth classicism and managed to look like the clay studies of his friend Saint-Gaudens. His winged figures were made for flying in the same allegorical skies as the Shaw Memorial angel; Thayer's appealing young virgin, with a child at either side, moves with the springing grace of the Sherman *Victory*. The painter could complete a head but less often a body to go with it, and there are passages in his work whose sketchy and unsubstantial quality would explain the fits of dejection of which John Jay Chapman wrote.

Not far from Thayer lived George de Forest Brush, who specialized in Madonnas and in American Indians to which he gave the high finish and cold finality of Gérôme. "We must not run after new things," he said, "we must find out what the masters knew"; and Brush had found out precisely how the Italians modeled their maternities. The light in his *Mother and Child* is the light of the studio, and it was painted with obviously tender feeling but with a forced chiaroscuro and over-precise contours.

As one recalls the conversing girls of Dewing, the virgins of Thayer, and the *Amor Caritas* of Saint-Gaudens, one sees the effort of a generation to embody its ideal of the young American woman. She was the same handsome self-possessed creature whether she posed for Sargent, played tennis in Howells' summer resorts, or moved through the novels of Henry James. One found the same long-limbed proportions and classic profile in the girl who trailed her satin train through a Gibson parlor and in the one who was poised as naked Diana on the top of Madison Square Garden. Henry Adams had shrewdly observed her when he wrote that American artists, with the exception of Walt Whitman, Bret Harte, and a few flesh painters, "had used sex for sentiment, never for force," concluding that American art was as far as possible sexless.

Certainly one found in the centers of art activity little evidence of the "peculiarly sensible carnality" which shocked Henry James in French painting. Out of the Paris studios of Boulanger, Lefebvre, and Carolus-Duran or the American classes of Duveneck, Weir, and Chase came dozens of young men and women whose work conformed to the cheerful average.

In Boston, for example, Joseph Rodefer De Camp quietly painted the light on women's shoulders with a solid craftsmanship he had learned from Duveneck but with a palette responsive to impressionism; his *Guitar Player* (Boston Mus. Fine Arts) was like an enlarged and more solid Dewing figure posed against a

Edmund C. Tarbell, *Josephine and Mercie*

Corcoran Gallery of Art, Washington, D.C.

pleasant gray wall. Frank W. Benson placed his children in frilled white summer dresses among the trees, and studied the play of light on ribbons and parasols. Edmund Tarbell revived the formula of Vermeer, the foreshortened windows at one side, the woman reading or knitting in profile against the far wall, the vase or bowl of flowers carefully placed; yet Vermeer defeats him with a keener eye for the play of light on forms and a more robust delight in the reality of common things.

Boston's most rigorous teacher of figure drawing since William Rimmer was Philip L. Hale, a draughtsman whose delicacy and sureness earned him the title of the "Bostonese Ingres." This son of Edward Everett Hale could provide Boston with Whistleresque portraits and with charming genre in a quasi-impressionist manner; but his enthusiasm for those "dinnerpail artists," the newspaper illustrators, and his zest for boxing matches and prize fights were departures from the Back Bay pattern. Hale's likeness of his father, done when the painter was in his early thirties, deserved to hang beside the solid and serious characterizations of Hunt and Duveneck. His *Between Rounds* provokes comparison with Eakins; the body of Hale's relaxed fighter was superbly drawn and knowingly painted; one misses only the sharper tang of actuality, the dust and sweat of the Philadelphian.

Philip Hale's naturalism seems robust beside the "idealizations" of Will H. Low, Edward E. Simmons, and Robert Reid, young men whose careers extended well into the twentieth century, and whose essential aimlessness was suggested by their titles: *Summer Idyll, Narcissus, Dolce Far Niente, The Iridescent Fan.* When de Kay called Ryder an idealist he was careful to ex-

Philip L. Hale, *Edward Everett Hale*
(American Academy of Arts and Letters)

Courtesy Mrs. Lilian Westcott Hale

plain that he meant something more difficult than most "idealizers" attempted. The aim of the latter was a pleasant dilution of meaning. Girls in Greek costumes posed listlessly for Low in the garden of MacMonnies, and in his *Woodland Glade* figures like those of Puvis strike attitudes in a setting where one cannot see the woods for the trees. Simmons drew peasants without a trace of the human sympathy of Millet and was ready in the nineties to paint the American girl nine times as the Muses in the Library of Congress. In the work of Reid the same female impersonated the Five Senses after she had posed à la Whistler in a kimono against a Japanese screen.

In Walter Shirlaw's *Dawn* a stout and boneless nude bent over a lily pond while doves circled above her head; in John W. Alexander's *Pot of Basil* the American miss became unsubstantial under the elegantly flowing lines of her classical gown. The *Cumaean Sibyl* of Elihu Vedder stalked with somewhat more energy across the smoking heath (Wellesley Coll.), and Vedder made lively illustrations for *Omar Khayyam.* But he unwisely challenged Blake with his *Soul in Bondage;* and when he assembled the faces of Burne-Jones in *The Soul between Doubt and Faith,* his tricks with line were obvious and his manner overcame his matter.

Low spoke for men like these in *A Painter's Progress* when he discussed the artist's problem in American society. For a few intelligent patrons, he said, there are many who look on art as a form of investment. Yet the artist must live, and to live must compromise with the taste of his Maecenas. Let him do so, consoling himself meanwhile with the thought that in the long run his art will refine and "spiritualize" the crudest customer.

The year of 1893 provided these idealizers with an opportunity to spiritualize the customers of the Chicago Fair; on its walls and ceilings they would demonstrate their incapacity to revive the art of Raphael, or even to rival the tepid Puvis.

CHAPTER 24 / THE WHITE CITY

As the Columbian quadricentennial approached, it might have been observed that the national festivals seemed to coincide with national disasters. The panic of 1873 had rumbled as an undertone to the shrill exhibitionism of the Centennial, and now there was panic again. Growth and the cultural fruits of prosperity were to be the Chicago theme, but there were signs not to be ignored that the economic structure as a whole was something like a skyscraper jerry-built and straining perilously on weak foundations. The price of iron and steel sagged in 1890; two years later, Henry Clay Frick attacked the minimum pay of Carnegie workers, and Alexander Berkman attacked Frick with a dagger and a revolver. In the West and South the farmer struggled against a long depression; in the East one great railway system after another failed. Banks closed their doors, and Coxey led his straggling army of the jobless toward Washington.

The willful optimist could turn to more pleasant subjects: the new game called basketball which someone had just invented; the appearance of the electric trolley in American streets; the quaint Rip Van Winkle which that old barnstormer Joseph Jefferson was still carrying up and down the country at the age of sixty-four. The grimy Chicago workmen were too busy preparing in 1893 for their battle with the Pullman Company to visit the palaces and gondolas on Lake Michigan; nor would visiting foreigners have time to note the contrast between the fair's ordered symmetry and the huddled tenements a few blocks away. The *Scribner's* reader had glimpsed four years before *How the Other Half Lives* in an article by Jacob Riis; but the artist Kenyon Cox, whose pen drawings of New York alleys, ragpickers, and flophouses had underscored the text, was soon to portray Metal Work and Textiles in the form of handsome goddesses on a dome at the Chicago festival.

Thanks to Chicago push and bluster, Congress decided in 1890 that the western city was to have the Exposition, and the first conception of its plan and color was in Root's mind and Burnham's. Chicago, as Root observed, had not only more ground and more money than were available to Paris for the Universal Exposition but a lake besides. On scraps of brown paper the partners sketched an ensemble whose parts would have no architectural uniformity, their unity being one of bright clashing colors, of "barges, gondolas, flags and flutter"; here Root saw a Romanesque tower, there a bristling structure not unlike the Kremlin. The Fine Arts Building was to be of pink granite and brown Spanish tiles, the rest avowedly impermanent, a lively promise of coming power, not a final commitment to any one form. While Root amused himself with turrets and spires, with mosques and Chinese pagodas, Frederick Law Olmsted and his young partner Henry Codman solved the problem of the site, a windbeaten tract of Jackson Park on the lakeside, with sand and water underneath—a chaos to be made orderly in less than two years and a half.

Chicago supposed in 1890 that its most noted firm would design the Exposition buildings; but Burnham and Root insisted that a national project called for national collaboration. Local architects were given five structures; for the rest, Burnham chose the dean of their profession, Richard Hunt, to plan the Administration Building; Boston was to be represented by Peabody and Stearns, Kansas City by Van Brunt and Howe, New York by McKim's firm and that of George B. Post.

When the experts gathered at Chicago in January, 1891, the question was whether John Root would convert the bookwise Easterners to the warmth and splendor of his conception of the fair. That brilliance would have bloomed for only a few summer days; it was destined never to bloom at all. Within a few days of the first conference Root was dead, and the cool formalisms of "McKim, White and Gold" were established as the Columbian theme. Diana was lowered from her New York tower and shipped west to preside over the McKim Building in Jackson Park, symbolizing that victory.

The Gilded Age was to receive a coating of plaster of Paris in the façades by the lake, whose symmetry was part Roman, part Greek, part Renaissance, and part Beaux-Arts of Paris. As Cortissoz observed, the tall hat, the tailor-made gown, and the hansom cab could never be reconciled to Bernini's colonnade or an authentic reproduction of the Loggia dei Lanzi; but one could discreetly temper the authentic, take classic buildings and "modernize" them with bright flags, minarets, and sculptural bustle, mingling the dignified with the piquant. One could use Root's general plan, shifting its details for greater formality. One axis was determined by a peristyle at the water's edge, a basin, and a Court of Honor as foreground to Hunt's main building; the second was formed by a canal with a colonnade and an obelisk at one terminus. The principal structures conformed to this geometry; the rest were more informally disposed.

As the framework of the architecture was made ready for its plaster façades, the artistic collaboration which the Boston Library had demonstrated brought more painters and sculptors to the shacks on Lake Michigan than had ever joined talents in America to create an ensemble. Directed by Frank D. Millet, the painters worked on huge cartoons for mural decorations; a small army of sculptors turned clay models into plaster casts under the generalship of Saint-Gaudens, who cried one day to Burnham, "Do you realize that this is the greatest meeting of artists since the fifteenth century?"

When Grover Cleveland opened the World's Columbian Exposition on the first of May in 1893, most Americans agreed with Saint-Gaudens' boast, "It seems impossible that such a vision can ever be recalled in its poetic grandeur and elevation." As L'Enfant had once turned swampy Goose Creek into Tiber Canal, so the resourceful Olmsted had made sure that all the major palaces would reflect themselves in water. Chicago's H. C. Bunner christened the ensemble "The White City," and New York's Richard Watson Gilder drew the inevitable parallel:

> Say not, "Greece is no more."
> Through the clear morn
> On light wings borne
> Her white-winged soul sinks on the New
> World's breast.
> Ah! happy West—
> Greece flowers anew, and all her temples soar!

If one came by train one stepped into the Court of Honor and looked from the terraces of Hunt's Administration Building down the wide lagoon. On one's right were the lacelike spires and domes of the Machinery Building and, beyond the three graceful arches of a

Chicago World's Fair, general view of the Court of Honor

Photo Forbes Library, Northampton, Mass.

bridge, the Agricultural pavilion of McKim with the borrowed Diana on its Pantheonlike dome; on the left, a colossal Franklin stood before the Van Brunt and Howe Electricity Building, and the long white bays of Machinery Hall prolonged the vista. At the end of the lagoon was the colossal golden *Republic* of French, a spear and a liberty cap in one hand, a globe raised in the other. Beyond her was the forty-eight-columned peristyle centered upon a triumphal arch with Columbus riding his four-horse chariot on its crest; between the columns and beneath the arch one saw the blue water of the lake.

One could arrive by boat and reverse the vista, finding an echo for French's gilded goddess in Hunt's great dome above the jets of the Columbian fountain, which MacMonnies had conceived as a vessel: a winged Fame stood at the prow; Father Time used his scythe for a tiller; ranks of maidens on either side gracefully swayed to their oars; cupids above them bore the pedestal where Columbia proudly sat; seahorses pranced before and behind through tumbling water and spray. From a gondola at night one could move in another direction from the obelisk north alongside the tall lighted windows of the Manufactures and Liberal Arts, the cornices outlined and the sculptures bathed by thousands of the new Westinghouse lights, and pass under a bridge into the north lagoon with its wooded island, where the glass dome of the Horticulture Building was like an enormous bubble above the trees. The artists of Gilder's *Century Magazine* showed stay-at-homes how French's *Republic* looked an hour after sunrise, or Hunt's dome by moonlight.

In the harsher daytime, the critical eye could see endless embroidering on what was a simple formula—the arcade, the triumphal arch, the saucer dome, the pediment, the long rows of windows with round heads. Like "not unfeared, half-welcome guests" stood Sullivan's Transportation Building with its unclassical cupola and its enormous round-arched Golden Door, and the Fisheries Building of Henry Ives Cobb which dared to be Romanesque and whose decoration had been molded on the shapes of starfish and lobsters, crabs and sea horses.

The White City owed its nimble air to the gay banners and the rippling reflections, the plash of water, and the cries of gondoliers. Taft and Bartlett, French and MacMonnies, Boyle and Potter and Martiny had labored for months with others to produce its white populace, mixing cement and fibers with plaster to make "staff," a substance which could resist weather for at least a few months. This sculptured multitude spread its wings at the base of domes, marched solemnly along the peristyle, rode the bridges, and rested in the pediments; it shouldered entablatures and thrust itself from the surface of lagoons. Its lavish half nudity would not have been welcomed seventeen years before at the Centennial.

Chicago was spared at least some of the sartorial horrors of Philadelphia. There was a mild distinction in the modeling of French's *Republic* and a degree of con-

Chicago World's Fair, Agricultural Building

Photo Forbes Library, Northampton, Mass.

trolled vitality in her pose and gesture. She was not the tallest goddess in America, for Bartholdi's *Liberty* had stood in New York harbor for seven years; but she was sixty-five feet from toes to laurel-crowned head, and in her classic solemnity there was no hint of the "smile of young presumption" which Tom Moore had once seen on Columbia's rising brow. Saint-Gaudens' huntress swung gracefully among the searchlights and so did Martiny's *Victory* on the dome of the Art Palace, fourteen feet six inches tall in her bare feet, as the guidebook said.

These were exceptions in a display which ranged from the banal to the ridiculous. American sculptors had seen statues by Jules Dalou in Paris which had the frivolity and flutter of the baroque. They had observed the frank sensuality of the Falguière nudes, and studied Mercié's design for the Paul Baudry tomb, where the painter's bust was crowned by a nervously modeled Angel of Glory while a limp personification of Grief mourned at the base of his pedestal. In Paris, Frederick MacMonnies had made a *Nathan Hale* whose feminine softness belied its bronze; and now the plaster horses and rowing maidens for his Columbia Fountain arrived in crates from abroad to be a mammoth centerpiece for the Chicago feast. Behind it in the Court of Honor was an enormous *Columbus* with the flag of Aragon and Castile in his hand, which a young pupil of Saint-Gaudens had contrived. Philip Martiny provided most of the embellishment for the Agricultural and the Art buildings; his *Four Continents* holding an astrolabe imitated the Car-

Daniel C. French, *The Republic*

Bogart Studio photo

peaux fountain in the Place de l'Observatoire, and his oxen and rams led by a classical farm girl were as detailed in execution as though they were a bronze mantel ornament, not a group sixty feet from the ground.

The four-horse chariot by French and E. C. Potter on the peristyle was another variant on the *quadriga* of antiquity, the Renaissance, and modern Europe. Both Janet Scudder and Bessie Potter Vonnoh did their first work at the Exposition, and it was Miss Scudder who helped Lorado Taft with the frieze of cupids which ran on all four sides of the Horticulture Building. For Sullivan's Transportation structure John J. Boyle tried the more difficult task of placing realistic figures among all these attributes and allegories—the inventors of twelve nations in proper historic dress, and a Muse of Transportation riding a cowcatcher. Karl Bitter's groups on the corner pavilions and around the base of Hunt's dome were neither coldly classical nor awkwardly naturalistic, but bristled with a certain festive energy. Bitter had been trained in Vienna, and there was fluency in his whipped-cream baroque. He had already worked for Hunt in the Fifth Avenue mansions, a cheerful plagiarist who copied Michelangelo's *David* for a pair of Vanderbilt andirons and misquoted Ghiberti on the bronze gates of Trinity Church.

In the large rotunda of the Art Building and in the four wings branching from it stood sculpture of a more permanent sort from half a dozen countries. Some of it was in stone and bronze, yet there was little to distinguish it from the white multitude outside. America showed nearly one hundred and fifty pieces, of which the *Buffalo Hunt* of Bush Brown and *Charles Dickens and Little Nell* by F. Edwin Elwell were typical in their fusion of sentiment with careful detail. Only an occasional work, like French's *The Angel of Death and the Sculptor,* which had received a Paris medal a few months before, revealed mildly sculptural qualities. The exhibit from France held casts of historic fragments from the Trocadero Collection, and one could admire the details of Amiens Cathedral; but it also held Michel's repulsive *Blind Man and the Paralytic* and a cheaply provocative *Phryne* by Hannaux. The Italian pieces, smaller in scale, fluttered and pranced "with an entire absence of idealism," as one visitor said.

While the sculptors had worked against time in their studios at Jackson Park, another small army of painters had climbed up and down ladders before the huge canvases which would be placed here and there to relieve the near whiteness of the fair buildings, or had drawn foreshortened figures directly on the plaster surfaces of domes. For the tympana of the Liberal Arts Building Walter McEwen did *Music* and *Life,* each forty feet long, while Gari Melchers, whose reputation was based on his accurate studies of European peasants, produced *The Arts of War* and *The Arts of Peace.* Design for both men consisted in loosely adapting the poses of their quasi-classical figures to the curve which bounded their spaces, upright in the center, kneeling or crouching at both ends, the colors pale, the forms anemic, the movement huddled and commonplace. In the porticoes of the Agricultural Building George Maynard was slightly more forceful with panels of the *Seasons,* of *Abundance* and *Fertility,* of *Cybele* and *Triptolemus,* in each of which the single figure in lively colors was placed against a deeper tone of Pompeian red.

Nearly three hundred feet above the floor of Hunt's building the Dodge brothers had worked on ladders and scaffolding in the dome to complete *The Glorification of the Arts and Sciences,* a multitude of larger-than-life figures in procession before Apollo's throne; and the curved surfaces of the entrance domes and pendentives for the Building of Manufactures and Liberal Arts had likewise to be painted *in situ.*

Most if not all the painters had seen how Tiepolo and Tintoretto, as well as Baudry in the ceiling of the Paris Opera, mastered similar problems. But none of the eight decorators of the Chicago domes had either the skill or the time for a like inventiveness, and their aim was rather "to show to the people who are too busy to go abroad what a powerful adjunct to architectural effect painting may be." Their formula was the same in all cases: a single figure occupying each of the four corner pendentives with scarcely more in the crest of the dome above them than an agreeably tinted surface. Each man worked out his mild variation: Edwin H. Blashfield gave his figures wings, and a few doves fluttered in his blue vault; swirling wires and an electric spark centered the dome of J. Carroll Beckwith; Kenyon Cox, Robert Reid, and Edward Simmons used graceful ribbons to fill their spaces and label their allegories; C. S. Reinhart broke his curves with potted plants; Alden Weir painted a sunburst over his ladies' heads; Walter Shirlaw's device was a huge cobweb. Thus was a problem in collaboration reduced to the lowest common denominator of the assembled talents, and the more difficult problems of mural design tactfully avoided.

Passing beyond the dozen structures whose cornices were all of equal height and whose tint was described as that of "time-kissed ivory," the visitor found himself among more familiar forms and colors: a British Building which was more or less Tudor, a German one which managed to look like both a castle and a beer garden, a Choral Hall severely Grecian, a Marine Café bristling with cone-shaped turrets. He discovered that the Florida Building was a replica of Saint Augustine's ancient fort, Indiana a French château, Iowa a squat Romanesque affair not unlike a railroad station, Virginia a new Mount Vernon. In the Midway Plaisance were Eskimo and Algerian villages, a ferris wheel, and a model of St. Peter's fifteen feet high.

The Exposition had other purposes than to demonstrate an architectural point, and the pavilions under the gaunt beams of the Manufactures Building held the expensive if tasteless products of all nations. The observer in search of novelty could admire a map of the United States which was made with pickles; the more artistic delighted in Sèvres porcelains and Gobelin tapestries;

Frank D. Millet painting a decoration for the N.Y. State Building, Chicago Fair

Art and Progress

the philosopher could observe with misgiving a Krupp gun worth a million dollars which weighed one hundred and thirty tons. The feminist could admire the evidence of skill and patience in the Women's Building; the man who remembered seeing a five-thousand horsepower Corliss engine at the Centennial could now see that power quadrupled as the thirty-foot flywheel of its Chicago brother revolved once in a second.

Henry Adams lingered among the dynamos, confronted with a display of sheer power which raised more questions in the historian's mind than he could answer. He had talked with the sculptors and painters who had gone West to create the Exposition and had found them doubtful whether their gifts would be appreciated in Chicago. They talked, he said, as though art to the Westerners was a stage decoration; a diamond shirt-stud, a paper collar. One glimpse of the Art Palace should have convinced them that such notions of art were not peculiar to the West, nor even to America. The nine thousand paintings, with a few distinguished exceptions, constituted a display of empty dexterity which knew no national boundaries. They hung three and four deep with no other principle of arrangement than a farmer uses to build walls with stones of different sizes.

For the French exhibit, which was twice as large as that of any other foreign country, the two principal artists' associations had offered three thousand paintings from which the American commissioners chose five hundred oils and one hundred water colors. The names were familiar to any tourist who had seen the Salons: the sturdy competence of Bonnat, the charm of Puvis, the sweetened peasants of Jules Breton, the city types of Raffaelli, the anecdotes of Ribot and Laurens.

There was no Daumier in the French rooms, nor any Courbet or Degas. One had to look in the exhibit of foreign pictures owned by Americans to find canvases by Corot and Manet.

Thanks to Sir Frederick Leighton, the British walls were heavy with products of the Royal Academicians, the tight naturalism of John Millais, and the pale echoes of Blake in Watts's *Love and Life*. Germany made up for her exclusion from the Paris show of 1889 by exhibiting hundreds of canvases as competently dull as those of France; Menzel was a favorite here, and also a monster *Apotheosis of Wilhelm the First* which covered one whole wall.

From Russia came the oversized historical paintings of Repin and Verestchagin; from Spain, the obviously sunny Sorolla and the deliciously clever Fortuny; from Italy, the dextrous and shallow Boldini. Sweden was represented by the broad but empty brushwork of Anders Zorn, and Holland by Mauve's genre and the tender sympathetic family scenes of the popular Josef Israels.

On the walls of the fifteen rooms which America had reserved for her own display was a demonstration that she could match European skill of the academic variety and on occasion be original. As in 1876, the largest number of paintings had come from the East: seven hundred and fifty from New York, Boston, and Philadelphia, and only seventy-five from Chicago. Again as at the Centennial a retrospective show surveyed the country's past from Smibert and Copley through Peale, West, Stuart, Allston, and Sully to Mount and Bingham. Thomas Cole's *Roman Aqueduct* was shown, and the work of Durand and Kensett. The sixty-eight-year-old Inness, who had been strangely snubbed at Philadelphia, came into his own with fifteen paintings, and among the "modern" landscapists were Hunt, Twachtman, Robinson, and Hassam.

The illustrators of the Golden Age were well represented, and the readers of *Century, Harper's,* and *Scribner's* could study the originals in a large group of illustrations by men like Remington, Gibson, and Frost, and turn from the large Abbey canvas of the *Holy Grail*—one of his series for the Boston Library—to his delightful drawings for the comedies of Shakespeare.

The American portraits ranged from a *Thiers* by Healy to the *Alice* of Chase and the nine Sargent likenesses, among them the lovely *Mrs. Inches* in her red-purple velvet and the charming portrait of the boy Homer Saint-Gaudens. In the field of genre, Eastman Johnson held his own with *Cranberry Harvest* and Eakins with his *Agnew Clinic.* A medal and a diploma went to Homer for his group of fourteen paintings which included *The Fog Warning* and *Eight Bells.*

Such work by no means set the average in Chicago. The most lavish praise was saved for Abbott Thayer's *Virgin Enthroned* and for Kenyon Cox's *Painting and Poetry,* a watered version of Titian's *Sacred and Profane Love.* Visitors whose taste had not advanced beyond the well-told story admired F. A. Bridgman's Algerian scenes, Walter Shirlaw's *Toning the Bell,* Frank Vincent Du Mond's *Monastic Life,* Vedder's *Lair of the Sea Serpent,* and *The Sculptor and the King* by George de Forest Brush.

It was the purpose of the White City to consecrate success, not to play dangerously with new forces in the world of art. Whether one walked from the French into the Russian rooms or wandered into the German, one saw the same mother crouched at the bedside of the dying child, the same naked young women in distress, the same peasants making hay, the same monks being quaint. One emerged at last from these five acres of floor space, these two hundred rooms under the great glass ceilings, with the conviction that the successful paintings of all countries were as much alike as the standardized products of their mills and factories.

Only a few eyes looked beneath the plaster surface of the Columbian Exposition. When Harry Thurston Peck described it fourteen years later he spoke for the majority: "It revealed to millions of Americans whose lives were necessarily colorless and narrow, the splendid possibilities of art, and the compelling power of the beautiful."

Henry Adams sat on the steps of Hunt's building and reflected more soberly that "since Noah's Ark, no such Babel of loose and ill-joined, such vague and ill-defined and unrelated thoughts and half-thoughts and experimental outcries . . . had ever ruffled the surface of the Lakes." Did the American people know where they were driving? Not by the evidence around him; nor did Henry know, though he would keep on trying. The McKim classicism yielded no answer to him: he dismissed it as "the Beaux-Arts artistically induced to pass the summer on the shore of Lake Michigan."

Charles Eliot Norton was more patient with the Chicago incongruities. "Not one of those great façades," he said, "was the expression of the plan, construction or purpose of the building behind it," nor an organic symbol of our own superabundant vitality. Yet "the great Fair was indeed a superb and appropriate symbol of our great nation, in its noble general design and in the inequalities of its execution; in its unexampled display of industrial energy and practical capacity; in the absence of the higher works of the creative imagination . . . in its refinements cheek-by-jowl with vulgarities, in its order and its confusion, in its heterogeneousness and in its unity."

To more recent critics the Exposition's importance lies not in itself but in the precedents it set; and although the verse-making Gilder saw the festival as a frail vision soon to fade forever, generations yet to come would witness its consequences. Olmsted had demonstrated the effectiveness of planning, and the lesson would be applied in careful symmetries throughout the country. The sculptures of Chicago were a generation born to die with the summer of 1893, but their tougher offspring in marble and bronze would soon preside at the gates of parkways and astride the cornices of railway stations from Boston to San Francisco. The triumphal arch of the Columbian peristyle with its quadriga was repeated a few years later when New York welcomed the victorious Admiral Dewey; in more durable stone, it rose in dozens of American cities or was embedded in the façades of new museums.

For the first time at Chicago large groups of painters had learned subjugation of self in a collective enterprise. They had also learned to subjugate form and color to what they believed the architecture demanded, but they had not managed to invent an American iconography.

In the years to come, one great building after another would perpetuate their fallacies on its walls—the relaxed postures, the legato rhythms, and the cautious interpolation of modern dress among the chitons and the togas.

There were few Americans wise enough in 1893 to know how much was blandly ignored in the Chicago painting exhibition. Some of them had read W. C. Brownell's articles in *Scribner's* the year before, where Manet and Degas, Monet and Pissarro were at least discussed, if not wholly approved. Brownell noted the frivolous undertone of the French modernists, but added: "One has the feeling that the future is pregnant with some genius who will out-Monet Monet" by submitting impressionism to a more rigorous discipline.

He need not have been prophetic. When he wrote, Renoir had painted *Madame Charpentier* and was working at his *Jeunes Filles au Piano* and his bathers. Van Gogh had been dead two years, and Seurat one, leaving his *Grande Jatte;* Cézanne was painting his several *Card Players*.

The visitor to the Chicago Exposition would have searched in vain for a sign that such men existed. They were to be tardily discovered by Americans who, if they went to the fair at all, went in velvet pants and lace collars for half fare.

The Dewey Triumphal Arch, New York City

Wurts Bros. photo

BOOK FIVE

PROGRESSIVISM, CULTURE, AND WAR

c. 1900 – c. 1930

Lewis Hine photograph, *Child in a Carolina Cotton Mill* ▶

Lewis Hine Memorial Collection, New York City

PART ONE

THE VOICE OF THE CITY

INTRODUCTION / THE GREAT STOCK-TAKING

While Columbia's festival drew its twelve millions in 1893, quieter voices could be heard whose pitch was not harmonious with the smug self-congratulatory chorus in Chicago. In that year Hamlin Garland published his *Prairie Songs,* and a young professor of history from Wisconsin read an essay to his colleagues whose title was *The Significance of the Frontier.* Turner understood the westward course of his country's growth and the new customs, the impatience with inherited ways, the release from an irrelevant past, the courage and freshness of Americans who had held the ever-retreating frontier, the hither edge of free land. "Since the days when the fleet of Columbus sailed into the waters of the New World," he declared, "America has been another name for opportunity. . . . And now, four centuries from the discovery of America, at the end of a hundred years of life under the Constitution, the frontier has gone, and with its going has closed the first period of American history."

Three years later McKinley defeated the Great Commoner Bryan, and it was obvious that the second period of American history was, for some time to come, to be shaped by the monopolists, the seekers of foreign markets and new areas for investment, who controlled the victorious party. Columbia, as Mr. Dooley said, had been satisfied to do up her hair in side combs; now she was a lady with maturer charms, "a knowledge of Europeen customs an' not averse to a cigareet." Commodore Dewey became a front-page hero when he destroyed the rickety Spanish fleet in Manila Bay, and Lieutenant Colonel Teddy Roosevelt when his Rough Riders charged up San Juan Hill. The island peoples, their revolt against ancient masters accomplished with American help, now found themselves regulated for their own good by a great neighbor who spoke of the "white man's burden"; and while Albert Beveridge told the Senators that "God has made us adepts in government . . . among savages and senile peoples," Mr. Dooley concluded that the people of Cuba had exchanged the tyranny of Spain for that of the sugar beet.

As the century turned, few Americans could hear the far-off skirmishes between our troops and Aguinaldo's rebels in the Philippines. McKinley easily won the 1900 election from the persistent Bryan, and when Roosevelt assumed the presidency a year later American diplomats opened the doors of China to American enterprise, got possession of the Isthmus where the Panama Canal would link two oceans, and sponsored a compromise peace treaty between Russia and Japan by which the balance of power in the Far East was maintained.

For this America the gilded goddess of Daniel Chester French was an appropriate symbol, bearing in one hand the liberty cap and in the other a globe on which an eagle perched. As the plaster deities of the Chicago Exposition came down they were given a permanent home in the new Library of Congress, their right to personify the accepted virtues having received the sanction of the government.

What matter if the Library's exterior walls were a mask for the reading rooms and stacks at the core of the building? Fifty sculptors and painters had encrusted every spandrel, niche, and vault of the Library with their work: MacMonnies and Olin Warner designed the bronze doors, Martiny the operatic staircase, Vedder and Alexander the semicircular panels. Around the base of the rotunda reading room stood figures of History, Art, Commerce, et cetera, which were a roll call of America's talent with clay and marble; in the collar and lantern of the dome was Blashfield's *Evolution of Civilization.*

Charles Caffin predicted that this ensemble would inspire a distinctively American school of mural painting to express the aspirations of a self-governing people. His optimism was scarcely justified when the full consequences of Chicago revealed themselves in state capitols and courthouses, at Bowdoin College, the University Club of New York, and in the Waldorf-Astoria Hotel. Before Howard Pyle died he painted several murals including a *History of the Hudson River* for Jersey City. When Edwin A. Abbey's delightful pen drawings for *The Deserted Village* appeared in 1902 he was at work on designs for the lunettes and circular panels for the capitol at Harrisburg, Pennsylvania. Neither Pyle nor Abbey could do more than make enlarged illustrations; and the ceiling of the Baltimore Courthouse by Frank D. Millet had the same vacuity and the same obviously pretty color which were in his New York State panel for the Chicago Exposition.

It was this mural ineptitude which the malicious Henry B. Fuller burlesqued in *Little O'Grady Versus the Grindstone,* where O'Grady dreamed of painting the Goddess of Finance in robes of saffron and purple declaring a quarterly dividend: "Gold background. Stockholders summoned by the Genius of Thrift blowing fit to kill on a silver trumpet. Scene takes place in an autumnal grove of oranges and pomegranates . . . Marble pavement strewn with fallen coupons." Some fifteen years later, Will H. Low was no less ridiculous in his *Sculpture,* one of thirty-six panels for the State Education Building at Albany: his goddess was a Venus de Milo, modeling with her restored arms the *Victory* of Saint-Gaudens, with the Parthenon behind her.

For the Dewey triumphal arch in 1899 old John Ward freely restored the *Victory of Samothrace,* and Daniel Chester French supplied a Peace group as one more reminder that the Columbian Exposition had set the sculptural fashions. French at fifty, with an income which in one year reached eighty thousand dollars, lived in the world of good clubs, distinguished friends, and safe reputations, a world which had its own iconography and managed to keep the important commissions in the proper hands. The technical labor of enlarging and cutting the French statues was done by the six Piccirilli brothers who had brought the Italian craft to New York in the eighties and to whom Bartlett, MacMonnies, and Saint-Gaudens also entrusted their clay models.

Thanks to the men who had planned and built the White City, the Washington of Roosevelt and Taft was purged of its Victorian confusions. The White House was discreetly remodeled, and in 1900 the Junior Olmsted urged, at a convention of the American Institute of Architects, a return to the straight symmetries of the town's original designer. The Institute agreed that nothing good is really new, and one member quoted Kipling's lines on Homer:

> An' what he thought 'e might require,
> 'E went an' took—the same as me!

Olmsted, Burnham, McKim, and Saint-Gaudens roamed Europe, measuring, photographing, and discussing the plans of Versailles and Fontainebleau, the tapis vert of Hatfield House, the Theresa Platz of Vienna, and the sequence of the Champs-Élysées. Out of this material they composed the McMillan plan for Washington, a thoroughly logical diagram. Its main axis imitated the Parisian scheme on ground which did not rise, like the Champs-Élysées, to a splendid climax. The off-

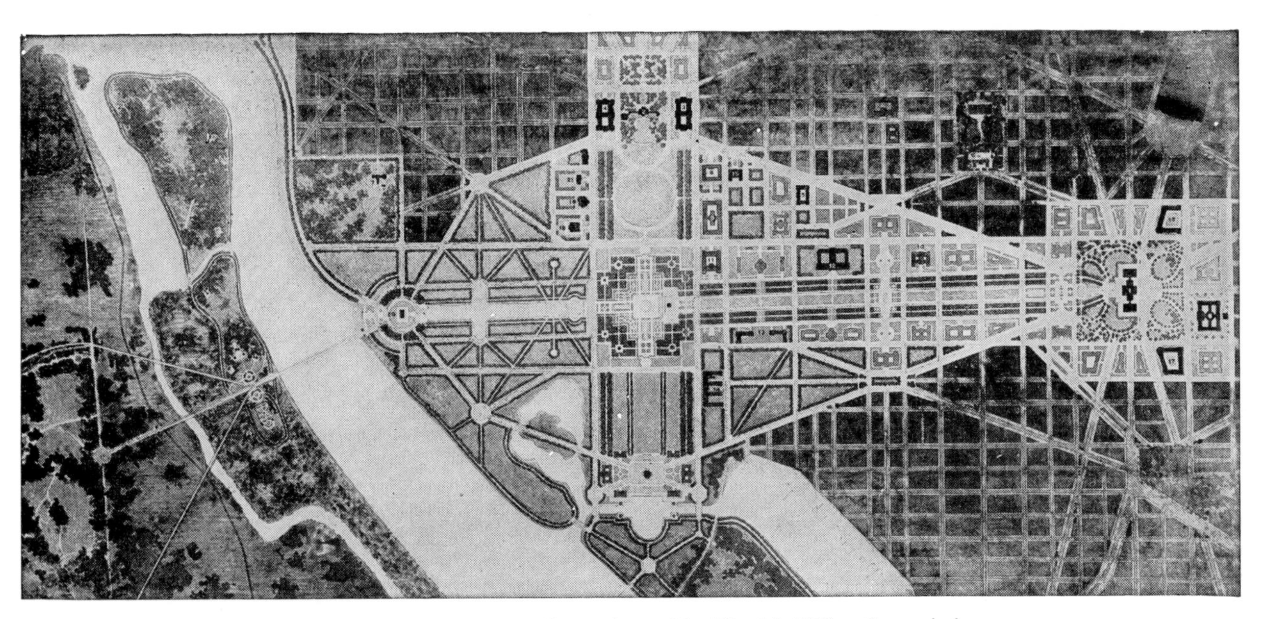

The Mall, Washington, D.C., as planned by The McMillan Commission

Courtesy National Commission of Fine Arts

centered location of the obelisk was to be concealed by steps, terraces, and a sunken garden, and the line of L'Enfant's "Grand Avenue" was to continue westward through a lagoon to a Lincoln Memorial and a bridge to Arlington. At the south end of the shorter cross axis was to be located another monument. The public buildings would be grouped, the legislative on Capitol Hill, the executive near the White House, the municipal in the reclaimed "Triangle."

Only the sense of human scale was missing; and in its absence these vistas became too long for the tired eye, the lines of buildings on either side a parade of chilly façades, a stretching of the Chicago formula to flabbiness. McKim died before the plan was fully realized, but he had perpetuated the philosophy which inspired it when he established the American Academy in Rome, which was made a national institution in the year 1905. From its villa on the Janiculum the young American painter, sculptor, or architect could look down on twenty centuries of art, and take from them "what he thought he might require."

Far more significant than these crystallizations of the accepted order was the resurgent liberalism of the century's first fifteen years, a mighty third effort, by men who remembered Jefferson and Jackson, to "put man above property," as Parrington has written. The progressive ferment was continuous and the pressure took a dozen forms: the rise of trade-union membership in these years; the ninety-six thousand votes for Debs and his Socialist party in 1900; Bill Haywood's militant I.W.W. four years later; the middle-class opposition to the expansionist program. Women acquired the vote in state after state, and liberals condemned the spoils system and pressed for pure food laws and the regulation of the hours and conditions of labor. Roosevelt brandished a big stick at the "malefactors of great wealth" and led the secession of the Progressives. The reforms of the Democrat Wilson owed much to a public conscience which the swashbuckling Teddy had helped to arouse.

As they had done in the age of Jackson, American philosophers, historians, and literary men played a major part in what Parrington called "the great stock-taking venture." *McClure's* published pieces by Lincoln Steffens and the other "muckrakers" who dissected the politics of cities with a clinical thoroughness. It was possible in 1908 for *Pearson's* to describe Morgan the Magnificent as a great man who had saved the nation from panic; three years later in Gustavus Myers' *History of the Great American Fortunes* he was conceded only the virtue of consistency. A new school of historians appeared who took seriously the remark of Turner that the economic questions were now the order of the day and that "the age of machinery, of the factory system is also the age of socialistic inquiry"; and in 1913 Charles A. Beard published his quasi-Marxian *Economic Interpretation of the Constitution.*

The writers of novels and essays meanwhile proved that they had read Tolstoy, Zola, and the plays of Ibsen. Hamlin Garland called attention to the new spirit which was reinvigorating art in Europe, and in *Crumbling Idols* called for the "veritist," the man whose version of what life might be gave him the power to write of it as it is, with sad severity. "Each age writes, paints, sings of its own time and for its time. . . . The surest way to write for all time is to embody the present in the finest form with the highest sincerity and with the frankest truthfulness." The coming author would be the localist whose work had a quality not possible to any other place or people than those around him.

When Garland's essays appeared, Hjalmar Boyesen had already seen life with sad severity in *The Mammon of Unrighteousness;* his touch was mildly Zolaesque, and *Mammon* was a picture of the petty compromises and small hypocrisies of life in a college town. The tough, cold-blooded naturalism of Zola was more painfully evident in Stephen Crane's *Maggie,* in the *McTeague* of Frank Norris, in Dreiser's *Sister Carrie* of 1900, and in Upton Sinclair's *Jungle* six years later.

These dissections of American life and of American men and women in grim struggle against environment and economic forces went far beyond Garland's veritism. They had the brutal objectivity which had shocked Howells in the French and Russian novels even while he praised them, and their effect on the reader was not the "vague discomfort" Howells had felt when he saw how people lived in the shadows of the Third Avenue Elevated. The mood of the new "city realists" bore somewhat the same relation to the mood of Garland and Howells as the I.W.W. to the followers of socialist Debs; and while city planners tore down a few slums to make broad white classic plazas, other men probed the slums beyond the plazas.

Two Americans, both men of an older generation, assessed the civilization of the Roosevelt era: Henry James and Thorstein Veblen, the former a "restless analyst" from the leisure class, the latter a ruthless critic of that class itself. James had been absent more than twenty-five years from the country which he explored from Maine to Florida and as far west as California in 1904 and 1905. His *American Scene* is the story of old idyls vanished, old steady ways replaced by "pompous, flagrantly tentative ones." The new city houses seemed vulgar to James after the old brick rows he had known as a child in New York, and those new mountains of steel and glass, the skyscrapers, were a "huge, continuous fifty-floored conspiracy against the very idea of the ancient graces." The palpable piles at Newport stood empty along the Drive. "Let them stand there always, vast and blank, for reminders to those concerned of the prohibited degrees of witlessness."

Money was being spent everywhere, James saw, for all the most exquisite things—except creation: the Metropolitan Museum, whose new east wing by Post and Hunt had the Roman solemnity, would provide a climate where Acquisition might bask, and James thought of the acres of canvas and tons of marble about to be turned out into the cold world as the penalty of old error and the warrant for a clean slate.

In Boston the tawny marble staircase and couchant lions of the new library bribed James to a mild emotion, though the building as a whole spoke more loudly of the purse than of Bostonian sensibility, and its murals were placed perilously close to the general public. At Harvard College he praised the refinement of the Union with its portrait of Henry Lee Higginson by Sargent—"a projection of genius which even that great painter has never outdone." Approaching Central Park, whose mixed population slightly alarmed him, James noted the "golden elegance" of the Saint-Gaudens *Sherman,* and its dauntless refinement amid the vulgar surroundings of an America which seemed to him "the triumph of the superficial and the apotheosis of the raw."

The reproofs of James were witty and well bred; Veblen's analysis of the life around him was quietly savage. The latter's phrase, "conspicuous waste," suggests a parallel with James; but the expatriate would never have asked, as Veblen did, whether the mechanization of labor and the reduction of the workman to an impersonal cog in the American machine did not render meaningless his claim to equality. Technical knowledge was for Veblen the core of a civilization; its ownership was now in the hands of a few whose aim in life he described as "an indefinitely extensible consumption of superfluities."

In *The Theory of the Leisure Class,* Veblen attacked the foundation of the kind of life which James lived in Europe and would like to have lived here, tracing the "classicism" of fashionable taste to the "protracted dominance of a predatory, leisure-class scheme of life." A page in his *The Higher Learning in America* sardonically explained the collegiate architecture of his time:

> It is in the eyes of the unlettered, particularly the business community, that it is desirable for the university to present an imposing front. . . . In recent scholastic edifices one is not surprised to find lecture rooms acoustically ill designed, and with an annoying distribution of light, due to the requirements of exterior symmetry . . . waste of space and weakness of structure, due, e.g., to a fictitious winding stair, thrown into the design to permit such a façade as will simulate the defensive details of a mediæval keep. . . . All of which may suggest reflections on the fitness of housing the quest of truth in an edifice of false pretenses.

The progressive spirit found a hundred tongues in the twenty years after the Chicago Exposition: the crude statistics of the muckrakers, the brutal prose of Jack London and Upton Sinclair, the fulminations of Roosevelt, the eloquence of La Follette, the cool idealisms of Wilson, the verbal surgery of Veblen. The smug acceptances of the Gilded Age were gone forever in an America whose mind and conscience had been stirred, as Parrington said, to their lowest sluggish stratum.

In the decade before 1913, the world of art knew the same ferment as the political world. It had its die-hard

Republicans, its mild Progressives, and its third-party secessionists, its trusts and its trust busters. The formation of the "Ten," for example, in 1898, was no effort to challenge the Academy, but a means for self-advancement of men whose work shocked nobody: Hassam, Tarbell, Benson, Alden Weir, De Camp, Metcalf, Dewing, Simmons, Reid, and Twachtman. By 1906 the Society of American Artists, which thirty years before had politely bolted the National Academy, as politely returned to the fold. Three years later, at a Washington convention called by the Academy and attended by eighty or more societies and institutions, was formed the American Federation of Arts, with the announced purpose of improving art conditions in America and molding public taste, of serving as a clearinghouse, of organizing exhibitions throughout the country, and of sending lecturers to American towns and cities.

The Chicago sculptor and teacher, Lorado Taft, published in 1903 *The History of American Sculpture;* two years later appeared Samuel Isham's *History of American Painting.* Neither was content with assembling biographical essays, and both discussed art in terms of movements as well as of men. Taft's conservatism was to be seen in his two paragraphs on Rimmer compared with a whole chapter on Powers; Isham's discussion of the Hudson River school was admirable, but he failed to grasp the quality of Thomas Eakins.

The critics of the daily and weekly press ranged from right to left, from the hack reporter to the scholarly stylist. The long career of Royal Cortissoz as art editor of the *New York Herald Tribune* began in 1891, and his world was that of the National Academy, the Century Club, and the Academy in Rome. He was the biographer of Saint-Gaudens in 1907, of La Farge in 1911, and his archconservatism was well served by his knowledge of the great past and his accomplished literary style. There was no clouding of the issues in Cortissoz, who declared war on the postimpressionist barbarians in his forties and thereafter yielded not an inch.

Trained in Berlin and Paris as a scholar, Frank Jewett Mather wrote with a lighter and more tolerant pen, and his *Nation* articles in the five years from 1901 were an antidote to such ventures into inaccuracy as Elbert Hubbard's bland assertion in 1899 that "Botticelli builded on Giorgione and Burne-Jones builded on Botticelli." Guy Pène du Bois returned from Europe in 1906 to be art critic for the New York *American,* to assist Cortissoz, and to write for the *Evening Post.* The critical columns of *Harper's Weekly,* the *Post,* and later the *Sun* were written by an Englishman, Charles Henry Caffin, who had arrived here in time to work on the decorations of the Chicago Exposition. When he discussed our leading artists in *The Story of American Painting, American Masters of Sculpture,* and other books, he made Homer, Inness, and Fuller live in his pages; and when he compared Sargent with the old masters of portraiture his criticism was both shrewd and just.

Some of the most vigorous comments on art, as Jerome Mellquist has reminded us, issued from men like James Gibbons Huneker, who were not exclusively art critics. Huneker was an unquenchable Bohemian whose long life was devoted to the discovery of new human oddities. A music teacher who had been trained in Europe in the eighties, he became music critic for the *Sun* in 1900, then its drama critic, and in the years before the war was the first American, he later claimed, to discuss Cézanne and Gauguin in a newspaper. This critical opportunist could write as brilliantly—and as superficially—of Matisse as of George Moore, of Richard Strauss and Whistler as of Picasso and Maeterlinck.

More steadfast if less clever was Sadakichi Hartmann, who published in 1901 the two volumes of his competent survey, *A History of American Art,* and whose *Forum* piece of 1910, "The American Picture World, Its Shows and Shams," bravely attacked the market concept. "The ludicrous height to which the prices of Inness landscapes soared after the artist's death," he wrote, "can only be compared to the shrewd operations in Spring wheat." Hartmann declared that the dealer's code of ethics was beneath that of the best department store; and he attacked the millionaire who bought Gainsborough's *Blue Boy* while the original still hung in London, the annual shows of art which the Academy hogged, the loaded juries, the morguelike museums with their empty walls, the chicanery and jockeying which forced an artist to imitate the flashy methods of a showman.

The critics and artists of this first decade of the century were girding their loins and sharpening their spears for the day when the war of the Ancients and the Moderns would be joined in earnest. In Philadelphia a militant squad of newspaper draughtsmen whose captain was Robert Henri and most of whom called themselves socialists were applying Hamlin Garland's veritism to slums, barrooms, and elevated railways. In New York another band enrolled with Alfred Stieglitz, a few "world-losers and world-forsakers" who proposed to revolutionize the American notion of form in art. The two groups seemed incompatible, yet they both belonged to an age whose critics included Teddy Roosevelt and Emma Goldman, Mr. Dooley and the I.W.W.

CHAPTER 25 / MOP, PAIL, AND ASHCAN

Sadakichi Hartmann's *Plea for the Picturesqueness of New York* was addressed in 1900 to the photographic brotherhood, but the more progressive novelists and painters would have agreed with him that "to give to art the complexion of our time, boldly to express the actual, is the thing infinitely desirable." Let the photographer observe the sunrise glittering on the Elevated rails, let him study Paddy's market on Ninth Avenue and watch the trains crawling like fantastic fireworms up the grade at One Hundred and Tenth Street. Let him discover the patterns of crisscrossed telegraph wires, the intricacies of Fulton Fish Market, the iron skeletons of half-finished buildings; or, if his mood is socialist, let him seek the inexhaustible misery of the slums. Hartmann predicted that in 1930 nobody would believe that his plea was necessary, for the beauty of New York would then have been explored by thousands. Who will now be the first? he asked. "May he soon appear!"

He had appeared ten years before in the person of Alfred Stieglitz, and *Camera Notes,* three months after Hartmann's piece, reproduced a New York street with an omnibus lumbering through a blizzard, together with a portrait of the man who had stood shivering for hours to record it on his plate—a hawk-nosed person with black tumbling hair, an aggressive mustache above his jutting chin, and a pair of eyes which one of his friends compared to powerful lenses surrounded by dark shades. Stieglitz had left Hoboken in 1881 for Germany, from which his father had migrated thirty years before, and in Germany had turned from engineering to a study of photography.

The orthochromatic plate was only one of many technical advances which now made the instrument of Mathew Brady seem crudely primitive. The new dry plate had shortened exposures, and there were improved papers for printing, better lenses, and the small Kodak with its roll of film. Thousands of amateurs pointed their cameras at everything within sight and hung the dubious results in exhibitions. Photography had become a trade, a sport, and a science.

Had it also become an art? Not in the minds of the German painters to whom young Stieglitz showed his prints and who cried, "What a pity it is that your photographs are not paintings!" Their minds contrasted the swift mechanical record of the commercial cameraman with the long sittings, the patient selection, the willful interpretations of their own craft. Ida Tarbell spoke for a minority in 1897 when she declared in *McClure's* that some of the greatest portraits of the time had been made by photographers. She discussed G. C. Cox, who, like Stieglitz, would not pose a sitter, nor dress him for the occasion, nor move him from his own surroundings. The Cox portraits no more pleased his customers than did the painted ones of Eakins; their penetration of character went too deep, and Cox was happiest with "decided" personalities like Richardson and Whitman, Howells and Beecher.

When Miss Tarbell wrote, rebel groups in Europe and America were calling themselves "pictorialists" and showing their work in a dozen cities; the Munich and Vienna enthusiasts called themselves "secessionists," and in England the "Linked Ring" included experimentalists from several countries. Unfortunately the "pictorial" photograph of the eighties and nineties, using the "hints on composition and chiaroscuro" to be found in the manuals of Henry Peach Robinson, borrowed the more obvious devices of painting and ignored the special character of the medium. What Robinson called "pictorial effect" was the placing of one's chief motive as Turner did, the imitation of Claude's landscape disposition, and the distribution of light in accordance with the schemes of Rembrandt.

The prints which Stieglitz brought home in 1890 after five years of travel and research surpassed everything America had seen. *Gossip-Katwyk* was no automatic record of facts: he had waited on the Dutch shore until a simple relationship of rolling surf, a snub-nosed sailing vessel, and two women was complete and satisfying, and his tones were exquisitely balanced, the lighter sky against the sands, the dark prow against the darker figures, his range brilliant and clean from the white head-dresses to the deepest folds in a dress. At Tynemouth Winslow Homer had shown no greater skill with the same elements.

Within two days in 1893 Stieglitz made his famous *Winter, Fifth Avenue,* and his *Terminal,* the latter a study of car horses drawn up before the Astor House in the snow and slush with steam rising from their flanks. He soon did what had seemed impossible by photographing wet New York pavements at night with people moving under the street lamps. Here obviously was the scientist-poet whom Hartmann sought, and Paul Strand has spoken of these early New York prints as "rich and lyrical gleanings from the city's turbulent life" by a man

G. C. Cox photograph of Walt Whitman

Library of Congress

who expressed a lively interest in simple human things.

Stieglitz, the natural leader of the American pictorialists, attacked the smug average competence of the commercial and the amateur, the complacent juries of the photographic salons; his opponents referred to his group as the Oscar Wildes of the camera and Charles M. Mitchell called them the Mop and Pail Brigade, perhaps because of Stieglitz' interest in the life of city streets. The painter William M. Chase pronounced their prints "artistic" but not works of art, and Dwight Tryon accused the medium of indiscriminate response to every detail.

Charles Caffin met this condescension with his *Photography as a Fine Art,* maintaining that the camera was like any other artistic tool with its own limitations which a creative person could overcome. It is only the best painting or sculpture that deserves to be called a work of art, he concluded, claiming the same right for the best photograph; to which Stieglitz added in an article for *Century* that there was no limit to individual expression in photography now that the man controlled the process from beginning to end.

When the Stieglitz piece appeared in 1902 he was the leader of the "photo-secession" and published in that year the first number of *Camera Work,* a beautifully designed quarterly. In 1905 he opened three small exhibition rooms in a brownstone front at 291 Fifth Avenue, where he hung the work of the secessionists. Many of these had been trained as painters, and in their effort to demonstrate their creativeness in the new medium they often imitated the tricks of light, the groupings, and the atmosphere of the painters. Clarence White's figures with their exquisite gradations were wraiths out of Thomas Dewing's world, and there was more than a hint of Twachtman's blurred forms in Steichen's landscapes, whose design suggested Inness. Gertrude Käsebier made studies of children which had the wistfulness of Abbott Thayer; she was much stronger when she studied the play of light on Indian faces, the shining skin drawn taut over the bones.

Some of the pictorialists worked in color; others secured unusual textures by printing on papers which ranged from extremely thin to roughly thick. Frank Eugene used an etching needle to enrich the darks of his negative; Joseph T. Keiley had special ways of manipulating his prints, using a brush on the platinum paper as the image slowly developed, to accent a contour here and remove a shape there, until the result looked like a photograph of a painting.

There were no such mannerisms in Stieglitz' study of the New York Central yards in 1903; crossing the ocean in 1907, he looked down at a huddled group of emigrants, rushed for his camera, and made that unposed masterpiece, *The Steerage.* Steichen's portrait of the elder Morgan bore no trace of his earlier lyricism. It was used by Carlos Baca-Flor when he painted the official likeness of the millionaire, but no painter would have dared to record the bead-bright eyes, ferocious eyebrows, and rubescent nose as Steichen's camera did.

As George Bernard Shaw observed in a talk to a camera club in London, there was a "terrible truthfulness" in their instrument. That truthfulness was in the documentary pictures of Lewis W. Hine. When the principal of the Ethical Culture School asked Hine in 1903 to make illustrations for the courses, Hine had never touched a camera. With a crude machine and a supply of flash powder Hine began his thirty-odd years of "terrible truthfulness" at Ellis Island, and in the tenements, factories, and mines of working America. There was no picturesque haze in his prints nor did he manipulate his negatives of an Italian immigrant family looking for its baggage, of begrimed children in southern cotton mills and in Pennsylvania coal breakers. Hine discovered something for which the word "picturesque" would have been an insult, and out of his deep concern with the lives he photographed came his *Washerwoman,* as nobly monumental as any Daumier.

The pen-and-ink men of America were meanwhile giving to art the complexion of their time in cartoons and illustrations. The best of graphic humor was at the disposal of the progressives: F. B. Opper created a gross image of Monopoly in the minds of a generation, crush-

Alfred Stieglitz photograph, *The Steerage*

Philadelphia Museum of Art

ing the Common People in his fat fist; Homer Davenport arrived in New York in 1895 and four years later drew the statue of George Washington being carted away to make room for Mark Hanna's effigy on the Sub-Treasury steps. Those amiable weeklies, *Judge, Puck,* and *Life,* kept T. S. Sullivant busy with his droll cows and Walt Kuhn with fantastic crocodiles; but *Puck* printed Art Young's grim sketch of tenement life under the title of *American Mothers,* and *The Verdict* used George Luks's pictures in its campaign against McKinley in 1900, while Luks still amused children every Sunday with his *Hogan's Alley* comics in color.

The *Collier's* of Norman Hapgood hired young Boardman Robinson to insult Joe Cannon at regular intervals and to indict the liquor industry in a drawing whose tense lines owed something to Daumier, while old hands like Frost and Gibson drew its indulgent full-page satires of country and city life. Many of the funny men would become painters, but Art Young remained a cartoonist to the end of his long days. As a pictorial reporter he sketched the Haymarket defendants and drew the first daily cartoons in the Midwest; as a middle-aged humorist with a bland line and a genial exaggeration he became a socialist, and his work for *Puck, Life,* and *Judge* acquired a keener sting, whether he attacked the venal press or the makers of war for profit.

The newspaper half-tone had not yet replaced the man with a sketch pad who worked up his rough notations with pen and ink in the office with the hum of the presses in his ear and printer's ink in his nostrils. If the Philadelphia *Press* needed an on-the-spot illustration of a tenement fire, a mine disaster, or an explosion in a delicatessen it was John Sloan who rushed to the scene with a pencil and a scrap of paper, or one of his cronies —George Luks, Everett Shinn, and William Glackens. All four were in their thirties when Gertrude Käsebier made their portraits: the rotund Luks of Pennsylvania Dutch stock with a lusty enthusiasm for Frans Hals, *Tristram Shandy,* and the bottle; the grave Glackens with his shrewd all-perceiving eyes; light-fingered Shinn from New Jersey with dapper suits and loud shirts; the handsome Sloan, whose finely chiseled face had some of the elegance of the posters he designed.

Their gods were Daumier, Hogarth, and Goya, for their training was of a similar sort—the daily encounters which gave them a keen and tolerant interest in plain people, the necessity which bred pictorial invention and a swift getting to the point. As they watched society indulging in various forms of lunacy they were "agin the government" all along the line, as Sloan once said; and they loathed the perfunctory "eyesight painting" of academies, where young people made "bromidic smudges" in classrooms with that old-cathedral smell. They would all have agreed that Robert Henri had formed their philosophy on Thursday evenings at Henri's house, when Luks made rarebits in a skillet over the gas jet.

There was French, English, and Irish blood in Henri, who, only two years older than the oldest of the three, had seen Hals and Velasquez, Rembrandt, Goya and

Art Young cartoon, *Respectability*

The Masses

Manet at first hand before he taught his first classes in Philadelphia. Anshutz had been his first master, in whom the tradition of Eakins lived. The fruits of Henri's more than thirty years of teaching would one day be gathered in that remarkable book, *The Art Spirit;* but Sloan and his comrades heard their earliest formulation. The "transparent honesty" that Henri looked for in the artist he also demanded of life, and he believed that the orderliness in nature, revealed by the painter, could rebuke the man-made chaos. When he looked at an individual it was in the "eager hope of finding there something of the dignity of life, the humor, the humanity . . . that will rescue the race and the nation." No arty-decorative painter could reveal these qualities, nor the academic hack; and as for the dexterity of a Chase, "there is nothing in the juggler's skill of copying things. . . . A good picture is a well-built structure."

Henri was what Garland called a veritist, and his conception had already been described in *Crumbling Idols:* "Art, I must insist, is an individual thing,—the question of one man facing certain facts and telling his relations to them." There was a swift and solid construction of landscape forms in *Far Rockaway,* a broad and spontaneous building of a head in *Mary,* with its bold darks and flatly painted lights, its vigorous characterization, its firm control of a few closely related colors, its technical frankness, and its disarming honesty. Henri was a lesser Hals when he made his portraits, and both

Robert Henri, *Mary*

Addison Gallery of American Art, Andover, Mass.

Pissarro and Sisley had shown him how to paint the rutted New York snow under a grimy sky, the blank brownstone fronts, and the scurrying small figures.

When Henri opened his classes at the Chase School in New York something of his temper was in the air of the metropolis. For Hutchins Hapgood's *The Spirit of the Ghetto,* a study of the Jew's effort to find a place in American life, a young artist named Jacob Epstein drew the people among whom he was born—the old Talmudic scholars, the pushcart men, the novelists, poets, and radicals. "There is no nature in the sweatshop," Epstein said, "and yet it is there and in the crowded street that my love and my imagination call me." One critic faintly praised Hapgood for his picture of a strange eddy in the current of things American, but the average reader doubtless turned with relief to the back pages where F. Hopkinson Smith's books were advertised—*In London Town, The Real Latin Quarter,* and *How Paris Amuses Itself.*

At the same time a former scene painter named Jerome Myers, who had studied at Cooper Union and returned from France with no enthusiasm at all for the real Latin Quarter, painted the first of his East Side genre, his interest divided between its people and the

Everett L. Shinn, *Revue* (detail)

Whitney Museum of American Art, New York City

George B. Luks, *The Spielers*

Addison Gallery of American Art, Andover, Mass.

Maurice B. Prendergast, *Central Park,* water color
Whitney Museum of American Art, New York City

patterns of shape and color they made upon his canvas —Italian children in their Sunday best before a gaudy street shrine or mothers and babies cooling off at night on a river pier. Against the dark shadows in *Madison Square Concert* his dresses and ribbons were brushed with the directness of his friend Sloan.

The color arabesques which Myers sought had already been found by the more sensitive and skillful Maurice Prendergast, who with his brother Charles made picture frames and showcards to keep himself alive. Maurice had painted at St. Malo and Dieppe in the eighties and on his return found similar themes at Marblehead, at Revere Beach, and in Central Park; he was a "confirmed and wary bachelor," as Van Wyck Brooks knew him, who resented short dresses and found nothing as graceful in his later days as the motion women had made at street corners when they lifted their skirts to cross the street.

In Venice, Carpaccio delighted Prendergast and in Paris the broad fresh color, the over-all interplay of the impressionists; and he learned to orchestrate his own tenuous but charming melodies of the early nineteen hundreds. Henry James's impression of Central Park was keyed to the same pitch: "The children at play, more particularly the little girls . . . frisking about over the greenswards, grouping together in the vistas, with an effect of the exquisite in attire . . . that might have created a doubt as to their popular affiliation." The best of the park scenes were not in oil but in water color, the forms of trees, of elegant carriages, of flowered hats, ruffled organdy and black-stockinged legs enclosed mosaiclike in their drawn contours, and each playing its part in the color life of the whole. (See color plate 15.)

Henri watched with pride the painterly achievements of his Philadelphia cronies. Shinn hacked for the New York *Herald* and the *World* and produced flashy murals for Stanford White houses; he discovered that the footlights at Keith's in Union Square shed the same garish light on frilled costumes and backdrops that had delighted him in London and Paris music halls, and played the same tricks with the pretty faces of the girls. Luks covered the Cuban unpleasantness for a Philadelphia newspaper, accomplished his weekly drudge with *Hogan's Alley* comics, and visited Paris before he settled down to painting. In 1905 he made good his boast that he could paint with a shoestring dipped in lard by producing the frowzy *Old Duchess* (Met. Mus.) and the gay *Spielers.* John Spargo, who wrote *The Bitter Cry of the Children,* praised Luks for his slum starvelings and outcasts.

Glackens' sense of the comic was as lively as that of Luks, and his drawings for *McClure's* reminded one of Charles Keene and Phil May, each pen or pencil stroke a witty summation of observed character. But when he

William J. Glackens, *Roller Skating Rink* (Ira Glackens coll.)

Courtesy Kraushaar Galleries, New York City

painted he never staked everything on one moment as Luks did, and it was a subtler brush that created *Chez Mouquin* (Chicago Art Inst.), a picture as knowingly composed as Manet's *Bar at the Folies-Bergère,* though with less originality. The still life on its table was a recollection of the bottles in the French picture; but Glackens' heavy-set and mustached drinker and the girl beside him with hourglass figure and picture hat were American types, modeled with a strong and supple hand in the rich tonalities of this relatively "dark phase" of Glackens. His *Roller Skating Rink,* close to Prendergast in its theme, found movement and space depth in a seeming spontaneity of crowd action where the Bostonian found only the patterns of tapestry.

John Sloan's first allegiance had been to the "decorative" ideas of the poster makers when the brilliant flat patterns of Toulouse-Lautrec and the rich elaborations of Mucha were revolutionizing the art of pictorial advertisement. The fat brush drawings of the Englishman William Nicholson and the linear gracefulness of Aubrey Beardsley had their effect on Americans in the nineties. Edward Penfield's posters and covers for *Harper's,* with their careful arrangement on the page and their simple color balances, were in this mode; and for the Merrymount Press Will H. Bradley imitated Beardsley and the curves of "Art Nouveau" in drawings whose rich borders by Bertram G. Goodhue resembled the products of Kelmscott. At Pratt Institute, Arthur W. Dow was revolutionizing instruction in design, for this former curator of Japanese art in Boston taught principles, not procedures, and his book *Composition* was a demonstration that the designer must begin with the whole before proceeding to the parts.

Sloan could have become a decorator in Bradley's or Penfield's sense. Alternatively, he could have joined the young men who followed the tradition of Pyle, Frost, and Abbey. In an old mill at Chadds Ford on the Brandywine, Pyle instructed a new generation—Violet Oakley, Jessie Willcox Smith, F. E. Schoonover, N. C. Wyeth, and Maxfield Parrish. This generation was com-

John Sloan, *The Wake of the Ferry*

Phillips Memorial Gallery, Washington, D.C.

posed of slenderer talents than its elders. Frank C. Yohn could not make history live as Pyle did, and neither J. Walter Taylor nor W. Appleton Clark worked with distinction. F. Hopkinson Smith was charming but on the softer side, and so were those minor Gibsons, Howard Chandler Christy and Harrison Fisher. In 1905 Edith Wharton's *House of Mirth* was illustrated without distinction by Arthur B. Wenzel, and her *Italian Villas* had colored half-tones whose mellow cypresses and exceedingly blue skies acknowledge the dexterity of Maxfield Parrish and reveal his indebtedness to photographs.

Sloan chose to be neither a posteresque designer nor a "refined" illustrator: his drawings of backstage life were in the *Collier's* serial, *The Making of an Actress,* and his "night vigils" at the back window of his Twenty-third Street studio bore rich and humorous fruit. One could not doubt the "popular affiliation" of the fat women and work-heavy men whose forms Sloan contrasted with deep shadows among the chimneys in his etching *Roofs, Summer Night,* nor resist the humor of *Fifth Avenue Critics.* (See color plate 18.)

The paintings of Sloan demonstrated Henri's principle that a good picture was a well-built structure. In 1904 he made his bow to Henri in the powerful darks and lights of his *Boy with a Piccolo,* and to Manet in the simple breadth of the boy's hands; and in the following year his *Spring, Madison Square* made Hassam seem tepid and fussy. *Dust Storm* of 1907 was a tour de force of wind-tossed trees, stalled automobiles, and scampering people under a false brown dusk (Met. Mus.).

The same fertile year saw two versions of *Wake of the Ferry,* a masterful design with a few elements: the post of the boat, the barrier at its stern, a corner of the upper deck, a lone passenger, and the oily harbor water swelling under a thick sky. Sloan painted his top-heavy ladies picking up their skirts to cross under the Elevated —and these were the days "when an ankle counted"— or a string of wash on a clothesline in the brilliant sun, or the city pavements in a spring rain, with a relish for

John Sloan, *Fifth Avenue Critics,* etching

Whitney Museum of American Art, New York City

Glenn O. Coleman, *Minetta Lane,* lithograph

Whitney Museum of American Art, New York City

texture and for character but also with a superb sense of his picture as a whole. A black cat prowling through snow in a Greenwich Village backyard was placed at the precise point which the canvas asked for, and the dark mass of the Third Avenue Elevated cleaves his *Six O'Clock, Winter* with a forward thrust as powerful as it is premeditated (Phillips Mem. Gall.).

The impact of Henri was to be seen among others than the ex-Philadelphians. He taught Guy Pène du Bois a firm grasp on space and volume; another of his pupils was Glenn Coleman, who lived in Greenwich Village and studied its odd types for drawings and lithographs which would soon appear in the *Masses* alongside Boardman Robinson, Art Young, and John Sloan. Close to the style of Luks was the broadly painted and fleshy *Stag at Sharkey's,* the work of twenty-seven-year-old George Bellows from Ohio, who found his subjects across the street from the Henri school at Sharkey's Athletic Club at a time when Edward Hopper, Rockwell Kent, and Eugene Speicher were his fellow pupils (Cleveland Mus. of Art).

The year 1908 gave the city veritists their first chance to be seen together. Sloan's offerings and those of Luks and Glackens had been rejected the previous year by the Academy and there was no room for them in the dealers' "plush grottos," as Shinn called them. William Macbeth was an exception, and it was Macbeth

Ernest Lawson, *Boat House, Winter, Harlem River*

Corcoran Gallery of Art, Washington, D.C.

who asked his friend Henri to organize a small exhibition of those men whom Henri most admired. It was a foregone conclusion that Sloan's *Hairdresser* and his *Election Night* would hang in the Macbeth Galleries along with Henri's own portrait of *Martche in a White Dress;* that Glackens would show his *Mouquin* and his Central Park coasters, Luks his *Old Duchess*, and Shinn his *White Ballet.*

Henri, however, was not concerned simply with his own disciples, but with individuals who had found free and independent language for personal expression. He therefore completed his group show with Maurice Prendergast's *Beach at St.-Malo* and his American playgrounds, with Ernest Lawson's snow scenes, and with Arthur B. Davies' exquisite pictures of pale dancers by blue seas in a world which only Davies had seen.

Lawson had earned his right to distinction by learning all that Twachtman and Weir could teach him of their impressionist procedures, and by his instinct for solid earth and the flavor of places he built a more robust impressionism than was theirs, in winter scenes along the Harlem and the Hudson. While others dissolved form and character to weave broken color tapestries Lawson maintained his grip on what was underneath the light-reflecting surfaces of old river cabins, boathouses, wet nights in Gramercy Park, and the converging tracks of the old Grand Central Station. From over one's head the span of a bridge thrust back toward its vertical pier in the middle distance, the straight top edge of the bridge threw diagonal shadows against the far abutment, its curve repeated in the water.

Davies had been a draughtsman for a civil engineering concern in Mexico, had studied painting in Chicago and at the Art Students League in New York, and had traveled in Italy. *Along the Erie Canal,* which he painted in 1890, had the charm of a landscape by Ralph Earl in the stiff clustered elms, the long quiet horizontals, the primly ordered hills (Phillips Mem. Gall.). Now his delicately moving nymphs who gleamed in the early morning light against green cliffs and reflected themselves in impossibly blue lakes were the fruit of endless studies made from life on faintly toned paper with a

Arthur B. Davies, *Crescendo* (detail)

Whitney Museum of American Art, New York City

deft crayon and touched with opaque white lights and thin colored washes. They must have seemed far from home among Shinn's variety stars and the corseted creatures of John Sloan.

Henri's gesture in withdrawing his own work from the Academy exhibition and in organizing a rival one was not lost upon the critics. One of them called his group "the Eight," and the name stuck to them even though they never held another show after this demonstration had been seen in New York, in Philadelphia, and in Chicago. The *Outlook* conceded that the vivacity and touch and go of such painting kept time with twentieth-century life; but it referred to Henri, Luks, and Bellows as extremists who "deliberately and conscientiously paint the ugly wherever it occurs."

This was a natural response from the America of 1908, where William Faversham played *Julius Caesar* and William Hodge *The Man from Home,* the Metropolitan Museum bought a Giovanni Bellini, *The Merry Widow* played "three hundred feet above the hot street," and O. Henry published his *The Voice of the City*. It should have been obvious that the men and women in Sloan's pictures had stepped from O. Henry's pages. Why, then, was one half of the Eight referred to as the "Ash Can School" and the "Revolutionary Black Gang"? The genre of Luks and Sloan, Glackens and Shinn was in the robust and heartily sentimental tradition of Mount and Bingham; the portraits of Henri had the honesty if not the tragic depth of Eakins; the snow in city backyards and on the Hudson Palisades was the same snow which Durrie had more carefully painted on Connecticut farms. Nor were these younger men pioneers of technique. As John Baur has observed, none of them brought unknown methods of form and color to his work. Duveneck had painted as broadly as they did, and Chase as swiftly, some twenty years before; Hassam and Twachtman had spoken the language of impressionism while the four were cub reporters.

What shocked the world of art was a preoccupation with types, localities, and incidents to which Americans were conveniently deaf and blind. A degree of strenuousness could be forgiven in the days of Teddy Roosevelt; but to paint drunks and slatterns, pushcart peddlers and coal mines, bedrooms and barrooms was somehow to be classed among the socialists, anarchists, and other disturbers of the prosperous equilibrium.

Unhurt by name-calling, the "Revolutionary Black Gang" campaigned against the entrenched monopolists of art. They knew that jury prizes still went to the safer people; they observed when the Charles T. Yerkes collection was sold in 1910 that a Ryder reached $260 but a Bouguereau $10,000; an Inness brought $8,400, and an Alma-Tadema over $22,000. In the spring of that year a larger group than the Eight assembled a Show of Independents which had no organizational motives and was open to all serious artists. More than five hundred paintings, drawings, and sculptures were hung without benefit of a jury.

Frank Jewett Mather of the *Nation* conceded that much of this work would have been unacceptable to the Academy and that its best pictures were by dissatisfied members or associates of that body. Here and there he detected the influence of the revolutionary moderns, and he observed that both Maurice Prendergast and Morton Schamberg were "wearing the shoes of Cézanne." For an old-fashioned person, he said, there was "more green, yellow and red sickness about than positive talent." The critic who recoiled before so mild a dose of modernism was ill prepared for the epidemic which was only three years in the future.

CHAPTER 26 / THE BOOK AND THE EDIFICE

The Putnams published in 1900 a volume with a pompous title which gave a more impressive account of what the nation had achieved in medicine and military science, in life insurance and libraries, in gold production, steel, women's rights, and psychic research than in the arts. Russell Sturgis was one of the contributors to *The Nineteenth Century, A Review of Progress during the Past One Hundred Years in the Chief Departments of Human Activity;* and Sturgis, the scholarly critic and historian of architecture, declared that new problems and new materials had found few architects intelligent enough to cope with them. This faithful Ruskinian knew his first principles and could never accept the clever plan on paper as a substitute for designing in three dimensions; he had written on an earlier occasion that no building could be judged by its outline on the ground, since it would never be looked into from above by a disembodied spirit to whom the roof was transparent. Now he saluted Sullivan's effort to design the exteriors of lofty steel-framed structures in accordance with their nature; but his report closed with a question: Would a community whose best energies were given to making money apply those energies in the next hundred years with serious purpose to architecture as an art? The nation's artistic mind, he concluded, had outgrown its callow, ill-bred youth, but in 1900 had not reached maturity.

Nothing could have been more immature, for example, than the country's attitude toward the planning and replanning of its towns. Nearly a century before, Owen's New Harmony had implied the value and beauty of a community whose life could proceed as an integrated whole; and in the mid-century there had been groups of cooperatively owned houses in the outskirts of American cities, like John Stevens' Industrial Homes Associations. No real effort had been made, however, to stem the tide of speculation and reckless concentration which had made the larger town a shapeless mass of factories, commercial buildings, residential oases, and shabby, depressing slums. It was now too late to do more than modify these features of the older cities; the alternative was to plan new ones. Ebenezer Howard had shown how this could be done in *Garden Cities of Tomorrow,* with its small industrial units surrounded by well-spaced homes and greenbelts, and the garden city of Letchworth in England rose in 1903 to demonstrate his principles. Six years later Raymond Unwin devoted his *Town Planning in Practice* to civic art as an expression of the total life of the community, surveying the history of that notion from Egypt to Sir Christopher Wren.

This book and Patrick Geddes' *City Development* of 1904 would be a challenge and an inspiration to the few American designers of vision in the nineteen twenties; but meanwhile what passed for "planning" in the century's first few years was a shallow solution on the aesthetic level, a tactful mitigation of a disorder which had its roots in the national attitude toward private property and the inalienable right to speculate with land.

There was a flurry of municipal planning in the first decade of the century: a scheme for Los Angeles with an avenue a mile long and two hundred feet wide ending in a plaza. Olmsted and Cass Gilbert were trying to restore order out of chaos at New Haven; Burnham drew a plan for Chicago and another for Cleveland, in the latter case assisted by Carrère and Arnold Brunner. San Francisco failed to adopt a Burnham scheme. When the Columbus, Ohio, Commission discovered that a new skyscraper stood on the edge of its proposed long mall to the state house, it recommended that a companion be built for the sake of symmetry. Such planners did their best to plant a miniature version of the Chicago Exposition in the midst of some urban tangle and thus to present as dignified a front as possible to the world.

No one could complain in the early nineteen hundreds that architecture was not taken seriously. Up and down the land courses were being given in colleges and universities; the Society of Beaux-Arts Architects conducted extension courses and organized ateliers; every important structure was described, illustrated, and criticized in the professional periodicals. The *American Art Annual* published in 1900 a directory of architects which was far from being complete, since it was drawn from the membership lists of seven professional societies, yet the roster had nearly twelve hundred names and in 1910 had risen to over twenty-six hundred.

The work of most of them suffered not so much from what Sturgis called immaturity as from premature senility. The shingled "Richardsonian" of Babb, Cook, and Willard, for example, and the railway stations of the dead master's partners and pupils were thin variations on his sturdy theme; without his instinct for unity, their contrasts of light and dark stone defaced the solid wall, their careful asymmetry became a loose jumble of

McKim, Mead, & White, Columbia University Library, New York City

Wurts Bros. photo

parts. Their failure was written large and sprawling in schools, libraries, town halls, and courthouses in what Ralph Adams Cram calls a "love-feast of cavernous arches, quarry-faced ashlar, cyclopean voussoirs and seaweed decorations." Frank E. Case, a prosperous manufacturer of dental equipment, was one of countless citizens who built in this fashion, and whose mansion at Canton, Ohio, in the nineties bristled with gables, with turrets poked into angles, with monstrous chimneys erupting from sandstone façades, and with porte-cocheres huddling against them.

Large and small, in country and in suburb, thousands of competent men rang endless changes on the Romanesque, the Queen Anne, and a "Colonial" which reproduced the low ceilings, the boxlike rooms, the small windows of the age of fireplaces. In cities where the human stream wore deeper among man-made canyons with every year of "progress," firms like George Browne Post and Sons committed themselves to no one dialect but spoke loudly and fluently in all, clinging to the old three-part formula for the skyscraper which Sullivan had long since discarded. In the same years which saw Sullivan's Bayard Building in Bleecker Street praised by Montgomery Schuyler as architecture "founded on the facts of the case," the Posts raised New York's tallest structure, the St. Paul, whose twenty-two stories apologized garrulously for being so high. Their Prudential Insurance Building in Newark was lined with Caen marble, and Blashfield's *Prudencia* graced the ceiling of its board room; their huge hotels at Detroit and Cleveland in the century's second decade established a type but not a style.

As the states outgrew their old capitols the pattern of Thornton, Latrobe, and Walter on the Potomac was let out to fit them. The ungainly national dome was on McKim's state house at Providence in 1903, with four tourelles at its base which recalled the more florid ones on Madison Square Garden; it rode the crossing of the Posts' capitol at Madison, Wisconsin, and reared itself as the climax of the Wilder and White group in faraway Olympia in the State of Washington.

All these were monuments to the Easiest Way, like Francis Henry Kimball's Manhattan Life, the Metropolitan Life by Le Brun with its Venetian campanile, the pedimented Stock Exchange in New York by Post and Sons, the châteaulike St. Luke's Hospital by Ernest Flagg, the Waldorf-Astoria of Henry J. Hardenbergh—to choose at random among their kind. There were plan-and-elevation men in all cities, many of whom took their cue from McKim, Mead, and White, who had no peers in the art of the polished quotation. Having conquered the Chicago Exposition, the McKim idea proceeded to conquer the country. The firm produced another Pantheon with a dim reading room beneath its dome, the Columbia Library, and its Herald Building of 1894 was an exquisite near replica of the Consiglio Palace at Verona. Three years later the palazzo formula was used again in the University Club where H. Siddons

Mowbray plagiarized the Pintoricchio murals at Rome and Siena. The Baths of Caracalla became the Pennsylvania Station in 1903, its huge waiting hall of Roman travertine dwarfing the human passenger, the naked steel trusses of its concourse more impressive than the veneered tepidarium behind it.

The McKim example, in the words of Pope, "filled half the land with imitating fools"; and when Mr. Morgan's library in 1906 was housed behind the Palladian motif of the Villa Medici, Rochester copied it in the Art Gallery of Foster, Gade, and Graham.

McKim's young men had already been heard from when Cass Gilbert placed the dome of St. Peter's on his St. Paul capitol in 1896, and when John Merven Carrère and Thomas Hastings designed a public library in New York which was only a little better adapted to its purpose than the Boston one. Carrère and Hastings had been fellow students at the Beaux-Arts before they worked together for McKim and became partners on their own, designing a more or less Spanish hotel for Henry Flagler at St. Augustine. They rebuilt the Palace of Fontainebleau at Lakewood, New Jersey, as the Hotel Laurel-in-the-Pines. The rear façade of their New York Public Library suggested the life within as its three Roman arches on Fifth Avenue did not; their Frick house in the Louis XVI manner was as expensively simple as the Morgan pile; they made the Senate and House Office Buildings discreetly subordinate companions to the Washington Capitol.

In the century since Latrobe, America had always had its partisans of the crocket and the finial. Now Upjohn and James Renwick were dead, leaving Trinity, Grace Church, and St. Patrick's to remind younger men of their fine strength and independence. Charles Coolidge Haight designed the General Theological Seminary in the eighties, and his sober charm in these and his Yale buildings seemed the proper scholastic note. New Yorkers praised the skill with which J. Stewart Barney's massive tower—in fact, a five-story office building—rode the nave of his Broadway Tabernacle. What the Gothicists needed was a scholar-designer who could speak this language as authoritatively as McKim spoke another, and who could justify the flying buttress in the age of Bryan. This man was Ralph Adams Cram, whose Gothic quest had begun in the eighties.

Cram, Goodhue, & Ferguson, Post Headquarters, West Point, N.Y.

Photo Hillyer Art Library, Northampton, Mass.

Neither of Cram's partners shared his concern with the values beneath forms. The practical mind of Frank W. Ferguson occupied itself with problems of business, construction details, and efficient specifications, which he organized into systematic office files. Bertram G. Goodhue's mind was pictorial; dissatisfied with the hard, ruler-drawn lines of architectural rendering, and perhaps inspired by the brilliant pen-and-ink methods of Pennell and the illustrators, he made ingratiating sketches of the firm's projects. In the Goodhue drawings, details were tactfully suppressed to intimate how a structure would look when the sun played over its forms and patterned them with shadows. He had learned his Gothic from Renwick and practiced it with an eye for the handsome general effect. He built a church at Havana with the lush detail of an authentic Spanish mission, launched the California Renaissance with his Gillespie villa at

Santa Barbara, and gave the Romanesque a new twist in the brick vaults of St. Bartholomew's in New York. The gigantic reredos of St. Thomas' on Fifth Avenue was his, and much of the firm's work at West Point had his flair for the handsome site handsomely built upon.

Between the West Point commission of 1903 and the Princeton Graduate College ten years later it was Cram who talked and wrote of the principles behind the "Gothic Restoration." He shared Bergson's belief that man's effort to shape life by his intellect is bound to fail, since his creative powers transcend his reasoning; nor could Cram find in the recent history of his art any masterpiece which "crescent individualism" had built. His version of the past ran parallel to that of the younger Pugin: first the great periods when mankind built out of a compelling faith, a communal spirit, a soul and not a brain; then the decline with the Renaissance, to which Cram added Jefferson's "spacious and delusive imitations," the Graeco-Baptist style, the libelous Carpenter's Gothic, and the lumpy Romanesque.

One need look for no great architecture, no authentic style, Cram said, until a pagan society became a deeply and pervasively Christian one, until art ceased to serve the world and went back to serving God. In the meantime the buttressed barracks, the fortresslike Chapel and Post Headquarters at West Point could at least remind modern society of a unity and a motivation it had lost; at Princeton the quadrangle and English Perpendicular tower of the Graduate College could symbolize the nonmaterial ends of education; while churches at Pittsburgh, Cleveland, Chicago, and Houston made other men's Gothic seem shallow and crude. To the modern critic, Cram's distinction lies in his insistence that only a sound community can build noble architecture, and in his lifelong refusal to accept an easier ideal.

Only Frank Lloyd Wright could match this ardor and this courage, yet the creed which Wright expounded before women's clubs, fellow architects, and Daughters of the American Revolution was fashioned from far different materials and had quite other implications. It was not Thomas Aquinas whom he worshiped, but Thomas Jefferson and Thomas Paine. He could thank his Wisconsin forebears for his own foursquare self-reliance, though Shelley and Carlyle, Rousseau and Goethe loosened the grip of their Unitarian dogma from his mind; he absorbed in his years with Louis Sullivan the idea that life was integral and could have an organic quality of its own. Whitman added his spark to the flame of Wright's democracy; he read Tolstoy and Mazzini, and in a chapter of Victor Hugo's *Notre Dame* he found a magnificent tribute to the art he practiced. Under the title *One Shall Destroy the Other,* Hugo said that, before the printing press, the best of human thought had been inscribed in this great granite book. For the last three centuries architecture had declined as the colossal edifice of the printed word rose in its place; the book had destroyed the edifice, and architecture was dead, although "the advent of some architectural genius may startle us unexpectedly even in the twentieth century."

Wright was that genius, and before the century was ten years old had shaped his philosophy and plotted his course. At the core of that philosophy was the American proposition: democracy and its promise of unwarped growth for the individual. His ideal society would derive its unity not from submission to any authority, religious or secular, but from the laws of normal growth which Sullivan had helped Wright to discern in nature, and which the Chinese philosopher Lao-tse had once explained.

Whatever impeded that organic unfolding must be rejected. Wright never forgot the opening words of *Progress and Poverty,* where Henry George declared that Capitalism must have been stood on its head like a pyramid on its apex to produce a "progress" where luxury and destitution walked together and where the gulf widened between Dives and Lazarus. Even Anarchism, with its respect for the other fellow's rights, was preferable to this false Capitalism which could make empires, wars, and insolent bureaucracies but not creative personalities; nor could Wright accept what he called the "worm's-eye view" of the Socialists, whose concern for the mass of men he believed a threat to the free individual.

Wright's democratic citizen, in short, must build a true Capitalism whose basis was not the factory nor the shop but the land itself, owned and improved by the people, not gambled with by speculators. He gave Samuel Butler's name "Usonia" to his organic commonwealth where credit belonged to everybody; where production was determined by what the consumer needed; where the fruits of the age of invention belonged to the citizens; where education was free and cooperation the law of life; where only the people could vote a war; and where the congestion of human life in great ugly centers was reversed.

Wright's generous utopia was not built in a day, though its main outlines were clear before he reached thirty in Chicago. It was made, like his buildings, from the materials at hand, tested and tried, and his temper as he sought architectural forms for democracy was the temper of Henry George: "If the conclusions that we reach run counter to our prejudices, let us not flinch; if they challenge institutions that have long been deemed wise and natural, let us not turn back." Above all, there would be no turning back to the taste of any age; from the great Gothic, Wright would take its organic principle but none of its forms; and as for the

Frank L. Wright, Ward H. Willits house, Highland Park, Ill.

Fuermann photo, Chicago Architectural Photographing Co.

Renaissance, hatred grew in him as he studied its wanton destructiveness of the organic, its shapes put on from without; it was not a development but a disease, a soulless blight. In a sense which Hugo had not intended, the book had killed the edifice. The architecture which Wright proposed to build would be no better and no worse than the quality of life, private or communal, which it made possible.

He was not a lone reformer in the Chicago of the nineties over whose great checkerboard, as Henry B. Fuller wrote, "keenness and rapacity played their daring and wary game." The Studio Building was described by Fuller as a "rabbit warren" where Lorado Taft and his fellow sculptors upheld the Columbian classicism while Hamlin Garland urged them toward a greater interest in native themes and treatment. Most Chicago people behaved, to be sure, as though Oscar Wilde had never admonished them; Curtis Jadwin, who cornered wheat in Norris' *The Pit,* found rooms in his mansion that he had never seen and hung Bouguereau's bathing nymphs in an art gallery which was a two-storied rotunda with a dome of colored glass and an organ large and loud enough for a cathedral.

But Sullivan had meanwhile inspired a band of younger men to design homes and furnishings of an honest simplicity, and when a Chicago clergyman preached that a man's home was a place for simple and restful living, not for nervously expensive display, his sermon-essays were printed by hand in a volume designed by Wright, and their title, *The House Beautiful,* was borrowed by a new magazine where Eugene Klapp, Henry Harvey, and Herbert Stone campaigned for the simplifying of homes and their decoration. In Chicago, as elsewhere, William Morris had inspired Arts and Crafts circles whose members purged their rooms of bric-a-brac and found in the making of their own chairs, tables, and hangings some of the lost satisfactions of the premechanical age. "Dress reform houses" appeared on Chicago streets, the work of Myron Hunt, of George Mayer, of Hugh Garden, and of a dozen others, while Claude Bragdon became a missionary of the new gospel in Buffalo, and Harvey Ellis in Minneapolis.

The virtues of the "Chicago school" were largely negative ones, and from the beginning Wright's inventiveness, his imagination, and his dauntless individuality went far beyond their Spartan rigor. There was a faintly Richardsonian flavor in his own house of 1889 at Oak Park, but the original tang was here and in the Tudor shapes of the Nathan Moore house in 1895, in the compact strength of the somewhat "Colonial" Blossom house in 1892. These were brief stylistic gestures compared to the Charnley house; and when, in the year 1894, Wright declared his principles in a speech at Evanston, his just-completed house at River Forest for W. H. Winslow demonstrated them. "There is no one part of your building," he said, "that may not be made a thing of beauty in itself as related to the whole"; and those relationships were to be seen in the brickwork and the terra-cotta frieze above it, in the stone phrasing of the central door and windows, and in the interplay of polygon with semicircle, of clean vertical with jutting horizontal at the back of the Winslow house.

The word and the deed kept pace with each other in the years that followed. The masculine dignity of Wright's low-cost housing design for Francisco Terrace and his apartments on West Walnut Street, Chicago, underscored his remark that true simplicity was not the simplicity of the side of a barn; the sturdy shelves, tables, and benches which he made an integral part of

Frank L. Wright, Interior, Darwin Martin house, Buffalo, N.Y.

Courtesy Henry-Russell Hitchcock

his own studio in 1895 were his substitute for the "machine-carved and over-wrought," the "cold molasses, piano-finished" furnishings he condemned in his talk of that year for the University Guild.

In 1900 he wrote about Japanese prints, whose subtle ordering of nature he had first experienced at the Chicago Exposition. That order was in his two houses at Kankakee: his Bradley dining room was conceived as a unit whose shapes and proportions reappeared in the chairs and tables; almost the whole ground floor of the Hickox home was one space, with only that hint of division to be found in Japanese houses, and on its exterior Wright used dark vertical strips of wood against plaster with the skill of a Hiroshige.

A Hull House audience of 1901 heard him announce that the machine was here to stay and that one must use it creatively, not prostitute it in the reproduction with murderous ubiquity of premachine-age forms. He told the Chicago Women's Club the following year that a home must in a special sense belong to its owner and belong to the land from which it rises, standing firmly in its socket on the earth, and built of gold-colored or ruddy tan brick, "the choicest of all earth's hues." The stance of his Ward Willits house in Highland Park was of that sort, its amplified cross plan and the rhythm of its projections the culmination of his essays toward the prairie house.

In the year 1904, when *House Beautiful* reproduced the gaudy interiors of the best Chicago people in a series called *The Poor Taste of the Rich,* Buffalo saw Wright's superb Darwin Martin residence and his Larkin Administration Building. He had never contrived as fine a continuity of inner spaces, nor handsomer chairs and tables than in the Martin design, nor so subtly locked the various units together: the main house with long banked windows, porches, and porte-cochere, the gallery to the conservatory, the terraced flower beds and urns whose living masses of green were as essential to the whole as the stone and yellow brick above them. The exposed piers of vitreous brick in the Martin house were an integral part of the decorative scheme, and over the living room fireplace the fumed white oak was en-

Frank L. Wright, Larkin Building, Buffalo, N.Y.

Fuermann photo, Chicago Architectural Photographing Co.

riched with gold wistaria forms against a duller gold mosaic.

One could conjure the ghost of Downing to admire this interweaving of natural with man-made beauty, and one could see at last, after fifty years and more, the principles of Horatio Greenough given form. That remarkable man had once observed that nature made the laws of building and that a ship was a marvel of construction because it had to meet the dread test of wind and water. As for our blunders on terra firma, Greenough had written: "Instead of forcing the functions of every sort of building into one general form, adopting an outward shape for the sake of the eye or of association, without reference to the inner distribution, let us begin from the heart as a nucleus, and work outwards."

The heart of the Larkin Building was a many-galleried court lighted from above and from windows on the sides that were sealed from the dirt and noise of the near-by railroad yards. Clerks sat before built-in files which were part of the wall. Clean and majestic rose the brick piers from floor to skylight around this nucleus, and the piers on the exterior spoke of the interior divisions, at each corner a massive unbroken tower of brick which housed a stairway and an intake for fresh air; a fireproof structure clean, efficient, and gracious with its banked shrubs, its elaboration of the pier tops with simple ornamental forms, its entrance at the side with a fountain and a door which was a huge sheet of plate glass, its iron fence where the big shapes of the whole were repeated on a lesser scale.

If Wright's projected row of houses for the Larkin employees had been built they might have saved many a later blunder on terra firma, for Wright had achieved a rhythm of banked casement windows, shadowed by cantilevered roofs, of recurrent chimneys and doorway recesses; and his compact two-story units proved that repetition need not be monotony.

As with wood, stone, and brick, so with the new material of poured concrete, Wright found appropriate textures, silhouettes, and volumes in Unity Church at Oak Park, which he designed for the Universalists in

1905: two buildings with a linking unit, the great cube-like masses unbroken save by clerestories whose piers had severe ornament on their upper faces, and by the powerful shadows cast by thick projecting slabs of roof. When the structure was done his dubious clients conceded his success and found in their auditorium that "sense of happy cloudless day" which he had predicted.

For Wright as for the cause of American art in general, the year 1908 turned out to be a pivotal one. In that year, Macbeth's gave Robert Henri's group its exhibition, and Alfred Stieglitz hung the strange drawings and stranger paintings of Rodin and Matisse at "291." Cram built his handsome West Point Gymnasium; the Union Station at Washington by Daniel Burnham stood complete in all its pseudo-Roman elegance. Carrère published *City Improvement from the Artistic Standpoint,* revealing how superficial was his approach to a problem of desperate importance. The *Architectural Record* debated the value of a Beaux-Arts training to a young American, one of its experts concluding that native schools were superior, since new types of building made claims on the designer for which Paris had no solution.

The world seemed to have forgotten Louis Sullivan, except for Schuyler and Sturgis and a handful of young Westerners who read his *Kindergarten Chats* and his *Craftsman* articles on the American people and their architecture. His commissions were now few and far between: his pioneering design for the Schlesinger-Mayer department store in Chicago, his small banks which Hugh Morrison calls "jewels on the shoddy main streets of the prairie towns," and in 1907 his Babson house at Riverside. The *Architectural Record* drew a close parallel between the Babson home and Wright's Coonley residence of the same time and place, concluding that Sullivan's smaller and simpler scheme would appeal to a more normal taste than that of his former assistant.

It was in 1908 that Sullivan wrote *Democracy: A Man-Search,* unpublished for more than thirty years, asserting that "democracy is ever a revolution . . . an aspiration, a great instinctive reality pushing up through the heavy overlay of illusion, and seeking form for its superb and calm spirit." And with more precision and concreteness Frank Lloyd Wright in 1908 wrote for the *Architectural Record* a full statement of his belief and practice, *In the Cause of Architecture,* with eighty-seven reproductions of his work. He reaffirmed his belief in nature's law, observing that nature rarely says a thing and tries to take it back at the same time; he acknowledged his debt to Louis Sullivan and then proceeded to state his own propositions. To achieve that simplicity and repose which were the true measure of his art a building should contain as few rooms as intelligent living asked for; openings must be part of the structure, not holes punched in it; "decoration" had best be eliminated unless it be wrought in the warp and woof of the structure; all appliances or fixtures must be assimilated into the design of the whole; a picture not part of the structural whole was a defacement of good walls; the best furniture is built into a house as part of the original scheme; a house should be as individual as its owner and should grow easily out of its site, as did his own Coonley house of that year and his Robie house of 1909.

Go not to the ribbon counter for your color schemes, he wrote, but to the autumn woods and fields; develop what is the natural texture of wood or plaster, brick or stone; make use of the machine, for it is the normal tool of our civilization; "give it work that it can do well." In words whose modesty concealed their radical significance he quietly explained what he had done in these fifteen years. "As for the future, the work shall grow more truly simple . . . more fluent . . . more organic . . . for only so can architecture be worthy of its high rank as a fine art."

The man who thus designed his own future was no honorless prophet in his own country. To be sure, the greater number of his fellow architects behaved as though he had not cut the ground from beneath their practices. McKim died in 1909 and Cortissoz in *Scribner's* pronounced his eulogy, but there remained a host of what Wright called the "voluntary pall-bearers for the remains of Thomas Jefferson," and the gigantic colonnade of the New York State Education Building by Palmer and Hornbostel went up at Albany in the year of McKim's death. Even the perceptive Sturgis, in one of his last articles in the *Architectural Record,* pronounced the Larkin Building an extremely ugly affair, though he sympathized with Wright's attempt to make comely a hard-working and economical structure. After praising the intelligence of Wright's internal planning, he condemned the whole for its failure to produce graceful and simple combinations of light and shade, its knife-like edges, its planes unmodified by projecting bands, corbels, moldings, or color patterns. The architect had gone beyond even this enlightened critic's power to follow him.

Yet as early as 1902 Chicago had given Wright's work an exhibition; the readers of half a dozen periodicals were familiar with his designs; imitators were already cribbing what they called his "style"; and the list of his projects and realized structures before 1910 contains nearly two hundred items and includes houses, apartments, commercial buildings, and housing schemes for town and country. That English preacher of Arts and Crafts, C. R. Ashbee, visited Wright; Kuno Francke saw his Chicago work and urged him to go to Germany;

Berlage talked with him in 1910 and returned to lecture on his work before German architects at a time when isolated reformer groups were busy with like experiments in France, Holland, Austria, and Scandinavia. When Wasmuth of Berlin published two handsome monographs on Wright in 1910 and 1911, in which much of his projected and completed work was illustrated, his enormous influence on Europe began.

At forty, Frank Lloyd Wright, like Martin Luther, had posted his principles. "Architecture by now was mine," as he later said; and in the years that followed, while the "rubbish heap of the styles" mounted around him, there issued from his workroom designs of inexhaustible originality. Their character had been predicted when he wrote of his work: "It shall grow not only to fit more perfectly the processes that are called upon to produce it, but shall further find whatever is lovely or of good repute in method or process, and idealize it with the cleanest, most virile stroke I can imagine."

Frank L. Wright, F. C. Robie house, Chicago, Ill.

Fuermann photo, Chicago Architectural Photographing Co.

Mervin Jules, *Museum of Modern Art* ▶

Mr. and Mrs. Paul Seton coll.

PART TWO

ART'S COMING OF AGE

INTRODUCTION / ART AND MR. PODSNAP

If Sullivan, Wright, and Stieglitz played John the Baptist in their time, it was the time which cast them in that role. The egoism of his master, Wright said, had been more armor than character. The time was out of joint, the world no longer moving steadily and sanely toward purposes commonly willed, toward the fulfillment of man's powers and his desires. "Here is no body of culture," Wright once said of Sullivan's work, "evolving through centuries of time a scheme and 'style' of plastic expression but an Individual working away in the poetry-crushing environment of a more cruel materialism than any seen since the days of the brutal Romans."

This sense of alienation from the world's people was to permeate the modern effort. The very terms the artists and their spokesmen used — terms like "plastic equivalent" and "significant form"—drove artist and layman further apart. A multitude of "isms" developed as numerous branches and shoots put forth from the trunk of this modern tree, sect warred upon sect, and manifestoes became wordy skirmishes on the battleground of aesthetic theories.

Half a century later one can see a common effort and a pervasive character in all this pioneering. In peculiarly bleak circumstances the painter and architect, the sculptor and stage designer can be seen struggling to regain lost ground and to re-establish what had always been their function in the world. Since time began, the artist's emotions have run deeper than the average, his imagination has ranged further, his eye has seen more clearly, his brain and hand have been capable of perceiving and of setting forth relationships of which most men were oblivious. His special act has been the making of forms through which others shared with him the meaning of experiences common to all. Such was Giotto, summing up all that religious men once believed, and Goya making the *Disasters of War* to chastise men for being barbarians; such was Daumier, going blind in his sixties over the lithographic stones which bore his passionate belief in justice and the essential decency of the small citizen.

In the mind of the true artist there has been a tension when the traditional and familiar forms of art, which have been socially shaped and are persistent, meet the changing experiences of the present moment. From this tension he creates a synthesis; he must make new forms because old ones are inadequate for new content. To ask that he do anything less is to ask that he cease to be an artist.

The world of Wright, Cézanne, and Van Gogh set a premium on the pseudo artist with his facile solution and his shallow grasp. The fruitful continuity between art and the normal experience of mankind had broken down, though philosophers differed on when, how, and why. Henry Adams concluded it had happened when the Virgin ceased to be a power and became a picture; Tolstoy said it was when the artist forgot his fraternity with suffering men; Veblen, when art became a showy index of superfluous wealth.

Faced with the dislocation between art and non-art, a man could move into the more comfortable past and stay there. He could rebuild the Parthenon as the First National Bank, place a mortarboard on Athena's head and call her the Spirit of Education, or attempt nothing less than the rehabilitation of the artist as a maker of forms of and for his time. In the latter case he would claim certain drastic freedoms, personal and artistic, in the teeth of convention and of visual habit.

First of all, the modern would reject the so-called "imitation of nature." For roughly five hundred years artists had objectified their vision in forms which corresponded more or less with what every man saw about him. The worst of them had been content with painted equivalents of this "nature"; the best of them sought something more, knowing that no artist can literally imitate nature even if he wishes, and that nature and art may overlap but never coincide. When the modern compared Rembrandt, Poussin, and Veronese with the "naturalism" of his own day, he found in the latter a transcription of observed fact into which the artist had put no thought, feeling, or personal conviction, and from which the layman derived only the lazy pleasures of recognition.

Once more the balance would have to shift toward those elements in a work of art which result directly from the play of the artist's intellect, his emotions, his human sympathies upon his visual material. This revolution would bring gain and loss; it would restore to the artist his reason for being but it would make shapes and colors so new and unfamiliar as to provide small ground for mutual understanding between artist and public. The consequent estrangement could be charged to modern society itself, or it could be rationalized by the notion that art by its nature can never appeal to the many. The artist could be socially hopeful though independent or he could deny his responsibility to any but himself.

If Van Gogh and Gauguin, Cézanne, Seurat, and Renoir were the patron saints of the moderns it was because each of them managed to be in his own way a fully creative artist. None of them was content with a passive reflection of the external world; each of them used the impressionist freedoms to gain still greater freedoms.

Cézanne was too humble a worshiper of nature to seek the momentary play of light over her forms but probed for the permanent relationships of field and mountain, tree and cloud, for greater amplitude of volumes, for continuities beneath the accidental. He sat for hours in the sunshine before the Mont Sainte-Victoire in the effort to build up from nothing on his canvas a world of planes and volumes as organically complete as the one he saw before him.

When he was lucky he found the red and yellow, the blue or violet that would define the position of each object in space and clarify its relation to all other objects, whether or not that color was the one his eye received from the object; he found correspondences of direction between the edge of a hill and a bending tree branch, between the slope of a roof and the slope of a cliff, between the long horizontal of an aqueduct and the edge of a pasture. He built paintings as Frank Lloyd Wright built houses, and his language was equally new: sequences of color on a mountain or an apple devoid of the gray-brown shadows hitherto considered essential to rounding a volume; simplifications which said one forceful thing and refused to take it back. These were Cézanne's "distortions," his means for telling all-inclusive truths while others spoke half-truths.

The livid yellows, the searing blues, and flaming vermilions of Van Gogh were no closer to "nature" than Cézanne's architectural colors, but he wanted them to suggest "any emotion of an ardent temperament." There was a violence in his traffic with things and people which shocked the prudent and strained his own mind beyond sanity. His was the "mental labor of balancing the six essential colors—sheer work and calculation, with one's mind utterly on the stretch," the very antithesis of Cézanne's plodding; and in those moments of terrible concentration he found the majestic sweep of meadows, the almost painful tangibility of potatoes, the torment of cypress trees, the rock shapes which seemed to writhe in the process of being created, the flame and heat of sunflowers, the peasant disfigured by his labor.

Van Gogh's "distortions" were the swirling contours, the stabbing colors, the powerful brush accents, the stark confrontations of one area with another which were his symbols for the human meaning these things

Paul Cézanne, *Poor House on the Hill*

Metropolitan Museum of Art, New York City

had for him. The faces of his potato eaters had the rich browns of the earth from which they dug their food; Roulin's beard bristled with his own republicanism, and his postman's uniform took the shapes of his "gestures in the manner of Garibaldi." No painter since Rembrandt had so humbly, so insistently evoked what was invincible in the plainest of people.

Seurat's integrity was of a colder kind; he was an engineer with horizontal and vertical stress and counterpoise, with subtle permutations of broken color. The people of his *Grande Jatte* sit or lie or stand in the spaces he made for them on the bank of the island, each in his necessary place, no slightest shape of bonnet or umbrella without its calculated relation to the whole, no scrap of color which does not at once harmonize and contrast with every other.

Gauguin's island was in the South Seas, not the Seine, and of his palpitant greens and his hot brown flesh he said that "the cold calculations of reason have not presided at this birth." This broker renounced money and found poverty a torment; this rebel against domesticity went haunted by the thought of wife and children; this enemy of prudery and the Church lived among Tahitians perverted by missionaries and soiled by petty French officials. With a reckless courage he left the Philistine mainland only to find that his island was a peninsula; and the brilliant patterns of his painted world were as much the projections of his own spirit as of the realities around him.

Gauguin allowed nothing to stand between his images and the thought they bodied forth, and that thought sometimes came to the painter as he worked, idea and form developing together in mutual reinforcement. A Tahitian girl lying naked on her bed became *The Spirit of the Dead Watching,* the primitive terror of Tupapau. In Gauguin's forests there were no deep-thrusting spaces but a tapestry of brilliance spread on the canvas, a balanced interplay of shapes and intensities; the roundness and weight of the breasts and legs of his grave, impersonal islanders were in their contours and their mass. Gauguin could not find a nineteenth-century Paradise but he could paint one.

The Paradise of Renoir, as Wilhelm Hausenstein said, was in Paris, and a plump housemaid in a brook was for him what Venus had been for Titian and Boucher. This lover of cities was no man of ideas; he loved the healthy human animal and had a great gift for shaping its forms vigorously under the impact of the sun. Renoir's overdressed children and his bathing women had nothing in common with the broken-down and vicious people whose silhouette Lautrec drew with such malicious truth, nor would he suppress the physical abundance of their bodies to make a pattern, as Gauguin, Lautrec, and Whistler did, and before them the Japanese. Out of the impressionist play of pure, half-mingled colors, Renoir made, as Cézanne had made, something more solid and enduring like the old masters; Renoir's masters were the great flesh painters of history, and he chose the moments when the urban bourgeois forgot the office desk and the kitchen for the seashore, the boating party, and the dance hall under the trees.

The four Frenchmen and the one Hollander were not the only artists who declared a private war on public standards of truth and taste. The unbearable intensity of Van Gogh found an echo in *The Cry* of the Norwegian Edvard Munch, where the landscape writhed as if in response to the lone figure's distress, and in his woodcut *The Kiss,* where man and woman were fused by their mutual feeling into one block of form. Under the impact of Gauguin, the Swiss Ferdinand Hodler achieved broad color arabesques of tree and cloud. Adolphe Appia in the nineties purged operatic scenery of its naturalistic clutter, designing a sacred forest for *Parsifal* which had no painted leaves or pretended bark but nobly ascending forms molded by light—the most living force in the theater next to the human protagonist. The scenes of Gordon Craig grew not only out of the play but from "broad sweeps of thought" which the play had conjured up in him. As antidote to the stale sculptural routine of the Beaux-Arts a young Jew from New York named Jacob Epstein learned first principles from the archaic Greek and the Egyptian statues in the Louvre, and from the African and Polynesian figures in the British Museum; while in France the animal strength of Renoir was in the first small bronzes of Aristide Maillol. A young woman from San Francisco, Isadora Duncan, danced the *Seventh Symphony* as sculpture in motion, revealing how a human body unfettered by technical discipline in the older forms of the art could respond directly in time and space to an all-possessing emotion.

The modern movement, however, was not simply a pendulum swing from the conventional to the personal, from the descriptive to the expressive; its history cannot be told as a series of individual rebellions. Those rebellions and their theoretical justifications followed logically enough one from another. But art like other forms of living does not develop in a vacuum; in the first decade and a half of the new century its inconsistencies were no more blatant than those of Europe as a whole. In that Europe reformers and scientists promised a better world, and belligerent nationalisms threatened to destroy it. Alfred Dreyfus made racial hatred a world issue and British policemen wrestled with suffragettes while the French occupied Morocco and the Italians fought the Turks over Tripoli. Briand broke the French railway strike; Nicolle announced that typhus could be controlled; and Norman Angell wrote *The Great Illusion.*

In such a world the artist, unless a complete anarchist, asked himself how his forms could be used for more humane living and for enlightened social purposes. The problem of the designed community, for instance, absorbed Englishmen and Continentals; the garden cities of the former remained dreams unless a wealthy individual was on hand to build them; the German liberals faced the fact that only the municipality or the state could instrument such planning. Just as the painters had to free themselves from the bond of literal imitation, so the designers and craftsmen had to break with the historic "styles." John Ruskin and William Morris had taught them that art's function is to serve man, but since the nineties it had been clear that no revival of the guild system could provide an honest three-dimensional environment for more than a few men, nor could the handmade article defy the machine-turned piece.

When Victor Horta designed a house in 1893 whose decoration had no reference to any previous style but was composed of graceful, easily interflowing lines like those of flowers and plants, Europe seized upon "Art Nouveau." These slim and graceful elaborations appeared in the shapes of chairs and tables, in bowls and vases of glass, on department store façades, on the covers of art magazines, and in the lines of the illustrators. But "Art Nouveau" soon proved to be no more than a stylistic moment. Reluctantly, men of the Arts and Crafts movement like C. R. Ashbee and Lewis F. Day accepted mechanical mass production as a potential instrument for progress.

The forms which this acceptance made possible were developed in the minds of a few individuals: Otto Wagner asserted that modern life must be the point of departure for the artist; Henry Van de Velde emphasized a logical honesty in architectural structures which carried him far beyond his early devotion to "Art Nouveau"; H. P. Berlage in Holland spoke in the nineties of a pure art of utility for an age which he later called the century of socialism. Practice often lagged behind theory, but Romanesque forms had nearly disappeared from the Amsterdam Beurs which Berlage designed in 1898, and its broad stone surfaces and the naked metal trusses of its great hall were engineering made art. That monumentality and subordination of the lesser detail to the volume as a whole was in the work of Peter Behrens of Germany, of Nyrop in Copenhagen, of Østberg in Stockholm, despite the persistence of the historic reference and the naturalistic overtone.

The turn of the new century saw an occasional structure of startling originality. The austure gables and severe rounded bays of Voysey's country houses almost disowned their Tudor lineage; the stone and glass façade of Charles Dennie Mackintosh's Art School in Glasgow owed nothing to tradition, and in its interior the posts and horizontal supports of galleries made their own ornament in a manner which recalls the rooms of Wright. A Parisian house by Auguste Perret in 1903 made no apology for being constructed of concrete, since the material had determined the shape and scale, the projections and recessions. Seven years before Wright's Unity Temple, Josef Maria Olbrich's *Sezession* Building in Vienna had a plain gravity of joined blocks nearly devoid of surface elaboration; the Convalescent Home which Josef Hoffmann built at Purkersdorf in 1903 had a Spartan simplicity which one would not have expected from this Viennese eclectic.

The new leaven was soon at work through the whole complacent mass in London, Paris, Berlin, Vienna, Rome, and Moscow, and new content burst old forms in every one of the arts. Resistance to change came from two sources: from the vested interests of the academies and schools, and from the disinclination of the vast public to new ways of seeing. The needs of defense and offense drew rebellious individuals into groups which formed, dissolved, and re-formed in the twenty years before the first World War; and as the painters, architects, writers, and musicians perceived their common aims, their exchange of ideas became international.

Russian artists, dissatisfied with the aristocratic overtones and the backward-looking folkish accent of the "World of Art" group, formed the "Blue Rose" and the "Knave of Diamonds" and carried the gospel of Cézanne and later of Picasso to a country which had lost touch with Parisian innovations, while Diaghilev prepared his Ballet Russe for the export trade.

In England Roger Fry attacked the inmovable middle class, with its admiration for shop finish and for the "scented soap atmosphere" of Tadema's Roman scenes. Fry attempted to convince the plein-airists of the New English Art Club, itself a mild rebellion against the Royal Academy, that innovation in painting had not come to an end with Monet and Pissarro, Manet and Degas; in 1910 and twice in the following years he defied

Henri Matisse, *The Red Madras Headdress*

Barnes Foundation, Merion, Pa.

the "materialism of Mr. Podsnap" by bringing to the Grafton Galleries Cézanne and the other men who were now called postimpressionists.

In Germany Edvard Munch gathered artists of the "Junge Kunst" about him to preach the new freedoms and in 1904 launched the "Bridge" group; four years later the Berlin secession was led by Otto Kokoshka; three years more, and Karl Hofer, Franz Marc, and Wassily Kandinsky were among the "Blue Riders" of Munich, joined in 1913 by American-born Lyonel Feininger.

From Italy to Paris came young Italians in violent reaction against their country's past, to discover new forms with which they could symbolize their belief that an automobile at full speed was more beautiful than the *Victory of Samothrace* and to teach Italians how to be themselves, not ancestor worshipers, "armed, up-to-date, hostile to everybody" but above all to the common man. Paris in turn first saw their work in 1912, and Fernand Léger and Marcel Duchamp were not the only Frenchmen whose art was affected by it.

During these busy exchanges the forms of art were moving further from that parallelism with nature which had been the aim of the first moderns. In 1905 the Russian revolution was no more startling than the irruption of the "wild men"—the *Fauves*—at the Autumn Show in Paris; here were the massive and flowing shapes of Rouault, the lean geometry of Dérain, the flowing patterns and audacious color contrasts of Matisse, the fantasies of Dufy, and the architectural still lifes of Braque. When Picasso began his *Demoiselles d'Avignon* in 1906, the curves of his bodies changed to angles, their features became masklike, their gestures and proportions were stretched out of "normality" to make a total construction in which color balanced color, form flowed into form, and lines moved in rhythms and cross rhythms imposed on his material by the painter.

Cézanne had urged that artists keep the cube, the cone, and the cylinder in their consciousness as they worked; in the paintings of the cubists were roof tops, trees, mandolins, and faces reduced to those primal forms. Writers like Guillaume Apollinaire, who sought to liberate words from their conventional meanings, helped the painters to explain their "methodical and complex disintegration" of familiar things, which the artist reassembled freely as his mind suggested and his work proceeded. The shape and color of an arm or a fruit bowl were determined by the weight it must exert in his pictorial structure, its contour was straightened or curved to continue or oppose others, its planes overlapped other planes, its perspective abandoned the accepted rules until one looked down upon, into, and through, not simply toward the object.

Whatever could be made to play its full part in this "self-sufficient" ordering of experience was assimilated to the whole: a dark shadow tone deserting its object, a colored thing taking over the color proper to another thing; an applied fragment of newspaper, tin, glass, or sandpaper raising the cross play of textures to a more nervous intensity; a shape of ear, nose, or foot borrowed from the newly discovered art of the Africans without much thought of what the African's motive had been; an independence of scale and shape which these sophisticates admired in the modern "primitive" Henri Rousseau, whose ignorance of the accepted rules of art seemed bliss to the cubists.

Germans meanwhile saw the Van Goghs at Berlin in 1901 and found coolheaded Cézanne less appropriate to their expressive purposes than the Dutchman, who had once written, "For me the drama of storm in nature, the drama of sorrow in life, is the most impressive." Here, too, the movement which called itself "expressionism" had both pictorial and literary adherents. The former transformed the world into the image of their scorn for bourgeois smugness or their private fears and obsessions, their social and political radicalism; and each of them stamped his own personality on what he did, with an intensity which made the Paris group seem coldly intellectual. All of them believed that what was in one man's mind could discharge itself directly into the mind of another, dispensing with that ancient intermediary, the known appearance of physical things.

More frankly political and more rankly patriotic was the Italian group, whose speeches, writings, and pictures had the recklessness and fury of a demonstration in a city square: denial of the past and its iconography; contempt for the public which thinks in terms of logic and mere intelligibility; assertion of the beauty and the necessity of violence in politics and art. The course of Cézanne had been a middle path between representation and the work of art; these young men looked forward, calling themselves "futurists," to a resumption of that conflict without compromise; to revolution, not reform; to war which called forth the heroic and the creative in man. Henceforth the speed and the flashing perfection of yachts, automobiles, and skyscrapers must dictate the painter's forms. Cubism had frozen life into immobility; the futurists made it writhe and stamp and shout upon their canvases and painted a trotting dog with eight tails and a cloud of legs.

In a mood less stridently anarchistic, and radical in a far different sense, other men perceived the parallel between pictures like Picasso's *Factory at Horta* and the machine-accepting structures of a few architects—the sequences of cubelike volumes, the intersections of one mass with another, the planes devoid of anything but the strength with which they sliced and molded space. In Holland the austere geometry of Piet Mondrian had something in common with J. J. P. Oud and other rationalists of architecture who would join Mondrian during the war to publish *De Stijl.* In France the point of cubism was not lost on Le Corbusier, who worked for Perret in the year Picasso painted the *Woman with a Mandolin;* in Russia the painter Malevich pushed his own cubism toward a more absolute purity which he called "suprematism" while others made three-dimensional objects of wire, glass, wood, and paper which contained within themselves their own logic of parallel and related planes, of counterthrust and equipoise, of texture and color contrast.

This "constructivism" was in the minds of Peter Behrens and Hans Poelzig, whose German factories at the end of the first decade of the century reduced form to its simplest terms. It inspired Walter Gropius to build the Fagus factory at Alfeld in 1911, the most "modern" of these efforts to crystallize in steel and glass the victory of the machine over weight and tradition, of calculated precision over fumbling sentiment. Another German named Hermann Muthesius had given the deathblow to the handicraft obsession by accepting the notion of standardized machine manufacture, and artists and craftsmen were busy designing simple furniture and industrial objects in a dozen workshops in Switzerland, Austria, and Sweden, in emulation of the *Deutscher Werkbund* of 1907. In the art schools progressive teachers were replacing the academic oldsters, and Walter

Walter Gropius, Fagus Factory, Alfeld-an-der-Leine

Courtesy Museum of Modern Art, New York City

Gropius organized the best of these at Weimar—the Bauhaus, which for a decade after 1914 would be the focus of European modernism.

By 1913 every large city from Moscow to New York had seen the work of the postimpressionists, the *Fauves,* the cubists, the expressionists, and the constructivists. Into the surface of what had been the quiet pool of art, it seemed as though mischievous boys were throwing bigger and bigger stones, shattering its reflections into blinding fragments. In 1913 Stravinsky's *Sacre du Printemps,* with its massive blocks of sound, its strange rhythms and harsh dissonance, was a celebration of their success; in the same year, Alma-Tadema died, and Roger Fry wrote a piece in the London *Nation* which proved that he had come to bury the Academician, not to praise him.

The modernists now made no concessions to their opponents, and in 1914 Clive Bell published his book *Art,* in whose chapters he gave representational content an even smaller place than Fry was yet ready to give. Discarding the art of the Renaissance and most of what intervened between it and postimpressionism, Bell asked: "What quality is common to Sta. Sophia and the windows at Chartres, Mexican sculpture, a Persian bowl, Chinese carpets, Giotto's frescoes at Padua, and the masterpieces of Poussin, Piero della Francesca, and Cézanne?" His answer was "Significant Form"—the relations of lines and colors which stir our aesthetic emotions when those emotions are free from all associations. "The representative element in a work of art may or may not be harmful; always it is irrelevant. For, to appreciate a work of art we need bring with us nothing from life, no knowledge of its ideas and affairs, no familiarity with its emotions. Art transports us from the world of man's activity to a world of aesthetic exaltation . . . It is a world with emotions of its own."

At Florence in 1913 the futurist Soffici spoke in the same vein, declaring that pure painting derives from the study of forms alone, is regulated by its own laws, and exists for its own sake. In Paris in 1913 Apollinaire published *The Cubist Painters: Aesthetic Meditations,* in which he declared that the world was moving toward a new and a pure art which would stand, with respect to painting, as music stands to literature.

And finally, in 1914 came the English translation of Kandinsky's *Art of Spiritual Harmony.* In his own painted improvisations this expressionist had externalized his "inner need" in absolute patterns. Now he explained that the psychic and spiritual vibration of color has nothing to do with the colors we see with our eyes. All outer supports having failed mankind—religious dogma, scientific laws, and moral precepts—man turns in upon himself; Maeterlinck and Débussy, Picasso and Matisse move toward the nonmaterial, the abstract, raising a spiritual pyramid which shall reach toward heaven.

The base of the pyramid had now been laid, and the modern theory of form and content, art and society, present and past, would not henceforth be greatly changed. The nations went to war, and in the brutality and the illogic of the conflict more than one modern saw proof of the arguments by which he had rationalized his alienation from the common aims and his contempt for man in the mass.

CHAPTER 27 / RUCTIONS IN THE HENNERY

To Americans the phenomenon of modernism was more revolution than evolution, and few of them understood that these strange works had had their beginnings nearly thirty years before, when Cézanne and Van Gogh, Seurat and Gauguin found their alternatives to impressionism. In America no pioneers like these had steadily undermined the naturalistic idea; and how was the connoisseur to bridge the gap between the bathing nymphs of Bouguereau and the bathers of Cézanne, only to be confronted with Picasso's girls of Avignon? In the decade between the first issue of Stieglitz' *Camera Work* and the Armory Show of 1913, Americans tried to catch up with what had been in France and Germany a continuous experiment. The American lag was obvious; and in the year 1909, when Marin and Maurer showed their work in New York, the American Federation of Arts published the first number of *Art and Progress,* whose articles and pictures suggested that Monet had been the last word in artistic innovation.

The Federation, as Richard Watson Gilder said, was in "good hands." In the year of Wright's Robie house, *Art and Progress* published the "classical" new Boston Art Museum; while London raged in 1910 over Epstein's figures on the British Medical Association Building, the magazine presented the reliefs of Daniel Chester French as "a new development in monumental sculpture."

The American modern faced a public wholly unprepared for what he did; his opponent in the world of art was an academism less official in its monopoly than in European countries, but none the less powerful. He would speak with his own personal accent the form languages which Frenchmen and Germans and Italians had fashioned, and for that reason speak them often with less conviction. He could rely on only a few kindred spirits to understand him.

Among those kindred spirits were rebels in other fields of life, men and women who welcomed a strike, a Freudian theory, a suffragette, or a cubist as signs of healthy unrest. These idealists often underestimated the powers they opposed, identifying themselves with the "movers and shakers" of Arthur O'Shaughnessy's poem, who with a new song's measure "can trample an empire down." When Hutchins Hapgood saw the work of the postimpressionists it spelled agitation to him, a phenomenon as disturbing in one field as the I.W.W. was in another. "It shakes the old foundations," he wrote at the time, "and leads to new life, whether the programs and ideas have permanent validity or not."

For secessionists like these the gallery at 291 Fifth Avenue was indeed, as Hartley said, "the largest small room of its kind in the world," and a port of call for people at sea, tacking each in his own direction and none too sure where his course lay. One of them called that gallery a cooling oasis of the spirit in the desert of American ideas; to another, its spirit fostered liberty, defined no methods, never pretended to know, but always encouraged the enemies of convention.

The genius of the place was Alfred Stieglitz, who swayed in and out of its doorway, refusing to explain what hung on its walls, refusing to be commercial, refusing to accept less than the finest in craftsmanship. He reminded Sherwood Anderson of an old wagon maker in Ohio demonstrating how the rim of a wooden wheel should be made. Stieglitz was beginning his long and stubborn fight for the artist's right to be himself. Bill Haywood found him indifferent to wider problems; let Haywood fight the people's battles, he said, and he would defend the creative artist. Within the world which Stieglitz thus circumscribed, his were a tongue and a pen to be reckoned with by the sleazy technician, the connoisseur with money standards, or the museum director who shunned the moderns; and the volumes of *Camera Work* are a record of his courage and his integrity.

The early numbers of that quarterly reproduced the work of Käsebier, White, Steichen, and Stieglitz in superb photogravures and its articles discussed photography; as time went on, however, its contributors wrote essays of a more general character.

In Number 18, *Camera Work* explained that the idea of secession could not be limited to one medium. Steichen shortly declared that the very success of photography had thrown into relief the falsity of the naturalistic idea in painting. This was the mood in which Frank Lloyd Wright, twelve years before, had said that, if you saw a cow in a painting which looked out at you as "real as life," you had better buy an actual cow, because the painting was probably worthless.

Two years after its opening, "291" was ready to demonstrate other than photographic forms of secession. For a time in 1908 and again in 1910 the camera studies were replaced by Rodin drawings whose swiftly traced lines and summary color washes were something new in America. The sitting and reclining nudes of

Matisse in crayon, pen, and water color were hung in 1908, 1910, and 1912, and Frank J. Mather described them as in the high tradition of figure draughtsmanship, with the *furia* of a modern Pollaiuolo, even though their sketchlike quality annoyed him.

The color lithographs of Toulouse-Lautrec were seen at "291": the magnificent silhouette of Aristide Bruant and the lanky Yvette Guilbert with her long black gloves and her maliciously pointed features. There was an obvious parallel between these and the color prints of Japan which were shown the same year. Two lithographs by Cézanne, shown in 1910, were the first work of that master which the public had seen. The Cézanne water colors which followed were too starkly simple in their suggestion of earth forms and foliage to seem anything but childish daubs to most of the people who saw them; but Stieglitz met that point in 1912 by exhibiting the drawings of children. There was a glimpse in 1910 of Renoir's fleshiness and shimmer; and in 1911 Stieglitz pushed defiance to its limits by showing Picasso.

Meanwhile Americans who were destined to be called the pioneers of native modernism had seen the European revolutions at first hand. Alfred Henry Maurer was among the first of them and stayed the longest until the war forced him to come home. His father, Louis Maurer, painted accurate genre scenes for Currier and Ives; Alfred's early gods were Chase and the smooth technicians of the National Academy, and his *Carrousel* had the charm and freshness of a John Sloan (Brooklyn Mus.). "Alfy" was the little dark dapper man who came often to Gertrude Stein's house and whose solemn humility amused her. He saw the Japanese prints come down from her walls to be replaced by Cézannes and Renoirs, by the vivid and splashy arabesques of Matisse's *Bonheur de Vivre,* and by Picasso's rocklike portrait of his hostess.

Bernard Karfiol knew the moderns, too, and his work was shown in the Salon d'Automne of 1904. When he came home about three years later the Russian-born Samuel Halpert had already deserted the Beaux-Arts discipline for the rigors of Cézanne; Charles Demuth from Lancaster, Pennsylvania, was learning that master's way with apples; Maurice Sterne, trained in the National Academy, had begun the ten years of roaming in Europe, Greece, Egypt, and Bali which broke that discipline; and a young cartoonist from San Francisco named Walt Kuhn was ready to return after three years or more of Europe.

When the *Fauves* exploded their group show in 1907 Marguerite Zorach of California was in Paris and Max Weber had begun his three years' friendship with the innovators, with Henri Rousseau and Matisse, learning from these and from the work of El Greco, Cézanne, and the early Italians, from African sculpture and the

Abraham Walkowitz, drawing of Isadora Duncan

Courtesy of the artist

Oriental art of the Musée Guimet a more daring conception of design and form than Arthur Dow had taught him. In 1905 a lean New Jersey man reached Paris who had studied at the Pennsylvania Academy and the Art Students League and who was expected to be an architect; John Marin's six years abroad left him with a sense of his vocation as a painter but with no special indebtedness to any of the moderns. Even his etching of a cab horse and a glimpse of a Paris street revealed that his powers of selection were his own, and in Venice his plates went far beyond Whistler in condensation, in quick personal response to palace fronts and the sheen of canal water.

The trickle of Americans became a small stream in the first decade of the century. The year of Cézanne's death saw Abraham Walkowitz in Europe, finding in the master's terse landscape an inspiration for his fresh and verdant nature paintings and in the dynamics of Rodin and Matisse a rhythm which would inspire hundreds of studies of the "divine" Isadora Duncan. When more than fifty canvases by Cézanne were assembled for the great memorial show of 1907 Walter Pach saw them and forgot his work with Chase and Henri. Arthur G. Dove was in Paris that year, a compe-

Andrew Dasburg, *Landscape*

Courtesy of the artist

tent New York illustrator who discovered how little of himself had gone into his hack work and who moved "from form to plane to first flash" when he painted *The Lobster* in 1908. Stanton Macdonald-Wright began in 1907 the six years of apprenticeship to the moderns which culminated in his "synchromism."

When the *Fauves* became cubists and the Italians screamed their futurist doctrine, Thomas Hart Benton of Missouri and Preston Dickinson of New York were in Paris; Morton Schamberg and Charles Sheeler were traveling in France and Italy, both of them ex-pupils of William Chase in Philadelphia. Joseph Stella, who had drawn the smoke and grime of Pittsburgh, awoke to a new sense of color through friendship with Picasso, Matisse, and Modigliani, and in Rome and Florence caught a spark from the futurist bonfire. Young Andrew Dasburg abandoned the tepid manners he had learned from Kenyon Cox and soon painted a vase of tulips with the rugged force of Cézanne and reduced American trees and roof tops to their underlying shapes and colors as the man from Aix had done with the vineyards and slopes of the Mont Sainte-Victoire.

Edward Steichen in Paris watched these transformations of his countrymen abroad; Alfred Stieglitz at the little gallery in New York showed their work and defended it. On the third floor of "291" the returning travelers could find the fellowship and the sense of a common effort which they had known in the studio of Gertrude Stein, the bistros of Montparnasse, and the German beer gardens. One of the Stieglitz "bunch" was a Mexican caricaturist, Marius de Zayas, and in 1910 de Zayas made fifteen brilliant portraits of the photographers, painters, and writers who constituted the advance guard of modernism. A few years later Stieglitz characterized them with his camera with a penetration which has never been surpassed, transforming even the backgrounds of his prints into symbols of personality.

The de Zayas drawings could have been used to illustrate Temple Scott's description in the *Forum* of Stieglitz' comrades quarreling over roast beef and potatoes at the Holland House. Scott's names only half concealed their identities: "Michael Weaver," who walked Fifth Avenue and remembered the Boul' Mich', was Max Weber; "Seaman" was Marin with a long pointed nose and keen eyes under a mat of hair; Finch, with a pince-nez and a ruffled gray mane, was Stieglitz himself. Under the name of Church, Scott taxed the "bunch" with a notion of beauty so far above common comprehension that they were in danger of becoming the victims of their own Frankenstein. Why this contempt of money, he asked, and why this scorn for the public of America?

When Scott's piece appeared the public had seen Marin's water colors at "291" and the oils of Hartley and Maurer; in the next two or three years Walkowitz, Dove, and Weber were given one-man exhibitions.

Hartley was the only man in the group who at thirty-two had not seen Europe. In the early nineteen hundreds, that "gnarled New England spinster man" from Lewiston, Maine, was painting his native mountains with an impressionistic breadth, and the yellows and crimsons of his autumn were laid against the bulk of his hills with bold square touches; his gnarled cloud shapes bore witness to his admiration for that other solitary, Albert Ryder, whom he called "the painter poet of the immanent in things."

Hartley stated his creed in *Camera Work:* until the public understood what art could be, it was at least a matter of private aristocratic satisfaction to the artist. The repressed and brooding Yankee met the Blue Riders in 1912, the expressionists a year or two later, and found an explosive release in brilliantly colored pictures whose shapes had little resemblance to known things—crosses, checker patterns, and concentric rings held in suspense by their hot yellows and vermilions, their grass greens and acid blues. Hartley spoke of the modern idea as a "fresh relationship to the courses of the sun and to the living swing of the earth"; but he had not yet discovered that relationship in himself.

The eye of Alfred Maurer gleams from his self-portrait with a mild ferocity; the long tight mouth and the square jaw below are those of a man whose unbearable private conflict ended only when he took his life at sixty-four. He broke with his father's realism, with his own academic past, and for a decade with the life of his country; and the landscapes of his early forties, with their dense and thrusting tree forms and their rude greens, blues, and purples, were his response to the *Fauves.*

Dove's palette included strong earth yellows, blacks, and grays; his curvatures were robust in *Team of Horses.* One did not see the straining beasts with their heavy cart on the hill but the shapes of black and yellow, red, and gray pastel which stood for the weight they pulled, the resistance of the earth, the counterthrust of their burden. The impact of Dove's sweeping curvatures, his strenuously molded clouds, his large flaunting shapes of pure flat color, was like the impact of nature on him —all sufficient for the moment, with no afterthoughts. Franz Marc and the Blue Riders were as bold as Dove with color but more resourceful in the patterns and rhythms they made.

More complex of purpose and more subtle in design was Max Weber, whose problem was to discover at twenty-four what he wanted to say and in this tower of Babel which was modern art to find his own tongue. Now he attempted the fluidities of Matisse; now he sculptured in paint the heavy breasts, bellies, and legs of women as Cézanne had done; now the shapes of his Chinese ladies lost and found themselves in long looping curves which swung through his canvas, cubist-fashion. His friend Rousseau had created a world out of his own integrity, and the down-to-essentials character which Weber sought was in the Oriental bronzes at the Musée Guimet; he found it in the African idols, in the elongations of El Greco, and in the unshakable dignity of Piero's *Resurrection.*

Back in New York, Weber prolonged his researches among the totem poles and Mayan gods of the museums. His problem was that of many moderns. The very richness of their knowledge, their sensitive perception of past greatness, seemed to stand between them and the one thing that had given their artistic gods a form-making power—a deep attachment to their own time and place. Where find the equivalent of Cézanne's passion for trees and apples, for Giotto's

Marsden Hartley, *Forms Abstracted* (Hudson Walker coll.)

Courtesy M. Knoedler & Co., New York City

Max Weber, *Chinese Restaurant*

Whitney Museum of American Art, New York City

faith, for the philosophy of China, for the fervor of El Greco?

John Marin needed no reassurance from history, and he could understand the motives of the moderns without becoming less sure of his own. He was as delicately put together as Hartley and Maurer, but would bend and not break under strain. His affection for the shapes of earth, cloud, and river was as virile as that of Dove, but he was a more resourceful suitor. There were willful touches in the skies of his first Paris etchings which must have annoyed the dealers for whom he was working; and in his water color of the Pont Alexandre he massed his shadow tones to say one thing, once and for all. His *Mountain, Tyrol,* done during his last year abroad, was scarcely "drawn" at all; its blue snow-shadow and sharp pine-greens were color gestures, so to speak, with a white pause between them.

Stieglitz already knew that he had found an authentic individual when Marin, returning to New York in 1911, painted the sky-piercing Woolworth Building, and a St. Paul's tower which seemed in the midst of an angry dialogue with the clouds and the crowding skyscrapers. He had not yet found his full range but already he could paint not things but the experience of things, not the structure of the Elevated but its speed and clatter, not the height of a building but its will to outreach. One October day in 1914 Marin told Stieglitz that he had just given a thousand dollars for a few tree-covered rocks off the Maine coast; and Stieglitz wondered at his simplicity, not knowing that three water colors would soon pay for Marin's island.

For almost a decade before this conversation took place, the storms of controversy had shaken that other island which was "291." For one champion among the newspaper and magazine critics there were a dozen whose purpose was to be cleverly derisive. The New York *Evening Mail* inquired what a gob of Maurer's color represented: was it a burst tomato or a fireman's

John Marin, *Marin's Island, Maine,* water color

Philadelphia Museum of Art

hat? One could guess either; but there were Maurers, the writer said, which made even guesswork impossible. As for Max Weber, the *Globe* called his work travesties of the human form by a man seemingly out of his mind, and the *World* concluded that such grotesquerie could only be acquired by long and perverse practice. Arthur Dove was more tolerantly received in 1912, and one critic condescended to see his color as a child would look through a kaleidoscope—the weirder the better.

Such comments were republished in *Camera Work* alongside those of the more patiently discerning. James Huneker of the *Sun* was welcomed as a friend because he called Marin a harmonist in an attenuated scale, a symbolist above all else. His reviews of Stieglitz' shows were at least tolerant and he declared that he preferred plunder to paralysis.

The modernists gained support from Walter Pach, who wrote articles on Monet and Cézanne for *Scribner's* in 1908, and from tolerant and witty Henry McBride, who had been a painter and a teacher of life drawing at the Art Alliance when he became art critic for the *Sun* in 1912; but in the first tempestuous years it was Hartmann and Caffin who defended Stieglitz' island. When Maurer's freedom with color was scorned by others, Hartmann upheld his "scarlet departure"; in Weber he saw architectural solidities like those of old mural paintings. He summed up the main issue by declaring that "the love for exactitude is the lowest form of pictorial gratification." While others ridiculed Alfred Maurer, driving him deeper into seclusion, Caffin compared his art to music, and put nature in its place as "the scaffold on which to hang the decoration of a color fantasy."

It was natural that the men who had fought these early skirmishes with Stieglitz should think of him as a prime mover and shaker. The historian will not diminish the stature of the man when he records that there were others in these years who moved and shook the complacent. The Misses Cone, encouraged by Gertrude Stein, brought the work of Matisse to Baltimore as early as 1906, and Buffalo was introduced to Hartley and Dasburg by Nina Bull. The Haas Gallery in New York, which was scarcely more than a picture-framing shop, showed Walkowitz and Weber. In 1910, John Cotton Dana included John Marin in his modern show at the Newark Museum.

That remarkable director knew that most people had no share in the art experience, and his years at Newark were a brilliant and courageous effort to bring the two together. He saw his galleries as a place "where actual life reported . . . where nothing was shown merely because it was ancient, but only because it had authentic power to open men's eyes to the movement and meaning of the stream of life." Dana displayed the experiments of the *Deutscher Werkbund* and brought home his point with textiles, wallpaper, and kitchenware made in New Jersey, including bathroom fixtures. His was the first public institution to give Henri and his group a showing. Two years after Stieglitz, Dana gave Weber a one-man exhibition; and while the wealthy Metropolitan Museum ignored the contemporary Americans, Dana spent his small funds to acquire their work.

In the year 1908 Gertrude Vanderbilt Whitney opened a small gallery which was to become the Whitney Studio Club and a haven for the nonacademic. Many a young independent whose work was snubbed by the dealers had Mrs. Whitney and Mrs. Juliana Force to thank for his chance to be seen and for his opportunity to study abroad. The valiant work of these two women is an important chapter in the history of American art, although it was less dramatic than the crusade of Stieglitz.

That crusade was in full swing when Caffin tried in 1908 to summarize what "291" had accomplished. The advance guard had needed above all a man whose individuality was as truculent as their own, who was a master of his own art, and who bolstered their morale and helped them to stay alive. Stieglitz was that man, and Caffin's tribute was serious beneath its barnyard metaphors. He described the official world of art as the finest hennery on earth where the cocks and hens sunned themselves in the warmth of self-admiration, led the pleasant routine of laying eggs, and fattened themselves for the market. Into that hennery Stieglitz had come with a fluffed and aggressive topknot. "He made flights into far-off potato patches" and "from his wanderings he brought back strange ideas . . . possibilities of life hitherto undreamed of by poultry. . . The roosters he exasperated by his extra-cocky airs; for he declared their complacency had made them careless in their personal habits, so that bare spots in unbecoming places showed through the dowdiness of their feathers. This was bad enough, but his treatment of the hens was worse. He brought them to a pitch of bewilderment . . . by maintaining they ought to make the laying of eggs an act of personal expression."

In short, "he made ructions in the hennery."

CHAPTER 28 / EXPLOSION IN THE ARMORY

When Frank Jewett Mather wrote *Separatist Art Bodies* for the *Nation* in 1912 he had heard a new group was forming which called itself The Association of American Painters and Sculptors. Why not remain with the National Academy, he suggested, rather than sap its strength by leaving? And he reminded these malcontents that the Society of American Artists, after some thirty years of independence, had finally returned to the Academic fold.

The new association had no such hope of thawing the Academy. What united them was their awareness of a progressive movement among American artists and their impatience with the museums, dealers, and critics whose smugness denied it an opportunity to be seen and judged by the public. They had no intention of becoming a clique, and they were, as one of them said, "persons of varying tastes and predilections." Walt Kuhn was their secretary and the wealthy John Quinn was drawn into the circle as legal adviser. Frederick James Gregg of the New York *Evening Sun* was made an honorary member, and among the artists were men as diverse as Maurice Prendergast and Robert Henri. Jo Davidson the sculptor was there, and Henry Fitch Taylor, who not only painted but directed a small art gallery.

Into this group came Arthur B. Davies, whose knowledge of contemporary art in Europe would never have been guessed from his own exquisite painted idyls. The association planned to hold an exhibition of the Ameri-

The Armory Show, New York City

Courtesy Walter Pach

can moderns; but Davies as president persuaded them to enlarge their original scheme and to illustrate modernism as a whole, from its beginnings, on a world scale. No international exhibition in America had yet included the challengers and the dissenters. In 1876 the men of Barbizon and Fontainebleau had been conspicuously absent from Philadelphia; in 1893 Chicago had snubbed impressionism and everything to the left of it. When Walt Kuhn sailed for Europe in the summer of 1912 it was to borrow the work of men whose one common trait was their nonconformity to Academic routine. Money had been loaned for the enterprise and a building had been found large enough to hold the show—the Sixty-ninth Regiment Armory at Lexington Avenue and Twenty-fifth Street.

Kuhn scurried from Cologne to Munich and Berlin and from Paris to London, delighted with the response to his request for paintings and sculptures. He met Lehmbruck and borrowed his *Kneeling Woman;* he obtained lithographs by Edvard Munch; he found several Van Goghs and enough paintings by Odilon Redon to fill a room. Through Alfred Maurer and Walter Pach in Paris he met the sculptor Raymond Duchamp-Villon, whose austere forms had nothing in common with the surface subtleties of Rodin, and Raymond's two brothers, Jacques and Marcel, the latter of whom was to provide the loudest explosion on Lexington Avenue. From the studio of Brancusi the Americans obtained several pieces.

Matisse, the *Fauves,* and the cubists would outnumber the Italian futurists and the English progressives in the show because its organizers believed Paris to be the heart of the revolution. Marinetti and his friends were too busy to lend their work; and when the Americans saw the Grafton Show in London they found its modernism only skin-deep; Vanessa Bell and Duncan Grant reminded them how much better Frenchmen did these things, and Wyndham Lewis' iron-hard shapes and machine lusters seemed cubist in name only.

In New York the public was being prepared for the show by Gregg and by du Bois, who explained its purpose in the newspapers and magazines. Debts piled up unpaid; a catalogue was prepared which was inadequate by the time the works were shown; the grim brick walls of the Armory were hung with green garlands, and the huge drill hall was divided by burlap-covered partitions into corridors and cubicles. The pine tree of the American Revolution was printed on badges and stationery

André Dérain, *The Window on the Park*
Museum of Modern Art, New York City

as the emblem of the association; in March it appeared on the cover of *Arts and Decoration* with the legend "The New Spirit."

Just what the new spirit was, du Bois attempted to define as a rebirth which began when Delacroix challenged the cold classicism of Ingres, and Courbet filled the gap between them. He explained how Cézanne, Seurat, and Van Gogh had restored to art its primitive force, its vigorous response to life. Even Picasso and the cubists, whose extremism the writer could not wholly accept, should stimulate the healthy American appetite for change. John Quinn added that we had had in art as in law too much government of the living by the dead. "American art," he wrote, "needs the shock that the work of some of these men will give." Much of it would hurt the optic nerves, but "better crude life than sickly or sentimental decay."

New Yorkers first exposed their optic nerves to the Armory Show on the night of February 17, 1913, and for four weeks afterward. Everything possible had been done to ease the shock: in the entrance corridor stood Barnard's colossal *Prodigal Son;* near by stood the vigorous but naturalistic portrait heads of Jo Davidson, and delightfully whimsical screens by Robert Chanler with swans and leopards in blue, white, and silver on black. The French display began with Ingres, Delacroix, Daumier, Corot, and Courbet; after Monet, Manet, and Degas came Cézanne with *The Poor House on the Hill.*

The visitor passed from the austerity of Seurat to Renoir's vibrant *Boating Party* and from the coolness of Puvis to a Gauguin frieze where tawny Samoans stood beneath trees and vines heavy with brilliant fruits. The blue eyes of Van Gogh fixed one from his self-portrait and his ravine at Arles writhed with its own torment. In contrast to the finality of Ingres was a group of Rodin drawings; a strange fancy was at work among the Redons, which had a room of their own, where the flower pieces glowed like sparks of many-colored fire.

With Rouault's *Parade* one was suddenly among the wild men. Here stood the iron-hard jug on Dérain's window sill, its shadow cutting knifelike across a table whose horizontals had straightened a bowl's ellipse out of "correctness," while trees beyond rose stiff and bare as the frame of the window. Matisse in the dancing nudes of *Nasturtiums* was a man as obsessed with surface shape and pattern as Gauguin; but the pattern seemed to have a dynamics of its own which oddly reshaped the dancing legs and the clasped hands.

One entered the Cubist Room for the ultimate shock: Picabia's *Dance at the Spring* shattered the identity of two figures; the dance was there in the flash and counterthrust of angular shapes, but not the dancers. In the face of Picasso's *Woman with a Mustard Pot* the painter had made accents and shadings which refused to become in the familiar sense a three-dimensional form; he merely stated that here was a bossing outward, there a channel, and never allowed one to forget that this was a flat painted surface. Finally Marcel Duchamp, in *Nude Descending a Staircase,* forbade all reconstruction of the lady herself and boldly translated her downward motion in a complex of flashing shapes and lines. One had crossed a century from Ingres to Duchamp, and one asked: At what point had the hot water become steam?

The same question was posed by the marbles and bronzes. To one who knew Rodin, the soft white limbs of Barnard's *The Birth,* encased in the still rough block of marble, brought no surprise. Lachaise gave promise of great vigor, and there was a nervous intensity in Epstein, a sturdy resolution in Maillol of the lesser into the greater forms. There was a linked musical rhythm in the Lehmbruck *Kneeling Woman* as one saw her from the side, and an odd grace and tenderness in her body, gaunt and elongated as she was. A few feet away, however, stood Brancusi's *Mademoiselle Pogany,* her features merely a modification of the smooth, white egg-shaped head. The sculptor had begun with a portrait study in which nose, eyes, hair, head, and hands were differentiated; his second version had suppressed particularities, and this final one was Brancusi's effort, as he said, to get all the forms into one form.

There was little to shock the optic nerves on the walls of the American rooms. If one granted Matisse his freedom to play with line and shape one granted it to Walkowitz; if one found a reassuring steadiness in Cézanne's hills one responded similarly to those of Andrew Dasburg. Alfred Maurer's trees, to be sure, thrust themselves brutally from the earth; and one felt that the skyscrapers of Marin might presently be shattered into something as unrecognizable as the Kandinsky *Improvisation* on a neighboring wall. But the mild and pretty *Naples* of Childe Hassam was here, and a quarry by Jonas Lie in pleasantly broken color, together with Twachtman's more rugged *Coronation Week in Madrid.*

The bright pinks and yellows of street urchins danced to a hurdy-gurdy before brick fronts in a Jerome Myers study; John Sloan's girls dried their hair on a roof top in the sun; Robert Henri's gypsy was painted with as few broad strokes as possible; Luks was at his flashing best in the portrait of Huneker; George Bellows presented prize fighters in rapid pencil notation, and constructed in solid, lively paint the snow-covered docks along the river, the stevedores working, the tugboats sending white puffs into a crisp blue sky.

From the opening day these sixteen hundred pictures and sculptures drew crowds from every social level. The millionaire came and so did his cook; the Academicians and the "movers and shakers" from "291," the dealers and the museum directors, the top-string critics and the nosing reporters. Ancients descended from the uptown clubs, and whole classes of children flocked from the schools, eager to win a newspaper prize for the best "explanation" of the Duchamp nude. Davies helped Albert Ryder to make the rounds, a bearded patriarch of sixty-six whose *Pegasus* was in the show. Otto Kahn appeared one day as though on a slumming expedition, and wealthy Miss Lillie Bliss was guided by her friend Davies.

Most Armory visitors refused to accept the more brutal works as the last term in an historical evolution. Kenyon Cox, whose frozen *Judicial Virtues* at Wilkes-Barre had recently won him a Medal of Honor from the Architectural League, fumed that the Matisse drawings were the scrawls of a nasty boy. The trouble began, he cried, when the impressionists lost their respect for tradition and discipline; here were the results in a painted anarchism which overthrew all the laws and utterly abolished the art of painting in order to deify a whim and make insanity pay.

A more sympathetic visitor could view the marble ovoid of Brancusi with Jo Davidson and share his tolerance, his belief that one must see these innovations again and again until one's accumulated notions of form could be at least for the time forgotten. Davidson's plea was for an honest effort to see what the new men were driving at, since "it is as much a mistake to accept a thing without understanding it as to reject it without understanding it."

Norman Hapgood reviewed the show for the *Globe* as though it were a fire or an earthquake; Mabel Dodge allowed her reason to fall asleep and at once the pattern of Picasso filled her consciousness; she was reminded of the prose of Gertrude Stein, whose sensuous music rose from the inherent qualities of words and not their accustomed meanings.

Somewhere between the shrill fury of Kenyon Cox and the mindless ecstasy of Mabel Dodge ranged the pamphlets, editorials, and reviews provoked by the show. Theodore Roosevelt in the *Outlook,* after claiming that his own Navajo rug surpassed the cubism of Duchamp and the other Knights of the Isosceles, expressed his

Marcel Duchamp, *Nude Descending a Staircase* (Walter Arensberg coll.)

Courtesy Museum of Modern Art, New York City

gratitude for a show which had nothing commonplace and much of extraordinary merit, including Cézanne's *Woman with a Rosary.* In the *International Studio* Christian Brinton subtly considered the aesthetic questions raised at the Armory; in the *Nation* Frank Mather's tone was one of bland reassurance: art was safe in the long run; why be disturbed by the clever hoax or the negligible pedantry of the cubists?

It was not expected that Royal Cortissoz would be amused. One remembered his praise for Abbott Thayer and for Dewing's "expression of impalpable loveliness," his aversion to the "garish crudity" of George Luks. Cortissoz wrote in the *Century* that he had carefully studied the modern hypothesis, and he concluded that Cézanne was a complacent ignoramus, Van Gogh a crazy incompetent, and Picasso a man whose unadulterated cheek resembled that of Barnum. In a piece called *Ellis Island Art* Cortissoz warned that the United States was being invaded by aliens who threatened the body politic; modern art he found likewise foreign-born, and just as dangerous. In the *Forum* for July, 1913, W. D. MacColl replied that art criticism has other business than name-calling and tried to explain what an abstraction really is. The dictionary said it was the name of a quality apart from the thing. The abstract painter was evidently seeking to personify a thing, to characterize it, not to name it.

Meanwhile the Armory Show had come to a riotous close in New York. Nobody knew how many had seen it; one said a hundred thousand, another claimed a fourth of a million. The committee marched up and down the hall with fife and drum to celebrate what seemed their victory, and John Quinn quoted the words of Captain Philip when he sank a Spanish ship at Santiago: "Don't cheer, boys, the poor devils are dying." The pictures and statues came down, and a selection from them was sent to Chicago, where the Law and Order League campaigned against its "obscenities." In Chicago, the show kept its place in the newspapers in spite of a local tornado and the rival attractions of Lily Langtry in vaudeville and George M. Cohan in *Broadway Jones.* In June the Copley Society of Boston housed the exhibition with no such ill-bred protests, and then the whole affair became an historic moment. The Association of American Painters and Sculptors melted away, and Davies and his friends managed to pay the bills.

In the months and years that followed one could measure the aftereffects of the Armory explosion. Between two and three hundred works had been bought from its walls; among them was *The Poor House on the Hill,* which entered the Metropolitan Museum as the first Cézanne to be acquired by a public institution. Thanks to the persuasiveness of Kuhn, John Quinn's purchases amounted to five or six thousand dollars, and he soon acquired not only the French masters but Hartley and Marin, Prendergast and Weber. Five years after the Armory Show, Duncan Phillips incorporated his Memorial Gallery in Washington, which he later described as an intimate museum combined with an experiment station where the work of young men would submit to an endurance test; the Phillips home displayed the American impressionists but also the work of Demuth and O'Keeffe, of Dove, Karfiol, Karl Knaths, and Sheeler. Under the guidance of Davies, Lillie M. Bliss steadily built her collection until it contained twenty-four of the finest Cézannes and superb paintings by Seurat, Matisse, and Picasso.

There were few signs of experiment in the great Art Palace of the Panama-Pacific International Exposition two years after the Armory. The buildings beside the blue Golden Gate in San Francisco had at least the courage to modify the Chicago formulas and to substitute pleasant blues, pinks, and yellows for the whites of the White City; but Henry Bacon designed the Court of the Four Seasons as a faithful follower of McKim, and the statues—more than fifteen hundred of them—proclaimed their Chicago parentage. In the American section of the Palace of Fine Arts, certain recently dead painters were given abundant room—Homer and La Farge, Twachtman and Robinson. Duveneck came into his own along with Sargent, Chase, Alden Weir, Tarbell, Whistler and Hassam. The Eight were well represented. Maurer and Prendergast were the most radical artists there, although the foreign rooms displayed Kokoshka and also the work of Balla, Boccione and other Futurists.

The modern terrain was far wider in 1915, however, than Stieglitz' rooms. Further uptown his friend Marius de Zayas displayed Van Gogh and the recent work of Picasso at the Modern Gallery. At the Montross Gallery one saw Max Weber struggling with his accumulated knowledge. Durand-Ruel placed Monets beside the bathers of Renoir and his *Seine at Argenteuil.* Away from Fifth Avenue the People's Art Guild of John Weichsel oranized six exhibitions for the settlement houses.

Weichsel, a wordy Hegelian who believed the work of Picasso, Kandinsky, and Picabia was the first step toward "cosmic heights," announced the purpose of his Guild: "To reclaim the people's life for self-expression in art and to make it an hospitable ground for our artists' work." Weichsel would take art to those who were never seen at the uptown salons, and he would ask the artists to explain their aims in simpler language than the critics used. Sloan's etching of his mother was shown at the University Settlement in 1915 together with the work of Myers, Bellows, and Hassam;

Wilhelm Lehmbruck, *Kneeling Woman*

Museum of Modern Art, New York City

and the Guild also took Hartley, Marin, and Walkowitz hopefully to the Bowery and the East Side.

Three years after the Armory, Willard Huntington Wright was godfather to the *Forum* show, assisted by Christian Brinton, Henri, Stieglitz, and Weichsel. Such a concerted effort would have been impossible in the pre-Armory days, and this exhibition of seventeen progressives was what Jerome Mellquist has called it, "the first thorough cross-section of the newer American endeavor."

Here, in addition to the work of Stieglitz' "bunch," were newcomers making an obvious effort to find original expression through mainly borrowed language: in Ben Benn one saw the ruggedness of Van Gogh and the naïve specifications of Henri Rousseau; in McFee, the planes and edges of the cubists which had replaced his earlier impressionism. Sheeler's austerity was already evident, both in his still lifes and in more rigorously geometrical studies almost devoid of natural references. Man Ray, who had met Duchamp the previous year, was ordering cool colors and broad shapes in two dimensions. The figure studies of Thomas Benton bulged and writhed, and the observer could find in them some of the hot color of the synchromists, some of the brusque simplifications of Picasso, and some of El Greco's dynamics.

The synchromists themselves, Morgan Russell and Stanton Macdonald-Wright, here flaunted their shapes and colors boldly, and Americans could judge their effort to complete the modern cycle, the ultimate purification. Cézanne, the synchromists explained, had devised color sequences to express degrees of force in light but always with a recognition of the local colors of things. The synchromists freed color from this double obligation, abandoned all semblance to natural form, and made whirling shapes of brilliant hues, for every one of which they claimed an absolute spatial character, an absolute degree of volume.

While this latest heresy reverberated in the world of art the echoes of the Armory could be detected in the new confidence with which the designers of hats and hardware played with bold shapes and brighter color schemes. The *Craftsman* had foreseen this greater liberty, this shattering of the vogue for pastel tones, in an article written by Mary Fanton Roberts while the Armory Show was still current. In Vienna the textile makers were already audacious with patterns, as was Paul Poiret in Paris with his clothes; we shall soon, the *Craftsman* said, have color in our homes. Walt Kuhn recalls that business was quick to appropriate the Armory innovations and that Brancusi's metallic shapes, the cubist angularities, and the gaudy Matisse patterns eventually were reflected in the design of milliners' dummies, streamlined trains, airplanes and automobiles, furniture and posters, gas pumps, clothing, and beach umbrellas.

The American artists asked themselves the sober question: What had the Armory Show done for their work and for their place in the American scheme of things? As Frederick Gregg wrote, with their eyes open they had risked the deadly comparison between their effort and the achievement of the Europeans. Gregg had prophesied that the exhibition would at least shake the lethargy of local men: better an uncertain future, he said, than no future at all. Uncertainty grew when John Quinn persuaded the United States Senate to remove the customs duty on European art which was less than twenty years old. The dealers flooded the market with these duty-free importations until more than one native painter believed, as Jerome Myers said, that Davies had "unlocked the door to foreign art and thrown the key away."

On the other hand, John Sloan concluded that much could be learned from the European canvases. It was Sloan and his friends who established the Society of Independent Artists in 1917 to preserve the innovating spirit; there were no prizes and no juries, and the society hung its first show democratically in the alphabetical order of the artists' names. Robert Henri urged his fellows to pierce to the core of the modern movement and not be confused by its sensational exterior.

This tolerant effort to penetrate beneath labels to principles was supported by the written commentaries of Leo Stein, Walter Pach, and Willard Huntington Wright. Soon after the *New Republic* began publication in 1914 Stein wrote its art commentaries with subtlety and shrewdness. In *Century* and *Harper's* Pach explained the motives of modern art in the light of his long acquaintance with the innovators here and abroad. Wright was the most dogmatic of all the interpreters and the most brutally outspoken; he had championed the synchromism of his brother Stanton and of Morgan Russell, and he came to New York in 1915 to write for the *Forum*.

Wright paid his compliments to the Academicians when he reviewed one of their shows under the title of *Morituri Salutamus,* describing it as a grand saturnalia of sentimentality, bad craftsmanship, incompetent drawing, and crude, insensitive color. The brickbats which had been thrown at the Armory were now hurled back through the Academy windows. He denounced the empty fluency of artists who painted as easily as the layman butters his bread in summer; he mocked the bravado of "these radicals who have come abreast of Monet and Pissarro." Their days were numbered; for every person who began to understand the newer men, some Academician lost a client.

But Wright's indictment of the critics was more

savage still, and he called the roll of their inadequacy: Cortissoz, "clinging with a kind of desperate fear to the established and accepted past"; Kenyon Cox, whose "aesthetic ossification" was mistaken for taste and logic; Mather, the scholastic pedant splashing about disconcertedly in water which was not over his head; Caffin, presumably converted to modern art by Stieglitz' hypnotism, whose books were a storehouse of facts but, to the seeker of mental food, an empty larder. In Europe, Wright maintained, there were German psychologists of art, serious analysts like Meier-Graefe, Roger Fry, Clive Bell, and Guillaume Apollinaire, who at least took modern art seriously.

In his *Forum* notes and in his book *Modern Painting* of 1915, Wright attempted that coldly rational analysis whose absence he deplored in others, stripping art of its intriguing charm and its soothing vagueness and tracing form to its psychological roots. He wrote that, with Cézanne, the *Fauves,* and the cubists, art moved toward its only legitimate goal, which was to stimulate an aesthetic emotion by pure and absolute relationships of form. When the synchromists abandoned the last trace of natural form, the great cycle of a century was completed; the extraneous had been purged away and art could be as pure as music. To this art one could react with an aesthetic faculty insulated from all other experiences. Wright praised the People's Art Guild but had no interest in what he called its "socialistic" side. No more than Clive Bell, Roger Fry, or Guillaume Apollinaire was he concerned with what lay outside the aesthetic moment in the lives of people. Like a modern Moses he proclaimed the laws of art, and it remained only for artists to create in obedience to those laws.

From conciliation to a dogmatic truculence, the sequence of modernism now included the first appearance of Henri's group in 1908, the Stieglitz demonstrations, the Independent Show of 1910, the Armory shocker of 1913, and the first exhibition in 1917 of Sloan's Society of Independent Artists. Would the conflict in Europe, as the conservatives hoped, destroy the new cults and isms and restore the *status quo?* The answer would have to wait; three days before the Independents opened their doors the United States was at war with the German Empire.

Stanton Macdonald-Wright, *Far Country—Synchromy*

Detroit Institute of Arts

Wassily Kandinsky, *Improvisation no. 30: Warlike Theme* ▶

Art Institute of Chicago

PART THREE

DECADE OF DISILLUSION

INTRODUCTION / A RACE OF HAMLETS

Kandinsky wished his *Improvisation No. 30* to speak directly through its lines, shapes, and colors; he called it his "cannon picture" but explained that this title had no significance for anyone but himself, and that his image had been doubtless suggested by the constant talk of war in 1913. Three years later, when talk had given way to action, Willard Huntington Wright believed that the European conflict would slow the modern current but not deflect it from its course. He found Picasso working peacefully and observed that Matisse and others, now in uniform, looked forward to the day when they could take up the brush or the chisel again. He reported that the war issue of *Blast,* published by the vorticists of the Rebel Art Centre, was as "vortiginous" as ever.

The events of the next few years proved how premature that confidence had been, as the catchwords of the prewar idealists acquired new and sinister connotations. The consciousness of nationality fed the flames of war; science became the means for more efficient destruction; socialism discovered its powerlessness to sway the middle class. As one historian has said, this was a generation which spoke eloquently of humanity and progress, yet drove millions of young men to their death. Among those young men were French cubists, Italian futurists, Dutch and German theorists of the "new plasticism," expressionists of Germany, and constructivists of Russia. Some of them died in battle; for others the war was a "violent interruption," as Gropius called it; still others tried, at a distance from the battle, to transact the unfinished business of modernism.

How could one close what Gropius called the "disastrous gulf" between reality and idealism? Or could it be closed at all? To ask these questions was to become painfully aware that the alienation of the artist from the more general purposes of his time had not diminished but increased since the day of Cézanne and Van Gogh.

The prewar achievement of the moderns could now be regarded as one of the great historic assertions of man's potentialities. Had such a demonstration occurred in societies intelligently planned and humanely motivated the artist would have regained that place in human affairs which had once been his. But his own relentless pursuit of new forms, his own aversion to the collectivity as such had contributed to his isolation. He had claimed freedom only to discover that freedom is a brittle thing amid the unfreedom of others.

He was free, indeed, to choose one of three courses. He could stay in the arena where larger issues were being fought out; he could set up a laboratory on its margin; or he could take to the well-known ivory tower. Faced with the starvation of whole peoples by blockade, the bitter consequences of the peace treaty, and the no less bitter struggle of political factions, he was lucky if he could prevent the prewar gains from being altogether lost, much less extend and complete them.

In France and Russia the collaboration between art and politics was a shallow opportunism. Sant' Elia, whose drawings of futurist cities anticipated the shapes of later building, was killed at twenty-eight, Boccioni was another casualty, and Marinetti was given a medal for heroism. History records that by their hatred of popular government, their blind nationalism, and their glorification of blood and battle the futurists helped to prepare the cowardly victory of Mussolini's march on Rome.

The Russian advance guard, having freed art, as Malevich said, from the ballast of the objective world, was preparing to soar in the realms of proletarian culture and to identify their revolution with that of Lenin. Their effort failed for reasons which Lenin himself suggested when he observed that proletarian culture could not be manufactured in studios by specialists. "Why worship the new as a god to be obeyed because it is new?" he asked. "We are too much iconoclasts."

To the German idealists it seemed for a brief moment that there was a parallel between the "direct action" of the expressionists—man speaking to man without intermediaries—and "aktivismus" in politics and the social movement. After the revolution which failed and in the uneasy years of the Weimar Republic it seemed that the creative will had found many an eloquent voice—in the mystical poems of Stefan George and Rainer Maria Rilke, in the deep humanism of Thomas Mann's novels, the terrible concentration of Jessner's *Richard the Third,* the mordant line of George Grosz, the lunar magic of Hindemith's music. Not since Daumier and Goya had man's bestiality found such images as now in the war drawings of Otto Dix. The compassionate Käthe Kollwitz racked the world's conscience with her lithographs and woodcuts of children whose hunger was in their eyes. At Weimar until 1925 and then at Dessau the "orchestral cooperation" of sculptors, painters, architects, and designers at the Bauhaus symbolized, as Gropius said, the cooperation possible in society as a whole.

Farther and farther in the nineteen twenties the spectacle of greed and folly, of national and international selfishness drove European artists toward the outer fringe of human affairs. They were disabused of their faith in leaders who became misleaders, and even in the people themselves, apparently so willing to be misled. They had even lost faith in their own past, and Franz Marc looked on the war as a deserved affliction. In *Massemensch* Ernst Toller dramatized the intolerable dilemma of the individualist and the social man trying to be one; the plays of Kaiser showed man as a victim of his own machines, and the letters of Rilke announced his surrender: "Let us remain each on his *still* quiet, *still* trustworthy little island of life." If the drawings of Grosz became more cruel year by year it was because, as he said, "I saw a blinded raging people destroy what had taken centuries of building."

In the shattered economy of Europe even the Bauhaus workers could only remind the world that rational minds still existed, and there was a cold logic in much of their work which seemed overcompensation for the prevailing senselessness. That austerity was in the neoplasticism which Piet Mondrian announced in his Paris manifesto of 1920, and in his paintings, where a few rectangular shapes and primary colors found an absolute perfection of interrelation. One saw it also in the canvases of Lyonel Feininger and the architecture of Ozenfant and Le Corbusier, Oud and Miës van der Rohe. Feininger had turned from his brilliant cartooning to the construction of paintings whose formal integrity was complete, creating relationships of semiabstract ships and buildings with ruler-straight lines and with colors of extraordinary delicacy. Such painting and building seemed appropriate to a century whose cold precision, in the words of Nikolaus Pevsner, leaves "less space for self expression than did any period before."

With one half of its artistic mind the Continent seemed bent on preserving reason at all costs; with the other half it reacted from the present misuse of intelligence by dismissing reason, and sought those states of mind—primitive, childlike, dreaming—in which consciousness of the real world has little or no place. As a young man, Paul Klee had written in his diary, "I want to be as though new-born, knowing nothing, absolutely nothing, about Europe"; in his maturity he improvised a delightfully quizzical picture-writing to symbolize a world not already formed but in the process of creation, not only the visible but the "antecedents of the visible."

The war had stimulated the irresponsibilities of the *Dada* group, exasperated spirits half-serious in mood, who dispensed wholly with logic; and the painted fantasies of Miro, Ernst, Tanguy, and Masson in the postwar years seemed to be derived, by a process like automatic writing, from the subconscious. As time went on, this movement baptized itself with the term which Apollinaire had used to describe one of his plays as *surréaliste*, and strove to synthesize inner with outer reality. "We believe," André Breton declared, "in the future transmutation of those two seemingly contradictory states, dream and reality, into a sort of absolute reality, a super-reality, so to speak." The consciousness of individual man was to be liberated from fears and obsessions by the surrealists as a step toward the winning of his social and political freedom.

While these former nihilists struggled with their own contradictions, Picasso showed no interest in theories, and seemed indifferent to the world around him. The clothes of his *Seated Pierrot* had the fluted ponderability of a classical column, and his *Seated Woman* was painted with a cool impersonality. The *Seated Woman* of 1927 was something else, however, with her terrifying profile, as though Picasso sensed the fear and brutality of the time, its monstrous behavior; and the bleak cruelty of the late twenties was in the hard bonelike structures of his "metamorphoses." While Picasso worked to "unload himself of feelings and visions," other cubists like Fernand Léger manipulated heavy shapes of a quasi-machine character in patterns of strong color as though to bridge the gap between painting and architecture.

The postwar decade, in sum, saw many efforts to integrate the artist with the movement of society, and saw them frustrated. The close of that decade found the surrealists at a moment of crisis in the effort to improvise a social philosophy for their unsocial art. It found Grosz, Dix, and other Germans fusing expressionist distortion with fragments of harshly realistic detail and calling the result the "New Objectivism." It heard Stravinsky's music, which one of his followers praised for "inherent musical weight rather than intensity of utterance," impersonal and self-sufficient.

Roger Fry called himself an anarchist in his letters of 1925, voicing his fear and hatred of the "herd" with its immense gullibility, its emotional unreason. He had come around to Bell's insistence on a pure aesthetic emotion of no ethical or practical value, something which felt important but could not be explained. In his mind as in the art of half a dozen countries a kind of polarization had taken place, and the extremes of self-preoccupation and cold factualism seemed farther apart than ever. In *The Hollow Men,* T. S. Eliot wrote:

> Between the idea
> And the reality
> Between the motion
> And the act
> Falls the Shadow.

There were hollow men in America, too, but they were a minority. As the country drifted toward the crisis of 1917 the socialists and near socialists of the *Masses* denounced war and the makers of war. Its humor was mild in George Bellows' ridicule of the human types he found in gymnasiums; it stung when Art Young portrayed the members of the press as inhabitants of a brothel; its aim was deadlier when Robert Minor drew a giant with a naked torso and no head before whom the army doctor cries, "At last a perfect soldier!" Only in the old files of *Charivari* where Daumier lashed the war-hungry Third Napoleon could one find scorn and anger so completely fused with the biting pen line and the brutal shading of the crayon.

Boardman Robinson in the *Masses* for October, 1916, drew the European ass moving toward a precipice, astride his back the dark hooded figure of Death holding the carrot of Victory before his nose. Within six months America was at war and the machinery of national unity in full swing: the terrifying newspaper stories, the numberless forms of social pressure, the feverish war loan speeches in the shadow of the Sub-Treasury statue, the Draft Law, the Espionage and the Sedition Acts. John Reed visited the Balkan front as a reporter for the *Metropolitan Magazine* and Boardman Robinson went with him to send home drawings of the face of war itself—the filth and stench of typhus wards in Serbia, the bombed ruins of Belgrade, and the half-buried piles of dead on Gontchevo Mountain. When Art Young sketched ministers, editors, profiteers, and politicians "having their fling" while Satan led the orchestra, he was tried for conspiracy; and although the jury twice failed to convict him and the *Masses,* the magazine was destroyed.

Stieglitz held his island at "291" until the war came; taking a nickel out of his pocket, he reflected that this was what the war was about. At fifty-three he saw a world seemingly bent on self-destruction, which held no place for the values he had so stubbornly defended. Up to the last moment, however, he upheld the right of the individual to his vision, showing in 1916 the camera work of Paul Strand and the highly personal drawings of Georgia O'Keeffe.

After the war tensions came the disintegration of Wilson's presidency and the generous vision on which it had been based; the Republican faction scuttled the treaty in its haste to repeat the good times of McKinley. One learned of the new millionaires and saw in peace the growth of intolerances such as war had not known. The decade of disillusion opened on January second of 1920 with Mitchell Palmer's agents breaking into the homes of suspected aliens. President Harding assured the country that the war had been no crusade but an offensive defense of national rights, and for five years

Boardman Robinson cartoon, 1916

The Masses

the newspapers recounted the scandal of Teapot Dome and the oil reserves which had enriched public officials and their friends.

Negro, Jew, and Catholic alike were victims of the Ku Klux Klan as its membership spread through the nation. A society for the suppression of vice tried to prevent Cabell's *Jurgen* from being read, while Bruce Barton wrote a book to prove that Christ had been the very pattern of the business executive. National Prohibition was first made lawful and then by every illegal means evaded; in Tennessee, where it was a crime to teach the theory of evolution, the brilliant lawyer and agnostic Darrow made the Great Commoner Bryan a figure for ridicule. In Massachusetts a poor shoemaker named Sacco and a fish peddler named Vanzetti were electrocuted for murder, and many fair minds shared these men's belief that their crime had been their anarchist opinions.

Alfred Kazin has written that "nothing was so dead in 1920 as the crusading spirit of 1910," yet the note of black despair was not the dominant note of these years. The nation's economy had not collapsed but seemed more secure than ever. There was no hunger by blockade, as there had been no invading armies; nor had American cities cracked and re-formed and burst in the violet air like those in Eliot's *Waste Land*. The post-war plot unrolled, among its characters the stony Coolidge and the bloody Al Capone, the clergyman discoursing on spiritual principles in advertising, and the booster proclaiming that Rotary was a manifestation of the Divine. This was not so much a catastrophe as a grotesque carnival; not a civilization crumbling into chaos but a civilization making a fool of itself.

Could one blame the thoughtful man for deciding that such an era called not for jeremiads but for Dunciads? One could find no trace of the epic in the citizen who wept as the soft face of Lillian Gish emerged from the Limehouse fog in Griffith's moving picture *Broken Blossoms;* who saw American life overindulgently with Booth Tarkington, put on radio earphones to hear "Barney Google," and sang "I'll Say She Does"; who thought the scented romances of Joseph Hergesheimer were literature, and turned from the harsh truth of Dos Passos' *Three Soldiers* to the drolleries of Old Bill in the comedy *The Better 'Ole.*

The cartoonists of the twenties spared no current imbecility. There was no kindness in Ralph Barton's drawings for *Vanity Fair* nor in the acid profiles of theatrical people by Alfred Frueh in *The New Yorker.* That urbane weekly published full-page black-and-whites by Gluyas Williams, whose ridicule of the suburbanite or the smug man of business was as mild as his exquisite thin line; but it also presented Peter Arno's crackling burlesques of lustful clubmen and mink-heavy dowagers. The anatomical liberties of Arno reminded one of Rowlandson, but not the harsh mockery of these bold lines and brilliantly summary washes.

Sharp literary scalpels probed American self-deceptions and bared the ugliness of the middle-class environment: Sinclair Lewis wrote *Main Street* and *Babbitt* and Upton Sinclair wrote *The Goose Step.* In *The American Mercury* Henry L. Mencken explored the anatomy of the moron and with more wit than democratic faith upheld the "civilized minority" against the "booboisie."

These smart and cynical new liberals made the middle-aged Vernon Parrington feel like a mourner at his own funeral. In 1927 he published the first two volumes of his *Main Currents in American Thought,* a brilliant study of the native mind; and in his half-completed final volume he wrote *finis* to a chapter in American liberalism, sadly comparing the "brilliant coruscations" of the younger writers with the sturdy idealism of the prewar men. All was not lost, however, and Parrington reserved a place of honor for a few poets, novelists, and critics who probed beneath the surface of American behavior—Sandburg, the lusty champion of individual dignity, and Dreiser, "a heavy-footed peasant with unslaked curiosity and a boundless pity," who tramped on the neat little garden beds of convention. Parrington argued even that Sinclair Lewis, that Diogenes, betrayed some lingering faith in man; and Sherwood Anderson at least believed that the big ugly towns, the factories, and the prosperity of the country were part of her earnest effort to build a land to the glory of Man, even though he concluded that the affair blew up in the process.

Parrington considered Randolph Bourne an important critic because Bourne and a few others not only asked what was wrong with civilization in the United States but offered answers: Bourne in the *New Republic,* and Van Wyck Brooks, Lewis Mumford, Waldo Frank, and Paul Rosenfeld in the short-lived *Seven Arts.*

Randolph Bourne was a hunchback with a "peculiarly acute mechanism for suffering," whose opposition to the war was proof against conversion, and who died at twenty-eight in the last year of the conflict after prophesying a "fatal backwash and backfire" upon creative and democratic values in his country. Bourne reminded Americans that the European notion of culture had been torn to shreds; why believe that it would serve better here? "To have learned to appreciate a Mantegna and a Japanese print, and Dante and Débussy, and not to have learned nausea at Main Street, means an art education which is not merely worthless but destructive."

Van Wyck Brooks recoiled also from the pseudo culture around him but his was a sturdier constitution than Bourne's. In *The Wine of the Puritans* and in *America's Coming of Age* he traced the American dividedness back to Jonathan Edwards and Benjamin Franklin, to the transcendentalist and the catchpenny opportunist, concluding that there was no ground in common between the Highbrow and the Lowbrow, art and business, honor and graft, theory and practice. In *Letters and Leadership* he declared that the young artists of America, with no sense of a collective spiritual life to work for, were becoming a race of Hamlets, and he called for a Whitman to reaffirm a humanity which was older than Puritanism. Walt, too, had known misgivings in the after years of an earlier war, but his belief in people was more robust than that of Brooks's generation. The man who wrote *A Song for Occupations* would never have called his country, as Brooks did, a "vast undifferentiated herd of good-natured animals"; and the tone of *Letters and Leadership* was a discouraged one, as though its author doubted whether new leaves of grass could grow in America.

For the figurative arts the postwar decade was neither as feverish as the pre-Armory days had been nor as desperate as the depression years would be. The war itself had produced little of significance in painting and sculpture, in spite of the energy with which the spokesmen for the arts threw themselves into the cause. The Federation of Arts renamed its magazine the *American Magazine of Art,* and in its pages Duncan Phillips called on painters to help win the conflict. England had sent her best draughtsmen to the front to record battles; America had produced scarcely more than the flimsy posters of Howard Chandler Christy. The Federation promoted a traveling show of the lithographs which Joseph Pennell made of work in the dry docks and arsenals; John Sargent painted Wilson's portrait; Childe Hassam's impression of Allies' Day on Fifth Avenue was gay with the flags of nations. Adeline Adams summoned the sculptors to do their best for Pershing's crusaders and to prevent the national emotion from begetting shapeless memorials and mean portrait statues when the victory had been won. Otto Kahn in the early twenties explained that the common people needed the solace of art in such troubled times and that no Bolshevik could rob us of the dividends we receive from Botticelli's *Spring.*

Of the two insurgent groups of the early nineteen hundreds, the progressives moved more securely in the twenties than the radicals. The opinions of Henri, which had influenced so many American careers, were collected by Margery Ryerson and published in 1923 as *The Art Spirit.* When Allen Tucker marked the fiftieth year of the Art Students League in 1924, praising the unique methods by which its own pupils managed its affairs, not only Henri but Luks, Sloan, and Schnakenberg were on its faculty. Three years later Sloan and other members of the Independents refused the National Academy's invitation to contribute to its spring annual. Forbes Watson denounced the maneuver as an effort to make hospitality pay dividends; and the work of those who accepted gave the event an unaccustomed and undeserved distinction.

Mrs. Whitney continued to be hostess and counsellor to a growing number of artists, and in 1928 the Whitney Studio Club was replaced by the Whitney Studio Galleries for the exhibition and sale of work by young men who had no dealers. It was a sign of progress when J. G. Butler, an industrialist of Youngstown, Ohio, replaced his first dubious collection, destroyed by fire, with another which was exclusively American; and although the Butler Art Institute in the twenties acquired Alexander and Abbey, Sargent and Tryon, it also bought Henri and Lawson, Davies and Twachtman.

The progressives had a valiant spokesman in Forbes Watson. When this critic of the *World* assumed the editorship of *The Arts* in 1923 that genteel magazine changed its tone; the work of experimentalists appeared among its illustrations and there was a single trenchant page in each issue by Watson himself. He had no respect for native collectors who snubbed their own countrymen, and he found a modern potboiler as objectionable as an academic one. The internationalism of the Armory days had in some respects been harmful to the native, and a mild isolationism was implied in Watson's first editorial: *The Arts* would do no flag waving, but would stand with the American artist against both timidity and snobbery.

This concern with the native inspired Lewis Mumford, whose *Sticks and Stones* and whose *Brown Decades* reinterpreted the arts from a liberal point of view in essays which were among the most perceptive yet written in the United States. Suzanne La Follette's *Art in America* (1929) restored to painting, sculpture, and building their social context and their national motivations.

American research had begun in earnest. A group of enthusiasts, among them John Hill Morgan, Frederick F. Sherman, Charles K. Bolton, and William Kelby, investigated the colonial and the republican men, while others studied wall paintings and gravestones, wood carving and prints. In 1922 appeared the scholarly survey by Fiske Kimball of *Domestic Architecture of the American Colonies and of the Early Republic.* The twelfth volume of *The Pageant of America* was given to *The American Spirit in Art,* and the Whitney Museum published Virgil Barker's short but stimulating *Critical Introduction to American Painting.*

As this exploration of the national past went forward, the literary friends of modernism discussed its problems less violently than in the days before the war. Sheldon Cheney's *Primer of Modern Art* codified the modern theories in chapters directed to the layman's comprehension. Walter Pach wrote skillfully of the great tradition from Ingres to Renoir and Picasso, a tradition which had nothing to do with conservative painting; his *Freeman* essays were collected for *Masters of Modern Art* in 1925; his *Ananias* in 1928 demolished such national idols as John Sargent and Daniel Chester French. With a bantering humor and a touch of Mencken's sarcasm, Henry McBride assured his *Dial* readers in one of his monthly essays that America was in no imminent danger of catching up with the moderns.

Many veterans of the Armory days had either disappeared or deserted. Caffin was dead, and Willard Wright published essays on literature and philosophy before turning himself into the "S. S. Van Dine" of the murder mysteries. James Huneker in 1916 advised John Quinn, "Don't buy crude American art or cubist junk. This new crowd is already ancient. Buy a few great pictures and sculptures—like Puvis. . . ." And Huneker assured Cortissoz that he was no longer a Cézannist; that grumpy old bird was a third-rater. As for the crew of modernity yowlers, Huneker was dead sick of them all.

One had to read the little magazines—the *Bookman,* the *Dial,* and *Seven Arts*—to find champions of those artists who remained incorrigibly experimental. Beneath the rather lush prose of Paul Rosenfeld were his subtle insights into the work of painters, sculptors, and photographers whose portraits he drew in *Port of New York,* and all of whom produced their own principles from out of themselves. Most of his subjects were intimates of Stieglitz. Their personalities had no protective shell against life in the nineteen twenties, and if several of them suffered a more than normal insecurity and dividedness of mind, it was no mere coincidence. Stieglitz moved uptown in 1925 to a room in the Anderson Building which he called the "Intimate Gallery"; in 1929 he opened "An American Place." Stanton Macdonald-Wright was shown in these years, Hartley, Demuth, and Marin, the sculpture of Élie Nadelman and Gaston Lachaise, the paintings and drawings of Oscar Bluemner and Peggy Bacon. Equally receptive to eccentricity were Katherine Dreier and Marcel Duchamp, whose Société Anonyme gave Eilshemius his first one-man show in 1920.

Despite such occasional support the innovators among painters and sculptors discovered that the doors of the museums were as firmly closed against them as the minds of the directors. The Metropolitan showed the postimpressionists on a huge scale in 1921 but there was no sign of a desire to hang them permanently, much less to support their American cousins. Two years later the formation of the Barnes Collection was announced, with many of the masterpieces of Cézanne and Renoir. Matisse hung on the walls of Walter Arensberg's apartment with Brancusi, Braque, Gris, and the famous descending nude of Duchamp. It seemed that the country was tied more firmly than ever to what McBride called the apron strings of Paris.

The radicals of the Armory Show now learned that one trumpet blast had not destroyed the walls of academism or the walls of ignorance and suspicion which stood between the artist and his people. The war had not made the world appreciably safer for the more venturesome. Under these circumstances many an artist in the twenties attempted to find continuity with the best in the native tradition, aided by the new interest in America's old masters. Others found time, after demanding formal freedom, for considering what use they wished to make of that freedom. There is a time for biting off and a time for chewing. This decade was the digestive period for the American modern.

CHAPTER 29 / DISTORTION DOMESTICATED

On the tenth anniversary of the Armory Show Forbes Watson wrote that he could see few signs of American talent in the galleries. He may have noticed that in the forthcoming Carnegie International Marquet and Signac would represent the "newer school"; perhaps he had read a review of the Independents' seventh show whose author noted with relief that no "freaks" had been included. According to the *Art News* the Metropolitan had bought a Goya *Bullfight;* Great Britain had exported to this country in 1922 eight million dollars' worth of "art."

The painters of academic portraits at least had no complaint; as in the wake of older wars, they were now deluged with commissions. Charles S. Hopkinson was chosen by the government to paint the Versailles delegates; he had acquired from Twachtman and from Denman Ross a clean and orderly palette, a vigorous naturalism, and a skill in placing his figure within its rectangle, and his eye for personality was sharp if not searching. For most of the specialists in this genre, John Sargent had established the tone of the sprightly portrait, and his influence persisted long after he died in 1925. The painter of *El Jaleo* had passed sixty when he sketched on the French front in 1918, and the strength of his early work contrasted with the shallow and clever likenesses of his later years. There had been at least a robust color in his decorations for the Boston Public Library, but in the rotunda and stair hall of the Boston Art Museum his deities postured in wan flesh tones and chalky whites against a pretty blue; and one turned in relief to the vigorous landscapes of the Canadian Rockies which he did in his off moments.

Among the veterans, Gari Melchers still won medals in his sixties for sentimental genre pieces whose flimsiness had little in common with his earlier *Fencing Master,* a portrait with something of Manet's breadth and directness. *The Age of Gold,* by Bryson Burroughs, Curator of Paintings at the Metropolitan Museum, was a charming thin echo of Puvis. It was now almost forty years since impressionism had seemed an innovation, and both Melchers and Burroughs had made decorous use of its free handling and its color methods. The brood of Monet was indeed both numerous and popular in the 1920's. Twachtman and Metcalf were dead, but Hassam and Lawson would see the middle thirties, and there were quaint harbors, picturesque farmlands, and melodramatic deserts from Ogunquit to Santa Fe for colonies of painters to render in broken hues and a mild luminism.

The layman whose eye had caught up with those simplifications and whose mind asked for no deeper penetration of familiar forms delighted in such landscapes. He noted that Birge Harrison's *Meadows in Winter* was like Twachtman's frozen brooks, without observing that it lacked the latter's sensitiveness; and it was easy to compare the lively marines of Frederick J. Waugh with Winslow Homer, though the storm and surge of the ocean found a thinner orchestration in Waugh. Younger than most of this group was the Norwegian Jonas Lie, whose dazzling white sailboats against ice-blue water compelled attention on the walls of the National Academy.

Here and there the language of academic naturalism was spoken with a mildly modern accent by men who could rely on a solid old-fashioned discipline in drawing but who, like Russell Cowles, "took some liberties with the facts." The quiet unity and the mild rhythms in the wistful nudes of Bernard Karfiol and in his tender and

Jonas Lie, *Deep River*

Courtesy Grand Central Art Galleries, New York City

sympathetic studies of children were not derived from his Academy training. It was perhaps Cézanne who showed James Chapin how to pose his farmers in their kitchen chairs and how to build with verticals and horizontals. The suave eliminations in the nudes of Robert Brackman were achieved without sacrifice of meticulous craftsmanship, and in his portraits of handsome and prosperous people a tendency toward type was to be seen.

Leon Kroll developed his own idealization of human form, whether a girl posed for his deft pencil on the rocks of Cape Ann or strode as Justice Triumphant through a mural. Kroll's backlog was his work in Paris with Laurens, and his brush had been enlivened through friendship with Henri and Bellows. Kroll worked with a dignity and grace, an insistence upon wholes which distinguished him from the merely clever transcribers of nature. His orderliness was matched by the less lyrical Eugene Speicher, the forceful disposal of whose portrait figures and whose emphasis on mature human shapes owed a little to Cézanne and Renoir. Speicher resolved detail into generalized contours and broad facial planes, practicing his mild modernism coolly and with workmanlike precision in such handsome portraits as the full-length *Katharine Cornell.*

A somewhat ruder strength was in Henry Varnum Poor's Matisse-like early drawings and in the abrupt simplifications of his *Boy with a Bow* (Newark Mus.). There was a Ryderesque drama in the sea pictures of Henry Elis Mattson, who took liberties with the shapes of rock and wave. Walt Kuhn gave a monumental dignity to his clowns, his acrobats, and his guides, making rich patterns of the circus costumes against dark backgrounds, and sculpturing the whitened faces boldly under harsh light. When Maurice Sterne resolved the houses of Italian towns into their basic planes, one recalled the Provençal farms of Cézanne; for Sterne, a ring of people watching a night show in the square at Anticoli was a means of repeating the ellipse of a fountain. Stefan Hirsch was as sharply definitive as an architect's draughtsman in his views of New York skyscrapers; under the clear sky of a Maine winter, Niles Spencer revealed the essential structure of rocks and fishermen's houses at Ogunquit with the rigor of Seurat, but with a sharper focus.

To paintings like these the quarrelsome word "abstract" could be applied only in its milder meaning—to summarize, to abridge; it also suggested a less lively concern with subject matter than had moved Henri and his veritists. The painters of the twenties seemed to take more interest in the construction of a head than in what went on inside it; the still lifes of the period had no such delight in fruit and flowers as one found in the Peale pictures; there were figures in many a landscape whose reason for being there was less than urgent. Henri's group, which had once challenged the Academy, was now challenged by artists who took a more detached view of what he had called the building materials of a work of art.

Henri worked with his earlier strength when a good subject was before him: the rutted features of an old Spaniard, the firm cheeks of an Indian girl at Santa Clara, the whiskered Gael of his *Guide to Croaghan,* whom he treated with Dickensian breadth and humor. His faces of children were built with a few planes of fresh color but seemed often to rely more on the charm of childhood than was safe. When Henri died in 1929 Forbes Watson observed that his ex-pupils were everywhere and that their work was sometimes sloppy.

George Luks had his sloppy moments, but not when he built a firm space for *Mrs. Gamely* and placed the old crone with her white rooster solidly in it (Met. Mus.). William Glackens under the spell of Renoir was learning not only that master's luminous way with flesh, his rounding of breasts and buttocks, but something of his over-all pictorial rhythm.

It was John Sloan, however, in his fifties who had most deeply pondered the Armory lessons. "Looks like" was no longer for him the test of good painting, since it "shows that the artist has not put his brain to work." The charm of a decade already remote was in his Times Square shoppers, his variations on *McSorley's Bar,* and his children scampering in the shadows of the Washington Arch; but his forms were now firmer, his mind was more deliberate. By the end of the twenties Sloan was painting nudes with the cool sculptural quality of Italian masters, having found new media and a new handwriting of the brush to emphasize roundnesses and concavities, the rhythms made by bodily gestures.

Bernard Karfiol, *Standing Nude*

Estate of the artist, courtesy Downtown Gallery

Still more self-conscious in his concern for the dynamics of picture making was George Bellows, younger than Sloan by eleven years. That concern marked the difference between his Luksian slapdash prize fights of 1909

Leon Kroll, *A Farm in Maine* (private coll.)

Courtesy Whitney Museum of American Art, New York City

Eugene E. Speicher, *The Blue Necklace*

Toledo Museum of Art

and his more drily calculated *Dempsey and Firpo* of 1923. The people in his lithographs moved like well-directed actors through the spaces of their settings, and when Bellows composed his triple portrait of *Eleanor, Jean and Anna* he had discovered in the "dynamic symmetry" of Jay Hambidge a system for placing his figures and locating his main points (Albright Gall.). The canvas itself was half of what Hambidge called a "root five rectangle," and the proportions and shapes of the child and the two old ladies coincided with subdivisions of this area, with its diagonals and their reciprocals. One felt the vigor and affection of Bellows' characterizations but a certain stiffness in his conscientious geometry. Would he have regained his early vitality if he had not died at forty-three?

A more deliberate stylization of forms was in Guy Pène du Bois, whose French years gave him an abiding love for the backstage subjects of Steinlen and for Daumier's stubby bourgeois pretending to be connoisseurs of pictures. Not Daumier's tolerant humor, however, but a cool dislike seemed often to model the tight bodies, the bald heads, the corseted breasts, and the hard flanks of du Bois' creatures. His *Waiter!* reminds

George W. Bellows, *Dempsey and Firpo*

Whitney Museum of American Art, New York City

one of Sloan's freshness; his *Jeanne Eagels* (Whitney Mus.) was a clever life-size caricature; his men and women of the 1920's moved in the hard light as though they were mannequins or dolls, and in *Masked Ball* of 1929 they were perilously like wax dummies artfully disposed.

Both Edward Hopper and Rockwell Kent were thirty-eight years old when the twenties opened, and both acknowledged their debt to Henri. The impressionism of Hopper's early Paris street scenes gave place to a firmer grip on space and a harsher translation of sunlight on white clapboards and lighthouses. There was a prose thoroughness in his *Automat* which reminded Virgil Barker of Pieter De Hoogh. In the Alaska scenes of Rockwell Kent, his Monhegan marines, and his Berkshire snow scenes, earth forms had been strengthened and simplified in the modern manner, the figures rendered with powerful light-and-shade divisions. He soon found special shapes for clouds and cliffs, and a crisp sculptural manner in his black-and-white illustrations as the formalizing of his work progressed.

For much of the intellectualism which, Jerome Meyers said, was a consequence of the Armory, Kenneth Hayes Miller was responsible both as artist and as teacher. Persistent in his mind was a perfectionism which can perhaps be traced to his Congregational ancestors and the Oneida Community where Miller was born. His romantic *Serpent* of 1911 was a strange Pan-like figure brooding darkly against clouds, and Miller never lost his affection for Albert Ryder; but when Renoir inspired him in his forties, Paul Rosenfeld wrote that he lacked the opalescence and fluidity of the Frenchman and suggested that Miller was tempted to overmodel. That tendency was in his shoppers and working girls, and one looked vainly for an interest in the human which would differentiate between a face and a fur coat. Younger men could at least learn from Miller to dislike the sentimental and easy solution and to practice a scrupulous craftsmanship.

That discipline helped Yasuo Kuniyoshi to paint *Boy Stealing Fruit* with its wiry primitive quality, where the artist used the stark shapes and knife edges of Jack-

Guy Pène du Bois, *Opera Box*

Whitney Museum of American Art, New York City

Kenneth H. Miller, *The Shopper*

Whitney Museum of American Art, New York City

Yasuo Kuniyoshi, *Stove and Bouquet*

Murdock Collection, Wichita Art Museum, Kansas

Henry L. McFee, *Still Life—Oranges*

Whitney Museum of American Art, New York City

Charles Demuth, *Acrobats,* water color (detail)

Museum of Modern Art, New York City

Preston Dickinson, *Bridge,* water color

Newark Museum

sonian stencil painting (Columbus Gall.). At the Art Students League Kuniyoshi became familiar with the works of Daumier and Delacroix, and gradually his metallic smooth rendering gave way to a relaxed and more humorously personal form. Thanks also to Miller, Henry Ernest Schnakenberg in his twenties made a careful arrangement of window frame, cloth, and fruit bowl and painted it with more energy than sensitiveness. A masculine vigor was in the brush of Alexander Brook, another Miller pupil who showed his work in the twenties alongside the mischievous caricatures by his wife, Peggy Bacon. Brook's response to the character of Raphael Soyer gave warmth and humor to that portrait, but the Brook still lifes were as laconic as they were sturdy; his *Girl with Flowers* was a skillful exercise in the dynamic balancing of a body, the curves of a wicker chair, and the line of a floor (Met. Mus.).

Most of these young men would have concurred in Henry Lee McFee's statement of his purpose at the time of the *Forum* Show: to find "a plastic unit expressive of the form life of the collection of objects." His own search for that unit led him all the way from the impressionist Birge Harrison at Woodstock to a mildly cubist preoccupation with planes, textures, and interpenetrations, and thence to a digesting of Cézanne. McFee had read Bernard Berenson, and there were "tactile values" in his still lifes, viewed from above as Cézanne viewed his table tops, with each fold of cloth, bottle, and fruit given its due volume and its relation to all other objects in his space.

Although McFee declared that a painter must love his subject if his form-making capacities were to be stirred, his own canvases suggest a love for autumn leaves and pastures which was cool and platonic. One must look elsewhere to find a sprightlier imagination at work and a more personal response to experience. One finds them in the crisp and delightful still lifes of Charles Demuth and in his vaudeville acrobats. There was a dainty athleticism in this man whose fruit and flowers made exquisite clean use of water color and whose factory chimneys and New England cupolas were charmingly disjointed in a pseudo-cubist fashion. Before Charles Burchfield produced his somber streets and drab Victorian façades there was a moment when his child fantasies took form in an expressionism of his own making—thunder clouds "black as a tar barrel," strange jagged trees and gaping caves, and woods where terrifying plants and flowers grew.

Charles Burchfield, *The First Hepaticas,* water color

Museum of Modern Art, New York City

Georgia O'Keeffe, *Skunk Cabbage*

Collection of the artist, courtesy Downtown Gallery

There was no such emotional charge beneath the crisp paintings and pastels of Preston Dickinson, who played like an Oriental with formalized trees and houses as detached motifs against white snow, the ordering lines of his pictures compelling the shape and position of these units. The tugboats and thrusting bridges of Dickinson were half description, half symbolic pictograms, a quaint abstraction-once-removed. Karl Knaths called himself an expressionist, and the humorous simplifications of shape and tone in his *Cock and Glove* of 1927 had something of Braque's interest in assimilating volumes and colors to the two-dimensional canvas (Phillips Mem. Gall.). Stuart Davis saw the Place Pasdeloup in Paris the next year and compressed its forms into a few flat areas to emphasize color-shape relations which he considered beautiful independently of the house fronts, iron balconies, and café signs themselves.

"Clean-swept as though by a strong wind" was the phrase of Alexander Brook for the paintings by Georgia O'Keeffe at the Anderson Galleries in 1923. Her barns, trees, hill slopes, and low-hanging clouds were somber in color, impeccably brushed and locked inviolably together by a controlled intensity, as though her relation

Joseph Stella, *Brooklyn Bridge* (base of panel omitted)

Newark Museum

Alfred H. Maurer, *Abstraction*

Phillips Memorial Gallery, Washington, D.C.

to things was more intimate than that of Davis or Dickinson and her seeming "objectivity" a mask for deeper feeling. In her 1921 show *Black Spot* was a contrast of a few hard shapes embedded in softer white roundnesses, and Paul Rosenfeld praised her fusion of the passionate and the chaste. One could not doubt the part which emotion played in Morris Kantor's *Haunted House,* a strange room into which the outdoors penetrated in surrealist fashion, and into the making of which had gone his early devotion to Seurat, his cubist experiments, and his own romantic fancy (Chicago Art Inst.).

There is no substitute, after all, for the strong initial experience either of the inner or the outer world which summons the artist to make images and, merging with his form-making powers, determines the result. The point was demonstrated to New York in 1923 by five large panels called *New York Interpreted* which in no literal way described their subjects. The artist was an Italian, Joseph Stella, who returned from Europe after knowing the futurists, and found New York " a monstrous steely bar elevated by modern Cyclops to defy the gods." Exhilarated by his theme, Stella composed the movements of a visual symphony in which night, the glare of electricity, the sheen of steel, and the roar of the subway train played their parts. At the base of each panel were abstracted shapes derived from subways; above, the relentless vertical stacks of Manhattan became the prow of a vessel, or the cables of Brooklyn Bridge swung majestically upward. Stella's pictures had the intensity of stained glass and the monumentality of murals, every form whether minute or gigantic living the life of the whole.

It was Stella who discovered the self-made Vincent Canadé, likewise an Italian, and called attention to the harsh intensity of the man's self-portraits. Canadé, who painted to forget his own tragedies, was "modern" without knowledge of the moderns; and so, in a sense, were those other "primitives," Horace Pippin and John Kane. The former, a negro who had worked as a farm boy, coal loader, and railway porter, made Bible scenes with crayons on paper doilies and in the late twenties turned to scenes of the war in which he had fought for two years. "Pictures just come to my mind," he said, "and then I tell my heart to go ahead"; and Pippin went ahead with a directness which the sophisticated envied. And even the Carnegie Institute showed John Kane in 1927 when the ex-miner and ex-house painter was nearly seventy and for nearly a decade had been turning out Scottish picnics and views of Turtle Creek Valley, whose firm colors and precise details, whose delight in pattern, and whose independence of orthodox pictorial rules reminded Americans of Henri Rousseau.

Too many paintings of the nineteen twenties implied that "abstraction" was a mold into which content could be poured, a garment to be either worn or put aside. Against this shallow synthesis stood older men who had borne the full stress of modernism's early battles. The struggle toward new expression seemed to take place on a deeper personal level in such men. Most of the American impressionists, for example, looked lazy and uninventive beside Maurice Prendergast; before he died in 1924 the separate forms in his yachting scenes and his promenades in parks and on seashores had lost some of their identity, had grown heavier and richer, less specific in drawn outline; they had become strands in a sturdier and more subtly integrated whole.

Alfred Maurer had known the cubists before the war sent him home to practice their dislocations and reassemblings. Braque and Picasso had made their pictorial structures of edges and planes whose relationships were more rigorously logical because nearly devoid of contrasting colors; Maurer's palette was bright with yellows, greens, and fresh pinks, and he managed to combine in one canvas semiabstract and wholly abstract motives. His still lifes were not profound explorations of volume and space, but lively and often beautiful patterns; and in a less familiar series of nude studies he sturdily integrated the shapes and rhythms of the body with its surroundings. One compared the staring eyes and long sharp noses of his female heads, their waxen flesh tones and tubular necks, to the creatures of Modigliani; but this vision was Maurer's own, inspired by his response to girls whom he knew. Some of these paintings are poignant and tender; in other works the image becomes huge, masklike, and rather terrifying. She stands alone, or in twos, threes, or fours, and haunts the observer as she doubtless haunted Maurer.

At An American Place one could see the fruit of Dove's effort, in the intervals of farming and illustrating, to give back in bold colors and half-abstract shapes his enjoyment of life's "highest instances" — and as the years went on he created his fantasies of rock and waterfall, of trees whipped by a "golden storm," of thawing snow.

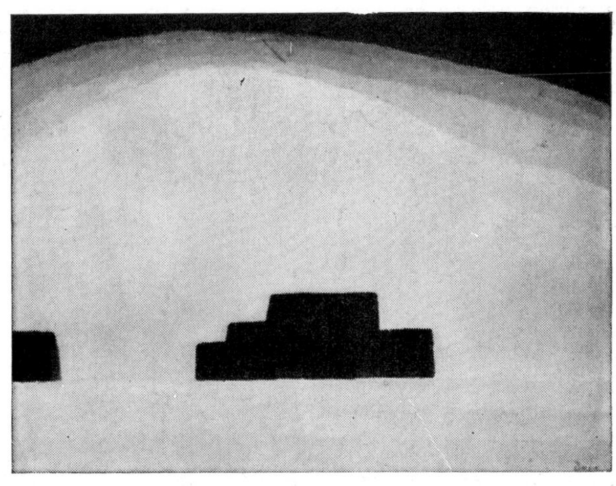

Arthur G. Dove, *Snow Thaw*

Phillips Memorial Gallery, Washington, D.C.

Max Weber, *The Red Cap,* gouache

Whitney Museum of American Art, New York City

After Max Weber published his *Essays on Art* in 1916 there was no full-length showing of his work until 1923, and his seven lean years were a time for self-exploring. The results were contradictory; his superb *gouaches* of 1918, scarcely larger than a postal card, characterized human types with sympathy, humor, and pathos. He found in the experience of Jews what he called a religious-archaic subject, and the blocklike faces and reaching hands of his *Invocation* conveyed the intense mysticism which was part of Weber. In other works the subject became wholly the servant of form and the artist disclaimed a merely emotional interest, explaining that sculpturesque-spatial values and plastic necessity had determined their nature.

John Marin, *Mountain Top,* water color

Cleveland Museum of Art

In letters and published essays one could follow Marsden Hartley's conflict. Mabel Dodge observed that he had known terrible hours of shadow in the war years; now he rejected the materialism of America and Europe, and held in contempt the public's fear of change. Life was all right, he wrote, but he resented the price one had to pay to get a simple vision of it. As he struggled for that vision the artist moved from New Mexico to Berlin, Florence, Vienna, and Rome, from Paris to London, and from London back to New England. He wrote essays on the power of Audubon and on the masculinity of Courbet, and dedicated his *Adventures in the Arts* to Stieglitz.

Hartley believed that Whitman and Cézanne had done most to "clarify the sleeping eye" of his time and it was at Aix that he renounced his expressionism. As he painted the Mont Sainte-Victoire the American declared, "I would rather be sure that I had placed two colors in true relationship to each other than to have exposed a wealth of emotionalism gone wrong in the name of richness of personal expression." Hartley went to New Hampshire in 1930 scarcely aware that suddenly awakened Yankee qualities, and not pure intellectualism, would soon clarify his sleeping eye.

The eye of Marin never slept, nor was he given to pondering on the state of civilization. He wrote letters, to be sure, in which phrase and thought flicked back and forth like a fisherman's fly. He cheerfully conceded that "we are all a bunch of dubs," but he would go about his business "saying a real say." When others talked of their inner vision, Marin said "rubbish" and explained that he was no different from other men save that he had his own intensity, his own direction. For him the dip and flash of a sailboat, the stirring of pines in the wind, the pounding of waves on a shore made "the heart, liver, lungs, everything, the whole human critter expand nigh to bustin' point"; and Marin's relation to such things was original in Emerson's sense. "To the attentive eye, each moment of the year has its own beauty, and in the same field, it beholds, every hour, a picture which was never seen before, and which shall never be seen again."

If Marin's pictures seemed incoherent it was because the man was compelled to paint equivalents of his exhilaration, to give the movement of water and wind in a medium which could not move, to catch immensity in a small rectangle, and thrusting space on a flat sheet of paper. There were more verbs than nouns in his language, more adverbs than adjectives, and no clichés whatever; and he moved outside the accepted rules of "grammatical" construction. Yet, as he once said, "this seemingly crazy stroke is put down with deliberate, mulish willfulness" to define not things but their qualities and their response to one another—an island sailing like a boat, a boat jumping like a fish, an undulant cloud taking the curves of the hills, a gray sea chopped into white which keeps on chopping. (See color plate 17.)

In Marin's water colors of the twenties his mind dictated nothing which his hand could not do, from the rough-fibered broad stroke to the silk-fine line, from the sonorous brown rock to the delicately washed pale sky; and he had found devices of his own which were like comments under the breath: "This is what your eye does when a Penobscot buoy lurches in spray or when you see six or seven thunderstorms going on at the same time in New Mexico." His *Midtown, New York* was like a geologist's cross section sliced through subway, five-story block, and skyscraper. When Stonington village in Maine got him "by the scruff of the neck" he enclosed its prim white houses and small gardens with brushed lines which formed a polygonal frame-in-frame and served as a mental and visual preparation for the angularities of the theme itself. In *Boat Fantasy* the enframing shape had the character of a visual joke, like a ship inside a bottle; in other sea paintings it closed in on wave and sails, forcing their rhythm to become more insistent. When Marin faced the immensity of Taos, he made pictures like maps of the tableland sliced by canyons and ridden by mountains. He specified trees with small black-and-green dot shapes against the general pinkness; and the few seemingly casual spots of blue above the hills not only said sky and cloud but in some extraordinary way gave scale and substance to the whole valley.

Set beside a Marin schooner, Charles Sheeler's *Pertaining to Yachts and Yachting* seemed at first more "realistic"; yet in spite of Sheeler's sharp drawing and the impeccably smooth gradation of light on his sails, his boats were no more real than Marin's. Sheeler objected when people spoke of his style as "photographic," and turned the tables on his critics by claiming that the camera could transcribe and fix abstract qualities. As proof he cited those photographs by Stieglitz which their maker called "equivalents"—studies of the nude body and of sky and cloud which were the symbols of a mind turning inward. Still further removed from "nature" in the 1920's were prints which Man Ray produced by "solarization," and the "Rayographs" he made by placing objects of varying opacity on sheets of light-sensitive paper.

Paul Strand believed in the essential objectivity of the camera, controlled by a conception in the artist's mind prior to his exposure. He, too, had experimented with the generalization of objects in the interest of design, and his *Abstraction* of 1915 wove the shadows and lights of bowls into a compelling counterpoint; but in the same year he also snapped the creased and weary features of old men and women who did not know that they were being photographed. The prints of Strand showed people hurrying through the chasms of New York and across the blank fronts of stores and banks; his portrait of Marsden Hartley was a study of suffering and tension. In Number 49 of *Camera Work* Strand urged photographers to respect what was in front of them and to express it through an almost infinite range of tonal values. In the 1920's he explored that range with subtlety in his own close-ups of machines, of blasted trees in Colorado, of rocks in Maine, and of plants whose cobwebs enmeshed drops of rain.

When Strand and Sheeler showed their film *Manahatta* in 1921 it was the fact creatively presented, not the manipulative trick, which had inspired them. The motion picture in America, after one or two shallow efforts to match the expressionist distortions of the German *Doctor Caligari,* employed a documentary

Charles R. Sheeler, *Church Street El*

Courtesy of the artist

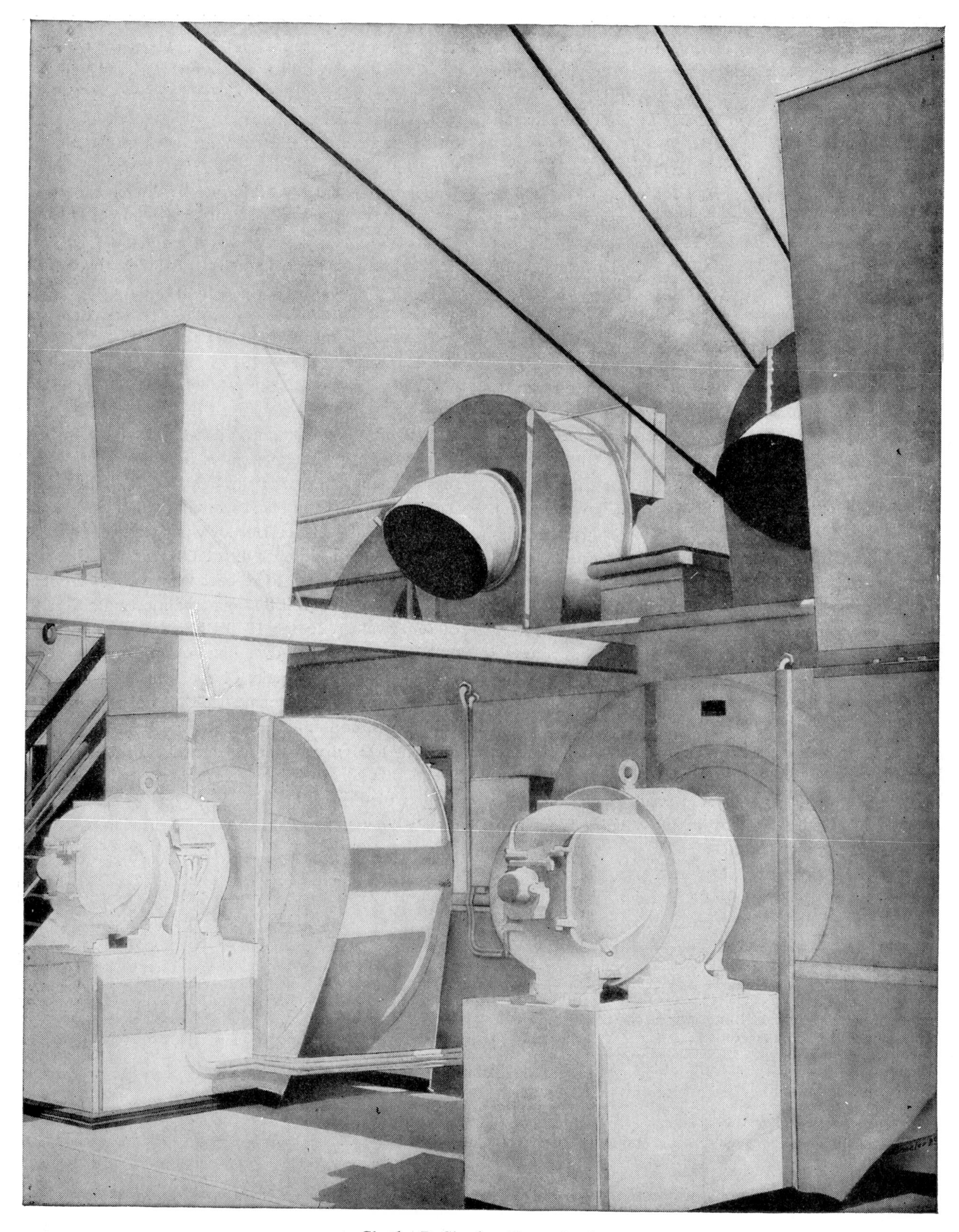

Charles R. Sheeler, *Upper Deck*

Fogg Museum of Art, Harvard University, Cambridge, Mass.

Louis Eilshemius, *Approaching Storm*

Phillips Memorial Gallery, Washington, D.C.

truthfulness in James Cruze's *Covered Wagon* and in Robert Flaherty's *Nanook of the North.* The Strand-Sheeler film was less self-conscious than *Caligari* and more deliberately selective than the work of Flaherty; it was a masterly orchestration of forms and movement with captions from Walt Whitman—the ferryboat discharging its people, the docking of a great liner, the shafts of buildings "slender, strong, splendidly uprising toward clear skies."

In 1921 Sheeler's canvas of *Church Street El* seemed like a still from that motion picture with its "camera angles" and its rather abstract rendering of skyscrapers, tracks, and trains. His work now included both painting and photographs. Without sacrifice of descriptive detail he interpreted the final unity, the irreducible rightness of Pennsylvania farm buildings and Shaker furnishings. At River Rouge in the late twenties and in his Chartres prints he found the same organic perfection under complex details. *Upper Deck* was the culmination of his effort to paint a picture which had "the structural design implied in abstraction" yet was presented through "realistic" detail. He had organized it as though designing a watch or an aeroplane, every least part of which must do its work in the whole, and then painted the white shapes and the sharp shadows with a relentless clarity as though to force these extremes to meet and reconcile what others had held irreconcilable.

Poles apart in temperament, Marin and Sheeler had this in common: in an age of groping, each found a belief and a focus. Marin discovered it in the response of the whole personality to the beauty and power of the all-embracing outdoor moment; Sheeler, in the permanent object, the mind's satisfaction in the faultless articulations of a machine, the lean athleticism of a Shaker chair, the clean intersections of a Pennsylvania barn. (See color plate 25.)

Two personalities of the time stood in contrast with the passionate Marin and the imperturbable Sheeler: Louis Eilshemius, with his eccentric blend of the primitive and the sophisticated, and the raucous, incorrigible George Overbury Hart. The former, who called himself Master of Art, Doctor, Mesmerist, Mahatma, and Supreme Protean Marvel of the Ages, had once been a pupil of Kenyon Cox in New York and of Bouguereau in Paris. The connoisseurs of the naïve admired the artless way in which his *Plaza Theatre* was put together; the bare stretches of his *Central Park West* were compared to the bleak avenues of Utrillo, and his moonlight had a Ryderesque glimmer. The man was most authentically a primitive in his visions of nude creatures bathing or dancing, and he had his own forceful way of cradling a nymph in the clawlike branches of a tree. One expected the unexpected from Eilshemius—a mass of foliage superbly studied and exquisitely rendered in a landscape otherwise half-formed and tenuous; a road in Tennessee whose dusty warm indolence communicated itself; a *Sunburst* in which his mastery of trees, mountains, and sky was for once complete. His anarchic personality would not attach itself to principles of growth, in spite of his fresh insights into nature and his delightful lyricism.

"Pop" Hart from Illinois roamed his own country, then France and Italy, Egypt and Mexico, Iceland and the South Seas, before settling down in a shack on the New Jersey shore. In water colors, etchings, and lithographs Hart caught the excitements of a Mexican cockfight or a baptism in Trinidad with nimble fingers and, when he was lucky, with a knack for holding his episode together with a curving wall or the downsweep of a tent. Hart in his late fifties came to be recognized as a Yankee in the old boisterous genre tradition; and his sprawling script was a relief among the neat Spencerians.

The unpredictable Eilshemius and the rowdy Hart were exceptions whose warmth only emphasized the prevailing coolness of the post-Armory climate. In general, an imbalance between form and content suggested that the time was out of joint. The antisepticism of Sheeler and O'Keeffe implied a kind of visual efficiency and could be taken as a symbol of intellectual honesty and frankness, but it did not necessarily lead toward intensification or clarification of human meanings. More than one painter of the period would have agreed with Russell Cheney when he wrote, "My picture . . . looks as if it were done at too low a temperature."

CHAPTER 30 / REASON IN BRONZE AND CONCRETE

Half a mile down the Washington Mall from the Smithsonian alcove where Greenough's *Washington* gathers dust, Abraham Lincoln sits in his Greek temple, a somewhat more successful effort to measure a great man in feet and inches. The first President looks cramped in his Neo-Gothic surroundings; behind the forty-four-foot columns of Henry Bacon's memorial the *Lincoln* of Daniel Chester French shares a vast space with the murals of Jules Guérin. The memorial was to be "as simple as his life, as beautiful as his character, as refined as his nature, as dignified as his bearing, as pure as his thoughts, and as noble and great as his life work"; and the architect, the painter, and the sculptor produced a handsome symbol of this somewhat expurgated Abraham.

As the temple rose at the end of its axis during the war years Guérin, a minor Puvis known for his pale tinted renderings in the magazines, enlarged his designs upon two canvases, each sixty feet long and twelve feet high: groups of allegorical people standing under the outstretched wings of a presiding deity with blue sky and russet-colored poplar trees behind them. Beneath the murals were huge tablets bearing the Gettysburg Speech and the Second Inaugural Address. Facing the Capitol sat the French *Lincoln,* thirty feet high with its pedestal, and cut from Georgia marble.

French was sixty-five when he began this statue; it was forty years since the Concord *Minute Man* had been unveiled, and the sculptor had achieved fluency and grace. His relief maidens on the bronze doors of the Boston Public Library had the easy rhythms of "Art Nouveau"; his various memorials were in the mood of Saint-Gaudens' *Grief.* His symbolic groups for the Custom House in New York were neither too vague nor too specific; his *Africa* was half nude with drapery as vigorously modeled as her body and with an arm

Daniel C. French, Lincoln Memorial statue (model)

Bogart Studio photo

resting upon a sphinx. French could speak the language of crisp naturalism which Saint-Gaudens spoke, and his portrait figures of Civil War generals in Massachusetts, his seated statues of John Harvard and Emerson, his standing Lincoln for the Nebraska capitol had the controlled vitality of the *Farragut* if not its nervous intensity.

The French *Lincoln* progressed from a small clay sketch less than three feet high to an eight-foot plaster model which was enlarged by the Piccirilli brothers and carved by them from twenty-eight blocks of marble. In the first study only the gaunt form, the powerful hands, and ridges of folds in trouser and coat were indicated. The final plaster model sharpened details and slightly modified the pose of legs and hands. When a cast of the eight-foot *Lincoln* was placed in Bacon's temple, it proved insignificant in scale and had to be enlarged to nineteen. French also discovered, as Greenough had before him, that the lighting from the thin marble slabs of the ceiling was too weak to mold his forms, and from the polished floor and from outdoors a conflicting light robbed the statue of its plasticity. It was only after seven years of anxious experiment that French saw his *Lincoln* illuminated by powerful electric floodlights concealed behind louvers in the roof. The impressiveness of the figure derives as much from this stagy artifice as from monumentality in conception, and one concludes that an architect and a sculptor could more successfully collaborate in ancient Greece than in modern America.

When the bronze *Diana* came down from her dismantled Madison Square Tower in 1925 it seemed that an age had ended, yet Saint-Gaudens still ruled the sculptural heavens. The Corcoran had assembled more than one hundred of his pieces for its memorial show in 1908; his suave lyricism and his lively surfaces inspired many of the pediments of stock exchanges, the memorials to new heroes, the park fountains, and capitol reliefs of the postwar years.

The prolific Karl Bitter provided four quotations from Goujon for the façade of the Metropolitan Museum. There was unaccustomed restraint in his *Carl Schurz* on Morningside Drive above the archaistic reliefs, but his *Thanatos* at Montpelier was a theatricalized version of Saint-Gaudens' *Grief*. For the pedestals before the Boston Public Library, vacant for fifteen years, Bela Pratt made lumpy figures of *Science* and *Art* which huddled down into their granite blocks lest they hide one's view of the McKim portals. The flutter and prettiness of Frederick MacMonnies' Chicago fountain reappeared in his Brooklyn sculptures—the quadriga on its triumphal arch at the entrance of Prospect Park, his *Horse Tamers,* and his *Triumph of Mind over Brute Force*. *Civic Virtue* in New York was a young Hercules whose flabby nakedness stirred a livelier controversy than had the Boston *Bacchante*.

Mahonri M. Young, *Groggy*

Whitney Museum of American Art, New York City

When John Ward died in 1910 there were few signs that his homely realism had once been part of the American tradition, and the Piccirillis were completing a *Maine* monument for Columbus Circle in New York whose allegorical figures maintained no consistent scale, aped the poses of Michelangelo, and looked as though they had been hastily assembled from the contents of the studio to stand, crouch, and gesticulate for the occasion.

One could admire at least the craftsmanship of Paul Bartlett, although his pediment for the House of Representatives tactfully conformed to precedent; George Barnard carved directly in stone, even if the result had a softness which evaded light. Barnard's two huge groups before the Harrisburg capitol, with thirty-one figures, needed more than the play of sun on white marble to give them strength and scale, and one cannot regret that his colossal memorial arch of the first World War, with more than fifty figures, never got beyond the model stage. One can be grateful instead for the specimens of Gothic carving and architecture which he collected through the years and which were built into the magnificent Cloisters above the Hudson River.

At thirty-three Lorado Taft had modeled a fountain for the Chicago midway. His beardless *Lincoln* at Urbana had an impressive dignity, and his *Solitude of the Soul* reminded one of Rodin's practice, with smooth figures emerging from roughened stone. Many young sculptors learned their Beaux-Arts lessons from Taft at the Chicago Art Institute, and his lectures and writings had the authority of experience behind them, if his practice seldom exceeded competence.

Hamlin Garland, who accused his brother-in-law of being a Greek-worshiper, would doubtless have approved A. Phimister Proctor, Cyrus Dallin, and the Borglum brothers, who specialized in western subjects. Proctor's *Indian Warrior* stood before the Brooklyn Institute, and Dallin, who had been born in Utah and was familiar with the red man, provided no less than four Indians on horses for Boston, Chicago, Philadelphia, and Kansas City, all conscientiously executed. The stampedes and bucking broncos of Solon Borglum were furious small bronzes, and the sketchlike intensity of Gutzon's *Mares of Diomedes* could be attributed both to his training under Rodin and to an exuberance of character which, in the twenties, attacked two mountains, shaping their flanks into colossal images of famous Americans. Borglum's head of Robert E. Lee adorned Stone Mountain in Georgia, and his four great Presidents on the face of Mount Rushmore in South Dakota were described as "sculpture with dynamite" by a man who discarded drills and blasted the stone within a few

Richmond Barthé, *Blackberry Woman*

Whitney Museum of American Art, New York City

Robert Laurent, *Kneeling Figure*

Art Institute of Chicago

inches of the desired contour, signing himself "sculptor and engineer."

Among the sculptresses, Anna Hyatt Huntington made a *Joan of Arc* for Riverside Drive which seemed one of an endless series of Joans traceable to Paris; Taft's pupil Janet Scudder modeled a charming *Frog Fountain;* and Bessie Potter Vonnoh, who had also begun with the Chicago Exposition, produced statuettes in the Tanagra tradition, with mothers and children whose faces were softly shadowed. Malvina Hoffman's graceful *Pavlova Gavotte* won a Paris prize in 1915; from Rodin she learned the translucent marble nudities of her *Offrande;* and there was a trace of the aquiline mannerisms of Mestrovic in her *Four Horsemen of the Apocalypse*. When the Field Museum of Chicago decided in 1930 to represent the world's ethnic types in a series of bronze statues for a Hall of Man, Miss Hoffman's technical skill and her personal energy made her the inevitable choice for the assignment.

The Indian groups by Mahonri Young in the Museum of Natural History, like the Hoffman series, had more ethnographic than artistic value; but Young could draw ditchdiggers and prize fighters with a swift vitality like that of Daumier, and out of those drawings he created sturdy bronzes, *Groggy, The Driller, The Digger,* which had weight and sinew under their surfaces and a muscularity out of proportion to their size. One found similar qualities in the mature work of Richmond Barthé, who had grown up with the New Negro movement after the war and who had overcome his "African" mannerisms when he made his bronze *Blackberry Woman*.

There was no flattery in Jo Davidson's busts, for which most of the world's famous people sat; his head of Anatole France was full of sculptural quirks, and his seated *Gertrude Stein* was a wise and humorous statement of her sturdy personality—the knees apart and the hands between them, the body and round head indomitably chunky. If the *Stein* looked mildly modern against the melodrama of the Rodinesques and the prettiness of the frog fountains and small maternities it was because its forms had a simpler and stronger core of substance and character.

A modern consciousness of medium was to be felt in Robert Laurent's *Charity,* cut from oak, whose volumes and directions had been suggested by the shape and grain of the original slab; and when Laurent turned to bronze in the *Kneeling Figure* he delightfully exploit-

Paul Manship, *The Indian Hunter*

Photo Smith College Museum of Art, Northampton, Mass.

ed the planes and surface textures inherent in that material. When W. Hunt Diederich reduced a jockey and his prancing horse to a few bronze planes and nervous curves it was in the interest of a decorative silhouette.

Manner in such work always threatened to become mannerism. From Minnesota came Paul Manship to work in New York with Solon Borglum, then with the fastidious Grafly in Philadelphia, and at twenty-three in the American Academy at Rome. Kenyon Cox praised his talent when he returned, observing that his *Duck Girl* fountain was neither pseudo-classic nor realistic. Chandler Post found his taste impeccable in 1921 and called him the most hopeful figure in native sculpture. Within the limits of frontality Manship could compose a *Centaur and Dryad,* a *Dancer and Gazelles* in graceful rhythm, curve answering curve, and one could read the history of sculpture in his exquisite drapery lines, his archaistic beards and ringlets, the neat articulation of breast and thigh. One thought of Benvenuto Cellini and one delighted in his bronze melodies, not listening for deeper sonority.

The more rigorous exploration of form by a few sculptors of the twenties had its risks and could rely on little public or private encouragement. Americans seemed nearly as impervious to what makes sculpture sculptural as in the days of Hiram Powers; and when the museum public was asked to decide by vote on the basis of competitive models who was to execute a colossal *Pioneer Woman* for the State of Oklahoma, they chose the Englishman Bryant Baker in preference to the stylized Maurice Sterne and the rugged Jo Davidson; and Baker's figures had the banality of a lesser John Rogers.

Only a few Americans understood that sculpture is something toward which and away from which the layman moves, conscious of the core or axis which motivates its bossing out and its recessions, its lesser within its greater rhythms, its continuities and its oppositions, its hard and soft, its light and heavy. Gaudier-Brzeska had said that sculptural feeling was the appreciation of masses in relation, sensuous and immediate, and he described the sculptor's task as the defining of these masses by his planes. Reacting against shallow emotionalism and tricky imitation, Joseph Hudnut declared that not life but a mathematics to which life had been reconciled should be the sculptor's first concern.

In the best modern work, however, no contradiction existed between life and the science of form-making. At the heart of Maillol's great nudes was the same worship for the health and strength of women that one found in Renoir, and in the "Gothic" attenuations of Lehmbruck a compassionate humanism. Jacob Epstein had

Jo Davidson, *Dr. Albert Einstein*

Whitney Museum of American Art, New York City

studied the Chaldeans, the Egyptians, and the Orientals as diligently as Manship but with a deeper purpose, and his heads of children were not variants on Verrocchio and Della Robbia but strenuously alive creatures. His brooding *Night* owed something to primitive ways of cutting stone but more to his forceful imagination. With pellets of clay Epstein built the aggressive surfaces of his portraits as externalizations of his intense response to people, and cast them in bronze without further smoothing down their fierce play of light.

While the English Philistines vented upon Epstein their ignorance, their anti-Semitism, their prudishness, and their pride of nationality, Americans learned from Alfeo Faggi, from Alexander Archipenko, and from Constantin Brancusi how to escape the tyranny of past forms. The lean concavities of Faggi derived their power from a religious attitude which had more in common with the earliest Christians than with his country's Renaissance. When Archipenko established his New York school in 1923 he had renounced his own Beaux-Arts training, and his abstractions of the human body were intended, as he said, to reveal "nothing but its constructive law and function."

Brancusi's *Bird in Flight,* a swelling shaft of polished metal with no resemblance whatever to a bird, arrived in New York in the twenties, to be denied free entry by a customs collector whose literal mind classified the *Bird* as dutiable according to the laws affecting metal utensils for hospital and household use. Modernists claimed for their work the same final perfection that was in machine parts and industrial implements, and now one of them had to sue the government to prove that he had made a work of art. Two notions of art faced each other in a court of law, until the law decided reluctantly that Brancusi's word had to be taken.

William Zorach, who turned from painting to sculpture in the twenties, saw in Brancusi a vision of a new age where everything had a new constructive form, new values. But "suddenly the vision begins to pall. The sleekness, the perfection, the nicety becomes as overwhelming as a mid-Victorian atmosphere." Sculpture, he knew, did not have to obey the laws of living flesh and blood, but he wished for it the strength of his own feelings for women, children, and animals. A sculptor could make half a dozen life-size figures in clay a year to be copied by others in stone; Zorach preferred to spend a year in carving one of his own in order to be the sole master of the work from first conception to last detail. His wood carvings of his own children kept their forms in alignment with the block itself; and his *Mother and Child* in Spanish marble revealed, as one moved around it, a constantly changing interplay of volumes and rhythms charged with a feeling both masculine and tender.

A more complicated personality was Elie Nadelman, whose work Stieglitz showed in the winter of 1915 and who came to America two years later. He had worked in Paris during the cubist ferment and his drawings oddly combined geometrical rigors with a lyricism which was also to be seen in his rather Grecian marble heads. His restless mind turned from the making of elegant small studies of animals to the carving of droll figures in wood, and from his own experiments to the collecting of American and European folk art for a "museum" at his home in Riverdale. Nadelman studied old dolls and toys, and some of their smooth eliminations reappeared in his wooden dancers, musicians, and people sitting in chairs, their features and clothes painted on the sleek surfaces as cigar-store Indians were painted.

Miller, du Bois, Bellows, and Kent were among the painters who seem to have learned something from the Polish sculptor's way of shaping a skull and of phrasing noses and lips, breasts and arms. Nadelman's life in the twenties and thirties was largely his own secret, for he worked alone at Riverdale, an aristocrat who was almost the first to appreciate the art of the common people. In his studio were hundreds of small figures of papier-

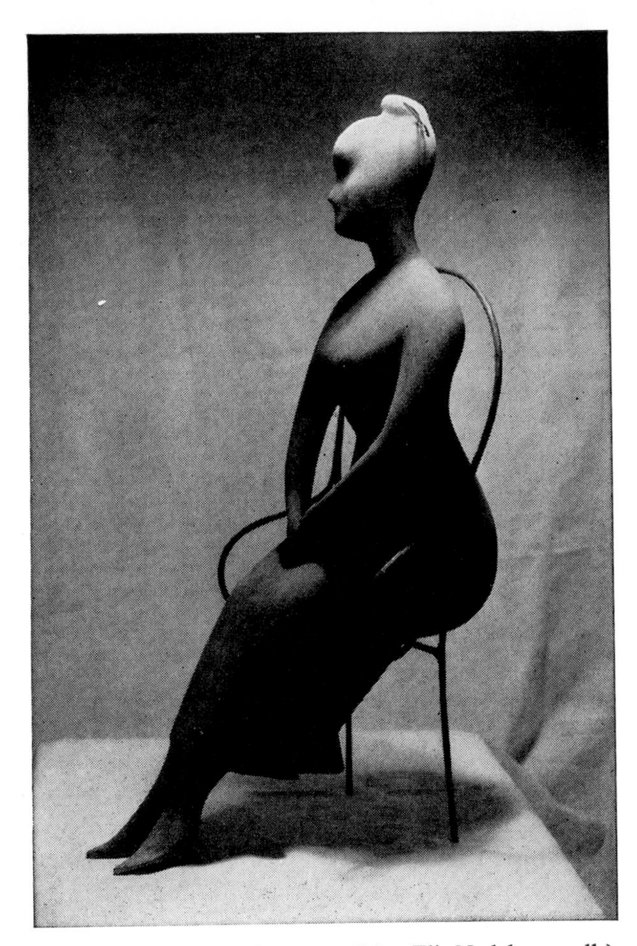

Elie Nadelman, *Seated Woman* (Mrs. Elie Nadelman coll.)

R. V. Smutný photo, courtesy Lincoln Kirstein

Chaim Gross, *Mother and Child at Play*

Newark Museum

mâché and of terra cotta in which the grace and vitality of Tanagra were born again. It was said that he intended these to be made in quantities for the grandchildren of Americans who had owned china dogs and cheerfully colored figurines; their final form, however, eluded this perfectionist to the end of his days.

The *Mother and Child at Play* of Austrian-born Chaim Gross dates from the year of Zorach's marble on the same theme. The spiraling movement and flow of energy from one body into another shaped this piece and the wooden figurines which followed. A stubby child acrobat of Gross, with glistening lights on nose, lip, and breast and along its stout legs, keeps the vitality and hardness of the block from which he shaped it, whether one sees it from front, side, or back. Tait McKenzie also knew the anatomy of muscular exercise but his athletes were three-dimensional illustrations beside those of Gross.

John B. Flannagan, *Chimpanzee*

Whitney Museum of American Art, New York City

In the field of animal sculpture one could compare the competent naturalism of Chester Beach and Frederick Roth with the *Young Calf* of Reuben Nakian and the *Chimpanzee* of John Flannagan. The essence of the calf's structure and action was humorously summed up in a few bulges and twisting ovoids; the crouched forms of the monkey were suggested to Flannagan by the rock shape he had found in a field and were completed by a few indentations which retained the strength and character of the original fragment.

The Armory Show had seen a small plaster by Gaston Lachaise, who had been in America only a few years assisting Henry Kitson in Boston and Manship in New York. He was as gracefully sleek as the latter when he made his bronze *Peacocks* and carved Manship's de-

Reuben Nakian, *Young Calf*

Museum of Modern Art, New York City

sign for the Morgan relief in the Metropolitan Museum; and he made a brief gesture toward the conventional with a projected figure for the Telegraph Building which had more than a hint of the Delphi Charioteer. But the zest of Lachaise for what Hartley called the joyous moment broke through such formalisms and no sculptor in America could match the voluptuous rhythms and superb rotundities of his standing *Woman,* completed in 1927 after fifteen years of work.

Here was a complete synthesis of the sculptor's passion for his subject, his skill with gleaming bronze, his genius for directing and shaping the movement which springs from the toes barely touching the earth to the proud head and the curling finger tips. The sculptured woman in America had had to endure a boneless adolescence and then a sedentary young middle age before she reached opulent maturity and a commanding grace in this figure. Among the few critics who could accept so Whitmanesque a poem was E. E. Cummings, who dismissed Manship's titillation of the "highly sophisticated unintelligence," and wrote that the Lachaise woman tantalized the beholder with her "magnificently conjugated largeness."

In the building as in the sculpture of the 1920's, commissions and prizes went to those whom Cummings called Gentleman Dealers in Second Hand Thoughts.

Gaston Lachaise, *Woman*

Albright Art Gallery, Buffalo, N. Y.

Two architects died in the year 1924, Henry Bacon at the summit of his reputation and Louis Sullivan destitute and broken, with the first copy of his *Autobiography* at his bedside in a shabby Chicago hotel.

Frank Lloyd Wright sat with the "beloved master" on the day before he died, and in the *Western Architect* he wrote more in anger than in sorrow of America's

Frank L. Wright, Press Building, San Francisco (project)

Courtesy Henry-Russell Hitchcock

blind infatuation with the expedient, which had forced Sullivan to give up architecture for writing—a medium which was the all-devouring monster of the age. Wright himself was fifty-five, and in the thirty years since the Winslow house had burst on a provincial suburb "like the Prima Vera in full bloom" his crusade against blind imitation and safe commercialism had run parallel with Stieglitz' rebellion against the trade conception of photography and Henri's denial of the juggler's skill in painting. While Bacon built his Lincoln Memorial of Georgia marble, Wright quarried Wisconsin limestone to make Taliesin of its hill, not on it. While Cass Gilbert's Woolworth tower of steel, fifty-six stories high, clothed itself in terra-cotta gargoyles and flying buttresses, Wright projected a concrete skyscraper for San Francisco as nobly severe as the Wainwright.

On the eve of the war Ralph Adams Cram built All Saints at Peterboro, New Hampshire, a small "gem" of the English parish type, and the suave Perpendicular tower and quadrangle of the Princeton Graduate College, whose hall bore the carved heads of students on its corbels. High above Morningside Drive in New York stood the unfinished apse of St. John the Divine; it had been planned by Heins and Lafarge as a free mingling of Romanesque and Gothic, but when Cram assumed their task in 1911 a "purer" Gothic inspired the drawings for its nave and towers. Wright in the meantime designed the terraces and towers of Midway Gardens in Chicago with festive shapes and brilliant colors which shamed the middle-aged frivolity of Madison Square Garden and suggested what he could have done for the Exposition of 1893. He raised his second Taliesin from the ashes of the first, as he conquered his private tragedies and faced a world more interested in his personal than in his artistic defiance of conventions.

For Cram the war of 1914 was a demonstration that society had taken a wrong turn. A civilization which could produce this catastrophe, he declared in his *Ministry of Art,* must yield to something older and better. The pacifist Wright was as harsh in his condemnation, yet the antithesis was complete between the man who urged the artist to serve God through forms which faith had consecrated and the man who wrote, "The conditions and ideals that fixed the forms of the twelfth are not the conditions and ideals that can truthfully fix the forms of the twentieth century."

The war years found Wright designing a great concrete mansion for Aline Barnsdall on Olive Hill in Los Angeles and the mighty Imperial Hotel for Tokyo, the one as austerely monolithic as the other was exquisitely elaborate. The Oriental art of elimination, studied over the years, helped the architect to resolve flower forms into geometric shapes—the famous "stone hollyhocks" whose beauty was made by the shadow and light upon Hollyhock House. For the hotel he devised a method of construction not to defy earthquakes but to outwit them. A building rigidly anchored risked being shattered; Wright's H-shaped structure was planned to absorb movement and yield to it, like the interlocking fingers of a hand. His short foundation pins were cushioned in the Japanese mud, his floors were balanced, cantilever fashion, as a waiter balances a tray; his walls of brick were lively with carved forms of lava both Japanese and profoundly original in their abstract shapes. When the test came in 1923 the Imperial Hotel rode out an earthquake.

The postwar years brought Wright few commissions but instead the odd experience of being called the father of a modern style which, codified in Europe and superficially understood here, he was at some pains to repudiate in the twenties. Did the work of Europeans, collectively considered, constitute a "style" at all? One could certainly find common characteristics in the Bauhaus of Gropius at Dessau, whose workshop walls were of sheer glass; in the smooth ribbonlike balconies of the long horizontal workmen's houses by Oud in Hook of Holland; in the concrete planes of Le Corbusier which laconically defined spaces; in the cantilevered parapets of Miës van

Frank L. Wright, Living room, "Taliesin," Spring Green, Wis.

Courtesy Henry-Russell Hitchcock

der Rohe and his great windows which made corners without benefit of masonry.

Henry-Russell Hitchcock and Philip Johnson did not hesitate to describe the totality of these efforts as the "International Style," and they defined its characteristics: the abandonment of weight and mass for thin weightless walls as boundaries and mediators between inner and outer space; the substitution of a subtle and varied regularity for the obvious traditional symmetries; the exploitation of whatever qualities, surfaces, and colors were to be found in the materials themselves.

Into that synthesis had gone the words and work of Frank Lloyd Wright as they became known through articles and essays. But the philosophy of the "International Style" was shaped also by men who were close to the cubists, and the writings of Ozenfant and Le Corbusier had a dogmatic finality not to be found in America. For these logicians cubism had created a new optics, a new way of being affected by pure form. As yet, only airplanes, automobiles, grain elevators, bridges, and ocean liners had brought that perfection close to the lives of people. The modern house should be as fully harmonized with the needs of man as the motor car with his wish to travel or plumbing with his hygienic necessities. A house-machine designed on this principle could be built in three days, its walls and openings submitting to a single unit of measurement, its woodwork put in place before its concrete walls were poured, its window frames as standard as those of factories. Le Corbusier's *Citrohan* house and his four-story block with its hundred *maisonnettes* serviced in common were intended to be as practical as a typewriter, and his villa at Garches in the Paris suburbs proved that engineering principles in the hands of an artist need not produce a barren uniformity. The "Internationalists" believed that the clean satisfactions of healthy living, of sunlight, and of spatial coherence were more than adequate as a substitute for the clutter and sham of the uniquely individual habitation.

No such relentless logic could rule American building in the twenties. Where could one look in America for great industries willing to cooperate with designers as they did for the German Bauhaus? Where was a group of architects willing to work as a disciplined unit? What American sociologist would attribute mass unrest to the contradiction between men's working and their domestic environment? How convert truculent individuals to communal planning, and how persuade the reformer that, as Le Corbusier had written, "big business is today a healthy and moral organism"?

Frank Lloyd Wright had worked for more than thirty years to rescue the individual from becoming a mechanical human unit. That insistence had been necessary to survival in Wright, as in Henri and in Stieglitz; it was their strength, and in so far as it bred overconfidence in the power of a few creative minds to change the taste and habits of thousands, it was their weakness too. Looking about him in the 1920's Wright could see no evidence of a true style in the making. Cass Gilbert's public buildings were as pompous as Gilbert himself; Raymond Hood's Chicago *Tribune* Tower was muffled in Gothicism; James Gamble Rogers was archly medieval in the calculated dilapidation of his Harkness Quadrangle at Yale. If the builders of skyscrapers could ridge their shafts with vertical lights and shadows they believed they had symbolized American aspirations; and when the zoning laws required that the upper portions of tall buildings recede as they grew higher, the setback was a new device for playing variations on a shaft—in Ralph Walker's Telephone Building in New York, in the Chicago work of Holabird and Root, in every city from east to west.

Wright's deepest scorn was saved for the "modernistic," which he saw everywhere about him. In 1914 he had disclaimed responsibility, in a new *Cause of Architecture* paper, for either a school or a style, finding his half-baked imitators as mediocre as any old-fashioned revivalist. For him, style remained the by-product of a process and came of the man or the mind in the process. He rejected the "form-and-function mechanism" of the European rationalists and their "cardboard box for boxing up space . . . sans ornament, sans souci, sans culotte." He had no more use for Miss Flat-Top than for her elder sisters, Mrs. Plasterbilt and Mrs. Gablemore. And Lewis Mumford, although he conceded that subways and automats had the chaste, inevitable beauty of a Euclidean demonstration, and that in a sense Childs Restaurant was superior to St. John's Cathedral, warned that more attention should be paid to the vagaries of the human mind.

In fairness to the European pioneers one recognized that Miss Flat-Top was not their child but the American offspring of visits to the Paris fair of 1925, which called itself the International Exposition of Modern Decorative and Industrial Arts. Amid that hodgepodge were buildings as stubbornly florid as the Italian Pavilion but also structures of a shallow and *chic* modernity. The Russian Pavilion looked as though a constructivist had been asked to be as eccentric as possible; the Porte de la Concorde was a circle of cement piers which looked like chimneys; the cornices and fluted pilasters of the Pavillon de l'Élégance had been tactfully slimmed down; queer "trees" by Mallet-Stevens were a cubist's dream of trunks and foliage; and the interiors proved how Lalique with glass and Ruhlmann with furniture could reconcile the curves of Louis XVI and of "Art Nouveau" with the new sophistications.

While Americans hung their windows with Paul Rodier's textiles, whose motives came from machine pistons and driving wheels, and built "skyscraper" bookcases into their walls; while the "modernistic" multiplied on Fifth Avenue shopfronts and in dime store bric-a-brac, Frank Lloyd Wright designed a skyscraper which was never built. It was no thrusting symbol of the boom-and-bust age but a cantilevered structure whose backbone was like that of a human being, with walls of copper and glass hung upon it. In the Millard house, "La Miniatura" at Pasadena, and in similar homes he explored the beauty of concrete blocks with ornament of shape and color cast into their faces and riveted at their joints with metal rods. Toward the end of what Hitchcock has called Wright's "ten dull years," when most of his projects were confined to paper, he turned to the unsolved problem of group living, with the preliminary studies for Broadacre City.

The American metropolis had stood condemned since Lewis Mumford's essay in 1922 for *Civilization in the United States*. He drew the contrast between America's provincial towns, which were true communities in every sense, and the gridiron plans and commercial stacks of the industrial age, "a rabble of individuals on the make." The City Beautiful movement which the Chicago Exposition had inspired was a mere front, its beauty a cosmetic. One had the choice, Mumford said, of humanizing the city or dehumanizing the population; and America had done the latter. There could be no reform of cities until one reversed those economic forces which drained money, strength, and brains into a dozen cities and thence into New York. "Our metropolitan civilization," he concluded, "is not a success." Wright's condemnation was equally final, and as for Hugh Ferris' drawings of the city of the future, where fantastic cubist forms rose through a mist of romance, they were "standardization upon stilts," new monstrosities on the sites of the old ones where the poor would be built in as a fixture.

At least a few Americans could have clean air at night, quiet schools for their children, and green fields for their holidays in the satellite towns of the twenties. Another Wright whose name was Henry planned Chatham Village with Clarence Stein for the architects Ingham and Boyd on a site two miles from the business center of Pittsburgh. Less than a third of its area was given to houses, the rest to trees, lawns, and gardens; and traffic was restricted to its residents, whose rows of pleasant homes, two to eight in each unit, descended in terraces, their style suggestive of colonial Williamsburg. Radburn, on the Hackensack meadows twelve miles from Manhattan, was described as a town for the motor age. Its designers, among whom were Wright and Clarence Stein, made sure that no pedestrian need cross a traffic road; set among parks and playgrounds, each of its dwellings was reached by car from dead-end branches of the main artery or on foot through an independent pattern of sidewalks. Radburn was one of the earliest and best towns designed for the health and safety of its people and built for families whose budgets provided for only moderate rental costs.

Communities like these, with their social-democratic and even socialist connotations, could be only oases in the United States of Coolidge and Hoover, like honest houses and unpretentious public buildings. The humanist in three dimensions, like his brother in two, discovered that planlessness, dishonesty, and pretense were in the majority. It seemed as though nothing less than a national calamity could bring a demand for his full powers, his reason, and his imagination. When Frank Lloyd Wright and his pupils sat down to put on paper their vision of Broadacre City that calamity, unlike Mr. Hoover's prosperity, was just around the corner.

Radburn, New Jersey, in 1929

Courtesy City Housing Corporation, New York City

BOOK SIX

NEW HORIZONS

c. 1930 — c. 1960

William Gropper cartoon ▶

The New Masses

PART ONE

THE AGE OF ROOSEVELT

INTRODUCTION / IN THE SHADOW OF WAR AND FASCISM

In the nineteen-twenties T. S. Eliot had written of the shadow which fell between idea and reality; during the next decade that shadow took on a clear and menacing shape. In 1931 the democrats of Spain launched their republic, while Japan invaded Manchuria. In 1933 Hitler was Chancellor of Germany; in 1935 the League of Nations failed to keep Mussolini out of Ethiopia; a year later a Socialist was at the head of France, supported by a "Front populaire," and the rightists of Spain, with the help of Germany and Italy, provoked a civil war.

The European artist who wished to be neutral in these circumstances must walk a tightrope. The masters of taste in Nazi Germany turned her clock back to the insipidities of the age of Bismarck, and modernism was destroyed as the work of "degenerates" by men who knew the real meaning of that word. To the Venice Exposition of 1936 France sent pictures by Degas and Marie Laurencin, Belgium a few imitations of Van Gogh, Switzerland sugary landscapes, and Hungary romantic ones. Only Spain, not yet "coordinated," showed surrealist paintings, and the Italian exhibit combined futurism with photographic "realism" to glorify the face of Benito and his African campaign.

Against the nationalist hysteria, the superstitions of race, the annihilation of independent thinking, and the brutal transformation of the human being into a mechanized warmaker, the intellectual seemed powerless. Eliot himself delivered an indictment of liberal democracy, which he accused of destroying social habits, licensing the opinions of the most foolish, and preferring cleverness to wisdom—in short, of producing a trashy and meaningless individualism which prepared the way for the brutal controls under which so many Europeans now had to live. His alternative was a community of

Christians regulated by an elite, where the masses would behave according to religious codes and where standards of art would be established by a cultural dictatorship of Anglo-Catholics. This contempt for the common man, alone or in the mass, was shared by Igor Stravinsky; in Paris, surrounded by upper-class adulation, he made music whose continuity was with the great classics, music of elegant sound and no depth of feeling, music whose lines were as chaste and cool as Picasso's etchings for Ovid.

Not every voice in Europe was tuned to despair and retrogression. In contrast to Stravinsky's fastidious art-for-art, W. H. Auden declared that the composer who feared losing his artistic integrity through contact with a mass audience no longer understood the meaning of the word "art." It was for such an audience that Prokofieff and Shostakovich worked, wishing at once to be understood by that audience and to enrich its powers of understanding.

In the France of the Popular Front aesthetic debate had the violence of politics. Wearied by the endless tracts and café discussions, the fly-by-night movements, and the mercantilism which had made Paris the stock exchange of art, Élie Faure concluded that painting no longer had any reason for existing. It had once been the instrument for lyrical individualism; now the place of the individual in art as in politics was steadily shrinking. Let painting and sculpture give place to the perfection of bridges, the integrities of Le Corbusier, and the dynamism of the motion picture.

Even the surrealists were forced by the crisis to justify their existence on something more solid than anarchic eccentricity. Salvador Dali remained incorrigible, and having rejected the "nauseating and sterile" purism of the cubists he invented a "photographic" realism to objectify his dreams. He believed it was intellectual and moral suicide to follow any social group, and his hatred for revolution of any kind became, he said, almost pathological. The civil war in his own Spain he described as a deluge of archbishops, grand pianos, and rotten donkeys; in another mood it meant to him the recovery of Spain's authentic Catholic tradition.

The left wing of surrealism saw matters differently; and when the French rightists attempted to seize power in 1934 many of them rose to defend the shaky republic. André Breton explained that his comrades worked to liberate the mind by breaking down the distinction between inner and outer reality, a process which he compared with the dialectic of Karl Marx. And Herbert Read in 1936 insisted that surrealism was performing a social task in revealing the latent content of the age, resolving contradictions in order to rid mankind of its anxieties and its imbalance.

Breton's former partner, Louis Aragon, turned against the movement. He now believed that it had undermined the capacity of men to change the real world because it had made that world seem an illusion; and the so-called radicalism of Breton looked to him like a mere play on words. At the Maison de la Culture in 1936, Aragon urged his colleagues to stop playing childish games and act like men, to become engineers of the soul and not mere entertainers. Painting had once been a supreme expression, a great and sacred thing. "And now, see what they have done with painting, the masters of this world on whom you have strangely depended during these last years. . . . Your pictures became the cards in this baccarat of the period of prosperity. And when the black and uncertain days of the depression arrived, your patrons discarded you as stable owners might discard worn-out horses."

Yet art is as essential to man, Aragon declared, as the necessities of life for which men were fighting at that moment throughout the world. The time had come for the painter to interpret the realities of that struggle, a task for which the mere imitation of nature was no more adequate than the inventions of the *Fauves* and cubists. And when the latter expostulated, he replied, "It displeases you today that the great social upheavals disturb the pattern of your chimeras, the sluggishness of your pictorial meditations. What can I do about it? That's how things are. . . . You have passed thirty years curled up comfortably on your treasures, on your discoveries. . . . What danger do you run and where is your importance?"

One year later German and Italian bombs destroyed a Spanish town and Picasso painted his *Guernica.* The weird dislocations and the gratuitous horror of his previous work here found their reason for being in a large mural where one heard the snort and stampede of frightened horses, the shrieks of children, the roar of planes, and the artist's own cry of compassion and horror. Here was neither cold imitation nor capricious invention, but a symbol of what man was doing to man in the Europe of 1937.

These foreign conflicts and disasters caused only a muted reverberation in the minds of most Americans. William Carlos Williams once predicted that if the citizens of the United States ever stopped making money their whole conception of reality would have to be changed, yet few of those citizens in 1929 could foresee that such a test was at hand. The Hollywood conception of reality seemed as profitable as ever, and Warner Brothers were planning a theater for Newark in the Austrian baroque style which would cost two million and a half and seat four thousand people. On two weeks' notice American composers made motion-picture scores whose pseudo-symphonic measures massaged the listening ear and whose leitmotifs, as Aaron Copland said, dogged the heroine like a shadow. Imitation Tudor cottages bloomed in American suburbs and the boom in real estate had deposited great Spanish hotels and Venetian lagoons in California and Florida towns. Cass Gilbert was completing his handsome elevation of the Supreme Court for Washington with its huge Corinthian portico and its implication that, as the *New Freeman* said, Form Follows Formula.

New Haven undergraduates played squash in a gymnasium which was a cathedral tower, and discovered that the quaintness of Rogers' quadrangle had been purchased at the cost of eternal darkness. The new capitol at Lincoln, Nebraska, stood complete, its Greek cross form enclosed in a square which made four inner courts and its central pylon rising four hundred feet above the mass. The monstrous portal below and the small domes above were evidence that Goodhue had nourished himself too long on the older styles; his realization that steel and concrete abrogated practically all historic forms had come too late. The same half-digested modernism was in the ceilings which Hildreth Miere designed for its vestibules and rotunda, where variously shaped and colored tiles were used like mosaic. The sculpture by Lee Lawrie was intended not only to decorate but to be comprehensible at a glance; and Lawrie's buffalo heads, ears of corn, and prairie wagons were fluent, hard, and quite devoid of feeling, a synthesis of Assyrian work with the chic modernism of the Paris Exposition.

In 1929 one could contrast the intelligence of Radburn with the accumulated discomforts and the accepted inequalities of Middletown, the unidentified village whose sociological portrait was drawn by Robert and Helen Lynd. In its leisure time Middletown improved its mind with Rotary speeches and club papers on Ruskin, Bolshevism, and the Birds and Flowers of the Bible; one or two citizens painted or collected pictures as a furtive hobby. As the town grew, the "ragged, unsynchronized movement" of its institutions was a poor substitute for reconsidering the very basis of those institutions; and if one multiplied Middletown by thousands one knew the enormous discrepancy between the vision of the creative American artist and the lives of his fellow citizens.

The rule, in short, was each man for himself. For each group its own taste; and in the prosperous summer of 1929 few Americans could imagine limits to the moneymaking on which this diversity was founded. In the fall of that year a noted economist told them that stock market prices were on a permanently high plateau. A few weeks later there was sudden panic: traders dumping their shares, banks foreclosing mortgages, millions bereft of their jobs. The plateau had been the peak of a shaky pyramid, and the families of the Middletowns had nothing left but their disillusion. In the two dark years which followed, the American conception of reality was profoundly altered.

The election of Franklin D. Roosevelt in 1932 implied a determination to grapple with the disaster, rejecting half measures, and attacking collective problems by collective methods. Here too, as in Europe, were many bewildered idealists. Some American liberals, like those abroad, abandoned earlier positions, and Walter Lippmann, ex-Socialist, produced a *Preface for Morals,* which was a ghostly philosophy for men of good will, since he believed that liberalism was a "genial spook" worth having around.

The human predicament nagged the conscience of Americans; and as the "epidemic of world lawlessness" spread from one people to another, they asked themselves whether isolation would keep them uncontaminated; and those who urged detachment could support their argument in a country which still remembered the rewards an earlier conflict had brought to profiteers and munition makers and which now observed the odd complacency of the free nations of Europe toward the fascist aggressions. In such an atmosphere many a writer and painter went forward with what Waldo Frank in 1929 called *The Rediscovery of America.* That exploration of the national past had been a phenomenon of the twenties; now, as Newton Arvin observed in the *New Freeman,* "it is the American desire, of course, in the thick of so crazy a present, to have a 'past' as firm as may be beneath one's feet; to affiliate oneself locally and personally with whatever forces may have once worked toward something besides business success and technical efficiency."

A firm past was no guarantee of a firm future, and the danger of cultural self-preoccupation soon became obvious. In the meantime the Museum of Modern Art, established by seven wealthy art collectors in 1929 with Lillie Bliss as vice-president, showed *Living American Painters* in its first year, and also the work of Eakins, Ryder, and Homer. The Whitney Museum, opened in 1930, was the first institution wholly devoted to this country's art, and Forbes Watson wrote that "nothing will keep the Whitney Museum . . . more certainly alive . . . than the continued desire to take risks by making those discoveries which committee-ridden institutions never make." The Whitney was soon showing Marsh, Burchfield, Benton, and other painters of the "American scene" and publishing its monographs on contemporaries, while the College Art Association issued its *Index of Twentieth Century Artists,* precious material for the historian and biographer collected while most of its subjects were still alive.

In the year of the Whitney opening, Matthew Josephson explored the causes and results of artistic emigration in his *Portrait of the Artist as American.* Eugen Neuhaus' *History and Ideals of American Art* in 1931 accented the native tradition as Isham and Cortissoz had not. In *The Roots of American Culture* Constance Rourke studied the "fresh configurations" imposed on foreign models by American conditions, contrasting the European notion of culture as imitation with that of culture as tillage by men whose first allegiance was to the native soil. She believed that creative forces peculiar to America had shaped much of its art.

One of the fruits of the new movement was the delight in "folk art" newly discovered, whether of the past or of the present. Shows of American "primitives" were organized by Holger Cahill for the Newark Museum in 1930 and 1931; John Kane was presented at the Museum of Modern Art. Two years later, in his introduction to the Folk Art Exhibition at the latter institution, Holger Cahill wrote an admirable brief history of the art of the common man in this country during a century and a half, surveying its achievements in a dozen media and explaining as no critic had yet done its importance as a field for future study and as an expression of the national experience.

Thanks to the rediscoverers, neglected masters came into their own and the history of native art was told not in terms of a few conspicuous examples but as the total expression of a developing society. The Whitney Museum displayed *American Genre* in 1935 and surveyed a century of landscape painting in 1938 with sensitive critical commentaries by Lloyd Goodrich; in 1939 the Metropolitan's *Life in America* was a superb panorama. During the same ten years Suzanne La Follette restored to art its social setting; Alan Burroughs pioneered in the application of a critical scholarly method to problems of quality and attribution in the early chapters of *Limners and Likenesses;* Holger Cahill and Alfred H. Barr, Jr., edited a series of essays called *Art in America* which gave motion pictures, photography, the stage setting, and the art of the untaught their place in the total picture. James T. Flexner and Oskar Hagen discussed colonial painting; Alain Locke evaluated the Negro's contribution to art; Homer Saint-Gaudens surveyed *The American Artist and His Times.*

America's rediscovery was a blend of rhapsody, ridicule, and nostalgia, of hopeful self-glorification, sober pride, and sheer curiosity. It included Benét's operetta *The Devil and Daniel Webster* and Aaron Copland's score for *The City*. Among its plays were *Tobacco Road* and *Awake and Sing;* among its films, the magnificent *River* and the trashy *Gone with the Wind.* Its novelists explored the Iowa farmer, the Chicago slum boy, and the Georgia cracker; for its scholars, a seventeenth-century limner or a Shaker barn became as legitimate an object for study as a Florentine palace or a Byzantine mosaic. Its critical temper ranged from the modest to the truculent, and in the summer of 1936 one could read Virgil Barker's essay on *Americanism in Painting* and Thomas Craven's *Nationalism in Art.* Barker defined the colonial, the frontier, and the urban mind as part of the historical total and concluded that American culture had not yet achieved full fusion and maturity. Craven raised immaturity to a first principle by defining the true American artist as a stubborn provincial cultivating his own "rich singularities," his scorn of formula, his rough-and-tumble originality, his aversion for Old World sophistications, his refusal to make "propaganda" by his art.

Another group of Americans concluded that a stubborn provincialism was no healthier in art than in politics. Among the rich singularities of the moment were Huey Long's dictatorship in Louisiana and Father Coughlin's Union for Social Justice, where discontent with the nation's inequalities was turned into channels of hate for the Jew and the "radical." There was something more sinister than "rough-and-tumble originality" in the Silver Shirts, the Khaki Shirts, the Order of '76, and the revived Ku Klux Klan. At the A.C.A. Gallery of Herman Baron one could see the work of artists who were not afraid of what Craven called propaganda and who rejected the notion of irresponsibility behind his definition of Americanism. For two years on Madison Avenue and seven on Eighth Street this "people's gallery" hung pictures whose themes were of concern to people: drawings of Hoovervilles; antifascist prints by members of the Artists' Congress; the paintings of William Gropper and Philip Evergood; the cartoons of Art Young.

The social horizon widened in other artists' minds when the depression robbed them of their wealthy patronage. They had asked the museums to pay them a rental fee for showing their work and had been refused; dealers had raised commissions and asked them to lower prices; paintings and sculptures were not protected by copyright. Out of these dissatisfactions came in 1929 the American Artists Professional League, directed by Academicians. A few years later the members of the American Artists Group designed Christmas cards in the effort to take lithographs and etchings out of the luxury class; the Associated American Artists marketed original prints for five dollars to a wide public; and the aggressive Artists' Union did not hesitate to walk the picket line, identifying its battle for economic and artistic freedom with that of other workers.

The socially inclined American painter had watched the Obregon Revolution in Mexico with its collaboration between government and artist. For more than ten years at Chapingo, Cuernavaca, and Mexico City the beauty of the Mexican land, the dignity of the peon, the power of religion, and the disasters of war had become themes for murals in true fresco by the famous "Syndicate," whose manifesto in 1922 hailed the monumental expression of art because "such art is public property." Among the Syndicate men were Rivera, Siqueiros, and Orozco. In the courtyards of the Ministry of Education Rivera told the story of his people as simply and sturdily as Giotto had once told the life of Saint Francis. When Rivera built his Detroit murals on the industries of that city in 1932 and Orozco at Dartmouth exposed the modern barbarities of American civilization in menacing shapes and strident color, the pale classical amenities of academic mural painting, its literary evasions, and its inert symmetries received a blow from which they could never recover. And it was the Mexicans who taught their would-be emulators the dangers of the enterprise, as outraged Dartmouth graduates protested the brutality of Orozco's work, and the patriots of Detroit charged the museum director with selling out its walls to "an outside, half-breed Mexican Bolshevist." The demonstration was completed when the owners of Rockefeller Center discovered a portrait head of Lenin in Rivera's *Man at the Crossroads of Life*, removed him from his scaffold, paid him off, covered the offending wall with plain canvas, and subsequently destroyed it.

The movement toward a more explicitly social art drew its greatest strength not from Mexico City but from Washington. After years of devil-take-the-hindmost the New Deal of Roosevelt had declared itself responsible for the welfare of the least citizen. Its program of Relief, Recovery, and Reform took shape in new agencies with bewildering alphabetical designations —the CCC, the NYA, the WPA, the PWA, the TVA. These were the instruments by which at least for a time the young were given training and morale, the old and the out-of-work were freed from their worst anxieties, the ill-housed were better housed, the farmers relieved of their occupational hazards. The victim of unemployment became a self-respecting beneficiary who earned his benefits by work he was qualified to do, and the victim of floods and drouth saw the transformation of earth's and water's power from a menace to a servant of his needs.

The impact of these new forces was immediate on the smaller world of art. A new confidence replaced cynicism in much of the writing of these years. The artiness of the Washington Square Players gave place to a vigorous realism when the superb acting company of the Group Theatre played Clifford Odets' *Awake and Sing;* Mordecai Gorelik's skeletonized scenery for *Let Freedom Ring* made its own grim comment on life in a Carolina mill town; and the music of Marc Blitzstein for *The Cradle Will Rock* was savage beneath its mocking humor.

Through the federal programs for slum clearance and rehousing, the architect and the town planner for the first time could attack those problems from the roots and demonstrate on a national scale the humane validity of their ideas. To painters, sculptors, and designers was given the opportunity to participate in a countrywide experiment whose scale and purpose were something new in the world—the Federal Art Projects. These were the culmination of previous gestures toward patronage by a country which had no Department of Fine Arts. For more than a century such matters had been handled by ten different committees, officials, and departments, most recently by Edward Bruce under the Civil Works Administration and then by the Fine Arts Section of the Treasury Department. It was obvious by 1935 that no present plan could absorb the thousands of jobless writers, musicians, sculptors, painters, designers, photographers, and actors; and in the summer of that year the Federal Arts Projects of the Works Progress Administration were established not only to give these people work and relief but, as one of the directors said, to feed the hunger of millions for music, books, plays, and pictures.

The structure of all the projects was essentially the same: a general policy shaped by Harry Hopkins, Holger Cahill, Hallie Flanagan, and others, with regional direction and a local administration in each of the states. The movement of the arts toward a few cities was to be reversed in the hope that art would become the possession of a whole people. Thanks to FAP, the states had their Federal Writers guidebooks, and towns which had never heard music at first hand listened to orchestras. Plays were produced for people to whom actors had been shadows on a screen. The decorative arts of the nation were recorded in thousands of drawings by the Index of American Design. In hundreds of villages there were new post offices, schools, and small art galleries with murals, sculptures, and easel paintings. Talented children were taught to make pictures, and older men and women learned how to plan homes and to weave, spin, or carve their own furnishings.

On the rolls of Federal Art were many of the ultramoderns, for the projects drew no more distinction on grounds of style than of race, religion, or politics, and the abstract painter was as truly a victim of the depression as his more naturalistic brother. The more uncompromising moderns were joined in these years by foreign recruits; Pavel Tchelitchew was as much at home in New York as in London and Paris, and in *Phenomena* represented himself at his easel among the mutilations of a crazy world. When the Bauhaus closed in 1934 some of its leaders came here—Gropius, Moholy-Nagy, and Josef Albers. After nearly fifty years in Germany, Lyonel Feininger returned to America, bringing his austere and exquisite gifts to the country of his birth.

At the Museum of Modern Art in 1936 one could see the work of men whom, by implication, Aragon had accused of sitting idly on their formal discoveries: the nervous patterns and insistent flat colors of Miro's *Person Throwing a Stone at a Bird,* the alarmingly empty spaces of Tanguy's *Mama, Papa Is Wounded!* the paradoxical objects which Pierre Roy assembled in *Daylight Saving Time* and painted with the deceptive brush of a Harnett; a woman by Max Ernst whose head became a fan and through whose perforated torso one saw a distant shoreline; Masson's *Battle of Fishes* with scribbled shapes of brush and pencil on canvas and sandpaper; the flaccid watches of Dali with bugs swarming over them in *The Persistence of Memory*.

One did not expect in such men an emphasis on content, social or otherwise. Albert E. Gallatin, whose Museum of Living Art at New York University displayed Picasso, Braque, Gris, and Léger and gave first showing to Arp, Miro, and Hélion, declared that subject was negligible in making American art American and that the highly socialized state managed by plebeian and vulgar tyrants was inimical to art; Gallatin's opinion of the New Deal was implied in his repetition of a famous remark that the least governed state is the best state.

Equally contemptuous of mass enterprises was Baroness Hilla Rebay, who presided over the collection of Solomon R. Guggenheim. In silver frames against the gray walls of this Museum of Non-Objective Painting hung the brilliant arabesques of Kandinsky, the glowing folk songs of Marc Chagall, and the ascetic spheres and pyramids of Rudolph Bauer, to demonstrate the baroness's claim that nonobjectivity was the great historic step from the materialistic to the spiritual. At Taos and Santa Fe in the same year the "Transcendental Group" took that step, disclaiming all concern with the political, the economic, or the social, and finding a pathway to the cosmic through their new discoveries of space and color.

Baroness Rebay believed that Bauer's and Kandinsky's intuitive sense of the cosmic order was a special gift of God to the elite. Their art need not be understood, she asserted, and it would blossom as inevitably as a flower, heedless of criticism. Culture is always created by great personalities who are neither helped nor understood as a rule by their fellow men; and the masses, though they proudly enjoy a nation's fame for culture, are usually the last to deserve it. In the far future, however, the people of the world who had slowly learned from nonobjective masterpieces to develop their spiritual power might learn to live in harmony together. In the meantime the baroness compared the works on the Guggenheim walls with the pitiful mass exhibitions of painting to be seen elsewhere, and concluded that what thousands of people painted could not be art.

More broadly than the Gallatin and Guggenheim collections, the Museum of Modern Art surveyed the movement as a whole. A large part of the Bliss collection had gone to this institution, where the Cézannes and other pioneering works could serve as a touchstone for evaluating more recent artists shown in temporary exhibitions. Here was a place where the wheat and the chaff could be separated, and where one could decide whether the theories of the first revolutionaries were still tenable. Each showing at the Modern was accompanied not only by a catalogue but by a scholarly and thoughtful essay.

This attempt to define the modern effort through the written word was typical of an unstable period when art seemed to fortify itself verbally and when a multitude of literary specialists toiled to give every little movement a meaning all its own. Peyton Boswell maintained in the *Art Digest* that there should be no Right, Left, and Middle in aesthetic matters, yet the articles and criticisms of the time seemed the counterpart of those divisions.

Margaret Bruening spoke for conservatives when she assured the readers of the New York *Post* that modernism was a momentary fad; and one could rely on Royal Cortissoz in the *Herald Tribune* for the same denunciation of modern "vulgarity" and the same unyielding defense of good old times that he had written thirty years before. He would shortly celebrate his half century as a critic with an exhibition of his favorite paintings assembled by Knoedler's in which the most "modern" canvas was a Renoir dated 1879.

Edwin Jewell of the *Times* occupied the middle ground and Ralph Pearson called him the diplomat among critics. Lewis Mumford was the most thoughtful of the liberal commentators, alive not only to formal qualities but to the human connotations in the arts which he discussed. The painters of the American scene, who disliked equally the cubists and the socialists, found praise in C. J. Bulliet's chatty column in the Chicago *Daily News.* That journalist with a gift for phrases, Thomas Craven of the New York *American,* denounced Picasso's portrait of Gertrude Stein as a "lifeless old squaw" and accused the extremists of "psychic smudges," "laboratory equations," "esoteric riddles," and "psychological balderdash."

The social artists had a discerning champion in Jerome Klein of the New York *Post.* The writers of *Art Front,* official organ of the Artists' Union, assailed Dali as a scientist of corruption and claimed that flights into fantasy were as complete an evasion of the artist's task as the pedestrian reproduction of the objective world. Where, they asked, was the alleged "social symbolism" of Breton's umbrella and sewing machine meeting by chance on an operating table? Was man to be liberated by "unremitting defeatism, demoralization and aggressiveness"? Surrealism might be the symptom of the century's illness but assuredly not its cure.

The weaknesses of the art critics, as Ralph Pearson surveyed them in three *Forum and Century* articles, derived from their misunderstanding of the true relation of form and content. That relation was explored more thoroughly by a group of scholars, philosophers, and museum specialists which included John Dewey, Walter Abell, Sheldon Cheney, Albert Barnes, James Johnson Sweeney, Alfred Barr, James Thrall Soby, Edward Rothschild, and Meyer Schapiro. Dewey's *Art As Experience* established the continuity between man's aesthetic and his nonaesthetic life; Abell attacked the fallacies of both the abstract and the representational schools; Cheney made it possible to understand in some degree what the ultramodern believed he was doing. The language of Dr. Barnes was not calculated to warm the layman, and his monographs on Cézanne, Renoir, and Matisse subjected those masters to a dissection which, although skillful and sensitive, often became tiresome; nor would the average person find clear answers to his questions in Sweeney's *Plastic Redirections in Twentieth Century Painting.*

The writing of these experts was solidly documented and always provocative; its purpose was not so much to pronounce judgment as to "undermine prejudice, disturb indifference and awaken interest," in the words of Alfred Barr. In a brilliant essay on *The Meaning of Unintelligibility in Modern Art,* Rothschild regretted that "we want the artist to scratch our backs in the old familiar places when we should be eager to mount behind him on his Pegasus" to explore an age which has been revolutionized by science, an age of speed, jazz, and psychic tensions. Each individual, he concluded, must judge the result of this exploration for himself; and since the quality of a work of art is unique in the experience of the individual, not one intelligible word can be said about it. In a similar vein Barr wrote that excellence is a matter of the quality of the work of art as a whole—something which "cannot be measured or proved or even analyzed with any logical satisfaction."

When Soby introduced Dali at the Museum of Modern Art he called Dali's art neurotic for a neurotic age; he described superbly its sensuous qualities and left open the verdict on its value, suggesting that there were parallels between the painter's eccentricities and those of the current world, between his double images and the double-talk of diplomats. When Barr wrote the essay for *Fantastic Art, Dada and Surrealism* he gave that movement a distinguished ancestry which included Blake and Goya, Giovanni di Paolo, Hogarth and Thomas Cole. In his *Cubism and Abstract Art* he conceded that the term "abstract" was ambiguous, but maintained that ambiguity was inseparable from the subject. Its antinaturalism implied impoverishment, but the abstract artist, Barr explained, preferred impoverishment to adulteration.

In "The Nature of Abstract Art" Schapiro sought to explain why the modern movement took place when it did, avoiding the mechanical theories of exhaustion, boredom, and reaction. He explained that "literal representation" was a straw man of the modernist, since no such enterprise was possible; on the other hand, there could be no "pure" forms unconditioned by experience and by concerns outside the realm of art. As for the much-discussed freedom of the modernist, Schapiro had written in 1936 that such an art cannot really be free because it is so exclusive and private: "There are too many things we value that it cannot embrace or even confront. An individual art in a society where human beings do not feel themselves to be most individual when they are inert, dreaming, passive, tormented or uncontrolled, would be very different from modern art."

The healthy society of which Schapiro spoke seemed remote indeed in the autumn of 1939. Mussolini had raped Ethiopia while the League of Nations turned its back; America's false neutrality had helped Franco's victory in Spain; European appeasement produced the betrayal at Munich and prepared the *blitzkrieg* in Poland. And Americans chose this awkward moment to open two world's fairs at the opposite ends of the continent.

The Golden Gate exposition, with its emphasis on the nations of the Pacific, was a modest and graceful ensemble which Talbot Hamlin contrasted with its aggressively modernistic rival on Flushing meadows. The New York Fair intended to show science and power as the servants of man; it became, Hamlin decided, a department store on a world scale in which every nation called attention to its wares in what another critic called the Corporation Style. Abandoning the flowery language of earlier expositions, "The World of Tomorrow" made abstraction the medium of advertising: the Maritime Building of Ely Jacques Kahn had the shapes of two prows embedded in it, and Witwold Gordon's stylizations covered the façade of the Coca Cola Building.

Nearly half a century before, Henry Adams had sat on the steps of Hunt's edifice at Chicago, looked down the lagoon and asked himself whether the American people knew where they were driving. He had promised, in the closing lines of his *Education,* to come back in 1938, on the centenary of his birth, to learn whether the world was now one that he and his friends "could regard without a shudder." One can imagine him now, a few months late for the rendezvous, on the steps of Howard Cheney's Federal Building with its stark cubes at his back, ironically observing the Court of Peace at his

Howard Cheney, Federal Building, New York World's Fair

Bogart Studio photo

feet and, beyond the Lagoon of Nations with its fountains, the Constitutional Mall.

Would he have considered Dali's "Dream House" in the amusement section an improvement on the Eskimo village of 1893, or the livelier colors of these façades as more than a device for shriller competition? Would he not have seen, behind the formality of the vista before him, a planless and competitive confusion? The statues on the Mall had no relationship of scale or style, and the shapes of the Perisphere and the Trylon were grotesquely out of place in their surroundings. At his left, the stainless steel worker raised his star from the top of the Soviet Pavilion, and the carillon tower rose from the Belgian Building; on his right, colossal lions roared the prestige of Great Britain. France was modern in better taste; but on the crest of the melodramatic Italian structure sat a goddess who seemed to have survived from Chicago days, with a waterfall flowing beneath her feet.

Within a few weeks the conflicts beneath these seemingly harmonized abstractions would be sufficiently obvious, and Henry Adams would have rejoined his ancestors convinced that this was not yet a world for "sensitive and timid natures."

CHAPTER 31 / AMERICAN SELF-PORTRAIT

Ten years after their first visit to Middletown the Lynds re-examined it. To be sure, the motion-picture palaces were bigger now but their offerings had not changed; the citizen was still afraid of sharp thinking, still relied on "reluctant adaptation" to new forces. Yet fifty-nine out of a hundred Middletowners voted the New Deal in 1936; Federal funds built a swimming pool and a park there, and an Art Building to house the local collections; and something like a local school of painting was to be discerned in the community.

The arts were finding deeper roots in native soil when Holger Cahill reviewed a year of Federal Art in 1936. Nearly four hundred and fifty murals had been completed for schools, armories, post offices, city halls, prisons, and hospitals; in twenty-five states the Index of American Design was in action; half a million Southerners had visited nineteen community art centers, and many were enrolled in classes where painting, sculpture, and the handicrafts were taught. Beyond statistics Cahill saw the beginning of the end of that aloofness

Paul S. Sample, *Maple Sugaring in Vermont*

Courtesy Encyclopaedia Britannica, copyright William Benton

between artist and community which had plagued the nation's culture; his essay and the exhibition at the Museum of Modern Art were entitled "New Horizons in American Art."

The painter viewed those horizons for the most part not as a tourist in search of a picturesque motive but as an artist born and bred into the ways of a region. Sheldon Cheney remarked that one had to travel far in the nineteen thirties to understand American paintings; and at the close of the decade Roland McKinney covered three million square miles to find representative work for the San Francisco Fair, while a network of regional juries sifted twenty-five thousand local offerings for the rival exhibition in New York, a procedure which the *Times* criticized as "dangerously democratic." The American scene was being portrayed in terms evasively academic and starkly modern; in terms of nature alone or nature as the focus of man's work and recreation; in the print, the small panel, and the enormous mural, in modest pride and in nationalistic swagger.

A tour through the American scene, in other words, was a journey through more than half a century of painting methods. Neat and close-mouthed were Paul Sample's maple sugar scenes from Vermont with spare tree branches against snow and fresh colors he had learned from Jonas Lie. "Superclarity" was the word for Luigi Lucioni when he painted the brilliant greens of those same pastures and woods in summer in all their sharpness of detail; the Connecticut anecdotes of Lauren Ford were garrulous in the manner of Gothic illuminations. Thomas W. Nason and John J. Lankes described the New England countryside in superb woodcuts.

The great red barns of the Illinois wheat country and the mounds of yellow grain were painted with a metallic prettiness by Dale Nichols against skies which were too blue, while Aaron Bohrod more sensitively explored Chicago suburbs where a woman waited for a train. With rude dynamics and a bold brush, Joe Jones of St. Louis recorded the work rhythms of wheat farmers.

J. J. Lankes, *Haying,* woodcut

Courtesy Carl Zigrosser

As the traveler drove through the green-yellow fields of Minnesota, with red silos, golden haystacks, and white farms scattered over the rolling earth under vast and thunder-heavy skies, it seemed as though nature were imitating the water colors of Adolf Dehn.

There was something of Dehn's breadth in the landscape of John Steuart Curry, whose father had been a stockman in Dunavant and whose *Baptism in Kansas* was one of the first experiments of the new regionalism. Curry in 1928 grouped Signorelli nudes around a circular bathing pool; a few months later, the pool became a wooden tank and the figures inside it a Baptist preacher and a country girl. From that moment, although he was to paint circus acrobats and the epic of John Brown, he was best known for canvases interpreting, as he said, the struggle of man with nature—line storms, floods, and tornadoes. That struggle took place in a fertile country whose hills and farms Curry rendered with more sympathetic warmth than firm underlying form. He could design with occasional strength, as he did in *Roadworkers' Camp* of 1929 (Univ. of Neb., Lincoln), but his *Mother and Father* of that year had less vitality than Ralph Earl's portrait of the colonial Ellsworths, which it oddly resembled with its two figures seated beside a window from which barn, silo, and windmill were to be seen.

The Southwest demanded a more muscular treatment, and received it in Boardman Robinson's lithographs of Colorado and in those of Adolf Dehn. An impeccable craftsmanship modeled the flanks of New Mexico hills in Peter Hurd's paintings and drew the cowboys raising dust in rodeos under a glittering June sky; Ward Lockwood, on the other hand, could find nothing more personal than a variant of Marin's symbols for the shapes of earth which one saw so clearly at far distances in the atmosphere of this country. Perhaps Orozco suggested to Jerry Bywaters how the shapes of cactus could be made to writhe against Texas cliffs, and there was more than a hint of Maxfield Parrish in Maynard Dixon's desert scenes in southern Nevada, Arizona, and California, the pink-orange lights and intense blue shadows of his naked lava ridges no more incredi-

Aaron Bohrod, *Oak Street Platform*

Museum of Fine Arts, Boston, Mass.

ble than reality itself but seen with an eye for the obvious. Alexandre Hogue painted the Texas panhandle, the dunes ridged by the dry wind where starving cattle left their tracks, the abandoned windmill, the sand heaped on railway tracks, the whole anatomy of the Dust Bowl exposed with a surgeon's scalpel.

The camera challenged the brush in this western record; and what painter could match the desolation of Paul Strand's photograph of a ghost town, *Red River,* in 1930, or in the next year his *Ranchos de Taos Church* whose adobe planes had been molded by Indian hands before the sunlight and shadow added their subtle interplay with volumes? Strand believed with Thoreau that "you cannot say more than you see," and Strand's vision penetrated the picturesque to disclose the mind and the life of those who fashioned the terraced pueblos and the mining towns of the Southwest.

The great desert skies with clouds piling up in them were photographed by Ansel Adams, and his study of Laguna Pueblo and of an old woman at Coyote in New Mexico were "straight" photography at its most brilliant and most lucid. Before Edward Weston made his series at Oceano, California, in the thirties, his camera work in Mexico had been a significant part of the Renaissance there; into his *Death Valley* went rhythms of incredible beauty which wind had sculptured in sand; and Weston's eye discovered the very pattern of desolation in a few white scratches and blisters on the side of an automobile abandoned on the Mojave Desert.

Artists in the South could face realities or sentimentalize them. In the untidy suburbs of Washington Nicolai Cicovsky found red cliffs, a glimpse of the Potomac, and a brick carrier, and painted them with harsh and lively simplifications. The most prominent object in Lamar Dodd's view of Athens, Georgia, was a railway embankment cutting like a knife across its foreground. Alexander Brook's *Family Unit* was a Negro group standing before their small cabin with its enclosing fence, a quiet canvas of low browns and grays brushed with unsentimental simplicity. Both strength and spontaneity were in the studies which Arnold Blanch made in the swamps of the Carolina low country and the

Joe Jones, *Wheat Farmers*

Courtesy Encyclopaedia Britannica, copyright William Benton

Georgia jungle, loose juxtapositions of Negro shacks with brackish yellow streams, the rusty brown earth, the barbed wire fence, and the spindly black children whose poverty had shocked this artist from Minnesota. For Hobson Pittman the deep South with its high-ceilinged plantation houses was a dream in vague colors and evanescent forms where moonlight shone through translucent walls and the wraiths of ante bellum ladies sat in the ghosts of rocking chairs.

Among the most conspicuous of the painters of the American scene were Thomas Benton and Grant Wood. They owed their prominence in part to Thomas Craven, who called the former the "foremost exponent of the multifarious operations of American life"; the latter, Copley's superior in design and in subtlety of characterization. Benton of Missouri, truculent and vocal, had little in common with the plodding and unpretentious man from Cedar Rapids, Iowa; yet both artists had sown wild oats in Montparnasse: Benton's synchromist moments produced bulging half-abstract nudes, and Iowa neighbors were puzzled for a time with Wood's effort to translate music into concentric circles of bright color.

Both men renounced these earlier indiscretions. Before the Federation of Arts in 1932 Benton declared that "no American art can come to those who do not live an American life, who do not have an American psychology, and who cannot find in America justification of their lives." In a pamphlet of 1935 Grant Wood more temperately argued that each section of the land had a personality of its own, that there was less temptation in the country regions for art to imitate art; without being dogmatic or sentimental, Wood recommended the common-sense utilization by the artist of those native materials which he knew best.

Benton's Americans, "living an American life," were to be seen on walls and in easel paintings. His Negro preachers and gamblers, cowboys and dancing Indians, racketeers, crooners, and strip teasers writhed and pranced in panels whose unity was a unity of the emphatic: the repeated serpentine contour, the balancing of one vortex of energy against another, the strident color oppositions, the modeling which emphasized bulging muscles, the elongated figures which looked like people seen from the side on motion-picture screens. His smoke plumes, saloon fronts, overalls, and flivvers all seemed to be made of the same material, and this man who despised formula had found a means of wrenching the observer from one episode to another which was itself a formula.

Grant Wood never tried, as Benton did, to sketch the nation as a whole. From Iowa towns and country-

Grant Wood, study for mural, *Dinner for Threshers* (detail)

Whitney Museum of American Art, New York City

side came his *American Gothic* (Chicago Art Inst.) and *Dinner for Threshers.* The spongelike trees of his landscape he had borrowed from his mother's china plates; the patient procedure of building a glassy-smooth paint structure with layers of glaze he owed to his study of Dutch and Flemish primitives. If his faces looked rather stony and his rounded hills monotonous and hard, Iowans explained that these qualities were indigenous ones in a country where a hen's shadow at noon fell sharp as a cut silhouette on the barnyard. If *Dinner for Threshers* recalled *Last Suppers,* the row of backs with crossed suspenders was nonetheless a local phenomenon. And the satire of his *Daughters of Revolution* became effective through the painter's refusal to be more than mildly resentful.

The artists who drew the American city at full length in these years did not share Benton's scorn for it as a "coffin for living and thinking." To Ralston Crawford the engineering of its bridges offered new sensations of movement and perspective to be distilled in a few thrusting dark shapes and austere patterns; to Louis Lozowick the clustered stacks of Manhattan were knife-edged and rich in detail as they stood against storm clouds in his lithographs. Francis Speight painted train yards in winter, and Burchfield made use of his dark palette to convey the monumentality of a drawbridge.

Ernest Fiene was occupied for several years with his series of eighteen city paintings; they were movements of a well-orchestrated suite; and although one of them was called *Nocturne* it suggested Copland rather than Chopin. Fiene knew his Manhattan as thoroughly as Daumier knew his Paris and he painted its demolitions, its sudden exposure of bedroom wallpaper, the forlorn masses of its half-dismantled buildings. His bold colors and hard contours clothed his affection for the play of weather and season over the skyscrapers, the white isolation of Washington's statue under the arc lamps in Union Square.

The city, however, is the people, as Henry Churchill reminds us, and most of the city paintings swarmed with them. As a visitor to Wilson, North Carolina, Lawrence Beall Smith found humor in Negro children lounging in their best dresses before a rundown brick corner store; as a man who intimately knew southern towns, Robert Gwathmey massed the roofs of Negro cottages to form dense walls of segregation and placed the same children in his dark and narrow spaces. In the North the city painters were now harsh and now indulgent: Louis Guglielmi carved an opening in a brick wall to show a relief client being bulldozed by an official, while a man and his wife bleakly pushed their groceries home in a gocart; out of "small truths" and an affection for fa-

John S. Curry, *Baptism in Kansas*

Whitney Museum of American Art, New York City

miliar places Louis Bouché painted his *Barber Shop* with its tin ceiling, tiled floor, and polished white cuspidors; out of his distaste for false Bohemia, Paul Cadmus made his Greenwich Village cafeteria as meticulous as a Crivelli in its cruel itemizations of drunks and blowsy women. In *Billiards at Julian's,* Joseph de Martini made much of the brilliant green table under garish light, as Van Gogh had done at Arles (Boston Mus. Fine Arts).

"Well-bred people are no fun to paint," said Reginald Marsh, and they were conspicuously absent from his canvases. He had tried many subjects and many media; he had been a pupil of Sloan and a parlor socialist, a cartoonist and a scene designer, an illustrator of *The New Yorker* and a technical experimentalist with Kenneth Miller and Thomas Benton. Now he had his own way of manipulating tempera, a medium which had built the closed forms and clean depths of Italian painting. In the relatively simple spaces of his *High Yaller* he modeled coherently, but the line of derelicts in his *Holy Name Mission* was a dingy mass of undistinguishable shapes. Plump bathers tossed in air or massed crowds before a Coney Island sideshow called for a baroque master's skill with a complex interlocking movement. Too often the dynamism of Marsh failed to "jell," his whirling merry-go-rounds stalled, and his massed sunbathers became a lumpy swarm of breasts, rumps, and legs. Into the browns and grays of his palette seemed to have gone the body sweat and the coal dust of New York, and out of that veil emerged the powder-white bellies of his nightclub dancers, the letters of street signs, and the faces of his blonde dolls and unshaven bums.

In the medium of photography and with the support of the New York City Federal Art Project, Berenice Abbott made her extraordinary portrait of the New York boroughs for the Museum of the City of New York. Many of her prints were reproduced in *Changing New York* in 1939 with the incisive commentaries of Elizabeth McCausland. Here was the lumpy statue of De Pey-

Thomas H. Benton, *Agriculture and Logging* (detail of mural, New School, New York City)

Peter A. Juley & Son photo

ster at Bowling Green, which Miss Abbott opposed to the clean dark shadows of skyscrapers, and the stacked Napoleonic masonry of the old Post Office against the Gothic filigree of the Woolworth Tower. The icy dignity of the eighties was in her houses at Fifth Avenue and Eighth Street; in *Warehouse* she made superb use of the line of paint which separated a brick wall into two bands, and the pattern of half-opened shutters throwing knifelike shadows along its front as counterpoint to the huge painted coffee advertisement.

"These States are the amplest poem," Whitman once wrote, and their amplitude inspired the mural artists in the New Deal years, who now possessed hundreds of walls where there had been only a few before. Here and there the decorous platitudes of Puvis de Chavannes and Blashfield found their imitators: Harry Louis Freund designed lunettes at Clinton, Missouri, where the nymphs of Puvis had become farmers and his classic hedges were transformed into stands of grain. But beyond these evasions in time were the great Renaissance solutions which had recently inspired the Mexicans—the solidities of Giotto, the stately grace of Ghirlandaio, the poised bodies of Piero della Francesca in their defined spaces, the controlled tumult of Michelangelo's hurtling bodies.

The American could not learn in a day what these masters knew of size and monumentality, of volume and weight on the large vertical painting plane. Much of his work was done in the studio for buildings long since completed, not on the scaffold as the structure itself took shape, reminding him constantly of its color, scale, and proportions, modifying his scheme, and suggesting bolder interpretations. Under these circumstances it was inevitable that America's mural renaissance should have a "middle layer of mediocrity," as E. M. Benson conceded, with too great a reliance on illustrative excitements.

One could date the new murals from 1930, when Benton summarized native activities at the New School for Social Research in New York, and Boardman Rob-

Paul Strand photograph, *Red River, New Mexico*

Courtesy of the artist

inson produced ten panels on the history of commerce for the Kaufmann Department Store in Pittsburgh. The unity of Benton's walls was a unity of feverish action and intense color, nervous linear contours and harsh oppositions of scale. Their loose separate energies were held in equilibrium by means of moldings which half

Ralston Crawford, *Whitestone Bridge*

Courtesy Encyclopaedia Britannica, copyright William Benton

separated one episode from another, a device which resembled the make-up of a page in the *Police Gazette*. Robinson's forceful tones were achieved with automobile paint; his Carthaginians, Venetians, and Dutchmen, his Englishmen in China, and his American slave traders and clipper ships were modeled in semiabstract planes and edges, their monumentality purchased at some cost of the flow and freedom of his first drawings.

Reginald Marsh, *The Bowery*

Metropolitan Museum of Art, New York City

Ernest Fiene, *Self-Portrait*

Courtesy of the artist

The Kaufmann murals had a certain rigidity and crampedness but testified to Robinson's search for first principles and his rejection of the pretty posture and the tactfully empty space.

A few years later the Mexican example bore fruit in murals of genuine monumentality, many of them executed in true fresco. Among the best of these were Edgar Britton's series in the Lane Technical High School of Chicago, the harvesters of Karl Kelpe in the Hawthorne School at Oak Park, Illinois. William C. Palmer narrated *The Development of Medicine* on the walls of Queens County General Hospital with the explicitness of Rivera at Detroit; and Charles Alston's panels on primitive and modern medicine in the cramped lobby of the Harlem Hospital were solidly painted in clean quiet tones. In the Evander Childs High School, New York, James Michael Newell's five episodes, *Evolution of Western Civilization,* owed much to Rivera.

It was the Missouri River which suggested to Mitchell Siporin and Edward Millman the panoramic design of their mural for the St. Louis Post Office, nearly three thousand feet of wall space which required three years for its completion. The green banks and the blue river connected a series of group episodes painted in terse forms and earthy colors: Indians, French fur traders,

Berenice Abbott photograph, *Warehouse, Water and Dock Streets, Brooklyn*

Courtesy of the artist

Dred Scott, Thomas Hart Benton, Carl Schurz, and Mark Twain. In Washington George Biddle used the skeletonized architecture and the cross-sectioned walls of Giotto to describe the lives of tenement people for the Department of Justice. At New London, Connecticut, Thomas La Farge solved a difficult problem by adapting whaling episodes to spaces which were long and narrow.

Too often a horror of the conventional vacuum caused artists to compress their volumes into hot and overcrowded designs, as Umberto Romano did in the post office at Springfield, Massachusetts; at the opposite extreme a baroque looseness weakened Palmer's episodes of western travelers slaughtered by Indians and highwaymen, and Joe Jones's vigorous *Threshing* for the Charleston, Missouri, Post Office seemed indifferent to its surroundings. There was more coherence and monumental force in Curry's Topeka mural of John Brown, with the free-soilers and the proslavery men facing each other beside him, the westward moving pioneers in a more distant plane, the far tornado and forest fire, and below Brown's feet on the "dark and bloody ground" the bodies of the northern and the southern soldier. One could only regret the indecisive modeling and the smothered color of *The Tragic Prelude,* whose realization called for the fierce clarity of Orozco.

Philip Evergood was among those who knew that a mural was not an enlarged picture and that it need not state its case with cold formality. *The Story of Richmond Hill* had a triple theme: the benefactor who planned this garden community, the country pleasures of Richmond Hill, and the harsh city life from which it offered a release. On the right side were the rigid horizontals and verticals of steel and cement, the confined spaces of life in the shadow of the Elevated; on the left, the free relaxed motion of men and women under the open sky; mediating between these and resolving their antithesis, the founders of the community. Two doors—a dingy broken one on the right and a clean white one on the left — were familiar objects which became fresh symbols. There was antithesis of

Boardman Robinson mural, *The Dutch in the Baltic*

Courtesy Kaufmann's Stores, Pittsburgh, Pa.

Mitchell Siporin, detail Siporin-Millman mural, St. Louis Post Office

Courtesy Public Buildings Administration, FWA

color too: the Richmond Hillers danced among vigorous greens, clean blues, yellows, and bright vermilions; in the city streets men went quietly to work among dark blues, metallic grays, and somber browns. Evergood's wall orchestrated work and play, a young gaiety and a tired maturity, a dream and a reality.

Less explicit in content but often sturdier in design were murals which preferred semiabstract to descriptive forms, and symbol to narrative. The *Electrical Research* of Henry Billings was composed of retorts and test tubes, and Eric Mose arbitrarily assembled parts of automobiles, airplanes, and locomotives for his decoration at the Samuel Gompers High School in New York. At the Newark Airport, Arshile Gorky proved that his abstract shapes and ingenious rhythms could be as entertaining on a large as on a small scale.

Edward Hopper, *The City*

University of Arizona Art Collection, Tucson, Arizona

One of the finest achievements of the period was Philip Guston's group *Maintaining America's Skills,* with its interlocking themes and the clean smoothness of its painted forms seen in silhouette against the concave entrance wall of the WPA Building at the New York World's Fair.

The painter of these years could sing the raucous present or he could remind his fellow citizens of a past which soon would disappear, discovering new subjects on Main Streets where the history of the country's architecture could still be read. The bristling mansards of Edward Hopper became an American staple with their malapropisms exposed to the glare of hot sunlight. His *Adams's House* at Gloucester was the ubiquitous clapboarded white box behind its picket fence, a bracketed cornice over its front door, a hydrant on the sidewalk, and a tipsy telephone pole with sagging wires behind which lay the town. In *The City* he contrasted a monotonous brick block with a mansarded survivor of the 1870's. (See color plate 20.)

Hopper could provide moments of amused nostalgia but not always establish more permanent integrations; Burchfield struck a deeper note. On a page of *Hello, Towns!* Sherwood Anderson wrote that houses had faces which smiled or frowned; there were proud ones with a keep-off-the-grass expression and darkly secretive ones where one heard no laughter and no singing. Burchfield and Anderson were natives of the same part of northern Ohio; the former knew the decayed verandas of "Winesburg," the shambling unpainted farmhouses on side roads off Trunion Pike, and the monstrous brick mansions of the bankers on Buckeye Street. His *House by a Railroad* was as swiftly brushed in water color as Hopper's Gloucester scene and had the same elements—house front, sidewalk, and pole—yet managed to convey more connotations of bleakness, of autumn rain and wind. With a rank garden, rotting boards, and sagging branches, Burchfield painted the end of life for old people in rocking chairs under ragged pines; he conveyed the warmth of Indian summer, the soggy bleakness of a mining town whose houses descended a long, slush-bordered street. Once he had pic-

Walker Evans photograph, *Two-Family Houses in Bethlehem, Pa.*

Courtesy Farm Security Administration, Washington, D.C.

tured houses which were the monsters of a child's imagining, and something of that empathy persisted in the naturalism of his mature years. (See color plate 21.)

Comparing these painted records of American survivals with those of Walker Evans, the photographer, one asks whether the camera did not more insistently remind one of past ugliness and its human overtones. Evans recorded an ungainly soldiers' monument, hard white against a spider web of wires; the gingerbread squalor of a Birmingham boardinghouse; a Louisiana plantation rotting in the sun behind an uprooted tree; the same lumbering cast-iron façades which Hopper painted in *Williamsburg Bridge* and Burchfield in *Promenade* but with every least ugliness exposed by sharp light; the same Alabama country store one found in Benton but more dismally weathered by rain, more relentlessly baked by the sun.

Relics of another sort were meanwhile being studied by hundreds of artists in thirty-one states and preserved in the form of amazingly accurate drawings and water colors for the Index of American Design. Here in something like twenty thousand plates was proof that thousands of nameless Yankees had wrought superbly in wood and iron, silver and wool: the gaudy crispness of carved circus wagons and cigar-store Indians, the reticence of samplers, the slim perfection of Shaker cupboards, the prancing silhouette of the farmer's weather vane, and the florid tulips of the Pennsylvania potter.

The Index reminded Americans of a people's art in the past but also fostered their interest in contemporary work which preserved that tradition. A hod carrier named Mike O'Brien won a first prize at Denver in 1935 for a landscape painted on the remnants of a cardboard box, and Richmond gave the first show a Virginia Negro had ever received to Leslie Bolling, who carved small genre pieces in wood. Max Schallinger of Baltimore assembled his odd wooden figures in groups with ingenious mechanisms to make them gesture, pivot, and play harps; the same carved creatures navigated a delightful vessel which he contrived from the fragments of a real ship discovered on a beach.

Charles E. Burchfield, *Evening,* water color

Newark Museum

When the Negro Horace Pippin was "discovered" in 1937, one compared the naïve fervor of his Biblical scenes with that of Edward Hicks, and praised the incredibly rich pattern, the monumentality of design in his flower pieces and interiors. But "primitive" was an inadequate word for this veteran of the first World War who worked all day and far into the night on a canvas, his injured right hand gripped by his left to steady the meticulous brush. There was a grave eloquence in his three tributes to John Brown which no other version of that much-painted subject could equal, and a searing intensity which was the projection of a sure intelligence and a noble depth of feeling.

In 1939 the Museum of Modern Art showed sixteen self-taught painters whom Sidney Janis had collected. Among them was Morris Hirshfield, whose shapes resembled the cut patterns of the coat factory where he worked, and who used a comb to paint a lion's mane. One saw Patrick J. Sullivan devising strange imagery to make people think: in *Man's Procrastinating Pastime* a forest stood for the unconscious mind, and its fallen trees and branches meant major and minor sins. A cabinetmaker named Bernard Freuchtben who had lost his business in the depression and whose wife had left him gave poignant form to his misfortune in *Lonely Man on a Lonely Road.*

Ten years after the crash of 1929 could one doubt that in painting, sculpture, and the graphic arts, as in the TVA, the country had reclaimed and put to work her vast creative resources? In the Palace of Fine Arts at San Francisco were four hundred works gathered from every region; at the New York Fair Holger Cahill directed the exhibition of more than a thousand entries, *American Art Today.* With all this evidence before him the citizen could attempt to answer Edward Alden Jewell's question, "Have We an American Art?" The labels on the frames in these exhibitions reminded one from how many foreign lands the artists or their parents had come and how many young talents like that of the Negro Jacob Lawrence had found instruction and encouragement during this decade; they proved that the history of native art could not be written in terms of the eastern seaboard. If any common denominator emerged it was a fresh consciousness of the American environment and a greater emphasis on factual content than on form.

The extreme nationalist argued that we had an art

Horace Pippin, *The Trial of John Brown* (Arnaud d'Usseau coll.)

Percy Rainford photo

whose character distinguished it from that of other peoples, and he often spent more words in advertising this product than in improving its quality. Jewell's question could be more profitably answered if phrased in a different way: "To what degree had the experience of a people found forms to express its deeper meanings?" Was it enough that the "stubborn provincial" had exchanged the brandy fumes of Montparnasse for the smell of western earth and manure if he could penetrate no deeper into native soil? Was his provincialism as healthy in the modern world as that of fifteenth-century Florence? Artists like Benton had made what Craven called a "swift and fearless plunge into life," but had they not landed in rather shallow water? Could John Curry give the grandeur to his *John Brown* which Michelangelo gave to his *Moses*, in a community which celebrated Brown as a hero but half feared him as a demagogue and a radical?

For that matter, were the faces of patient travelers waiting for buses in American cities essentially different from those of Romans and Parisians? Was not Curry's "struggle of man against nature" much the same wherever there were farmers, and the Irving Place "Burlecue" of Marsh very much like the Folies-Bergère? The artists of the American scene had discovered one truth: that healthy art springs from its own soil and is nourished by its own climate. There was another truth: that the deeper art penetrates, the closer it comes not to what makes peoples different but to what they have in common. There was an obvious antithesis of South and North in America, of city and country, of farm and tenement, of wide and congested spaces, of naïveté and sophistication. Men who concentrated upon these often ignored the deeper contrasts and conflicts in the nation's life. To deal with these latter was the task of the so-called "social conscience" artists.

CHAPTER 32 / COMMON CAUSE

"We are gathered together tonight for the first time partly because we are in the midst of what is plainly a world catastrophe." With these words Lewis Mumford on February 14, 1936, opened the first Artists' Congress in New York. Between three and four hundred painters, designers, photographers, and sculptors, among them a dozen Mexican visitors, heard Mumford say that fascism, war, and economic depression were at odds with all the forces of human culture: "The time has come for the people who love life and culture to form a united front against them, to be ready to protect, and guard, and if necessary, fight for the human heritage which we, as artists, embody."

Mumford declared that dictatorships fear art. A few months after he spoke, Hitler's oration at the Munich House of German Art proved his contention: the Nazi referred to the republican years as an era of shame and of artistic Bolshevism created by Jewish art dealers and critics, and exhibited the "degenerate" art of Grosz, Kokoschka, and Feininger, with Jews segregated even on the gallery walls.

Nothing but a world emergency could have brought together in New York men of such divergent personal philosophies and artistic principles as Peter Blume and Moses Soyer, Stuart Davis and Arnold Blanch, George Biddle and Hugo Gellert, Paul Manship and William Gropper. These men were willing to exchange an idle "freedom" for a concerted effort as artists to embody in form, line, and color the new aspirations and the old injustices, and to build a united bulwark against the powers of darkness at home and abroad. Stuart Davis, who was National Executive Secretary of the Congress, declared that this conference would be the biggest event since the Armory Show. Peyton Boswell, on the other hand, was dubious. He refused to believe that artists could organize as other workers did, since "genius is not a walking delegate." To F. Gardner Clough collective action meant regimentation and suggested communism.

Among the photographers at the Congress were Paul Strand, Margaret Bourke-White, and Ben Shahn. Strand had made a superb film of the revolt of Mexican fishermen, *The Wave,* as head of the Department of Photography and Cinema in the Department of Fine Arts of Mexico; and he had worked with Ralph Steiner and Leo Hurwitz in 1935 on *The Plow That Broke the Plains.* Bourke-White and Shahn had seen the look of men whose last possessions had gone down a flooded river, and the sightless eyes of houses abandoned to sun and sand. Many of their prints would soon bet published in *Land of the Free:* Ben Shahn's West Virginia deputy with his back, buttocks, and holstered pistol filling the page; the faces of men and women who asked, in the words of Archibald MacLeish,

> . . . If there's liberty a man can mean that's
> Men: not land
> We wonder
> We don't know
> We're asking.

In the sessions of the Congress sat painters who had learned that art is not made in a social vacuum. Joe Jones had fought Jim Crow at St. Louis to teach black and white children together; Paul Cadmus had seen his *The Fleet's In* removed from the Corcoran because an admiral denounced it as an insult to the Navy. A caricature of Hitler as a cloven-footed creature was banned by the Metropolitan Museum for its "bad taste"; Evergood's mural at Richmond Hill was barely saved from local critics of its "gross corporeal references." Colorado objected to the blood Curry painted on John Brown's hands; the Reverend Ignatius Cox denounced the Whitman quotation on a Ben Shahn mural as an affront to religion, and New York's Art Commission refused to accept Shahn's mural designs for the Riker's Island Penitentiary on the grounds of their "psychological unfitness."

The Congress not only discussed concrete issues but larger questions. They attacked the self-perpetuating board of trustees at the Mellon Gallery; they supported the Federal Art Projects. Like the Society of Painters, Sculptors, and Gravers they demanded a small rental fee for the showing of their work by museums which spent vast sums on the dead. Doris Lee criticized the false isolation of art colonies, and Lynd Ward reminded the nationalistic artists that a similar attitude had paved the way for Hitler in Germany. They sent exhibits of prints—*America Today* and *Against War and Fascism* —touring through the country, and at their second meeting in 1937 showed Picasso's *Dream and Lie of Franco* while church ladies picketed their hall.

There were more than six hundred members in that year, and within the Congress was a smaller group who had made the antifascist issue the core of their own work as avowed propagandists with brush and pen. The social artist, as Herman Baron remarked in later days, seemed to concentrate on three themes: policemen beating strikers, lynchings, and bloated capitalists. The danger for such an artist was the convenient stereotype which generations of cartoonists had made familiar to readers, and the urgency of the situation, which produced the violently obvious rather than the thoughtfully original. "His whole practice of art," as Thomas Willison observed, "has unfitted him for the representation of a large field, dense in meanings with interacting, changing, differentiated human beings. He must create for the first time images of great occasions," not simply render them as a spectacle whose composition "predominates over its inner life, its psychological tensions and latent meanings."

The cartoon was the most effective medium for social art in black and white, together with the cheap and easily distributed print. The democratic character of a lithograph, an etching, or a woodcut consists, as Elizabeth Olds has pointed out, in the fact that prints are in a sense original works of art, yet can be owned by many. The age of Jackson had richly made use of this fact, and now the print maker of the Federal Art Projects was finding a larger audience not only for conventional processes but for such unfamiliar ones as the silk screen color print, a stencil method explored by the Projects. The print was no longer a precious collector's item, and one artist declared that he would rather be owned by large numbers of people because his work was good than by one or two because it was rare.

The titles of prints shown by the Congress in 1936 indicate their content: Harry Gottlieb's *Coal Pickers,* Hugo Gellert's *Pieces of Silver,* Louis Lozowick's *Lynching,* Fletcher Martin's *Trouble in Frisco.* Three years later the New York World's Fair saw James Egleson's lithograph of workers crowding through factory gates, the chained Negro prisoner of Julius Bloch, the pinched complacency of Mervin Jules's *Rugged Individualist* standing beside his ticker. There was no subtlety here, nor in the acid line of Art Young's cartoon of the gorilla of war stealthily moving again after twenty years. Robert Minor had learned about socialism from the grizzled driver of a freight wagon, and he used the broad side of a lithographic crayon with a tiger's strength. Firmly and a little coldly Hugo Gellert modeled the portrait head of Paul Robeson; Adolf Dehn drew the grotesque obesities of wealthy opera patronesses and connoisseurs of art.

What William Gropper had to say often required crayon, pen, and brush in the same cartoon. For twenty years he had been making at least one drawing a day. If his East Side garment workers haunted the observer it was because he had worked in sweatshops and had struggled with the same noisome bundles which he drew on men's and women's shoulders. He had been well paid for his caricatures in the *Tribune* and the *Dial,* and his prophetic *Vanity Fair* lampoon on Hirohito provoked a diplomatic incident six years before Pearl Harbor; but his best energies were given to the radical press, where he toiled like Daumier to interpret history as it happened. One could rediscover Daumier in Gropper's terrible figure of black-robed Death with a swastika on his sleeve, sharpening his scythe, and in the movement of his figures across the white page, in the reduction of a hated face to a few bony sockets and bosses. Out of Goya's nightmares had come the flying woman in his *Tornado,* skirts blown over head; and the plump manikins of Brueghel were the ancestors of his farmers and stockbrokers. In the manner of the modern *collage* he papered the wall behind his gaunt tenement wife with newspaper clippings which made their own comment; his gnarled and crackling dry brush strokes reminded one of Hokusai.

Out of many languages Gropper made one peculiar to himself: the gross bodies straining at their clothes, the iron-hard contours, the stippled textures, the corroding pen accent, the over-all design which drove his meaning into one's mind. A row of huge armored tanks thrusts straight to the edge of a page, and an angel of

George Biddle, *William Gropper*

Courtesy Associated American Artists, New York City

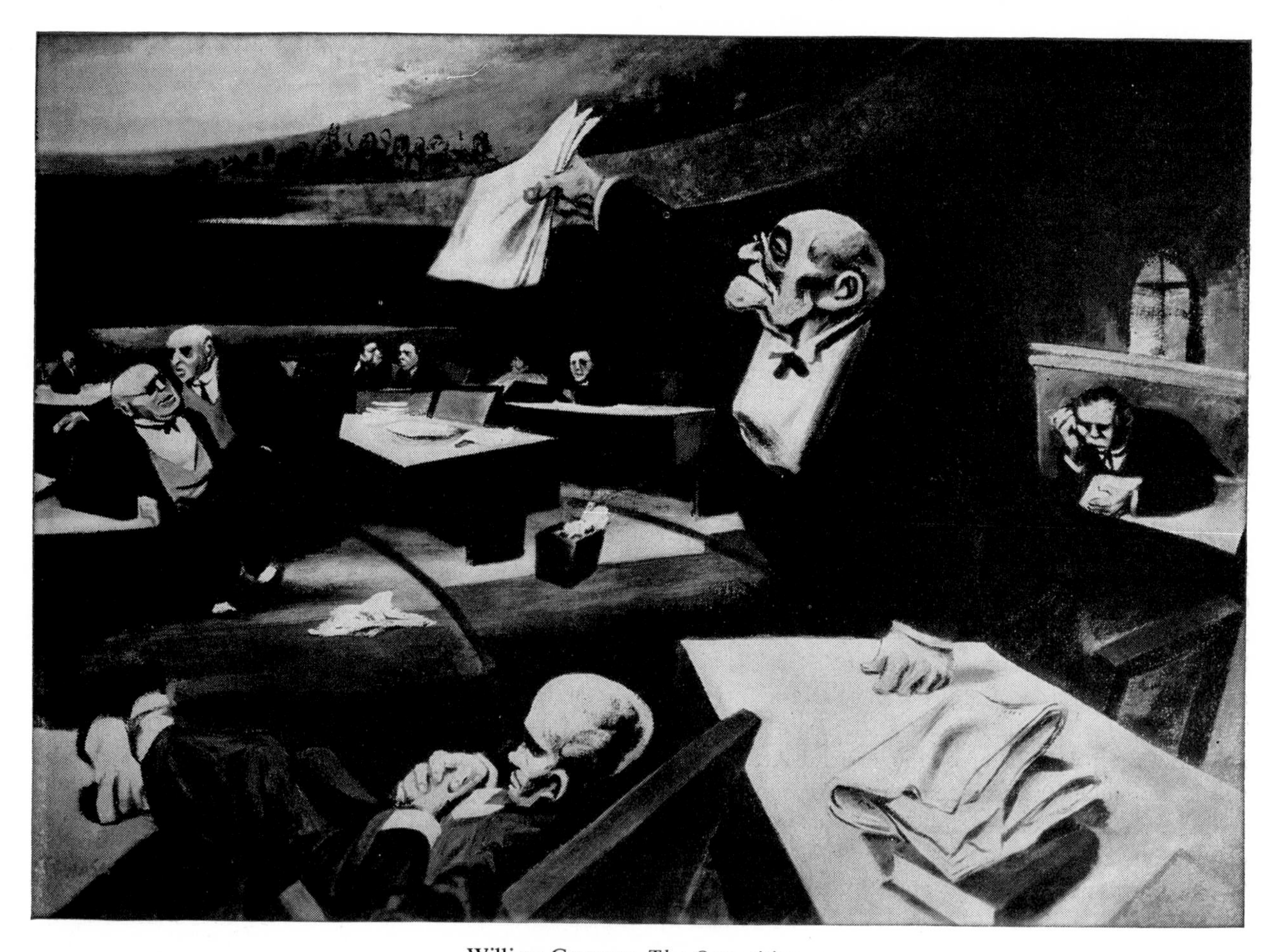

William Gropper, *The Opposition*

Courtesy Encyclopaedia Britannica, copyright William Benton

Peace forlornly thumbs a ride; the grinning Chamberlain cranks the triple grindstone for the knives of the Axis partners; lowered over a cliff by Hitler, a diminutive Daladier chips with his hatchet at the noble figure of Marianne, the French Republic. The man's power to give new forcefulness and mockery to the old pictorial clichés of cartooning was matched by an inventiveness of new symbols which seemed never to be exhausted.

When Gropper's canvases were shown in 1936 he had been painting fifteen years. One could see Brueghel in the turbulence of his *Wine Festival,* Goya in his *Bulldogging;* and the boldly silhouetted horses and upturned pushcarts of his *Strike* had the controlled disorder of the silk scrolls on which Oriental artists spread disaster. His senators thrashing the air among their desks reminded one of that rogue's gallery, the *Legislative Paunch* of Daumier. But here too Gropper had his own incisiveness of form, his own way of giving massive weight to rocks and a fearsome vitality to blasted trees. Every least shape worked for him; the hard edges of red congressional chair backs, the swift curve of a balcony, the gesture of a dead tree branch, the soiled white of poor men's shirts. On some occasions he could compose these elements with a terse finality; on others his impatience and his acquired fluency were too easily satisfied with forms which had been flung upon canvas before his mind discovered the relation between form and meaning.

George Biddle, whose portrait of Gropper was one of his most incisive characterizations, hoped that one of the effects of the depression would be a socially conscious art that transcended the literal and the accidental. Only out of deep personal conviction, it seemed, and with more than the illustrator's skill could one create images of great occasions. The thrusting diagonals of bayonets and falling pickets in a painting by Jacob Burck seized the dramatic moment but could not prolong it. The angularities of Orozco built to no climax in Adelyne Cross's *CIO at Inland Steel,* and James Turnbull's *Chain Gang* was no more than a statement of facts. Rouault's bestial lawyers found a weaker echo in the satirical *Clergyman* of Benjamin Kopman, whose brush laid the rich pigment on canvas without the Frenchman's passionate conviction.

The three Soyer brothers — Moses, Raphael, and Isaac — reached further back in time for suggested

Raphael Soyer, *Waiting Room*

Corcoran Gallery of Art, Washington, D.C.

forms and more quietly identified themselves with their subject. Their father had been a Hebrew scholar in Russia before the family came to New York's East Side, where the boys got such training as poverty allowed. "Our message," Moses said, "is People"; and he traced the tired lean gestures of ballet students against bare walls as Degas had done. As Daumier's crowds peered into print shops, so the shop girls of Moses Soyer stood before mannequins in department store windows; he built the head of an old worker with planes of thick ridged pigment and nervous linear accents, Daumier-fashion. The same quiet tones and reticent sympathy were in Raphael Soyer's *Waiting Room* and the *Employment Agency* of Isaac, whose gaunt men and stout women sat with a stubborn patience on hard benches among the shadows.

Would not the expressionist intensities or the surrealist's fusion of fact with nightmare better serve the social painter? The acid pen of George Grosz had once been the scourge of German profiteers, and his water colors, done with a blurred technique and colors which looked like bloodstains on the paper, had held a distorting mirror, as he said, to the face of hideous reality. Now he found refuge in America and although there was some of that earlier ferocity in his overdressed Manhattan promenaders, the American Grosz was done with politics; his thoughts turned inward and his vitriol was diluted. He painted his own face brooding among the smoke and ruins of a Europe he could not forget; in his *Wanderer* an old man stumbled through iridescent mud among thickets and brambles, a human spirit in a world of terror, behind him an explosion like a burst of bleeding flesh (Encyc. Brit.).

Peter Blume's immaculate white factories had the cubist austerity and he assembled girders, tugboats, and scows with an engineer's logic, but his *Parade* of 1930 at least hinted the present conflicts (Mus. Mod. Art). Its brick walls, machines, and ventilators were as relentlessly drawn as those of Sheeler in glaring whites, blacks, and brilliant reds, but more arbitrarily rearranged; and along the high wall with its purple door moved a workman holding above his head a glistening suit of armor—a riddle whose meaning was not obscure. The Corcoran Gallery refused in 1939 to hang the result of three or four years' work by Blume, the large and intricate *Eternal City*. It was a composite "painted essay," as

Peter Blume, *The Eternal City*

Museum of Modern Art, New York City

one critic said, on life under Mussolini, and Dali himself could not have surpassed its jewel-hard brilliance: the fragments of white marble torsos, the ruins of the Forum, the garish shrine with its Crucifixion, the beggar woman crouched over her brazier, and lurching out of corruption and decay the jack-in-the-box head of a livid green Mussolini.

Blume was only thirty-three when he completed *The Eternal City;* at the same age Anton Refregier abandoned the delightful themes he had painted for stylish interior decorators and chose the subject of human rehabilitation for a Federal Art mural at Riker's Island. When the occasion called for flippancy, as it did in the mural commission for Café Society Uptown, he could set weird flying figures and crazy balloons among high clean arches like a Miro of the nightclubs; when he designed panels for the San Francisco Post Office or painted a modern madonna in *Heir to the Future,* his bold emaciations and the harsh geometry of his light and shade spoke his pity for suffering and his reverence for the courage of pioneers. In smaller scenes where men built stone walls, farmers pruned trees, and their wives churned butter, Refregier was close enough to the event in time, place, and sympathy to make genre in the best American tradition.

One could apply the term "modern" to Robert Gwathmey's *Across the Tracks,* where he found the very pattern of segregation. Here was no circumstantial and picturesque South but a region of brassy sun and hard flat earth, of shanties with garish circus posters which said one thing, and drab cotton pickers who said another. Gwathmey used the colors of the red earth, astringent green plants, blistering whites, and brown-black flesh not merely to weave a pattern but to make an ironic point. He was an eighth-generation Virginian who knew the difference between cheap fancy and brutal fact; and in *Non-Fiction* he set two black children, their feet enmeshed in barbed wire, before a gaudy canvas with its minstrel caricature of the Negro.

The world of Joseph Hirsch and of Jack Levine was the northern city where slick lawyers whispered confidences and policemen hobnobbed with ward politicians in back rooms; and both were in their twenties when Federal Art gave them encouragement and support. Hirsch sculptured the huge muscles, bulging paunch, and muscled legs of *Masseur Tom* as though he had been

Robert Gwathmey, *Across the Tracks* (Arnaud d'Usseau coll.)

Courtesy A. C. A. Gallery, New York City

Daumier at a bourgeois swimming tank, and when his *Two Men* (Mus. Mod. Art) was voted first place by visitors to the New York World's Fair it was because the white worker and his Negro companion had found the shapes for their tension—the huge fist slapping the palm, the taut planes of the speaker's face, the triangulations of the listener's effort to understand. Hirsch had been a pupil of George Luks and he had seen men toiling at Ceylon and Shanghai before he came home to Philadelphia to paint the theme of work for the meeting hall of the Amalgamated Clothing Workers. He was trying, he said, to castigate the things he hated and build monuments to what he felt was noble: "The great artist has wielded his art as a magnificent weapon truly mightier than the sword. . . . So it strikes me that a reaffirmation by today's sincere artist of his faith in the common ordinary man will be as natural as was, for example, the emphasis by El Greco, in his day, on faith in the Church."

Jack Levine's castigations lost none of their force for being wryly humorous. He worked with the thick pigment of a Rouault or a Soutine; and out of the black-brown shadows of his *Feast of Pure Reason* three faces glowed like live coals. Three pairs of hands, a glint of white spats, a striped shirt sleeve and a decanter bring to life his "urbane and case-hardened cronies" in the back room of a pawnshop. When Levine painted a slum street, he wished "to be a steward of its contents, . . . to present this picture in the very places where the escapist plans his flight," challenging the observer to read its implications. (See color plate 28.)

Thanks also to the Art Projects, the Negro painter found his voice in the thirties. As one watched his effort to rid himself of the picturesque stereotype of the black man, and the notion that Africa had provided him with authentic racial forms, one saw that his form was no different from that of the white artist nor, save in details, his fundamental content. Hale Woodruff's *Card Players* was scarcely more than a cubist fantasy, and his strenuous elongations were as brittle as Benton's before

Jack Levine, *The Feast of Pure Reason*

Museum of Modern Art, New York City (*on extended loan from WPA Art Program*)

he rose to the occasion with his Amistad mural. Aaron Douglas was among those who issued the invitation to the Artists' Congress, but his lunette in the Harlem Y.M.C.A. was scarcely more than a pleasant decoration in cool greens, and the Negroes who danced in his panels were shadow shapes gesticulating behind a gauze curtain under pink or blue lights as they did in the island scene of *Porgy and Bess.* A harsh insensitivity pervaded the Harlem genre scenes of Motley; Charles White's *Fatigue* had the glistening lights and brutal voluminosity of Orozco's screaming child. The Mexican painter's hard abstractions of form and face appeared in White's portraits of Sojourner Truth and Booker T. Washington in a mural for Hampton Institute, a design whose sweep and strength made the figures of Romare Bearden seem stiffly archaic and willfully primitive.

At once more personal and more inventive, a twenty-one-year-old Negro, Jacob Lawrence, painted *Firewood* as a Project artist in 1938, the crisp flat shapes of the woman, cart, hatchets, and kindling like the scissored shapes of brightly colored paper, the whole pattern brilliantly alive. A later critic smugly missed the point of Lawrence when he wrote: "Long after . . . the inhabitants of Harlem have risen to affluence . . . these water colors may continue to give pleasure just because of a certain handsomeness they have." Precisely because Lawrence knew that that time showed no signs of coming, he worked at his picture-narratives, the lives of Toussaint L'Ouverture, of Frederick Douglass, of Harriet Tubman, of John Brown—each episode told with the simple directness of a child but with a man's love for the greatness of great men and his hatred for their persecutors. To praise Lawrence for his ingenious

Joseph Hirsch, *The Senator*

Whitney Museum of American Art, New York City

patterns was to belittle their meaning as the shapes of tortured and congested living, the arabesques of white brutality. Few mural artists could have built such nervous and powerful commentaries as Lawrence did on small panels in the *Harlem* and the *Migration of the Negro* series.

There was no dearth of talent among all these painterly consciences, white and black, old-timers and newcomers. What they seemed to lack was time for the event to ripen in their minds, for the image to gather about itself richer implications and deeper human meanings. That maturity, however, was in the best of Ben Shahn and Philip Evergood. Shahn had been a lithographer's apprentice and had spent four years abroad, where he saw foreign crowds march in protest against the execution of Sacco and Vanzetti in Charlestown, Massachusetts. Five years of thinking shaped his feeling on that subject and defined the symbols of the twenty-odd paintings he showed in 1932—the governor's top-hatted committee above the two coffins, the pedimented courthouse, the stony face of the judge, the two Italians manacled to each other. The painted tones were nearly flat, and out of all possible contours Shahn abstracted the few meaningful lines of a creased coat, a black judicial robe, a malignant eye. Here was no blast of explosive hatred but a counterpoint of humor and compassion, of irony and anger.

Many of Shahn's details came from his photograph files but their authenticity went beyond fact, and his apparently mechanical vision, as Jean Charlot said, was "heavily loaded with moral values." When Shahn painted *Vacant Lot* with a lonely young ballplayer in

Jacob Lawrence, *Most of the People Are Very Poor,* gouache

Courtesy Downtown Gallery, New York City

Anton Refregier, *Heir to the Future*

Courtesy A. C. A. Gallery, New York City

Charles White, mural design for Hampton Institute (detail)

Newark Museum

a bare yard with a vast brick wall behind it, he said what the writers needed thousands of words to say about life in big cities. Some of his confrontations were as unexpected as those of the surrealists but served to deepen, not disperse, the human meanings: an acrid pink-purple satin shirt against tenderly painted autumn leaves on a hillside where a man played *Pretty Girl Milking the Cow* on his harmonica; the microscopic realism of a campaign poster against broadly painted boards in *Sunday Football.* Shahn's people were done with the freedom from visual consistency of a "primitive"; yet one had only to walk Seventh Avenue to see these people made flesh.

The murals of Shahn in Roosevelt, New Jersey, in the Bronx Post Office, and in the Social Security Building at Washington never mistook size for greatness or nervousness for strength. On the west wall of the Bronx building Whitman was quoted: "Democracy rests finally upon us"; and Shahn explained "us" in thirteen panels, assisted by his wife, Bernarda Bryson. His color was low-toned and on the warm side with earth-reds, green-yellows, and browns against the gray interior. His figures were greater than life-size, and one of them sometimes filled a whole panel. No American could use fresco with such monumental simplicity; Shahn conveyed the stress and power of human effort without bulging biceps, giving a man's strength through the shape of his back, not the details of his garments. Here a nation of engineers, haymakers, steel and telephone workers went about their tasks steadily and with confidence. One massive girder with strong metallic reds told the story of construction; his textile maker was framed within the fine radiating threads of the machine itself—man, work, and instrument being one. Only the Italian masters of the fourteen hundreds could thus have achieved monumentality without monstrosity, graveness instead of melodrama, with a total absence of those hackneyed devices which lesser men used to "hold a wall together."

Philip Evergood was as talkative as Shahn was reticent. His men and women, like those of Shahn, had the force of symbols but were also remembered as people one had known—the pale girl at the tenement window, the boy soldier of Stalingrad, the fierce old lady ignoring a hurricane. Whitman's hearty affection for the children of Adam moved Evergood to paint "the play of masculine muscle through clean-setting trousers and waist-straps" and "the little plentiful manikins skipping about in collars and tailed coats." Living in a world of uncertainty, of conflict, of death and destruction, but believing it also a world of hope, he could not passively imitate its shapes or find escape in formal purity, form and content being one and inseparable in his mind. There was plenty of scope for invention, he

Ben Shahn, *Vacant Lot*

Wadsworth Atheneum, Hartford, Conn.

said, in the objective world we have in common; and one found no well-tested cliché, no reassuring formula in what he did, but astonishing originality of theme and of plastic invention, joyousness hard to resist, explosive ridicule, fierce indignation, simple affirmation of plain realities, and undertones of fear, of dream, and of fantasy.

There were paintings where Evergood's desire to insist resulted in overemphasis, others whose powerful tensions he could not resolve. His spaces sometimes refused to hold their human content and a figure seemed to arrive too early or too late to find its place. His failures, however, were more honorable than the failure of the "successful" to do more than repeat themselves ad infinitum; and his aim was high, being nothing less than "the prodigious feat of combining art, modernity, and humanity."

Still life for Evergood was not an excuse for playing with forms; the fruit on a table in *Expectation* was the materialization of a child's hunger. The red-brown shafts of trees and the moist greens in *Mill Stream* evoked not so much the image of a place where people lived as their affection for its ugliness and charm. In *Suburban Landscape,* with its sober row of stunted and standardized houses against snow, he not only recalled what each of us has seen from trains but quietly suggested the life behind those yellow-shaded windows. His brick factory became a shabby framework for toil, and each of its many windows opened on the life of the men and women who sat at its benches or stood among its machines.

Many a modern painter, faced with the discrepancies between man's capacities and his achievements, has imposed on his images of men the hard logical perfections of nonliving objects. Evergood reversed this process. He charged a brown wall with the bleakness in the mind of a man who has just received his dismissal slip, and made a brick one glow with the delight of Lily feeding spar-

Philip Evergood, *My Forebears Were Pioneers* (Mrs. Bruce E. Ryan coll.)

Courtesy A. C. A. Gallery, New York City

rows; his locomotives were not the sleek constructions of Sheeler nor the frenzied, snorting engines of Benton, but they had the chunky and cheerful strength of the men who climbed over them or stood beside them.

My Forebears Were Pioneers was no scribbled message but a picture as rich in implications as in color. On a lawn which the hurricane had ravaged sat an old lady in a rocker, ramrod-straight. Beyond her the great boles of uprooted trees had fallen on a Victorian mansion which had the same battered dignity as its owner. Its colors were the faded yellow and dull green of her own flesh; like her, it stared defiantly at disaster, proclaiming its immunity to change. One could read here the story of unshakable courage, or a tragicomic reminder that men have a knack of averting extinction by the skin of their teeth.

Gropper, Shahn, and Evergood represented "social art" at its most eloquent and most convincing. The artist with a conscience, however, could reach only a few minds compared to those huge shapers of public opinion, the newspaper, the radio, and the motion picture. On the few occasions when New Deal agencies made documentary films the motion pictures achieved maturity; and maturity, as Harry Alan Potamkin wrote, "demands not illusions but realities." In 1937 Pare Lorenz produced *The River* for the Farm Security Administration with a score by Virgil Thomson. It was the story of a great valley destroyed and rebuilt; word followed imagery and image was reinforced by music in a remarkable synthesis, poetic and forceful. Its proud enumeration reminded one of Whitman:

> Down the Rock, the Illinois and the Kankakee,
> The Allegheny, the Monongahela, Kanawha, and
> Muskingum . . .
> The Mississippi runs to the Gulf. . . .

One saw man's greed and his fear destroy the forests and build levees to keep back the flood; one watched the precious soil washed into the sea, and the poor land which made poor people. One saw man's intelligence create the Tennessee Valley Authority, build great dams to store the water in flood time and release it in time of need, to make electric power for the people of Tennessee while new trees were planted to hold the water in the earth and new houses replaced the old hovels.

The mural painters must have envied the epic proportions of *The River* and similar works; and one could only imagine what men like Gropper would have done through the medium of the animated cartoon. Walt Disney had established the latter as a true art form; from the early film *Plane Crazy* to the sound picture *Steamboat Willie* and from the first colored Silly Symphony to the full-length *Snow White,* he never forgot that his medium had gifts of its own for the fantastic and the droll, that his creatures need not obey the laws of gravity or the logic of space, scale, and time. Mickey Mouse joined Paul Bunyan in the world of the fabulous, and Disney's brilliant translucencies offered new and lighthearted satisfactions to millions of eyes.

In sober fact, however, the documentary films of the 1930's were but a brief moment in Hollywood time; and the Disney enterprise, with its split-second planning and its correlation of the separate efforts of an enormous staff, was too expensive to encourage experiment in any profound sense of the word. The artist with a message had to preach to a far smaller audience, while those instruments which were capable of changing the lives of everyone remained in the hands of men who insisted that Americans never would pay to be treated as though they had minds.

CHAPTER 33 / THREE-DIMENSIONAL CONSCIENCES

Only a few feet away from Evergood's *Forebears* in the New York World's Fair showrooms were two hundred and fifty sculptures, a cross section of the nation's effort to express itself in stone, wood, and bronze. Their final selection was made by John Gregory, Paul Manship, and William Zorach, presumed to represent the Right, the Middle, and the Left; and they ranged from Gertrude Whitney's Rodinesque entwined lovers to David Smith's enameled-steel *Blue Construction.* Here and there among the clever nudes and delightful children was the figure of a sharecropper, a refugee, a washerwoman, or a black pugilist to emphasize by contrast the prevailing view of the American as a handsome blond athlete with a Greek body and an Anglo-Saxon face. There were both dignity and depth of feeling in Maurice Glickman's *Negro Mother and Child,* and Minna Harkavy had cast not only shape but character in her taut, astringent *New England Woman,* being an ex-

Minna Harkavy, *Hall Johnson*

Courtesy of the artist

preferred the talent of Henry Hering, who sculptured a twenty-two foot *Pro Patria* for the War Memorial at Indianapolis, and the terra-cotta quotations from archaic Greek by Paul Jennewein for the Philadelphia Museum of Art.

From these ponderous platitudes one group of sculptors turned to a small and intimate scale while others sought a closer relation to their medium. Out of his patient observation on an Ohio farm Harry Wickey sculptured his small *Sulking Bull* with a nervous muscularity. Carl Walters fashioned ceramic cows, horses, and roosters of droll shape and lively surface decoration which seemed the modern offspring of the old Pennsylvania German cattle. The same intense life on a miniature scale was in Heinz Warneke's granite *Wild Boars* and his *Iron Worker,* but their elongations and near geometry were the result of a more conscious will to abstract. In contrast to Malvina Hoffman's *Elemental Man* with its mannerisms of Bourdelle, Oronzio Maldarelli's *Mother and Child* seemed to emerge slowly from its marble. The polished heads of José de Creeft kept the hard glint of the material which he attacked directly with his chisel, and all the compact density of the original block. Samuel Cashwan's *Adam* had the spare incisiveness of the Romanesque and Hindu works he so admired.

ception among sculptors in her concern with working people, whom she modeled with unsentimental strength in the bronze *Miner's Family* (Mus. Mod. Art).

Two years before the Fair, fifty artists in wood, bronze, and stone had formed the Sculptors' Guild in order to show their work and had been loaned a vacant lot on Park Avenue. Few were their opportunities to be seen by the general public either outdoors or in galleries, and the sculptor of the thirties shared certain social and economic liabilities with the painter. A controversy over a stone cat from ancient Egypt which the St. Louis City Art Museum bought for fourteen thousand dollars underlined the indifference of public institutions to contemporary carvers. The *Pioneer Family Group* by Zorach won first mention in a Dallas competition but succumbed to the public's aversion to nudity, and even in New York his aluminum *Spirit of the Dance* was banished for a time from Radio City Music Hall. In 1935 Lincoln Kirstein wrote that America had raised no monuments to Eakins and Homer, Melville and John Reed; he reminded the country that Lachaise had years before him, and wrote, "Not to make the fullest use of such a talent would be heartless waste." Within a few weeks of Kirstein's essay Lachaise was dead. Americans

Heinz Warneke, *Wild Boars*

Art Institute of Chicago

This consciousness of medium distinguished the *Boxers* of Ahron Ben-Shmuel, who had been a granite carver in Vermont, it resolved the lesser forms into the larger masses of child and animal in Zorach's *Affection* (Proctor Inst.), and it prompted Isamu Noguchi to choose whatever wood, metal, or stone was best suited to each of the fifteen people whose portrait heads he exhibited in 1930. Donald Hord preferred to work out of doors in the hard California light, using diamond points and air drills to cut the hard obsidian and diorite of the Southwest into shining Indian heads. From the rose-colored sandstone and white limestone of Texas the Mexican-born Indian, Octavio Medellin, shaped the *Thinking Girl* with the power of his ancestors.

To the mediocrity of public sculpture the City of St. Louis made an exception when it asked the Swedish-American Carl Milles to model a fountain, *The Marriage of the Rivers*. When Milles came in 1931 he had a brilliant reputation for monumental enterprises in his own country, and one could find Rodin's better qualities in him, a baroque grace and largeness inspired by his Italian journeys, and a humor which was his own. The nymphs and Tritons in St. Louis made similar work by Americans look joyless and anemic, and Meyric Rogers called attention to the rhythmic life, the fine craftsmanlike sense of hard bronze, softer wood, and subtle stone in the work of Milles. There were mannerisms of plane and edge in his St. Paul Peace Monument and in his Orpheus fountain for Stockholm, but they were at least sculptural ones; and Milles communicated his own hard strength to his American pupils.

On the Mall at the World's Fair in New York one could compare the clean forms of Milles' *Astronomer* with the cleverly festive men who remained in the tradition of 1893. It was difficult to find unity between James Earle Fraser's *George Washington,* sixty feet of

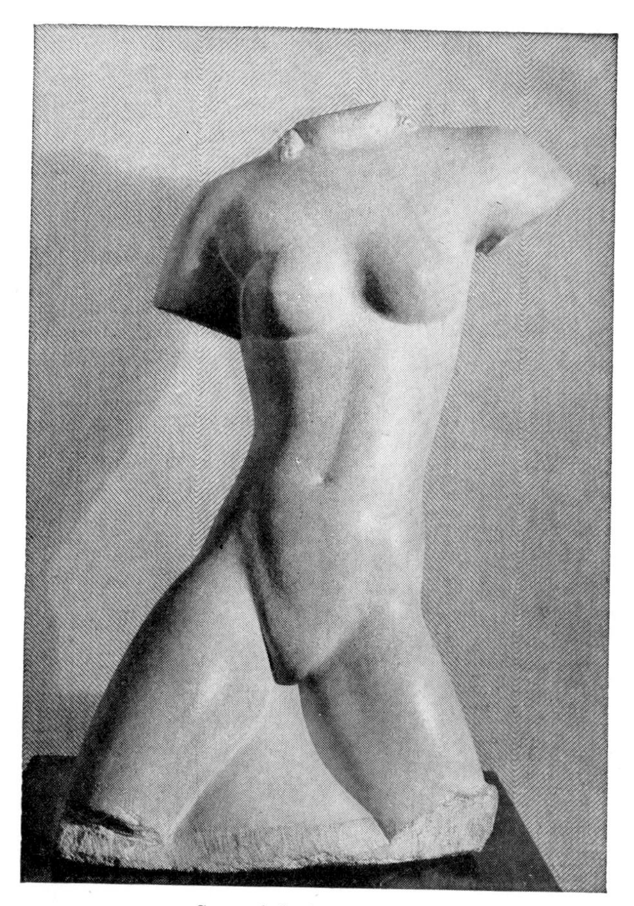

Samuel Cashwan, *Torso*

Vassar College Art Gallery, Poughkeepsie, N.Y.

William Zorach, *Affection* (Proctor Institute, Utica, N. Y.)

Courtesy of the artist

solemn flatulence, and Paul Manship's four *Moods of Time,* whose bodies arched gracefully in sprays of water; or between these and the smart stylizations, the tepid gestures, of Leo Friedlander's *Four Freedoms*. The florid Chester Beach group, *Riders of the Elements,* was ill at ease before the austere circular portal of the Aviation Building; the Leo Lentelli nudes exhibited more modern standards of female beauty than the plaster Gibson girls of Daniel Chester French had done, and those newer standards had also chosen the bathing girls of Billy Rose's Aquacade in the amusement area near by. The sculptured reliefs at the fair, like those of Carl Schmidt, acquired a momentary interest from being trickily lighted from behind. One left the Fair with the impression that the sculptor's place in American life was as marginal as it had been half a century before, when he was hired by Columbia to decorate her four-hundredth birthday cake.

The architect of the depression years could not evade their implications, his theory and practice both deeply involved in the way men live, singly or in groups. In the year of the Artists' Congress Ralph Adams Cram stated his belief for the last time in *My Life in Architecture;* but few younger men could share his convic-

Carl Milles, *Dancing Girls,* Bloomfield Hills, Mich.

Harvey Croze photo

Frank L. Wright, "Falling Water," Bear Run, Pa.

Hedrich-Blessing photo

tion that the art of Modigliani, Epstein, Orozco, Stravinsky, and the architectural functionalists was a passing fashion, a temporary aberration. In the following year a modernist would have considered irrelevant the dispute over John Russell Pope's design for a Jeffersonian Memorial, Fiske Kimball defending its Pantheon form and the Fine Arts Commission visualizing a plainer structure in the style of the early republic. Neither symbol would stand for the pioneering mind from Monticello, and the Pope temple was to be three million dollars' worth of smooth white reminiscence.

In speeches and articles Frank Lloyd Wright left no doubt of his scorn for these evasions, nor would he accept the "slick architectural salesmanship" of men like Raymond Hood, whose tall buildings were modern only in the pictorial sense. Hood discarded the Gothic trimmings of his *Tribune* Building and the black-and-gold cleverness of the Radiator Building for the *Daily News* and McGraw-Hill skyscrapers, whose effect of clustered verticals and horizontals was achieved by surface variations of color, not so much three-dimensional masses as paintings against the Manhattan sky. Wright had been snubbed again when four hundred acres of Burnham Park were laden with mock modernism for the Century of Progress Fair, an enterprise in which Hood played a dominant part; and at a Town Hall meeting to protest Wright's nonemployment the honored guest amused himself by designing in words not one Chicago Fair but three—a huge skyscraper, grouped pylons with a canopy swung between them, a festival floating on pontoons.

The next few years saw Wright's Administration Building for the Johnson Wax Company at Racine, Wisconsin. Its walls of brick lined with cork and concrete were sealed against fire, noise, and dirt, and the heating of its air-conditioned spaces was synchronized with the movement of the sun. A soft, even light penetrated the bundles of thin glass rods which formed its ceilings and the upper portions of its walls, and from its floor sprang pillars only a few inches thick at their base which mushroomed in great disks against the glass sky. Before it was completed in 1939 Wright had created beauty on a

Richard J. Neutra, Emerson Junior High School, Los Angeles, Cal.

Wayne Andrews photo

modest scale in his Jacobs house at Madison with walls of wood in three layers and heat from concrete floor slabs, at a total cost of fifty-five hundred dollars; and for the wealthy Kaufmann he had swung the cantilevers of Falling Water over the rocky stream at Bear Run in Pennsylvania. This house over a waterfall was anchored in pylons of the near-by stone, and its structure, as Henry-Russell Hitchcock has observed, was "crystalline," an interpenetration in space of the rough masonry core with the vertical planes of glass and the smooth white terraces upon which they opened; this critic called the house a matchless fusion of fantasy and engineering.

That balance between weight and lightness, between prose and poetry, was in the houses which Richard J. Neutra built on California hillsides. Neutra had been one of the younger innovators of Berlin before he visited Taliesin and established himself in Los Angeles, where his Garden Apartments found strong cubic forms for the balconies and terraces which Westerners liked. The cement-covered horizontals of his Lovell house riding its hill were supported by steel which did not disguise itself; and in his Experimental School at Los Angeles Neutra used wood forms which were exquisite yet strong.

The more sophisticated patron no longer recoiled before the "new vision" which Lewis Mumford explained in *Technics and Civilization,* the fresh qualities of shape, edge, and surface which mechanical forms and mechanical lighting now made possible. There was an aesthetic of the hard repeated unit, he contended, a beauty of precise calculation, of flawless economy, of sheer repetition, as well as an aesthetic of the unique and the unrepeatable.

At Brno in Czechoslovakia the houses of Miës van der Rohe had this quality, and Americans now learned to phrase interior space as he did with curtains on tracks, to employ the ramp which Le Corbusier substituted for the staircase, to accept the austere wall surfaces of Alvar and Aino Aalto in Finland and of Walter Gropius and Marcel Breuer in eastern Massachusetts. Paul Nelson had Miro, Arp, Léger, and Calder as his collaborators when he designed a "suspended house" in 1938—a row of steel arches from which hung glass-enclosed rooms.

The beauty of the Chamberlain house at Wayland, Massachusetts, was the satisfaction of its smooth surfaces of unpainted wooden sheathing, the one-floor structure extending for eight feet over a rough stone basement. Maine shingles and clapboards covered George Howe's summer home for Clara Fargo Thomas

William Lescaze, Edward A. Norman house, New York City

Gottscho-Schleisner photo

on Mount Desert Island, but no down-Easter had seen a living room thrust over the water's edge on a concrete cantilever. Frank Lloyd Wright summarized the best of his domestic achievements in the small and compact "Usonian" dwellings at Okemos, Michigan; his superbly intersecting cubes were in the Winkler-Goetsch house: brick contrasted with wide horizontal slabs of redwood on its exterior, and a low clerestory of glass provided extra light. For Edward A. Norman in New York William Lescaze brilliantly defeated the narrowness of a city lot, causing space to flow into space from street side to garden and creating a front of white brick, transparent and translucent glass whose proportions and subdivisions would have delighted Mondrian.

Other men in their early thirties were building one-story horizontal houses, usually without cellar or attic, with long ranges of glass toward the south, and curtains which were movable partitions. Their structural elements were prefabricated, and roof overhangs were a protection from the summer sun. John Funk set the glass panels of his Heckendorf house directly into its wooden framing at Modesto, California; Carl Koch used the stone hillside for one interior wall of a house at Belmont, Massachusetts.

It was a sign of these times that arguments among architects no longer dealt with purely stylistic questions. The series of articles which began in *Pencil Points* in March, 1932, reconsidered the larger problem of the architect's job in the America of the New Deal. George Howe had begun his partnership with the Swiss designer Lescaze, and their Oak Lane Country Day School near Philadelphia demonstrated the cool rationalism of the one and the resourceful imagination of the other. The architect, Howe maintained in *Pencil Points*, must conform for better or worse to the standards of society, and the only satisfaction he could provide, or ever had provided, was through forms which expressed the life process carried on inside and around buildings. This dogmatic functionalism was attacked by Robert L. Anderson as a "revealed religion," and Anderson resented the hint that the architect should concern himself with the social order, which it was his task to reflect but not to mold. Henry S. Churchill even wondered if function, as narrowly defined, had anything to do with architecture except to enthrone the machine as God. It was easy to function, he wrote, but hard to create beauty. If architecture was not to vacillate eternally between two extremes, "a philosophy must underlie the life of multitudes."

Lewis Mumford, in his essay for the Museum of Mod-

Walter Gropius and Marcel Breuer, Gropius house, Lincoln, Mass.

Wayne Andrews photo

ern Art that year, boldly met the criticism that he turned architecture into sociology by pointing out that as the single expensive American house became a thing of beauty the main quality of the nation's homes deteriorated. At their most prosperous only one third of the people earned more than two thousand dollars a year, which could build only substandard homes for substandard living. For most of his countrymen, therefore, the gospel of individualism did not provide individual satisfactions; and Mumford asked the profession to face the fact that there were only two escapes from this impasse: economic revolution or governmental subsidy.

During the first five years of the Roosevelt administration it was the government which financed many of the dwellings American architects designed for the ill-housed one third of a nation. The Carl Mackley houses at Juniata Park in Philadelphia were shrewdly placed to receive a maximum of light and air through large windows, and their interiors were well planned although the ensemble had a somewhat bleak effect. Lescaze broke the gridiron pattern with his Williamsburg dwellings, an oasis in the Brooklyn slums, in order that sixteen hundred families might have sunlight in summer and in winter. The long parallel rows in Trumbull Park, Chicago, of which Holabird was chief architect, were uniform but not monotonous. In the more open country near Norris Dam, Stonorov and Kastner built a community whose units were modernized versions of the traditional "dogtrot" house of Tennessee. At Berwyn, Maryland, the roads and footpaths of "Greenbelt" ran among trees and followed the natural slopes and contours of the site, the row houses informally placed. The poorest of these new communities were of a drab uniformity; the best of them placed single dwellings, stores, and nurseries of delightful originality on locations as bare and flat as Woodville in California.

Before Henry Wright died in 1936 he could observe in these garden towns and in these cities-within-cities the boldness, the humanism, and the hardheadedness which made his Radburn a superb achievement. His mind had not quailed before statistics in its search for the apartment forms which lower-income people could afford. He believed that the American notion of each family self-contained in its own house was capable of being changed; and those who lived comfortably in the group dwellings he devised, each two or three stories high and within the human scale, would have supported his contention.

Henry Wright remained this side of Utopia; Frank Lloyd Wright created structures in his mind whose intelligence and humanism were a prophecy of social structures far in the future. His model of Broadacre

Rockefeller Center, New York City

Thomas Airviews photo

City was a vision of how fourteen hundred families could live decently within four square miles which provided a complete existence: a few industries set apart from the residential sections, homes for single families and apartment houses, dwellings for men with five cars and for men with no cars; a theater, college, school, hospital, stadium, and airport; long- and short-distance traffic separated. Only through an organic statesmanship, Wright believed, could such a plan be realized; but he found no such statesmen in the world of the 1930's.

As that decade came to an end New York saw the completion of the Bronx-Whitestone Bridge in which the designer Aymar Embury and the engineers Allston Dana and O. H. Amman achieved a superb economy of arching roadway, steel cables, and towers. It also saw Rockefeller Center, an ensemble of skyscrapers which impressed one by sheer bulk and the multiplication of shafts and windows rather than by imagination in design, its collaborators including Henry Hofmeister, Harvey Wiley Corbett, and Raymond Hood. To the ranks of the moderns had come Marcel Breuer and Walter Gropius, doctrinaires of the Bauhaus, and the two Aaltos from Finland, Alvar and Aino, whose laminated wood furniture was seen in New York in 1938.

The ideas of the best modern men too often had to be studied on paper, not in brick and stone. Eliel Saarinen's design for the Chicago *Tribune* Building had been set aside in the twenties in favor of a bastard Gothicism; and his subsequent work at Cranbrook in Bloomfield Hills, Michigan, underlined that error. Would the Smithsonian Art Gallery, as Eliel and his son Eero designed it with the help of J. Robert Swanson for a first prize in the competition of 1939, ever be allowed to spread its clean, interlocked forms among the sprawling whited sepulchers of the Washington Mall? Would the competitive designs for a new art center at Wheaton College, displayed at the Museum of Modern Art, survive the outraged protests of Wheaton alumnae?

In the fateful autumn of 1939 Frank Lloyd Wright stood before a London audience and said that the modern city must disappear, and with it most of the mental habits, ethical notions, and modes of conduct on which it was based. He calmly suggested that London rid itself of all its slums and dreary rows of houses, plant lawns and trees around its fine old monuments, and become a park. When Englishmen objected that their country was too densely populated to hold Broadacre cities, Wright reminded them that some Englishmen owned four-thousand-acre estates. When they argued that the huddled life of the working class bred qualities of courage and endurance, he retaliated that his own country was founded by Englishmen who said "No" to that battleship notion of existence. "Really there is no reason," he concluded, "why a democracy should not have, and be free to will and to possess the best." We must get people, states, and buildings not taste-built but thought-built. Since architecture is life itself taking form, and since form and function are one, "some deeper thought on our part . . . must get inside, penetrate, and from the inside work out the practical new forms suited to democratic life," and make democracy not something merely on the lips, but "an actual way of life and work, *alive,* and affecting, throughout, every human being today right where he stands."

CHAPTER 34 / STATE OF HIGH CONCENTRATION

The painters of the American scene and the dramatists of social conflict accused their abstract brethren of evasion, yet could not the accusation be reversed? Too many of these lynchings, prairie wagons, and barroom carousels possessed an energy that was simply of the nerves and muscles; the portrait of America, like the *U.S.A.* trilogy of Dos Passos, threw a multitude of vivid facts together in the hope that they would form a pattern. Surely there were more things in heaven and earth than these Horatios dreamt of, too few beings on these canvases to remind one of Hamlet's exclamation, "What a piece of work is man!" Could not the painter suggest even through recognizable forms the infinite complexity of the mind, and make rocks and trees the symbols of his convictions and his fears?

When Henry McBride saw Georgia O'Keeffe's painting in 1937 of a ram's skull with a hollyhock he wrote that perhaps the artist was a Hamlet. On the objective level one delighted in its clean, superbly painted whites against gray clouds with the New Mexican hills far beneath. Her lilies and purple petunias had velvet-smooth surfaces and depth of hue, but one could not dismiss them as magnificent still lifes in which objects had been oddly brought together. To one, her bleached skull spoke of the death of animals who, because they live grandly, die grandly; to another, her dark hills held that permanence and patience of the earth which was man's reassurance; to still another, the convolutions of her flowers suggested fertility and birth.

The same hills had been painted by Marsden Hartley in *Cash Entry Mines* of 1920, but with restless curvatures which reminded one of Dove's dynamics. The next ten years had been roving and experiment in Berlin and Vienna, Florence, Rome and the Cézanne country; and when Hartley wrote from Gloucester in 1931 that he was clearing his mind of all art nonsense,

Marsden Hartley, *Smelt Brook Falls*

City Art Museum, St. Louis, Mo.

he had found his authentic voice. On Dogtown Common he saw and pictured a monstrous rock thrusting like a whale's jaw against a blue sky and a hard white cloud. There would be no more hesitation nor self-defeating in the twelve years Hartley now worked among the Nova Scotia fishermen, under Mount Katahdin, and along the Penobscot. When he said, "I wish to declare myself the painter from Maine," he had learned

Walt Kuhn, *Roberto*

Courtesy of the artist

to identify himself with the sensuous qualities of icy lake water, gray-white boulders, whipped sea, and deep black-green pine woods; into these at sixty he could put all of himself.

There was a majestic certainty in the blue shape of Katahdin and the fiery autumn reds below its flanks, no hesitation in reducing clouds, hills, trees, and lake shore to the simplest and boldest contours. Quieter tones sufficed for the still lifes which he made from objects to be found along the shore; and no American had played richer variations on white, black, and brown than were to be found in *Black Duck* (Boston Mus. Fine Arts). Hartley wrote poems during these years, and the single plumed wave springing like a column from tawny rocks in one of his canvases reminds one of his "wind pounding sea-froth into frozen curds." His hard-faced fishermen were like the three old men he once described under the gas globes of a Maine parlor, who

> . . . seemed to be saying
> nothing at all
> violently.

His rocks were "these volcanic personal shapes," his log jams tumbled down over the waters "settling into jackstraw patterns."

Such paintings as *The Wave* (Worcester Art Mus.) and *Fishermen's Last Supper* were the fruit of Hartley's splendid last five years when, thanks to his friend Hudson Walker, Americans rediscovered a painter-poet whose imagination could match Ryder's and whose waves moved with the power of Winslow Homer's,

> playing about like lion cubs over
> the loins of these stone lionesses. . . .

Hartley's path toward certainty had been a tortuous one, with forms assimilated and forms discarded; Walt Kuhn, another veteran of the first modern battles, was only three years younger than Hartley, and his work was a steady and patient reiteration of his early premises, with the intensification which maturity made possible. His *White Clown* of the late twenties and his *Roberto,* nearly two decades later, are similar in pose and costume. The pattern of forms in the latter, however, against a dark background, is more insistent; a greater tension runs through the arms, legs, and gripping hands; the mask and cranium are more powerfully carved by Kuhn's brush.

It was not easy for younger men to state personal convictions with the power of a Hartley. *Quiet Evening,* by his admirer John Edward Heliker, found similar hard shapes for the cut edges of quarry granite, but with a more obvious calculation. There were strenuous concentrations in the *Fence Builders* of Everett Spruce, who had lived in the Ozarks as a child and who worked as an attendant in the Dallas Art Museum while he learned how to paint a watering trough in a desert or a blasted tree on a pile of boulders with some of the terrifying emptiness of Chirico. Raymond Breinin was a young Russian whose long horizons on which solitary houses stood or a single figure moved had the mystery of folk legends; and Julian Levi's mind dwelt on the lonely beaches where fishermen prepared their nets under vast skies. The smooth trees of Helen Lundeberg, who termed herself a postsurrealist, were intended to stimulate "an ordered, pleasurable, introspective activity" which should depend on both her subject matter and her form. The forlorn birds of Morris Graves enmeshed in white threads of moonlight were painted "to rest from the phenomenon of the outer world." At twenty Graves had journeyed to Japan, at twenty-seven to New York; back home in Seattle the Oriental collection of the Art Museum encouraged his nervous calligraphy with *gouache* and with brush lines of silk-thread fineness on thin sheets of paper. Out of his solitary contemplation came the strange textures and rhythms of his *Wounded Gull* and his *Joyous Young Pine,* and a bird in a Graves painting was a "little known bird of the inner eye." (See color plate 22.)

The work of Hyman Bloom was the result of the same inward looking and he pictured the rich Torah scrolls and vestments of synagogues, with the dense glowing pigments of Rouault and with as much religious conviction and tragic solemnity. Both Darrel Austin and Paul Burlin painted tigers; the glaring eyes of Austin's large cats crouched on impossibly green grass were the creatures which haunt a child the morning after nightmare, by an artist who never concerned himself, he said, with what his pictures would look like to others. Burlin, too, "went out on a limb" for sheer imaginative design, for automatic inspiration, but the beast in his *Tiger, Tiger* was the artist disgorging a world he could not digest, his hide "armored against bourgeois taste."

In America as in Europe of the mid-thirties the abstract painters and the surrealists were at some pains to claim a social value for their art; and Walter Quirt attempted to prove that a healthy offspring could be expected from what someone called the marriage of surrealism with the class struggle. Quirt condemned "Americana" painting as a futile effort to prolong a tradition valid only in the previous century, when people were more sensitive to literary than to plastic values. The middle class, he wrote, "could not tolerate an art which wished to find new meanings in life, but wanted

Morris Graves, *Blind Bird,* gouache

Museum of Modern Art, New York City

Walter Quirt, *Tranquility of Previous Existence*

Museum of Modern Art, New York City

one which assured it that its values and *status quo* were absolutes." But Quirt saw this class now more emotionally stable, more cognizant that free emotion was an important element in man's life, with a logic of its own which was not hurtful to man but an aid in explaining him.

"Americana," in short, denied the existence of man's complexities, his weaknesses, and his mistakes, hiding the real human being behind a smoke screen of patriotic anecdote; its worship for the object confessed the poverty of its soul. Now, said Quirt, "we are going to explore the subjective self as it stands in relation to reality, and out of it produce a pattern for the future." Such an art will thrust the spectator back into himself, rasp him into a consciousness of his emotional ingredients, and since the experience will be a new one for most men, this art will not be at once intelligible. The new surrealist could thank the older ones for having discovered a creative mechanism, free association, and an imagery which stood for neurotic elements in man; but that treasure, Quirt maintained, had been squandered by Dali and others when they made their discovery an end and not a means. Now it was time to use free association positively to "explore the language of the emotions on problems the public feels but has not the means for projecting into actualities"—in short, to psychoanalyze society for its own good.

As this program of "Social Surrealism" crystallized in Quirt's mind, he painted *The Future Belongs to the Workers* and exhibited it with the John Reed Club in 1933, a design of the mural type in which three tense groups—a wounded worker, a funeral, and a crowd holding up a red flag—were neither formally nor ideologically connected. More successful in 1935 was his *Morals for Workers,* where his Daliesque sharpness underlined the mockery of those conceptions—patriotism, virtue, education, cleanliness, and thrift—which were empty catchwords in the mouths of reformers and reactionaries. A monstrous watch depended from a worker's neck in this painting as though to suggest his bondage to the time clock. Six years later, when Quirt painted *The Tranquility of Previous Existence,* his colors had grown more brilliant and his trenchant anecdotes had given way to swirling shapes which the *Art Digest* called "enigmatic" (Mus. Mod. Art).

Most of the abstract and nonobjective artists were less specific and less confident than Quirt with regard to the importance of their art to other men. Dane Rudhyar spoke of a minority of creative personalities whose historically fated task was to embody the "polar attitude." In John Flannagan's carved chicken, half emerged from its egg, Wilhelm R. Valentiner was to find a symbol of vital forces in the act of creating life, and more than one "creative personality" thus played God. Some of them belonged to the "Transcendentalists," who claimed indifference to social, economic, or political problems and whose membership included Bill Lumpkins and Raymond Jonson. In *Chromatic Contrasts* and in *Peace and Equipoise* Jonson traced "the rhythms that flow into and through matter picking up essences and spiritual feelings" in the effort to state at least a portion of life's meaning. Lumpkins' *Form Synthesis* represented this group at the World's Fair, its dry swirling shapes suggestive of the grain and knots of weathered wood.

The Fair jury also chose a *Jersey Landscape* by Eugene Morley which closely resembled the manner of Stuart Davis. Jean Xceron's laconic *Painting* was there, Arthur Carle's *Episode of the Mantis,* and Byron Browne's *Forms on Black Space,* whose relation to Paul Klee was obvious. Balcomb Greene's *Composition* was a group of bald shapes seen through a tipped picture frame; Gertrude Green played curves against right angles in the interlocking shapes of her *Construction;* Elise Armitage modeled spherical pellets and truncated pyramids against vague darkness and called the result *Out of Space.*

The verbal explanations of such painters were seldom helpful to the layman. Charles Howard, for example, who had been trained as a decorator and made abstract murals for the Federal Art Projects, said simply that he relied on his obsession to dictate his forms, that *Trinity, The Cage,* and *Generation* were titles which had no explanatory function, and that he intended to recall the shapes and relations of things which were common to all mankind. Knud Merrild modestly earned his living as a house painter and decorator in Los Angeles, though his unconventional forms had caused his expulsion from a Danish art school. This friend of D. H. Lawrence hoped, he said, that life would be richer for a few as the result of his *Synthesis* and his *Mirage;* they were efforts toward absolute beauty, but he would never be sure he had reached it.

George L. K. Morris spoke more confidently. He had been one of the founders of the Abstract American Artists and he saw no alternative but to abandon art, as Frank Lloyd Wright would abandon cities, and build on wholly new foundations. The old styles were dead past reviving; let art be stripped to its bones and begin again. He worked in the early thirties in Paris with Ozenfant and Léger, and announced on his return to America that the elusive and reticent compositions of Hans Arp were among the purest and most authentic comments on troubled Europe. Against a severe flat background Arp had been placing his rounded shapes cut from thin wood and variously colored; and to those who saw nothing but shape and pattern in these reliefs Morris explained that "a broken piece of pottery will

Irene R. Pereira, *Yellow Oblongs*

Courtesy A. C. A. Gallery, New York City

often bring us closer to Greece than the Laocoön," leaving for further discussion the question whether an unbroken pot would not serve the purpose even better.

The painted comments of Morris were as enigmatic as those of Hans Arp, his coeditor of *Plastique,* and much resembled them. One could see them as natural forms which had been reduced to a final purity or as invented symbols of the first step toward living nature, bold fragmentary bits of matter against a darker void with serpentine lines leading one's eye among them.

Beside the machinelike construction of Morris' *Mural Composition,* a canvas by Irene Rice Pereira was more richly inventive with the same terms. By a stretch of the imagination her forms could be likened to grilles and ladders, fire escapes, and building scaffolds, but they were not so intended. Her work was first seen at the A.C.A. Gallery in 1933, and her laboratory experiments with new materials — glass, parchment, gold leaf, cement, and glyptal paint — constantly enriched her work in color, texture, and complexity of construction. Her titles had no hint of the metaphysical: *Orange Rhomboids, Radium Diagonals, Blue Predominates, Diffraction.* Hers was a fascinating polyphony for the eye, far more elaborate than that of Mondrian: square and curved shapes of subtly varied hue and surface character seen on one ground or through several superimposed layers of glass, each transparent or translucent plane bearing its own pattern and playing its part in the intricate play of light. Pereira drew with the precision of an architect and planned her balances and counterthrusts as an engineer would plan. (See color plate 19.)

Pereira's philosophy, however, looked beyond the composition of visual fugues, in which she had no peer. For her, the Renaissance and the present were both periods of shattering new discoveries which art could not ignore. The arena of the artist's action in the fifteenth century had been three-dimensional space, and linear perspective his expressive instrument. The new science had given him the means for describing and measuring concavities and depths, and the solid bodies which moved in them: Masaccio's crucified Christ beneath his receding arch would have been impossible in the flat medieval world. Five centuries later, science has again revolutionized man's conception of the world with the notion of a fluid, ever-changing space-time continuum; parallel lines no longer meet in infinity and the new mathematics has "destroyed the old shape of the universe." Pereira's effort was frankly a laboratory experiment to find new forms by which this revolution could be expressed.

Not only man's environment but man himself was changing, and Pereira was deeply aware that an accelerating tempo in human relations, a tension in social relationships, had reached a climax in the struggle between freedom and slavery. Picasso's *Guernica* marked this crisis in human liberty, and in it space and time had been united to make what Thomas Mann called a "universal feast of death." But out of the laboratories which perfected the bombs of a fascist could also come instruments for the fashioning of a decent world. Although one found in Pereira no reference to the creatures who lived between despair and hope in the present world, one could read in her *Quadrigraph* and her *Yellow Oblongs* at least a reminder that the mind and the hand could plan as well as destroy, be rational rather than brutish, and as capable of integrity as of deceit.

The patterns of Stuart Davis more broadly hinted their origins in the familiar factual world than those of Quirt and Pereira in the late thirties; his free association was less turbulently emotional than the former's, and the ordering of his motives had not the intricacy and rational perfectionism of the latter. It was over twenty years since the Armory Show had plunged Davis into his search by trial and error for relationships which should have their justification within themselves. There had been a brief period when Gauguin and Van Gogh looked over his shoulder, a time in the twenties when he assembled cigarette papers and the labels of tobacco tins in the manner of *papiers collés,* and painted them with careful sobriety in low tones. For a year he had discovered a multitude of possible designs in a fan, a glove, and an egg beater variously disposed, and had used heavy contours and dense colors like those of Léger to play variations on his theme.

Davis was trying to locate that point where generalized forms would not have to depend for their vitality on one's recollection of the natural objects which had inspired them; he wanted "is like" to become "is." The Paris street scenes of the late twenties and the Gloucester landscapes of 1930 stripped the subject down, he explained, to the real physical source of its stimulus, the source in this instance being French *kiosques,* tobacconists' windows, plaster house fronts, iron balconies, Cape Ann cottages, and sailboats drawn with as few lines as possible and filled with a minimum of unshaded hues—what Davis called the common denominators of color-shape. These he recomposed to make a more exciting visual whole than the subject itself had been able to provide—cleaner and fresher greens, blues, vermilions, and whites, a purer balance from left to right and from top to bottom, more vigorous sequences for the eye to move in than through the cluttered detail of the original "reality." As he worked, the local color of one object transferred itself to another, houses crossed streets to occupy a better pictorial position, boats sailed not only behind headlands but through them.

Davis once listed the things which constituted the first step toward these disintegrations and reintegrations:

Stuart Davis, *Cape Ann Landscape* (Harry A. Solomon coll.)

Courtesy Museum of Modern Art, New York City

American ironwork, gasoline stations, the fronts of Woolworth stores, kitchen hardware; and he added the music of Bach and Earl Hines's hot piano. He was in effect composing a visual jazz with piquant references to the above elements, moving from the rather banal and obvious counterpoint of his Paris and Gloucester days to the more complicated and sharp-toned dissonances of his *Swing Landscape* and his murals for Radio City and the New York City broadcasting station, whose shapes had given up more of their own character than his early ones in order to be more like one another and to move with a more insistent tempo. Davis called his fantasy of 1940 a *Hot Still-Scape for Six Colors*, in whose brassy yellows and writhing black lines one could hear an echo of Louis Armstrong and Eddie Condon. It was modern swing as Milton Mezzrow described it, frantic, savage, berserk, "the music of tics . . . and jump and rib-bop." And Mezzrow's warning was apropos: "Let yourself get blown into a thousand jagged fragments, like the world around you, and you can't pour harmonious New Orleans music out of your soul . . . high-spirited but pervaded all through with a mysterious calm and placidity—the music of a personality that hasn't exploded like a fragmentation bomb."

Samuel Kootz described the paintings of Stuart Davis as self-sufficient symbols; and Davis, like Quirt and Pereira, claimed more than private meaning for his work. All three were members of the Artists' Congress, and Davis for a time played a principal part in its activities, having become, he later said, "socially conscious as every one else was doing in those days." Art for him was a form of communication by a man who wants to say something to others through his work. He denied that the work of Dali was in any sense revolutionary, being a commonplace calendar art in which "we contemplate a desert of the familiar bric-a-brac of human hopes and realities. . . . In these scenes a man looks only backward and the sun is setting. Artists who intend to continue will have to change cars."

Davis had changed cars more than once. Five years after the first Artists' Congress he insisted that art has a function in society but an indirect one—to use as its subject matter "new and interesting relations of form and color which are everywhere apparent in our environment," forms which were bound to have political, psychological, and utilitarian associations. The modernist was to play, as it were, his own obbligato in the social symphony.

The abstract-minded sculptor of these years, possessing a medium which, as John Sloan once said, one could

Alexander Calder, *Lobster Trap and Fish Tail*

Museum of Modern Art, New York City

stumble over in the dark, could scarcely claim nonobjectivity for his art, nor vaporous transcendental values. He could, however, follow Brancusi's example and fashion shapes whose appeal was almost exclusively to the sense of touch, the perception of dynamic swellings and contours, the pleasure in textures meeting light. At the New York World's Fair the bronze *General* of Hugo Robus had bosses and archings which had been abstracted from its subject, and it was the suave curvatures of his white plaster *Girl Washing Her Hair,* not the hint of back, breasts, and arms, which remained in the mind. In the late twenties Noguchi exchanged the tutelage of Gutzon Borglum for that of Brancusi, and the result was obvious in the almost-abstraction of his *Miss Expanding Universe,* in his machinelike *Chassis Fountain* for the New York World's Fair, and in the stone *Capital* (Mus. Mod. Art) which made no reference to the classical orders.

The resemblance of Emma Lu Davis' "handies" to any other objects was purely coincidental; they were small fragments shaped to give tactile pleasure to the hands which held them, as a small boy fingers a pebble in his pocket or an old man the knob of his walking stick. They were the result of her effort to bring sculpture closer to the average moment, and to provide the first step in the layman's sense of what sculpture is. They were gadgets, like the metal shapes of Alexander Calder's "mobiles," with which the observer could design arabesques in space and time by touching the subtly balanced mechanism from which they hung. Calder's mobiles of the nineteen thirties added a mild new visual excitement to an art which needed relief from a weightiness which was too often purely physical.

When one drew up the balance sheet of abstract and nonobjective art for this decade of the thirties one found that it numbered more friends among collectors, critics, and even museum experts than in previous years. Jean Hélion defined abstraction as a "state of high con-

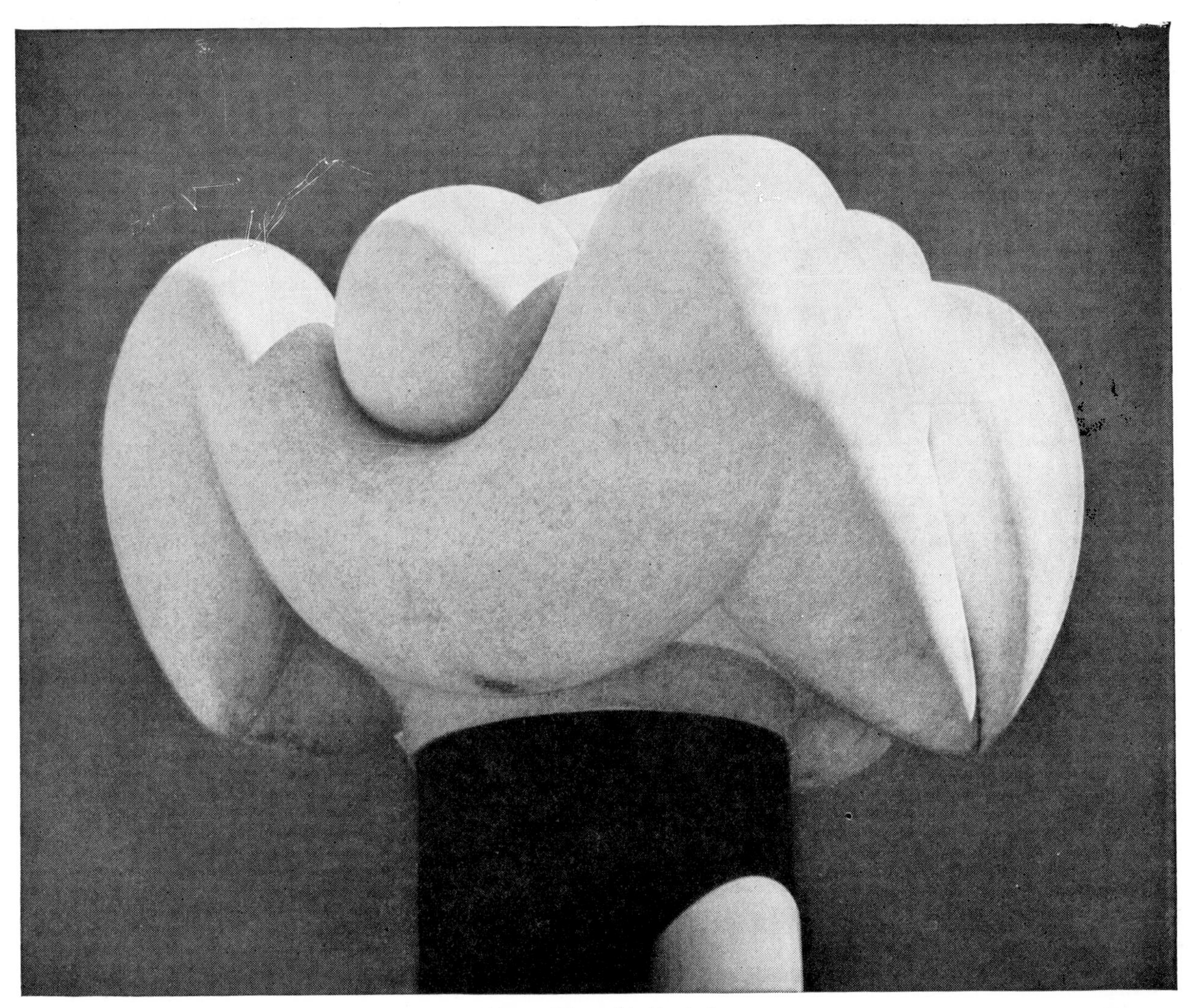

Isamu Noguchi, *Capital*

Museum of Modern Art, New York City

centration" in men who wished to liberate art from the mania of representation, men who discovered new qualities for painting, new relationships to intrigue the mind, and new intensities of feeling. There were some critics who accepted the modern because, for better or worse, it was the inevitable product of a society in turmoil and confusion. Others insisted upon weighing the better and the worse, and questioned inevitability in a realm where human will and reason were supposed to play their part. One had doubtless to accept the universe as Margaret Fuller did, but must the artist's role be limited to bearing witness against what mankind had made of it?

The formalist had established beyond a doubt that unless a painting or a sculpture speaks to our form-perceiving faculties it has no right to call itself a work of art; and he had provided those faculties with new matter on which to exercise themselves. The observer could simply enjoy this music for the eye or he could believe that Quirt was a seismograph recording psychic tremors. These artists, however, made further claims for what they did. The exquisite blue spheres of Rudolf Bauer, weightless in darker blue space, were for Hilla Rebay sources of spiritual inspiration; a Davis "still-scape" aimed to increase man's understanding of his world; Pereira believed that she expressed that world as Piero and Uccello had expressed an earlier one; Quirt's effort was to release people from hidden conflicts which were harmful to themselves and others.

Put to the test of experience, these claims raised more questions than they answered. How could the works of Baroness Rebay's protégés inspire the world, since admittedly they had been created by a few geniuses for the few who could rise to their heights? Was not the "self-sufficient symbol" of Davis a contradiction in terms, since a form which had wider connotations than its own color, size, and outline was no longer self-sufficient? The artist of the Renaissance had not only worked to

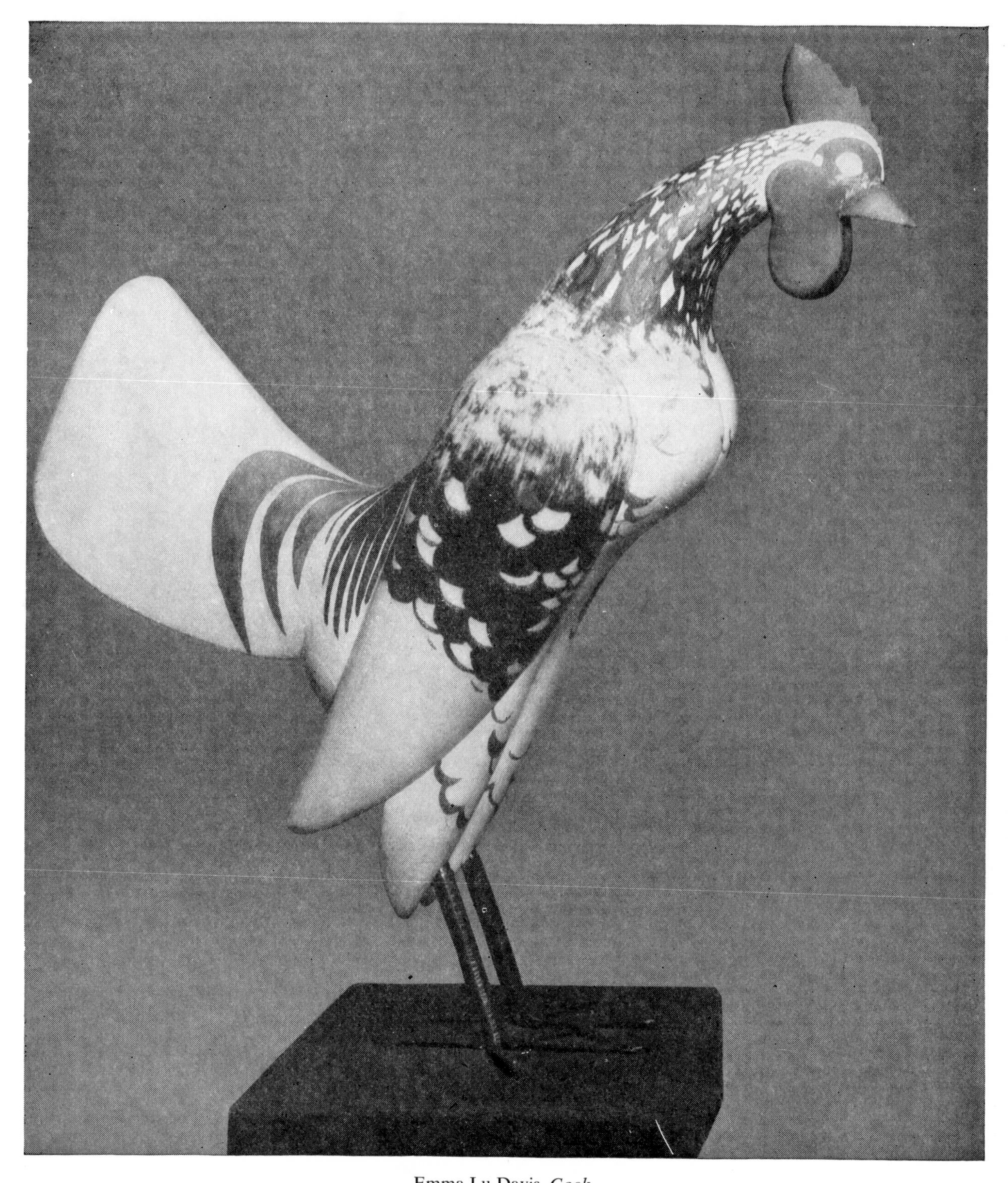

Emma Lu Davis, *Cock*

Whitney Museum of American Art, New York City

"express" the spatial and scientific notions of his time, but also to give form to the thoughts, feelings, and values of Humanism. And how was the new surrealist to be sure that, in purging himself of his obsessions, he had provided a clue for the self-liberation of others?

The abstractionist had made his own dilemma. If his elements resembled even slightly the world from which he had abstracted them, he struggled against an obstinate human habit of reading the natural and the familiar into them, and against the layman's discomfort when he found himself frustrated. The work of art which, on the other hand, made no concessions to recognition and was therefore "pure" was likely also to be dull. Walter Abell denied in *Representation and Form* that form and content were separable and competing sources of effect, and showed that the richness and amplitude of great art depend on a multitude of associations, a chain reaction, so to speak, released by their forms. A picture by Morris, for example, could do one thing efficiently, being an object where "every disturbing element has been controlled and measured," a machine for seeing; yet it was difficult in 1940 to accept Rhodes Johnson's dictum that the functioning of a machine represents the essence of truth and beauty, so logical that "it will not even serve a false economy."

When the abstract and the surrealist artist tried to combine, in Evergood's words, Art, Modernity, and Humanity, his interpretation of the third was likely to be meager and ambiguous to other human beings. It was often the work of a "social surrealist" who had not socialized himself, of a mind whose symbols were too private for sharing and whose internal contradictions made it incapable of clear affirmation.

When Georges Lemaître surveyed the theory and the performance of writers and artists from the first cubists to the most recent surrealist, he wrote that one could understand the general purpose of this movement without grasping the meaning of any specific work it had produced. Its nightmarish shapes had not given him a glimpse of the "higher universe." He was impressed by the theories of the advance guard yet found almost no successful embodiment of those theories in its poems and paintings. "In any case," he concluded, "it would be a mistake to consider modernistic theories either as a passing fashion or as the product of a few exceptional and pathological minds. The continuity of their development and their persistency under various forms throughout several anxious generations show conclusively that they correspond to something really deep and important in contemporary life. . . . Whatever their intrinsic worth, they express strikingly a genuinely pathetic reaction to the stress of our times."

The integration of art presupposes a personal integration in the artist, as lively a curiosity about others as about himself, and a willingness to surrender a degree of his mental and aesthetic autonomy. Otherwise he remains a voice eloquent with words which few others can understand. He is like a painted island by Hartley which, the author said, "wants itself and hates to give it up."

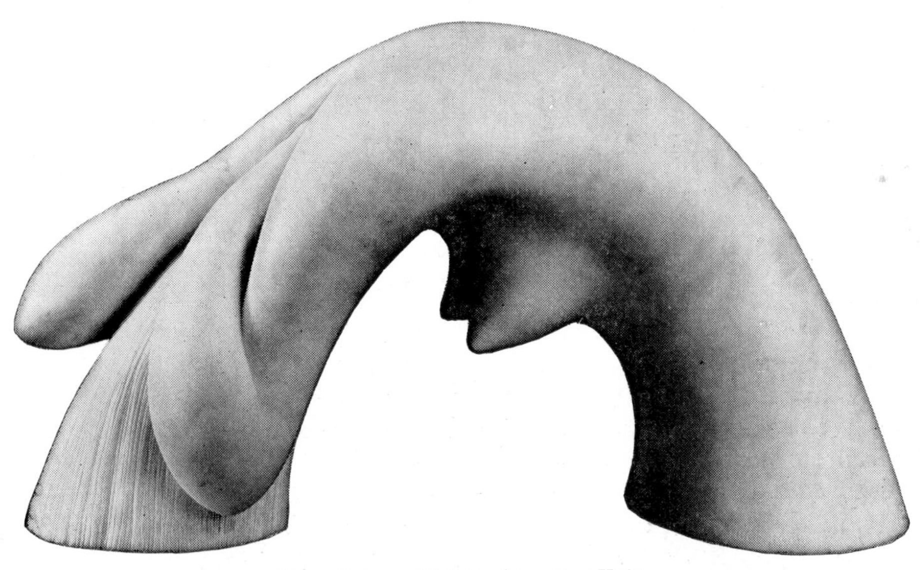

Hugo Robus, *Girl Washing Her Hair*

Museum of Modern Art, New York City

Ben Shahn, *The Welders,* tempera ►

Museum of Modern Art, New York City

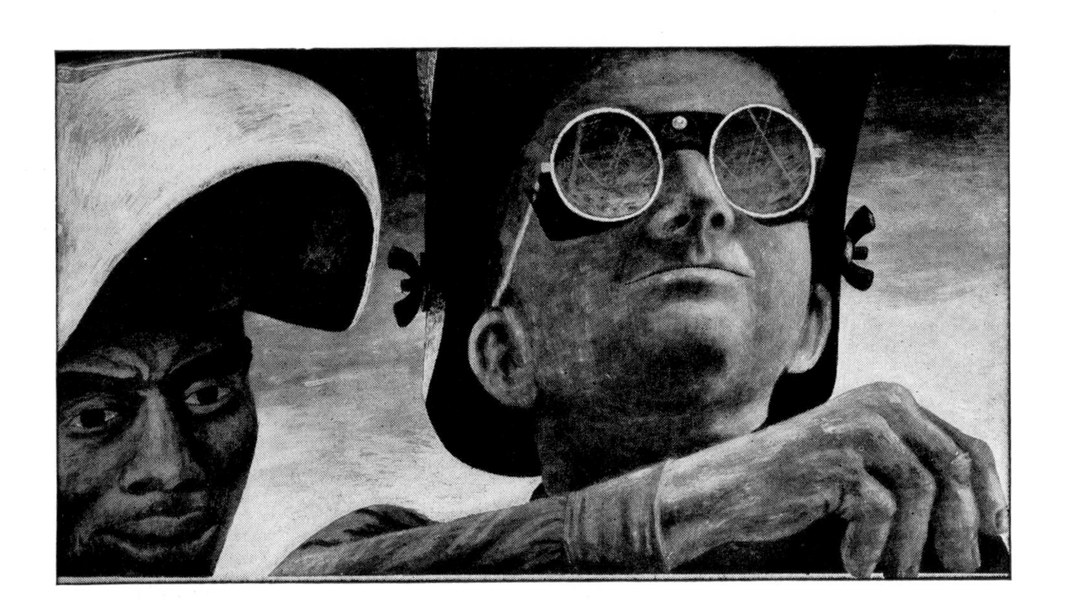

PART TWO

POINT OF PROMISE AND OF DANGER

INTRODUCTION / COLD WAR CLIMATE

In the fall of 1939 the Art Institute of Chicago surveyed *Half a Century of American Art* and Daniel Catton Rich summed up the meaning of the show, concluding that "much is expected of America and much will come forth, particularly if our artists heed the counsel of Thomas Eakins to 'peer deeper into the heart of American life.' " Two months before, Hitler had unleashed his *blitzkrieg* on Poland, and Americans for the next six years would have no time for national introspection. In offices, factories, and shipyards they created an "arsenal of democracy" and hoped that Lend-Lease would discharge their obligations toward the conflict. That hope diminished as the area of Nazi victory spread like a bloodstain over the maps in the newspapers; and many an artist and patron asked himself whether this country, having shaped a democratic conception of the arts out of the economic and social turmoil of the thirties, could now defend that conception in a war which threatened to engulf the world.

The notion of the artist as citizen, as spokesman for collective ideals and purposes, owed much of its vigor to the Artists' Congress and the Federal Art Projects; yet in this crucial moment both of them proved to be experiments stillborn. The former, whose motive had been the prevention of what had now taken place, was divided by the question of America's relation to the war; the latter was confronted with accusations of disloyalty from a Congress unimpressed by its accomplishments and appalled by its expenditure of the taxpayer's money for such intangible benefits as puppet plays and murals. By the beginning of 1939 the Projects were employing about five thousand artists in more than forty states, and more than a million works of art had been placed in public institutions. Lewis Mumford declared the Projects had "planted the seed of the fine arts, hitherto raised under glass in a few metropolitan hothouses, in every village and byway in the country, renovating soils that have become sour with neglect, and opening up new areas for cultivation." Art, like education, he wrote, must be given active and constant public support; but when Representative Coffee introduced a bill in August of 1937 which would establish a permanent Bureau of Fine Arts, the attack on his proposal and three similar proposals left no doubt that Mumford's view was an exception. Letters blossomed in newspapers which attacked the sponsors of a federal art: "Under the smokescreen of elevated verbiage," one of them cried, "they hide the bitter envy and the implacable hatred they bear toward inherent superiority of every kind," and Francis Henry Taylor referred to the "cesspool of art politics from which this lotus of the American Renaissance has come to flower."

Against these shrill outcries the friends of the Projects raised their voices: Sherwood Anderson and Holger Cahill, Burgess Meredith and Paul Manship supported a Public Use of Art Committee; even Broadway, which had not given Federal Art its unreserved support, now sent Tallulah Bankhead, Helen Hayes, Brooks Atkinson, and Eddie Cantor to Washington to defend it before congressmen. Their last-ditch effort failed. In June, 1939, the Fine Arts Bill was tabled by the House amid derisive references to the teaching of ballet dancing to twelve million unemployed. Federal Art was allowed to limp for a while longer on reduced funds and carefully planned restrictions. The price of one battleship was evidently too high a price to pay for the greatest experiment in democratic culture the world had ever seen. The Art Projects, which would have contributed more than any other artistic enterprise to a sense of the common cause, were still alive in forty states on the day of Pearl Harbor; eighteen months later they were ended. Thousands of canvases, rolled into bundles, were sold at auction and could later be discovered in junk shops.

Meanwhile the separate energies of millions were being fused in the most gigantic effort which this Hercules had ever attempted, and one which demanded a level of productive collaboration by labor, management, and government undreamed of in their past. Many Americans who had convinced themselves that the first World War was a conflict of greedy imperialisms did not find it easy to support the second one without misgivings; for most democrats, however, the struggle was clearly one for survival. It had been called a People's War, and it had to be so fought. This conviction was nowhere stronger than among artists. When Earl Robinson composed "Ballad for Americans" he declared that "music as usual" was out of the question and that his colleagues would never have a greater theme to celebrate than now, or a better opportunity to prove that private satisfaction was not the only motive for writing music. In a similar mood eleven hundred artists responded in 1942 to the call for pictures of the country's defense effort issued by the Office for Emergency Management, and a somewhat larger number submitted work in the Red Cross competition.

Civilian Defense, the War Production Board, and the Office of War Information were among the several agencies which sponsored the making of posters, and many Americans came to know Joseph Hirsch through the rugged figure of a G.I. on the war bond poster of 1943, and Ben Shahn through his magnificent study of two welders, one white and one black, published by the Political Action Committee of the C.I.O. The Museum of Modern Art, exhibiting two hundred posters, revealed how great had been the progress in that art since the efforts of Howard Chandler Christy, Charles Dana Gibson, and Joseph Pennell in the earlier war. Modern simplifications helped most of them to make their point: the brutal mask of a German officer with a gallows and its victim reflected in his monocle, the work of Karl Koehler and Victor Ancona; Seymour Fogel's haunting image of a gaunt child in *Deliver Us from Evil.* In Rockland County, Maine, Waldo Peirce was one of a group who made war posters for local use.

Other forms of propaganda were exploited by the Artists League, whose Victory Workshop carried the war issues directly into trade-unions, air-raid posts, and other vital areas and whose exhibition in 1941 was called *This Is Our War.* In Kansas City, Missouri, Thomas Benton finished his *Year of Peril* paintings as a contribution to "a unity of all-out practical, purposeful and realistic seeing and doing." The War Department in 1942 chose forty-two artists to provide a pictorial documentation, and many of them were in the war areas when Congress cut off the project's funds and forced them either to come home or to continue under private auspices. *Artists for Victory* was the united effort of some twenty or thirty art societies to aid the national effort by assembling exhibitions, holding poster competitions, and auctioning pictures for the War Fund.

In sum, the war activities of artists reflected their own sense of responsibility rather than wide official recognition of their usefulness. Yet the implications of the Federal Art years were not forgotten, and discussions of large-scale public patronage continued during the war. In 1943 George Biddle published in *Harper's* his scheme for resuming the federal experiment with modifications designed to meet its critics. Although Charles Beard, Van Wyck Brooks, and others approved his plan, opponents were dubious of any procedure in which the notion of relief, not purely artistic competence, played a part; and Stuart Davis felt sure that the proposed Bureau of Fine Arts would discriminate against the painter of abstractions.

Before the war ended, two sources of support for artists had developed—business and the trade-unions. The employment of painters to reinforce the advertiser's slogans was no new thing in America, but it reached new proportions in the nineteen-forties, when Abbott Laboratories, Standard Oil, the Container Corporation, and the International Business Machines Corporation were buyers of art to be used directly for advertisement or indirectly for prestige, and Pepsi-Cola announced the winners of a competition which had drawn five thousand canvases from every state but one. The president of Pepsi-Cola hoped that other concerns would follow this example and carry American art to the public in the original and through color reproductions, not requiring artists to paint any particular theme but selecting good canvases of every kind, paying well for them, and using them in a variety of ways. In the same year, *Encyclopaedia Britannica* began a collection of contemporary art which was reproduced in its volumes and in a special book; it also toured the museums and schools of the country. Thanks to its art director Glenn Price, the *Britannica* pictures made good their claim to be a faithful cross section.

Was this new alliance the answer to the artist's problem? Thomas Benton welcomed business patronage as a means of helping the artist to get into contact with the living world. "Historically, art has always been supported by the dominant economic and social interests. . . . Now, in the United States, who are the dominant interests? Free enterprise."

In a more reserved commentary Elizabeth McCausland applied arithmetic to the question, observing that ten thousand Pepsi-Cola contests would be required each year to keep alive the fifty-thousand practicing artists of America. To those who believed that the "art boom" of the forties proved the adequacy of private patronage Miss McCausland offered the results of her own survey among artists. Studying the results of a questionnaire sent to a representative group, she discovered that the average male artist was forty-five years old with four years of training and twenty of practice behind him and that his annual income from art was $1,150. A woman was even less fortunate, with an income from her art of a little more than $500. These unrewarded people relied on teaching, inherited funds, commercial hack work, and investments to keep themselves alive.

Meanwhile, at the opposite extreme of society from the large business patron, a few artists had found rewards both material and mental in working for the trade-unions. During the political campaign of 1944 Ben Shahn directed a squad of cartoonists and poster makers for the Political Action Committee of the C.I.O. On the theme of the "Four Freedoms" Hugo Gellert was engaged to paint murals for the Hotel and Club Employees Union of the A.F.L. and for the National Maritime Union. In the auditorium of the Central Needle Trades High School in New York Ernest Fiene celebrated *The Victory of Light over Darkness.* Even the Metropolitan Museum sponsored a series of discussions on Labor and Art and dispatched a few exhibitions to the union halls.

The most significant result of the painter's and the sculptor's activity among working people was the stimulus, through classes and recreational groups, to the creative powers of workers themselves. With the help of the United Seamen's Service the merchant seamen of several nations showed in 1943 the paintings and drawings they had made in studios on land and at moments aboard ship, and critics were amazed by the sureness, the grasp of form and incident revealed in the exhibition. Here and in the A.C.A. presentation two years later of the National Maritime Union no common subject and no predominant style could be discovered; there were both "primitives" and men of sophisticated vision, their common denominator a force and an independence which derived from first-hand experience directly translated into forms. Walter Abell wrote that "both the making and the possession of art are on their way to becoming again a normal part of the lives of industrial workers."

For the great majority of Americans, now as before, familiarity with art was based, not on originals, but on printed reproductions. Too often the layman assumed that his framed reproduction of Michelangelo or Grant Wood was faithful to the colors of its original. The reproductive techniques had advanced far since Currier and Ives, but the world of art-at-second-hand still had its aristocrats and its poor relations. *Life* magazine used a halftone process whose accuracy was limited by inferior paper, coarseness of the screen, unskillful choice of the four inks which had to provide all the range of hue and chiaroscuro, and the use of these basic colors for several reproductions on a single page until the distinctive quality of each artist was lost in an averaging of tonality.

You paid your money and you took your choice; for ten dollars a man could buy Thomas Craven's *Treasury of Art Masterpieces,* whose one hundred and forty-four plates varied from accuracy to misrepresentation. The *Fortune* subscriber enjoyed illustrations whose excellence had been achieved by offset lithography; the buyer of large individual prints found that the "gelatones" issued by the Associated American Artists were

Julio de Diego, *They Shall Sail the Seven Seas*

Courtesy Encyclopaedia Britannica, copyright William Benton

an appropriate vehicle for the thin washes of a Benton or a Dehn water color. Most sensitive of all processes, and most expensive, was the collotype, which involved no screen and in which a dozen or more color plates were sometimes used. If the contemporary painter looked with some reservations on this proliferation of imagery, one could not wholly blame him. It was pleasant to know that approximately twenty million people each week were seeing his work, but his pleasure was qualified by the filtering out of his artistic personality by the machinery of mass production. He wondered if a generation which fed upon facsimiles would develop a regard for originals, however inexpensive. And when books were published with a minimum of text and a maximum of reproductions for which he received no fee, he was expected to rejoice that his work was being kept in the public eye.

In spite of the nation's inability to support her artists, of official antipathy to forms of public support, and of the willingness of many Americans to content themselves with art at secondhand, that curiosity, that growing sense of the excitement and satisfaction of art for which the maligned Federal Art Projects had been largely responsible, continued through four years of tension and struggle. How much in turn did artists accomplish by way of interpreting this struggle during its progress?

The record is an honorable one, including not only the vivid posters, cartoons, and documentary paintings but also works in which the imagery of warfare had a less obvious and less directly utilitarian place: a suggestion of torpedoed ships in Bradley Walker Tomlin's *To the Sea;* the plates and bolts of uncompleted vessels in Julio de Diego's fantasy, *They Shall Sail the Seven Seas.* The theme of homelessness was not new to Mitchell Siporin, but his life as a member of the Engineer Corps had intensified it when he painted *Night Piece.* Jacob Lawrence's life in the Navy inspired another of his brilliantly inventive series, and Bernard Perlin's *After an Ambush* was based on his own experience on Samos; in Louis Guglielmi's *Odyssey for Moderns* featureless men crawled from a broken ship's hull on a lonely beach to gaze at a sun low in the sky; in Philip Guston's canvases of the war years, children with paper caps and carnival masks played soldier amidst the litter of a world which had no place for them. And a veteran of house-to-house fighting would respond coolly if at all to George Morris' abstraction of that title, which had begun with an episode in France, then shifted to the Orient, its forms reduced to mere hints of falling window blinds, Chinese shop signs, and the guns and teeth of Japanese soldiers.

But the full impact of the war years on the minds of

artists was only afterward and slowly to reveal itself. In the meantime it seemed that the camera was readier than the brush to record the immediate moment, and the makers of documentary films rose superbly to the occasion, Paul Strand with *Native Land* in 1942, and Frank Capra in 1943 with a series compiled largely from newsreels to be shown to soldiers under the caption *Why We Fight*. Walt Disney contributed to the education of fighting men with an ingenious animated cartoon, *The Grain That Built a Hemisphere*, suggesting a new use for this medium. Among the films for whose circulation the OWI was responsible, *Bomber* had a running commentary which Carl Sandburg had written; John Ford's Technicolor *Battle of Midway* was made during the engagement; the Army's *Memphis Belle*, also in color, was the story of a flying fortress in action. Here were motion pictures with a new and shattering dynamism, a split-second brilliance of light and color, a masterly perception of how images can be built toward a climax of meaning. These films came nearer perhaps than any of the visual arts to taking the full measure of this great epic of human agony, strength, and courage.

The epic was near its close when President Roosevelt, just two months before he died, spoke his prophecy and his warning on the twelfth of February, 1945: "The point in history at which we stand is full of promise and of danger. . . . We have a chance . . . to use our influence in favor of a more united and cooperating world." On August 6, the atomic bomb burst over Hiroshima, and on the same day the UN established an Educational, Scientific and Cultural Organization one of whose aims was to help the artist find his place in a single world.

These two events could stand as symbols of the contradictory years that followed, years which saw Truman's effort to keep alive the idealism and the farsightedness of New Deal days, America's generous assumption of her responsibilities as a great and prosperous nation to those less privileged; saw also the inconclusive war in Korea, the struggle to contain a former ally turned enemy as the tide of Russian power and influence advanced in Eastern Europe and Asia, the national elections which brought to politics men of narrow concepts and demagogic motives, the honest fears bred by the race for superiority in new weapons which could wipe man from the earth. War, one had once more to realize, is no mere interruption of the nation's life, and nothing afterward can be what it was. War had taught people to see in black and white, had summoned energies which could now be misdirected, had suppressed freedoms which were not easily restored, had led men to think in terms of power rather than of ideas and moral values. The liberal who now surveyed America was inclined to agree with Max Lerner's conclusion of 1957 that the nation was on "the descending arc of its inner social and moral vigor."

This Cold War climate, in which a Senator could disrupt whole departments of government with reckless charges of subversion and his imitators could destroy those whose task is the development of men's power to think for themselves; in which, as Waldemar Kaempffert said, "the exigencies of war determine the course that science seems destined to pursue"; in which those mighty instruments for mass information, the press, radio, and television, were becoming instruments for mass persuasion—this climate was not one in which the artist could feel at home, as he had in the 1930's, or think any longer that he was responsible, in the words of MacLeish in that period, for providing "an image of mankind in which man can again believe."

The architect, the painter, the sculptor found themselves in a society which no longer regarded art as a public necessity but as a private luxury. In spite of a wide and growing awareness of art by the great public, that public was, as Lloyd Goodrich observed, a spectator rather than a supporter; the contemporary artist must rely for the actual purchase of his work on the small minority of Americans which comprised the museums, schools, colleges, foundations, and private collectors. A Joint Artists-Museums Committee, formed in 1950, worked out a code for remunerating the artist for the public exhibition of his work, and ways and means were discussed by which he could also benefit from its commercial reproduction; books and articles multiplied in the effort to extend public knowledge of what he was trying to do; meanwhile the boom in business of the 1950's was reflected in the doubling of the number of commercial galleries in Detroit and Chicago, in the twenty-five in Los Angeles, the five in Seattle, the twenty-five in Dallas and Houston. Nevertheless, Bernard S. Myers' survey discovered in 1957, as Elizabeth McCausland had in 1946, that the majority of artists were unable to support themselves by their art alone.

One fact was clear: no artist need dream of that large-scale encouragement of art by government which marked the age of Roosevelt. Delegates from a dozen art organizations formed in 1948 a Committee on Government and Art under the chairmanship of Lloyd Goodrich, and six years later submitted a report to President Eisenhower with the establishment of a Federal Advisory Commission on the Arts as its central idea; but when appropriate bills were introduced in 1955 and in revised form a year later, action upon them was frustrated by the old familiar arguments. To read the report of the hearings by a House Committee is to find one's self back in the days which preceded the death of the Federal Projects: this was not a proper area for the expenditure of federal funds; mediocrity would become the standard; the hard competitive way to success was the best way; in short, no budgetary arguments were justified on behalf of an activity which could not prove its "absolute necessity."

When the government did sponsor art in the form of exhibitions which were intended to help in explaining ourselves to other peoples of the world, these shows sometimes bore the marks of a timidity bred by previous attacks by cultural vigilantes upon the State Department, or failed, because selection was entrusted to people of strong stylistic bias, to be a fair cross section of American achievement. A London show of American art in 1955 oddly ignored several artists of major talent who graced the 1930's, in its apparent effort to emphasize the most advanced and daring of the experimentalists; and Emily Genauer's strictures on the Brussels Fair exhibit of 1958, which by its one-sided choice missed an opportunity "to demonstrate to many millions of visitors from all over the world the importance, the vitality and the diversity of creative life in America today," applied in some degree to previous official efforts of this kind. The paintings sent in the summer of 1959 to the American exhibition in Moscow were admirably chosen by a jury of impartial experts, but they were bitterly attacked in Congress.

The creative freedom of the wide-ranging prewar years no longer existed when the Nebraska legislature exploded in anger over a "square bull" in its mural, when San Francisco patriots objected to a reference to Russia in a painting whose theme was the formation of the UN, and when citizens of Dallas tried to suppress an exhibition because it included the work of artists whose political ideas had been questioned. For the victims of the new Philistinism, Huntington Hartford's complaint that artists were too indifferent to the taste of the average man had a hollow ring, as did the pronouncement of one politician that those who failed to describe the beauty of America in a simple style that everyone could understand were enemies of their country.

Small wonder that the most obvious and pervasive aspect of the arts in the postwar period was a deepened sense of alienation, and the artistic practices which that sense engendered; some of the most bitter condemnations of our time came from the mouths and pens of writers and artists. When Stephen Spender compared the 1950's with the 1930's he concluded that his generation had been fortunate to be young at a time when it was possible to commit one's self to a great human cause without loss of individuality; the painter Robert Motherwell wrote that the modern states as we have known them have all been enemies of the artist, whose refusal to identify himself with the aims and values of modern society left him with no vital connection to it save that of opposition.

For Motherwell, as for other troubled artists, there was no alternative to formalism and the isolated development of his own vision, so long as society was dominated by the love of property and the pursuit of power. Clement Greenberg in 1949 declared that the only important movement of the time was an abstraction purged of all irrelevant context whether religious, poetic, or mystical. Its practitioners, as Adolph Gottlieb saw them a few years later, would seek no help from groups outside their own circle, or from a public which seemed to feel no need for the artistic expression of its needs and purposes, but they would accept as a fact "the stony ignorance of aesthetic illiterates" and would cheerfully exercise a freedom whose other face was alienation.

When the artists and writers of the avant-garde came to consider that popular culture which depends on the mass media for its diffusion, they took a dim view of its present qualities and future prospects, echoing the conviction of André Malraux that, in the absence of a collective faith, there can be no "people," hence no modern art for the masses, but only the trashy arts of delectation, the momentary pleasure of the motion picture palace, the sentimental sex appeal of the magazine illustration. The indictment was more explicit on some of the pages of *The Scene before You,* a series of essays by several authors who probed the nation's culture in 1955: the mannerisms of the highbrow motion picture, its effort to transform a simple, direct, and popular medium in order to "improve the world through art"; the radio soap dramas "where the drabness and stupidity of life are celebrated"; "the magnetic emptiness" of most comic strips; the "glossy mediocrity" of *Time* and *Life,* which contained the "best imitation of thought and feeling that the machine can produce."

Greenberg regretted the modern breakdown of cultural authority and the unwillingness of a swollen public to abide by the judgment of its betters. Perhaps it was the effort to restore this authority which gave the critic of the 1950's so prominent a part, and impelled Randall Jarrell to call ours an Age of Criticism in which the writer, once a mediator between art and the layman, had become a joyless, long-winded and self-important oracle, speaking a jargon as institutionalized as that of a sociologist, until the clues to a labyrinth had themselves become a labyrinth. This was the New Criticism, frequently obscure, whose practitioners behaved as though a work of art were a body to be coldly dissected with much learned talk of symbols and a degree of psychoanalysis.

Philip Guston, *Martial Memory*

City Art Museum, St. Louis, Mo.

Too often critics whose loyalties were to the avant-garde wrote comments which were the literary equivalent, rather than the clarification, of complex and difficult paintings and sculptures. And their sharpest weapons were reserved for that persistent group of artists for whom the word "humanist" was not a term of reproach. In the *Art News,* Manny Farber characterized Jack Levine as a tired cartoonist with "hackneyed, politically-toned images . . . a cliché-slanted criticism of politicians, law enforcers, high society, criminals and well-fixed business men"; Adolph Gottlieb, in words attributed to him by Selden Rodman, put the issue even more sharply: "The social realist wants to charm you or win you over. But the abstract expressionist says to the public (more honestly): 'You're stupid. We despise you. We don't *want* you to like us.' "

This unsocial mood, although prevalent in the world of art, was by no means universal. Against the exclusiveness of the doctrinaires could be set the far-ranging discernment of James T. Soby's comments on contemporary work; and a fair description of the postwar climate should include David Riesman's observations on popular taste. He found a surprisingly rapid growth of sophistication in the motion picture and its audiences; he noted the sale of good books in drugstores, the diffusion of the best music through records, affording to thousands the satisfaction once enjoyed by the cultured few. "My effort," he wrote at the end of *The Lonely Crowd,* "has been . . . directed to closing the gap generally believed to exist between high culture and mass culture." And Jacques Barzun, conceding that machine technologies were being used to produce what was cheap, standardized, and predictable, reminded his readers that the same techniques made possible a democratic culture. Our commitment, he said, was to freedom, but also to equality. "The first thing democracy has to be is inclusive."

A vigorous affirmation of the artist's responsibility appeared rather inconspicuously at a time when collectors avidly patronized the most daring of the experimentalists, when museums featured their works, dealers shrewdly promoted them, and such publications as the *Art Digest, Art News,* and *Art in America* gave increasing space to their ideas and achievements. In 1953 a group of artists published the first of three small brochures, under the name *Reality.* Its contributors were as diverse in style and conception as Ernest Fiene, Reginald Marsh, William Thon, Isabel Bishop, Edward Hopper, and Leon Kroll; what united them at this moment was an unabashed "respect and love for the human qualities in painting" and a resentment against museums and critics who in their opinion were making of art "a thing of cults and fads, of obscurity and snobbery." All the possibilities of art must be explored; but

> we nevertheless believe that texture and accident, like color, design, and all the other elements of painting, are only the means to a larger end. . . . We are asked to believe that art is for the future, that only an inner circle is capable of judging contemporary painting, that everybody else must take it on faith. . . . The dogmatic repetition of these views has produced in the whole world of art an atmosphere of irresponsibility, snobbery and ignorance. . . . We will work to restore to art its freedom and dignity as a living language.

Clearly, it was the nature of the artist's function in America which had become the central issue. On the one hand we have the dictum of Greenberg, "The naturalistic art of our time is unredeemable," his brilliant championing of "an art which refuses to serve ends other than itself." On the other hand there is Ben Shahn's rejoinder to a group of young abstract expressionists, "You guys are just afraid of being emotionally involved in anything bigger than yourselves. Is Giotto's *Entombment* more meaningful if you don't know who's being buried and what the angels are lamenting about?" and his belief that, in a period which negates human sovereignty and reduces men from their status as ultimate value to that of industrial and political particles, the natural reaction of the artist would be strongly toward bringing man back into focus as the center of importance.

Between these two conceptions lies all that was daring, obscure, sensational, stirring, compassionate, hateful, sharply intellectual, violently expressive, or warmly fraternal in the art of the Cold War years. Any reconciliation between the two seemed as remote as the "united and cooperating" world of Roosevelt's dream.

CHAPTER 35 / ARCHITECTURE OF LOGIC AND IMAGINATION

Building activity in wartime America was largely confined to the speedy erection of homes for the workers who converged on factory centers and shipyards; as often as not, these structures were architecture without architects. Eighty-five individual houses at Windsor Locks, Connecticut, in 1942 were trimly designed by Hugh Stubbins, Jr., with vertical sidings of redwood in contrast to sun blinds of white, but there was neither time nor money to create a landscape environment for them. More permanently planned in 1943 were the six hundred units at Los Angeles whose shapes and proportions Richard Neutra had skillfully adapted to the sloping ground toward the shipyard and the sea. At Clifton, New York, the three hundred and fifty families of "Aquackanonk," thanks to Henry Churchill, could enjoy some of the physical and mental satisfactions which prewar experiment had made possible: informally curving streets, parking spaces near houses, blind roads, and shrubbery screens for neighborhood privacy. With variously colored roof shingles and exterior wall panels Churchill gave individuality to structures whose basic plan was similar.

These were years not so much for building as for planning, for consolidating modern principles and recent experience, for anticipating future needs; and the published comments on the art of building acquired a cutting edge. The Metropolitan Life Insurance Company announced that it would build Stuyvesant Town for twenty-four thousand New Yorkers; and in the *Architectural Forum* for June, 1943, Henry Churchill described the project as a walled company town with no provision for civic or educational activities, a pseudo community to replace eighteen blocks of slums, and an unsound financial venture save from the short-range view of the Metropolitan. G. E. Kidder Smith documented with photographs his "Tragedy of American Architecture"—museum steps which exhausted the visitor before he reached the classic portal, whole streets of boxes with holes for windows, the incoherence of San Francisco and the visual torment of Times Square. In the last year of the war Frank Lloyd Wright once more condemned the city as a "man-trap of monstrous dimensions" and rejected as aids to architecture the arrogant scientist, the too machinelike government, and that man of makeshifts, the politician.

It was expected that, when, the war ended, more than a million new homes would be required each year; and one could predict the character of the best of them from the house which Philip Johnson designed for himself at Cambridge, Massachusetts, during the war years, with prefabricated walls and with columns and beams of laminated wood, and from the work of John Funk, Carl Koch, Fred Keck, Gardner Dailey, John Yeon, and Harwell Harris, which set a high standard for the dwelling of moderate size. These and others were finding a synthesis between geometry and feeling. The color and texture of native materials enlivened surfaces which the first modernists had made coldly austere; glass was used with less extravagance and mannerism; space was articulated as much for privacy as for continuity. Lescaze spoke for this generation of designers when he defined the artist-architect as a man with a passion for his art, a profound concern for other men and the kind of lives they lead, and a mastery of his craft. Both reason and imagination have played their part in what he has done; "architecture is the art of producing beautifully what is useful."

This concept found rich expression in the renewed activity of the prosperous postwar years, when the demand for new homes, for industrial and commercial structures, for schools and churches, seemed insatiable. Surveying them as a whole, Henry-Russell Hitchcock was to find no fundamental feature which had not been foreshadowed in the years before the war; as Philip Johnson said, "The battle of modern architecture has long been won." King Canute, to be sure, is always with us, and in *The Golden City* Henry Hope Reed, Jr., announced that the modernist tide was ebbing and saw the city of the future as a formalized group of monumental structures in the Beaux-Arts style with neoclassical colonnades, porticoes, and sculpture-laden façades.

No such attacks, however, could shake the position of those acknowledged major figures, Le Corbusier, Gropius, Mies, and Wright, the average of whose ages at the close of the war was nearly sixty-seven and each of whom embodied a ripened concept of the art: Le Corbusier in the massive forms of his apartment building for Marseilles; Gropius subordinating his own personality to the teamwork of his Architects' Collaborative and urging the designer to be the master and not the slave of technology; Mies achieving an austere and puritanical perfection of line, mass, and proportion to prove his dictum, "Less is more"; Wright the romantic individualist designing the Johnson Wax Company research tower with a spinal column, ribs, and a

Kennedy, Koch, De Mars, Rapson and Brown,
Eastgate Apartments, Cambridge, Mass.
Ezra Stoller photo

skin of brick and glass, giving the First Unitarian Church at Madison, Wisconsin, the gesture of praying hands, and writing articles and books whose central ideas he had set forth half a century before.

Each of these men grappled in his own way with an age whose technical inventiveness exceeded its power to assimilate, to humanize invention; and the alternatives were sharply defined: Wright scorned the "boxation" of Mies and Philip Johnson, while the latter called Wright the greatest architect of the nineteenth century, a pure poet who had not, like Mies, created a style. Surveying our "current drab disorder," Richard Neutra found it conducive to endless nervous strain and recommended that the designer make use of new scientific knowledge of the structure and functioning of the human organism to help man's "search in space for happiness and equilibrium" and to save the race from the fatal consequences of a misguided industrial technology. A similar recognition inspired Sigfried Giedion to write *Mechanization Takes Command* and the essays of *Architecture, You and Me.*

For critics and planners alike, these issues found their most insistent form in what the editors of *Fortune* called "the exploding metropolis." Condemnation of the large American city was based on its failure to achieve a wholesome balance between private and community living. Apartment life, for example, was not to be judged by the fortunate tenants of Mies' shimmering towers on the shore of Lake Michigan, or of 100 Memorial Drive in Cambridge, designed by Kennedy, Koch, De Mars, Rapson and Brown, whose balconies overlooked the broad Charles River Basin. The average apartment offered only a cramped and robotlike existence to the tenants in their cells; and for those of still lower income dilapidated structures were replaced by bleak and monotonous new buildings which increased the former congestion and would themselves soon acquire dilapidation. Meanwhile that American obsession, the motor car, demanded traffic "improvements" which only intensified the creeping paralysis of cities. As the metropolitan chaos spread outward to engulf former suburbs, bulldozers destroyed more than a million acres each year of fields and woods on the fringes of big towns.

By way of solution Wright called for the total dispersal of cities and offered as alternative his Broadacre City, which would space people too widely for genuine community; more reasonably, Lewis Mumford urged that cities be replanned with sane limits set upon density and with a decentralizing of commercial and industrial activities. Studying those new communities, privately financed, which were rising in the postwar years, Mumford found in "Fresh Meadows," built in Queens by Vorhees, Walker, Foley and Smith for the New York Life Insurance Company, an exhilarating antidote to Stuyvesant Town. It covered an area one-fifth as large as Central Park and was spaciously and imaginatively planned for those who occupied its varied and organically related houses and apartments and walked its intervening lawns and parks to well-designed stores, nursery school, and community garages.

By contrast, Levitt and Company transformed a Long Island potato farm into a huge pattern of nearly identical houses, thanks to mass-production techniques and a highly organized system for planning, building, and marketing homes with incredible speed. The more than thirty thousand Americans who had bought or rented houses there by 1949 for a surprisingly low cost could enjoy radiant heating, built-in kitchen equipment, and many other conveniences, but not individual variations of design, intervals of space and light, which would have been too slow and too expensive to manage. An air view of Levittown in that year bore the alarming caption: "Will be three times as big by 1950." Wider lots and more variety in the relation of house to lot were in the plans of 1951 for a second Levittown near Morrisville in Bucks County, Pennsylvania; and a third was to be built in New Jersey a few years later.

In these quick-profit developments and along the streets of American towns the "magazine houses" were a familiar sight during these years, houses which embodied new devices for comfort and health, for less cluttered and messy living, but whose design, at the hands of men who had no real sense of proportion,

Karl Koch and Associates, Parton House, Dorset, Vermont

Ezra Stoller photo

Twitchell and Rudolph, W. R. Healy House, Sarasota, Fla.

Ezra Stoller photo

texture or color, was usually commonplace and frequently ugly and ill-adjusted to the site, with picture windows which had no picture to justify them. They were the diluted and distorted versions of the homes designed by architects who were creative artists for more affluent and sophisticated clients throughout the country, and to survey the work of Yeon, Harris, Neutra, Eames, and their like is to measure the difference between expressive utterance and stammering misquotation. These structures had in common a fine integration with the natural site, a delicate and lively sense of color which owed something to modern painting, a fondness for the single story, a tendency to make space flow rather than to chop it up with partitions, and to relate indoors more intimately with outdoors by means of large glass areas.

What gave these structures their variety was the skill and inventiveness with which their designers used the materials native to a given location, combined them with new materials, revived local building traditions, and took advantage of topographical and climatic peculiarities. Some of the ideas which, in thoroughly modern form, gave distinction to the Smith House in Stockton, California, by Wurster, Bernard and Emmons, came from the early ranch houses of that region and the bungalows of a later day; Harwell Harris made superb use of the Californian redwood, and his Los Angeles house for Ralph Johnson, half concealed by the luxuriant foliage of its three-level sloping site, effectively exposed its wooden framing both inside and out. In Portland, Oregon, John Yeon gave character to houses by the varied use of plywood sheathing and vertical battens; at Siesta Key in Florida, Ralph Twitchell and Paul Rudolph designed the W. R. Healy house to resist insects and hurricanes with a single floor of concrete raised on posts and a curving roof of steel bars covered with a flexible and weatherproof plastic and anchored down with tie-rods. The board-and-batten siding of the Parton house at Dorset, Vermont, by Carl Koch and Associates, was in the native vernacular, but not the cantilever which suspended its living room over a mill stream.

Charles Eames' Case Study House for *Arts and Decoration* was built on the Pacific shore at Santa Monica as an experiment in getting a maximum of space at minimum cost, using for its steel frame the standard elements produced in factories and enlivening this frame with panels of plywood, glass, and stucco whose bright reds, blues, and whites suggested a three-dimensional Mondrian. At Montecito, California, Richard Neutra devised a pinwheel plan for the Tremaine house, whose masonry was of the local sandstone, whose great glass spaces under sweeping horizontals gave breathtaking glimpses of the great trees and boulders of the near distance and of the sea and mountains beyond them, and whose subtle transitions of plan and of materials outward from its core seemed to join it imperceptibly with nature.

Aristocrats among these dwellings were Philip Johnson's own house at New Canaan and the Farnsworth House by Mies at Fox River, Illinois: the former was a glass box whose only inner divisions were suggested by the arrangement of its furnishings and sculpture, save for a cylindrical brick core with bathroom and fireplace—a tour de force which practically eliminated the distinction between indoors and out; also mainly of glass, the Mies house suspended its roof and floor from eight white columns of steel, and its exquisite proportions and Italian marble steps and flooring gave it, in the words of Hugh Morrison, "an Olympian serenity."

When the architect of the late forties and the fifties turned from the designing of homes to that of factories, industrial research centers, department stores, office

Richard Neutra, Warren Tremaine House, Montecito, Cal.
Wayne Andrews photo

buildings, and banks, his problem was to produce not only a structure beautiful in itself through scale, proportion, line, and color but one which would symbolize activities of an impersonal, sharply defined, and practical nature. Here the clean, efficient, orderly, repetitive, and solidly secure forms of the modern were peculiarly appropriate; and the predominant type of these years came to be the tall smooth slab which owed much to Le Corbusier and Mies and whose curtain walls were of thin metal sheets or great expanses of glass reflecting its neighbors and the sky. Since, as Lewis Mumford reminds us, no basic advances in skyscraper engineering have been made since the turn of the century, the new look was mainly the result of ingenious but skin-deep changes.

Pietro Belluschi's office building of 1948 for the Equitable Savings and Loan Association in Portland, Oregon, had a sheath of aluminum and glass of which no part projected more than seven-eights of an inch. Wallace Harrison and Max Abramowitz achieved another surface variation by clothing their Alcoa Building in Pittsburgh in 1952 with prefabricated sheets of aluminum, stamped with a repeat pattern, each of which was one story high and could quickly be set in place from inside. To secure more light and visual effect, Skidmore, Owings and Merrill, with Gordon Bunshaft as chief designer, used less than half their site in New York in 1952 for the tower of Lever House, raising it upon stainless steel piers which left an open arcade at street level; their twenty-four stories of blue-green glass were open on three sides to air and sun. Quality of space, as Mumford said, here took precedence over mere quantity. Facing Lever House on Park Avenue in 1959 was the Seagram Building by Mies and Philip Johnson, standing back from the street on a pink granite platform with pools and shrubs to modify the austerity of a shaft of thirty-eight stories with amber-grey glass and with mullions, spandrels, and portico columns of dull bronze.

When Skidmore, Owings and Merrill designed the Fifth Avenue branch of the Manufacturers Trust Company, they dared to set a five-story bank with a façade of glass among the shadows of far taller structures and proclaimed its function by giving the passer-by a glimpse of the great door of its vaults. In spite of the difference in style, Henry James might have praised this luminous and handsome structure, as he had praised the New York Public Library, for its "willingness to present itself as seated rather than as standing." One other commercial structure of modest dimensions, Wright's V. C. Morris store of 1949 in San Francisco's narrow Maiden Lane, teased the shopper by giving him only a glimpse, through the round entrance doorway of its otherwise unbroken buff brick front, of the wide graceful ramp that curled upward around its circular space to a second floor under a ceiling of plastic bubbles.

Wright's hatred of architectural slabs was no secret, and in the 1950's other and less arbitrary minds were beginning to judge their limitations. When the most ambitious of them all, the United Nations Secretariat, was completed in 1950, the work of nine architects whose chairman was Wallace Harrison, Mumford attacked its "arid neutralism." This forty-story slice whose narrow ends were covered with grey-green marble and whose east and west façades were huge sheets of green-tinted glass, impressed many with its hard and glittering perfection; but Mumford accused it not only of functional inadequacies but of failure to express in any degree the high and humane purposes the UN was supposed to serve.

A similar revulsion led Allan Temko some years later to ask if there were not some golden mean between skin-and-bones architecture and the exuberance of Wright. Considering recent work by SOM, including a Connecticut General Life Insurance Building near Hartford which was a horizontal version of their formula, Temko decided that a packaged article was being supplied for all regions and for many uses. There was something phantasmal, he wrote, about buildings which owed much to the almost fanatical puritanism of the Miesian aesthetics.

Skidmore, Owings and Merrill, Lever House, N.Y.C.

Wayne Andrews photo

One brilliant effort to modify chill perfection was the General Motors Technical Center at Detroit by the

Saarinen, Saarinen and Associates, General Motors Technical Center, Detroit, Mich.

Wayne Andrews photo

Eero Saarinen and Associates, T.W.A. Terminal, Idlewild Airport, N.Y. (model)

Richard Knight photo, courtesy of the architects

Saarinens, whose well-ordered units had a sharp severity of outline but whose exterior walls were given panels of glazed brick in bright blue-greens, chartreuse, and burnt orange which suggested the art of ancient Persia; along the sides of the dynamometer building the exhaust stacks of blue-black formed a handsome and monumental colonnade. Another architect who could clothe usefulness with beauty was Edward Stone, devising perforated grilles of cast stone to create flickering patterns of light and shadow. These lacelike screens encircled his American pavilion for the Brussels Fair of 1958; in delicate white and gold behind slender gilt columns they were reflected in the lagoon of his American Embassy at New Delhi, a structure thoroughly contemporary yet magically suggestive of the Taj Mahal. And when the Museum of Modern Art showed four models in 1959 under the title, "Architecture and Imagery," including a T.W.A. terminal for Idlewild Airport by Eero Saarinen whose winglike roofs suggested the excitement of flying, not one of them had a trace of the slab formula.

In the same year Richard Buckminster Fuller designed a sports stadium for Oklahoma City; and his gold-tinted "geodesic" dome for the main display of the American Exhibition in Moscow, with its seemingly weightless web of metal in patterns which suggested those of molecules and crystals, was a contribution to the aesthetics as well as the engineering of structure. Since 1927, when Fuller's design for an octagonal house hung from a central mast offended conservatives, he had devised one startling scheme after another in his effort to enclose great spaces with a minimum weight of material and expenditure of time, basing his work on intricate mathematical calculations and what he called "good geometry"; in the 1950's he came into his own when his spidery domes were put to many uses—a restaurant at Woods Hole, Massachusetts, a rotunda for the Ford Motor Company at Dearborn, Michigan, shelters for State Department exhibitions in faraway countries, mobile military shelters, and Air Force radomes. In the work of Fuller, as in that of Stone and others, new structural devices were being

Caudill, Rowlett, Scott and Associates, Central High School, San Angelo, Texas

Ulrich Meisel photo

used to create a "shape-architecture" of bold and complex originality.

This liberation from cliché helped the architects of schools, museums, and churches, whose functions are often complicated, whose human connotations are subtle, whose values and aspirations elude sharp definition. No traveler who remembered the drab and dangerous schoolhouses of the past and our falsely classical high schools could fail to conclude that here our best designers had surpassed themselves. These thousands of new schools met the practical needs of education, and their orientation was wisely related to climate, light, and traffic; a one-story scheme eliminated stair-climbing and reduced fire hazards; study and play areas were well integrated; structure was frankly revealed; glass was abundantly but not excessively used; the clean and well-ventilated classrooms could easily be changed in size and shape, and had a controllable balance of lighting from windows, clerestory, and ceiling; covered walks gave shelter.

The best of these schools, like the series in Sarasota, Florida, were the result of cooperation between educators and designers who could give an individual character to such institutions. A long vaulted canopy of concrete with low-rounded arches to shelter arriving pupils distinguished the High School at West Columbia, Texas, by Donald Barthelme and Associates in 1952; in the Elementary School at Vista, California, Maynard Lyndon used gay colors and scaled his details to the size of small children; at San Carlos, San Mateo, Campbell, and San Louis Obispo, Ernest Kump and Mark Falk found ingenious and unexpected ways to use new material. The pictures of eighty-nine recent American schools shown in 1957 at the International Conference on Public Education in Geneva suggested, however, that in the hands of less gifted men the average school had the uniformity of a closely followed formula and a modern version of the institutional look.

When a contemporary building was to be placed on an existing university or college campus, the architect was sure to be criticized for shattering a stylistic "harmony" which did not exist, and attacked by nostalgic graduates for whom education was symbolized for eternity by Georgian brick, McKim colonnades of marble and granite, or ivy-carpeted Gothic. Walter Gropius had been thus defeated in 1938 by ignorant alumnae of Wheaton College; twelve years later there was a mixed but less hostile response to his Graduate Center for Harvard University, eight severely designed buildings of buff brick and stone forming several courtyards, linked by covered walks and enlivened by the decorations of Miró, Arp, and Albers. On the steeply sloping campus of the University of California at Berkeley in 1941, William Wurster had managed to give his women's Dormitory a sense of belonging graciously to its verdant location; on the shore of the Charles, the Senior Dormitory of Massachusetts Institute of Technology, the work of Alvar Aalto in 1948, had the plan of a letter W; thanks to its serpentine façade of rather blank brick, all its rooms looked on the river. For Sarah Lawrence College in Bronxville, New York, Marcel Breuer designed a Students Art Center whose compact interlocking shapes moved upward from a glass-fronted one-story living room to the stage house at the rear.

It seldom falls to the lot of an architect to design a whole college from the ground up; yet Mies and Wright were engaged at about the same time to do just that and, in so doing, to demonstrate the polarity of their attitudes. In a flat area cleared of Chicago slums, the

Mies van der Rohe
Illinois Institute of Technology, Chicago, Ill.
Hedrich-Blessing photo

Frank L. Wright, Administration Bldg.,
Florida Southern College, Lakeland, Fla.
Wayne Andrews photo

Illinois Institute of Technology was conceived by Mies as a group of buildings whose proportions were variations of a module and whose relationship was determined by an invisible but felt geometry of space. On this rectangular campus of one hundred and ten acres, the apartment buildings for students and faculty, the commons, the school of architecture, the buildings for metallurgy and engineering, the alumni hall, the chapel, played subtle variations on a single theme; their beauty was the abstract beauty of austere and perfect form.

In an entirely different setting among orange groves beside a lake, Florida Southern College became in the hands of Wright an informally spaced group of buildings connected by winding covered walks, whose unity was that of bright foliage, blue water, and the white of cement blocks out of which the architect shaped a library, a chapel, an administration building, and many other structures each of which had its own free and utterly unexpected shapes. Euclidian intellect and romantic imagination could have found no more startling a contrast than that between Chicago and Lakeland. The one embodied man's ability to give his chaotic and ugly environment the shapes of reason and logic; the other found a happy synthesis between man and nature at her most luxuriant and prodigal.

Related to the architecture of education was that of the museum. When the Whitney Museum of American Art moved uptown to a site adjoining the Museum of Modern Art, the chief problem of Auguste Noel was to find a tactful relation to the latter; the pleasant interiors were designed by Bruce Buttfield, and the galleries were lighted with fluorescent units through a ceiling, although daylight was available on three sides of this four-story building. A new Community Art Center of the fifties at Fort Worth, Texas, by W. G. Clarkson and Company, was less remarkable for its severe, blocklike exterior than for its spacious and well-integrated studios, workshops, galleries, library, and theater, all planned to serve a progressively-minded city of three hundred thousand.

The Guggenheim Museum in New York was the final major project of Frank Lloyd Wright, who did not live to see its inauguration. Its last scaffolding was being removed in April of 1959 when the master, who a few weeks later would have reached ninety, was carried to his grave at Taliesin on a farm wagon with family, friends, and students walking behind him. With undiminished audacity he had made the main structure of this gallery for nonobjective art a huge concrete mass whose shape was determined by a continuous spiral ramp expanding as it rose toward the light of a glass dome. Edgar Kaufmann, Jr., found here a complete unity between the free forms, the ever-changing natural light, the novel handling of interior space, and the modern works of art to be seen in it; for him it was "the clearest and most powerful statement of architectural and artistic liberation" yet made by Wright.

Eero Saarinen, Chapel, Mass.
Institute of Technology, Cambridge, Mass.
Wayne Andrews photo

The prospects of a free and modern approach to the designing of religious edifices had greatly improved between the time when Wright's design for Unity Temple provoked parish opposition and the year which saw the Madison Unitarians helping to build his church there; but the architect's problem was still one of difficult resolution between the wish to be contemporary in spirit and the attachment to traditional forms by which a given faith had been ritualized. The simplest solution was to modernize without basically changing the general shape and interior features, as the Saarinens did at Columbus, Indiana, or Belluschi in the Central Lutheran Church at Eugene, Oregon, with its severe and spaciously proportioned interior of brick and stained firwood, or John Carter in Saint George's Episcopal Chapel at Durham, New Hampshire, where arches of laminated wood framed a chancel window by Robert Sowers with blue and white rectangular shapes of glass in abstract patterns. Philip Johnson designed a ceiling of ethereal lightness, a series of gracefully curving vaults, for a synagogue at Port Chester, New York.

Among the more venturesome concepts was the design by Harrison and Abramowitz for a church at

Stamford, Connecticut; and Eero Saarinen's chapel for Massachusetts Institute of Technology in Cambridge, completed in 1956, was a windowless brick cylinder intended for quiet individual meditation. Around its base ran a moat whose reflected light, through round arched openings at the base of the chapel, tinged the lower walls of an interior whose plainness was relieved by Harry Bertoia's abstract altar screen of bright metal fragments on vertical wires. The spire by Theodore Roszak suggested religious aspiration without denominational connotations. Saarinen shut out the world; at Madison, Wisconsin, Wright welcomed it with an auditorium filled with light from the high glass windows behind the podium, with surfaces which sloped inward as they went up to meet an oddly peaked roof and gave the entire structure, the less respectful said, the look of a sitting hen. For Wright, this was but one of many possible forms for churches: the most striking feature of his design for Beth Sholem Synagogue in Philadelphia was a luminous prism with a copper crown; his Greek Orthodox Church for Milwaukee was drawn as a small and dignified building of surprisingly classical feeling; for the Christian Science Church at Bolinas, California, he planned two reinforced concrete domes the lower of which was the reverse of the upper. Meanwhile, the inevitable copyists vulgarized the tentlike shape of his Madison Meeting House by scattering devotional wigwams over the country.

In the course of its postwar development, American architecture proved that it had lost that fear of embellishment which had marked its previous and more narrowly dogmatic phase, and its makers called more often upon the sculptor for collaboration, sensing a kinship with the latter's desire to exploit unfamiliar materials and new techniques for constructing three-dimensional patterns in space. Bertoia's screen for the Manufacturers Trust Company was sixteen feet high and seventy in length and fashioned of steel fused with brass, copper and nickel. Richard Lippold's skeletonized *World Tree* of stainless steel matched the spare reticence of Gropius' Graduate Center at Harvard University; Roszak's aluminum spire rose forty-five feet above the M.I.T. chapel; Percival Goodman commissioned Herbert Ferber's relief, *Burning Bush,* whose writhing shapes of soldered copper, brass, lead, and tin sharply defined themselves against the wooden façade of B'Nai Israel Synagogue at Millburn, New Jersey, as did Ibram Lassaw's welded bronze *Pillar of Fire* on the wall of Temple Beth El in Springfield, Mass.

This new collaboration, with mutual benefit to architect and sculptor, was an important phenomenon of the time, proving that modern sculpture need be no mere graceful addition to structure but rather an integral part of it, its abstract or semiabstract shapes and its variously gleaming textures a completion of the structure's meaning.

CHAPTER 36 / PAINTING AND SCULPTURE AT MIDCENTURY

The wandering critic who studied the annual Whitney survey in the fall of 1945, the huge compilation at the Carnegie Institute, *Painting in the United States,* and other shows of the moment, might search for a direction, a predominant approach, but find none. A portrait by Alexander James, a snow scene by Hobart Nichols reminded him that the academic naturalists are always with us; such artists of originality as Gropper and Guy Pène du Bois seemed caught in the meshes of their own style; a likeness by Eugene Speicher, clean, methodical, and workmanlike, was a reassurance that one need expect no surprises from him. The champions of the regional movement of the thirties seemed to have spent themselves, as national self-preoccupation gave place to something else in American minds. Marsh contributed another Burlesque scene to the Whitney show, and Hopper's familiar yellow-greens and acidulous blue shadows were in *August in the City*. Ivan Le Lorraine Albright created a new shudder with figure studies in which every physical blemish was patiently and ruthlessly itemized, and exhibited a painting with a funeral bouquet against a door which also suggested a coffin lid; and Emerson Burckhart's study of a Negro was likewise done in the varicose vein.

There was evidence of the continued vogue of the "primitive" in works by Grandma Moses, who at seventy-eight had begun her delightful snow scenes, with more than a casual reference to the Currier and Ives prints which she had known all her life. She believed in 1945 that she had made more than a thousand landscapes and genre scenes, and she produced them with the same regularity and tidy competence which lined her shelves with jam. A more rugged touch was in the portraits and street scenes of the ex-prize fighter and ex-saloonkeeper Mickey Walker. Far less authentic than either Grandma or Mickey were the church picnics and Arbor Day celebrations of Doris Lee, whose naïveté was of the voluntary sort.

Here and there among the exhibitions one found affirmations of the painter's affection for common men and his anger and pity for their present condition. In Jack Levine's *The Passing Show* (Mus. Mod. Art) a tired old man led his grandchild through the reek and decay of slums; Gregorio Prestopino, with a chunky strength which suggested Brueghel, painted episodes in the lives of men who caught streetcars in winter half-daylight and ate their sandwiches in the refuse of excavations. Abraham Rattner in 1939 had created color chords and variations in *Springtime Showers* of which few Americans were capable and a fascinating rhythm of repeated heads and umbrellas; now the debris of mutilated towns was piled up in his *City Still Life* (Walker Art Center). The eyes of Evergood's homeless children stabbed one's conscience; men and women moved with a forlorn dignity among the gutted buildings of Shahn's Italian landscapes, and on his poster of 1946 a boy with sleepless dark eyes and a face which hunger had aged before its time held out his empty hand.

In spite of these reminders that mankind had just faced one of its crucial moments, it seemed that for most painters the war and its memories were a mental ballast to be cast overboard as one rose above the immediate past. And it could not be said in 1945 that recent events had reconciled opposing factions in the world of art. Into the ranks of native experimentalists had come fresh recruits from Europe: Pavel Tchelitchew enriching surrealist imagery with his incredible draughtsmanship, and the Swiss Kurt Seligmann filled with images of horror, whose *Carnivora* (Smith College) was a nightmare in lurid pale tones; Amédée Ozenfant discovering here new shapes of cloud, waterfall, and mountain to be rendered with a cold clarity; Max Ernst, whose work was to be seen at Peggy Guggenheim's Gallery; Marc Chagall, who continued in America to weave his dreams of peasant childhood; André Masson with his "emblematic" landscapes of the new country; Fernand Léger, delighted by the superfluous energy and frankly bad taste of Americans; Yves Tanguy, whose brush responded to wider and emptier spaces than he had known before; Roberto Matta from Chile, whose white lines crackled like gunfire and whose shapes burst with the intolerable brilliance of bombs at night; Jean Hélion retaining in his new work the prison pallor of his days in a Nazi prison; the German expressionist Max Beckmann, once labeled "degenerate" by Hitler, coming when he was sixty-three with only three more years in which to teach and to paint his dense and monumental compositions.

Although America would not fundamentally change the art of these men, their work and that of other Europeans noticeably affected native painters. One could not fail to be reminded of Hans Arp by George L. Morris, to observe that Picasso's stark resolutions of form were in Byron Browne and the shrillness of his *Guernica* in the work of Stanley William Hayter. Would Milton Avery repay his debt to Matisse, and Arshile Gorky to Miró? The hostile critic saw weakness and danger in this emulation; the friendly one insisted that the language of art had become international. One thing was certain: the work of the innovators held the focus of attention in the galleries of 1945 by its intensity of utterance and by its liveliness of execution. Few canvases could hold their own beside Byron Browne's *Still Life in Primary Colors* or the strident reds and searing greens of Walter Quirt's intricate *Carnival.*

Four years of so-called "peace" had gone by when sixteen experts surveyed "The State of American Art" in the pages of the *Magazine of Art;* their comments were as varied as their points of view, but there was general agreement that no one style prevailed in America and that this pluralism was healthy. George H. Hamilton detected a search for the "delicate and often perilous equilibrium . . . between abstract design and expressive content"; and this greater subjectivity, this concern with intangibles beneath and beyond the fact, was indeed the main observable tendency of the years that followed.

Even painters who continued to practice a comparative naturalism came to be revalued in other terms, and the commentators on Edward Hopper, for example, spoke of his spiritual affirmation, his sensitiveness to "those hidden tensions which exist below the level of human intercourse," his "enigmatic drama," and the "alienating quality of his light." The pantheism and childlike fantasy of Charles Burchfield's earliest work now reappeared in more mature form after the interlude of robust and often satirical regionalism which had seen his *Promenade* and his *Civic Improvement;* the large watercolor of 1945, *An April Mood,* was a metaphor of decay and renewal, the brown earth waiting and the twisted trees gesturing toward ponderous and swollen clouds. (See color plate 21.)

The titles of Charles Sheeler's new canvases suggested a similar change of emphasis—*Incantation* in 1946 (Brooklyn Museum), *Architectural Cadences* in 1954. (See color plate 25.) There persisted the Yankee coolness, detachment, and bold confidence in the rational, the cleanly functioning, but Sheeler now played more freely with his barns and factories, whose shapes interpenetrated and whose colors more subtly provided the chords for an intricate visual music. Although there was no modification of previous method in *The Rock,* which kept Peter Blume busy from 1945 to 1948, its theme was more general than that of *Eternal City:* man's violent struggle to tear from the reluctant earth the materials for his building, in this case Wright's masterpiece "Falling Water."

Two younger artists, Irene Pereira and Loren MacIver, whose ages at the war's end were forty and thirty-six, had something in common in spite of the obvious contrast of their styles. The former was careful to distinguish her own art of abstraction, the natural human effort to summarize experience, to extract and distill its meaning, from that "abstract expressionism" of the moment which seemed to her fragmentary and nihilistic, a kind of subtraction. (See color plate 19.) Her "inquiry into the heart of meaning," her effort to help man to understand his place in the great scheme of things gave greater warmth and luminosity, less geometrical finality to such works as *Spring, Twelve O'Clock,* whose pale greens and fresh yellows were those of the hopeful season. The delicate art of MacIver explored the often deep and mysterious associations stirred by things as ordinary as a window shade, a battered shoe, a child's hopscotch pattern in chalk on the sidewalk. As though to say, there is more in these than meets the eye, she began with simple things to lead the observer, she explained, "by means of various manipulations of colors, objects and tensions toward a transformation and a reward." That reward was in *Oil Splatters and Leaves,* in *Naples Aquarium,* and in a magical *Venice* which was not a description of that golden city but its dreamlike reflection in one's memory. (See color plate 23.)

Dreams of a more horrible kind might have inspired a series of paintings done at the close of the war by Hyman Bloom, nightmares of flesh blasted by bombs or decomposing at Buchenwald. Bloom's synagogues with their crowded figures and hot colors now gave place to less sharply defined images and a palette which held the livid reds and purples of decomposition. In *Female Corpse,* in *The Anatomist* (see color plate 24), and in *Slaughtered Animal* (U. of Cal. at L.A.) he produced images of a terrible beauty.

A more delicate and elusive poetry was to be found in two painters whose otherworldliness and whose tendency to see with the mind's eye were fostered by contact with Oriental philosophy and art, Morris Graves and Mark Tobey. The former renewed these contacts after the war in Honolulu and Japan; the latter spent some time in a Zen Buddhist monastery. Graves' subtle intuition, his sense of the mystery of man's inner life, had already found a metaphor in forlorn winged creatures; now these emerged mysteriously from the shapes of Chinese ceremonial bronzes or stood in ethereal majesty against backgrounds of exquisite color, drawn with the swift grace and elegance of a master, an Audubon of the psyche. (See color plate 22.) Tobey, who noted that the "Pacific hiatus" was closing, found a parallel between the Zen pursuit of Enlightenment, a liberation of the self achieved through identification with all that one knows or sees, and the modern artist's effort to assimilate and to master the intricacies of his life and to find a path through the endless continuities of what Tobey called the geography of the imagination. His "white writing" caught the convulsive turmoil of city crowds, the enveloping silence of fog, the uncountable stars in the vast night sky, the spinning surface of the earth. (See color plate 26.)

This struggle to relate the self with the non-self carried many a painter irresistibly toward a directness of expression which for many observers was enigmatic and visually unrewarding. The children of Philip Guston's *Martial Memory,* for example, were still entities in the livelier and more complex work, *If This Be Not I;* figures and their surroundings fused more intimately in *Night Children* and in the *Somersault* paintings of 1946. The painter was trying, he said, to fashion plastic images strong enough to hold the terrifying and contradictory spirit of the age. A few years later he was working with weightless, undefined areas of softly brushed pigment which held no reference to his earlier human forms, as in *Summer.* One asked whether the drastic change of Bradley Tomlin in the last decade of his life was not too sudden to be healthy, in rich and complicated interwoven patterns of ribbonlike calligraphic motifs of restrained color, canvases whose obsessive similarity was underscored by the fact that Tomlin gave them numbers rather than names. Another man who, having kept to the middle of the road, now veered to the aesthetic left, was Ralston Crawford, whose *Aircraft Factory* (Cinc. Mus.) had the clean precision and clear flat color areas of his *Whitestone Bridge* but less of interest for the eye and the mind.

This was what John Baur has called the third wave of abstraction which only after the war gathered full force and impact. The old accusations of insincerity, of technical incompetence, of mental instability were leveled against it, and hostile critics attributed its prominence to the museum director's quest for novelty, the dealer's promotion, the collector's pride in the latest thing, and the praise of the tractable critic.

There was a degree of truth in these observations, but not enough for a blanket condemnation. Among the avant-garde were undisciplined and anarchic spirits whose crude slashes and splashes of pigment exploded

Adolph Gottlieb, *The Seer*
Phillips Memorial Gallery, Washington, D.C.

on the walls of exhibitions and whose own comments on their work had little or no meaning; but there were also thoughtful men who, like Balcomb Greene, maintained that life when honestly seen presented a contradictory, tragic, and almost meaningless pattern, and who refused to produce forms ritualized by custom in order to encourage people's emotional laziness and false comfort.

In the decade which followed the war the cool geometry of Greene's earlier style gave way to something which was described as "between evocation and dissolution," a quality suggesting clouds, waves, and mist, as in *Composition: The Storm* (Whitney Mus.). The shapes of William Baziotes had the stark and rather terrifying grotesquerie one finds in the art of primitive people; his titles, *Moon Forms, Dragon, Jungle,* suggested a "subject" which, the painter explained, developed itself in the process of painting and sometimes was not known to him until after the work was done. One

Willem de Kooning, *Asheville*
Phillips Memorial Gallery, Washington, D.C.

also thought of primitive pictographs when one saw the symbols of Adolph Gottlieb in their compartmental framework, but the device was his own, and perhaps a metaphor of simultaneous isolation and connectedness. His red velvet curtain appliquéd with religious symbols hung before the ark in the Millburn Synagogue, and his stained glass covered the façade of the Steinberg Memorial Center in New York.

A more nervous intensity was in the sardonic and witty "improvisations" of Arshile Gorky, who shortly before his death in 1948 proved that, mainly with the help of Kandinsky and of Miró, he had developed his own way of spinning fantasies of rich textures and strident color in *Agony* (Mus. Mod. Art), *The Betrothal* (Whitney Mus.), and *The Liver Is the Cock's Comb.* (See color plate 27.) In that same year a first show presented the explosive Willem de Kooning, whose brush attacked the canvas with the force of a Van Gogh but with more anger, it seemed, than pity. His shapes for a time were rather suggestive of living organisms, and in 1950 an obsessive female figure emerged from his slashing strokes and shrill dissonances, in a series called *Woman.*

When Robert Motherwell painted a mural for B'Nai Israel Synagogue, the big abstract shapes in strong flat colors were, so to speak, predetermined symbols; in *Western Air* (Mus. Mod. Art), in *Five in the Afternoon,* and in *Fishes, with Red Stripe,* it was his own subconscious that supplied the matter with which he consciously made his compositions. When Franz Kline used only stark black and white for his boldly aggressive statements, the gesture itself was the intended means of expressiveness. This effort, as Sam Hunter described it, "to give powers of speech to the absolutely rudimentary elements of the painting process," led Jackson Pollock to weave his fascinating and seemingly endless fabric of colors by dribbling them from a brush or vessel which moved above a horizontal canvas. He was one of the many younger painters directly or indirectly influenced by the work and teaching of the German-born expressionist Hans Hofmann, who had come to America in 1930 and established his classes in New York and Provincetown a few years later. The intricacies of Pollock were for some observers superb decoration and no more; for James Soby they held troubling allusions which actively involved the observer, and Parker Tyler found in them "the universe in totality of being." (See color plate 29.)

The term, "abstract expressionist," was as suitable as any for most of these men and as well for Clyfford Still, Theodore Stamos, Byron Browne, and Mark Rothko. They could claim to practice a kind of art which no longer depended on European precedent and which indeed, as "American-type painting," received

Theodoros Stamos, *Lupine*
Phillips Memorial Gallery, Washington, D.C.

Andrew Wyeth, *Northern Point*
Wadsworth Atheneum, Hartford, Conn.

the tribute of transatlantic emulation. What they shared in varying degrees was a sense of separateness, ranging from Still's belief that demands for communication were both presumptuous and irrelevant to Greene's statement that it did not matter that John Doe, with nothing but mediocre and destructive prejudices to guide him, could not understand this art.

When these painters spoke of the "average man," they were creating an abstraction; and history might well record that their wholesale condemnation of the public was as unintelligent and as ill-considered as was the obstinate intolerance of the most hidebound Philistine. Indeed, there were signs in the late 1950's that some artists were no longer satisfied to stake everything on the immediate impact of a work. Peter Selz pointed out the clear human implications of Leon Golub's *Damaged Man,* and in order to demonstrate the emergence of the specifically human in paintings and sculpture organized "New Images of Man" for the Museum of Modern Art in the fall of 1959. The exhibition was welcomed even by those critics for whom its dominant tone was one of agony, hopeless despair, and bitter anger. Elsewhere, however, the mood of the humanists ranged from tragedy to good-humored satire, from grim reminders of man's plight to the affirmation of his powers.

Scorning the abstract expressionists as "space cadets," Jack Levine refused to believe that cubes, planes, and alarm clocks could conquer life's problems, and went on painting his Hogarthian genre scenes with wry humor and solemn-faced mockery—*Welcome Home* (Brooklyn Museum), *Gangster Funeral* (see color plate 28), *The Trial* (Chic. Art Inst.), *Election Night* (Mus. Mod. Art). *The American Shrimp Girl* of Philip Evergood, with sturdy white limbs and scarlet sweater, in a seascape which bristled with boats and circling seagulls, was a tender, odd, and strangely monumental figure. *The Acrobat* and *Carnival* (Mus. Mod. Art) of Alton Pickens were painted in seemingly realistic manner to convey "the feeling of imminence and threat that follows the life of any sentient man." Rico Lebrun believed that artists could survive this age only as spokesmen, not as entertainers; his *Migration to Nowhere* of 1941 had been inspired by firsthand experience of warfare, and nine years later, what Soby has called his "compassionate dramaturgy" found its theme in a large triptych of the *Crucifixion* (Syracuse Univ.).

In the art of Honoré Sharrer and of Andrew Wyeth the patient and meticulous handling of Raphaelle Peale and of William Harnett reappeared. Sharrer's *Tribute to the American Working People,* whose many small and exquisitely drawn figures kept her busy for several years, was an infinitely detailed report on every aspect of the lives of ordinary people, a humorous and healthy genre painting in the native tradition. The son and pupil of a noted illustrator, Wyeth developed a microscopic realism in tempera and water color at Chadd's Ford in Pennsylvania and at Cushing in Maine, paintings which went below surface actuality to suggest the loneliness, the fears and troubled depths of his men and women, giving a bleak poetry to a cracked ceiling, a shingled barn roof, a dim hayloft, the drab windbeaten houses of *Christina's World.* Another "realist" was Walter Stuempfig, whose sharply defined details in *The Wall* held their place in a broadly and firmly conceived design, and whose *Manayunk,* a study of a factory neighborhood near Philadelphia, was oddly suggestive of Canaletto.

Leonard Baskin, woodcut, *Poet Laureate*

Courtesy of the artist

Both Stephen Greene and Bernard Perlin had been strongly affected by the art of Ben Shahn without loss of their own qualities—the religious intensity of Greene and the gift of Perlin for stating the familiar and the obvious fact with new implications and unexpected overtones. For Shahn himself the postwar years saw an increasing subtlety of design, form, and color, a multiplicity of suggested meanings, but no weakening of his belief that "man is of ultimate value." He said of his *Miners' Wives* (Phila. Mus.), "I do assume that most people are interested in the hopes, fears, dreams and tragedies of other people, for those are the things that life is made of." Shahn knew that this assumption set him apart from artists who, in this time of turmoil and of fearful change, concerned themselves with purely abstract forms. "Art," he wrote, "has no reason to go on if it has nothing further to express."

Shahn agreed with Jack Levine that the growth and maturity of an artist bring with them the pitfalls of complexity, and in the 1950's he did not always escape these pitfalls; but although one had to work harder now to grasp his whole meaning, it was there, in *Cybernetics, The Blind Botanist* (see plate 30), and *Allegory*. This last painting, as he explained in his Norton lectures at Harvard, was a synthesis of many elements—the image of Romulus and Remus suckled by a wolf, a lionlike beast which in the artist's mind had become a symbol of primitive fear, the story of a Chicago fire in which a Negro's children were destroyed, and Shahn's own dread of fire since his slum childhood. As he worked at *Allegory* his "inward demon," the critic inside the artist, ruthlessly rejected what was irrelevant and kept what gave the completed work its searing unity and its rich variety of implication.

At a time when painters like Shahn and Evergood were in the minority, brilliant and perceptive photographers continued to document the beauty of the land and the faces of her people. Alfred Stieglitz, to be sure, had no greater sense of "fitting into the scheme of things" than in the first world conflict; and at the end of the second war one saw a tired man of eighty-one moving in a long cloak among the O'Keeffes, the Doves, and the Marins of his gallery. "In my own way," he said, "I have also given my life to my country"; and his life ended in 1946.

Younger men and women, however, were now proving that the instrument whose expressive powers owed much to Stieglitz was in capable hands. No finer portrait characterizations had been made in America than Berenice Abbott's, as final in their factual statement as they were penetrant of personality. Arthur Fellig, known as "Weegee," was on hand when a brooding ill-dressed woman glared at the mink and diamonds of two patronesses, and his *Opening Night at the Opera* became a classic of its kind. Barbara Morgan's interpretations of Martha Graham miraculously caught not only the sculptural forms of her body but, in one recorded instant, the design of a whole dance in space and time. Ansel Adams wrote the text for his book of prints in 1949, *My Camera in Yosemite Valley,* and a year later Nancy Newhall edited passages from American documents to accompany the photographs of Paul Strand in *Time in New England.* Superbly displayed at the Museum of Modern Art in 1955 was *The Family*

David Smith, *Cockfight Variation*

Whitney Museum of American Art, New York City

Theodore J. Roszak, *Anguish*

Courtesy of the artist

of Man, described by its creator Edward Steichen as the most ambitious project that photography had ever attempted, more than five hundred prints chosen from two million by professionals and amateurs throughout the world to show that the cycle of life is the same for all men. This extraordinary exhibition was subsequently seen by people of other countries and was also published as a book.

Among the print makers of the postwar years one found more concern with technical experiment, with intense and vigorous personal statement, than with the family of man. One of the exceptions among younger graphic artists was Leonard Baskin, also a gifted sculptor, avowing in the former field his kinship with the "moralists and political partisans," with Callot, Goya, Kollwitz, and Rouault, and using the ancient medium of woodcut in his *Man of Peace,* a figure nearly life-size with sinewy old legs behind barbed wire, gnarled hands grasping a dead bird, and haunted eyes in deep sockets. Here and in *Frightened Boy and His Dog* were the torments and anxieties of present man but also his unquenchable dignity and his patient endurance; and Baskin's unsentimental loyalty to the human creature, his anger toward those who warp and destroy, spoke through the stark contrasts of black and white, the lines which now stated contours with a harsh and bitter finality, now subtly were interwoven to suggest what time had done to a man's head and panic to a child.

Baskin's woodcuts were part of a remarkable renaissance of print-making which marked the afterwar period. One of the signal achievements of the Federal Art Projects had been the revival of the graphic arts and the exploration of such new procedures as the silk screen print. Since 1947 the Brooklyn Museum held a Print Annual which encouraged similar enterprises throughout the country; another stimulus was the work and teaching of the Englishman Stanley William Hayter at his Atelier 17 in New York.

In this renaissance a few of the older men and women kept alive earlier modes: the wood engravings of Asa Cheffetz, Fritz Eichenberg, and Thomas W. Nason achieved rich tone and texture by minute and patient means; Ellison Hoover's lithograph, *Dancers in a Moonlit Garden,* had the luminous mist of a Fantin-Latour; Stow Wengenroth in the same medium was a master of objective description. Far more typical of the period, however, were the innovators whose exploration of new visual possibilities was parallel to that of the avant-garde in painting, and many of whom had worked with Hayter. Alice T. Mason in drypoint etching developed amoebic, Miróesque themes; the color woodcuts of Louis Schanker were alive with flowing abstract forms; Sue Fuller and Leo Katz were equally resourceful. Old techniques were often ingeniously combined in a single print; at other times, new textures were secured by pounding bits of wire screening into the printing surface, or by applying bits of cloth, string, and other materials. Some artists managed with electric hand drills to get a singing calligraphic line, some cut relief prints from Lucite. Seong Moy found ways of making prints of many colors from one or two blocks; Boris Margo made "cellocuts" by coating his plate with a varnish of liquid plastic before working it with his tools. Thanks to these innovators the American print often achieved an entertaining complexity of line, a subtlety of texture and of color, and a busy interaction of abstract or nearly abstract shapes which made many efforts of the time on canvas seem uneventful.

In sculpture during these years, as in the graphic arts and painting, one found an increasing preoccupation with new concepts of form and space rather than with the communication of meaning through familiar content; and the architect's avid experiment with new materials also found its counterpart here. The anthropomorphism of the past persisted, and with it the conception of sculpture as solid mass displacing space and reflecting light from hard continuous surfaces, not only in the tepidly academic output of the National Sculpture Society but in the work of bolder and more original men. The *Himalaya* of José de Creeft (Whitney Mus.), its bosses hammered into relief from a sheet of lead, had both intensity and strength, likewise William Zorach's porphyry *Head of Christ* (Mus. Mod. Art); and Leonard Baskin's figures carved in wood pressed forward with the dignity of Egyptian gods but with the weary fortitude of modern creatures.

For an increasing number of sculptors, however, space was infinite and volumes could swing, swell, and contract, not in harmony with man's proportions, but as the artist willed. Space could be snared in an intricate network or filtered through unexpected voids; light gained force and variety when it was reflected by rods and wires or entangled in the pocked and pitted surfaces of welded and brazed metals. Such ideas had become familiar before the war in the work of Brancusi, Archipenko, Arp, Gabo, Pevsner, Giacometti, and Moore. Jacques Lipchitz had come to New York in 1941 to work on his bronze *Pegasus*. The visual geometry of the constructivists, the beauty of machinery, the free manipulation of shapes by abstract and surrealist painters, all played a part in the contemporary sculptural aesthetic.

David Hare's *Young Girl* hinted at lips, teeth, breast, and thigh, but these were marginal references; the curving sheets of painted metal in José de Rivera's *Black, Yellow and Red* (Miller Co.) were completely abstract. In monument yards and boiler factories David Smith had learned ways of cutting stone and of welding and forging metal when he fashioned his humorous *Home of the Welder* and assembled the sharp steel plates of *Cockfight* (Whitney Mus.). He had sketched from the Albany train before making his *Hudson River Landscape* but had no intention of describing a place, and one who saw its rhythmic loopings and straight bars against the Maine sky in the courtyard of the Ogunquit Museum was welcome to make his own journey to his own destination. The blind brutalities of the time led an angry Theodore Roszak in 1945 to abandon his coolly reasoned constructions for the clawlike shapes of *Transition;* his *Anguish* writhed and shrieked as light fell on metal which had been brazed to the texture of torn flesh. A decade later the jagged rocks and gnarled shrubs of the New England coast inspired his *Sea Sentinel* (Whitney Mus.).

Such works and the still more novel works to come made no effort to meet the traditional idea of what a sculpture ought to be. People accepted Bertoia's screen in a Fifth Avenue bank because it was a sculptured decoration, but recoiled from a twelve-foot *Rape of Lucrece* which Reuben Nakian made from sheets of black welded steel; and the City Council of Los Angeles urged that Bernard Rosenthal's skeletonized figures for their Police Building be melted down for scrap. As late as 1959, when corrective legislation was passed, our tariff laws defined sculpture as the imitation of natural objects in their "true" proportions and consequently denied free entry to works which they classified as hardware. Certainly a sculptor's workshop in the 1950's bore no resemblance to those romantic places where, a century before, artists in smocks and velvet caps molded their portrait busts and marble nudities. It was likely to be a bare brick loft with a formidable array of rasps, wire cutters, drills, blowtorches, anvils, and small forges.

Yet out of these shops in the years after the war came work of exquisite complexity and sometimes of deep feeling by Ibram Lassaw, Gavor Peterdi, Louis Schanker, Peter Grippe, Seymour Lipton, Herbert Ferber, and Richard Lippold. In *Jungle-Bloom* (Yale Univ.) and *Sanctuary* (Mus. Mod. Art) Lipton shaped the forms of growing things into symbols of hope and regeneration among the agonizing tensions of the present; he worked with variously shaped thin sheets of monel metal brazed at their joints and given a fascinating line and texture by melting bronze or nickel-silver over them. Herbert Ferber's *Burning Bush* was designed, he hoped, to give a sense of its "ultimate involvement" with the architecture of the Millburn Synagogue; Richard Lippold's *Aerial Act* (Wadsw. Ath.), *Gemini* (Proctor Inst.), and *Full Moon* (Mus. Mod. Art) were part of this announced effort to capture space with the most seductive material he could find. Among his admirations were fine machinery, the fragility of snowflakes, the sparkling and dangerous cobweb; less violent than many of his colleagues, he believed that patience was as important as passion in controlling the "little delicate relationships of life," which had their parallel in his intricate constructions of chromium and silver wire. Incredible patience and craftsmanship went into his series of *Variations within a Sphere.* Suspended by stainless steel wires from the corner of a room at the Metropolitan Museum was his *Sun,* begun in 1953, of innumerable shimmering gold wires, its core slowly revolving within a weblike corona.

The student who, some fifteen years after the war's end, wished to assess the value of what our painters, print makers, and sculptors had accomplished during that period, could profitably note the response of Europeans to such traveling exhibitions as "Modern Art in the United States," shown in 1956 at the Tate Gallery in London, and "The New American Painting," which three years later moved from Basel to Milan and Madrid, and thence to Berlin, Amsterdam, Brussels, Paris, and London. Among the varied reactions there was hearty praise for Hopper, Shahn, Tobey, Wyeth, Graves, and MacIver, who seemed to have forged distinctive styles to convey original and penetrating views of man and nature. Foreign observers were impressed by the resourcefulness of our print makers, from the "heroic scale and assurance" of Baskin to the rich inventions of Sylvia Ward, Leona Pierce, and Walter Rogalski. A French critic had called Alexander Calder "le poète des formes aériennes et des courbes subtiles," and for most Europeans his devices embodied the ceaseless dynamism of the Yankee.

The canvases of our abstract expressionists, now often called the action painters, were dismissed by the *Spectator* in 1956 as "extraordinarily slight . . . for all their size, energy and assurance"; in 1959 *Le Figaro Littéraire* deplored "the terrible danger which the publicity given to such examples offers," but the London *Times* decided that "the quality of adventure, of individual striving, of hammering out modes of expression with a pioneering sense of independence, lends these personal utterances a forceful, easily communicable vitality." Pollock, Kline, Motherwell, de Kooning, and their associates were, for the *Times,* the shock troops in the American invasion of painting, a school of artists which "has put the nose of Paris out of joint and is leading artistic fashion."

Carl Sandburg has written of the scroll which records "what the people learn out of lifting and hauling and waiting and losing and laughing." From John White's drawings of the Indians to Lippold's *Sun* and Shahn's *Allegory*—a span of some three hundred and seventy years—the carved stone, the built structure, and the painted canvas have been part of that scroll.

One looks back over it to provincial America, unconscious of its separate destiny but being reshaped by local circumstances into the character which looks from Anne Pollard's likeness and the faces of Ralph Earl and John Singleton Copley. The scroll turns, and a new nation not too sure of its prestige in the world, or of its own capacity to invent republican forms, drapes a toga over its coat and breeches and transacts new business in Jeffersonian temples and rotundas. Hero worship produces her great portraits of Lafayette and Washington; an equally enduring belief in the character of the least citizen is in the spare-time portraits of Jonathan Fisher. Her will to peace forms Quaker Hicks's modest allegories and the elaborate histrionics of Cole's *Course of Empire.*

The pattern of the scroll becomes complicated when Jacksonian ideas of equality fight to survive in an age of factories, railroads, and banks. Out of that struggle comes further clarification of purposes and preferences. One finds a zest for the rational, the organic, the enlargement of man's knowledge, and his grasp of constructive materials in the words of Horatio Greenough, the engineering of Latrobe, Strickland, and Mills, the photographs of Brady, the bridges of the Roeblings, and later in the tall buildings of Louis Sullivan, the paintings of Sheeler, the prints of Stieglitz and Paul Strand. After the fumblings of eclectics toward better homes for a democratic people comes the architecture of Frank Lloyd Wright. America's pleasure in her own rocks and hills calls for Doughty, then Durand and Inness, and after them Marin and Hartley.

The beauty of America's new cities has been recorded by her print makers, the squalor of her old ones indulgently set forth by John Sloan and his ashcan realists. When she has been in a mood to love the concrete she has possessed a Bingham or a Homer; Eakins and Lachaise have both helped her to understand that the body is as important as the soul. From Allston to Ryder, and from Ryder to Morris Graves, her imagination has discovered images of storm and symbols of private conflict. And lest she forget the unfinished business of perfecting a democracy, Thomas Nast and Art Young have underlined her mistakes, Jacob Lawrence has reminded her of John Brown, and Jack Levine has mocked her moments of pretension.

One approaches the blank space on the scroll reserved for the future with hope and with misgivings, at a moment when man's very survival depends upon his ability to control and direct the terrible new energies his own knowledge has set loose in the world. One knows that America will never again be conceivable as an independent fragment of human experience, and that her artists, although they speak with an unmistakeable accent, voice thoughts and emotions shared by other peoples. The intricate *Sun* of Lippold tells of her concern with technologies, her bold and inventive use of new materials, her skill in organization; the *Allegory* of Shahn embodies her primitive fears and her ready compassion; yet both have world-wide meaning as symbols of a generation which can launch glittering mechanisms into outer space and plan to set foot on other planets but has not yet succeeded in making a safe or happy home for itself on this one. While some of our artists make of their work a defiant gesture of individual freedom in a world which seems to ignore the individual, others more actively and more specifically concern themselves with that struggle in which democratic man, as Tocqueville said, "forever seeking, forever falling, to rise again, often disappointed, but not discouraged, . . . tends unceasingly towards that unmeasured greatness so indistinctly visible at the end of the long track which humanity has yet to tread."

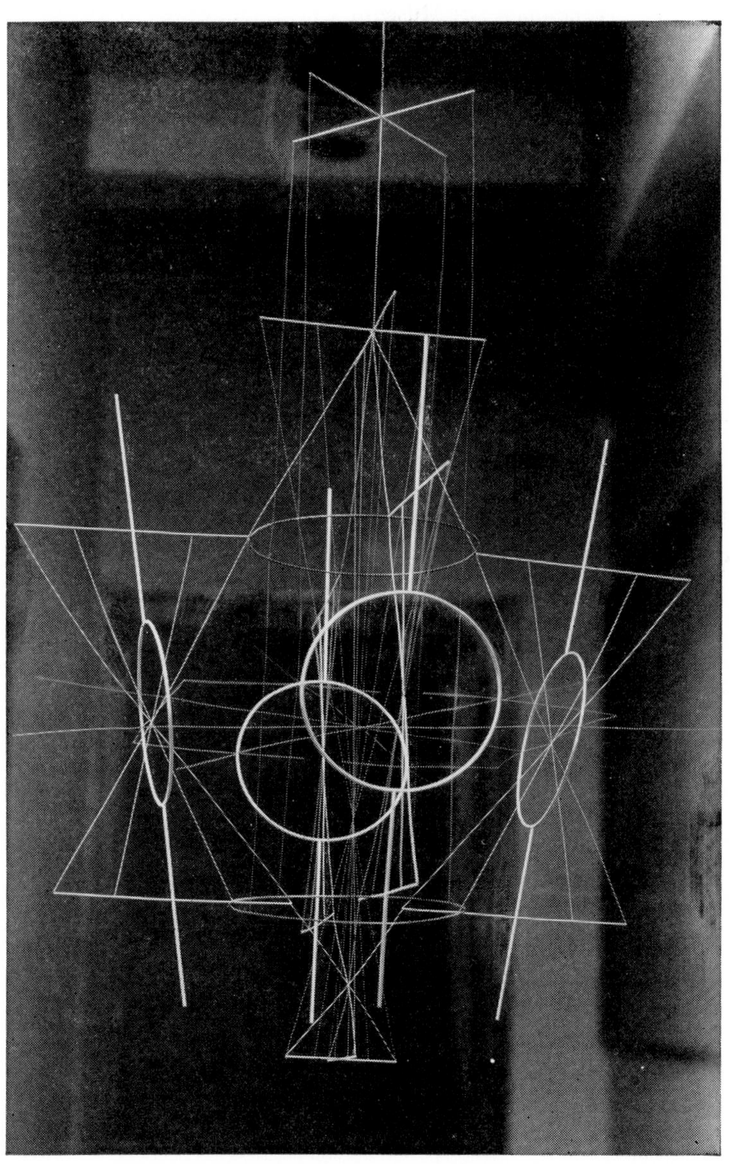

Richard Lippold, *Aerial Act*

Wadsworth Atheneum, Adolph Studly photo

INDEX OF ABBREVIATIONS

Adams Mem. Soc.	Adams Memorial Society, Quincy, Mass.
Addison Gall.	Addison Gallery of American Art, Andover, Mass.
Albany Inst.	Albany Institute of History and Art, Albany, N. Y.
Albright Gall.	Albright Art Gallery, Buffalo, N. Y.
Am. Antiq. Soc.	American Antiquarian Society, Worcester, Mass.
Boston Ath.	Boston Athenaeum, Boston, Mass.
Brookline Hist. Soc.	Brookline Historical Society, Brookline, Mass.
Chic. Art Inst.	Art Institute of Chicago, Ill.
Cin. Mus.	Cincinnati Art Museum, Cincinnati, Ohio
Columbus Gall.	Columbus Gallery of Fine Arts, Columbus, Ohio
Conn. Hist. Soc.	Connecticut Historical Society, Hartford, Conn.
Corcoran Gall.	Corcoran Gallery of Art, Washington, D. C.
De Young Mus.	De Young Memorial Museum, San Francisco, Cal.
Encyc. Brit.	Encyclopaedia Britannica Collection of Contemporary American Painting
Essex Inst.	Essex Institute, Salem, Mass.
Fort Worth Mus.	Fort Worth Museum, Fort Worth, Texas
Freer Gall.	Freer Gallery of Art, Washington, D. C.
Litchfield Hist. Soc.	Litchfield Historical Society, Litchfield, Conn.
Mass. Hist. Soc.	Massachusetts Historical Society, Boston, Mass.
Md. Hist. Soc.	Maryland Historical Society, Baltimore, Md.
Met. Mus.	Metropolitan Museum of Art, New York City, N. Y.
Miller Co.	The Miller Co., Meriden, Conn.
Minn. Inst. of Arts	Minneapolis Institute of Arts, Minneapolis, Minn.
Mus. Mod. Art	Museum of Modern Art, New York City, N. Y.
Natl. Acad.	National Academy of Design, New York City, N. Y.
Natl. Coll. of Fine Arts	National Collection of Fine Arts, Washington, D. C.
Natl. Gall.	National Gallery of Art, Washington, D. C.
Natl. Mus.	National Museum, Washington, D. C.
Natl. Statuary Hall	National Statuary Hall, U. S. Capitol, Washington, D. C.
N. E. Hist. Gen. Soc.	New England Historic Genealogical Society, Boston, Mass.
New Haven Col. Hist. Soc.	New Haven Colony Historical Society, New Haven, Conn.
N. Y. Hist. Soc.	New York Historical Society, New York City, N. Y.
N. Y. State Hist. Assoc.	New York State Historical Association, Cooperstown, N. Y.
Pa. Acad.	Pennsylvania Academy of the Fine Arts, Philadelphia, Pa.
Pa. Hist. Soc.	Pennsylvania Historical Society, Philadelphia, Pa.
Peabody Mus.	Peabody Museum, Salem, Mass.
Phila. Mus.	Philadelphia Museum of Art, Philadelphia, Pa.
Phillips Mem. Gall.	Phillips Memorial Gallery, Washington, D. C.
Pilgrim Hall	Pilgrim Hall, Plymouth, Mass.
Proctor Inst.	Munson-Williams-Proctor Institute, Utica, N. Y.
Redwood Lib.	Redwood Library and Athenaeum, Newport, R. I.
Smith Mus., Springfield	George Walter Vincent Smith Art Museum, Springfield, Mass.
Wadsw. Ath.	Wadsworth Atheneum, Hartford, Conn.
Whitney Mus.	Whitney Museum of American Art, New York City, N. Y.
Yale Univ.	Yale University Art Gallery, New Haven, Conn.

BIBLIOGRAPHICAL NOTES

Explanation:

Sections 1–8 list works on American life and surveys of American art as a whole.

Section 9 is a bibliography of the whole period covered by Book One. (Colonial Arts)

Sections 10, 11, 12 follow the sequences of the actual text, chapter by chapter.

The same procedure is followed with regard to Books Two–Six.

In a work of this scope, bibliographical lists must be selective. An effort has been made to include interpretations of movements and artistic personalities and problems which contrast with those of the author, and also to direct the reader to works of art and to artists not discussed in this book.

The sources of significant quotations, if not indicated in the main body of the text, are included here.

Certain books are mentioned repeatedly. The second and subsequent citations of such works are abbreviated.

SECTION 1

Dictionaries, Encyclopedias, and Other Reference Works

Many artists are included in *Appleton's Cyclopaedia of American Biography,* 1887–1900, and in *Dictionary of American Biography,* 1928–1936, with supplementary volume 1944. *Artists of the Nineteenth Century and Their Works,* edited by Clara E. Clement and Laurence Hutton, 1889, includes Americans, as do Thieme and Becker, *Allgemeines Lexikon der Bildenden Künstler,* 1907–1948, and Bryan's *Dictionary of Painters and Engravers,* 1903 and later editions.

Exclusively American are Mantle Fielding, *Dictionary of American Painters, Sculptors and Engravers,* 1926; *Who's Who in American Art,* 1936 to date; Ralph C. Smith, *A Biographical Index of American Artists,* 1930; Isabel S. Monro and Kate M. Monro, *Index to Reproductions of American Paintings,* 1948. The best dictionary is George C. Groce and David H. Wallace, *The New-York Historical Society's Dictionary of Artists in America, 1564–1860,* 1957.

Information on art schools, museums, exhibitions, sales, art societies, lists of artists, etc., is in the *American Art Annual,* 1898 to date; since 1937 it has appeared biennially.

The introductory chapters of the Federal Writers Guides to the several states provide excellent summaries of local art history.

The Archives of American Art, established by Edgar P. Richardson at the Detroit Institute of Arts, is an invaluable collection of letters, diaries, catalogues, and other material related to this subject.

A special number of *Art in America,* vol. 33, Oct., 1945, edited by Lloyd Goodrich, discusses the problems of scholarly research in American art.

SECTION 2

The History of American Society, Its Thought and Taste

Among the best of social histories are Harold U. Faulkner, *American Political and Social History,* 6th ed., 1952; Charles and Mary Beard, *The Rise of American Civilization,* 1937; Ray Billington, Bert Loewenberg, and Samuel Brockunier, *The United States: American Democracy in World Perspective,* 1947. Arthur M. Schlesinger and Dixon R. Fox have edited a twelve-volume series, "A History of American Life," 1927–1944, with useful bibliographies in each volume. Social behavior is discussed in Dixon Wecter, *The Saga of American Society,* 1937, and William E. Woodward, *The Way Our People Lived,* 1944. Marshall B. Davidson, *Life in America,* 1951, is a reconstruction of American life in pictures, with useful text; see also *American Processional, 1492–1900,* 1950, catalogue of an exhibition commemorating the 150th anniversary of Washington, D. C., with an historical essay by Elizabeth McCausland.

The mental life of our people is discussed in Merle Curti, *Growth of American Thought,* 1943, and Howard M. Jones, *Ideas in America,* 1944. See also Ralph H. Gabriel, *The Course of American Democratic Thought,* 1940; and Avery Craven, *Democracy in American Life,* 1941.

On literary expression: *Literary History of the United States,* 3 vols., 1948, edited by Robert E. Spiller and others, is a record of cultural-literary history by fifty-five scholars; vol. 3 is a bibliography. A stimulating critical survey is Vernon L. Parrington's *Main Currents in American Thought,* 1927 and 1930. Briefer studies are Bernard Smith, *Forces in American Criticism,* 1939; and Ferner Nuhn, *The Wind Blew from the East: A Study in the Orientation of American Culture,* 1942.

The influence of religion is surveyed in Thomas C. Hall, *The Religious Background of American Culture,* 1930.

SECTION 3

Surveys of the Arts in America

The first is William Dunlap's *A History of the Rise and Development of the Arts of Design in the United States,* 2 vols., 1834, an indispensable reference work; Frank W. Bayley and Charles E. Goodspeed have edited a revised three-volume edition, 1918. See also Rilla E. Jackman, *American Arts,* 1928; Suzanne LaFollette, *Art in America,* 1929; Holger Cahill and Alfred H. Barr, Jr. (eds.), *Art in America; A Complete Survey,* 1935.

SECTION 4

General Works on American Architecture

Talbot Hamlin, *The American Spirit in Architecture,* 1926 (vol. 13 in "The Pageant of America" series); Fiske Kimball, *American Architecture,* 1928; James M. Fitch, *American Building; The Forces That Shape It,* 1948; Wayne Andrews, *Architecture, Ambition and Americans,* 1955; Christopher Tunnard and Henry H. Reed, *American Skyline: The Growth and Form of Our Cities and Towns,* 1955. Henry-Russell Hitchcock, *American Architectural Books,* rev. ed., 1946, lists books, pamphlets, etc., published in America before 1895.

For the history of American rooms and furnishings, see Meyric R. Rogers, *American Interior Design,* 1947

SECTION 5

General Works on American Painting

Nineteenth-century works include Charles E. Lester, *The Artists of America,* 1846; Samuel G. W. Benjamin, *Art in America; A Critical and Historical Sketch,* 1880; Henry T. Tuckerman, *Book of the Artists,* 1867 (includes sculptors). More recent surveys: Sadakichi Hartmann, *A History of American Art,* 2 vols., 1902; Samuel Isham, *The History of American Painting,* first published in 1905, new edition with supplementary material by Royal Cortissoz, 1927; *The American Spirit in Art,* edited by Frank J. Mather, Jr., Rufus Morey, and William J. Henderson, 1927 (vol. 12 in "The Pageant of America" series), mainly on pictorial art, with some sculpture; Eugen Neuhaus, *The History and Ideals of American Art,* 1931; Alan Burroughs, *Limners and Likenesses,* 1936; Homer Saint-Gaudens, *The American Artist and His Times,* 1941. Virgil Barker, *American Painting: History and Interpretation,* 1950, and Edgar P. Richardson, *Painting in America,* 1956, are the best critical surveys. Alexander Eliot, *Three Hundred Years of American Painting,* 1957, is illustrated wholly in color.

Useful for their illustrations are *Life in America,* catalogue of a Metropolitan Museum exhibition in 1939; and *Great American Paintings from Smibert to Bellows,* edited by John Walker and Macgill James, 1944.

SECTION 6

On American Sculpture

No comprehensive recent work has been published. See Lorado Taft, *The History of American Sculpture,* 1903; and Chandler R. Post, *A History of European and American Sculpture,* 2 vols., 1921.

SECTION 7

The Graphic Arts

David M. Stauffer, *American Engravers upon Copper and Steel,* 2 vols., 1907; supplementary volume by Mantle Fielding, 1917; Frank Weitenkampf, *American Graphic Art,* 1912; I. N. Phelps Stokes and Daniel C. Haskell, *American Historical Prints* (1497 to 1891), 1933. William Murrell, *History of American Graphic Humor,* 2 vols., 1933 and 1938, is an admirable study of social and political satire.

SECTION 8

Other Aspects of American Art History

Jean Lipman, *American Primitive Painting,* 1942, and *American Folk Art in Wood, Metal and Stone,* 1948; Jean Lipman and Alice Winchester, *Primitive Painters in America, 1750–1950,* 1950; Erwin O. Christensen, *The Index of American Design,* 1950; Wolfgang Born, *Still-Life Painting in America,* 1947, and *American Landscape Painting,* 1948; Walter Pach, *The Art Museum in America,* 1948; Eliot Clark, *History of the National Academy of Design, 1825–1953,* 1954; John A. Kouvenhoven, *Made in America,* 1949; Russell Lynes, *The Tastemakers,* 1954; Aline B. Saarinen, *The Proud Possessors,* 1958, a study of American collectors.

SECTION 9

Book One / The Colonial Arts

THE PERIOD IN GENERAL

On English backgrounds: B. Sprague Allen, *Tides in English Taste,* 2 vols., 1937 (the seventeenth and eighteenth centuries); C. H. Collins Baker, *British Painting,* 1933; Thomas E. Tallmadge, *The Story of England's Architecture,* 1934; J. Alfred Gotch, *The Growth of the English House,* 1909; Horace Field and Michael Bunney, *English Domestic Architecture of the Seventeenth and Eighteenth Centuries,* 1928; Herbert Cescinsky, *English Furniture from Gothic to Sheraton,* 1929.

On colonial America: Curtis P. Nettels, *The Roots of American Civilization,* 1945; Herbert M. Morais, *The Struggle for American Freedom,* 1944; James T. Adams, *Provincial Society,* 1927 (vol. 3 in the "History of American Life" series); Parrington, *Main Currents,* vol. 1; *Literary History of the United States,* vol. 1, sections 1–8.

On colonial architecture: Harold D. Eberlein, *The Architecture of Colonial America,* 1915; Joseph Jackson, *American Colonial Architecture,* 1924; Fiske Kimball, *Domestic Architecture of the American Colonies and of the Early Republic,* 1922, a scholarly study. The best of all surveys of architecture in the seventeenth and eighteenth centuries is Hugh Morrison, *Early American Architecture,* 1952. See also Thomas T. Waterman, *The Dwellings of Colonial America,* 1950. Colonial buildings are included in Frank J. Roos, Jr., *Writings on Early American Architecture,* 1943, an annotated list relating to structures in the eastern half of the U.S.A. before 1860; also in *Historic American Buildings Survey,* 1941, a catalogue of photographs and measured drawings made by the Survey and now deposited in the Library of Congress. An issue of *Art in America,* vol. 43, May, 1955, is given to Williamsburg, Sturbridge, and other "restoration villages."

On the planning of colonial towns: See Henry S. Churchill, *The City Is the People,* 1945; chs. 1–2; Anthony N. B. Garvan, *Architecture and Town Planning in Colonial Connecticut,* 1951.

On furnishings and crafts: See Luke V. Lockwood, *Colonial Furniture in America,* 1902; Scott G. Williamson, *The American Craftsman,* 1940. *The Homes of Our Ancestors,* by R. T. H. Halsey and Elizabeth Tower, 1935, is a valuable study based on the American Wing of the Metropolitan Museum.

On colonial painting: James T. Flexner, *First Flowers of Our Wilderness,* 1947.

On the graphic arts: Stauffer, *American Engravers;* Weitenkampf, *American Graphic Art,* ch. 3.

SECTION 10

Book One / Part One / Saints and Traders

Introduction / *A Sensible People*

Herbert I. Priestley, *The Coming of the White Man,* 1929 (vol. 1 in the "History of American Life" series), deals with the Spanish, French, and Dutch. See also John H. Inness, *New Amsterdam and Its People,* 1902; Ellis L. Raesly, *Portrait of New Netherland,* 1945. Thomas J. Wertenbaker, *The First Americans,* 1927 (vol. 2 in the "History of American Life" series), deals with the English. See also his *The Founding of American Civilization: The Middle Colonies,* 1938. James T. Adams, *The Founding of New England,* 1921; Philip A. Bruce, *Social Life in Virginia,* 1907; Louis B. Wright, *The First Gentlemen of Virginia,* 1940.

The work of John White and Jacques Le Moyne is reproduced in Stefan Lorant, *The New World: The First Pictures of America,* 1946.

On aesthetic attitudes: Louis Wright, *Middle-Class Culture in Elizabethan England,* 1935; Perry Miller, *The New England Mind,* 1939; Ralph Barton Perry, *Puritanism and Democracy,* 1945; George G. Coulton, *Art and the Reformation,* 1928; Thomas J. Wertenbaker, *The Puritan Oligarchy,* 1947, ch. 4.

"The Good Hows-holder" (1607) is quoted from Louis B. Wright, *Middle-Class Culture,* p. 187.

The comparison between the plowman and the painter, the carpenter and the carver, occurs in an anonymous pamphlet of 1719, *An Addition to the Melancholy Circumstances of the Province Considered.*

Morton's description of Massachusetts Bay is in *The New English Canaan,* 1632, Book 2, ch. 1 (Prince Society edition, 1883).

Chapter 1 / *The Serviceable Carpenter*

On Spanish beginnings: See Rexford Newcomb, *Spanish Colonial Architecture in the United States,* 1937. The seventeenth century is discussed in Kimball, *Domestic Architecture,* pp. 3–52; Jackson, *American Colonial Architecture,* chs. 1–5; Morrison, *Early American Architecture,* parts 1, 2.

Howard C. Forman treats the first English buildings in the Carolinas, Virginia, and Maryland in *The Architecture of the Old South,* 1948. See also Trent E. Sanford, *The Architecture of the Southwest: Indian, Spanish, American,* 1950.

Edward Johnson's description of Salem is in his *Wonder-Working Providence of Sions Saviour in New England,* 1654, book 1, ch. 9. See also George F. Dow, "The Colonial Village Built at Salem, Mass. in the Spring of 1930," in *Old Time New England,* vol. 22, July, 1931, p. 3. John Hammond's description of southern houses is in *Leah and Rachel,* 1656 (see Peter Force, *Tracts,* vol. 3, no. 14, p. 18, reprint of 1947).

On log houses: See Henry C. Mercer, "The Origin of Log Houses in the United States," in *Old Time New England,* vol. 18, July and Oct., 1927, pp. 3, 51; Louis

W. Flanders, "The Garrisons of Ancient Dover, New Hampshire," in *Old Time New England,* vol. 17, Oct., 1926, p. 51; Harold R. Shurtleff, *The Log Cabin Myth,* 1939.

On early New England buildings: Antoinette F. Downing, *Early Homes of Rhode Island,* 1937, chs. 1–2; Antoinette F. Downing and Vincent J. Scully, *The Architectural Heritage of Newport, Rhode Island, 1640–1915,* 1952, chs. 1, 2; Norman M. Isham and Albert F. Brown, *Early Connecticut Houses,* 1900, chs. 1–3, 5, 6; J. Frederick Kelly, *The Early Domestic Architecture of Connecticut,* 1924 (emphasizing construction methods).

For notes on some early structures discussed here: See *Old Time New England,* vol. 11, p. 3; vol. 21, p. 19; vol. 23, p. 131; vol. 29, p. 75.

On the South: George C. Mason, *Colonial Churches of Tidewater Virginia,* 1945; Thomas T. Waterman, *Domestic Colonial Architecture of Tidewater Virginia,* 1947, and *The Mansions of Virginia,* 1946, chs. 1–2.

On New Holland and the middle colonies: Inness, *New Amsterdam;* Raesly, *Portrait;* Harold D. Eberlein, *The Manors and Historic Homes of the Hudson Valley,* 1924; Helen W. Reynolds, *Dutch Houses in the Hudson Valley before 1776,* 1929; Wertenbaker, *The Middle Colonies;* Philip B. Wallace, *Colonial Churches and Meeting Houses of Pennsylania, New Jersey and Delaware,* 1931.

Christopher White's house is described in *Pennsylvania Magazine of History and Biography,* vol. 10, 1886, p. 164.

On seventeenth-century furnishings: Lockwood, *Colonial Furniture;* Wallace Nutting, *Furniture of the Pilgrim Century,* 1921; Thomas H. Ormsbee, *Early American Furniture Makers,* ch. 1; Williamson, *The American Craftsman.*

On the carvers: See the article by Erich A. O'D. Taylor in *Old Time New England,* vol. 15, p. 59; and articles by Harriette M. Forbes in the same, vol. 16, p. 138; vol. 17, p. 125; vol. 19, p. 159.

Chapter 2 / *The Limner*

On English portraiture: C. H. Collins Baker and W. G. Constable, *English Painting of the Sixteenth and Seventeenth Centuries,* 1930.

The first American portraits are discussed by Burroughs, *Limners and Likenesses,* ch. 1 and ch. 2, sections 4 and 5; Oskar Hagen, *Birth of the American Tradition in Art,* 1940, chs. 1–7; Flexner, *First Flowers of Our Wilderness,* chs. 1–3. Louisa Dresser, *Seventeenth Century Painting in New England,* 1935; Waldron P. Belknap, Jr., *American Colonial Painting, Materials for a History,* 1959.

The *Catalogue of American Portraits in the New York Historical Society,* 1941, reproduces many early portraits of the New York region, with the aid of William Sawitsky on questions of attribution.

JUSTUS E. KÜHN (flourished c. 1708–1717) is discussed by Dr. J. Hall Pleasants in *Proceedings of the American Antiquarian Society,* vol. 46, Oct., 1936, p. 243.

SECTION 11

Book One / Part Two / Margin for Leisure

Introduction / *Niceties and Curiosities*

On Spanish-American architecture and crafts: Newcomb, *Spanish Colonial Architecture;* George Kubler, *The Religious Architecture of New Mexico,* 1940; Sanford, *Architecture of the Southwest;* Mitchell A. Wilder and Edgar Breitenbach, *Santos: The Religious Folk Art of New Mexico,* 1943.

On the French: Charles E. Peterson, "French Landmarks along the Mississippi," in *Antiques,* vol. 53, Apr., 1948, p. 286; Samuel Wilson, Jr., "New Orleans Ironwork," in *Magazine of Art,* vol. 41, Oct., 1948, p. 214.

On the English colonies: Adams, *Provincial Society;* Morais, *The Struggle for American Freedom,* ch. 4; Charles M. Andrews, *Colonial Folkways,* 1921; Parrington, *Main Currents,* vol. 1, book 2.

Nathaniel Ames (1758) is quoted from Samuel Briggs, *The Essays, Humor and Poems of Nathaniel Ames,* 1891. Hempstead's activities are summarized from *The Diary of Joshua Hempstead* (1711–1758), 1901.

On English taste in the eighteenth century: Allen, *Tides in English Taste;* J. Steegman, *The Rule of Taste from George I to George IV,* 1936; Field and Bunney, *English Domestic Architecture;* Gotch, *Growth of the English House;* Cescinsky, *English Furniture.*

On English aesthetic doctrines: Rensselaer W. Lee, *Ut Pictura Poesis,* 1940; Charles-Alphonse Dufresnoy, *The Art of Painting* (here quoted from William Mason's translation, 1783); *Discourses . . . by Sir Joshua Reynolds,* edited by Roger Fry, 1905.

On English painting: Collins Baker, *British Painting,* 1933; Tancred Borenius, *English Painting in the Eighteenth Century,* 1938.

On furniture and the crafts in America: Lockwood, *Colonial Furniture;* Ormsbee, *Early American Furniture Makers,* ch. 2; Williamson, *The American Craftsman;* George F. Dow, *The Arts and Crafts in New England,* 1927; Alfred C. Prime, *The Arts and Crafts in Philadelphia, Maryland and South Carolina 1721–1785; Gleanings from Newspapers,* 1929; George S.

and Helen McKearin, *American Glass,* 1941; Henry C. Mercer, *The Bible in Iron,* 1914; Henry Kauffman, *Pennsylvania Dutch American Folk Art,* 1946; Frances Lichten, *Folk Art of Rural Pennsylvania,* 1946.

Chapter 3 / *Tidewater Classicism*

General surveys: Kimball, *American Architecture,* chs. 4–6; Eberlein, *Architecture of Colonial America;* Jackson, *American Colonial Architecture;* Kimball, *Domestic Architecture,* pp. 53–141. *The Georgian Period,* 3 vols., edited by William Rotch Ware, 1899–1902, a pioneering work, is valuable for its measured drawings and photographs of eighteenth-century buildings.

Fiske Kimball's "Romantic Classicism in Architecture," in *Gazette des Beaux-Arts,* vol. 25, Feb., 1944, p. 95, is an effort to place classicism within the larger romantic movement.

On religious architecture: Mason, *Colonial Churches of Tidewater Virginia;* Frances B. Johnston (photographs) and Thomas T. Waterman (text), *The Early Architecture of North Carolina,* 1941; Philip B. Wallace, *Colonial Churches . . . of Pennsylvania, New Jersey and Delaware,* 1931; Aymar Embury II, *Early American Churches,* 1914. See Embury's studies of Christ Church, Philadelphia, in *Architectural Record,* vol. 32, p. 88; on St. Michael's, Charleston, in the same, vol. 31, p. 424; on King's Chapel, Boston, in the same, p. 418; on St. Paul's, New York, in the same, vol. 32, p. 81. See also Horace H. F. Jayne, "Cloisters at Ephrata," in *American Magazine of Art,* vol. 29, Sept., 1936, p. 594.

On PETER HARRISON (1716–1775): See Carl Bridenbaugh, *Peter Harrison, First American Architect,* 1949.

On domestic architecture: See references in first paragraph above. For New England: John M. Howells. *The Architectural Heritage of the Piscataqua,* 1937, and *The Architectural Heritage of the Merrimac,* 1941; Isham and Brown, *Early Connecticut Houses,* chs. 4, 7–8; Downing, *Early Homes of Rhode Island,* chs. 3–4; Henry-Russell Hitchcock, *Rhode Island Architecture,* 1939; Downing and Scully, *The Architectural Heritage of Newport,* chs. 3–6. Thomas T. Waterman discusses the Savage house, Boston, in *Old Time New England,* vol. 17, Jan., 1927, p. 107. On the Hancock house, see Walter K. Watkins in the same, vol. 17, July, 1926, p. 3, and Donald Millar in the same, Jan., 1927, p. 121.

On wall decorations: Kate Sanborn, *Old Time Wall Papers,* 1905; Edward B. Allen, *Early American Wall Paintings,* 1926; Edna Donnell, "The Van Rensselaer Wall Paper and J. B. Jackson," in *Metropolitan Museum Studies,* vol. 4, 1932, p. 77.

On domestic architecture: See references above in section 10, ch. 1; see also Eberlein, *Manors and Historic Homes of the Hudson Valley,* chs. 15–45; Reynolds, *Dutch Houses;* Frank Cousins and Philip M. Riley, *The Colonial Architecture of Philadelphia,* 1920. On the group of houses in Fairmount Park, see Marie G. Kimball in *Architectural Record,* vol. 62, July, 1927, p. 1. See also Rosamond J. Beirne and John F. Scarff, *William Buckland, 1734–1774; Architect of Virginia and Maryland,* 1958; Deering Davis, *Annapolis Houses,* 1947; Waterman, *Domestic Architecture of Tidewater Virginia,* and *The Mansions of Virginia.* William Byrd is quoted from John S. Bassett, *The Writings of Colonel William Byrd,* 1901. See also Johnson and Waterman, *Early Architecture of North Carolina;* Alonzo T. Dill, Jr., "Tryon's Palace," in *North Carolina Historical Review,* vol. 19, Apr., 1942, p. 119; Alice R. H. and D. E. H. Smith, *The Dwelling Houses of Charleston,* 1917; Beatrice St. J. Ravenel, *Architects of Charleston,* 1945.

On the beginnings of American sculpture: See references under section 10, ch. 1; also Pauline A. Pinckney, *American Figureheads and Their Carvers,* 1940. On wax portraits, see Ethel S. Bolton in *Old Time New England,* vol. 13, July, 1922, p. 3. On the Drownes, see J. Rayner Whipple, "Old New England Weather Vanes," in *Old Time New England,* vol. 31, Oct., 1940, p. 45.

Chapter 4 / *Likenesses in a Proper Manner*

On the pre-Revolutionary painters: Fourteen artists are included in Cuthbert Lee, *Early American Portrait Painters,* 1929, with useful lists of works in public collections. See also Burroughs, *Limners and Likenesses,* ch. 2; Flexner, *First Flowers;* Barker, *American Painting,* divisions 1–3; Richardson, *Painting in America,* chs. 1–5; *From Colony to Nation,* 1949, catalogue of an exhibition at the Art Institute of Chicago; Belknap, *American Colonial Painting.* William Kelby in *Notes on American Artists,* 1922, compiles evidence of the artists' activities from newspapers. See also Anna W. Rutledge, *Artists in the Life of Charleston,* 1949.

William Byrd's characterization of Bridges is quoted from the *Virginia Magazine of History and Biography,* vol. 36, 1928, p. 211.

On individual artists: (Since few of them have as yet received exhaustive, full-length treatment, one must consult magazine articles, essays, exhibition catalogues, and the publications of historical societies.)

On JEREMIAH THEUS (1719–1774): Margaret S. Middleton, *Jeremiah Theus, Colonial Artist of Charles Town,* 1953.

On JOHN WATSON (1686–1768): John Hill Morgan

in *Proceedings of the American Antiquarian Society,* vol. 50, Oct., 1940, p. 225, and vol. 52, April, 1942, p. 126.

On J. COOPER (not discussed here): See Bartlett Cowdrey, "J. Cooper, an Early New England Portrait Painter," in *Panorama,* vol. 1, Nov., 1945, p. 15. Cooper was active 1714–1718.

On HENRIETTA JOHNSTON (active c. 1708–1728/9): Anna W. Rutledge, "Who Was Henrietta Johnston?" in *Antiques,* vol. 51, Mar., 1947, p. 183.

On JOHN SMIBERT (1688–1751): Henry W. Foote, *John Smibert, Painter,* 1950; Hagen, *Birth of the American Tradition,* ch. 2. Mather Byles's poem on Smibert here cited is quoted in full by Henry W. Foote in "Mr. Smibert Shows His Pictures," in *New England Quarterly,* vol. 8, Mar., 1935, p. 14.

On GUSTAVUS HESSELIUS (1682–1755): See catalogue of exhibition at the Philadelphia Museum of Art, 1938, with foreword by Christian Brinton.

On ROBERT FEKE (1706[?]–1752[?]): Henry W. Foote, *Robert Feke,* 1930; the essay by Lloyd Goodrich in the catalogue of the Feke exhibition at the Whitney Museum of American Art, N.Y., 1946.

On PETER PELHAM (1697–1751): William H. Whitmore, *Notes Concerning Peter Pelham,* 1867; also the article on Pelham as an engraver by Anne Allison in *Antiques,* vol. 52, Dec., 1947, p. 441.

The work of CHARLES BRIDGES (active 1735–c. 1740) is discussed by Harry B. Wehle, "A Portrait by Charles Bridges," in *Metropolitan Museum Bulletin,* vol. 20, 1925, p. 197; Flexner, *First Flowers,* ch. 4, pp. 103–108, and p. 294.

On JOHN WOLLASTON (active here c. 1749–c. 1767): See notes by John H. Morgan in *Brooklyn Museum Quarterly,* vol. 10, Jan., 1923, p. 1; and article by Theodore Bolton and Harry L. Binsse in *Antiquarian,* vol. 16, 1931, p. 30.

On JOHN HESSELIUS (1728–1778): See Theodore Bolton and George C. Groce, Jr., "John Hesselius: An Account of His Life and the First Catalogue of His Portraits," in *Art Quarterly,* vol. 2, 1939, p. 77.

On WILLLIAM WILLIAMS (flourished 1740–1794): William Sawitzky, "William Williams, First Instructor to Benjamin West," in *Antiques,* vol. 31, May, 1937, p. 240; and "Further Light on the Work of William Williams," in *New-York Historical Society Quarterly Bulletin,* vol. 25, 1941, p. 101.

On JOSEPH BADGER (1708–1765): Lawrence Park, *Joseph Badger,* 1918; and Joseph Badger of Boston and His Portraits of Children," in *Old Time New England,* vol. 13, Jan., 1923, p. 99.

On JOSEPH BLACKBURN: Lawrence Park, *Joseph Blackburn,* 1923; and John H. Morgan and Henry W. Foote, "An Extension of Lawrence Park's Descriptive List of the Work of Joseph Blackburn," in *Proceedings of the American Antiquarian Society,* vol. 46, Apr., 1936, p. 15.

On JOHN GREENWOOD (1727–1792): Alan Burroughs, *John Greenwood in America,* 1943 (with a check list).

See also, Lila P. Lyman, "William Johnston (1732–1772), Forgotten Portrait Painter of New England," in *New-York Historical Society Quarterly,* vol. 39, Jan., 1955, p. 62; Susan Sawitzky, "The Portraits of William Johnston: A Preliminary Checklist," in the same, Jan., 1955, p. 79; Helen B. Smith, "John Mare (1739–c. 1795), New York Portrait Painter," in the same, vol. 35, Oct., 1951, p. 354.

On miniatures: See Harry B. Wehle, *American Miniatures* (1730–1850), 1927.

SECTION 12

Book One / Part Three / The Revolutionary Generation

Introduction / *Emergence of the Yankee*

On the historical movement: See Nettels, *Roots of American Civilization;* Evarts B. Greene, *The Revolutionary Generation,* 1943 (vol. 4 in the "History of American Life" series); Morais, *Struggle for American Freedom,* chs. 5 and 6.

The Revolutionary writers (Paine, Trumbull, Freneau, *et al.*) are discussed in vol. 1 of *Literary History of the United States;* selections from their work appear in Robert E. Spiller, *The Roots of National Culture,* 1933 (vol. 1 of *American Literature: A Period Anthology*).

Beginnings of the graphic arts: Weitenkampf, *American Graphic Art;* Stokes and Haskell, *American Historical Prints;* Stauffer, *American Engravers* (brief biographies and check lists); Carl W. Drepperd, *Early American Prints,* 1930, chs. 2–3; Charles A. Munn, "Some Pre-Revolutionary American Engravers," in *Art and Progress,* vol. 5, Oct., 1914, p. 407; Henry W. Cunningham, *Christian Remick,* 1904.

On Copley see references under ch. 5 in this section; on Peale, under ch. 6; on Trumbull, under section 15, ch. 11.

Chapter 5 / *Fair Fraud and Vulgar Imitation*

On BENJAMIN WEST (1738–1820): John Galt, *The Life, Studies and Works of Benjamin West,* 1820; Burroughs, *Limners and Likenesses,* ch. 3, section 10; Flexner, *America's Old Masters,* ch. 1; Lee, *Early American Portrait Painters,* p. 79; William Sawitzky,

"The American Work of Benjamin West," in *Pennsylvania Magazine of History and Biography,* vol. 62, Oct., 1938, p. 433; catalogue of the West exhibition at the Philadelphia Museum of Art, 1938, with an essay and notes by Henri Marceau; Charles H. Morgan and Margaret C. Toole in *Art in America,* vol. 38, Dec., 1950; Grose Evans, *Benjamin West and the Taste of His Times,* 1959.

For European aesthetic doctrines which affected West, see references above in section 11, "Introduction"; also Hagen, *Birth of the American Tradition,* ch. 5.

The Death of General Wolfe is variously discussed by the following: Agnes Addison in *College Art Journal,* vol. 5, Nov., 1945, p. 23; Charles Mitchell in *Journal of the Warburg and Courtauld Institutes,* vol. 7, Jan.–June, 1944, p. 20; Edgar Wind in the same, vol. 10, 1947, p. 159.

On JOHN S. COPLEY (1738–1815): Augustus T. Perkins, *A Sketch of the Life and a List of Some of the Works of John Singleton Copley,* 1873; Martha B. Amory, *The Domestic and Artistic Life of John Singleton Copley, R.A.,* 1882. More recent and more reliable: Copley is discussed by James T. Flexner in *America's Old Masters,* ch. 2; *First Flowers,* chs. 9–10; *John Singleton Copley,* 1948. See also John H. Morgan's "Notes on Copley," in *Antiques,* vol. 31, Mar., 1937, p. 116; and his *John Singleton Copley,* 1939. Copley's American work is fully presented by Barbara N. Parker and Anne B. Wheeler, *John Singleton Copley,* 1938, with excellent illustrations, and notes on portraits and their subjects.

The Copley and Henry Pelham quotations are from "Letters and Papers of John Singleton Copley and Henry Pelham," in *Collections of the Massachusetts Historical Society,* no. 71, 1914.

The letter from Copley to Samuel Adams in 1795 (Ms. Room, New York Public Library) was first mentioned by Flexner in *America's Old Masters.*

Chapter 6 / *Sons of Liberty*

On CHARLES W. PEALE (1741–1827): Flexner, *America's Old Masters,* ch. 3; Theodore Bolton and George C. Groce, Jr., "Charles Willson Peale: The First Catalogue of His Portraits," in *Art Quarterly,* vol. 2, 1939, p. 417; Theodore Bolton, "Charles Willson Peale, an Account of His Life and Work," in the same, p. 354. The most complete and authoritative work is the two-volume biography by Charles C. Sellers: vol. 1, *The Artist of the Revolution; The Early Life of Charles Willson Peale,* 1939; vol. 2, *Charles Willson Peale, Later Life,* 1947. See also catalogue of an exhibition, "Paintings by the Peale Family," at Cincinnati Museum of Art, 1954.

On RALPH EARL (1751–1801): Frederic F. Sherman, "Ralph Earl: An Eighteenth Century Connecticut Portrait Painter," in *Art in America,* vol. 22, June, 1934, p. 81; and "The Painting of Ralph Earl," in the same, vol. 27, Oct., 1929, p. 163. See also the catalogue of the Earl exhibition at the Whitney Museum of American Art (N.Y.), 1945, with an essay by William Sawitzky; and Lloyd Goodrich, "Ralph Earl," in *Magazine of Art,* vol. 39, Jan., 1946, p. 2. Sawitzky's definitive work on Earl was incomplete at his death, and has not yet been published.

On JOHN DURAND (active 1767–1782): The Rapalje portrait, see *Antiques,* vol. 51, Mar., 1947, p. 174; the Ray portraits, see John W. Myer in *Bulletin of the Museum of the City of New York,* vol. 5, Jan., 1942, p. 27. See also Thomas Thorne, "America's First Nude?" in *William and Mary Quarterly,* vol. 6, Oct., 1949, p. 565.

The authority on WINTHROP CHANDLER (1747–1790) is Nina F. Little, guest editor of the special issue of *Art in America,* vol. 35, Apr., 1947, on Chandler's work. See also her supplementary article in the same, vol. 36, Apr., 1948, p. 81.

On other painters in this group: Charles H. Hart, "Edward Savage," in *Proceedings of Massachusetts Historical Society,* vol. 19, 1905, p. 1; Louisa Dresser on Savage in *Art in America,* vol. 40, no. 4, Autumn, 1952; Harriette M. Forbes on Gullager's portraits of the Salisburys in *Old Time New England,* vol. 21, July, 1930, p. 3; Louisa Dresser on Gullager, in *Art in America,* vol. 37, July, 1949; William Sawitzky, *Matthew Pratt, 1734–1805,* 1942; Susan Sawitzky (ed.), "Portraits by Reuben Moulthrop: A Checklist by William Sawitzky," in *New-York Historical Society Quarterly,* Oct., 1955, p. 385; William Roberts, "Henry Bembridge," in *Art in America,* vol. 6, Feb., 1918, p. 96.

On the Jennys family: See references under section 15, ch. 10.

SECTION 13

Book Two / Self-Conscious Republic

The Period in General

On republican America: Beard, *Rise of American Civilization,* chs. 7–11; Morais, *Struggle for American Freedom,* ch. 7; John A. Krout and Dixon R. Fox, *The Completion of Independence,* vol. 5 in the "History of American Life" series; Francis Franklin, *The Rise of the American Nation,* 1943.

On literature and taste: Parrington, *Main Currents,* vol. 1, book 3; Spiller, *The Roots of National Culture. Literary History of the United States,* vol. 1, sections 9–15.

On architecture and crafts of the period: Morrison, *Early American Architecture,* part 3; Andrews, *Archi-*

tecture, Ambition and Americans, ch. 3; Roos, *Writings on Early American Architecture; Historic American Buildings Survey;* Kimball, *Domestic Architecture,* p. 145, "Houses of the Early Republic"; Hamlin, *The American Spirit in Architecture;* Williamson, *The American Craftsman;* Halsey and Tower, *The Homes of Our Ancestors;* Rogers, *American Interior Design,* ch. 3; Charles O. Cornelius, *Furniture Masterpieces of Duncan Phyfe,* 1922.

Regional and local studies which include this period: Rexford Newcomb, *Architecture of the Old Northwest Territory,* 1950, and *Architecture in Old Kentucky,* 1953; Frederick D. Nichols, *The Early Architecture of Georgia,* 1957; Downing and Scully, *The Architectural Heritage of Newport;* Richard H. Howland and Eleanor P. Spencer, *The Architecture of Baltimore,* 1953.

On painting: Isham and Cortissoz, *History of American Painting,* chs. 5–9; Burroughs, *Limners and Likenesses,* ch. 4; ch. 5, sections 16–18; Neuhaus, *History and Ideals of American Art,* chs. 3–6; Cuthbert Lee, *Early American Portrait Painters,* sections on the Peales, Stuart, Trumbull, Joseph Wright, Robert Fulton, with notes on their works in public collections; Barker, *American Painting,* division 4; James T. Flexner, *The Light of Distant Skies, 1760–1835,* 1954, the second in a series on the history of American painting; Richardson, *Painting in America,* chs. 6, 7.

SECTION 14

Book Two / Part One / The Jeffersonian Promise

Introduction / *Christians, Mohawks, Democrats*

Moore's verses on Buffalo are quoted from *The Poetical Works of Thomas Moore,* 1881, vol. 2, p. 95. For Audubon's impressions, see his *Delineations of American Scenery and Character.* Freneau's poem, "Lines Intended for Mr. Peale's Exhibition," is quoted from *The Poems of Philip Freneau,* 1903, vol. 2, p. 246.

On the Adamesque in England: *The Works in Architecture of Robert and James Adam,* 3 vols. 1778–1822; John Swarbrick, *Robert Adam and His Brothers,* 1915; James Upton, *The Adam Style,* 1917; Mowbray A. Green, *Eighteenth Century Architecture at Bath,* 1904.

On CHARLES BULFINCH: See references under this section, ch. 7. The authority on Jefferson's architecture is Fiske Kimball; see his *Thomas Jefferson, Architect,* 1916, and his *Thomas Jefferson and the First Monument of the Classical Revival in America* (on the Richmond Capitol). See also Ihna T. Frary, *Thomas Jefferson, Architect and Builder,* 1931; Karl Lehmann, *Thomas Jefferson, American Humanist,* 1947; Eleanor D. Berman, *Thomas Jefferson among the Arts,* 1947.

On Jefferson's activities concerning the Houdon statue: See *The Writings of Thomas Jefferson* (Paul L. Ford, ed.), vol. 4, pp. 26–28, 72–75. See also Charles H. Hart and Edward Biddle, *Jean Antoine Houdon,* 1911.

Chapter 7 / *The Adamesques*

On CHARLES BULFINCH (1763–1844): Ellen S. Bulfinch (ed.), *The Life and Letters of Charles Bulfinch,* 1896; Charles A. Place, *Charles Bulfinch, Architect and Citizen,* 1925; John M. Howells, "Charles Bulfinch, Architect" in *American Architect and Building News,* vol. 93, June, 1908, p. 195; Martha Shannon, "The Architecture of Charles Bulfinch," in *American Magazine of Art,* vol. 16, Aug., 1925, p. 431. On the Harrison Gray Otis house, see *Bulletin of the Society for the Preservation of New England Antiquities,* no. 17, Oct., 1926, and no. 36, April, 1946.

On ASHER BENJAMIN (1773–1845): F. T. Howe, "Asher Benjamin," in *Antiques,* vol. 40, Dec., 1941, p. 364; John G. Greene on the Charles Street Church in *Old Time New England,* vol. 30, Jan., 1940, p. 87.

On SAMUEL MCINTIRE (1757–1811): Fiske Kimball, *Mr. Samuel McIntire,* 1940; Essex Institute, Salem, Mass., *Samuel McIntire: A Bicentennial Symposium,* 1957. McIntire's furniture designs and decorative carvings are discussed by Kimball in *Antiques,* vol. 18, Nov., 1930, p. 388, Dec., 1930, p. 498; vol. 19, Jan., 1931, p. 30, Feb., 1931, p. 117, Mar., 1931, p. 207; vol. 23, Feb., 1933, p. 56; see also Mabel M. Swan in the same, vol. 26, Oct., 1934, p. 130.

On the Derby mansion: Fiske Kimball, *The Elias Hasket Derby Mansion in Salem* (reprinted from *Historical Collections of Essex Institute,* vol. 60, 1924); Mabel M. Swan, "Where Elias Hasket Derby Bought His Furniture," in *Antiques,* vol. 20, Nov., 1931, p. 280. Eliza Southgate's description of the mansion is in "A Girl's Life Eighty Years Ago," in *Scribner's,* vol. 2, 1887, p. 78.

On the Gardner-Pingree house: See Pauline S. Chadwell in *Antiques,* vol. 47, May, 1945, p. 282.

On the Adamesque in other regions: Hitchcock, *Rhode Island Architecture;* Howells, *Architectural Heritage of the Piscataqua* and his *Architectural Heritage of the Merrimac;* Samuel Green, "Thomas Lord, Joiner and Housewright," in *Magazine of Art,* vol. 40, Oct., 1947, p. 230; Ravenel, *Architects of Charleston;* I. T. Frary, *Early Homes of Ohio,* 1936.

Chapter 8 / *From Goose Creek to Tiber*

On L'Enfant's plan: *Columbia Historical Society, Records,* vol. 6, 1903, p. 1; vol. 12, 1909, p. 1; Fiske Kimball, "Origin of the Plan of Washington," in *Archi-*

tectural Review, vol. 7, Sept., 1918, p. 41; Elizabeth S. Kite, *L'Enfant and Washington,* 1929.

Moore's lines on the Capital are quoted from *The Poetical Works of Thomas Moore,* 1881, vol. 2, p. 83.

On the evolution of the U.S. Capitol: Glenn Brown, *History of the U.S. Capitol,* 1900, vol. 1; Charles E. Fairman, *Art and Artists of the Capitol of the U.S.A.,* 1927; I. T. Frary, *They Built the Capitol,* 1940; Fiske Kimball and Wells Bennett, "William Thornton and His Design for the National Capitol," in *Art Studies,* vol 1, 1923, p. 76; Talbot Hamlin, "The Birth of American Architecture," in *Parnassus,* vol. 10, Nov., 1938, p. 8. See also Roger H. Newton, "Bulfinch's Design for the Library of Congress," in *Art Bulletin,* vol. 23, Sept., 1941, p. 221.

On BENJAMIN H. LATROBE (1764–1820): The authoritative work is Talbot Hamlin, *Benjamin Henry Latrobe,* 1955; see also *Journal of Latrobe,* 1905; Ferdinand C. Latrobe II, "Benjamin Henry Latrobe," in *Maryland Historical Magazine,* vol. 33, 1938, p. 247; also Talbot Hamlin in the same, vol. 37, Dec., 1942, p. 339. Latrobe's ms. notes, "Ideas on the Encouragement of the Fine Arts in America," are in the Maryland Historical Society. See Fiske Kimball on the Bank of Pennsylvania in *Architectural Record,* vol. 44, Aug., 1918, p. 132. On the Pump House, see Costen Fitz-Gibbon in *Architectural Record,* vol. 62, July, 1927, p. 19. Latrobe's remarks on Greek architecture are quoted from his *Anniversary Oration for the Society of Artists of the U.S.,* May 8, 1811 (a pamphlet). On the Bank of the United States, see Fiske Kimball in *Architectural Record,* vol. 58, Dec., 1925, p. 581.

On William Strickland and Robert Mills, see references under section 17, ch. 13.

On the Fairmount Water Works: See Harold D. Eberlein in *Architectural Record,* vol. 62, July, 1927, p. 57. Philip Hone's remarks are quoted from his *Diary* for June 6, 1838 (original ms. in the New York Historical Society).

On the University of Virginia: See Lewis Mumford, *The South in Architecture,* 1941, lecture 12.

On Union College: See H. A. Larrabee, *Joseph Jacques Ramée and America's First Unified College Plan,* 1934 (a pamphlet). On ITHIEL TOWN, see Roger H. Newton, *Town and Davis, Architects,* 1942. On GIDEON SHRYOCK, see Alfred Andrews in *Antiques,* vol. 48, July, 1945, p. 35. On the Salisbury mansion, see Harriette M. Forbes in *Old Time New England,* vol. 20, Jan., 1930, p. 99.

On early Gothic Revival buildings: See references under section 17, ch. 14; see also William S. Rusk, "Godefroy and St. Mary's Chapel, Baltimore," in *Liturgical Arts,* vol. 3, 1933, p. 140.

On early industrial buildings: Hitchcock, *Rhode Island Architecture;* John Coolidge, *Mill and Mansion,* 1942.

On New Harmony: Julia L. Knox in *Indiana Magazine of History,* vol. 32, Mar., 1935, p. 52.

On Shaker art: Marguerite F. Melcher, *The Shaker Adventure,* 1941; Edward D. Andrews, "Communal Architecture of the Shakers," in *Magazine of Art,* vol. 30, Dec., 1937, p. 710; Elizabeth McCausland, "The Shaker Legacy," in the same, vol. 37, Dec., 1944, p. 287; Edward D. and Faith Andrews, *Shaker Furniture,* 1950.

Chapter 9 / *Sculpture's Wooden Age*

References to late eighteenth-century carvers occur in Lorado Taft, *History of American Sculpture,* 1924, ch. 1; Albert T. Gardner includes a list of men before 1800 in *Yankee Stonecutters,* 1945, p. 59. Many craftsmen are discussed in Pauline A. Pinckney, *American Figureheads and Their Carvers,* 1940.

On the figure carvings of McIntire and the Skillins: Mabel M. Swan in *Antiques,* vol. 20, Dec., 1931, p. 338; Homer E. Keyes in the same, vol. 23, Apr., 1933, p. 142; Leroy L. Thwing in the same, vol. 33, June, 1938, p. 236.

On the Italian carvers in America: Brown, *History of the U. S. Capitol,* vol. 1, ch. 7; Fairman, *Art and Artists of the Capitol, passim.*

On carved and modeled profile portraits: Fiske Kimball, "Joseph Wright and His Portraits of Washington," in *Antiques,* vol. 17, Jan., 1930, p. 35; A. J. Wall, "Wax Portraiture," in *New-York Historical Society Quarterly Bulletin,* vol. 9, Apr., 1935, p. 3, and "Joseph Valaperta, Sculptor," in the same, vol. 11, July, 1927, p. 53; Ethel S. Bolton, *American Wax Portraits,* 1929.

The *Portfolio,* vol. 4, July, 1814, p. 94, has an unsigned review of the Columbian Society and the Pennsylvania Academy exhibition with comments on Miller, Rush, and other carvers.

On WILLIAM RUSH (1756–1833): See catalogue of the Rush exhibition at the Philadelphia Museum of Art, 1937, with introduction and notes by Henri Marceau. References to Rush works occur in J. Thomas Scharf and Thompson Westcott, *History of Philadelphia,* 1884. Latrobe's tribute to Rush is quoted from his *Anniversary Oration for the Society of Artists of the U.S.,* 1811 (a pamphlet).

On JOHN FRAZEE (1791–1858): His autobiography was published in *North American Quarterly Review,* vol. 6, 1835, p. 1; excerpts are in the *American Collector,* vol. 15, 1946, Sept., p. 15, Oct., p. 11, Nov., p. 12.

For information on HEZEKIAH AUGUR (1791–1858) the author is indebted to notes for a thesis loaned by

Prof. George H. Hamilton of Yale University. The *American Journal of Science and Arts,* vol. 9, June, 1825, p. 173, has references to Augur.

On JOSEPH WILSON and other carvers of his region: see Mabel M. Swan, "Ship Carvers of Newburyport," in *Antiques,* vol. 48, Aug., 1945, p. 78.

On JOHN HENRI ISAAC BROWERE (1792–1834): Charles H. Hart, *Browere's Life Masks of Great Americans,* 1899; Knoedler and Co., catalogue of an exhibition, *Life Masks of Noted Americans of 1825,* 1940.

SECTION 15

Book Two / Part Two / *Republican Painting*

Introduction / *Museums, Academies, and Panoramas*

Dunlap lists several American art collections in his *History,* vol. 3, ch. 14 (Goodspeed ed.). See also T. B. Thorpe, "New York Artists Fifty Years Ago," in *Appleton's Journal,* vol. 7, May 25, 1872, p. 573. Van Wyck Brooks discusses the literary and artistic life of this period in the early chapters of *The World of Washington Irving,* 1944.

On JOHN J. AUDUBON (1785–1851): Francis H. Herrick, *Audubon the Naturalist,* 2d ed., 1938; Donald A. Shelley, "John James Audubon, Artist," in *Magazine of Art,* vol. 39, May, 1946, p. 171.

On Saint-Mémin (1770–1852): See references under this section, ch. 10.

On still life: Born, *Still-Life Painting in America,* 1947; John I. H. Baur, "The Peales and the Development of American Still Life," in *Art Quarterly,* Winter, 1940, p. 81.

On panoramas: S. Hausmann, "Die Erfindung der Panoramen," in *Kunst für Alle,* vol. 4, Mar., 1889, p. 198; also Germain Bapst, *Essai sur l'histoire des panoramas et dioramas,* 1891. Dunlap's remarks on panoramas are in his *History,* vol. 2, p. 165 (Goodspeed ed.).

On the printed view: Drepperd, *Early American Prints,* chs. 4–6; Stokes and Haskell, *American Historical Prints;* Sydney Kellner, "Early Aquatints in America," in *Prints,* vol. 6, 1935–1936, p. 143.

On cartoonists: Murrell, *A History of American Graphic Humor,* vol. 1, chs. 1–6.

On Charles W. Peale's museum: Harold S. Coleman, "Peale's Museum," in *Popular Science Monthly,* vol. 75, Sept., 1909, p. 221; see also Peale's correspondence in *Pennsylvania Magazine of History and Biography,* vol. 9, 1885, p. 121. A full account is in vol. 2 of Charles C. Sellers' biography of Peale. Faux's description is reprinted in *Early Western Travels* (Reuben G. Thwaites, ed.), 1905, vol. 12, p. 67.

On academies: Peale's efforts are described in Sellers' biography of Peale, vol. 2; his statement of purpose is quoted from Helen W. Henderson, *The Pennsylvania Academy of the Fine Arts,* 1911, p. 5. See also Anna W. Rutledge, *Cumulative Record of Exhibition Catalogues: The Pennsylvania Academy of the Fine Arts, 1807–1879,* etc., 1955; historical essay on the American Academy by Theodore Sizer in vol. 1 of Mary B. Cowdrey, *American Academy of Fine Arts and American Art-Union,* 1953; Clark, *History of the National Academy of Design.* For the Morse-Trumbull controversy, see Morse's Anniversary Discourse before the National Academy of Design, 1827 (a pamphlet); also his reply to Trumbull, 1833 (a pamphlet). On the Boston Athenaeum, see Mabel M. Swan, *The Athenaeum Gallery,* 1940.

On the beginnings of art criticism: Caroline V. Davison, "Maximilian and Eliza Godefroy" in *Maryland Historical Magazine,* vol. 29, 1934, p. 1; William D. Hoyt, Jr., "Eliza Godefroy: Destiny's Football" in the same, vol. 36, Mar., 1941, p. 10; Harold E. Dickson, *Observations on American Art; Selections from the Writings of John Neal,* 1943. On William Dunlap, see references below, under section 17, "Introduction."

Chapter 10 / *Portraits*

For refereinces to Charles W. Peale: See above, under section 12, ch. 6. On James Peale, see Cuthbert Lee, *Early American Portrait Painters,* p. 263. On Rembrandt Peale, see catalogue of 1923 exhibition at the Pennsylvania Academy of the Fine Arts.

On miniatures: See Theodore Bolton, *Early American Portrait Painters in Miniature,* 1921; Harry B. Weyle and Theodore Bolton, *American Miniatures, 1730–1850,* 1927; Ruel P. Tolman, *The Life and Works of Edward Greene Malbone,* 1958. Virgil Barker discusses several miniaturists of this period in *American Painting,* ch. 39.

On profile portraits: K. M. Knox, *The Sharples,* 1930; John H. Morgan, "The Work of M. Févret de St.-Mémin," in *Brooklyn Museum Quarterly,* vol. 5, Jan., 1918, p. 5; Fillmore Norfleet, *St.-Mémin in Virginia,* 1942; Mable M. Swan, "Master Hubard, Profilist and Painter," in *Antiques,* vol. 15, June, 1929, p. 496, and "A Neglected Aspect of Hubard," in the same, vol. 20, Oct., 1931, p. 222. On the physionotrace, see Rembrandt Peale's note in the *Crayon,* vol. 4, 1857, p. 307.

On John Trumbull: See references under this section, ch. 11.

On JOHN VANDERLYN (1775–1852): No satisfactory study has been published. Marius Schoonmaker included a biographical sketch in his *History of Kingston, N.Y.,* 1888. The author is indebted to John J. Vrooman for the use of typed copies of notes by Robert Gosman for an unpublished life of Vanderlyn; the original ms. is in the New-York Historical Society, N.Y. See John E. Stillwell, *History of the Burr Portraits,* 1928; Theodore Bolton, "Vanderlyn and American Panoramania," in *Art News,* vol. 55, no. 7, part 1, Nov., 1956, p. 43.

On the nonprofessional portrait painters: Mary E. Chase, *Jonathan Fisher,* 1948; Clara E. Sears, *Some American Primitives,* 1941; Fannie H. Eckstorm, "Jeremiah Pearson Hardy," in *Old Time New England,* vol. 30, Oct., 1939, p. 41; Frederic F. Sherman, *Richard Jennys, New England Portrait Painter"* 1941; Agnes M. Dods on the Jennys family, especially J. William Jennys, in *Art in America,* vol. 33, Jan., 1945, p. 4, and vol. 34, Apr., 1946, p. 114; William L. Warren, *"The Jennys Portraits,"* in *Connecticut Historical Society Bulletin,* vol. 20, no. 4, Oct., 1955; Nina F. Little on Dr. Rufus Hathaway in *Art in America,* vol. 41, Summer, 1953; J. Hall Pleasants, *Joshua Johnston,* 1940.

On GILBERT STUART (1755–1828): Lawrence Park, *Gilbert Stuart,* 1926, 4 vols. (a pictorial record of his work); William T. Whitley, *Gilbert Stuart,* 1932; Mantle Fielding, *Gilbert Stuart's Portraits of George Washington,* 1923; Frank J. Mather, Jr., "The Origin of Gilbert Stuart's Style," in *Art Studies,* vol. 4, 1926, p. 3; Flexner, *America's Old Masters,* ch. 4, and *Gilbert Stuart,* 1955.

Svinin's description of old Stuart is quoted from Avrahm Yarmolinsky, *A Memoir on Paul Svinin,* 1930, p. 34.

On the Stuartesques: See John H. Morgan, *Gilbert Stuart and His Pupils,* 1939; catalogue of Matthew H. Jouett exhibition at J. B. Speed Memorial Museum, Louisville, Ky., 1939; Edgar P. Richardson, "Portraits by Jacob Eichholtz," in *Art in America,* vol. 27, Jan., 1939, p. 14; Cuthbert Lee on Mather Brown in *Early American Portrait Painters,* p. 279; Theodore Bolton and Irwin F. Cortelyou, *Ezra Ames of Albany,* 1955.

On CHESTER HARDING (1792–1866): See his own account, *My Egotistography,* 1866; also Margaret E. White (ed.), *A Sketch of Chester Harding, Artist,* 1890.

On THOMAS SULLY (1783–1872): See his own *Hints to Young Painters,* 1873; Edward Biddle and Mantle Fielding, *The Life and Works of Thomas Sully,* 1921; catalogue of exhibition, the Pennsylvania Academy of the Fine Arts, 1922; Charles H. Hart (ed.), *A Register of Portraits Painted by Thomas Sully, 1801–1871,* 1909.

On PHILIP TILYARD (1785–1830): See article by Wilbur H. Hunter, Jr., in *William and Mary Quarterly,* vol 7, July, 1950, p. 393.

On SAMUEL F. B. MORSE (1791–1872): Carleton Mabee, *The American Leonardo,* 1943; Oliver W. Larkin, *Samuel F. B. Morse and American Democratic Art,* 1954.

On JOHN WESLEY JARVIS (1780–1840): See Theodore Bolton and George C. Groce, Jr., "John Wesley Jarvis, an Account of His Life and the First Catalogue of His Work," in *Art Quarterly,* vol. 1, 1938, p. 299; Harold E. Dickson, *John Wesley Jarvis,* 1949. Audubon describes Jarvis in his *Delineations,* 1926 ed., p. 86.

On JOHN NEAGLE (1796–1865): See Virgil Barker in the *Arts,* vol. 8, July, 1925, p. 7; also the catalogue of the Neagle exhibition at the Pennsylvania Academy of the Fine Arts, 1925, with biographical sketch by Mantle Fielding.

Chapter 11 / *The Dying Hercules*

On JOHN TRUMBULL (1756–1843): Theodore Sizer, *The Works of Col. John Trumbull,* 1950, and (ed.) *The Autobiography of Col. John Trumbull,* 1953. Jefferson's opinion of Trumbull as a historical painter is quoted from a letter to James Barbour, Jan. 19, 1817, in the Barbour papers, New York Public Library (called to the attention of the author by Professor Karl Lehmann). For the history of Trumbull's rotunda pictures, see Brown, *History of the U.S. Capitol,* vol. 1, ch. 7, and Fairman, *Art and Artists of the Capitol, passim.*

On WASHINGTON ALLSTON (1779–1843): Jared B. Flagg, *Life and Letters of Washington Allston,* 1893; Edgar P. Richardson, *Washington Allston,* 1948, an authoritative treatment of the artist in relation to his age.

For the controversy over Wertmüller's *Danaë* and Rembrandt Peale's *Io:* See the *Portfolio,* vol. 3, Jan., 1814, p. 35, and Feb., 1814, p. 154.

The episode of the mastodon is related in vol. 2 of the Sellers biography of Charles W. Peale, pp. 124–135. Peale's letter to West on his picture is in the *Pennsylvania Magazine of History and Biography,* vol. 9, 1885, p. 130.

Rembrandt Peale is here quoted from his pamphlet, *Account of the Skeleton of the Mammoth,* 1802–1803.

On Rembrandt Peale's *Court of Death:* This account is based on a pamphlet by Rembrandt Peale, *Peale's Court of Death,* 1845.

Chapter 12 / *The Rise of Landscape*

On landscape painting in Europe: Prosper Dorbec, *L'art du paysage en France,* 1925; M. H. Grant, *A Chronological History of Old English Landscape Painters in Oil,* 2 vols., 1926; C. Lewis Hind, *Landscape Painting,* 1923, vol. 1, part 3. Aesthetic theories: Edmund Burke, *An Essay on the Sublime and Beauti-*

ful, in *Cassell's National Library,* 1887, vol. 2, no. 88; Uvedale Price, *An Essay on the Picturesque,* 1794.

On WILLIAM WINSTANLEY, WILLIAM GROOMBRIDGE, THOMAS BECK, and FRANCIS GUY: J. Hall Pleasants, "Four Late Eighteenth Century Anglo-American Landscape Painters," 1943 (reprint from *Proceedings of the American Antiquarian Society,* Oct., 1942). See also "A Biographical Memoir of the Late George Beck," in the *Portfolio,* 3rd series, vol. 2, Aug., 1813, p. 117. Guy's remark on Americans is quoted from Faux's journal in *Early Western Travels,* vol. 12, p. 90.

On printed views: Stokes and Haskell, *American Historical Prints;* Frank Weitenkampf, "Early American Landscape Prints," in *Art Quarterly,* vol. 8, 1945, p. 40.

On marine painting: Catalogue by John I. H. Baur for "The Coast and the Sea," an exhibition at the Brooklyn Museum, 1948. Corné's landscapes in the Sullivan-Dorr house, Providence, R.I., are reproduced in Allen, *Early American Wall Paintings.*

On ROBERT SALMON (c. 1785–after 1840): See W. G. Constable in *Bulletin of Boston Museum of Fine Arts,* vol. 41, Feb., 1943, p. 2; also Charles D. Childs, "Robert Salmon, a Boston Painter of Ships and Views," in *Old Time New England,* vol. 28, Jan., 1938, p. 91.

On the Hudson River Portfolio: See *Old Print Shop Portfolio,* vol. 3, Sept., 1943, p. 3.

On the first American landscape school: Sydney Kellner, "The Beginnings of Landcape Painting in America," in *Art in America,* vol. 26, Oct., 1938, p. 158; *The Hudson River School and the Early American Landscape Tradition,* 1945, catalogue of an exhibition at the Art Institute of Chicago and the Whitney Museum, with an introduction and notes on the artists by Frederick A. Sweet, and many illustrations; Clara E. Sears, *Highlights among the Hudson River Artists,* 1947.

On Doughty, Cole and Durand: See references below, under section 18, ch. 16.

SECTION 16

Book Three / Democratic Vistas

The Period in General

Jacksonian America: Beard, *Rise of American Civilization,* chs. 12–16; Carl R. Fish, *The Rise of the Common Man,* 1927, vol. 6 in the "History of American Life" series; Arthur M. Schlesinger, Jr., *The Age of Jackson,* 1945; Curti, *The Growth of American Thought,* 1943, parts 4–5.

Literature: Parrington, *Main Currents,* vol. 2; Tremaine McDowell (ed.), *The Romantic Triumph: 1830–1860,* 1933; *Literary History of the United States,* vol. 1, sections 16–37 and vol. 2, sections 38–45; Van Wyck Brooks, *The Flowering of New England.* 1937.

Architecture: Roos, *Writings on Early American Architecture;* Kimball, *American Architecture,* chs. 8–9; Rogers, *American Interior Design,* pp. 95–140; Andrews, *Architecture, Ambition and Americans,* ch. 4; Henry-Russell Hitchcock, *"The Development of the Detached House in England and America,"* in *Architecture, Nineteenth and Twentieth Centuries,* 1958, ch. 15.

Painting: Isham and Cortissoz, *History of American Painting,* chs. 13–15; Neuhaus, *History and Ideals of American Art,* chs. 4–7; Saint-Gaudens, *The American Artist and His Times,* pp. 61–113; Barker, *American Painting,* division 5; *The M. and M. Karolik Collection of American Paintings, 1815 to 1865,* 1949, with an excellent essay by John I. H. Baur; Lipman and Winchester, *Primitive Painters in America;* Richardson, *Painting in America,* chs. 7–9.

Sculpture: Taft, *History of American Sculpture,* chs. 2–12; Gardner, *Yankee Stonecutters,* with brief essays on sculptors of this period and a biographical dictionary of sculptors born between 1800 and 1830.

Some art books of the period: Charles Lanman, *Letters from a Landcape Painter,* 1845; Charles E. Lester, *The Artists of America,* 1846; Henry T. Tuckerman, *Artist-Life,* 1847, and *Book of the Artists,* 1867; James J. Jarves, *Art Hints,* 1855, *The Art Idea,* 1864, and *Art Thoughts,* 1869. Valuable material is to be found in the periodical, the *Crayon,* published 1855–1861.

A useful reference book for this period is *National Academy of Design Exhibition Record, 1826–1860,* compiled by Bartlett Cowdrey, 2 vols., 1943. See also: Kouwenhoven, *Made in America;* Lynes, *The Tastemakers;* Lilian B. Miller, "Patronage, Patriotism and Taste in Mid-Ninteenth-Century America," in *Magazine of Art,* vol. 45, Nov., 1952, p. 322.

SECTION 17

Book Three / Part One / Jacksonian Ferment

Introduction / *Shapes of Democracy*

Foreign visitors and their impressions: Thomas Hamilton, *Men and Manners in America,* 2 vols., 1833; Frances Trollope, *Domestic Manners of the Americans,* 1832; Frances Kemble, *Journal,* 1835; Harriet Martineau, *A Retrospect of Western Travel,* 1838, and *Society in America,* 1839; Alexis de Tocqueville, *Democracy in America,* 1838; Charles Lyell, *Travels in America in the Years 1841–42,* 2 vols., 1852.

Self-appraisals by Americans: Cooper's remarks are

in *The Sea Lions,* 1849, ch. 1; his letter to Greenough is in his *Correspondence,* vol. 1, p. 358. Greenough on English misconceptions: "Remarks on Art," in *U.S. Magazine and Democratic Review,* vol. 13, 1843, p. 45.

Emerson's definition of art is in "Thoughts on Art," in the *Dial,* vol. 1, Jan., 1841, p. 367. His challenge to the American artist is in "The Poet," in *Essays,* vol. 3, edition of 1903, p. 37.

Art patronage: Private collections are described by Samuel F. B. Morse in his *Address to the National Academy of Design,* May 3, 1827 (a pamphlet). The *Crayon,* vol. 3, 1856, contains a series of articles, *Our Private Collections,* pp. 27, 57, 123, 186, 249, 394, with information concerning prices paid. See also the auction sale inventory of Philip Hone's collection (a pamphlet), 1852. Thomas S. Cummings, *Historic Annals of the National Academy of Design . . . from 1825 to the Present Time,* 1865, has material on this subject.

The anonymous article on the art dealer is in the *Crayon,* vol. 7, 1860, p. 37.

The American Art-Union and its activities are here summarized from notes loaned to the author by Mr. Howard N. Doughty. For the history of the Art-Union, see essay by Charles E. Baker in vol. 1 of Cowdrey, *American Academy and American Art-Union.* (Vol. 2 is an exhibition record, 1816–1852.)

The memorial of artists to Congress and the reaction of a congressional committee are discussed in the *Crayon,* vol. 6, 1859. See also House Report No. 198, 35th Congress, 2nd session.

On WILLIAM DUNLAP (1766–1839): Theodore S. Woolsey, *William Dunlap, Painter and Critic,* 1914; Oral S. Coad, *William Dunlap,* 1917; catalogue of the Dunlap exhibition at Addison Gallery, Andover, Mass., in 1939, with an essay by Winslow Ames. Dunlap's ideas on art and democracy are in his "Essay on the Influence of the Arts of Design" in *American Monthly Magazine,* vol. 7, Feb., 1836, p. 113.

On CHARLES LANMAN, CHARLES EDWARDS LESTER, HENRY T. TUCKERMAN, and JAMES JACKSON JARVES: See references above, under Section 16, "The Period in General." On Jarves, see also Francis Steegmuller, *The Two Lives of James Jackson Jarves,* 1951.

For contrasting interpretations of romanticism in America: see Parrington, *Main Currents,* introduction to vol. 2; George Boas (ed.), *Romanticism in America,* 1940; Howard M. Jones, *Ideas in America,* 1944, chs. 6–7; Wolfgang Born, "Sources of American Romanticism," in *Antiques,* vol. 48, Nov., 1945, p. 274.

Chapter 13 / *Templed Hills*

Surveys of the Greek Revival, with varying interpretations: Kimball, *American Architecture,* ch. 8; Howard Major, *The Domestic Architecture of the Early American Republic: The Greek Revival,* 1926; Lewis Mumford, *Sticks and Stones,* ch. 3. Talbot Hamlin, *Greek Revival Architecture in America,* 1944, the most complete and authoritative book on this subject, discusses and illustrates all types of structure, with regional variations. It includes a valuable list of articles on architecture published in American periodicals before 1851.

George Tucker's opinions are here quoted from "Thoughts of a Hermit," in the *Portfolio,* vol. 4, Dec., 1814, p. 559.

For the principal handbooks used by builders: See Appendix 4 in Hamlin, *Greek Revival Architecture,* which describes the American modifications of Greek forms; see also Thomas E. O'Donnell, "The Influence of the Carpenters' Handbooks on the Early Architecture of Ohio," in *Architecture,* vol. 55, Mar., 1927, p. 169.

For articles on specific buildings: See Roos, *Writings on Early American Architecture.* Measured drawings and photographs are listed in the catalogue of the Historic American Buildings Survey, 1941.

On the revivalists: The work and influence of ITHIEL TOWN (1784–1844) and ALEXANDER J. DAVIS (1803–1892) are fully discussed in Roger H. Newton, *Town and Davis, Architects,* 1942. Thomas E. O'Donnell writes on ASHER BENJAMIN (1773–1845) in *Architecture,* vol. 54, Dec., 1926, p. 375. On ROBERT MILLS (1781–1855), see H. M. Pierce Gallagher, *Robert Mills,* 1935. On WILLIAM STRICKLAND (1788–1854), see Agnes A. Gilchrist, *William Strickland,* 1950. See also the *Autobiography* of JAMES GALLIER, SR. (1798–1868), 1864; on GIDEON SHRYOCK (1802–1880), see A. Andrews in *Antiques,* vol. 48, July, 1945, p. 35; on THOMAS U. WALTER (1804–1887), see William S. Rusk, "Thomas U. Walter and His Works," in *Americana,* vol. 33, Apr., 1939, p. 151, with bibliography. As a type of the more modest builder, see Samuel M. Green, "Thomas Lord, Joiner and Housewright," in *Magazine of Art,* vol. 40, Oct., 1947, p. 230.

Regional and local studies which include this period: Downing and Scully, *The Architectural Heritage of Newport;* Theo. B. White (ed.), *Philadelphia Architecture in the Nineteenth Century,* 1953; Walter H. Kilham, *Boston after Bulfinch,* 1946; Newcomb, *Architecture in the Old Northwest Territory* and *Architecture in Old Kentucky;* Frary, *Early Homes of Ohio;* Lee Burns, *Early Architects and Builders of Indiana,* 1935; John Drury, *Historic Midwest Houses,* 1947; Howland and Spencer, *The Architecture of Baltimore;* Johnston and Waterman, *The Early Architecture of North Carolina;* Ravenel, *Architects of Charleston;* Nichols, *The Early Architecture of Georgia;* Nathaniel C. Curtis, *New Orleans, Its Old Houses, Shops, and Public Build-*

ings, 1933. See also Thomas T. Waterman, "Notes on Decorative Cast Iron," in *Magazine of Art,* vol. 32, Oct., 1939, p. 584, with photographs by Frances B. Johnston; Samuel Wilson, Jr., "New Orleans Ironwork," in the same, vol. 41, Oct., 1948, p. 214; Lyle Saxon, *Old Louisiana,* 1929; J. Frazier Smith, *White Pillars,* 1941; Harnett T. Kane, *Plantation Parade,* 1945; Catharine Van Court, *In Old Natchez,* 1937.

On the structural experiments of Mills and others: See Louise Hall, "Mills, Strickland and Walter: Their Adventures in a World of Science," in *Magazine of Art,* vol. 40, Nov., 1947, p. 266. Mills's unfinished essay, "The Progress of Architecture in Virginia," is quoted by H. M. Pierce Gallagher in *Robert Mills,* p. 154.

Horatio Greenough's comments on "Aesthetics at Washington" were first published in pamphlet form in 1851; they are included in Harold A. Small, *Form and Function,* 1907.

Chapter 14 / *A Few Crockets and Finials*

English books which influenced the Gothic Revival in America: Augustus C. Pugin, *Specimens of Gothic Architecture,* 1821–1823; Augustus W. N. Pugin, *Contrasts,* 1836; *Gothic Furniture in the Style of the Fifteenth Century,* 1835; *True Principles of Pointed or Christian Architecture,* 1841; Peter F. Robinson, *Domestic Architecture in the Tudor Style,* 1837.

Coleridge's remarks on the Gothic in his London lecture of 1818 appear in *Coleridge's Essays and Lectures on Shakespeare,* etc., 1907, p. 219. See also Agnes Addison, *Romanticism and the Gothic Revival,* 1938, which discusses the movement in Europe and America.

Robert D. Owen's attack on Greek Revival buildings is in *Hints on Public Architecture,* 1849. Arthur D. Gilman criticizes the "five-order men" in a review of Shaw's *Rural Architecture,* in *North American Review,* vol. 58, Apr., 1844, p. 436. Mark Twain's comments on Gothic in the South are in the chapter, "Enchantments in Enchanters," in *Life on the Mississippi.*

For the Gothic work of Town and Davis: See Newton, *Town and Davis, Architects.* See also Edna Donnell, "A. J. Davis and the Gothic Revival," in *Metropolitan Museum Studies,* vol. 5, Sept., 1936, p. 183. Hone's remarks on the Paulding Villa are in his *Diary,* Nevins ed., vol. 2, p. 550.

On the work of other Gothicists: Everard M. Upjohn, *Richard Upjohn, Architect and Churchman* (1802–1878), in 1939; Geoffrey Baker, "The Smithsonian" (by James Renwick, 1818–1895), in *Magazine of Art,* vol. 34, March, 1941, p. 128; Robert D. Owen also discusses the Smithsonian in the work cited above.

For regional and local studies which include this period: See references above, under ch. 13.

Articles on specific buildings are cited in Roos, *Writings on Early American Architecture.*

The growth of eclecticism: Thomas Hope is here quoted from his *Historical Essay on Architecture,* 1835, vol. 1, p. 561; the work of A. J. DAVIS in a variety of manners is described and illustrated in Newton, *Town and Davis,* chs. 7 and 8. On HENRY AUSTIN (1804–1891), see Austin's contribution to 1846 edition of Chester Hills, *The Builder's Guide.* Yale University Library has many original designs by Austin. See also Clay Lancaster, "Italianism in American Architecture before 1860," in *American Quarterly,* vol. 4, Summer, 1952, p. 127.

On ANDREW J. DOWNING (1815–1852): See Carl Carmer, *The Hudson,* 1939, ch. 21. Some Downing works: *A Treatise on Landscape Gardening Adapted to North America,* 1841; *Cottage Residences,* 1842; *The Architecture of Country Houses,* 1850; *Rural Essays,* 1853 (a posthumous collection of essays). On Llewellyn Park, see Christopher Tunnard, "The Romantic Suburb in America," in *Magazine of Art,* vol. 40, May, 1947, p. 184.

On the octagonal house: See Orson S. Fowler, *A Home for All,* 1848 and later editions; Walter Creese, "Fowler and the Domestic Octagon," in *Art Bulletin,* vol. 28, 1946, p. 89; Clay Lancaster, "Some Octagonal Forms in Southern Architecture," in the same, p. 103.

Gervase Wheeler's remarks on the architectural Babel are quoted from *Homes for the People in Suburb and Country,* 1855 and later editions.

Chapter 15 / *The White Marmorean Flock*

Ship carvers of the nineteenth century are discussed in Pinckney, *American Figureheads and Their Carvers.*

Richard Guggenheimer on the form problems of the sculptor is quoted from *Sight and Insight,* 1945, p. 176. For Margaret Fuller's ideas on sculpture, see her *Memoirs,* 1852, vol. 1; also the *Dial,* vol. 1, 1840, p. 260, and vol. 3, Apr., 1843, p. 454 (quoting Canova). See also Erastus D. Palmer, "Philosophy of the Ideal," in the *Crayon,* vol. 3, 1856, p. 18. Hawthorne discusses the problem of nudity in *The Marble Faun,* 1860, ch. 14.

Gardner, *Yankee Stonecutters,* is the best recent study of sculptors of this period. See also the following:

On WILLIAM W. STORY (1819–1895): Henry James, *William Wetmore Story and His Friends,* 2 vols., 1903; and Story, *Conversations in a Studio,* 1890.

On HARRIET HOSMER (1830–1908): Cornelia Carr, *Harriet Hosmer, Letters and Memories,* 1912.

On WILLIAM H. RINEHART (1825–1874): William S. Rusk, *William Henry Rinehart, Sculptor,* 1939; Marvin

C. Ross and Anna W. Rutledge, *A Catalogue of the Work of William Henry Rinehart,* 1948.

On HORATION GREENOUGH (1805–1852): Taft, *History of American Sculpture,* ch. 2.

Hawthorne's impressions of the expatriate sculptors are in his *Italian Notebooks,* 1858–1859.

On HIRAM POWERS (1805–1873): Taft, *History of American Sculpture,* ch. 3; and Edna M. Clark, *Ohio Art and Artists,* 1932, ch. 6. Philip Hone's praise of the *Greek Slave* is in his *Diary,* Nevins ed., vol. 2, p. 818; Henry James's recollection of the *Slave* is quoted from *William Wetmore Story,* vol. 1, p. 114.

On Greenough's statue of George Washington: Tuckerman's visit to Greenough's studio is described in *American Monthly Magazine,* vol. 7, Jan., 1836, p. 53. Work on the statue is described in unpublished letters in the Massachusetts Historical Society and the Boston Public Library. His petition to move the statue is quoted by Fairman, *Art and Artists of the Capitol,* p. 102. Hone's adverse comment is quoted from the microfilm of the original *Diary* for April 29, 1844, in the New York Historical Society. Greenough's letter to Winthrop is quoted by Tuckerman in *Book of the Artists,* p. 405.

On Greenough's writings on art: See *Letters of Horatio Greenough to His Brother Henry Greenough,* edited by Frances B. Greenough, 1887. The essays were first published in various magazines; several were reprinted in Horace Bender (pseudonym for Horatio Greenough), *The Travels, Observations and Experiences of a Yankee Stone Cutter,* 1852; also in Tuckerman, *A Memorial of Horatio Greenough,* 1853; eight of them appear in *Form and Function,* edited by Harold A. Small, 1947. "Observe a ship at sea," etc., is quoted from the essay, *American Architecture,* which appears in *Form and Function.*

The work of THOMAS CRAWFORD (1813–1857) is discussed in Fairman, *Art and Artists of the Capitol,* and in Taft, *History of American Sculpture,* ch. 4. Equestrian statues are evaluated in William R. Valentiner, *Origins of Modern Sculpture,* 1946, ch. 6; see also THOMAS BALL (1819–1911), *My Threescore Years and Ten,* 1892.

On JOHN ROGERS (1829–1904): Dorothy C. Barck, "John Rogers, American Sculptor," in *Old Time New England,* vol. 23, Jan., 1933, p. 99; Mr. and Mrs. Chetwood Smith, *Rogers Groups,* 1934.

On JOHN WARD (1830–1910), see Taft, *History of American Sculpture,* ch. 12; also Russell Sturgis, "The Work of J. Q. A. Ward," in *Scribner's,* vol. 32, Oct., 1902, p. 385; and Adeline Adams, *J. Q. A. Ward; An Appreciation,* 1912.

On WILLIAM RIMMER (1816–1879): Truman H. Bartlett, *The Art Life of William Rimmer,* 1882; Lincoln Kirstein, catalogue of Rimmer exhibition at the Boston Museum of Fine Arts in 1947. By Rimmer himself: *Elements of Design,* 1864 and 1879; *Art Anatomy,* 1877, 1884, and later editions.

Jarves' comments on contemporary sculpture are in *The Art Idea,* ch. 16. His conclusions, here quoted, are on p. 285.

SECTION 18

Book Three / Part Two / At the Feet of the Familiar

Introduction / *Paint for the Many*

On WASHINGTON ALLSTON: See references above, under section 15, ch. 11. Margaret Fuller appraises Allston in the *Dial,* vol. 1, July, 1840, p. 73; see also Elizabeth Peabody, *Last Evening with Allston,* 1886.

On SAMUEL F. B. MORSE: See references above, under section 15, ch. 10.

On JOHN TRUMBULL: See references above, under section 15, ch. 11. The rotunda paintings are discussed in Fairman, *Art and Artists of the Capitol,* ch. 3.

On JOHN VANDERLYN: See references above, under section 15, ch. 10. Benjamin Champney's recollections of Vanderlyn are in his *Sixty Years' Memories of Art and Artists,* 1900.

On still-life painting: See Born, *Still-Life Painting in America.*

On portraits: The work of many portrait painters of this period is reproduced in Edgar P. Richardson, *American Romantic Painting,* 1944. See also references to THOMAS SULLY above, under section 15, ch. 10.

On photography: Beaumont Newhall, introduction to catalogue of Museum of Modern Art exhibition, *Photography,* 1937; *Masters of Photography,* edited by Beaumont and Nancy Newhall, 1958; Robert Taft, *Photography and the American Scene,* 1938. On MATHEW BRADY (1823–1896): Roy Meredith, *Mr. Lincoln's Camera Man,* 1946. Early discussions of photography as art: C. E. Lester, "M. B. Brady and the Photographic Art," in the *Photographic Art Journal,* vol. 1, Jan., 1851, p. 36; unsigned article, "The Photographic Portrait," in the *Crayon,* vol. 4, 1857, p. 154; Rembrandt Peale's article in the same, p. 44.

Portrait painting in the second half of the century: On WILLIAM PAGE (1811–1885), see "Our Artists in Italy," in *Atlantic Monthly,* vol. 7, Feb., 1861, p. 129, and Joshua C. Taylor, *William Page, the American Titian,* 1957; on CHARLES L. ELLIOTT (1812–1868), see the article by C. E. Lester, in *Harper's,* vol. 38, Dec., 1868, p. 42; on THOMAS B. READ (1822–1872), see Alice E. Smith (ed.), "Letters of Thomas Buchanan Read," in *Ohio State Archaeological and Historical Quarterly,* vol. 46, 1937, p. 68, here quoted; on GEORGE

PETER ALEXANDER HEALY (1813–1894), see his *Reminiscences of a Portrait Painter,* 1894; also Marie de Mare, *G. P. A. Healy, American Artist,* 1954. On THOMAS HICKS (1823–1890), see George A. Hicks, "Thomas Hicks, Artist," in *Collections of Bucks County Historical Society,* vol. 4, 1917, p. 89.

On the influence of Couture and Millet: See Thomas Couture, *Art Methods,* 1879; see also references to ROBERT L. NEWMAN and WILLIAM M. HUNT under section 21, ch. 21.

Tuckerman is here quoted from *Book of the Artists,* p. 39.

Chapter 16 / *Westward the Course of Landscape*

On THOMAS DOUGHTY, THOMAS COLE, and ASHER DURAND, see Sydney Kellner, "The Beginnings of Landscape Painting in America," in *Art in America,* vol. 26, Oct., 1938, p. 158. See also Sweet, *The Hudson River School;* Isham and Cortissoz, *History of American Painting,* ch. 13; Sears, *Highlights among the Hudson River Artists,* 1947; Born, *American Landscape Painting,* chs. 2–3; Howard M. Jones, "James Fenimore Cooper and the Hudson River School," in *Magazine of Art,* vol. 45, Oct., 1952, p. 243; Charlotte B. Johnson, "The European Tradition and Alvan Fisher," in *Art in America,* vol. 41, Spring, 1953, p. 79.

This account of THOMAS DOUGHTY (1793–1856) is based on unpublished notes for a life of Doughty, loaned to the author by Mr. Howard N. Doughty.

On ROBERT W. WEIR (1803–1899), see Irene Weir, *Robert W. Weir, Artist,* 1947.

On THOMAS COLE (1801–1848): See Louis L. Noble, *The Course of Empire, Voyage of Life, and Other Pictures of Thomas Cole,* 1853; Walter L. Nathan, "Thomas Cole and the Romantic Landscape," in *Romanticism in America;* catalogue by Esther I. Seaver for Cole exhibition at the Wadsworth Atheneum, Hartford, Conn., and the Whitney Museum in 1949; Everett P. Lesley, Jr., "Some Clues to Thomas Cole," in *Magazine of Art,* vol. 42, Feb., 1949, p. 42; Donald A. Ringe, "Kindred Spirits: Bryant and Cole," in *American Quarterly,* vol. 6, Fall, 1954, p. 233.

The passage from Volney's *Les ruines,* 1826 edition, ch. 1, is translated by the author. Cole's indebtedness to Burford is discussed by Wolfgang Born in "Sources of American Romanticism," in *Antiques,* vol. 48, Nov., 1945, p. 274. Cole's "Essay on American Scenery" was read at the American Lyceum and published in *American Monthly Magazine,* vol. 7, Jan., 1836, p. 1. Bryant's tribute is in a funeral oration before the National Academy of Design, May 4, 1848, published as a pamphlet.

On makers of landscape and urban views: Drepperd, *Early American Prints,* chs. 5–7; Weitenkampf, *American Graphic Art,* chs. 4, 6, 10; Stokes and Haskell, *American Historical Prints.*

On Ruskin's philosophy of art: See Henry Ladd, *The Victorian Morality of Art,* 1932; on his influence, see David H. Dickason, *The Daring Young Men: The Story of the American Pre-Raphaelites,* 1953. The "Letters on Landscape Painting," by ASHER B. DURAND (1796–1886) are in the *Crayon,* vol. 1, 1855, pp. 1, 34, 66, 97, 145, 209, 273, 354, and vol. 2, 1856, p. 16. See also John Durand, *The Life and Times of A. B. Durand,* 1894.

See Champney, *Sixty Years' Memories* on the early painters of the White Mountain region. See Sweet, *Hudson River School,* for brief sketches of Kensett, Cropsey, and others of this group. GEORGE H. DURRIE (1820–1863) is discussed in Mary C. Durrie, "George Henry Durrie: Artist," in *Antiques,* vol. 24, July, 1933, p. 13; Bartlett Cowdrey, introduction to catalogue of the Durrie exhibition at the Wadsworth Atheneum in 1947.

On painters of the West: On GEORGE CATLIN (1796–1872): see Loyd Haberly, *Pursuit of the Horizon,* 1948; Harold McCracken, *George Catlin and the Old Frontier,* 1959. Hone's remarks on Catlin are in the *Diary,* Nevins ed., vol. 1, pp. 290, 434. Bernard De Voto, in *Across the Wide Missouri,* 1947, includes material on ALFRED J. MILLER (1810–1874) and reproduces many paintings by Miller and Bodmer. See also R. W. G. Vail, "The First Artist of the Oregon Trail," in *New-York Historical Society Quarterly,* vol. 34, Jan., 1950, p. 24; Marvin C. Ross (ed.), *The West of Alfred Jacob Miller,* 1951. On SETH EASTMAN (1808–1875), see Bartlett Cowdrey in *Panorama,* Feb., 1946; on JOHN M. STANLEY (1814–1872), see W. Vernon Kinietz, *John Mix Stanley and His Indian Paintings,* 1942. See also Perry T. Rathbone, "Charles Wimar, Indian Frontier Artist," in *Magazine of Art,* vol. 40, Dec., 1947, p. 315; on GEORGE WINTER, see Mary Q. Burnet, *Art and Artists of Indiana,* 1921; catalogue of the Winter exhibition at the Herron Institute, Indianapolis, in 1939; Indiana Historical Society, *The Journals and Indian Paintings of George Winter, 1837–1839,* 1948. On GEORGE HARVEY (c. 1800–after 1877), see Barbara N. Parker in *Bulletin of Boston Museum of Fine Arts,* Feb., 1943, and Donald A. Shelley, "George Harvey and His Atmospheric Landscapes of North America," in *New-York Historical Society Quarterly,* vol. 32, Apr., 1948, p. 104. See also *Mississippi Panorama,* 1949, catalogue of an exhibition at City Art Museum of St. Louis.

On photographers of the frontier: Taft, *Photography and the American Scene,* chs. 14 and 15, discusses these men. The work of WILLIAM H. JACKSON is described and illustrated in Clarence S. Jackson, *Picture Maker of the Old West,* 1947.

On Henry Lewis' panorama: Bertha L. Heilbron (ed.), *Making a Motion Picture in 1848: Henry Lewis' Journal of a Canoe Voyage from the Falls of St. Anthony to St. Louis,* 1936.

On the panoramic painters: See Sweet, *Hudson River School,* on ALBERT BIERSTADT (1830–1902), WORTHINGTON WHITTREDGE (1820–1910), THOMAS MORAN (1837–1926), and SANFORD R. GIFFORD (1823–1880); also Fritiof Fryxell (ed.), *Thomas Moran, Explorer in Search of Beauty,* 1958, and catalogue of Gifford memorial exhibition at the Metropolitan Museum in 1881. On THOMAS HILL (1829–1908), see *Historical New Hampshire,* Feb., 1946, p. 11; on WILLIAM KEITH (1838–1911), see Eugen Neuhaus, *William Keith, the Man and the Artist,* 1938, and Brother Cornelius, *Keith, Old Master of California,* 1942.

Exotic landscapes: Victor W. von Hagen, "F. Catherwood, Archt," in *New-York Historical Society Quarterly,* vol. 30, Jan., 1946, p. 17; and "Mr. Catherwood's Panorama," in *Magazine of Art,* vol. 40, Apr., 1947, p. 143. See also the catalogue of FREDERICK E. CHURCH (1826–1900) exhibition at the Metropolitan Museum in 1900. Comments on Church by his contemporaries: Louis L. Noble, *Church's Painting: The Heart of the Andes,* 1859 (a pamphlet); Adam Badeau in *The Vagabond,* 1859.

On MARTIN J. HEADE (1819–1904): See Elizabeth McCausland in *Panorama,* Oct., 1945, p. 1, and Robert G. McIntyre, *Martin Johnson Heade,* 1948.

On WILLIAM M. HUNT, JOHN LA FARGE, and GEORGE INNESS: See references below under section 21, ch. 21 (Hunt and Inness) and section 22, Introduction (La Farge).

Chapter 17 / *Art for the People*

On genre painting: See introductory essay by Lloyd Goodrich for catalogue of *American Genre* exhibition at the Whitney Museum in 1935.

On cartoons and illustrations: See Murrell, *History of American Graphic Humor;* Theodore Bolton, *American Book Illustrators,* 1938.

On prints: See Harry T. Peters, *America on Stone,* 1931, and *Currier and Ives, Printmakers to the American People,* 1942; Russel Crouse, *Mr. Currier and Mr. Ives,* 1930; Morton Cronin, "Currier and Ives," in *American Quarterly,* vol. 4, no. 4, Winter, 1952, p. 317.

The painters of genre: On JEREMIAH HARDY (1800–1888), see Fannie H. Eckstorm, "Jeremiah Pearson Hardy," in *Old Time New England,* vol. 30, Oct., 1939, p. 41; on JOHN QUIDOR (1801–1881), see John I. H. Baur's catalogue for Quidor exhibition at the Brooklyn Museum in 1942, and his article in *American Collector,* vol. 11, Mar., 1942, p. 6; on DAVID G. BLYTHE (1815–1863), see Dorothy Miller, *The Life and Work of David G. Blythe,* 1950; also catalogue of the Blythe-Beale exhibition at the Whitney Museum in 1936. The definitive work on WILLIAM S. MOUNT (1807–1868) is Bartlett Cowdrey and Herman W. Williams, Jr., *William Sidney Mount; An American Painter,* 1944, with a catalogue of Mount works and a bibliography. For a comment on Mount, see *Uncollected Poetry and Prose of Walt Whitman,* 1921, vol. 1, p. 238. On GEORGE C. BINGHAM (1811–1879), see Fern H. Rusk, *George Caleb Bingham, the Missouri Artist,* 1917; Albert Christ-Janer, *George Caleb Bingham of Missouri,* 1940; Virginius C. Hall, "George Caleb Bingham, the Missouri Artist," in *Print Collector's Quarterly,* vol. 27, Feb., 1940, p. 9; John F. McDermott, *George Caleb Bingham, River Portraitist,* 1959. On RICHARD C. WOODVILLE (1825–1856), see Tuckerman, *Book of the Artists,* p. 408. See also Theodore Sizer (ed.), *The Recollections of John Ferguson Weir,* 1957.

Lesser men: On ENOCH W. PERRY (1831–1915), see Bartlett Cowdrey, "The Discovery of Enoch Wood Perry," in *Old Print Shop Portfolio,* Apr., 1945; on EDWARD L. HENRY, see Elizabeth McCausland, *The Life and Work of Edward Lamson Henry, N.A., 1841–1919,* 1945; on JOHN W. EHNINGER (1827–1889), see Tuckerman, *Book of the Artists,* p. 461. On EASTMAN JOHNSON (1824–1906), see John I. H. Baur, *An American Genre Painter, Eastman Johnson,* Brooklyn Museum, 1940.

On WINSLOW HOMER: See references below under section 21, ch. 21.

Chapter 18 / *Art by the People*

This phase of art in America is described and evaluated from various points of view by Carl Drepperd, *American Pioneer Art and Artists,* and by Jean Lipman and Holger Cahill. See Lipman, "A Critical Definition of the American Primitive," in *Art in America,* vol. 26, Oct., 1938, p. 171, *American Primitive Painting,* 1942, and *American Folk Art in Wood, Metal and Stone,* 1948. See Cahill, catalogues of exhibitions, *American Primitives,* 1930, and *American Folk Sculpture,* 1931, at the Newark Museum; *American Folk Art: The Art of the Common Man in America,* at the Museum of Modern Art in 1932; see also Cahill's articles in *American Mercury,* vol. 24, Sept., 1931, p. 39; in *Parnassus,* vol. 4, Mar., 1932, p. 1; and in *Creative Art,* vol. 11, Dec., 1932, p. 255. See also John M. Graham, *Popular Art in America,* 1939.

Important collections of folk art are in the Philadelphia Museum of Art, at the New York Historical Society, at Harvard, Mass. (Clara E. Sears), and at Colonial Williamsburg, Va.; also in various state and municipal historical societies. See Nina F. Little, *The Abby Aldrich Rockefeller Folk Art Collection,* 1957.

The Index of American Design, a pictorial record of art objects made by the American people, is deposited in the National Gallery of Art, Washington, D.C.

Types of folk art: E. Boyd, *Saints and Saint Makers of New Mexico,* 1946. On Shaker arts, see references above under section 14, ch. 8. See also Henry Kauffman, *Pennsylvania Dutch American Folk Art,* 1946, and Frances Lichten, *Folk Art of Rural Pennsylvania,* 1946; James A. Porter, *Modern Negro Art,* 1943, chs. 1–3.

On portrait painting: Clara E. Sears, *Some American Primitives,* 1941; Henry W. Belknap, *Artists and Craftsmen of Essex County,* 1927 (material on CHARLES O. COLE); *Somebody's Ancestors,* catalogue of an exhibition of Connecticut Valley portraits at the Springfield Museum of Fine Arts, Springfield, Mass., in 1942; Lucy B. Mitchell on James Sanford Ellsworth in *Art in America,* vol. 41, Autumn, 1953; Nina F. Little, "William M. Prior, Traveling Artist," in *Antiques,* vol. 53, Jan., 1948, p. 44; Jean Lipman, "I. J. H. Bradley, Portrait Painter," in *Art in America,* vol. 33, July, 1945, p. 154.

Landscapes: Allen, *Early American Wall Paintings,* 1926; Esther S. Brazer, "Murals in Upper N.Y. State," in *Antiques.* vol. 48, Sept., 1945, p. 148; Nina F. Little, "Thomas Chambers, Man or Myth?" in *Antiques,* vol. 53, Mar., 1948, p. 194; Jean Lipman on Rufus Porter, in *Art in America,* vol. 38, Oct., 1950.

On EDWARD HICKS (1780–1849): See his own *Memoirs of the Life and Religious Labors of Edward Hicks,* 1851; Frederic N. Price, *Edward Hicks,* 1945 (a pamphlet, here quoted); Alice Ford, *Edward Hicks: Painter of the Peaceable Kingdom,* 1952.

On Erastus S. Field: See Frederick B. Robinson, "Erastus Salisbury Field," in *Art in America,* vol. 30, Oct., 1942, p. 244; and a check list of Field paintings by Agnes M. Dods in the same, vol. 32, Jan., 1944, p. 32.

SECTION 19

Book Four / Between Two Panics

The Period in General

Charles and Mary Beard, *The Rise of American Civilization,* ch. 25; Billington, Loewenberg, and Brockunier, *The United States,* chs. 13–22; Allan Nevins, *The Emergence of Modern America, 1865–1878,* 1927, vol. 8 in the "History of American Life" series; Arthur M. Schlesinger, *The Rise of the City, 1878–1898,* 1933, vol. 10 in the same.

Thought and literary expression: Merle Curti, *The Growth of American Thought,* parts 5–6; Lewis Mumford, *The Brown Decades,* 1931; Parrington, *Main Currents,* vol. 3; Louis Wann (ed.), *The Rise of Realism, 1860–1888,* 1933; Alfred Kazin, *On Native Grounds,* 1942, part I, chs. 1–2. *Literary History of the United States,* vol. 2, sections 48–56.

On taste and design: Lynes, *The Tastemakers;* Kouwenhoven, *Made in America.*

Architecture of the period: Kimball, *American Architecture,* chs. 10–13; Hamlin, *The American Spirit in Architecture,* chs. 12–13; Andrews, *Architecture, Ambition and Americans,* chs. 5, 6; Vincent J. Scully, Jr., *The Shingle Style: Architectural Theory and Design from Richardson to the Origins of Wright,* 1955.

For regional and local studies which include this period: See references above, under ch. 13, also Oscar Lewis, *Here Lived the Californians,* 1957, part 4.

Painting: Sadakichi Hartmann, *A History of American Art,* 1902, vol. 1, ch. 4, vol. 2, chs. 3–4; Neuhaus, *History and Ideals of American Art,* chs. 8–21; Isham and Cortissoz, *History of American Painting*, chs. 16–27; Burroughs, *Limners and Likenesses,* chs. 24–25; Saint-Gaudens, *The American Artist and His Times,* pp. 115–208; Barker, *American Painting,* divisions 6, 7; Richardson, *Painting in America,* chs. 10–12.

Sculpture: Taft, *History of American Sculpture,* chs. 15–22; Loring H. Dodd, *The Golden Age of American Sculpture,* 1936; Adeline Adams, *The Spirit of American Sculpture,* 1923.

Some art books of the period: George W. Sheldon, *American Painters,* 1879, and *Recent Ideals of American Art,* 2 vols., 1888–1890; Samuel G. W. Benjamin, *Our American Artists,* 1879, and *Art in America,* 1880.

Articles on the men of the period, and essays by Benjamin, Norton, and other critics, are in the *American Art Review,* 2 vols. only, 1880 and 1881. See also comments on artists of the 1870's in Henry James, *The Painter's Eye,* 1956.

SECTION 20

Book Four / Part I / A Chromo Civilization

Introduction / *The Spirit of '76*

Arthur M. Schlesinger, Jr., on the conservative triumph, is quoted from *The Age of Jackson,* p. 518.

John Stafford on Joel C. Harris is in "Patterns of Meaning in *Nights with Uncle Remus,*" in *American Literature,* vol. 18, May, 1946, p. 89.

John Frankenstein's warning is in his *American Art: Its Awful Altitude,* 1864, p. 87.

Art patronage: Benjamin J. Lossing, *History of New York City,* 1884, p. 840, lists many pictures in private collections, with prices paid. See also the catalogue of the A. T. Stewart sale, 1887. Edward Strahan (Earl Shinn) reproduces typical works from private collections in *Art Treasures of America,* 3 vols., 1879.

On George P. A. Healy: See references above under section 18, Introduction. The figures in *The Arch of Titus* were identified for the author by David Huntington.

On structural experiments with metal and glass: See Sigfried Giedion, *Space, Time and Architecture,* 1941, pp. 164–211.

On the Philadelphia Centennial: *The Centennial Exposition Described and Illustrated,* 1876; Edward C. Bruce, *The Century: Its Fruits and Its Festival,* 1877, part 10; Edward Strahan, *The Masterpieces of the Centennial Exposition,* 1876–1878, vol. 1; *Official Catalogue of the Art Gallery and Annexes,* 1876; Mildred B. Matthews, "The Painters of the Hudson River School in the Philadelphia Centennial of 1876," in *Art in America,* vol. 34, July, 1946, p. 143; Clay Lancaster, "Taste at the Philadelphia Centennial," in *Magazine of Art,* vol. 43, Dec., 1950, p. 293.

William D. Howells is quoted from "A Sennight of the Centennial," in *Atlantic Monthly,* vol. 38, July, 1876, p. 93.

Chapter 19 / *False Front*

Greenough's comment on Trinity Church, the Astor House and the Reservoir is in his essay, "American Architecture."

On Bogardus' ideas: See James Bogardus, *Cast Iron Buildings: Their Construction and Advantages,* 1858; see also "Iron Buildings," in the *Crayon,* vol. 3, 1856, p. 84.

Building books of the period: Calvert Vaux, *Villas and Cottages,* 1867; Isaac Hobbs and Son, *Hobbs's Architecture,* 1873 and 1876; George E. Woodward and Edward G. Thompson, *Woodward's National Architect,* 1868 and later editions. For others, see Hitchcock, *American Architectural Books.*

Essays by several leading critics on city, suburban, and country houses were published as *Homes in City and Country,* 1893. Montgomery Schuyler traces the development of the brownstone front in "The Small City House in New York," in *Architectural Record,* vol. 8, Apr.–June, 1899, p. 357; his series, "The Architecture of American Colleges," is in the same, vol. 26, 1909, pp. 243, 393; vol. 27, 1910, p. 129; vol. 28, 1910, p. 425; vol. 29, 1911, p. 145; vol. 30, 1911, pp. 57, 549; vol. 31, 1912, p. 513. One hundred wealthy homes are illustrated in George W. Sheldon, *Artistic Country Seats,* 2 vols., 1886.

See *Dictionary of American Biography* on PETER B. WIGHT (1838–1925); GEORGE B. POST (1837–1913); HENRY VAN BRUNT (1832–1903); WILLIAM ROBERT WARE (1832–1915). On James Renwick, see Rosalie T. McKenna, "James Renwick, Jr. and the Second Empire Style in the United States," in *Magazine of Art,* vol. 44, Mar., 1951, p. 97.

On RICHARD MORRIS HUNT (1828–1895): Montgomery Schuyler, "The Works of the Late Richard M. Hunt," in *Architectural Record,* vol. 5, Oct.–Dec., 1895, p. 97, a long article with many illustrations; John Vredenburgh Van Pelt, *A Monograph of the William K. Vanderbilt House,* 1925.

Chapter 20 / *A Mighty Hankering*

A. B. Frost's cartoons of the Jones family were published in *Harper's Weekly,* Aug. 24 and Oct. 12, 1878.

Henry James is quoted from *The American,* vol. 2 in *Novels and Tales,* 1901, pp. 27, 29, 45.

Mark Twain's description of "The House Beautiful" is in *Life on the Mississippi,* ch. 38.

The American edition of Charles L. Eastlake, *Hints on Household Taste in Furniture, Upholstery and Other Details* is 1872.

On the Art Students League, founded in 1875, see Marchal E. Landgren, *Years of Art: The Story of the Art Students League of New York,* 1940. On Cooper Union, see three articles by Elizabeth McCausland in *Magazine of Art,* vol. 40, 1947, pp. 242, 282, and 322. On Norton and Moore: Kermit Vanderbilt, *Charles Eliot Norton,* 1959; Frank J. Mather, *Charles Herbert Moore,* 1957.

On the first art museums: William C. Bryant, address at the Union Club, N.Y., Nov. 23, 1869, in *Prose Writings,* 1884, p. 261; James J. Jarves, "Museums of Art, Artists, and Amateurs in America," in the *Galaxy,* vol. 10, July, 1870, p. 50; George F. Comfort, *Art Museums in America,* 1870 (a pamphlet); Charles C. Perkins, *Art Education in America,* 1870 (a pamphlet); Arthur Hoeber, *The Treasures of the Metropolitan Museum of Art of New York,* 1899; Winifred E. Howe, *A History of the Metropolitan Museum of Art,* vol 1, 1913.

On the wood engravers: Joseph Pennell, *Modern Illustration,* 1898, ch. 6; Alphaeus P. and Margaret W. Cole, *Timothy Cole: Wood-Engraver,* 1936; Elbridge Kingsley's unpublished autobiography, in the Forbes Library, Northampton, Mass.

Illustration in the eighties and nineties: Theodore Bolton, *American Book Illustrators,* 1938, a check list of over one hundred artists; Frank Weitenkampf, *The Illustrated Book,* 1938, ch. 9, and *American Graphic Art,* chs. 7–8; F. Hopkinson Smith, *American Illustrators,* 1892; Jerome Mellquist, *The Emergence of an American Art,* 1942, ch. 6. Henry James discusses

Abbey and others in *Picture and Text,* 1893. See also Robert Taft, *Artists and Illustrators of the Old West, 1850–1900,* 1953.

On EDWIN A. ABBEY (1852–1911): Edward V. Lucas, *Edwin Austin Abbey,* 2 vols., 1921; Yale University Art Gallery, *Paintings, Drawings and Pastels by Edwin Austin Abbey,* 1939 (items from the Abbey collection at Yale).

On ARTHUR B. FROST (1851–1928): See H. C. Bunner in *Harper's,* vol. 85, Oct., 1892, p. 699; also *A Book of Drawings by A. B. Frost,* 1904.

On HOWARD PYLE (1853–1911): Charles D. Abbott, *Howard Pyle; A Chronicle,* 1925; Wilmington Society of Fine Arts, *Catalogue of Pictures by Howard Pyle,* 1926.

On JOSEPH B. BEALE (1841–1926): See the catalogue of Blythe-Beale exhibition at the Whitney Museum in 1936.

On FREDERICK REMINGTON (1861–1909): See Robert Isaacson, *Frederick Remington, a Painter of American Life,* 1943; Harold McCracken, *Frederick Remington, Artist of the Old West,* 1947.

SECTION 21

Book Four / Part Two / Critics, Rebels, and Prophets

Introduction / *The American Conscience*

The cartoons of Nast, Keppler, and others are discussed in Murrell, *A History of American Graphic Humor,* vol. 2, chs. 3–4; see also J. A. Mitchell, "Contemporary American Caricature," in *Scribner's,* vol. 6, Dec., 1889, p. 728.

Comments by foreign visitors: James Bryce, *The American Commonwealth,* 1888; Lloyd Lewis, *Oscar Wilde Discovers America,* 1936; Matthew Arnold, *Civilization in the United States,* 1888, and *Discourses in America,* 1896.

John Hay and Henry Adams: See Hay, *The Bread-winners,* 1883; Adams, *Democracy,* 1881, and *The Education of Henry Adams,* 1918.

Walt Whitman is here quoted from "Democratic Vistas," in *Complete Poetry and Selected Prose and Letters,* 1938, pp. 697, 702.

On FREDERICK L. OLMSTED, SR. (1822–1903), and Central Park, N.Y.: See Frederick L. Olmsted, Jr., and Theodora Kimball, *Frederick Law Olmsted, Landscape Architect,* vol. 2, 1928; also *Description of a Plan for the Improvement of the Central Park,* by "Greensward" (Olmsted and Calvert Vaux), 1858 (a pamphlet).

Henry Van Brunt's essays are collected in *Greek Lines and Other Architectural Essays,* 1893. Montgomery Schuyler is here quoted from *American Architecture,* 1892, a collection of his articles. See Edward R. Smith, "Montgomery Schuyler and the History of American Architecture," in *Architectural Record,* vol. 36, Sept., 1914, p. 264, for a list of Schuyler's writings.

On the École des Beaux-Arts: See article by Henry O. Carey in *Scribner's,* vol. 2, Oct., 1887, p. 387.

Zola's art criticism is in the chapter, "Mon salon," in *Mes haines,* 1879.

On JAMES M. WHISTLER (1834–1903): See Elizabeth R. and Joseph Pennell, *The Life of James McNeill Whistler,* 2 vols., 1908.

On Leibl and the Munich group; Josef Stransky, *Modern Paintings by German and Austrian Masters,* 1916. On FRANK DUVENECK (1848–1919): Norbert Heermann, *Frank Duveneck,* 1918; catalogues of Duveneck exhibitions at the Cincinnati Art Museum in 1936 and at the Whitney Museum in 1938. Henry James's comment on Duveneck is quoted from the *Nation,* vol. 21, 1875, p. 5.

On J. FRANK CURRIER (1843–1909): See Nelson C. White, *Life and Art of J. Frank Currier,* 1936.

On the Society of American Artists: See Will H. Low in *A Chronicle of Friendships,* 1910, chs. 19, 20.

John F. Weir's defense of the young painters, here quoted, is in "American Art: Its Progress and Prospects," in *Princeton Review,* vol. 53, May, 1878, p. 115.

Chapter 21 / *Palpable Truth*

On WILLIAM M. HARNETT (1848–1892) and the other "eye-deceivers": See Alfred V. Frankenstein, *After the Hunt: William Harnett and Other American Still Life Painters, 1870–1900,* 1953; Edouard Roditi, "William Harnett: American Necromantic," in *View,* series 5, no. 4, Nov., 1945, p. 9; Wolfgang Born, "William M. Harnett: Bachelor Artist," in *Magazine of Art,* vol. 39, 1946, p. 248, and *Still-Life Painting in America,* ch. 5.

On WILLIAM M. HUNT (1824–1879): Helen M. Knowlton, *Art-Life of William Morris Hunt,* 1899; Martha A. Shannon, *Boston Days of William Morris Hunt,* 1923; Henry C. Angell, "Records of William M. Hunt," in *Atlantic Monthly,* 1880, vol. 45, pp. 559, 630, 753, and vol. 46, p. 75; Albert T. E. Gardner, "A Rebel in Patagonia," in *Metropolitan Museum of Art Bulletin,* vol. 3, May, 1945, p. 224; *William Hunt's Talks on Art* (Helen M. Knowlton, ed.), series one, 1875; series 2, 1883; Gibson Danes, "William Morris Hunt and His Newport Circle," in *Magazine of Art,* vol. 43; April, 1950, p. 144.

On the murals at Albany: Low, *A Chronicle of Friendships,* ch. 21; articles on the structural failure of the capitol vaulting at Albany in *American Architect,* vol. 15, 1884, p. 147; vol. 24, 1888, p. 117.

On GEORGE FULLER (1822–1884): *George Fuller,* 1886, a collection of essays by Howells and others; M. G. Van Rensselaer in *Century,* vol. 27, Dec., 1883,

p. 226; catalogues of Fuller exhibitions at the Boston Museum of Fine Arts in 1884 and at the Metropolitan Museum in 1923.

On RALPH A. BLAKELOCK (1847–1919): Elliott Daingerfield, *Ralph Albert Blakelock,* 1914.

On ROBERT L. NEWMAN (1827–1912): Frederic F. Sherman, *Landscape and Figure Painters of America,* 1917, p. 13; Marchal E. Landgren in *Magazine of Art,* vol. 28, Mar., 1935, p. 134; catalogue of exhibition at the Whitney Museum in 1935.

On ALBERT RYDER (1947–1917): Frederic N. Price, *Ryder,* 1932; Sadakichi Hartmann, "Albert Pinkham Ryder," in *Magazine of Art,* vol. 31, Sept., 1938, p. 504; William M. Hyde, "Albert Ryder as I Knew Him," in the *Arts,* vol. 16, May, 1930, p. 596; catalogue by Lloyd Goodrich for the Ryder exhibition at the Whitney Museum in 1947.

Charles de Kay's article, under the pseudonym of Henry Eckford, is "A Modern Colorist," in *Century,* vol. 49, June, 1890, p. 251.

Melville is here quoted from *Moby Dick,* 1851, ch. 9.

Elbridge Kingsley is quoted from his unpublished autobiography in the Forbes Library, Northampton, Mass.

On GEORGE INNESS (1825–1894): George Inness, Jr., *Life, Art, and Letters of George Inness,* 1917; Elliott Daingerfield, *George Inness; The Man and His Art,* 1911; Lloyd Goodrich, "George Inness and American Landscape Painting," in the *Arts,* vol. 7, Feb., 1925, p. 106. The best monograph is Elizabeth McCausland, *George Inness, an American Landscape Painter,* 1946.

On ALEXANDER H. WYANT (1836–1892): See Eliot C. Clark, *Alexander Wyant,* 1916.

On HOMER D. MARTIN (1836–1897): See article by Montgomery Schuyler in *Harper's Weekly,* vol. 41, Mar. 27, 1897, p. 323, here quoted; see also Frank J. Mather, Jr., *Homer Martin: Poet in Landscape,* 1912.

On J. ALDEN WEIR: See references below under section 22, ch. 23.

On EASTMAN JOHNSON: See reference above, under section 18, ch. 17.

On WINSLOW HOMER (1836–1910): William H. Downes, *The Life and Works of Winslow Homer,* 1911; Forbes Watson, *Winslow Homer,* 1942. The definitive work is Lloyd Goodrich, *Winslow Homer,* 1944. See also Van Wyck Brooks, *Indian Summer,* ch. 7.

Homer's description of his home at Prout's Neck is quoted from Goodrich, *Winslow Homer,* p. 108; his reference to his water colors is quoted from Goodrich, "Winslow Homer," in the *Arts,* vol. 6, Oct., 1924, p. 185.

On THOMAS EAKINS (1844–1916): Alan Burroughs, "Thomas Eakins, the Man," in the *Arts,* vol. 4, Dec., 1923, p. 303. The definitive work is Lloyd Goodrich, *Thomas Eakins: His Life and Work,* 1933. See also catalogues of Eakins exhibitions at the Metropolitan Museum in 1917, at the Pennsylvania Academy of the Fine Arts in 1918, and at M. Knoedler & Co., N.Y., in 1944. On Eakins' experiments with "moving pictures" see Charles Bregler, "Photos by Eakins," in *Magazine of Art,* vol. 36, Jan., 1943, p. 28; also Beaumont Newhall, "Photography and the Development of Kinetic Visualization," in *Journal of the Warburg and Courtauld Institutes,* vol. 7, Jan.–June, 1944, p. 40.

Eakins' letter to Dr. Da Costa is here quoted from Lloyd Goodrich, *Thomas Eakins,* p. 118. His comments on art instruction are in Charles Bregler, "Thomas Eakins as a Teacher," in the *Arts,* vol. 17, Mar., 1931, p. 376; and vol. 18, Oct., 1931, p. 27; his remarks on the future of American art are quoted from Goodrich, *Thomas Eakins,* p. 139.

On HENRY O. TANNER (1859–1937): Clara T. MacChesney in *International Studio,* vol. 50, July, 1913, p. xi; also James A. Porter, *Modern Negro Art,* 1943, p. 64.

On sculptors of the period: See references above, under section 19, "The Period in General"; also Charles H. Caffin, *American Masters of Sculpture,* 1913; J. Walker McSpadden, *Famous Sculptors of America,* 1924; Hartmann, *A History of American Art,* vol. 2, ch. 1.

On JOHN Q. A. WARD: See references above, under section 17, ch. 15; also "Conversations with Ward," in *Harper's,* vol. 57, June, 1878, p. 62.

On DANIEL C. FRENCH (1850–1931): Adeline Adams, *Daniel Chester French, Sculptor,* 1932; also Margaret F. Cresson, *Journey into Fame,* 1947.

On AUGUSTUS SAINT-GAUDENS (1848–1907): Royal Cortissoz, *Augustus Saint-Gaudens,* 1907; Homer Saint-Gaudens (ed.), *The Reminiscences of Augustus Saint-Gaudens,* 2 vols., 1913; C. Lewis Hind, *Augustus Saint-Gaudens,* 1908.

On GEORGE G. BARNARD (1863–1938): Taft, *History of American Sculpture,* ch. 19; Thomas Craven, *Modern Art,* 1934, p. 290.

On PAUL W. BARTLETT (1865–1925): Taft, *History of American Sculpture,* ch. 20.

On two equestrian statues by Eakins and William R. O'Donovan: See Cleveland Moffett, "Grant and Lincoln in Bronze," in *McClure's,* vol. 5, Oct., 1895, p. 419. Hamlin Garland's article on Edward Kemeys is in the same, July, 1895, p. 120.

Chapter 22 / *Architects with an Idea*

Greenough's criticism of academic training is quoted from Robert Goldwater and Marco Treves, *Artists on Art,* 1945, p. 284.

On the Brooklyn Bridge: See D. B. Steinman, *The Builders of the Bridge,* 1945 (here quoted from pp. 313, 407); Montgomery Schuyler's essay on the bridge is in his *American Architecture.*

On HENRY H. RICHARDSON (1838–1886): Mrs. Schuyler Van Rensselaer, *Henry Hobson Richardson and His Works,* 1888; Henry-Russell Hitchcock, *The Architecture of H. H. Richardson and His Times,* 1936, the most authoritative work on the subject.

On JOHN W. ROOT (1850–1891): Harriet Monroe, *John Wellborn Root,* 1896, here quoted. On DANIEL H. BURNHAM (1846–1912) see Charles Moore, *Daniel H. Burnham, Architect, Planner of Cities,* 2 vols., 1921.

On LOUIS H. SULLIVAN (1856–1924) the authority is Hugh Morrison, *Louis Sullivan, Prophet of Modern Architecture,* 1935; see also Claude Bragdon, "Letters from Louis Sullivan," in *Architecture,* vol. 28, Mar., 1935, p. 188; Henry R. Hope, "Louis Sullivan's Architectural Ornament," in *Magazine of Art,* vol. 40, Mar., 1947, p. 111; John Szarkowski, *The Idea of Louis Sullivan,* 1956.

Sullivan's writings: *Autobiography of an Idea,* 1924; *Kindergarten Chats and Other Works,* 1947. *A System of Architectural Ornament,* 1924, reproduces many of his designs for ornament.

Adler's article on the Chicago Auditorium is in *Architectural Record,* vol. 1, Apr.–June, 1892, p. 415.

The skyscraper: See Montgomery Schuyler, "The Skyscraper up to Date," in *Architectural Record,* vol. 8, Jan.–Mar., 1899, p. 232; Hugh Morrison, "Buffington and the Invention of the Skyscraper," in *Art Bulletin,* vol. 26, Mar., 1944, p. 1; also Dimitris Tselos, "The Enigma of Buffington's Skyscraper," in the same, p. 2; and Muriel B. Christison, "How Buffington Staked His Claim," in the same, p. 13. See also Louis Sullivan, "The Tall Office Building Artistically Considered," in *Kindergarten Chats.*

On the early work of Frank Lloyd Wright, see Henry-Russell Hitchcock, "Frank Lloyd Wright and the 'Academic Tradition' of the Eighteen-Nineties," in *Journal of the Warburg and Courtauld Institutes,* vol. 7, Jan.–June, 1944, p. 46.

SECTION 22

Book Four / Part Three / Cosmopolitans

Introduction / *The Renaissance Complex*

See Edward Strahan, *Mr. Vanderbilt's House and Collection,* 2 vols., 1883–1884 (the home of William H. Vanderbilt); also George W. Sheldon, *Artistic Country Seats,* 2 vols., 1886.

On the social satire of the cartoonists: See Murrell, *History of American Graphic Humor,* vol. 2, ch. 6.

On CHARLES D. GIBSON (1867–1944): See Charles B. Davis, "Mr. Charles Dana Gibson and His Art," in the *Critic,* vol. 34, Jan.–June, 1899, p. 48; also article in *American Artist,* vol. 20, Dec., 1956, p. 50.

On the Stewart collection: See catalogue of the A. T. Stewart sale, 1887.

On Morgan and Frick as collectors: See John K. Winkler, *Morgan the Magnificent,* 1930; and George B. M. Harvey, *Henry Clay Frick, the Man,* 1928.

On the Renaissance analogy: See Howard M. Jones, *Ideas in America,* ch. 8.

On CHARLES F. MC KIM, WILLIAM R. MEAD, and STANFORD WHITE: *A Monograph of the Works of McKim, Mead and White,* 2 vols., 1925. On CHARLES F. MC KIM (1847–1909), see Alfred H. Granger, *Charles Follen McKim,* 1913; also Charles Moore, *The Life and Times of Charles Follen McKim,* 1929. On STANFORD WHITE (1853–1906), see Charles C. Baldwin, *Stanford White,* 1931; *Sketches and Designs by Stanford White,* edited by Lawrence White, 1920. Hitchcock discusses some early developments in the work of McKim, Mead, and White in "Frank Lloyd Wright and the 'Academic Tradition,' " etc., cited above in section 21, ch. 22.

On JOHN LA FARGE (1835–1910): Royal Cortissoz, *John La Farge,* 1911; Cecilia Waern, *John La Farge, Artist and Writer,* 1896, with many illustrations of his stained glass. See also La Farge, *Considerations on Painting,* 1896 (his lectures of 1893 at the Metropolitan Museum); and Henry La Farge, "John La Farge and the South Sea Idyll," in *Journal of the Warburg and Courtauld Institutes,* vol. 7, Jan.–June, 1944, p. 34.

On AUGUSTUS SAINT-GAUDENS: See references above, under section 21, ch. 21.

On Madison Square Garden: M. G. Van Rensselaer, "The Madison Square Garden," in *Century,* vol. 47, 1894, p. 732; two articles in the *American Architect,* vol. 128, Dec., 1925, pp. 513, 519.

The designing of the Boston Public Library is discussed in Granger, *Charles Follen McKim,* ch. 3, and in Moore, *Life and Times of Charles Follen McKim,* ch. 7.

Henry Adams on "An American Virgin . . ." is quoted from the *Education,* p. 385.

Chapter 23 / *The More Smiling Aspects*

Howells on the "cheerful average" is quoted from *Criticism and Fiction,* 1891, ch. 21.

On FRANK DUVENECK: See references above, under section 21, "Introduction." Royal Cortissoz discusses Duveneck and Chase in *American Artists,* ch. 10.

On WILLIAM M. CHASE (1849–1916): Katharine

M. Roof, *The Life and Art of William Merritt Chase,* 1917; also *William Merritt Chase,* 1957, catalogue of exhibition, Parrish Art Museum, Southampton, L.I.

On JOHN S. SARGENT (1856–1925): William H. Downes, *John S. Sargent; His Life and Work,* 1925; Evan Charteris, *John Sargent,* 1927; Charles H. Mount, *John Sargent,* 1955. Henry James's comments on young Sargent, here quoted, are in *Picture and Text,* 1893, p. 92.

The resistance to impressionism: See Theodore Child, "Art in America," in *Harper's,* vol. 74, Jan., 1887, p. 313, here quoted; Charles H. Moore in *Atlantic Monthly,* vol. 68, Dec., 1891, p. 805.

Hamlin Garland's definition of impressionism, here quoted, is in *Crumbling Idols,* 1894, p. 122.

The American exponents: See catalogue by John I. H. Baur, *Leaders of American Impressionism,* Brooklyn Museum, 1937. On CHILDE HASSAM (1859–1935): Adeline Adams, *Childe Hassam,* 1938. On JOHN H. TWACHTMAN (1853–1902): Eliot Clark, *John Twachtman,* 1924, and Allan Tucker, *John H. Twachtman,* 1931. On J. ALDEN WEIR (1852–1919): Duncan Phillips and others, *Julian Alden Weir: An Appreciation of His Life and Works,* 1922. On THEODORE ROBINSON (1852–1896): John I. H. Baur catalogue, *Theodore Robinson,* Brooklyn Museum, 1946. On WILLARD L. METCALF (1858–1925), Catherine B. Ely, "Willard L. Metcalf," in *American Magazine of Art,* vol. 13, Oct., 1925, p. 332.

The "idealizers": Royal Cortissoz writes sympathetically of Thayer, Dewing, Brush, and others in chs. 2–7 of *American Artists.* On DWIGHT W. TRYON (1849–1925): Henry C. White, *The Life and Art of Dwight William Tryon,* 1930. On ABBOTT THAYER (1849–1921); see Nelson C. White, *Abbott H. Thayer, Painter and Naturalist,* 1951. On GEORGE DE F. BRUSH (1855–1941); see catalogue of retrospective exhibition, Grand Central Art Galleries, N.Y., in 1930.

Henry Adams on the sexlessness of American art is quoted from the *Education,* p. 385.

On the Boston group: See Isham and Cortissoz, *History of American Painting,* chs. 24, 25. See also Rose V. S. Berry, "Joseph de Camp, Painter and Man," in *American Magazine of Art,* vol. 14, Apr., 1923, p. 182; Low, *A Painter's Progress;* Edward E. Simmons, *From Seven to Seventy,* 1922; Elihu Vedder, *The Digressions of V,* 1910.

Chapter 24 / *The White City*

On the Columbian Exposition: See Tallmadge, *Story of Architecture in America,* ch. 8; Monroe, *John Wellborn Root,* ch. 7; Granger, *Charles Follen McKim,* ch. 5; Cortissoz, *American Artists,* ch. 15 (on Frank D. Millet); William Walton, *Art and Architecture at the World's Columbian Exposition,* 2 vols., 1893; *Official Catalogue of the Fine Arts Exhibition.*

The most complete pictorial record of the Fair is R. Hitchcock (ed.), *The Art of the World: Painting, Sculpture and Architecture at the World's Fair,* issued in 30 portfolios and also (1896) in 2 vols.

Contemporary illustrated articles in magazines: Henry C. Bunner, "The Making of the White City," in *Scribner's,* vol. 12, July–Dec., 1892, p. 399, and Frank D. Millet, "The Decoration of the Exposition" in the same, p. 692; Henry Van Brunt, "Architecture at the Columbian Exposition," in *Century,* vol. 44, new series, vol. 22, May–Oct., 1892, pp. 81, 385, 540, 720, and 897; W. Lewis Fraser, "Decorative Painting at the World's Fair," in the same, p. 14; Royal Cortissoz, "Decorative Color in the Court of Honor at the Fair," in the same, July, 1893, p. 323.

Gilder's poem appeared in *Century,* vol. 46, May, 1893, p. 22.

Comments on the Fair: Harry T. Peck (here quoted), *Twenty Years of the Republic,* 1907, p. 350; Henry Adams, here quoted from the *Education,* p. 340; Norton's estimate, from a ms. lecture, "Art in America," is here quoted from Moore, *Daniel H. Burnham,* vol. 1, p. 87.

W. C. Brownell's three articles, "French Art," appeared in *Scribner's,* vol. 12, July–Dec., 1892. The passage quoted here is from p. 627.

SECTION 23

Book Five / Progressivism, Culture, and War

The Period in General

See Billington, Loewenberg, and Brockunier, *The United States,* chs. 23–28; Beard, *Rise of American Civilization,* chs. 25–29; Harold U. Faulkner, *The Quest for Social Justice,* 1931, vol. 11 in the "History of American Life" series; and Preston W. Slosson, *The Great Crusade and After,* 1930, vol. 12 in the same.

Thought and literary expression: Oscar Cargill, *The Social Revolt,* 1933; Curti, *Growth of American Thought,* chs. 26–28; Henry S. Commager, *The American Mind,* 1950; Kazin, *On Native Grounds,* part 1, chs. 4–6, part 2; *Literary History of the United States,* vol. 2, sections 66–73.

Architecture, sculpture, and painting since c. 1900: Hamlin, *The American Spirit in Architecture,* chs. 14–23; Fitch, *American Building,* ch. 7; Agnes M. Rindge, *Sculpture,* 1929, parts 5 and 6; Post, *History of European and American Sculpture,* vol. 2, ch. 29; C. Ludwig Brummé, *Contemporary American Sculpture,* 1948; Jacques Schnier, *Sculpture in Modern America,* 1948;

Samuel M. Kootz, *Modern American Painters,* 1930; Richardson, *Painting in America,* ch. 13; Andrew C. Ritchie, *Abstract Painting and Sculpture in America,* 1951; Thomas B. Hess, *Abstract Painting, Background and American Phase,* 1951; John I. H. Baur, *Revolution and Tradition in Modern American Art,* 1951, and *Nature in Abstraction,* 1958; Ralph M. Pearson, *The Modern Renaissance in America Art,* 1954; Milton Brown, *American Painting from the Armory Show to the Great Depression,* 1955; Rudi Blesh, *Modern Art U.S.A.: Men, Rebellion, Conquest, 1900–1956,* 1956; John I. H. Baur (ed.), Lloyd Goodrich, Dorothy C. Miller, James T. Soby, and Frederick S. Wight, *New Art in America,* 1957, part I; Carl Zigrosser, *The Artist in America,* 1942, on twenty-four graphic artists.

On individual artists: Few references to individuals can be included in the modern sections of this bibliography. The reader is advised to consult the following:

Index of Twentieth Century Artists, published in four volumes by the College Art Association of America; each subject has a biographical sketch, a full bibliography, and lists of exhibitions and of works reproduced.

The American Artists Series of monographs issued by the Whitney Museum of American Art, most of them in 1931 and 1932 (to be indicated below by the intials WM). Each contains a short essay, a brief biography, and a bibliography.

A series of monographs published by the American Artists Group, chiefly illustrations, with brief forewords by the artists themselves.

Many modern Americans are discussed, singly or in groups, in the publications issued by the Museum of Modern Art in connection with its exhibitions (to be indicated below by the initials MMA).

Useful articles on this period are in magazines; see especially *Art and Progress,* vols. 1–6, 1909–1915, continued as *American Magazine of Art,* vols. 7–21, 1915–1930; also the *Arts,* 1921–1931.

SECTION 24

Book Five / Part One / The Voice of the City

Introduction / *The Great Stock-Taking*

Turner is quoted from "The Significance of the Frontier," an essay republished in *The Early Writings of Frederick Jackson Turner,* 1938.

On the Library of Congress: See Herbert Small, *Handbook of the New Library of Congress in Washington,* 1897, with a section by Charles Caffin, "The Architecture, Sculpture, and Painting."

On mural painting: See Edwin H. Blashfield, *Mural Painting in America,* 1913; *The Works of Edwin Howland Blashfield,* 1937, with introduction by Royal Cortissoz. On Abbey as a mural painter, see Cortissoz, *American Artists,* ch. 13. Henry B. Fuller's satire of mural allegories is in *Under the Skylights,* 1901.

On the Piccirillis and their work for French, Saint-Gaudens, and others: See Joseph V. Lombardo, *Attilio Piccirilli,* 1944.

On the replanning of Washington: Charles Moore, "The Improvement of Washington City," in *Century,* vol. 41, Feb., 1902, p. 621, and Mar., 1902, p. 747; Daniel H. Burnham, "White City and Capitol City," in the same, Feb., 1902, p. 619; Leila Mechlin, "The Washington Plan and the Art of City-Building," in *International Studio,* vol. 33, Jan., 1908, p. cix; Moore, *Life and Times of Charles Follen McKim,* ch. 15. For a modern evaluation, see Churchill, *The City Is the People,* p. 33.

Hamlin Garland defines the "veritist" in *Crumbling Idols,* ch. 3, here quoted.

Henry James's comments on New York, Boston, and Cambridge, here quoted, are in *The American Scene,* 1907, pp. 172, 186, 191, 248.

Veblen's characterization of college architecture is in *The Higher Learning in America,* 1918, p. 146.

On the critical writings of Caffin, Hartmann, Huneker, and others: See Mellquist, *Emergence of an American Art,* ch. 9.

Chapter 25 / *Mop, Pail, and Ashcan*

Hartmann's "Plea for the Picturesqueness of New York" is in *Camera Notes,* vol. 4, Oct., 1900, p. 91. Hartmann reports the comments of painters on photography in "A Photographic Enquête," in the same, vol. 5, Apr., 1902, p. 233. Other discussions of photography as an art: Ida Tarbell, "A Great Photographer," in *McClure's,* vol. 9, May, 1897, p. 559 (on G. C. Cox); Alexander Black, "The Artist and the Camera: A Debate," in *Century,* vol. 64, Oct., 1902, p. 813; and Alfred Stieglitz, "Modern Pictorial Photography," in the same, p. 822.

On the conventional approach to photography: See Henry P. Robinson, *Pictorial Effect in Photography,* 1881; for the new point of view, see Hartmann, "The Photo-Secession, a New Pictorial Movement," in the *Craftsman,* vol. 6, Apr., 1904, p. 33. On Keiley, Käsebier, and other photo-secessionists, see Caffin, *Photography as a Fine Art,* 1901; also Mellquist, *Emergence of an American Art,* ch. 4.

On Lewis Hine: See Marynn O. Ausubel, "Lewis Hine Memorial Collection," in *Photo Notes,* Aug.–Sept., 1947, p. 9.

On Stieglitz himself: See references below, under section 25, ch. 27.

Camera Notes was published in 1897–1902; *Camera Work* in 1903–1917, in fifty numbers.

On the cartoons and social satires of Opper, Davenport, Robinson, and others: See Murrell, *History of American Graphic Humor,* vol. 2, chs. 8–10.

On Henri and the Philadelphia illustrators: See "Artists of the Philadelphia Press," *Philadelphia Museum Bulletin,* vol. 41, Nov., 1945. On ROBERT HENRI (1865–1929), see Helen A. Read, *Robert Henri,* WM, 1931; Henri, *The Art Spirit,* rev. ed., 1930, here quoted, pp. 35, 43, 148, 152.

On JEROME MYERS (1867–1940): See his autobiography, *Artist in Manhattan,* 1940.

On MAURICE PRENDERGAST (1859–1924): William M. Milliken in the *Arts,* vol. 9, Apr., 1926, p. 181; Margaret Bruening, *Maurice Prendergast,* WM, 1931; *The Prendergasts,* catalogue of a retrospective exhibition of Maurice and Charles at Addison Gallery, Andover, Mass., in 1938.

Henry James on Central Park is quoted from *The American Scene,* p. 179.

On EVERETT SHINN (1876–1953) and the other members of the Eight: See Neuhaus, *History and Ideals of American Art,* ch. 22; *The Eight,* catalogue of Brooklyn Museum exhibition, 1944; Ira Glackens, *William Glackens and the Ashcan Group,* 1957; Guy Pène du Bois, *William Glackens* (1870–1938), WM, 1931; on JOHN SLOAN (1871–1951), see Edward Hopper, "John Sloan and the Philadelphians," in the *Arts,* vol. 11, Apr., 1927, p. 168; Sloan's autobiography, *Gist of Art,* 1939; Lloyd Goodrich (ed.), *John Sloan,* 1952. Van Wyck Brooks, *John Sloan, a Painter's Life,* 1955. On GEORGE B. LUKS (1867–1933): Elizabeth L. Cary, *George Luks,* WM; article by John Spargo in the *Craftsman,* vol. 12, Sept., 1907, p. 599; catalogue of Newark Museum exhibition, 1934. On ERNEST LAWSON (1873–1939): Guy Pène du Bois, *Ernest Lawson,* WM, 1932. On ARTHUR B. DAVIES (1862–1928): Royal Cortissoz, *Arthur B. Davies,* WM, 1931; Forbes Watson, "Arthur Bowen Davies," in *Magazine of Art,* vol. 45, Dec., 1952, p. 362.

Related figures: On GUY PÈNE DU BOIS (1884–1958): See his autobiography, *Artists Say the Silliest Things,* 1940; Royal Cortissoz, *Guy Pène du Bois,* WM; Walter Gutman in *Art in America,* vol. 18, Dec., 1929, p. 25. See also C. Adolph Glassgold, *Glenn O. Coleman,* WM, 1932. On GEORGE W. BELLOWS (1882–1925): George W. Eggers, *George Bellows,* WM, 1931.

The Independent Show of 1910 is reviewed by Robert Henri in the *Craftsman,* vol. 18, May, 1910, p. 160, with illustrations.

Chapter 26 / *The Book and the Edifice*

On architecture by older men in the early nineteen hundreds: James O. Post, "Recent and Current Work by George B. Post and Sons," in *New York Architect,* vol. 3, 1909; "The Work of Messrs. Carrère and Hastings," an entire issue of *Architectural Record,* vol. 27, Jan., 1910; see *Dictionary of American Biography* for HENRY J. HARDENBERGH (1847–1918) and CASS GILBERT (1859–1934); see also Herbert Croly, "Recent Works of John Russell Pope," entire issue of *Architectural Record,* vol. 29, June, 1911; Peter B. Wight, "Daniel Hudson Burnham and His Associates," entire issue of the same, vol. 38, July, 1915.

For a discussion of the value of Beaux-Arts training, see J. Stewart Barney in *Architectural Record,* vol. 22, Nov., 1907, p. 333; A. D. F. Hamlin in the same, vol. 23, Apr., 1908, p. 241; and Paul Cret in the same, May, 1908, p. 367.

Cram's description of the Richardsonesque is quoted from his *The Ministry of Art,* 1914, p. 33. Other Cram writings: *Church Architecture,* 1901; *The Gothic Quest,* 1907; *The Substance of Gothic,* 1917; *My Life in Architecture,* 1936. Montgomery Schuyler surveys the work of Cram's firm in "The Works of Cram, Goodhue and Ferguson," in *Architectural Record,* vol. 29, Jan.–June, 1911, p. 1. On BERTRAM G. GOODHUE (1869–1924), see Goodhue, *A Book of Architectural and Decorative Drawings,* 1914. On the Graduate College buildings at Princeton, see *Art and Progress,* vol. 5, June, 1914, p. 275; on West Point, see Cram, *My Life in Architecture,* ch. 6. For comments on the modern use of Gothic, see Charles R. Morey, "Mediaeval Art and America," in *Journal of the Warburg and Courtauld Institutes,* vol. 7, Jan.–June, 1944, p. 1.

FRANK LLOYD WRIGHT (1869–1959). The three most useful sources of information on his life, principles, and work are Wright's *Autobiography,* rev. ed., 1943; *Frank Lloyd Wright on Architecture,* 1941, a collection of his speeches and articles, edited by Frederick Gutheim; *In the Nature of Materials,* 1942, edited by Henry-Russell Hitchcock, a pictorial record of his projects and completed buildings, with critical commentaries. For further references, see below under section 24, ch. 26, and section 29, ch. 35.

Victor Hugo's "One Shall Destroy the Other" is in *Notre Dame de Paris,* Book 5, ch. 2.

Wright's speech at Evanston, here quoted, is from *Frank Lloyd Wright on Architecture,* p. 3.

Greenough's remarks on functionalism are quoted from Tuckerman, *Memorial of Horatio Greenough,* p. 125.

Wright's comments on Unity Temple are in his *Autobiography,* p. 153.

On Louis Sullivan: See references above, under section 21, ch. 22. Sullivan's *Craftsman* articles are in vol. 10, May–July, 1906. Excerpts from his *Democracy: A Man-Search* are in *Twice a Year,* no. V–VI, 1940–1941, p. 17, here quoted from pp. 22–23.

For the comparison between the Babson and Coonley houses, see "A Departure from Classic Tradition," in *Architectural Record,* vol. 30, Oct., 1908, p. 327.

Wright's article, "In the Cause of Architecture," is in *Architectural Record,* vol. 23, Mar., 1908, p. 155, and in *Frank Lloyd Wright on Architecture.* The phrases quoted here are from the latter, p. 45.

Sturgis' criticism of the Larkin Building is in *Architectural Record,* vol. 23, Apr., 1908, p. 311.

SECTION 25

Book Five / Part Two / Art's Coming of Age

Introduction / *Art and Mr. Podsnap*

Wright's characterization of Sullivan, here quoted, is from his *Autobiography,* p. 269.

The modern art movements in Europe are surveyed by Sheldon Cheney in *A Primer of Modern Art,* 1924, and *Expressionism in Art,* 1934. Other surveys in English: Willard H. Wright, *Modern Painting,* 1915; Walter Pach, *The Masters of Modern Art,* 1925. For critical interpretations of modern movements by Barr, Soby, Barnes, and others, see references below, under section 28, "Introduction."

Comments by modern artists on their own work are included in *Artists on Art,* edited by Robert Goldwater and Marco Treves, 1945.

On the revolution in architecture and allied arts: Nikolaus Pevsner, *Pioneers of the Modern Movement from William Morris to Walter Gropius,* 1937; Walter C. Behrendt, *Modern Building,* 1937; Henry-Russell Hitchcock, *Modern Architecture,* 1929; Sheldon Cheney, *The New World Architecture,* 1930; Sheldon and Martha Cheney, *Art and the Machine,* 1936. For other references, see below, under section 26, Introduction and ch. 30.

On the French moderns: See Georges Lemaître, *From Cubism to Surrealism in French Literature,* 1941, a discussion of both literary and visual-plastic arts. On the Italians, see Rosa T. Clough, *Looking Back at Futurism,* 1942. On the English, see Mary Chamot, *Modern Painting in England,* 1937. On the Russians, see Paul Miliukov, *Outlines of Russian Culture,* part 3, 1942, chs. 3, 4.

Aesthetic formulations: Clive Bell, *Art,* 1914, here quoted from pp. 8, 25, 26; Guillaume Apollinaire, *The Cubist Painters, Aesthetic Meditations,* 1913, translated by Lionel Abel; Wassily Kandinsky, *The Art of Spiritual Harmony,* 1914, translated by M. T. H. Sadler.

Chapter 27 / *Ructions in the Hennery*

On Stieglitz' gallery: See Mellquist, *The Emergence of an American Art,* ch. 9. A symposium of opinions was published in *Camera Work,* no. 47, July, 1914: "What Is 291?" Mather's comments on the Matisse show are in the *Nation,* vol. 90, Mar. 17, 1910, p. 272.

On ALFRED STIEGLITZ (1864–1946): *America and Alfred Stieglitz,* 1934, a symposium by several of his admirers. Much material on Stieglitz has appeared in *Twice a Year:* see no. I, 1938, p. 75; nos. 5–6, 1940–1941, p. 135; nos. 8–9, 1942, p. 105, 137; nos. 10–11, 1943, p. 245; nos. 14–15, 1946–1947, pp. 188, 203. Many photographs and paintings from Stieglitz' collection are in the Philadelphia Museum of Art: see the Museum catalogue of an exhibition, *History of an American, Alfred Stieglitz: "291" and After;* also "An American Collection," *Philadelphia Museum Bulletin,* vol. 40, May, 1945; and Newhall, *Masters of Photography.*

The pioneers of American modernism: See references below, under section 26, ch. 29. See also *Pioneers of Modern Art in America,* an exhibition at the Whitney Museum in 1946, with an essay by Lloyd Goodrich; Paul Rosenfeld, *Port of New York,* 1924, fourteen verbal portraits including many of the "291" group.

Temple Scott's article, "Fifth Avenue and the Boulevard Saint-Michel," is in the *Forum,* vol. 44, Dec., 1910, p. 665. Jerome Mellquist has provided the author with a key to the persons portrayed by Scott under fictional names.

Hartley's statement of his creed, here quoted, is in *Camera Work,* no. 22, 1908.

Weber's philosophy is stated by himself in the same, no. 31, 1910.

On John Marin: See references below, under section 26, ch. 29.

John Cotton Dana's pioneering work is summarized by Holger Cahill in his introduction to the catalogue of the Newark Museum, 1944, here quoted. Gertrude Vanderbilt Whitney's support of young innovators is described by Juliana Force in *Magazine of Art,* vol. 39, Nov., 1946, p. 271. Charles Caffin's piece, "Rumpus in a Hen-House," is in *Camera Work,* no. 22, 1908, p. 42, here quoted.

Chapter 28 / *Explosion in the Armory*

The best accounts of the Armory Show are Walt Kuhn, *Twenty-Five Years After: The Story of the Armory Show,* 1938 (a pamphlet); Walter Pach, *Queer Thing, Painting,* 1938, ch. 17; Mellquist, *Emergence of an American Art,* ch. 10; Frank A. Trapp (ed.), catalogue of "revival" of Armory Show at Amherst College, 1958.

Contemporary comments on the Armory Show from contrasting points of view: Theodore Roosevelt, "A Layman's View of an Art Exhibition," in the *Outlook,* vol. 29, Mar. 29, 1913, p. 718; Royal Cortissoz, "Ellis Island Art," reprinted as ch. 1 in his *American Artists;* W. D. MacColl, "The International Exhibition of Modern Art," in the *Forum,* vol. 50, July, 1913, p. 24; James F. Gregg (ed.), *For and Against,* 1913 (a pamphlet).

On the beginnings of the Phillips Memorial Gallery: See Duncan Phillips, *A Collection in the Making,* 1926.

On the Forum Show: See Oscar Bluemner, *The Forum Exhibition,* 1916; Mellquist, *Emergence of an American Art,* p. 247.

On the effect of the Armory on the decorative arts: See Mary F. Roberts, "Science in Art," in the *Craftsman,* vol. 24, May, 1913, p. 216.

On the Independent Show of 1917: See Pach, *Queer Thing, Painting,* ch. 20.

Willard H. Wright's attack on the critics is in the *Forum,* vol. 55, Feb., 1916, p. 201; his theories of art are in *Modern Painting,* 1915, and *The Future of Painting,* 1923.

SECTION 26

Book Five / Part Three / Decade of Disillusion

Introduction / *A Race of Hamlets*

Modern movements in Europe during and after the war: See references above, under section 25, "Introduction." See also the following: Herman G. Scheffauer, *The New Vision in the German Arts,* 1921; Amédée Ozenfant, *Foundations of Modern Art,* 1931; C. Giedion-Welcker, *Modern Plastic Art,* 1937, translated by P. Morton Shand; Joseph Hudnut, *Modern Sculpture,* 1929; Agnes Rindge, *Sculpture,* 1929, part 6; Walter Gropius, *The New Architecture and the Bauhaus,* translated by P. Morton Shand; *Modern Architecture,* MMA, 1932, with essays by Alfred H. Barr, Jr., Henry-Russell Hitchcock, Philip Johnson, and Lewis Mumford; Amédée Ozenfant and Le Corbusier, *Towards a New Architecture,* 1931, translated by Frederick Etchells; Le Corbusier, *The City of Tomorrow and Its Planning,* 1929, translated by Frederick Etchells; Henry-Russell Hitchcock and Philip Johnson, *The International Style: Architecture Since 1922,* 1932.

Rilke is here quoted from *Twice a Year,* no. VIII–IX, 1942, p. 97.

The characterization of Stravinsky's music by Roger Sessions, here quoted, is from Aaron Copland, *Our New Music,* 1941.

T. S. Eliot's poem, *The Hollow Men,* is quoted from *Collected Poems,* 1934, p. 104.

The war and its aftermath in the United States: On the anti-war cartoonists, see Murrell, *History of American Graphic Humor,* ch. 10. On ART YOUNG (1866–1943), see his *On My Way,* 1928, and his *Art Young, His Life and Times,* 1939. For Boardman Robinson's war drawings, see John Reed, *The War in Western Europe,* 1916. On the pictorial satire of Frueh, Arno, and others in the twenties, see Murrell, ch. 11.

Civilization in the United States, edited by Harold E. Stearns, 1922, is a critical symposium by thirty writers on American culture at this time.

Some literary dissenters: See Sherwood Anderson, *A Story Teller's Story,* 1924, and *Memoirs,* edited by Eleanor Anderson, 1942. On Randolph Bourne, see his own *History of a Literary Radical,* 1920, and *Untimely Papers,* 1919. Max Lerner discusses Bourne in *Twice a Year,* no. V–VI, 1940–1941, p. 54. Bourne is here quoted on the collapse of European culture from Louis Filler, *Randolph Bourne,* 1943.

Several essays of this period by Van Wyck Brooks are collected in *Essays on America,* 1934.

Art and critics in the post-Armory period: For Henry McBride, see the *Dial,* especially vol. 69, July–Dec., 1920. For Huneker's recantation, here quoted, see *Letters of James Gibbons Huneker,* edited by Josephine Huneker, 1922, p. 206. See also Duncan Phillips, "Fallacies of the New Dogmatism in Art," in *American Magazine of Art,* vol. 9, Dec., 1917, p. 43.

Chapter 29 / *Distortion Domesticated*

For references to individual artists: See suggestions above, under section 23, "The Period in General." Many artists of the twenties are included in exhibition catalogues of the Museum of Modern Art; see especially *Paintings by Nineteen Living Americans,* 1929; *American Painting and Sculpture,* 1932.

Some Whitney monographs: Jean P. Slusser on BERNARD KARFIOL (1886–1952); Frank J. Mather, Jr., on EUGENE SPEICHER (1883–   ); Virgil Barker on HENRY LEE MC FEE (1886–1953). On MORRIS KANTOR (1896–   ), see Forbes Watson in *American Magazine of Art,* vol. 28, Feb., 1935, p. 113.

On HENRY V. POOR (1888–   ), see Peyton Boswell, Jr., *Varnum Poor,* 1941; on MAURICE STERNE (1877–1957), see catalogue of retrospective exhibition, Museum of Modern Art, 1933. On WALT KUHN (1880–1949) see *Fifty Paintings by Walt Kuhn,* 1940, with comments by Paul Bird. On NILES SPENCER (1893–1952): See Holger Cahill in *Magazine of Art,* vol. 45, Nov., 1952, p. 313.

On HENRI, LUKS, BELLOWS, and DU BOIS: See references above, under section 24, ch. 25.

On EDWARD HOPPER (1882–   ): Guy Pène du Bois, *Edward Hopper,* WM, 1931; Lloyd Goodrich, *Edward Hopper,* 1950; Charles Burchfield, "Hopper: Career of Silent Poetry," in *Art News,* vol. 49, Mar., 1950, p. 15.

On ROCKWELL KENT (1882–): Kent and Carl Zigrosser, *Rockwellkentiana,* 1933.

On KENNETH H. MILLER (1876–1952): Rosenfeld in *Port of New York;* Alan Burroughs, *Kenneth Hayes Miller,* WM, 1931.

On YASUO KUNIYOSHI (1893–1953): Lloyd Goodrich, catalogue of Whitney Museum retrospective exhibition, 1948; notes on Kuniyoshi by Lloyd Goodrich, Robert Laurent, and Mary Meixner in *College Art Journal,* vol. 13, Fall, 1953.

On ALEXANDER BROOK (1898–): See his autobiographical notes in *Creative Art,* vol. 6, Oct., 1929, p. 715; Edward A. Jewell, *Alexander Brook,* WM, 1932.

On CHARLES DEMUTH (1883–1935): Forbes Watson in the *Arts,* vol. 3, Jan., 1923, p. 77; *Charles Demuth* (Albert E. Gallatin, ed.), 1927; William Murrell, *Charles Demuth,* WM, 1932; S. Lane Faison, "Fact and Art in Charles Demuth," in *Magazine of Art,* vol. 43, Apr., 1950, p. 123; Andrew C. Ritchie, *Charles Demuth,* MMA, 1950.

On PRESTON DICKINSON (1891–1930): Forbes Watson in the *Arts,* vol. 5, May, 1924, p. 285; Samuel M. Kootz in *Creative Art,* vol. 8, May, 1931, p. 339.

On KARL KNATHS (1891–): Lloyd Goodrich and John I. H. Baur, *Four American Expressionists,* 1959.

On GEORGIA O'KEEFFE (1887–): Waldo Frank, *Time Exposures,* 1926, p. 31; Rosenfeld, *Port of New York,* p. 199.

On the New York paintings of JOSEPH STELLA (1880–1946): See the catalogue of the Newark Museum, 1944.

On HORACE PIPPIN (1888–1946) and JOHN KANE (1859–1934): Selden Rodman, *Horace Pippin,* 1947; John Kane, *Sky Hooks,* 1938, an autobiography.

On MAURICE PRENDERGAST: See references above, under section 24, ch. 25.

On ALFRED MAURER (1868–1932): Elizabeth McCausland, *A. H. Maurer,* 1951.

On ARTHUR G. DOVE (1880–1946): Elizabeth McCausland, "Dove, Man and Painter," in *Parnassus,* vol. 9, Dec., 1937, p. 3; Frederick S. Wight, *Arthur B. Dove,* 1958.

On MAX WEBER (1881–): His own *Essays on Art,* 1916; catalogues of one-man exhibitions at the Museum of Modern Art in 1930 (with bibliography) and at the Whitney Museum in 1949.

On MARSDEN HARTLEY (1877–1943): See an early statement by him in *Camera Work,* no. 45, 1914, p. 17; his collected essays, *Adventures in the Arts,* 1921; his "Art and the Personal Life," in *Creative Art,* vol. 2, June, 1928, p. xxxi, here quoted; Elizabeth McCausland, *Marsden Hartley,* 1952. For further Hartley references, see below, under section 28, ch. 34.

On JOHN MARIN (1870–1953): Emanuel M. Benson, *John Marin, the Man and His Work,* 1935; H. J. Seligmann (ed.), *Letters of John Marin,* 1931; MacKinley Helm, *John Marin,* 1948, an extended discussion fully illustrated; catalogue of Marin exhibition at Institute of Modern Art, Boston, Mass., in 1947; *John Marin,* text by William Carlos Williams and others, 1956.

On photography in the twenties: See Beaumont Newhall, *Photography,* MMA, 1937, p. 67. Paul Strand states his principles in *Camera Work,* no. 49, 50, 1916–1917. The Strand-Sheeler motion picture, *Manahatta,* is reviewed by Robert A. Parker in *Arts and Decoration,* vol. 15, Oct., 1921, p. 369.

On CHARLES SHEELER (1883–): See the artist's early statement in the catalogue of the Forum Show, 1916; Forbes Watson, "Charles Sheeler," in the *Arts,* vol. 3, May, 1923, p. 345; catalogue of Museum of Modern Art exhibition, 1939; Constance Rourke, *Charles Sheeler, Artist in the American Tradition,* 1938; Frederick S. Wight, *"Charles Sheeler,"* in *Art in America,* vol. 42, Oct., 1954, p. 181.

On LOUIS M. EILSHEMIUS (1864–1941): See William Schack, *And He Sat among the Ashes,* 1939.

On "POP" HART (1868–1933): See *George O. "Pop" Hart,* 1928, with introduction by Holger Cahill.

Chapter 30 / *Reason in Bronze and Concrete*

On the Lincoln Memorial: See Jesse L. Williams' article on the Guérin decorations in *Scribner's,* vol. 66, Oct., 1919, p. 416; and W. M. Berger, "Making a Great Statue," in the same, p. 424. On Daniel C. French, see references above, under section 21, ch. 21.

Taft, Pratt, Dallin, Barnard, Bartlett, the Borglums, and others of this group are discussed in Post, *A History of European and American Sculpture,* vol. 2, ch. 29. See also William Walton, "Mr. Bartlett's Pediment for the House of Representatives," in *Scribner's,* vol. 48, July, 1910, p. 125; Ferdinand Schevill, *Karl Bitter,* 1917; Robert H. Moulton, "Lorado Taft, Interpreter of the Middle West," in *Architectural Record,* vol. 36, July, 1914, p. 13.

On MALVINA HOFFMAN (1887–): See her *Heads and Tales,* 1936. On Richmond Barthé and other Negro sculptors, see Porter, *Modern Negro Art,* chs. 6–8. On JO DAVIDSON (1883–1952) see his *Between Sittings: An Informal Autobiography,* 1951. See also Horace Brodsky, "Concerning Sculpture and Robert Laurent," in the *Arts,* vol. 1, May, 1921, p. 13.

On PAUL MANSHIP (1886–): Kenyon Cox, "A New Sculptor," in the *Nation,* vol. 96, Feb., 1913, p. 162; Edwin Murtha, *Paul Manship,* 1957.

On the more experimental sculptors: On WILLIAM ZORACH (1887–), see Paul S. Wingert, *The Sculp-*

ture of William Zorach, 1938; on ELIE NADELMAN (1882–1946), see Henry McBride in *Creative Art,* vol. 10, May, 1932, p. 393, and in the *Dial,* vol. 78, June, 1925, p. 528; see also Forbes Watson in *Magazine of Art,* vol. 28, May, 1935, p. 312. The most inclusive study is the Museum of Modern Art catalogue of a Nadelman exhibition in 1948, with text by Lincoln Kirstein. On CHAIM GROSS (1904–), see Lloyd Goodrich and John I. H. Baur, *Four American Expressionists,* 1959. On JOHN B. FLANNAGAN (1898–1942), see the *Arts,* vol. 15, Feb., 1929, p. 126; *American Magazine of Art,* vol. 27, Nov., 1934, p. 587; *The Sculpture of John Flannagan* (Dorothy C. Miller, ed.), MMA, 1942; Walter Pach, "John Flannagan, American Sculptor," in *Kenyon Review,* vol. 5, 1943, p. 384. On GASTON LACHAISE (1882–1935), see notes by E. E. Cummings in the *Dial,* vol. 68, Feb., 1920, p. 194, here quoted; introduction by Lincoln Kirstein for retrospective exhibition (MMA), 1935; a brief note by Marsden Hartley in *Twice a Year,* no. III–IV, 1939–1940, p. 260.

Comments on the death of Louis Sullivan: Frank Lloyd Wright, "Louis Henry Sullivan, Beloved Master," in *The Western Architect,* vol. 33, June, 1924, p. 64; and Fiske Kimball, "Louis Sullivan, an Old Master," in *Architectural Record,* vol. 57, Apr., 1925, p. 289.

For the work of Cram and Wright in this period: See references above, under section 24, ch. 26.

For the "international style" and the ideas of the most radical designers: See references above, under section 26, Introduction; see also Lewis Mumford, *Technics and Civilization,* 1934; and "Machinery and the Modern Style," in *New Republic,* vol. 27, Aug. 3, 1921, p. 263; Paul T. Frankl, *New Dimensions,* 1928.

On the problem of the city: See Lewis Mumford, *The Culture of Cities,* 1938, and *City Development,* 1945; Churchill, *The City Is the People.*

On Chatham Village: See Charles F. Lewis, "A Moderate Rental Housing Project in Pittsburgh," in *Architectural Record,* vol. 70, Oct., 1931, p. 217. On Radburn, see articles in the *American Architect,* vol. 137, Jan., 1930, p. 42; and in *Architecture,* vol. 60, Dec., 1929, p. 317. Several experiments in the designing of communities are described in Clarence S. Stein, *Toward New Towns for America,* 1957.

SECTION 27

Book Six / New Horizons

The Period in General

See Faulkner, *American Political and Social History,* chs. 39–41; Billington, Loewenberg, and Brockunier, *The United States,* chs. 29–32; Arthur M. Schlesinger, Jr., *The Age of Roosevelt,* vols. 1 and 2, 1957–1959; Kazin, *On Native Grounds,* part 3; *Literary History of the United States,* vol. 2, sections 74–81; Commager, *The American Mind.*

For references to books and articles on architecture, painting, and sculpture of this period: See *The Art Index,* 1929 to date.

Surveys of the arts: Zigrosser, *The Artist in America;* Ralph M. Pearson, *The Enjoyment of Art in America,* 1943; Kootz, *New Frontiers in American Painting;* Ritchie, *Abstract Painting and Sculpture in America;* Baur, *Revolution and Tradition in Modern American Art;* Pearson, *Modern Renaissance in American Art;* Blesh, *Modern Art U.S.A.;* Nathaniel Pousette-Dart (ed.), *American Painting Today,* 1956; Baur (ed.), *New Art in America;* Brummé, *Contemporary American Sculpture;* Fitch, *American Building,* ch. 8; Andrews, *Architecture, Ambition and Americans,* ch. 7.

Books with a minimum of text, but useful for their illustrations: *American Art Today,* reproducing works in various media shown at the New York World's Fair, 1939; *Contemporary American Painting,* edited by Grace Pagano, 1945 (the collection of the Encyclopædia Britannica); *American Painting Today,* 1939, with an essay by Forbes Watson; *Portrait of America,* edited by Aimée Crane with a preface by Bernard De Voto, 1945. See also the illustrated catalogues of the Carnegie Institute: *Directions in American Painting,* 1941; *Painting in the U.S.,* 1943, 1945. *Modern American Painting,* 1939, reproduces much work of this period in color plates, with text by Peyton Boswell, Jr.

For this period, the books issued by the Museum of Modern Art in connection with a series of one-man exhibitions and "theme" shows, are extremely valuable not only for their illustrations but for their informative notes and historical-critical introductions. Articles by and about contemporary artists are to be found in the periodicals *Art in America, Art News, Art Digest* (since 1955 called *Arts*), *College Art Journal,* and *Perspectives USA.*

SECTION 28

Book Six / Part One / The Age of Roosevelt

Introduction / *In the Shadow of War and Fascism*

T. S. Eliot's social views are in *The Idea of a Christian Society,* 1940. Élie Faure's discouragement is in "Contemporary French Art," translated by Walter Pach, in *Twice a Year,* no. V–VI, 1940–1941, p. 295; see also Faure's letter to Pach in the same, p. 308.

On the dispute among the surrealists: André Breton,

Le surréalisme et la peinture, 1928; also *Qu'est-ce que le surréalisme?* 1934; Herbert Read (ed.), *Surrealism,* a symposium by five writers; Louis Aragon, *Painting and Reality,* printed in *Art Front,* Mar., 1937, here quoted; Salvador Dali, *The Secret Life of Salvador Dali,* 1942.

On the Nebraska capitol: See Goodhue's designs in *Architectural Record,* vol. 48, July, 1920, p. 75; also Lee Lawrie, *Sculpture,* 1936, on his own work.

On increased interest in the American scene: See Waldo Frank, *The Rediscovery of America,* 1929; Cahill's essay in *American Folk Art: The Art of the Common Man in America,* MMA, 1932; Virgil Barker's article, "Americanism in Painting," in *Yale Review,* Summer, 1936; Thomas Craven, "Nationalism in Art," in the *Forum,* vol. 95, June, 1936. For Craven's views, see also *Men of Art,* 1931, and *Modern Art,* 1934, especially chs. 12–13, 17. Craven attacks certain modernists in *Modern Art,* chs. 8, 11.

On the influence of the Mexican renaissance on American art: See Diego Rivera, *Portrait of America,* 1934, on his work in the U.S. The new conception of mural art is illustrated in *Art in Federal Buildings,* 1936, which reproduces Treasury Department murals 1934–1936. See also *Murals by American Painters and Photographers,* with essays by Lincoln Kirstein and Julien Levy, MMA, 1932.

The Federal Art Projects of the WPA: See Holger Cahill, *New Horizons in American Art,* MMA, 1936; *Art as a Function of Government,* issued by the Supervisors Association of Federal Art Projects, 1937; Grace Overmyer, *Government and the Arts,* 1939. The history of the Federal Theatre has been brilliantly recorded by Hallie Flanagan Davis in *Arena,* 1940; a comparable survey of the Art Projects has not yet been made. For additional references on this subject, see below, under section 29.

The advance guard of modernism: See catalogues of the Albert E. Gallatin collection, opened 1927 as the Museum of Living Art at New York University; also catalogues of the Solomon R. Guggenheim collection of nonobjective paintings, written by Baroness Hilla Rebay.

Lloyd Goodrich's remarks on the opening of the Museum of Modern Art are in the *Nation,* vol. 129, Dec. 4, 1929, p. 664.

The critics and commentators: Ralph Pearson's three articles, "The Failure of the Art Critics," are in *Forum and Century,* vol. 94, Nov., 1935, p. 31, Dec., 1935, p. 373; vol. 95, Jan., 1936, p. 54.

The philosopher-critics: Albert C. Barnes, *The Art in Painting,* 1928; John Dewey, *Art as Experience,* 1934; Walter Abell, *Representation and Form,* 1936; James J. Sweeney, *Plastic Redirections in Twentieth Century Painting,* 1934; Edward F. Rothschild, *The Meaning of Unintelligibility in Modern Art,* 1934; Alfred H. Barr, Jr., *Cubism and Abstract Art,* MMA, 1936, *Fantastic Art, Dada, Surrealism,* MMA, 1936; *What Is Modern Painting?* MMA, 1943; James T. Soby, *After Picasso,* 1935; *Salvador Dali,* MMA, 1941; Meyer Schapiro, "The Nature of Abstract Art," in *Marxist Quarterly,* vol. 1, Jan.–Mar., 1937, p. 77; also "The Social Bases of Art," a paper for the First American Artists Congress, 1936, here quoted from the Congress report, p. 31.

On the two world's fairs: See special number of *Art Digest,* Mar. 15, 1939, on the Golden Gate Exposition. On the New York Fair: *Architectural Record,* vol. 86, Aug., 1939, p. 40; *Architectural Review,* vol. 86, Aug., 1939; *Magazine of Art,* vol. 32, May, 1939. Talbot Hamlin discusses both fairs in "Fair Comparisons," in *Pencil Points,* vol. 20, Oct., 1939, p. 641.

Chapter 31 / *American Self-Portrait*

The second study of Middletown by Robert and Helen Lynd is *Middletown in Transition,* 1937.

Kaj Klitgaard's regional study of American art is *Through the American Landscape,* 1941. The regionalists are discussed in Pearson, *Experiencing American Pictures,* ch. 7.

For most of the artists mentioned in this chapter: See bibliographical suggestions above, under section 27, "The Period in General."

On JOHN S. CURRY (1897–1946): Laurence E. Schmeckebier, *John Steuart Curry's Pageant of America,* 1943.

On THOMAS H. BENTON (1889–): See his *An Artist in America,* 1937; also Craven, *Modern Art,* ch. 13.

On GRANT WOOD (1892–1942): See his *Revolt against the City,* 1935 (a pamphlet); also Darrell Garwood, *Artist in Iowa, a Life of Grant Wood,* 1944.

Photographers of the American scene: See *Photographs, 1915–1945:* Newhall, *Masters of Photography; Paul Strand,* with an essay by Nancy Newhall, MMA, 1945; *The Photographs of Edward Weston,* with an essay by Nancy Newhall, MMA, 1946; *Walker Evans, American Photographs,* with an essay by Lincoln Kirstein, MMA, 1938.

The urban scene: Donald J. Baer, "Ernest Fiene's Paintings of New York," in *Magazine of Art,* vol. 30, Feb., 1937, p. 95. On REGINALD MARSH (1898–1955): article by Forbes Watson in *American Magazine of Art,* vol. 28, Jan., 1935, p. 62; catalogue of Marsh exhibition at Whitney Museum, 1955; Norman Sasowsky, *Reginald Marsh: Etchings, Engravings, Lithographs,* 1956.

Berenice Abbott's photographs of Manhattan are in

Changing New York, 1939, published by the New York City Federal Art Project.

On Benton's murals: See references above; also *The Arts of Life in America,* 1932, reproductions with a foreword by the artist. Lloyd Goodrich discusses Robinson's Pittsburgh murals in the *Arts,* vol. 16, Feb., 1930, p. 390. On other mural paintings, see references above, under section 28, "Introduction"; also Holger Cahill in *New Horizons in American Art,* p. 30.

On EDWARD HOPPER: See references above, under section 26, ch. 29.

On CHARLES BURCHFIELD (1893–); See catalogue of exhibition of his early water colors at the Museum of Modern Art in 1930; also article in *Creative Art,* vol. 3, Sept., 1928, p. xxii, and John I. H. Baur, *Charles Burchfield,* 1956.

The Index of American Design project is summarized by Holger Cahill in *New Horizons in American Art,* p. 24.

Sidney Janis discusses some recent primitives in *They Taught Themselves: American Primitive Painters of the Twentieth Century,* 1942.

Chapter 32 / *Common Cause*

Lewis Mumford is here quoted from p. 1 of *The First American Artists' Congress,* 1936, which includes the papers and discussions of the Congress.

Archibald MacLeish is quoted from p. 87 of *Land of the Free,* 1938, a series of documentary photographs with a "sound track" by the poet.

Elizabeth Olds discusses the social value of prints in "Graphic Art as a Democratic Medium," in *American Contemporary Art,* Aug., 1944. Thomas Willison on the responsibility of the social artist is here quoted from *New Masses,* Oct. 1, 1935.

Individual artists: See autobiography of GEORGE BIDDLE (1885–), *An American Artist,* 1944; on WILLIAM GROPPER (1897–), see *Gropper,* 1938, with introduction by Herman Baron; on MOSES SOYER (1899–), see A. C. A. (American Contemporary Art) Gallery catalogue, 1944, with comments by Bernard Smith; on GEORGE GROSZ (1893–1959), see his autobiography, *A Little Yes and a Big No,* 1946; John I. H. Baur, *George Grosz,* 1954; on PETER BLUME (1906–), see Kootz, *Modern American Painters,* p. 27; also Blume, "After Surrealism," in *New Republic,* vol. 80, Oct. 3, 1934, p. 338; on ANTON REFREGIER (1905–), see A. C. A. Gallery catalogue, 1942, with a foreword by Herman Baron; on ROBERT GWATHMEY (1903–), see the catalogue of the 1946 exhibition at A. C. A. Gallery, with an introduction by Paul Robeson.

JOSEPH HIRSCH (1910–) is here quoted from p. 62 of *Americans, 1942,* an exhibition at the Museum of Modern Art in 1942. JACK LEVINE (1915–) is quoted from p. 86 of the same. See also Frederick S. Wight, *Jack Levine,* 1952.

On JACOB LAWRENCE (1917–): See Elizabeth McCausland in *Magazine of Art,* vol. 38, Nov., 1945, p. 251.

On BEN SHAHN (1898–), James T. Soby, *Ben Shahn,* MMA, 1947; Selden Rodman, *Portrait of the Artist as an American: Ben Shahn, a Biography with Pictures,* 1951; Shahn, *Paragraphs on Art,* 1952, and *The Shape of Content,* 1957; James T. Soby, *Ben Shahn: His Graphic Art,* 1957.

On PHILIP EVERGOOD (1901–): *Twenty Years of Paintings by Philip Evergood,* with an essay by Oliver Larkin, 1947; Elizabeth McCausland, "The Plastic Organization of Philip Evergood," in *Parnassus,* vol. 11, Mar., 1939, p. 19.

Pare Lorenz and *The River:* Lorenz discusses films in the *Forum,* vol. 80, Sept., 1928, p. 364; see also W. H. White on Pare Lorenz in *Scribner's,* vol. 105, Jan., 1939, p. 7. *The River,* 1938, reproduces the words and some stills from the film, here quoted.

On the potentialities of the animated film: See Robin Feild, *The Art of Walt Disney,* 1942; also Jean Charlot, *Art from the Mayans to Disney,* 1939, chs. 25, 26.

Chapter 33 / *Three-Dimensional Consciences*

On the sculptors: Lincoln Kirstein is here quoted from his introduction to *Gaston Lachaise,* MMA, 1935. On HARRY WICKEY (1892–), see his autobiography, *Thus Far,* 1941. On ORONZIO MALDARELLI (1892–), see *American Magazine of Art,* vol. 21, July, 1930, p. 400; on CARL WALTERS (1883–), see *Creative Art,* vol. 10, June, 1932, p. 431; on HEINZ WARNEKE (1895–), see Emil G. Hutchings in *International Studio,* vol. 83, Feb., 1926, p. 35; see also Walter Gutman, "Four Potters," in the *Arts,* vol. 14, Sept., 1928, p. 154. SAMUEL CASHWAN (1900–), EMMA LU DAVIS (1905–), DONAL HORD (1902–), and OCTAVIO MEDELLIN (1908–) are discussed in *Americans, 1942,* MMA, 1942. Waylande Gregory discusses "The Present Impasse in Sculpture" in *First American Artists' Congress,* 1936. Sculptors of this period are included in *Painters and Sculptors of Modern America,* with introduction by Monroe Wheeler, MMA, 1942. On REUBEN NAKIAN (1897–), see *Creative Art,* vol. 12, Apr., 1933, p. 302; on ISAMU NOGUCHI (1904–), see the same, Jan., 1933, p. 29. A full-length study of CARL MILLES (1875–1955) is Meyric R. Rogers, *Carl Milles: An Interpretation of His Work,* 1940.

On the architects: See Baker Brownell and Frank

L. Wright, *Architecture and Modern Life,* 1937. On Wright's work at this period, see Hitchcock, *In the Nature of Materials.* On the work of other modernists, see *Built in the U.S.A., 1932–1944* (Elizabeth Mock, ed.), MMA, 1944; also *Tomorrow's Small House,* MMA, 1946.

On furnishings: *Organic Design in Home Furnishings* (Eliot F. Noyes, ed.), MMA, 1941; *Alvar Aalto, Architecture and Furniture,* MMA, 1938.

Cram's strictures on the modernists are in *My Life in Architecture,* ch. 16.

A series of twelve discussions on functionalism began in *Pencil Points,* Mar., 1932; see especially George Howe, vol. 13, Apr., 1932, p. 215; Robert L. Anderson in the same, July, 1932, p. 505; Henry S. Churchill in the same, Sept., 1932, p. 625.

HENRY WRIGHT (1878–1936): See his *Rehousing Urban America,* 1935; also "The Architect, the Plan, and the City," in *Architectural Forum,* vol. 54, Feb., 1931, p. 213; and an article on apartments for people with low incomes, in *Architectural Record,* vol. 71, Mar., 1932, p. 147.

Lewis Mumford's essays on planning are in *City Development,* 1945; see also *New Architecture and City Planning,* a symposium edited by Paul Zucker, 1944.

Frank L. Wright discusses his own "Broadacre City" in *Architectural Record,* vol. 77, Apr., 1935, p. 243. His Sulgrave Manor lectures in London are in *An Organic Architecture,* 1939, here quoted from p. 43.

Chapter 34 / *State of High Concentration*

On MARSDEN HARTLEY: See references above, under section 26, ch. 29; see also Hudson D. Walker, "Marsden Hartley," in *Kenyon Review,* vol. 9, Spring, 1947, p. 248. Hartley's remarks "on the subject of nativeness" are quoted on p. 65 of the Museum of Modern Art's Feininger-Hartley exhibition catalogue, 1944, which has a full bibliography. Hartley's verses are here quoted from *Selected Poems,* 1945.

Several artists discussed in this chapter, including Everett Spruce, Raymond Breinin, Helen Lundeberg, Morris Graves, Hyman Bloom, Darrel Austin, Charles Howard, Knud Merrild and Emma Lu Davis, are discussed in *Americans, 1942,* MMA. On HYMAN BLOOM (1913–   ), see Frederick S. Wight, *Hyman Bloom,* 1954. On MORRIS GRAVES (1910–   ), see W. R. Valentiner in *Art Quarterly,* vol. 7, 1944, p. 250, and Frederick S. Wight, *Morris Graves,* 1956.

Samuel Kootz includes abstract and surrealist painters in *New Frontiers of American Painting,* 1943; see also *American Realists and Magic Realists* (Dorothy C. Miller, ed.), MMA, 1943. Walter Quirt's point of view, here quoted, is set forth in "Wake over Surrealism," "Americana Painting or an Art," and "New Content, New Art Forms," issued by Pinacotheca Gallery (no date). On the founding of the Transcendentalist Group, see *Art Digest,* vol. 13, Mar. 15, 1939, p. 61.

GEORGE L. K. MORRIS (1905–   ) discusses his contemporaries in "Art Chronicle," in the *Partisan Review;* see especially his comments on Hans Arp in vol. 4, Jan., 1938, p. 32.

IRENE R. PEREIRA (1905–   ) explains her principles in "An Abstract Painter on Abstract Art," in *American Contemporary Art,* Oct., 1944, p. 3; see also John I. H. Baur, *Loren MacIver and I. Pereira,* 1953.

On STUART DAVIS (1894–   ): See James J. Sweeney, *Stuart Davis,* MMA, 1945. Samuel Kootz discusses Davis in *New Frontiers of American Painting.* Davis defines abstract art in his introduction to the Whitney Museum catalogue, *Abstract Painting in America,* 1935. His idea of the social value of abstract art is given in "Abstract Art in the American Scene," in *Parnassus,* vol. 13, Mar., 1941, p. 100.

Milton Mezzrow and Bernard Wolfe are here quoted from *Really the Blues,* 1946.

The nonnaturalistic approach to sculpture is discussed by William R. Valentiner in *Origins of Modern Sculpture,* 1946, and by Giedion-Welcker, *Modern Plastic Art.*

The sculpture of Hare, Roszak, and others is included in *Fourteen Americans* (Dorothy C. Miller, ed.), MMA, 1946. See also James J. Sweeney, *Alexander Calder,* 1951; H. H. Arnason, *Theodore Roszak,* 1956.

Debates on abstract art: William Schack, "On Abstract Painting," in *Magazine of Art,* vol. 27, Sept., 1934, p. 470; Walter Abell, "The Limits of Abstraction," in the same, vol. 28, Dec., 1935, p. 735; Rhodes Johnson, "In Defense of Abstract Art," in *Parnassus,* vol. 12, Dec., 1940, p. 7; "Life or Death for Abstract Art?" a debate by Lincoln Kirstein and George L. K. Morris, in *Magazine of Art,* vol. 36, Mar., 1943, p. 111.

Georges Lemaître's conclusions on some modern theories and modern accomplishments are in *From Cubism to Surrealism in French Literature,* here quoted from p. 217.

SECTION 29

Book Six / Part Two / Point of Promise and of Danger

Introduction / *Cold War Climate*

The collapse of Federal Art: See discussions by Forbes Watson, Francis H. Taylor, and others in *Magazine of Art,* vol. 31, Mar., 1938, p. 157; vol. 32, July, 1939, p. 389, and Dec., 1939, p. 677. See also

George Biddle, "Art under Five Years of Federal Patronage," in the *American Scholar,* vol. 9, July, 1940, p. 327, "Government and the Arts," in *Harper's,* vol. 187, Oct., 1943, p. 427; also Stuart Davis in the same, Dec., 1943, p. 16.

Artists and the war: George Biddle, *Artist at War,* 1944; Thomas Benton in *University Review,* University of Kansas City, Spring, 1942; Arnaud d'Usseau and others in *Contemporary American Art,* Winter, 1946.

The problem of patronage: Lee Simonson and Walter Abell, "Post War Artists and the People," in *Magazine of Art,* vol. 36, Feb., 1943, p. 52, and Apr., 1943, p. 148; Elizabeth McCausland, "Pepsi-Cola and Patronage," in *American Contemporary Art,* Aug.–Sept., 1944, and "Why Can't America Afford Art?" in *Magazine of Art,* vol. 39, Jan., 1946, p. 18; Walter Abell, "Art and Labor," in the same, Oct., 1946, p. 231.

Reproductions of art: Thomas M. Folds, "A Consumer's Guide to Color Prints," in *Magazine of Art,* vol. 36, May, 1943, p. 185.

Roosevelt is here quoted from his speech at the Bretton Woods Conference. On the postwar period, see Commager, *The American Mind,* ch. 20, and Max Lerner, *America as a Civilization: Life and Thought in the United States Today,* 1957.

On the Artists-Museums Committee: See its report, *The Museum and the Artist,* 1957. See also Bernard S. Myers, *Problems of the Younger American Artist,* 1957. On the work of the Committee on Government and Art, see Lloyd Goodrich in *College Art Journal,* vol. 14, Fall, 1954, p. 52, and vol. 15, Spring, 1956, p. 251.

Strictures on the period: Randall Jarrell, *Poetry and the Age,* 1955; Robert Motherwell, "The Painter and His Audience," in *Perspectives USA,* no. 9, Autumn, 1954, p. 107; Clement Greenberg, "The State of American Art," in *Magazine of Art,* vol. 42, Mar., 1949, p. 92; Adolph Gottlieb, "Artist and Society, a Brief Case History," in *College Art Journal,* vol. 14, 1955, p. 96; Chandler Brossard (ed.), *The Scene before You,* 1955; Manny Farber on Levine in *Art News,* vol. 54, Mar., 1955, p. 33. Gottlieb is quoted from Selden Rodman, *Conversations with Artists,* 1957, p. 89. For opposing views, see David Riesman, *The Lonely Crowd,* 1950; Jacques Barzun, *God's Country and Mine,* 1954; the brochure *Reality,* 3 nos. 1953–1955. Shahn is quoted from Rodman, *Conversations with Artists,* p. 228.

Chapter 35 / *Architecture of Logic and Imagination*

On architecture in the war period: Henry S. Churchill on "Acquackanonk," in *Pencil Points,* vol. 23, July, 1942, p. 35; on Stuyvesant Town in *Architectural Forum,* vol. 78, June, 1943, p. 34; G. E. Kidder Smith, "The Tragedy of American Architecture," in *Magazine of Art,* vol. 38, Nov., 1945, p. 255. William Lescaze is quoted from p. 157 of his essay, "These Documents Called Buildings," in *The Intent of the Artist,* 1941.

Architecture since 1945: *Built in USA: Post-War Architecture,* edited by Henry-Russell Hitchcock and Arthur Drexler, MMA, 1952; Hitchcock, *Architecture, Nineteenth and Twentieth Centuries,* ch. 25; Vincent J. Scully, Jr., "Archetype and Order in Recent American Architecture," in *Art in America,* vol. 42, Dec., 1954, p. 250; articles on contemporary work in the periodicals *Architectural Forum* and *Architectural Record.*

Henry Hope Reed, Jr., attacks the modern style in *The Golden City,* 1959.

The major figures: on WALTER GROPIUS (1883–), see his *The Scope of Total Architecture,* 1955, and Sigfried Giedion, *Walter Gropius,* 1954; on LUDWIG MIES VAN DER ROHE (1886–), see L. Hilberseimer, *Mies Van der Rohe,* 1956; on FRANK L. WRIGHT, see references above under section 24, ch. 26, and section 28, ch. 33; also his *When Democracy Builds,* 1945, *Genius and the Mobocracy,* 1949, *The Future of Architecture,* 1953, *A Testament,* 1957; on RICHARD NEUTRA (1892–), see his *Survival through Design,* 1954, and *Life and Human Habitat,* edited by Alexander Koch, 1956.

See references in the *Art Index* to other architects of the period, including ALVAR AALTO (1898–), GREGORY AIN (1908–), DONALD BARTHELME (1907–), PIETRO BELLUSCHI (1899–), MARCEL BREUER (1902–), GORDON BUNSHAFT (1909–), SERGE CHERMAYEFF (1900–), GARDNER DAILEY (1895–), CHARLES EAMES (1907–), JOHN FUNK (1908–), PERCIVAL GOODMAN (1904–), HARWELL HARRIS (1903–), WALLACE HARRISON (1895–) and MAX ABRAMOWITZ (1908–), HENRY HILL (1913–), PHILIP JOHNSON (1906–), FRED KECK (1895–), CARL KOCH (1912–), ERNEST KUMP (1911–), WILLIAM LESCAZE (1896–), MAYNARD LYNDON (1907–), AUGUSTE NOEL, EERO SAARINEN (1910–), LOUIS SKIDMORE (1897–), NATHANIEL OWINGS (1903–), and JOHN MERRILL (1896–), RAPHAEL SORIANO (1904–), EDWARD STONE (1902–), RALPH TWITCHELL (1891?–) and PAUL RUDOLPH (1918–), WILLIAM WURSTER (1895–), JOHN YEON (1910–).

For the ideas of Sigfried Giedion: See his *Mechanization Takes Command,* 1948, and *Architecture, You and Me,* 1958.

The problem of the city: *The Exploding Metropolis,* 1958, by the editors of *Fortune* magazine; Wilfred Owen, *Cities in the Motor Age,* 1959; Lewis Mumford,

From the Ground Up: Observations on Contemporary Architecture, Housing, Highway Building, and Civic Design, 1956, a collection of his *New Yorker* essays. The *Architectural Forum,* vol. 90, Apr., 1949, is given to the work of the Levitts and other "merchant builders."

Domestic architecture: Hugh Morrison describes several distinguished examples in "American Houses: Modern Style," in *Perspectives USA,* no. 5, Fall, 1953, p. 65; see also *A Treasury of Contemporary Houses,* by editors of *Architectural Record,* 1954.

The architecture of business and industry: on Lever House, see *Architectural Forum,* vol. 92, June, 1950, p. 84; on Seagram Building, see *Architectural Review,* vol. 118, July, 1955, p. 1; on Manufacturers Trust Co., see *Architectural Forum,* vol. 101, Oct., 1954, p. 47.

Lewis Mumford criticizes the UN Secretariat in *From the Ground Up.* Allan Temko discusses architectural puritanism in *Columbia University Forum,* vol. 1, Spring, 1958. On the General Motors Technical Center, see *Architectural Forum,* vol. 95, Nov., 1951, p. 111. On the work of Edward Stone, see *Architectural Record,* vol. 122, July, 1957, p. 153. On R. BUCKMINSTER FULLER (1895–), see the same, vol. 117, June, 1955, p. 155:

On the new "shape-architecture": See *Four New Buildings: Architecture and Imagery,* MMA, 1959.

Educational architecture: See Lawrence B. Perkins and Walter D. Cocking, *Schools,* 1949; article on Illinois Institute of Technology in *Architectural Record,* vol. 117, Jan., 1955, p. 126; on Florida Southern College in *Architectural Forum,* vol. 97, Sept., 1952, p. 120.

On the Guggenheim Museum: See Edgar Kaufmann, Jr., "The Form of Space for Art," in *Art in America,* vol. 46, Winter, 1958–1959, p. 75.

On religious architecture: See article in *Architectural Record,* vol. 118, Dec., 1955, p. 161, on six recent churches; also *Architectural Forum,* vol. 104, Jan., 1956, p. 116, on M.I.T. chapel.

On Harry Bertoia, Richard Lippold, and other sculptors who worked with architects: See references below under ch. 36.

Chapter 36 / *Painting and Sculpture at Midcentury*

Surveys which include this period: Baur, *Revolution and Tradition in Modern American Art;* Pousette-Dart, *American Painting Today;* Blesh, *Modern Art U.S.A.;* Hess, *Abstract Painting;* Baur (ed.), *New Art in America;* Baur and Rosalind Irvine, *The New Decade,* 1955. See also Herbert Read, Sam Hunter, and others, *Art since 1945,* essays on several countries, including America.

On the following painters, discussed or mentioned in this chapter, see three catalogues of the Museum of Modern Art, all edited by Dorothy C. Miller: ARSHILE GORKY (1904–1948), LOREN MAC IVER (1909–), ROBERT MOTHERWELL (1915–), ALTON PICKENS (1917–), HONORÉ SHARRER (1920–), and MARK TOBEY (1890–), in *Fourteen Americans,* 1946; WILLIAM BAZIOTES (1912–), JACKSON POLLOCK (1912–1956), MARK ROTHKO (1903–), CLYFFORD STILL (1904–), and BRADLEY TOMLIN (1899–1953), in *Fifteen Americans,* 1952; PHILIP GUSTON (1912–), FRANZ KLINE (1910–), and GRACE HARTIGAN (1922–), in *Twelve Americans,* 1956. On WILLEM DE KOONING (1904–) and RICO LEBRUN (1900–), see Baur, *New Art in America.* See *Art Index* for references to BYRON BROWNE (1907–), BERNARD PERLIN (1918–), THEODOROS STAMOS (1923–), and WALTER STUEMPFIG (1914–).

Statements by living painters about their work appear in the catalogues of the annual exhibitions of contemporary American painting at the University of Illinois, and in Baur, *Nature in Abstraction,* WM, 1958. On GRANDMA MOSES (1860–), see her autobiography, *My Life's History,* 1952. On ABRAHAM RATTNER (1895–), see Allen S. Weller (ed.), *Abraham Rattner,* 1956; Goodrich and Baur, *Four American Expressionists.*

On foreign artists working here, see "Eleven Europeans in America," in *Museum of Modern Art Bulletin,* vol. 13, nos. 4–5, 1946.

For the symposium, "The State of American Art," see *Magazine of Art,* vol. 42, Mar., 1949, p. 82.

For current evaluations of Hopper, Burchfield, and Sheeler, see references above, under section 26, ch. 29; on Pereira, see above in section 28, ch. 34, also her essay, *The Nature of Space,* 1956; on MacIver, see Baur, *MacIver and I. Pereira;* on Bloom, see Wight, *Hyman Bloom;* on Graves, see Wight, *Morris Graves;* on Tobey, see Kenneth Rexroth, "Mark Tobey of Seattle, Washington," in *Art News,* vol. 50, May, 1951, p. 17, also Tobey, "Reminiscence and Reverie," in *Magazine of Art,* vol. 44, Oct., 1951, p. 228; on Guston, see H. W. Janson, "Philip Guston," in *Magazine of Art,* vol. 40, Feb., 1947, p. 54; on Tomlin, see Baur, *Bradley Walker Tomlin,* 1957; on RALSTON CRAWFORD (1906–), see catalogue of exhibition at Milwaukee Art Center, 1958. On BALCOMB GREENE (1904–), see Elaine de Kooning in *Art News,* vol. 53, May, 1954, p. 34, and Greene, "The Artist's Reluctance to Communication," in the same, vol. 55, Jan., 1957, p. 44. On ADOLPH GOTTLIEB (1903–), see his article, "My Paintings," in *Arts and Architecture,* vol. 68, Sept., 1951, p. 20. On Gorky, see Ethel

K. Schwabacher, *Arshile Gorky,* WM, 1951, and notes by Stuart Davis and Lloyd Goodrich in *Magazine of Art,* vol. 44, Feb., 1951, pp. 56 and 59. Sam Hunter's essay on the action painters, "Painting by Another Name," is in *Art in America,* vol. 42, Dec., 1954, p. 291. On Hofmann, see Frederick S. Wight, *Hans Hofmann,* 1957. Parker Tyler comments on Pollock in "Jackson Pollock: The Infinite Labyrinth," in *Magazine of Art,* vol. 43, Mar., 1950, p. 92. Peter Selz discusses "A New Imagery," in *College Art Journal,* vol. 15, Summer, 1956, p. 290.

The humanists: on Levine, Evergood, and Shahn, see references above in section 28, ch. 32. On ANDREW WYETH (1917–), see Lloyd Goodrich in *Art in America,* vol. 43, Oct., 1955, p. 9. Shahn is here quoted from Rodman, *Conversations with Artists,* p. 192.

On the work of Adams, Strand, Steichen, and others: See Newhall, *Masters of Photography.*

On the graphic arts: Jules Heller, *Printmaking To-*
1949; *Bulletin of the Brooklyn Museum,* vol. 14, 1952;
day, 1958; Stanley W. Hayter, *New Ways of Gravure,*
Una E. Johnson, *Ten Years of American Prints, 1947–1956,* 1956; Albert Reese, *American Prize Prints of the Twentieth Century,* 1949.

On sculpture: See references above under section 28, ch. 34; also Carola Giedion-Welcker, *Contemporary Sculpture,* 1955, which includes several Americans. A special number of *Art in America,* vol. 44, Winter, 1956, is given to contemporary sculptors. On DAVID SMITH (1906–), see Sam Hunter (ed.), *David Smith,* MMA, 1957, and Smith, *"Thoughts on Sculpture,"* in *College Art Journal,* vol. 13, Winter, 1954, p. 97. See also Richard Lippold, "How to Make a Sculpture," in *Art in America,* vol. 44, Winter, 1956, p. 27.

On DAVID HARE (1917–) and THEODORE ROSZAK (1907–), see *Fourteen Americans;* on HERBERT FERBER (1906–) and RICHARD LIPPOLD (1915–), see *Fifteen Americans;* on IBRAM LASSAW (1913–), SEYMOUR LIPTON (1903–), and JOSÉ DE RIVERA (1904–), see *Twelve Americans.* See *Art Index* for references to other sculptors here mentioned: LEONARD BASKIN (1922–), LOUIS SCHANKER (1903–), PETER GRIPPE (1912–), GAVOR PETERDI (1915–), BERNARD ROSENTHAL (1914–), HARRY BERTOIA (1915–), and REUBEN NAKIAN (1897–).

American art shown abroad: See catalogues, *Modern Art in the United States,* 1956, the Tate Gallery, London, and *The New American Painting,* MMA, 1959. Quotations from European critics are mainly from the introduction to the latter.

Carl Sandberg is quoted from *The People, Yes,* 1936, p. 32. Tocqueville is quoted from *Democracy in America,* 1945 edition, p. 34.

INDEX

B

C

E

F

H

K

L

M

P

Q

R

T

U

V

W

X

Y

Z